1981
Malcolm Baldrige takes office as Secretary of Commerce. He supports Congressional interest in a national quality award.

Ford Motor Co. invites Deming to visit and explain quality control concepts

1985
Kaoru Ishikawa publishes in the U.S. *What Is Total Quality Control? The Japanese Way.*

David Packard sparks interest in TQM, Total Quality Management, as head of a commission to study defense management.

1989
Florida Power and Light becomes first company outside Japan to win the Deming Prize.

1990's
U.S. continues to incorporate Company-Wide Quality (CWQ) management techniques.

52
Genichi Taguchi ...s the U.S., ...ding ...&T's Bell ...oratories.

1979
Philip Crosby publishes *Quality is Free.*

0   1970   1980   1990

1972
Dr. Genichi Taguchi publishes *Quality Evaluations in Japan.*

1980
U.S. auto manufacturers enter a disastrous period. Chrysler Corp. is forced to acquire loan guarantees from the U.S. government and Ford Motor Co. loses $1.6 billion.

In June NBC airs documentary," If Japan Can...Why Can't We ?" Deming gains new recognition in the U.S.

1982
Tom Peters and Robert Waterman publish *In Search of Excellence.*

W. Edwards Deming publishes *Quality, Productivity, and Competitive Position.*

1987
On August 20, Congress creates the Malcolm Baldrige National Quality Award. Winners include:
1988
Westinghouse's Commercial Nuclear Fuel Division
Motorola, Inc.
Globe Metallurgical, Inc.
1989
Milliken & Co,
Xerox Corp's Business Products and Systems
1990
Cadillac Motor Car Division
IBM Rochester
Federal Express Corp.
Wallace Co., Inc.

1988
Secretary of Defense Frank Carlucci makes Total Quality Management official policy for the Department of Defense.

...ORPORATE
...ROL
...T ALL
...NAGEMENT

THE HIGH QUALITY OF JAPANESE CARS SPURS U.S. INDUSTRY

CONGRESS CREATES THE BALDRIGE NATIONAL QUALITY AWARD

Modern Management

Modern Management

Quality, Ethics, and the Global Environment

Fifth Edition

SAMUEL C. CERTO
Dean and Professor of Management
Roy E. Crummer
Graduate School of Business

ROLLINS COLLEGE

Allyn and Bacon   Boston   London   Toronto   Sydney   Tokyo   Singapore

Executive Editor: Richard Wohl
Series Editor: Susan Nelle Barcomb
Developmental Editor: Judith S. Fifer
Senior Editorial Assistant: Carol Alper
Production Administrator: Marjorie Payne
Editorial-Production Service: York Production Services
Text Designer: Deborah Schneck
Cover Administrator: Linda Dickinson
Cover Designer: Susan Slovinsky
Composition Buyer: Linda Cox
Manufacturing Buyer: Louise Richardson

Copyright © 1992 by Allyn and Bacon
A Division of Simon & Schuster, Inc.
160 Gould Street, Needham Heights, MA 02194

Previous editions were published as
Principles of Modern Management: Functions and Systems
Copyright © 1989 Allyn and Bacon

Copyright © 1986, 1983, 1980 by Wm. C. Brown Publishers

Library of Congress Cataloging-in-Publication Data

Certo, Samuel C.
    Modern management : quality, ethics, and the global environment /
Samuel C. Certo. — 5th ed.
      p. cm.
    Rev. ed. of: Principles of modern management. 4th ed. © 1989.
    Includes bibliographical references and index.
    ISBN 0-205-13154-9
    1. Management.   2. Industrial management.   3. Social
responsibility of business.   I. Certo, Samuel C.   Principles of
modern management.   II. Title.
HD31.C4125 1991
658—dc20   91-22793
                                              CIP

Printed in the United States of America

10 9 8 7 6 5 4 3 2   97 96 95 94 93

The credits and acknowledgments for figures, tables, boxes, and cases are found on pages 723–726. These pages should be considered extensions of the copyright page.

Photo Credits
Photo credits are found on page 726, which should be considered an extension of the copyright page.

To Mimi, Trevis, Matthew, Sarah, and Brian

About the Author

Dr. Samuel C. Certo is presently Dean and Professor of Management at the Roy E. Crummer Graduate School of Business at Rollins College. He has been a professor of management for over fifteen years and has received prestigious awards including the Award for Innovative Teaching from the Southern Business Association, the Instructional Innovation Award granted by the Decision Sciences Institute, and the Charles A. Welsh Memorial Award for outstanding teaching at the Crummer School. Dr. Certo's numerous publications include articles in such journals as *Academy of Management Review, The Journal of Experiential Learning and Simulation,* and *Training.* He has also written several successful textbooks including *Modern Management: Quality, Ethics, and the Global Environment, Strategic Management: Concepts and Applications,* and *Introduction to Business.* A past chairman of the Management Education and Development Division of the Academy of Management, he has been honored by that group's Excellence of Leadership Award. Dr. Certo has also served as president of the Association for Business Simulation and Experiential Learning, as associate editor for *Simulation & Games,* and as a review board member of the *Academy of Management Review.* His consulting experience has been extensive with notable experience on boards of directors.

Management success is what happens when preparation meets opportunity. Take advantage of this text and this course as a vehicle for preparing for management opportunities that you inevitably will have. Keep this text in your professional library as a *reference book*, which can be used to enhance your preparedness for opportunities throughout various stages of your future management career.

Contents

Preface

Consistent with previous editions, the purpose of this text is to prepare students to be managers. As the subtitle for this new edition implies, however, special excitement and contemporary relevance have been built into this new text version by emphasizing three important issues facing modern managers: quality, ethics, and the global environment. Through a realistic introduction to these and other management issues, students learn to appreciate the fact that management is much more than theoretical concepts. It is excitement, hard work, and challenge! This book continually emphasizes realism by carefully integrating cases and examples about actual managers and actual companies in order to help students see how management theories can be applied in the modern environment in which today's managers work.

This edition of the **Modern Management Learning Package**—this text and its related ancillaries—continues its distinctive tradition in management education. This tradition emphasizes clear, concise, and up-to-date coverage of critical management concepts, learning materials that are based on empathy for students and that enhance the student learning process, and instructional support materials that facilitate the design and conduct of only the highest quality principles of management courses.

Over the last fifteen years, changes to the **Modern Management Learning Package** have been guided by a single driving force: improving student learning. The continuing popularity of the package throughout the United States and many foreign countries has served to validate these learning-oriented improvements. Starting with the text, the following sections describe each major component of this newest learning package and explain how this tradition of improving student learning continues in this newest edition.

TEXT: THEORY OVERVIEW

The overall approach employed in this book is to emphasize the wisdom of both management scholars and practicing managers. Deciding on the management concepts that should be included in a text of this sort and on how they should be covered is probably the most difficult task an author faces. Much insight was gleaned through careful consideration of such materials as (1) reports and opinions of accrediting agencies—for example, the American Assembly of Collegiate Schools of Business (AACSB); (2) trends and issues in management research as highlighted by the work of management scholars; and (3) accounts by practicing managers emphasizing the contemporary organizational problems they face and how to deal with them.

Over all, management theory in this text is divided into six main sections: "Introduction to Management," "Planning," "Organizing," "Influencing," "Controlling," and "Topics for Special Emphasis." Naturally, updates of theories and examples have been extensively made throughout each section. More specifically, Section 1, "Introduction to Management," lays the groundwork necessary for studying management. Chapter 1, "Management and Management Careers" has been revised in this edition not only to better expose students to what management is, but also to give them a better understanding of special career issues such as the progress of women in management, dual career couples, and the multicultural workforce. This chapter also highlights Peters and Waterman's *In Search of Excellence*, which provides practical insights on how to manage a successful organization. Chapter 2, "The History of Management," presents several fundamental but different ways in which managers can perceive their jobs. The last chapter in this section, Chapter 3, "Corporate Social Responsibility and Business Ethics," discusses the responsibilities that managers have to society, and a discussion of business ethics and their applications to modern management. For this edition, this chapter has been moved from the last section of the book to the first section. In this way, students are able to reflect on societal implications of management action throughout their text and course.

Section 2, "Planning," elaborates on planning activities as a primary management function. This section begins with Chapter 4, "Organizational Objectives." In this edition, this chapter has been moved from the first section to the second in order to better emphasize the setting of organizational objectives as the beginning of the planning process. Chapter 5, "Fundamentals of Planning," presents the basics of planning. Chapter 6, "Making Decisions," discusses the decision-making process as a component of the planning process. Chapter 7, "Strategic Planning" has been significantly revised. Highlights of material added include coverage of Porter's model for industry analysis, the BCG Growth-Share Matrix, the GE Portfolio Matrix, strategy implementation, and strategic control. Chapter 8, "Plans and Planning Tools," discusses various managerial planning tools available to help formulate plans.

Section 3, "Organizing," discusses organizing activities as a major management function. Chapter 9 presents the fundamentals of organizing, and Chapter 10 elaborates on how to organize various worker activities appropriately. Chapter 11, "Managing Human Resources," discusses hiring people who will make a desirable contribution to organizational objectives. Chapter 12 is "Organizational Change and Stress." Coverage focuses on how managers change organizations and the stress-related issues that can accompany such action. The discussion highlights the definition of stress and the importance of studying and managing stress.

Section 4, "Influencing," discusses how managers should deal with people. The four chapters in this section (Chapters 13–16) respectively discuss the fundamentals of influencing and communication, leadership, motivation, and groups and corporate culture. The leadership chapter has been significantly revised with additional focus on more traditional concepts such as the Vroom-Yetton-Jago leadership model, the Michigan studies, and the Path-Goal Theory of Leadership, as well as more recently developing topics such as transformational leadership, and leadership and trust. New topics in the motivation chapter include equity theory, Alderfer's ERG theory, and monetary and nonmonetary incentives. New focus for the last chapter in this section emphasizes the role of corporate culture in managing groups.

Section 5, "Controlling," analyzes the performance of control activities as another basic management function. Chapter 17, "Principles of Controlling," presents the basics of controlling. Chapter 18, "Fundamentals of Production Management and Control," describes the basics of the production process, robotics, and a number of useful managerial tools for controlling production. Chapter 19, "Information," defines *information* and elaborates on its role in the controlling process. New coverage in this section emphasizes maintaining product quality in organizations. The relationship between quality and productivity is featured with special emphasis on the work of W. Edwards Deming.

The last section of this text is "Topics for Special Emphasis." Chapter 20, "International Management," discusses the basics of international and multinational organizations. Planning for multinational corporations, organizing multinational corporations, and influencing people in multinational corporations are all major topics. Special discussion focuses on learning from Japanese management techniques. Chapter 21, "Quality: Building Competitive Organizations," is a new chapter in this edition. This chapter focuses on building quality throughout all phases of organizational activity. Discussions focus on defining quality, achieving quality through strategic planning, and management skills necessary to build quality throughout an organization. The ideas of Philip B. Crosby, W. Edwards Deming, and Joseph M. Juran, internationally known quality experts, are highlighted.

TEXT: STUDENT LEARNING AIDS

Several features of this text were designed to make the study of management more efficient, effective, and enjoyable. A list of these features and an explanation of each follow.

LEARNING OBJECTIVES   The opening pages of each chapter contain a set of learning objectives that are intended as guidelines on how to study the chapter.

CHAPTER OUTLINES   The opening pages of each chapter also contain a chapter outline that previews the textual material and helps the reader keep the information in perspective while it is being read.

INTRODUCTORY CASES WITH "BACK TO THE CASE" SECTIONS   The opening of each chapter contains a case study that introduces readers to management problems related to chapter content. Detailed "Back to the Case" sections appear throughout each chapter, applying specific areas of management theory discussed in the chapter to the introductory case. All of these cases involve real companies such as Weyerhaeuser, Reebok, and Walt Disney Company, and highlight contemporary issues. All introductory cases are new to this edition.

CASE STUDIES   The concluding pages of each chapter contain a real-life case that further applies chapter content to related management situations. All end-of-chapter cases are based on real companies and are new to this edition. The cases cover a wide range of subjects, including recent accounts about business and government, and featuring accounts of managing cultural diversity. Among the companies focused on are Exxon, Pizza Hut, and Volvo.

CNN VIDEO CASES   A very innovative and exciting new feature of this edition is the CNN Video Case that follows each chapter. The case is comprised of textual material profiling management action in a real company as well as a specially edited CNN "Pinnacle" interview with a CEO or manager that is provided to the instructor for classroom viewing. The written and video materials were carefully designed to illustrate chapter material. Over all, the CNN Video Case makes management concepts "come alive" in the classroom. The textual material for each CNN Video Case concludes with discussion questions as well as in-class activities.

INTEGRATIVE CASES   Each of the six major parts of the text ends with a case relating to that section as a whole. These cases provide students with the opportunity to review and apply material from entire sections of the text. All integrative cases are based on real, undisguised situations and are new to this edition.

MARGIN NOTES   Each chapter contains margin notes that can be helpful in the initial reading and for review. A new margin note format for this edition highlights the key terms in each chapter and also provides brief definitions for the student's review.

MANAGEMENT HIGHLIGHTS   Management Highlights is another exciting new feature of this text. Management Highlights are extended examples emphasizing how modern managers face contemporary issues in real companies. Chapters have three highlights that illustrate the following timely and important management issues: quality, ethics, and the global environment. Companies featured in Management Highlights include Chrysler, PepsiCo, and Xerox.

ACTION SUMMARIES   Each chapter ends with an action-oriented chapter summary. In this summary, students respond to several objective questions that are clearly linked to the learning objectives stated at the beginning of the chapter. Students can check their answers with the answer key at the end of the chapter. This key also lists the pages in the chapter that can be referred to for a fuller explanation of the answers.

INTRODUCTORY CASE WRAP-UP   Each chapter ends with several questions about its introductory case. These questions provide the opportunity to apply chapter concepts directly to the case.

BUILDING ON WHAT YOU KNOW   One challenge that management students continually face is retaining what they learn. "Building on What You Know" is a new feature of this text designed to help management students meet this challenge. At the end of each chapter, the "Building on What You Know" section asks students to review a specified Management Highlight in the chapter and to then answer questions about that highlight that are based on material from a previous chapter. By using the "Building on What You Know" feature, students and instructors alike can systematically emphasize concepts covered in a previous chapter and consciously strive to retain what has been learned.

ISSUES FOR REVIEW AND DISCUSSION   The concluding pages of each chapter contain a set of discussion questions that test the understanding of chapter material and can serve as vehicles for study and for class discussion.

GLOSSARY   Major management terms and their definitions are gathered at the end of the text. They appear in boldface type along with the text pages on which the discussion of each term appears.

ILLUSTRATIONS   Figures, tables, and photographs depicting various management situations are used throughout the text to help bridge the gap between management theory and authentic situations.

SUPPLEMENTARY MATERIALS

A number of supplementary materials have been developed to complement the use of *Modern Management,* Fifth Edition. Although the text itself was designed to offer a desirable amount of material for a high-quality course in principles of management, special supplements are available to further enrich the learning situation in which the text is used.

EXPERIENCING MODERN MANAGEMENT: A WORKBOOK, FIFTH EDITION

This is a combination study guide and source book of more than sixty-five experiential exercises and is to be used in conjunction with the text. The fifth edition of this workbook, by Professor Lee Graf of Illinois State University and author Samuel C. Certo, contains a number of new and modified exercises that correspond to the revised text. Quality improvement, ethics, and international management are the dominant issues in these new exercises. Workbook elements that correspond to each text chapter include the following:

AN EXTENDED CHAPTER SUMMARY   Extended summaries are helpful for a quick review of text material. Summaries are keyed to chapter learning objectives in the text in order to facilitate student learning.

LEARNING ASSESSMENT ACTIVITIES   For each chapter of the text, the workbook contains a series of twenty-five objective questions that test the understanding of chapter content. Correct answers and the text page numbers on which answers are explained are furnished for all questions.

EXPERIENTIAL EXERCISES, ACTIVITIES, PROJECTS, CASES   A number of diverse in-class and out-of-class learning activities that further illustrate the content of each text chapter are provided. Exercises are provided for use in large classes, small classes, and for assignment to individuals. Figure 1 at the beginning of the activity manual/study guide outlines how each exercise can be best used. In addition, a suggested sequence for using the text and the workbook jointly is shown on the next page. Finally, the workbook table of contents identifies the topic and explains the fundamental objective of each of 65 or so exercises.

Computer Simulations in Management (CSM)

This software contains six computer-assisted experiential exercises designed to help students understand how software application programs can be used in practical

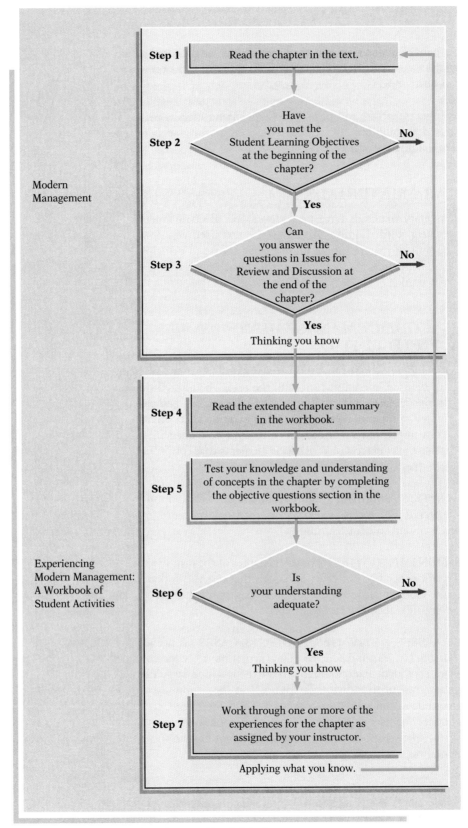

Modern
Management

Experiencing
Modern Management:
A Workbook of
Student Activities

FIGURE 1

Suggested sequence for using the text and student workbook jointly.

management situations. The exercises focus on major sections in the text; topics addressed in these exercises include using decision trees, assessing management style, and computer-assisted scheduling.

Profiles in Quality: Blueprints for Action from 50 Leading Companies

Available at a reduced price when packaged with *Modern Management,* this outstanding paperback highlights actual Quality Improvement Programs from well-known companies such as Federal Express, General Electric, Boeing, AT&T, Amana, and Hewlett Packard.

Other Instructional Aids

In addition to the supplements just described, several other ingredients of the *Modern Management* learning package also have been designed to enhance the learning environment in which this text is used. Detailed descriptions of these items are located in the Instructor's Resource Manual. These include

Instructor's Annotated Edition
Instructor's Resource Manual
Test Bank
Allyn and Bacon Test Manager, a computerized test bank
Acetate transparencies
CNN Videos
Video User's Manual
Video disc: Experiencing Management: What Managers Do
Classroom edition of the *Wall Street Journal*

Acknowledgments

Continued acceptance of the *Modern Management* learning package by management instructors throughout the United States and several foreign countries has been very satisfying. Undeniably, many professionals have played significant roles in the design and development of this package. It is with great pleasure that I recognize these people and extend to them my gratitude for their insight, expertise, and warm personal support and encouragement.

As with previous editions, Professor Lee A. Graf, Illinois State University, has been a major force behind this text and its accompanying experiential workbook. Professor Graf's conceptual and organizational skills have been critical in improving this learning package to the greatest degree possible.

Several other individuals have provided this text with valuable ancillary materials, and I would like to recognize each of them for their dedication and hard work:

Betty Pritchett of Kennesaw State College for preparing the annotations and instructor's section for the Instructor's Annotated Edition as well as revising the Instructor's Resource Manual.

Robert E. Kemper and Joyce Kemper of Northern Arizona University for revising the Test Bank.

F. Michael Kauffman of Santa Barbara City College for preparing the Video User's Manual.

The case studies, CNN video cases, and integrative cases were specially written for this text by the following team of case writers:

Michael Bowen, University of Notre Dame

Robert E. Kemper, Northern Arizona University

Sylvia Keyes, Bridgewater State College

Peter B. Petersen, The Johns Hopkins University

Charles B. Shrader, Iowa State University

Alice Smith, St. Louis Community College at Meramec

Mary S. Thibodeaux, University of North Texas

Leslie A. Toombs, University of Texas at Tyler

In addition, Leslie Brunetta, Robin Dechert Schachat, and Mary Walsh researched and made contributions to many of the case studies, CNN video cases, and integrative cases.

Every author appreciates the valuable contribution reviewers make to the development of a text project. Reviewers offer that "different viewpoint" that requires an author to constructively question his or her work. I again had an excellent team of reviewers. Thoughtful comments, concern for student learning, and insights regarding instructional implications of the written word characterized the high-quality feedback I received. I am pleased to be able to recognize members of my review team for their valuable contributions to the development of this text:

Robert J. Ash, Rancho Santiago College

Donald Baack, Pittsburg State College

Don B. Bradley III, University of Central Arkansas

Bob S. Bulls, J. Sargeant Reynolds Community College

Elizabeth A. Cameron, Alma College

Joseph E. Cantrell, DeAnza College

Justin Carey, St. John's University

D. Dexter Dalton, St. Louis Community College at Meramec

D. James Day, Shawnee State University

Robert L. Goldberg, Northeastern University

Sonia Goltz, University of Notre Dame

Dorothy Heide, California State University, Fullerton

Marvin Hill, Northern Illinois University

Marvin Karlins, University of South Florida

Robert E. Kemper, Northern Arizona University

Sylvia Keyes, Bridgewater State College

Arthur LaCapria, Jr., El Paso Community College

Daniel W. McAllister, University of Nevada, Las Vegas

E.S. Mills, Kendall College

R. Richard Sabo, California State Polytechnic University

Charles B. Shrader, Iowa State University

Mary S. Thibodeaux, University of North Texas

Leslie Toombs, University of Texas at Tyler

G.A. Vargas, California State University, Fullerton

Ronald Vickroy, University of Pittsburgh at Johnstown

Another source of valuable feedback that I have used for developing and implementing the *Modern Management* learning package has been the helpful comments from colleagues. These individuals have, over the years, provided reviewer comments or have responded to an opinion survey. This survey was conducted to expand the breadth of relevant feedback from colleagues about the instructional value of various components of the text as well as the *Modern Management* learning package as a whole. I would like to personally thank my colleagues who spent the time and effort to provide data that was critical in defining the character and scope of this text and its ancillaries.

Christopher Aglo-Ostoghile, *Prairie View Agriculture and Technology College*
Milton C. Alderfer, *Miami Dade Community College North*
Billie Allen, *University of Southern Mississippi*
Arturo Alonzo Jr., *St. Philip's College*
David Anstett, *College of St. Scholastica*
Donald L. Ashbaugh, *University of Northern Iowa*
Jack Ashmore, *Bee County College*
Lorraine Bassette, *Prince George's Community College*
David Baxter, *San Diego Mesa College*
Charles Beavin, *Miami-Dade Community College*
Lee A. Belovarac, *Mercyhurst College*
Jack Blanton, *University of Kentucky*
Pam Braden, *Parkersburg Community College*
Don B. Bradley, *University of Central Arkansas*
Terry H. Brattin, *Texas State Technical University–Harlingen*
William Brichner, *San Jose State University*
Duane Brickner, *Southern Mountain Community College*
John W. Jr. Brown, *SUNY Brockport*
W. Brown, *Berry College*
Robert Bruns, *Central College*
Shirley Bryan, *Pennsylvania State University–Berks*
F. M. Buchanan, *Salisbury State College*
Alison Buck, *Phillips University*
Robert S. Bulls, *J. Sargeant Reynolds Community College*
Ellen Burns, *Phillips University*
Thomas Burns, *Keystone Jr. College*
David T. Bussard, *Susquehanna University*
Dennis G. Butler, *Orange Coast College*
Austin Byron, *Northern Arizona University*
Edward Cahaly, *Stonehill College*
Robert E. Callahan, *Seattle University*
Perry Camingore, *Brazosport College*
Valeriano Cantu, *Angelo State University*
Mario Carrillo, *Colorado School of Mines*
Thomas Case, *Georgia Southern University*
Tommy Cates, *University of Tennessee at Martin*
C. Dale Caudill, *Morehead State University*
Herschel Chait, *Indiana State University*
Pamela Chandler, *University of Mary Hardin–Baylor*
John F. Chisholm, *Allegheny Community College*
Daniel W. Churchill, *Mount Ida College*
Robert A. Cisek, *Mercyhurst College*
Joseph Clairmont, *Bay De Noc Community College*
William Clark, *Leeward Community College*
Debra M. Clingerman, *California University of Pennsylvania*
Larry A. Coleman, *Indiana State University*
Terry Comingor, *Brazosport College*
John Coppola, *Cosumnes River College*
Pati Crabb, *Bellarmine University*
D. James Day, *Shawnee State University*
John R. Deegan, *Texas Wesleyan College*
Linda Dell'Osso, *California State Polytechnic University–Pomona*

Sezai Demiral, *Edinboro University of Pennsylvania*
Richard L. Dickinson, *California State University–Sacramento*
Dale L. Dickson, *Mesa College*
Daniel J. Duffy, *Loyola College–Evergreen*
Robert Dunn, *Alexander City State College*
John Eberle, *Embry-Riddle Aeronautical University*
Sidney W. Eckert, *Appalachian State University*
Jeb Egbert, *Ambassador College*
Randi Sue Ellis, *North Harris County Community College*
Chuck England, *Bridgewater State College*
Mary Sue Ewald, *Missouri Baptist College*
Vincent E. Faherty, *University of Northern Iowa*
Jeffrey W. Fahrenwal, *Central College*
Deborah Fajcak, *Harding Business College*
Jay Felton, *North Harris County Community College*
Judy Field, *Willmar Community College*
Stephen Field, *University of West Florida*
Richard Forsyth, *University of Wisconsin–Green Bay*
Paula S. Funkhouser, *Truckee Meadows Community College*
Dick Gardner, *West Virginia University*
Gerald Garrity, *Anna Maria College*
Carl Gates, *Sauk Valley College*
Pat Gaudette, *Pine Manor College*
Beth Gershon, *University of LaVerne*
Faith Gilroy, *Loyola College–Evergreen*
Carolyn Goad, *Oakland City Community College*
R. Goddard, *Appalachian State University*
Robert Goldberg, *Northeastern University*
David Goldenberg, *Bellarmine University*
Thomas Goodwin, *Johnson and Wales College*
Jack N. Grose, *Mars Hill College*
Raymond M. Guydosh, *SUNY Plattsburgh*
Luther Guynes, *Los Angeles City College*
James L. Hall, *University of Santa Clara*
Ed Hammer, *University of Tennessee–Chattanooga*
Kathleen Harcharik, *California State Polytechnic University–Pomona*
James Harvey, *University of West Florida*
D. B. Heide, *California State University–Fullerton*
Wayne Hemberger, *Edinboro University of Pennsylvania*
John W. Henry, *Georgia Southern University*
Bill Herlehy, *Embry-Riddle Aeronautical University*
Irving L. Herman, *California State University–Sacramento*
J. C. Hill, *Appalachian State University*
Robert T. Holland, *Woodbury University*
William Houlihan, *Detroit College of Business*
Fred House, *Northern Arizona University*
Edmund Hunter, *Delaware County Community College*
Warren Imada, *Leeward Community College*
William Jacobs, *Lake City Community College*
Ernest Jaski, *Richard J. Daley College*
David J. Jobson, *Keystone Jr. College*
Alan E. Johnson, *Embry-Riddle Aeronautical University*
Edwin Johnson, *Parkersburg Community College*

Karen R. Johnson, *University of New Hampshire*
Paul W. Joice Sr., *Walla Walla College*
Bette-Jean Jones, *Embry-Riddle Aeronautical University*
Charlie Jones, *East Central Oklahoma University*
Frazier C. Jones, *Montreat-Anderson College*
Frank Kattwinkel, *St. Leo College*
Fred Jeffrey Keil, *J. Sargeant Reynolds Community College*
Robert E. Kemper, *Northern Arizona University*
George Kevorkian, *Northern Virginia Community College*
Sylvia Keyes, *Bridgewater State College*
Scott King, *Sinclair Community College*
Jerome M. Kinskey, *Sinclair Community College*
Barney J. Klecker, *Normandale Community College*
John P. Kohl, *San Jose State University*
Bob Kovacev, *California State University–Fullerton*
Dennis Lee Kovach, *Community College of Allegheny North*
William Lacewell, *Westark Community College*
Patricia Laidler, *Massasoit Community College*
Philip M. Lee, *Campbellsville College*
Jery Lemmons, *State Technical Institute–Memphis*
Charles LePore, *Embry-Riddle Aeronautical University*
Robert Lerosen, *Northern Virginia Community College*
Ardyce S. Lightner, *D'Youville College*
Malcom H. Livick, *Blue Ridge Community College*
Mary Alice Lo Cicero, *Oakland Community College*
Chris Lockwood, *Northern Arizona University*
John F. Logan, *Thiel College*
David J. Lonergan, *Greater Hartford Community College*
David H. Lydick, *St. Leo College*
Robert J. Lyons, *Sweet Briar College*
Willard Machen, *Amarillo College*
Anita Marcellis, *College of St. Elizabeth*
John D. McCurdy, *Embry-Riddle Aeronautical University*
Barbara McDonnell, *College of Notre Dame of Maryland*
Robert L. McElwee, *University of Akron*
James L. McGuigan, *Community College of Allegheny County*
James M. McHugh, *St. Louis Community College–Forest Park*
Pat McLaughlin, *Merrimac College*
Edward Meier, *Concordia College*
Peggy C. Mifflin, *Indiana State University*
Robert A. Moore, *Southern Utah State*
James Moreau, *Rock Valley College*
Bill Morris, *Devry Institute of Technology*
J. B. Mosca, *Monmouth College*
Alexander Mosley, *Miami-Dade Community College*
Bonnie S. Moyers, *Blue Ridge Community College*

Eugene Murkison, *Georgia Southern University*
John E. Murray, *Massasoit Community College*
M. James Nead, *Vincennes University*
Thomas Nist, *La Roche College*
Janet M. Noble, *University of Maryland*
James Nordin, *Coffeyville Community College*
Christopher E. Nussbaumer, *Austin Peay State University*
Erna O'Connor, *Kishwaukee College*
Diana Page, *University of West Florida*
Karl Pape, *Embry-Riddle Aeronautical University*
Michael H. Parson, *Hagerstown Junior College*
John Paxton, *Southwest Missouri State University*
Joseph O. Pecenka, *Northern Illinois University*
Dennis Pennington, *Spartanburg Methodist College*
Shri Penugonda, *Wilkes College*
Joseph Platts, *Miami-Dade Community College*
Shane Premeaux, *McNeese State University*
Rebecca Pyrne, *Wilmington College*
William Racker, *Anoka-Ramsey Community College*
Kenneth J. Radig, *Medaille College*
Harry Ramsden, *University of LaVerne–NAS No. Island*
Richard Raspen, *Wilkes College*
Mary C. Raven, *Mount Mary College*
Wm. R. Rawlinson, *Solano Community College*
Morris Dale Reed, *East Central University*
Harriet Rice, *Los Angeles City College*
Charles A. Rickman, *University of Arts and Sciences*
Robert Roller, *Oral Roberts University*
Peggy Romanelli, *Oral Roberts University*
Stanford H. Rosenberg, *La Roche College*
Greg Runyon, *Trevecca Nazarene College*
Mary Beth Ruthem, *Jefferson Tech College*
Robb Ruyle, *Mesa College*
Madan Saluja, *Lake Superior State College*
Richard D. Sambuco, *West Virginia Northern Community College*
Cheryl Savage, *California State Polytechnic University–Pomona*
Clemmie Saxon, *Howard University*
Dietrich L. Schaupp, *West Virginia University*
Suzanne Seedorf, *Northeast Iowa Technical Institute*
Charles R. Schatzer, *Solano Community College*
David Shepard, *Virginia Western Community College*
Frederick Sheppard, *Bridgewater State College*
Steven Shiring, *Butler County Community College*
Sara Shryock, *Black Hills State College*
Jack Skaggs, *Oklahoma Christian College*

I have the deepest respect and warmest regard for my colleagues at the Roy E. Crummer Graduate School of Business at Rollins College. They continue to encourage and inspire me to develop the best possible *Modern Management* learning package. James M. Higgins, Theodore T. Herbert, and Max R. Richards, my management colleagues, have been especially supportive. Having recently been appointed Dean of the Crummer School, I look forward to the challenge of being both an administrator and a scholar. I am especially thankful for the support of Dr. Rita Bornstein, President of Rollins College, in providing me the opportunity to meet this exciting professional challenge. Meeting such a challenge will undoubtedly help me to better understand and maintain Crummer's fine tradition of excellence in management education and scholarship.

The support that Allyn and Bacon has given throughout this project has been invaluable. As editor, Rich Wohl has shown amazing insight and book savvy in helping me to develop this revision. Professionals such as Judy Fifer, Marjorie Payne, and Mary Beth Finch played critical roles in both the planning and evolution of this project. Mary Jo Gregory has ushered my manuscript through the production process smoothly and efficiently. John Isley and Bill Barke, respectively the president and vice president of Allyn and Bacon, have afforded me many important insights about the more general world of publishing that have helped me to improve this text. I thank the entire Allyn and Bacon family for its patience in listening to my ideas and appropriately improving, discarding, or accepting them. The healthy exchange of ideas between author and publisher that characterized this revision process is a primary reason that the text you see today is of such high quality.

From a more personal viewpoint, my family was always there to help me handle the difficult challenges that inevitably accompany the task of publishing a comprehensive text of this magnitude. My wife, Mimi, is simply the best! My children, Trevis, Matthew, Sarah, and Brian have no idea that the care they show is so inspirational to me. The strength shown by my father, Sam, and my mother, Annette, in handling personal challenges throughout their lives will always "show me the way."

IBM Rochester (Rochester, Minnesota) won the Malcolm Baldrige Award in 1990 in the manufacturing division of that award. The large Minnesota facility, home of the AS/400 family of computers and advanced direct access storage products, won the award for the combined excellence of all of its operations.

Introduction to Management

The purpose of this section is to introduce the field of management. In general terms, the introduction is accomplished through extended discussion on how management is defined, on various approaches to management that have evolved over the years, and on social responsibility and ethics. In more specific terms, this section offers a thorough explanation of the steps of the management process, of managerial effectiveness and efficiency, of the skills needed by managers, and of what can be expected from a management career. The explanation of different ways to perform the manager's job emphasizes the classical, behavioral, management science, contingency, and systems approaches. Last, this section discusses fundamentals of social responsibility, social responsiveness, social responsibility and management functions, and ethics.

As you study chapters in this section, keep in mind that this material is extremely important. An understanding of these foundation concepts will significantly influence your ability to understand the material in the remaining sections of the text.

Chapter 1

tudent Learning Objectives

From studying this chapter, I will attempt to acquire:

1. An understanding of the importance of management to society and individuals.

2. An understanding of the role of management.

3. An ability to define management in several different ways.

4. An ability to list and define the basic functions of management.

5. Working definitions of managerial effectiveness and managerial efficiency.

6. An understanding of basic management skills and their relative importance to managers.

7. An understanding of the universality of management.

8. Insights concerning what careers are and how they evolve.

Management and Management Careers

hapter Outline

CINEPLEX ODEON

When business was good, Garth Drabinsky, founder and chairman of the Cineplex Odeon movie-theater chain, was not shy about discussing his business accomplishments. According to Drabinsky, his company was more instrumental in determining how people saw movies than was any other company in the industry.*

The history of Cineplex Odeon is interesting. Drabinsky purchased his first movie theater in 1978. From this one facility, in a few short years Drabinsky built Cineplex Odeon to be one of the largest and most profitable movie chains in North America. The chain consisted of about 475 screens in Canada and 701 in the United States. Drabinsky seemed to be guided by one goal—"build, build, build." His

> Drabinsky seemed to be guided by one goal—"build, build, build."

aspirations were to have hundreds of screens in major metropolitan areas such as Chicago, Los Angeles, Seattle, and Minneapolis. As Drabinsky pursued his expansion, however, he needed about $125 million more than the $600 million that he had available for investment. He had to incur significant additional debt to make his expansion plans a reality.†

Drabinsky was employed as an entertainment attorney and real estate investor before buying his first theater. These experiences seemed to allow him to be more creative than his competitors in conducting business. As an example, in a very creative deal Drabinsky tied the First Chicago Bank in with Cineplex Odeon's 40 theaters and 150 screens in the Chicago area. When customers opened new accounts, they would receive $20 in gift certificates to be spent at Cineplex Odeon. As another testimony to his creativity, Drabinsky built his empire on the concept that part of the moviegoing experience is to see a movie in a large, elaborate building with an indoor cafe.** Initially, at least, customers seemed to respond positively to Drabinsky's concept.

Recently, however, the financial fortunes of Drabinsky and his Cineplex Odeon chain have turned. A 1988 earnings report for Cineplex Odeon showed a loss of $41 million. Part of the problem may be that the movie-house capacity of North America is quickly becoming saturated.†† Perhaps the most significant problem is that the Cineplex Odeon empire seems to have been guided by Drabinsky's financial expertise rather than his management expertise.

*Joshua Hammer, "Fast Fade for Cinema King," *Newsweek.* November 6, 1989, 61.
†Chuck Hawkins, "Umpteen Screens—and Oodles of Debt," *Business Week.* October 10, 1988, 148.
**Alex Ben Block, "Garth Drabinsky's Pleasure Domes," *Forbes.* June 2, 1986, 90–94.
††Dana Wechsler, "Every Trick in the Books," *Forbes.* May 29, 1989, 46, 48.

WHAT'S AHEAD

As discussed in the introductory case, the history of Cineplex Odeon is characterized by an accelerating as well as a more recent decelerating profit trend. The case ends with the thought that perhaps the company has recently become much less successful because Drabinsky, its chairman, lacks a basic understanding of what management entails. The information in this chapter is designed to help an individual like Drabinsky understand the basics of management. Management is defined through (1) a discussion of its importance both to society and to individuals, (2) a description of the management task, (3) a discussion of its universality, and (4) insights about management careers.

THE IMPORTANCE OF MANAGEMENT

Managers influence all phases of our modern organizations. Plant managers run manufacturing operations that produce our clothes, food, and automobiles. Sales managers maintain a sales force that markets goods. Personnel managers provide organizations with a competent and productive work force. The "jobs available" section in the classified advertisements of any major newspaper describes many different types of management activities and confirms the importance of management (see Figure 1.1 on page 6).

Our society simply could not exist as we know it today or improve its present status without a steady stream of managers to guide its organizations. Peter Drucker makes this point in stating that effective management is probably the main resource of developed countries and the most needed resource of developing ones.[1] In short, countries desperately need good managers.

In addition to being important to our society as a whole, management is vital to many individuals simply because they earn their living by being managers. Government statistics show that management positions have increased from approximately 10 percent to approximately 18 percent of the work force since 1950.[2] Managers typically come from varying backgrounds and have diverse educational specialties. Many individuals who originally trained to be accountants, teachers, financiers, or even writers eventually make their livelihoods as managers. In the short term, the demand for managers may vary somewhat from year to year. In the long term, managerial positions can yield high salaries, status, interesting work, personal growth, and intense feelings of accomplishment. To illustrate how substantial management salaries can be, consider the results of a 1990 poll by *Forbes* magazine ranking the highest total compensation amounts paid by organizations to managers.* Based on the results of the *Forbes* poll, Figure 1.2 on page 7 lists the top ten compensation packages paid to managers during 1989, the companies that paid them, and the managers who received them.[3]

---

*The *Forbes* poll defined *total compensation* as the total amount paid to a manager through salary, bonus, other sources like benefits, and value of company stock owned.

SR. MANAGEMENT DEVELOPMENT SPECIALIST

We are a major metropolitan service employer of over 5,000 employees seeking a person to join our management development staff. Prospective candidates will be degreed with 5 to 8 years experience in the design, implementation, and evaluation of developmental programs for first line and mid-level management personnel. Additionally, candidates must demonstrate exceptional oral and written communications ability and be skilled in performance analysis, programmed instruction, and the design and the implementation of reinforcement systems.

If you meet these qualifications, please send your resume, including salary history and requirements to:

Box RS-653
An Equal Opportunity Employer

BRANCH MGR–$30,500. Perceptive pro with track record in administration and lending has high visibility with respected firm.
Box PH-165

AVIATION FBO MANAGER NEEDED

Southeast Florida operation catering to corporate aviation. No maintenance or aircraft sales–just fuel and the best service. Must be experienced. Salary plus benefits commensurate with qualifications. Submit complete resume to:

Box LJO-688

DIVISION CREDIT MANAGER

Major mgf. corporation seeks an experienced credit manager to handle the credit and collection function of its midwest division (Chicago area). Interpersonal skills are important, as is the ability to communicate effectively with senior management. Send resume with current compensation to:

Box NM–43

ACCOUNTING MANAGER

Growth opportunity. Michigan Ave. location. Acctg. degree, capable of supervision. Responsibilities include G/L, financial statements, inventory control, knowledge of systems design for computer applications. Send resume, incl. salary history to:

Box RJM-999
An Equal Opportunity Employer

FINANCIAL MANAGER

CPA/MBA (U of C) with record of success in mngmnt positions. Employed, now seeking greater opportunity. High degree of professionalism, exp. in dealing w/financial inst., strong communication & analytical skills, stability under stress, high energy level, results oriented. Age 34, 11 yrs exper. incl. major public acctng, currently 5 years as Financial VP of field leader. Impressive references. **Box LML-666**

MARKET MANAGER

Major lighting manufacturer seeks market manager for decorative outdoor lighting. Position entails establishing and implementing marketing, sales, and new product development programs including coordination of technical publications and related R & D projects. Must locate at Denver headquarters. Send resume to **Box WM-214**
No agencies please

GENERAL MANAGER

Small industrial service company, privately owned, located in Springfield, Missouri, needs aggressive, skilled person to make company grow in profits and sales. Minimum B. S. in Business, experienced in all facets of small business operations. Must understand profit. Excellent opportunity and rewards. Salary and fringes commensurate with experience and performance. **Box LEM-116**

FOUNDRY SALES MANAGER

Aggressive gray iron foundry located in the Midwest, specializing in 13,000 tons of complex castings yearly with a weight range of 2 to 400 pounds, is seeking experienced dynamic sales manager with sound sales background in our industry. Salary commensurate with experience and excellent benefit package. **Box MO-948**

PERSONNEL MANAGER

Pubicly owned, national manufacturer with 12 plants, 700 employees, seeks first corporate personnel director. We want someone to administer programs in:

- Position and rate evaluation
- Employee safety engineering
- Employee training
- Employee communications
- Employee benefits
- Federal compliance

Qualifications: minimum of 3-5 years personnel experience in mfg. company, ability to tactfully deal with employees at all levels from all walks of life, free to travel. Position reports to Vice President, Operations. Full range of company benefits, salary $32,000-40,000. Reply in complete confidence to:

Box JK-236

FIGURE 1.1

The variety of management positions available

Company/chief executive	Compensation*			
	Sal + Bonus	Other	Stock Gains	Total
McCaw Cellular/Craig O. McCaw	$289	—	$53,655	$53,944
LIN Broadcasting/Donald A. Pels	1,363	—	21,428	22,791
Lotus Development/Jim P. Manzi	991	$49	15,372	16,412
Reebok International/Paul B. Fireman	14,606	—	—	14,606
BHC Commun/Herbert J. Siegel	13,687	14	—	13,702
Freeport-McMoRan/James R. Moffett	1,359	1,086	11,072	13,517
Torchmark/Ronald K. Richey	1,084	48	11,588	12,719
Great A&P Tea/James Wood	3,193	2,024	5,900	11,117
Coca-Cola/Roberto C. Goizueta	2,542	2,400	5,872	10,814
Walt Disney/Michael D. Eisner	9,589	6	—	9,595

* All dollar amounts in thousands

FIGURE 1.2
The ten highest total compensation amounts recently paid to managers

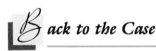 ack to the Case

The information just presented furnishes an individual like Drabinsky with insights concerning the significance of his role as manager. His role as a manager is important not only to society as a whole but also to himself as an individual. In general, as a manager he makes some contribution to creating the standard of living that we all enjoy and thereby earns corresponding rewards. Given the present status of Cineplex Odeon, the societal contributions that it can presently make will be fewer than it has made in the past. If the company becomes more successful, however, its positive effect on society will undoubtedly be more significant in the future.

THE MANAGEMENT TASK

Besides understanding the significance of being a manager and its related potential benefits, prospective managers should know what the management task entails. The sections that follow introduce the basics of the management task through discussions of the role and definition of management.

The Role of Management

Essentially, the role of managers is to guide organizations toward goal accomplishment. All organizations exist for some purpose or goal, and managers have the responsibility for combining and using organizational resources to ensure that the organizations achieve their purpose. Management moves organizations toward purposes or goals by assigning activities that organization members perform. If the activities are designed effectively, the production of each individual worker represents a contribution to the attainment of organizational goals. Management strives to encourage individual activity that will lead to reaching organizational goals and to discourage individual activity that will hinder organizational goal accomplishment. "There is no idea more important to managing than goals. Management has no meaning apart from its goals."[4] Management must keep organizational goals in mind at all times.

Defining Management

Students of management should be aware that the term *management* can be and often is used in several different ways.[5] For instance, it can refer simply to the process that managers follow to accomplish organizational goals. It can also be used to refer to a body of knowledge. In this context, it is a cumulative body of information that furnishes insights on how to manage. Management also can be the term used to pinpoint the individuals who guide and direct organizations or to designate a career devoted to the task of guiding and directing organizations. An understanding of the various uses and related definitions of the term should help students and practitioners eliminate miscommunication during management-related discussions.

As used most commonly in this text, **management** is the process of reaching organizational goals by working with and through people and other organizational resources. A comparison of this definition with the definitions offered by several contemporary management thinkers shows that there is some agreement that management has the following three main characteristics: (1) it is a process or series of continuing and related activities; (2) it involves and concentrates on reaching organizational goals; and (3) it reaches these goals by working with and through people and other organizational resources (see Table 1.1). A discussion of each of these characteristics follows.

Management is the process of reaching organizational goals by working with and through people and other organizational resources.

TABLE 1.1 Contemporary definitions of management

Management—
1. Is the process by which a cooperative group directs actions of others toward common goals (Massie and Douglas).
2. Is the process of working with and through others to effectively achieve organizational objectives by efficiently using limited resources in a changing environment (Kreitner).
3. Is the coordination of all resources through the processes of planning, organizing, directing, and controlling in order to attain stated objectives (Sisk).
4. Is establishing an effective environment for people operating in formal organizational groups (Koontz and O'Donnell).
5. Entails activities undertaken by one or more persons in order to coordinate the activities of others in the pursuit of ends that cannot be achieved by any one person (Donnelly, Gibson, and Ivancevich).

The Management Process: Management Functions

The four basic **management functions**—activities that make up the management process—are as follows:

1. *Planning.* Planning involves choosing tasks that must be performed to attain organizational goals, outlining how the tasks must be performed, and indicating when the tasks should be performed. Planning activity focuses on attaining goals. Managers, through their plans, outline exactly what organizations must do to be successful. They are concerned with organizational success in the near future (short term) as well as in the more distant future (long term).

2. *Organizing.* Organizing can be thought of as assigning the tasks developed during planning to various individuals or groups within the organization. Organizing creates a mechanism to put plans into action. People within the organization are given work assignments that contribute to goal attainment. Tasks are organized so that the output of individuals contributes to the success of departments, which contributes to the success of divisions, which in turn contributes to the overall success of organizations.

3. *Influencing.* Influencing is another of the basic functions within the management process. This function—also commonly referred to as motivating, leading, directing, and actuating—is concerned primarily with people within organizations.* Influencing can be defined as the process of guiding the activities of organization members in appropriate directions. An appropriate direction is any direction that helps the organization move toward goal attainment. The ultimate purpose of influencing is to increase productivity. Human oriented work situations usually generate higher levels of production over the long term than do work situations that people find distasteful.

4. *Controlling.* Controlling is the management function for which managers (a) gather information that measures recent performance within the organization; (b) compare present performance to preestablished performance standards; and (c) from this comparison, determine if the organization should be modified to meet preestablished standards. Controlling is an ongoing process. Managers continually gather information, make their comparisons, and then try to find new ways of improving production through organizational modification.

Management functions are activities that make up the management process.

Management Process and Goal Attainment

Although the four functions of management have been discussed individually, planning, organizing, influencing, and controlling are integrally related and cannot be separated. Figure 1.3 on page 10 illustrates this interrelationship and also that managers use these activities solely for the purpose of reaching organizational goals. Basically, these functions are interrelated because the performance of one depends on the performance of the others. To illustrate, organizing is based on well-thought-out plans developed during the planning process, and influencing systems must be tailored to reflect both these plans and the organizational design

---

*In early management literature, the term *motivating* was more commonly used to signify this people-oriented management function. The term *influencing* is used consistently in this text because it is broader and allows more flexibility in discussions of people-oriented issues. Later in the text, motivating is discussed as a major part of influencing.

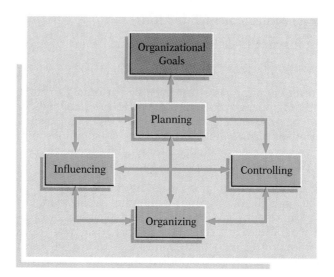

FIGURE 1.3

Interrelations of the four functions of management to attain organizational goals

used to implement them. The fourth function, controlling, proposes possible modifications to existing plans, organizational structure, or the motivation system to develop a more successful effort.

To be effective, a manager must understand how the four management functions must be practiced, not simply how they are defined and related. Thomas J. Peters and Robert H. Waterman, Jr., studied numerous organizations—including Frito-Lay and Maytag—for several years to determine what management characteristics best described excellently run companies. Table 1.2 contains the list and descriptions of characteristics finally developed by Peters and Waterman and published in their book *In Search of Excellence*. This list implies that planning, organizing, influencing, and controlling should be characterized by a bias for action; a closeness to the customer; autonomy and entrepreneurship; productivity through people; a hands-on, value-driven orientation; "sticking to the knitting"; a simple form with a lean staff; and simultaneous loose-tight properties.

The information in this section has been only a brief introduction to the four management functions. Later sections are devoted to developing these functions in much more detail.

Management and Organizational Resources

Organizational resources are assets available for activation during normal operations, including human resources, monetary resources, raw materials resources, and capital resources.

Management must always be aware of the status and use of **organizational resources.** These resources, composed of all assets available for activation during the production process, are of four basic types: (1) human, (2) monetary, (3) raw materials, and (4) capital. As Figure 1.4 on page 12 depicts, organizational resources are combined, used, and transformed into finished products during the production process.

Human resources are the people who work for an organization. The skills they possess and their knowledge of the work system are invaluable to managers.

TABLE 1.2 Characteristics of excellently run companies

1. *A bias for action,* for getting on with it. Even though these companies may be analytical in their approach to decision making, they are not paralyzed by that fact (as so many others seem to be). In many of these companies, the standard operating procedure is "Do it, fix it, try it." Moreover, the companies are experimenters supreme. Instead of allowing 250 engineers and marketers to work on a new product in isolation for fifteen months, they form bands of 5 to 25 and test ideas out on a customer, often with inexpensive prototypes, within a matter of weeks. What is striking is the host of practical devices the excellent companies employ to maintain corporate fleetness of foot and counter the stultification that almost inevitably comes with size.

2. *Close to the customer.* These companies learn from the people they serve. They provide unparalleled quality, service, and reliability—things that work and last. They succeed in differentiating—*à la* Frito-Lay (potato chips), Maytag (washers), or Tupperware—the most commodity-like products. IBM's marketing vice president, Francis G. (Buck) Rodgers, says, "It's a shame that, in so many companies, whenever you get good service, it's an exception." Not so at the excellent companies. Everyone gets into the act. Many of the innovative companies got their best product ideas from customers. That comes from listening—intently and regularly.

3. *Autonomy and entrepreneurship.* The innovative companies foster many leaders and many innovators throughout the organization. They are a hive of what we've come to call champions; 3M has been described as "so intent on innovation that its essential atmosphere seems not like that of a large corporation but rather a loose network of laboratories and cubbyholes populated by feverish inventors and dauntless entrepreneurs who let their imaginations fly in all directions." They don't try to hold everyone on so short a rein that creativity is stifled. They encourage practical risk taking, and support good tries. They follow Fletcher Byrom's ninth commandment: "Make sure you generate a reasonable number of mistakes."

4. *Productivity through people.* The excellent companies treat the rank and file as the source of quality and productivity gain. They do not foster we/they labor attitudes or regard capital investment as the fundamental source of efficiency improvement. As Thomas J. Watson Jr., said of his company, "IBM's philosophy is largely contained in three simple beliefs. I want to begin with what I think is the most important: *our respect for the individual.*

This is a simple concept, but in IBM it occupies a major portion of management time." Texas Instrument's chairman Mark Shepherd talks about it in terms of every worker's being "seen as a source of ideas, not just acting as a pair of hands"; each of his more than 9,000 People Involvement Program, or PIP, teams (Texas Instrument's quality circles) does contribute to the company's sparkling productivity record.

5. *Hands-on, value driven.* Thomas Watson Jr., said that "the basic philosophy of an organization has far more to do with its achievements than do technological or economic resources, organizational structure, innovation, and timing." Watson and Hewlett-Packard's William Hewlett are legendary for walking the plant floors. McDonald's Ray Kroc regularly visited stores and assessed them on the factors the company holds dear, Q.S.C. & V. (Quality, Service, Cleanliness, and Value.)

6. *"Stick to the knitting."* Robert W. Johnson, former Johnson & Johnson chairman, put it this way: "Never acquire a business you don't know how to run." Or as Edward G. Harness, past chief executive at Procter & Gamble, said, "This company has never left its base. We seek to be anything but a conglomerate." While there were a few exceptions, the odds for excellent performance seem strongly to favor those companies that stay reasonably close to businesses they know.

7. *Simple form, lean staff.* As big as most of the companies we have looked at are, none was formally run with a matrix organization structure, and some which had tried that form had abandoned it. The underlying structural forms and systems in the excellent companies are elegantly simple. Top-level staffs are lean; it is not uncommon to find a corporate staff of fewer than 100 people running multi-billion-dollar enterprises.

8. *Simultaneous loose-tight properties.* The excellent companies are both centralized and decentralized. For the most part, as we have said, they have pushed autonomy down to the shop floor on product development teams. On the other hand, they are fanatic centralists around the few core values they hold dear. 3M is marked by barely organized chaos surrounding its product champions. Yet one analyst argues, "The brainwashed members of an extremist political sect are no more conformist in their central beliefs." At Digital, the chaos is so rampant that one executive noted, "Damn few people know who they work for." Yet Digital's fetish for reliability is more rigidly adhered to than any outsider could imagine.

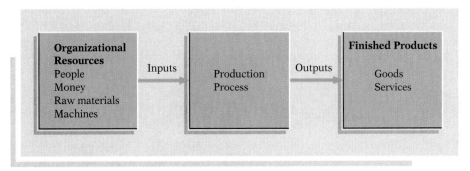

FIGURE 1.4

Transformation of organizational resources into finished products
through the production process

Monetary resources are amounts of money that managers use to purchase goods
and services for the organization. Raw materials are ingredients acquired to be
used directly in the manufacturing of products. For example, rubber is a raw
material that a company such as Goodyear would purchase with its monetary
resources and use directly in the manufacturing of tires. Capital resources are the
machines an organization uses during the manufacturing process. Modern machines, or equipment, can be a major factor in maintaining desired production
levels. Worn-out or antiquated machinery can make it impossible for an organization to keep pace with competitors.

Managerial Effectiveness. As managers use their resources, they must strive
to be both effective and efficient. **Managerial effectiveness** is defined in terms of
resource utilization in relation to organizational goal attainment. If organizations
are using their resources to attain their goals, the managers are effective. In reality,
there are degrees of managerial effectiveness. The closer that organizations come
to achieving their goals, the more effective the managers are said to be. Managerial
effectiveness can be depicted as being on a continuum ranging from ineffective to
effective.

Managerial Efficiency. **Managerial efficiency** is defined in terms of the proportion of total organizational resources that contribute to productivity during
the manufacturing process. The higher this proportion, the more efficient the
manager. The more resources wasted or unused during the production process,
the more inefficient the manager. As with management effectiveness, management
efficiency is best described as being on a continuum ranging from inefficient to
efficient. *Inefficient* means that a very small proportion of total resources contributes to productivity during the manufacturing process; *efficient* means that a very
large proportion contributes.

As Figure 1.5 shows, the concepts of managerial effectiveness and efficiency
are obviously related. A manager could be relatively ineffective, the organization
making very little progress toward goal attainment, primarily because of major
inefficiencies or poor utilization of resources during the production process. In
contrast, a manager could be somewhat effective despite being inefficient. Demand
for the finished goods may be so high that the manager can get an extremely high
price per unit sold and thus absorb inefficiency costs.

Managerial effectiveness is the
degree to which management
attains organizational objectives.
It is measured by how close organizations come to achieving
their goals.

Managerial efficiency is the degree to which organizational resources contribute to
productivity. It is measured by
the proportion of organizational
resources used during the production process.

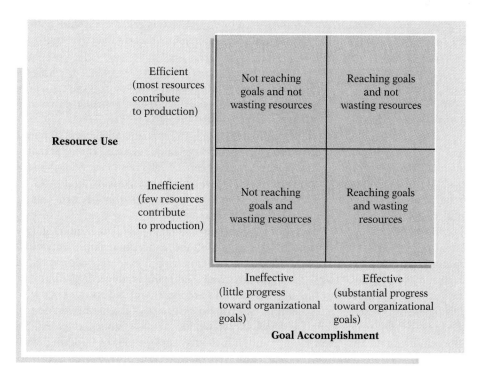

		Ineffective (little progress toward organizational goals)	Effective (substantial progress toward organizational goals)
Resource Use	Efficient (most resources contribute to production)	Not reaching goals and not wasting resources	Reaching goals and not wasting resources
	Inefficient (few resources contribute to production)	Not reaching goals and wasting resources	Reaching goals and wasting resources

FIGURE 1.5

Various combinations of managerial effectiveness and managerial efficiency

For example, some oil companies in Saudi Arabia could probably absorb many managerial inefficiencies when oil sells at a high price. Management in this situation has a chance to be somewhat effective despite its inefficiency. Thus, a manager can be effective without being efficient and vice versa. To maximize organizational success, however, both effectiveness and efficiency are needed.

 ack to the Case

The information just presented contains more specific information on what management is and what managers do. According to this information, as a manager Drabinsky must have a clear understanding of Cineplex Odeon objectives and guide the organization toward reaching these objectives. This guidance, of course, will involve his working more directly with other top managers at Cineplex Odeon headquarters as well as perhaps more indirectly with managers of specific theater locations throughout the country.

Drabinsky must be heavily involved in planning, organizing, influencing, and controlling. In other words, he will have to outline how jobs must be performed to reach objectives, assign these jobs to appropriate workers, encourage the workers to perform their jobs, and make any changes necessary to ensure reaching company objectives. As he performs these four functions at Cineplex Odeon, Drabinsky must remember that the activities themselves are interrelated and must blend together appropriately.

Wise use of organizational resources by Drabinsky is critical. He must strive to be both effective and efficient—to reach Cineplex Odeon objectives without wasting company resources.

Management Skills. No discussion of organizational resources would be complete without the mention of management skills, perhaps the primary determinant of how effective and efficient managers will be.

According to a classic article by Robert L. Katz, managerial success depends primarily on performance rather than personality traits.[6] Katz also states that a manager's ability to perform is a result of the managerial skills possessed. A manager with the necessary management skills will probably perform well and be relatively successful. One without the necessary skills will probably perform poorly and be relatively unsuccessful.

Technical skills are the ability to apply specialized knowledge and expertise to work-related techniques and procedures.

Human skills are skills involving the ability to build cooperation within the team being led.

Conceptual skills are skills that involve the ability to see the organization as a whole.

Katz indicates that three types of skills are important for successful management performance: technical skills, human skills, and conceptual skills. **Technical skills** involve using specialized knowledge and expertise in executing work-related techniques and procedures. Examples of these skills are engineering, computer programming, and accounting. Technical skills are mostly related to working with "things"—processes or physical objects. **Human skills** are skills that build cooperation within the team being led. They involve working with attitudes, communication, individuals and groups, and individual interests—in short, working with people. **Conceptual skills** involve the ability to see the organization as a whole. A manager with conceptual skills is able to understand how various functions of the organization complement one another, how the organization relates to its environment, and how changes in one part of the organization affect the rest of the organization.

As one moves from lower-level management to upper-level management, conceptual skills become more important and technical skills less important (see Figure 1.6). The supportive rationale is that as managers advance in an organization, they

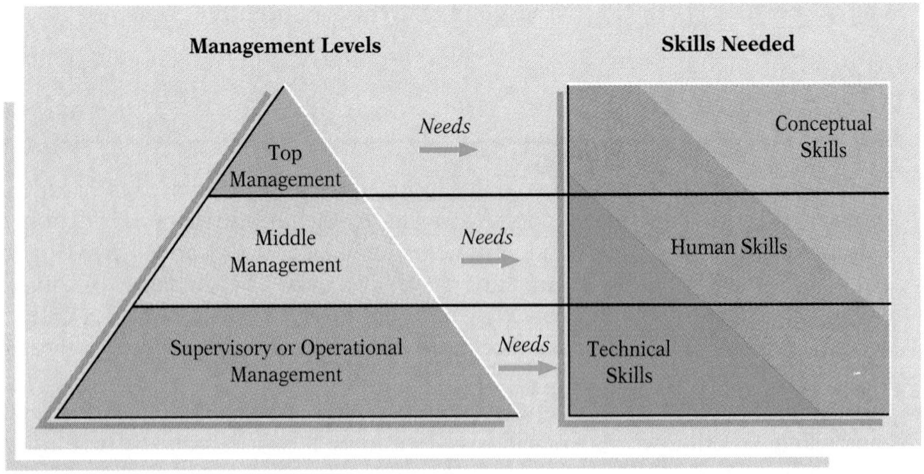

FIGURE 1.6

As a manager moves from the supervisory to the top management level, conceptual skills become more important than technical skills, but human skills remain equally important

become less involved with the actual production activity or technical areas and more involved with guiding the organization as a whole. Human skills, however, are extremely important to managers at top, middle,[7] and lower (or supervisory) levels.[8] The common denominator of all management levels is people.

THE UNIVERSALITY OF MANAGEMENT

Management principles are **universal;** that is, they apply to all types of organizations (businesses, churches, sororities, athletic teams, hospitals, and so on) and organizational levels. Naturally, managers' jobs are somewhat different in each of these organizations because each organization requires the use of specialized knowledge, exists in unique working and political environments, and uses different technology. However, job similarities also exist because of the common basic management activities necessary in all organizations: planning, organizing, influencing, and controlling.

Universality of management principles means that the principles of management are applicable to all types of organizations and organizational levels.

Henri Fayol, one of the earliest management writers, stated that all managers should possess certain characteristics, such as positive physical qualities, mental qualities, and special knowledge related to the specific operation.[9] B. C. Forbes, also describing managerial characteristics, has emphasized the importance of certain more personal qualities in successful managers. He has inferred that enthusiasm, earnestness of purpose, confidence, and faith in their worthwhileness are primary characteristics of successful managers. Forbes has described Henry Ford as follows:

> At the base and birth of every great business organization was an enthusiast, a man consumed with earnestness of purpose, with confidence in his powers, with faith in the worthwhileness of his endeavors. The original Henry Ford was the quintessence of enthusiasm. In the days of his difficulties, disappointments, and discouragements, when he was wrestling with his balky motor engine—and wrestling likewise with poverty—only his inexhaustible enthusiasm saved him from defeat.[10]

Fayol and Forbes can describe these desirable characteristics of successful managers only because of the universality concept: the basic ingredients of the successful management situation are applicable to organizations of all types.

ack to the Case

Drabinsky will be successful as the chairman at Cineplex Odeon only if he possesses technical skills, human skills, and conceptual skills. In order to be successful, a relatively low-level manager at Cineplex Odeon would generally need, probably in order of importance, first human skills, then technical skills, and finally conceptual skills. As a top manager at the company, Drabinsky would normally need, probably in order of importance again, human skills, conceptual skills, and then technical skills. In general, as lower-level managers in the company take over middle- and upper-level management positions, the ranking of skills importance changes by adding more importance to conceptual skills and less importance to technical skills.

A manager like Drabinsky usually finds that, as he gains experience in managing, his cumulative management experience is valuable in whatever management position he may hold either at Cineplex Odeon, in some other movie theater company, or even in some other business altogether. Drabinsky will also likely discover that, as his enthusiasm, earnestness, confidence, and faith in his own worthwhileness become more pronounced personal qualities, he will tend to become a more successful manager.

MANAGEMENT CAREERS

Thus far, this chapter has focused on outlining the importance of management to our society, presenting a definition of management and the management process, and explaining the universality of management. Individuals commonly study such topics because they are interested in pursuing a management career. This section presents information that will help students preview what might characterize their own management careers and describes some of the issues they might face in attempting to manage the careers of others within an organization. The specific focus is on career definition, career and life stages and performance, and career promotion.

A Definition of Career

A **career** is an individual's perceived sequence of attitudes and behaviors associated with the performance of work-related experiences and activities over the span of the person's working life.[11] This definition implies that a career is cumulative in nature. As individuals accumulate successful experiences in one position, they generally develop abilities and attitudes that qualify them to hold more advanced positions. In general, management positions at one level tend to be stepping-stones to management positions at the next higher level.

Career Stages, Life Stages, and Performance

Careers are generally viewed as evolving through a series of stages.[12] The evolutionary stages—exploration, establishment, maintenance, and decline—appear in Figure 1.7. This figure highlights the performance levels and age ranges commonly associated with each stage. The levels and ranges indicate what is likely at each stage, not what is inevitable.

Exploration Stage

The first stage in career evolution is the **exploration stage,** which occurs at the beginning of a career and is characterized by self-analysis and the exploration of different types of available jobs. Individuals at this stage are generally about fifteen to twenty-five years old and involved in some type of formal training, such as college or vocational education. They often pursue part-time employment to gain a richer understanding of what it might be like to have a career in a particular organization or industry. Typical jobs held during this stage might include cooking at Burger King, stocking at a Federated Department Store, or being an office assistant at a Nationwide Insurance office.

A **career** is an individual's perceived sequence of attitudes and behaviors associated with the performance of work-related experiences and activities over the span of the person's working life.

The **exploration stage** is the first stage in career evolution, which occurs at the beginning of a career and is characterized by self-analysis and the exploration of different types of available jobs.

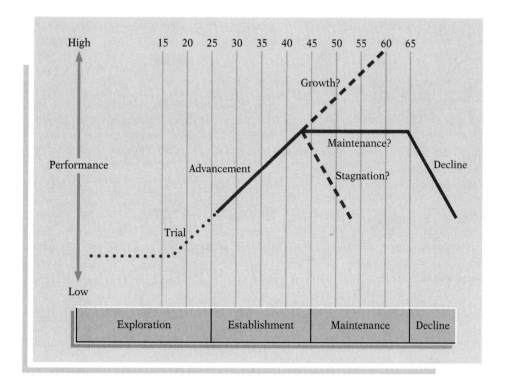

FIGURE 1.7

The relationships among career stages, life stages, and performance

Establishment Stage

The second stage in career evolution is the **establishment stage,** during which individuals who are about twenty-five to forty-five years old typically start to become more productive, or higher performers (as Figure 1.7 indicates by the upturn in the dotted line). Employment sought during this stage is guided by what was learned during the exploration stage. In addition, the jobs sought are usually full time. Individuals at this stage commonly move to different jobs within the same company, to different companies, or even to different industries.

The **establishment stage** is the second stage in career evolution, during which individuals of about twenty-five to forty-five years of age typically start to become more productive or higher performers.

Maintenance Stage

The third stage in career evolution is the **maintenance stage.** In this stage, individuals who are about forty-five to sixty-five years old show either increased performance (career growth), stabilized performance (career maintenance), or decreased performance (career stagnation).

From a managerial viewpoint, it is better to have growth than maintenance or stagnation. Some companies, such as IBM, Monsanto, and Brooklyn Union Gas, attempt to eliminate career plateauing.[13] **Career plateauing** is defined as a period of little or no apparent progress in the growth of a career. Table 1.3 on page 18 shows how Coca-Cola USA has tried to avoid career maintenance and stagnation by ensuring that employees know where to go for career development guidance, know what jobs are open within the company, and know what avenues are available for self-development.[14]

The **maintenance stage** is the third stage in career evolution, during which individuals of about forty-five to sixty-five years of age become more productive, stabilize, or become less productive.

Career plateauing is defined as a period of little or no apparent progress in the growth of a career.

TABLE 1.3 Aspects of Coca-Cola USA that help enhance career growth of employees

- *Newsmakers* is a monthly publication listing moves within Coca-Cola USA. This gives people information on the kinds and number of internal career moves taking place.

- Job posting and the Exempt Job Opening Listing indicate specific open positions of the lower and mid-level management levels.

- Career opportunities booklets provide a broad overview of each department, as well as specific qualifications for typical positions.

- The thirty-page *Career Planning Workbook,* designed specifically for Coca-Cola USA, gives individuals an opportunity to assess their strengths, values, and alternative career directions and provides a structured means of developing a career plan. A worksheet captures all the critical information in one place.

- Career planning can also be explored through a two-day "Career Strategies Workshop." Participants examine themselves, possible career options, and strategies for attaining their goals. A special feature of the program is the opportunity to meet key human resource people representing

each functional area in Coca-Cola USA as well as the larger structure of the Coca-Cola Company.

- The company helps employees develop their skills through an extensive in-house training program. The *Employee Training Catalog,* distributed annually with quarterly updates, lists courses offered by Coca-Cola USA by performance factor, such as organizing and planning. Therefore, if a particular skill area is identified during a performance evaluation or a career discussion, the appropriate course can easily be selected.

- A 100 percent reimbursement tuition aid program offers employees the opportunity to return to school to enhance their formal education.

- On- and off-the-job developmental activities are considered primary opportunities for growth. Employees may ask for feedback from their managers, act as an instructor or trainer, take on new projects, participate on a task force or project team, or join professional organizations. All of these activities allow the development of new professional skills and contribute to professional growth.

Decline Stage

The **decline stage** is the fourth and last stage in career evolution, which occurs near retirement and during which individuals about sixty-five years of age or older show declining productivity.

The last stage in career evolution is the **decline stage,** which involves people of about sixty-five years and older whose productivity may be declining. These individuals are either close to retirement, semiretired, or retired. People at this stage may find it difficult to maintain prior performance levels perhaps because they begin to lose interest in their careers or fail to keep their job skills up to date. As people live longer and stay healthier, many of them become part-time workers in businesses such as Publix supermarkets and McDonald's and in volunteer groups such as the March of Dimes and the American Heart Association. Some retired executives put their career experience to good use by working with the government-sponsored organization SCORE–Service Corps of Retired Executives. This program offers experienced management advice and consultation to small businesses trying to gain footholds in their markets.

Promoting Your Own Career

Practicing managers[15] and management scholars generally agree that careful formulation and implementation of appropriate tactics can enhance the success of management careers.[16] Planning your career path, the sequence of jobs that you will do along the course of your working life, is your first step in promoting your career. For some people this means planning to ascend the hierarchy of a particular organization. For others it will mean planning a career path within a particular

"As this is your proposal, Cosgrove, its failure could mean the end of your career. I think, however, that is an acceptable risk."

From Warren Keith Schilit, "What's the Logic of Strategic Planning?" *Management Review* (November 1988), 42. © Leo Cullum, 1991.

profession or series of professions. For everyone, however, career planning should be an ongoing process, beginning with the career's early phases and continuing throughout the career.

Your plan should not be seen as limiting your options. Consider both your strengths and your liabilities and assess what you need from a career. Then explore all the avenues of opportunity open to you both inside and outside the organization. Set your career goals, continually revise and update these goals as your career progresses, and take the steps necessary to accomplish these goals.

Another important tactic in promoting your own career is to work for managers who carry out a realistic and constructive role in the career development of their employees.[17] (The cartoon on this page lightheartedly depicts a manager who is *not* interested in the careers of his employees.) Table 1.4 outlines what career

TABLE 1.4 Manager and employee roles in enhancing employee career development

Dimension	Professional Employee	Manager
Responsibility	Assumes responsibility for individual career development	Assumes responsibility for employee development

Information	Obtains career information through self-evaluation and data collection:
	    What do I enjoy doing?
	    Where do I want to go?
		Provides information by holding up a mirror of reality:
		    How manager views the employee
		    How others view the employee
		    How "things work around here"

Planning	Develops an individual plan to reach objectives	Helps employee assess plan
Follow-through	Invites management support through high performance on the current job by understanding the scope of the job and taking appropriate initiative	Provides coaching and relevant information on opportunities

development responsibility, information, planning, and follow-through might include. This figure also contains an example of a complimentary career development role for a professional employee. Table 1.5 lists several additional tactics for enhancing career success.

To enhance their career success, individuals must be *proactive* rather than *reactive*.[18] That is, they must take specific action to demonstrate their abilities and accomplishments. They must also have a clear idea of the next position they are seeking, the skills they must acquire to function appropriately in that position, and a plan for how they will acquire those skills. Finally, they need to think about the ultimate position they will want and the sequence of positions they must hold in order to gain the skills and attitudes necessary to qualify for that position.

TABLE 1.5 Tips for enhancing your management career

- Remember that good performance that pleases your superiors is the basic foundation of success, but recognize that not all good performance is easily measured. Determine the real criteria by which you are evaluated and be rigorously honest in evaluating your own performance against these criteria.

- Manage your career; be active in influencing decisions, because pure effort is not necessarily rewarded.

- Strive for positions that have high visibility and exposure where you can be a hero observed by higher officials. Check to see that the organization has a formal system of keeping track of young people. Remember that high-risk line jobs tend to offer more visibility than staff positions like corporate planning or personnel, but also that visibility can sometimes be achieved by off-job community activities.

- Develop relations with a mobile senior executive who can be your sponsor. Become a complementary crucial subordinate with different skills from your superior.

- Learn your job as quickly as possible and train a replacement so that you can be available to move and broaden your background in different functions.

- Nominate yourself for other positions: modesty is not necessarily a virtue. However, change jobs for more power and influence, not primarily for status or pay. The latter could be a substitute for a real opportunity to make things happen.

- Before taking a position, rigorously assess your strengths and weaknesses, what you like and don't like. Don't accept a promotion if it draws on your weaknesses and entails mainly activities that you don't like.

- Leave at your convenience, but on good terms without parting criticism of the organization. Do not stay under an immobile superior who is not promoted in three to five years.

- Don't be trapped by formal, narrow job descriptions. Move outside them and probe the limits of your influence.

- Accept that responsibility will always somewhat exceed authority and that organizational politics are inevitable. Establish alliances and fight necessary battles, minimizing upward ones to very important issues.

- Get out of management if you can't stand being dependent on others and having them dependent on you.

- Recognize that you will face ethical dilemmas no matter how moral you try to be. No evidence exists that unethical managers are more successful than ethical ones, but it may well be that those who move faster are less socially conscious. Therefore, from time to time you must examine your personal values and question how much you will sacrifice for the organization.

- Don't automatically accept all tales of managerial perversity that you hear. Attributing others' success to unethical behavior is often an excuse for one's own personal inadequacies. Most of all, don't commit an act which you know to be wrong in the hope that your supervisor will see it as loyalty and reward you for it. Sometimes the supervisor will, but he or she may also sacrifice you when the organization is criticized.

Women in Management

Women in their roles as managers must meet the same challenges in their work environments as men do. However, because women have only recently begun to join the ranks of management in large numbers, they often lack the social network systems and mentor relationships that are so important in the development of a management career. Traditionally, women were also expected to manage families and households while simultaneously handling the pressures and competition of the work force. Some women also encounter sexual harassment in the workplace.

However, Tom Peters, author of the aforementioned classic management book *In Search of Excellence,* believes that women may have an enormous advantage over men in future management situations.[19] He predicts that, in the nineties, networks of relationships will replace rigid organizational structures and star workers will be replaced by teams made up of workers at all levels who are empowered to make decisions. Detailed rules and procedures will be replaced by a flexible system that calls for judgments based on a system of key values and for a constant search for new ways to get the job done. Strengths that are often attributed to women—placing high priority on interrelationships, listening, and motivating others—will be the dominant virtues in the corporation of the nineties.

Dual-Career Couples

Because of the growing number of women at work, many organizations need to consider how dual-career couples affect the work force. The traditional scenario in which a woman takes a supporting role in the development of her spouse's career is being replaced with one of equal work and shared responsibilities for both spouses. This requires a certain amount of flexibility on the part of the couple as well as on the organizations for which they work. Issues such as whose career takes precedence if a spouse is offered a transfer to another city, or who takes the ultimate responsibility for family concerns, point up the fact that dual-career relationships involve trade-offs and that it is very difficult to "have it all."

Studies of dual-career couples reveal that many people cope with their career difficulties in one of the following ways.[20] The couple might develop a commitment to both spouses' careers so that when a decision is made the right for each spouse to pursue a career is taken into consideration. Each member of the relationship is flexible about handling both home- and job-oriented issues. They work out coping mechanisms such as negotiating child care or scheduling shared activities in advance to better manage their work and their family responsibilities. Dual-career couples often find that they must limit their social lives and their volunteer responsibilities in order to slow the pace of their lives. Finally, many couples find that they must take steps to consciously facilitate their mutual career advancement. Organizations that want to retain an employee may find that they need to assist the employee's spouse in his or her career development as well.

A Multicultural Workforce

The term *multicultural* refers to the mix of many different ethnic groups that will be working in business in the United States in the 1990s. Various minority groups are included in that term, including African Americans, Hispanics, Asians, Africans, Native Americans, and Caribbean Islanders. The U.S. Department of Labor estimates that almost one-third of new entrants into the labor force in the 1990s will be members of various minority groups.

Minority groups are still underrepresented in management. The Rutgers University Graduate School of Management and the Program to Increase Minorities in Business found in a 1986 survey of 400 Fortune 1,000 corporations that less than 9 percent of all managers were members of a minority. One reason is a shortage of education among minorities in the fields most in demand by businesses: hard sciences, business administration, and engineering. As a result, many minority members end up in staff rather than line positions and are consequently more likely to be laid off in the event of a downturn. Finally, in some instances discrimination may be responsible for minority workers' being passed over for promotions.

As more and more of the new entrants into the labor market are members of various minority groups, it will be even more important for businesses to recruit talented minority workers. Building community visibility may be the first step a company can take to help minority applicants find them. Arranging internships and career fairs as well as providing financial support are concrete steps that a firm can take. Managers can look within the firm for people who can be promoted. Firms may need to conduct their own training and education programs to provide workers the skills they need to join the ranks of management.

Instead of looking for people who fit into the existing corporate culture, managers should consider talent and diversity. Some managers will be uncomfortable dealing with workers from different backgrounds and different cultures; corporations may need to provide support and reeducation for their own managers, to train them to be sensitive to other cultures. For example, much business jargon in the United States is sports-oriented, such as telling someone to "play hardball." Such terms can be confusing to those from other cultures.

Some American businesses are making a concerted effort to attract and promote minorities. A 1986 *Black Enterprise* magazine survey listed twenty-five firms that were rated by African Americans as good places to work. The survey included Xerox, IBM, Hewlett-Packard, Avon, Philip Morris, AT&T, and Equitable. The multicultural work force of the 1990s will need a new, more flexible and open style of management to reflect the new mix of backgrounds and cultures.[21,22]

MANAGEMENT HIGHLIGHTS: A SPECIAL FEATURE FOR THE REMAINING CHAPTERS

The **law of the situation** indicates that managers continually analyze circumstances within their organizations and apply management concepts to fit them.

The **law of the situation,** based upon the classic work of Mary Parker Follett, indicates that managers must continually analyze unique circumstances within their organizations and especially apply management concepts to fit those circumstances.[23] Managers can understand planning, organizing, influencing, and controlling, but unless they can apply these concepts to deal with specific organizational circumstances, the knowledge is of little value.

Management highlights, a special feature in the remaining chapters, focus on three key areas of management: ethics, quality, and management in a global environment. The feature provides a wealth of examples that show how chapter concepts can be applied to manage organizations. This feature has been purposefully designed to convey a practical understanding of chapter content by emphasizing the application of management concepts by real managers in real organizations. The management sections, titled "Global Highlight," "Ethics Highlight," and "Quality Highlight," offer an assortment of applications involving management positions and companies ranging from top-level to lower-level managers in organizations such as Motorola, Nike, General Electric, and Exxon. Application examples in each chapter emphasize issues related to three important contemporary management themes:

Global Highlights

Modern managers are faced with many challenges involving global business. Some such challenges involve building organizations in developing countries, fighting foreign competition, developing joint ventures with foreign companies, and building a productive work force covering several foreign countries. This management feature illustrates the application of management concepts in meeting international challenges.

Ethics Highlights

Modern managers face the challenge of developing and maintaining social responsibility and ethical practices that are appropriate for their particular organizations. Some such challenges involve issues like settling such questions as, Who within an organization should be involved in performing socially responsible activities, determining the role of ethics in an organization, encouraging ethical behavior in organizations, and determining internal funding for socially responsible activities? This management feature illustrates the application of management concepts in meeting a firm's social responsibility and ethical challenges.

Quality Highlights

Modern managers, perhaps more than any other generation of managers, face the challenge of developing and maintaining high quality in the goods and services they offer the marketplace. High-quality products are defined as goods or services that customers rate as being excellent. Most management theorists and practicing managers agree that if an organization is to be successful in the national and international business world of today, it must offer high-quality goods and services to its customers.

The maintaining of high-quality products has grown from an issue pertinent to the future success of individual businesses to an issue pertinent to the economic success of the United States as a whole. Congress passed the Malcolm Baldrige National Quality Improvement Act in 1987 to encourage a focus on quality products in business organizations throughout the United States.[24] This law establishes the granting of annual national quality awards, called the "Malcolm Baldrige National Quality Awards," to a company or companies doing exemplary work in the area of quality. The Baldrige award, named after the late U.S. Secretary of Commerce, is the highest level of national recognition that a company in the United States can receive, and it demonstrates the growing cooperation of business and government to improve the quality of U.S. goods and services.

Virtually every activity a manager performs can have some impact on the quality of goods or services that an organization produces. Activities such as developing organizational objectives, training organization members, strategic management, and designing organization structures can all affect the quality of goods offered by a company. This management feature illustrates how various management activities can affect product quality.

Studying all of these management highlights carefully will be valuable to you. They help you to build realistic expectations about what being a manager actually means. As applied to career-building, these cases illustrate that, as managers show the ability to solve various organizational problems, they become more valuable to organizations and are more usually recipients of organizational rewards such as promotion and significant pay increases.

 ack to the Case

As with managers of any company, managers at Cineplex Odeon are at various stages of career development. To exemplify how the stages of career development might relate to managers at Cineplex Odeon, let's focus on one particular manager, Martin Plane. Assume that Martin Plane is a regional manager within the company and oversees five of Drabinsky's theaters. He is forty-five years old and is considered a member of the company's middle management.

Plane began his career (exploration stage) in college by considering various areas of study and by holding a number of different types of primarily part-time positions. He delivered pizzas for Domino's Pizza and worked for Scott's, a lawn-care company. He began college at age eighteen and graduated when he was twenty-two.

Plane then moved into the establishment stage of his career. For a few years immediately after graduation, he held full-time trial positions in the movie entertainment industry as well as in the restaurant and retailing industries. What he learned during the career-exploration stage helped him choose the types of full-time trial positions to pursue. At the age of twenty-six, he accepted a trial position as an assistant manager in one of Cineplex Odeon's theaters. Through this position, he discovered that he wanted to remain in the movie entertainment industry in general and at Cineplex Odeon in particular. From the ages of twenty-seven to forty-five, Plane held a number of supervisory and middle-management positions within the company.

Now Plane is moving into an extremely critical stage in his career, the maintenance stage. He could probably remain in his present position and maintain his productivity for several more years. However, he wants to advance his career. Therefore, he must emphasize a proactive attitude by formulating and implementing tactics aimed at enhancing his career success, such as seeking training to develop critical skills or moving to a position that is a prerequisite for other, more advanced positions at Cineplex Odeon.

In the future, as Plane approaches sixty-five years of age (the decline stage), he may want to go from full-time employment to semiretirement. Perhaps he could work for the company or another company in the same industry on a part-time advisory basis or even pursue part-time work in another industry. For example, he might be able to teach a course in small business management at a nearby college.

Action Summary

Circle:

Reread the learning objectives that follow. Each objective is followed by questions. Answering these questions accurately will help you to retain the most important concepts discussed in this chapter. After answering each question, check your answer with the answer key at the end of this chapter. (*Hint:* If you have doubt regarding the correct response, consult the page whose number follows the answer.)

From studying this chapter, I will attempt to acquire:

1. **An understanding of the importance of management to society and individuals.**

T, F   **a.** Managers constitute less than 1 percent of the U.S. work force.

T, F   **b.** Management is important to society.

2. **An understanding of the role of management.**

a, b, c, d, e   **a.** The role of a manager is: (a) to make workers happy; (b) to satisfy only the manager's needs; (c) to make the most profit; (d) to survive in a highly competitive society; (e) to achieve organizational goals.

T, F   **b.** Apart from its goals, management has no meaning.

3. **An ability to define *management* in several different ways.**

a, b, c, d, e   **a.** Management is: (a) a process; (b) reaching organizational goals; (c) utilizing people and other resources; (d) all of the above; (e) a and b.

T, F   **b.** Management is the process of working with people and through people.

4. **An ability to list and define the basic functions of management.**

a, b, c, d, e   **a.** Which of the following is *not* a function of management: (a) influencing; (b) planning; (c) organizing; (d) directing; (e) controlling.

a, b, c, d, e   **b.** The process of gathering information and comparing this information to preestablished standards is part of (a) planning; (b) influencing; (c) motivating; (d) controlling; (e) commanding.

5. **Working definitions of managerial effectiveness and managerial efficiency.**

T, F   **a.** If an organization is using its resources to attain its goals, the organization's managers are efficient.

T, F   **b.** A manager who is reaching goals but wasting resources is efficient but ineffective.

6. **An understanding of basic management skills and their relative importance to managers.**

a, b, c, d, e   **a.** Conceptual skills require that management view the organization as: (a) a profit center; (b) a decision-making unit; (c) a problem-solving group; (d) a whole; (e) individual contributions.

T, F   **b.** Managers require fewer and fewer human skills as they move from lower to higher management levels.

7. **An understanding of the universality of management.**

T, F   **a.** The statement that management principles are universal means that they apply to all types of organizations and organizational levels.

T, F   **b.** The universality of management means that management principles are taught the same way in all schools.

8. Insights concerning what management careers are and how they evolve.

T, F   **a.** In general, as careers evolve, individuals tend to further develop job skills but show very little or no change in attitude about various job circumstances.

T, F   **b.** Individuals tend to show the first significant increase in performance during the establishment career stage.

T, F   **c.** Tips for enhancing the success of your career should not be seen as very useful over the long run.

Introductory Case Wrap-Up: Cineplex Odeon

"Cineplex Odeon" and its related back-to-the-case sections were written to help you better understand the management concepts contained in this chapter. Answer the following discussion questions about this introductory case to further enrich your understanding of the chapter content:

1. Would you like to manage one of Cineplex Odeon's theaters? Why?

2. What do you think you'd like most about being a manager? What would you like least?

3. You have just been appointed a regional manager at Cineplex Odeon with responsibility for supervising five theaters in Nashville, Tennessee. List and describe five activities that you think you'll have to perform as part of this job.

Issues for Review and Discussion

1. What is the main point illustrated in the introductory case on Cineplex Odeon?

2. How important is the management function to society?

3. How important is the management function to individuals?

4. What is the basic role of the managers?

5. How is *management* defined in this text? What main themes are contained in this definition?

6. List and define each of the four functions of management.

7. Outline the relationship between the four management functions.

8. List and describe five of Peters and Waterman's characteristics of excellent companies, and explain how each of these characteristics could affect planning, organizing, influencing, and controlling.

9. List and define the basic organizational resources managers have at their disposal.

10. What is the relationship between organizational resources and production?

11. Draw and explain the continuum of managerial effectiveness.

12. Draw and explain the continuum of managerial efficiency.

13. Are managerial effectiveness and managerial efficiency related concepts? If so, how?

14. According to Katz, what are the three primary types of skills important to management success? Define each of these types of skills.

15. Describe the relative importance of each of these three types of skills to lower-level, middle-level, and upper-level managers.

16. What is meant by "the universality of management"?

17. What is a career?

18. Discuss the significance of the maintenance career stage.

19. What tips for promoting the success of a career are most valuable to you? Explain.

20. What does the law of the situation tell you about the success of your management career?

Action Summary Answer Key

1. a. F, p. 5
   b. T, p. 5
2. a. e, pp. 7–8
   b. T, p. 8
3. a. d, p. 8
   b. F, p. 8
4. a. d, p. 9
   b. d, p. 9
5. a. F, p. 12
   b. F, p. 12
6. a. d, p. 14
   b. F, p. 15
7. a. T, p. 15
   b. F, p. 15
8. a. F, p. 16
   b. T, p. 17
   c. F, p. 20

Case Study

A Manager's Career:
Patricia Chadwick of Bloomingdale's

by Sylvia Keyes, Bridgewater State College

How does a manager survive, work with people, and even grow personally in a period of takeovers and bankruptcies? Patricia Chadwick, regional vice president of Bloomingdale's department store, did just that when Bloomingdale's parent company, Federated Department Stores, declared bankruptcy in 1990. Speaking of her survival, Chadwick says, "I have a belief that in any of our careers there will be cycles. There will be up cycles and down cycles, and when we hit a down cycle, we just have to get through it. . . . You perform the functions, you meet the challenges, and you look for advice from your mentors and your superiors."

During those crazy days, the company maintained a communicative and honest management style. Because of strong leadership, "incredible" customer loyalty, and a history of success, Bloomingdale's remained profitable. A key element of Bloomingdale's leadership was Patricia Chadwick's ability to motivate her employees by sharing information: "You continue to maintain your belief in the company, continue to communicate your belief in the company, and you continue to function in a business-as-usual fashion."

Chadwick began her career in a well-respected management training program at Jordan Marsh, a Boston department store. She describes that program as a "crash course" in two things: (1) retailing and merchandising, and (2) managing people. As in most such programs, she moved from hands-on merchandise selling into the central buying organization, where she learned to strategize, plan, and make purchases for the store. Of her five years at Jordan Marsh, she spent the last three as a buyer, which is the short-term goal of most people who enter a retail training program.

In 1980, Chadwick was approached by Bloomingdale's, which had opened a store in Boston in 1978 and had enjoyed uneven success. The Bloomingdale's management believed that the store could do better, and it sought to hire individuals with an understanding of the Boston market. Chadwick was asked to develop Bloomingdale's junior apparel business, which she did for several years before being given responsibilities as a divisional merchandise manager for all of ready-to-wear and children's apparel. In that position, she worked directly with the central buying organization in New York to plan, develop, and execute strategies to make the Boston store more successful.

In 1984, Chadwick became manager of Bloomingdale's apparel store, and in 1987, she took on management of the home furnishings store in Boston. In 1990, she was named regional vice president, with responsibility for overseeing two Bloomingdale's stores in Washington, D.C., as well as the Boston stores.

An interesting sidelight to Patricia Chadwick's career is that she has been able to pursue her career without relocating; she and her husband had agreed they would both stay in the Boston area. "The beauty of Bloomingdale's is that it is willing to allow me to continue to grow and to develop, yet all the while I am able to maintain my personal priorities of staying in one location."

In her current role, Chadwick executes plans developed by the central organization, but she also tailors those plans to meet the particular needs of Boston and of Washington, D.C. She is very involved in marketing strategies, including advertising, direct mail, and sales promotions. She is also a mentor for many people in the Boston stores. She is responsible for training, developing, and supervising divisional merchandise managers, department managers, the selling staff, and the sales support organization, with overall responsibility for the 400 staff employees and 50 executives who work in the Boston stores.

Looking ahead to the 1990s, Chadwick states, "There is no question that service is the key to success for the nineties; it has been found that customers will spend more money if they like the way they are treated." In keeping with the goal of high-quality customer service, Bloomingdale's recently switched to an incentive-based program for its sales employees: "We have really given our sales associates the opportunity to be professionals, to earn a good living, to be in a respected profession, and to be treated differently and to feel differently [from the sales clerks in other department stores]."

Patricia Chadwick maintains that one key to her success is her ability to communicate. "I have a very open-door policy. . . . Any person who wants to see me, I will always see within a day. I spend a lot of time talking [to employees] throughout the store, and I will also conduct ten- to fifteen-minute meetings, such as this morning, when I just updated them on what's happening this week and our plans for Christmas—a purely casual get-together."

Patricia Chadwick intends to work toward making Bloomingdale's one of the leading American retailers. She believes that to do so, she must attract customers who enjoy Bloomingdale's exclusive products, fashions, and service. On a personal level, she wants to learn and to grow in her career, and to find fulfillment by working with people, running a successful business, and mastering her new responsibilities as regional vice president.

Discussion Questions

1. Toward what organizational goals is Patricia Chadwick striving? How does she use the management functions to attain them?

2. Which management skills are most important to Patricia Chadwick in her current position at Bloomingdale's? Why?

3. How did Patricia Chadwick's management skills help Bloomingdale's weather bankruptcy proceedings and emerge as a profitable company? Which skills were most important in 1980? In 1990?

4. How does Patricia Chadwick's career illustrate the stages shown in Figure 1.7? In which stage is her career at present?

A Career in the Sun:
Ron Rice, Hawaiian Tropic

On a visit to Hawaii in the mid-1960s, Ron Rice observed the native Hawaiians cutting up baby coconuts and rubbing the gel on their skin. It gave him the idea for a natural suntan product that became Hawaiian Tropic, now the second largest tanning products company in the world.

It took Ron Rice three or four years to develop his first product, and he started small; he bought a garbage can, and paid two eleven-year-old kids to stir up the product with a broomstick and pour it into bottles. At first, he would sell a bottle and use the money to buy the ingredients for two more bottles, sell those and make four bottles, and so on. Hawaiian Tropic, his company, now has twelve manufacturing plants on five continents that produce several hundred thousand bottles a day of sun care products.

Ron Rice always had the entrepreneurial spirit. He grew up in Asheville, North Carolina, where his family lived on top of a mountain. Rice ran a roadside stand selling apples, berries, and other fruit grown on the mountain; he shelled walnuts and sold them in jars, and made apple cider to sell. At Christmas, he had his brother and sister help him make wreaths and sell them in nearby communities.

Rice's father was a perfectionist who always encouraged him to work harder. Rice himself had no particular plans to be in business; he was always interested in sports, and after flunking out of college he worked as a lifeguard and with football teams. Working as a camp counselor and lifeguard during the summer, he found that his skin continually burned from being out in the sun and that the existing sun-care products didn't seem to work for him. He believed that there was a need and a demand for a better product.

Rice takes a relaxed approach to management; he applies his fun-seeking philosophy to running his business. He likes a casual atmosphere where employees don't dress up; in fact, he says he doesn't care if they come to work at certain hours or not, so long as they get the job done. He describes his company as "beach-oriented" and "fun," and he consciously promotes a family atmosphere. On the other hand, Rice expects to be able to call employees at all hours and to have them respond immediately. When he is at his Daytona Beach headquarters, he holds informal staff meetings, often at his own home.

Rice describes his chief management skill as the ability to pick the right people, "the best people [he] can find." He objects to clock-watchers, and wants to hire people who enjoy working there and who appreciate the "beach-party" atmosphere. He feels that the human element is missing in much of big business.

Rice spent twelve years doing virtually nothing other than building Hawaiian Tropic into a successful company, where annual sales now top $200 million. Now, at age forty-nine, he has started to relax and enjoy his success. Meeting other successful people has helped him to put his own success into perspective; today, he believes that he would have been successful at whatever he tried, because of his inner drive. Rice's entrepreneurial spirit has created an American success story in Hawaiian Tropic.

Video Case Questions

1. Which of the three types of skills that managers use is most important to Ron Rice?

2. What does Ron say is his best ability as a manager? Is this an important ability? Why?

3. In the chapter section entitled "The Universality of Management" you read about certain managerial characteristics. From what you have read of Ron Rice, decide whether those characteristics describe him. Relate these to actual events in his life to support your decisions.

4. What were some of Ron Rice's jobs during the exploration stage of his career?

5. At what career stage is Ron Rice now?

Video Case Activities

1. Using the graph on page 17 (Figure 1.7), chart Ron Rice's career using the facts in the case just described. Indicate the exploration, establishment, and maintenance stages of his career. Does his career development fit the suggested pattern?

2. Imagine you are a manager with Ron Rice's company, and you are writing a handbook for new employees of Hawaiian Tropic. Write what you believe is the philosophy of the company, in about half a page. Then write what you think would be important traits for a successful manager in that company.

Chapter 2

Student Learning Objectives

From studying this chapter, I will attempt to acquire:

1. An understanding of the classical approach to management.

2. An appreciation for the work of Frederick W. Taylor, Frank and Lillian Gilbreth, Henry L. Gantt, and Henri Fayol.

3. An understanding of the behavioral approach to management.

4. An understanding of the studies at the Hawthorne Works of the Western Electric Company.

5. An understanding of the management science approach to management.

6. An understanding of how the management science approach has evolved.

7. An understanding of the system approach to management.

8. An understanding of how triangular management and the contingency approach to management are related.

The History
of Management

hapter Outline

*I*ntroductory Case

"MICKEY'S KITCHEN" AT THE DISNEY STORE*

You say you want a Mickey Mouse T-shirt and the kids are clamoring for a burger? Well, if you're in or near Montclair, California, The Disney Store has got you covered.

You can chow down on French fries shaped like Mickey or Donald or pig out on a Hot Diggity Dog.

In a shopping mall forty miles east of Los Angeles, The Disney Store, Inc. has opened Mickey's Kitchen. There, you can chow down on French fries shaped like Mickey or Donald or pig out on a Hot Diggity Dog, a meatless Mickey Burger, or the "Soup-a-Dee-Doo-Dah" garden soup.

And, in typical Disney style, the decor is more elab-

orate than that of the average burger joint. While they munch, diners will be seated in one of four themed areas that are mock sound stages—giant friezes, actually, where a famous Disney cartoon is being "filmed." No actual filming takes place.

The Montclair Mickey's Kitchen was recently joined by a second restaurant at The Disney Store in the Woodfield Mall in Schaumburg, Illinois. While it's likely that there will be more Mickey's Kitchens, "it's premature to announce more" now, said Chuck Champlin, spokesman for Disney's consumer products division headquartered in Burbank, California.

The Montclair Mickey's Kitchen has 190 seats and sells food items ranging from 50¢ to $3.45. The menu, which includes more low-fat items than typical fast-food fare, has been fine-tuned many times, but not substantially altered.

Pinocchio's Pizza includes three varieties of pizza: a cheese pizza or vegetable pizza that sells for $2.75 and barbecue chicken pizza for $2.95.

The PB&J Handwich, a pancake wrapped around a banana half and filled with peanut butter and jelly, has proved popular with children, Champlin said.

For those concerned about fat and calorie content, there is the Goofy Burger, with lean ground beef and fat content of less than 15 percent, which sells for $1.95 for adults and $1.25 for children. The Hot Diggity Dog is a turkey frank that sells for $1.50.

The meatless Mickey Burger consists of a blend of walnuts, mozzarella, bean curd, and vegetables. Rather than being fried, it is browned under a heat lamp.

Champlin said the lower-fat items aren't meant to be a subtle comment on the typically high-fat American diet but to offer diners a variety of choices.

"Our priority is to create fun . . . and the emphasis is to offer really good food with something for everybody."

*This case is from Vicki Vaughn, "Disney Testing Fast-Food Recipe," *The Orlando Sentinel,* November 4, 1990, D1, D2.

34

WHAT'S AHEAD

There are several different ways to approach management situations and to solve related organizational problems. Managers like the ones managing Disney's new Mickey's Kitchen must understand these approaches if they are to be successful in building successful organizations. This chapter explains five such approaches: (1) the classical approach, (2) the behavioral approach, (3) the management science approach, (4) the contingency approach, and (5) the system approach.

Chapter 1 focused primarily on defining *management*. This chapter presents various approaches to analyzing and reacting to the management situation. Each approach recommends a basically different method of analysis and a different type of action as a result of the analysis.

Over the years, disagreement on exactly how many different approaches to management exist and what each approach entails has been common. In an attempt to organize and condense the various approaches, Donnelly, Gibson, and Ivancevich[1] combined the ideas of Koontz, O'Donnell, and Weihrich[2] and Haynes and Massie[3] and offered these three: (1) the classical approach, (2) the behavioral approach, and (3) the management science approach. They stated that their objective was to simplify the discussion of the field of management without sacrificing significant information.

The following sections build on the work of Donnelly, Gibson, and Ivancevich in presenting the classical approach, the behavioral approach, and the management science approach. The contingency approach is also discussed as a fourth primary approach to analyzing the management task. The fifth approach, the system approach, is presented as a more recent trend in management thinking and is the approach emphasized in this text.

THE CLASSICAL APPROACH

The **classical approach to management** resulted from the first significant, concentrated effort to develop a body of management thought. Management writers who participated in this effort are considered the pioneers of management study. The classical approach recommends that managers continually strive to increase organizational efficiency to increase production. Although the fundamentals of this approach were developed some time ago, modern managers are just as concerned about finding the "one best way" to get the job done as were their predecessors.

For discussion purposes, the classical approach to management breaks into two distinct areas. The first area, lower-level management analysis, consists primarily of the work of Frederick W. Taylor, Frank and Lillian Gilbreth, and Henry L. Gantt. These individuals studied mainly the jobs of workers at lower levels of the organization. The second area, comprehensive analysis of management, concentrates more on the management function as a whole. The primary contributor to this category was Henri Fayol. Figure 2.1 on page 36 illustrates the two areas in the classical approach.

The **classical approach to management** is a management approach that emphasizes organizational efficiency to increase organizational success.

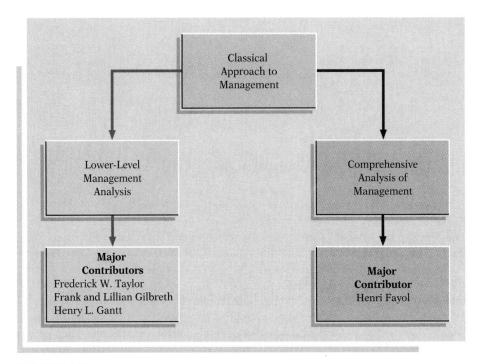

FIGURE 2.1

Division of classical approach to management into two areas and the
major contributors to each area

Lower-Level Management Analysis

Lower-level management analysis concentrates on the "one best way" to perform
a task; that is, it asks how a task situation can be structured to get the highest
production from workers. The process of finding this "one best way" has become
known as the scientific method of management, or simply, **scientific management.**
Although the techniques of scientific managers could conceivably be applied to all
management levels, the research, research applications, and illustrations relate
mostly to lower-level managers. The work of Frederick W. Taylor, Frank and
Lillian Gilbreth, and Henry L. Gantt is summarized in the sections that follow.

Scientific management emphasizes the "one best way" to perform a task.

Frederick W. Taylor (1856–1915)

Because of the significance of his contributions, Frederick W. Taylor is commonly
called the father of scientific management. His primary goal was to increase worker
efficiency by scientifically designing jobs. His basic premise was that there was one
best way to do a job and that that way should be discovered and put into operation.

Perhaps the best illustration of Taylor's scientific method and his management
philosophy lies in a description of how he modified the job of employees whose
sole responsibility was shoveling materials at the Bethlehem Steel Company.[4] During the modification process, Taylor made the assumption that any worker's job

could be reduced to a science. To construct the "science of shoveling," he obtained answers—through observation and experimentation—to the following questions:

1. Will a first-class worker do more work per day with a shovelful of five, ten, fifteen, twenty, thirty, or forty pounds?

2. What kinds of shovels work best with which materials?

3. How quickly can a shovel be pushed into a pile of materials and pulled out properly loaded?

4. How much time is required to swing a shovel backward and throw the load a given horizontal distance at a given height?

As Taylor began formulating answers to these types of questions, he developed insights on how to increase the total amount of materials shoveled per day. He increased worker efficiency by matching shovel size with such factors as the size of the men, the weight of the materials, and the height and distance the materials were to be thrown. After the third year that Taylor's shoveling efficiency plan was in operation, records at Bethlehem Steel indicated that the total number of shovelers needed was reduced from about 600 to 140, the average number of tons shoveled per worker per day rose from sixteen to fifty-nine, the average earnings per worker per day rose from $1.15 to $1.88, and the average cost of handling a long ton (2,240 pounds) dropped from $0.072 to $0.033—an impressive application of scientific management to the task of shoveling.

Global Highlight: Delta Faucet Company Competes Globally

When it became necessary to compete efficiently in the global manufacturing environment, managers at Delta Faucet Company in Chickasha, Oklahoma, recently focused their attention on automation to help them find the most efficient ways to perform jobs in Delta's manufacturing plant. This effort illustrates the scientific approach to management, which emphasizes finding the one best way to do a job—in this case, through the use of machines.

Experts analyzed the assembling and packaging of one of Delta's products, a faucet aerator. An aerator is a part attached to the end of a faucet that increases water pressure by introducing air into the stream of water. Delta's aerator consists of six plastic parts that fit together for easy assembly. With the help of the Kingsbury Machine Tool Company, Delta developed a special machine that assembles and packages about fifty aerators per minute. Once assembled and packaged, the aerators are placed on a conveyor belt for distribution to another part of the plant where they are made ready for shipment. This enables Delta to assemble, package, and distribute the aerators more efficiently.

One benefit of Delta's search for the most efficient and effective way to perform each of its jobs is that the company will be able to compete more effectively in an international marketplace. In Delta's case, finding the "one best way" to do a job is the key to successful expansion into international markets.

Frank Gilbreth (1868–1924), Lillian Gilbreth (1878–1972)

The Gilbreths were also significant contributors to the scientific method. By definition, therefore, they ascribed to the idea of finding and using the one best way to perform a job. The primary investigative tool in their research was **motion study**, which consisted of reducing each job to the most basic movements possible. Motion analysis is still used today to establish job performance standards. Each movement or motion that is used to do a job is studied in terms of how much time the movement takes and how necessary it actually is in performing the job. Inefficient or unnecessary motions are pinpointed and eliminated in doing the job.[5]

During a motion analysis, the Gilbreths considered the work environment, the motion itself, and behavioral variables concerning the workers. Table 2.1 lists the primary factors in each of these groups. The analysis of each of the variables in a task situation was obviously a long, involved, and tedious process.

Frank Gilbreth's experience as an apprentice bricklayer led him to do motion studies of bricklaying. He found that bricklayers could increase their output significantly by concentrating on performing some motions and eliminating others. Table 2.2 shows a portion of the results of one of Gilbreth's bricklaying motion studies. For each bricklaying activity, Gilbreth indicated whether it should be omitted for the sake of efficiency and why. He reduced the twelve motions per brick listed under "The Wrong Way" to the two motions per brick listed under "The Right Way." Gilbreth's bricklaying motion studies resulted in reducing the number of motions necessary to lay a brick by approximately 70 percent and tripling bricklaying production.

Lillian Gilbreth, in addition to collaborating with her husband, researched and wrote on motion studies after her husband's death. She applied the scientific method to the role of the homemaker and to the handicapped.

TABLE 2.1 Primary variables considered in analyzing motions

Variables of the Worker	Variables of the Surroundings, Equipment, and Tools	Variables of the Motion
1. Anatomy	1. Appliances	1. Acceleration
2. Brawn	2. Clothes	2. Automaticity
3. Contentment	3. Colors	3. Combination with other motions and sequence
4. Creed	4. Entertainment, music, reading, etc.	4. Cost
5. Earning power	5. Heating, cooling, ventilating	5. Direction
6. Experience	6. Lighting	6. Effectiveness
7. Fatigue	7. Quality of material	7. Foot-pounds of work accomplished
8. Habits	8. Reward and punishment	8. Inertia and momentum overcome
9. Health	9. Size of unit moved	9. Length
10. Mode of living	10. Special fatigue-eliminating devices	10. Necessity
11. Nutrition	11. Surroundings	11. Path
12. Size	12. Tools	12. "Play for position"
13. Skill	13. Union rules	13. Speed
14. Temperament	14. Weight of unit moved	
15. Training		

TABLE 2.2 Partial results for one of Gilbreth's bricklaying motion studies

Operation No.	The Wrong Way	The Right Way	Pick and Dip Method: The Exterior Four Inches (Laying to the Line)
	Motions Per Brick $\frac{1}{4}\ \frac{1}{2}\ \frac{3}{4}\ \frac{4}{4}$	Motions Per Brick $\frac{1}{4}\ \frac{1}{2}\ \frac{3}{4}\ \frac{4}{4}$	
1	Step for mortar	Omit	On the scaffold the inside edge of mortar box should be plumb with inside edge of stock platform. On floor the inside edge of mortar box should be twenty-one inches from wall. Mortar boxes never over four feet apart.
2	Reach for mortar	$\frac{4}{4}$	Do not bend any more than absolutely necessary to reach mortar with a straight arm.
3	Work up mortar	Omit	Provide mortar of right consistency. Examine sand screen and keep in repair so that no pebbles can get through. Keep tender on scaffold to temper up and keep mortar worked up right.
4	Step for brick	Omit	If tubs are kept four feet apart, no stepping for brick will be necessary on scaffold. On floor keep brick in a pile not nearer than one foot nor more than four feet six inches from wall.
5	Reach for brick	Included in 2	Brick must be reached for at the same time that the mortar is reached for, and picked up at exactly the same time the mortar is picked up. If it is not picked up at the same time, allowance must be made for operation.
6	Pick up right brick	Omit	Train the leader of the tenders to vary the kind of brick used as much as possible to suit the conditions; that is, to bring the best brick when the men are working on the line.
7	Mortar box to wall	$\frac{4}{4}$	Carry stock from the staging to the wall in the straightest possible line and with an even speed, without pause or hitch. It is important to move the stock with an even speed and not by quick jerks.
8	Brick pile to wall	Included in 7	Brick must be carried from pile to wall at exactly same time as the mortar is carried to the wall, without pause or jerk.
9	Deposit mortar on wall	Included in 7	If a pause is made, this space must be filled out. If no pause is made, it is included in No. 7.
10	Spreading mortar	Omit	The mortar must be thrown so as to require no additional spreading and so that the mortar runs up on the end of the previous brick laid, or else the next two spaces must be filled out.
11	Cutting off mortar	Omit	If the mortar is thrown from the trowel properly, no spreading and no cutting is necessary.
12	Disposing of mortar	Omit	If mortar is not cut off, this space is not filled out. If mortar is cut off, keep it on trowel and carry back on trowel to box, or else butter on end of brick. Do not throw it on mortar box.

Henry L. Gantt (1861–1919)

A third major contributor to the area of scientific management was Henry L. Gantt. He, like Taylor and the Gilbreths, was interested in increasing worker efficiency. Gantt attributed unsatisfactory or ineffective tasks and piece rates (incentive pay for each product piece an individual produces) primarily to the fact that they were set on what had been done in the past or on somebody's *opinion* of what could be done. According to Gantt, *exact scientific knowledge* of what could be done should be substituted for opinion. He considered this the role of scientific management.

Gantt's management philosophy is described by his statement that "the essential differences between the best system of today and those of the past are the manner in which tasks are 'scheduled' and the manner in which their performance is rewarded."[6] Following his own rationale, Gantt tried to improve systems or organizations through task-scheduling innovation and reward innovation.

Scheduling Innovation. The Gantt chart, the primary scheduling device that Gantt developed, is still cited as the scheduling tool that is most commonly and widely used by modern managers.[7] Basically, this chart provides managers with an easily understood summary of what work was scheduled for specific time periods, how much of this work was completed, and by whom it was done. The Gantt chart is covered in much more detail in chapter 7.

Reward Innovation. Gantt seemed more aware of the human side of production than either Taylor or the Gilbreths. He wrote that "the taskmaster (manager) of the past was practically a slave driver, whose principal function was to force workmen to do that which they had no desire to do, or interest in doing. The task setter of today under any reputable system of management is not a driver. When he asks the workmen to perform tasks, he makes it to their interest to accomplish them, and is careful not to ask what is impossible or unreasonable."[8]

Whereas Taylor had pioneered a piece-rate system under which workers were paid according to the amount they produced, and advocated the use of wage incentive plans, Gantt developed a system wherein workers could earn a bonus in addition to the piece rate if they went beyond their daily production quota. Gantt believed that worker compensation needed to correspond not only to production through the piece-rate system but also to overproduction through the bonus system.

 ack to the Case

The managers of Mickey's Kitchen, The Disney Store's new restaurants, could use a classical approach to management to stress organizational efficiency—the "one best way" to perform jobs at Mickey's Kitchen—to increase productivity. As a simplified example, Mickey's Kitchen managers might want to check whether the dispenser used to apply mustard and catsup is of the appropriate size to require only one squirt or whether more than one squirt is necessary to adequately cover the new lean ground beef Goofy Burger bun.

The managers also could use motion studies to eliminate unnecessary or wasted motions by their employees. For example, are Hot Diggity Dogs, french fries, and drinks located for easy insertion into customer bags, or must an employee walk unnecessary steps during the sales process? Would certain Mickey's Kitchen employees be more efficient over an entire working day if they sat, rather than stood, while working?

The classical approach to management might also guide Mickey's Kitchen managers in scheduling more efficiently. By ensuring that an appropriate number of people with the required skills are scheduled to work during peak hours and that fewer are scheduled to work during slower hours, managers would maximize the return on their labor costs.

Mickey's Kitchen managers also might want to consider offering their employees some sort of bonus if they reach certain work goals. But managers should make sure that the goals that they set are realistic, since unreasonable or impossible goals tend to make workers resentful and unproductive. For example, managers might ask that certain employees reduce errors in filling orders by 50 percent during the next month. If and when these employees reached the goal, Mickey's Kitchen managers could give them a free lunch as a bonus.

Comprehensive Analysis of Management

Whereas scientific managers approach the study of management primarily in terms of job design, managers who embrace the comprehensive view—the second area of the classical approach—are concerned with the entire range of managerial performance.

Comprehensive analysis of management involves studying the management function as a whole.

Among the well-known contributors to the comprehensive view were Chester Barnard,[9] Alvin Brown,[10] Henry Dennison,[11] Luther Gulick and Lyndall Urwick,[12] J.D. Mooney and A.C. Reiley,[13] and Oliver Sheldon.[14] Perhaps the most notable of all contributors, however, was Henri Fayol. His book *General and Industrial Management* presents a management philosophy that many modern managers still look to for advice and guidance.[15]

Henri Fayol (1841–1925)

Because of his writings on the elements of management and the general principles of management, Henri Fayol is usually regarded as the pioneer of administrative theory. The elements of management he outlined—planning, organizing, command, coordination, and control—are still considered worthwhile divisions under which to study, analyze, and put into action the management process.[16] (Note the similarities between Fayol's elements of management and the management functions outlined in chapter 1—planning, organizing, influencing, controlling.)

The general principles of management suggested by Fayol also still are considered by most managers to be useful in contemporary management practice. These principles follow in the order developed by Fayol and are accompanied by corresponding definitional themes:[17]

1. *Division of work*. Work should be divided among individuals and groups to ensure that effort and attention are focused on special portions of the task. Fayol presented work specialization as the best way to use the human resources of the organization.

2. *Authority*. The concepts of authority and responsibility are closely related. *Authority* was defined by Fayol as the right to give orders and the power to exact obedience. Responsibility involves being accountable and, therefore, is naturally associated with authority. When one assumes authority, one also assumes responsibility.[18]

3. *Discipline*. A successful organization requires the common effort of workers. Penalties, however, should be applied judiciously to encourage this common effort.

4. *Unity of command*. Workers should receive orders from only one manager.

5. *Unity of direction*. The entire organization should be moving toward a common objective, in a common direction.

6. *Subordination of individual interests to the general interests*. The interests of one person should not have priority over the interests of the organization as a whole.

7. *Remuneration*. Many variables, such as cost of living, supply of qualified personnel, general business conditions, and success of the business, should be considered in determining the rate of pay a worker will receive.

8. *Centralization*. Fayol defined *centralization* as lowering the importance of the subordinate role. Decentralization is increasing the same importance. The degree to which centralization or decentralization should be adopted depends on the specific organization in which the manager is working.

9. *Scalar chain*. Managers in hierarchies are actually part of a chainlike authority scale. Each manager, from the first-line supervisor to the president, possesses certain amounts of authority. The president possesses the most authority; the first-line supervisor possesses the least authority. The existence of this chain implies that lower-level managers should always keep upper-level managers informed of their work activities. Existence of and adherence to the scalar chain are necessary if organizations are to be successful.

10. *Order*. For the sake of efficiency and coordination, all materials and people related to a specific kind of work should be assigned to the same general location in the organization.

11. *Equity*. All employees should be treated as equally as possible.

12. *Stability of tenure of personnel*. Retaining productive employees should always be a high priority of management. Recruitment and selection costs, as well as increased reject rates, are usually associated with hiring new workers.

13. *Initiative*. Management should take steps to encourage worker initiative, which can be defined as new or additional work activity undertaken through self-direction.

14. *Esprit de corps*. Management should encourage harmony and general good feeling among employees.

Fayol's general principles of management cover a broad range of topics, but organizational efficiency, the handling of people, and appropriate management action seem to be the three general themes stressed. With the writings of Fayol, the study of management as a broad comprehensive activity began to receive the attention it deserved.

Limitations of the Classical Approach

Individual contributors to the classical approach were probably encouraged to write about their experiences largely because of the success they enjoyed. Structuring work to be more efficient and defining the manager's role more precisely yielded significant improvement in productivity, which individuals such as Taylor and Fayol were quick to document.

The human variable for the organization, however, may not be adequately emphasized in the classical approach. People today do not seem to be as influenced by bonuses as they were in the nineteenth century. It is generally agreed that critical interpersonal areas, such as conflict, communication, leadership, and motivation, were not emphasized enough in the classical approach.

THE BEHAVIORAL APPROACH

The **behavioral approach to management** emphasizes striving to increase production through an understanding of people. According to proponents of this approach, if managers understand their people and adapt their organizations to them, organizational success usually follows.

The behavioral approach is usually described as beginning with a series of studies conducted between 1924 and 1932. These studies investigated the behavior and attitudes of workers at the Hawthorne (Chicago) Works of the Western Electric Company.[19] Accounts of these studies are usually divided into phases: the relay assembly test room experiments and the bank wiring observation room experiment.

> The **behavioral approach to management** is a management approach that emphasizes increasing organizational success by focusing on human variables within the organization.

The Relay Assembly Test Room Experiments

The relay assembly test room experiments originally had a scientific management orientation.[20] The experimenters believed that if productivity were studied long enough under different working conditions (including variations in weather conditions, temperature, rest periods, work hours and humidity), the working conditions that maximized production would be found. The purpose of the relay assembly test room experiments was to determine the relationship between intensity of lighting and efficiency of workers, as measured by worker output. Two groups of female employees were used as subjects. The light intensity for one group was varied, while the light intensity for the other group was held constant.

The results of the experiments surprised the researchers. No matter what conditions employees were exposed to, production increased. A consistent relationship between productivity and lighting intensity seemed nonexistent. An extensive interviewing campaign was begun to determine why the subjects continued to increase production. The following are the main reasons, as formulated from the interviews:

1. The subjects found working in the test room enjoyable.

2. The new supervisory relationship during the experiment allowed the subjects to work freely, without fear.

3. The subjects realized that they were taking part in an important and interesting study.

4. The subjects seemed to become friendly as a group.

The experimenters concluded that human factors within organizations could significantly influence production. More research was needed to evaluate the potential impact of this human component in organizations.

The Bank Wiring Observation Room Experiment

The purpose of the bank wiring observation room experiment was to analyze the social relationships in a work group.[21] More specifically, the study focused on the effect of group piecework incentives on a group of men who assembled terminal banks for use in telephone exchanges. The group piecework incentive system dictated that the harder a group worked as a whole, the more pay each member of that group received.

The experimenters believed that the study would find that members of the work group would pressure one another to work harder so that each group member would receive more pay. To the surprise of the researchers, the opposite occurred. The work group pressured the faster workers to slow down their work rate. In essence, the men whose work rate would have increased individual salaries were pressured by the group, rather than the men whose work rate would have decreased individual salaries. Evidently, the men were more interested in preserving the work group than in making more money. The researchers concluded that social groups in organizations could effectively exert enough pressure to influence individuals to disregard monetary incentives.

Taken together, the series of studies conducted at the Hawthorne plant gave management thinkers a new direction for research. Obviously, the human variable in the organization needed much more analysis, since it could either increase or decrease production drastically. Managers began to realize that they needed to understand this influence in order to maximize its positive effects and minimize its negative effects. This attempt to understand people is still a major force of today's organizational research. The following cartoon humorously illustrates a manager whose lack of understanding of an employee results in employee discontent and perhaps eventually produces a relatively unproductive employee. More current behavioral findings and their implications for management are presented in much greater detail in later sections of this text.

ack to the Case

Comprehensive analysis of organizations implies that Mickey's Kitchen managers might be able to improve their restaurant by evaluating the entire range of their managerial performance—especially with regard to organizational efficiency, the handling of people, and appropriate management action. For example, Mickey's Kitchen managers should check with their employees to make sure they are receiving orders from only one source—that one manager hasn't instructed an employee to man the french fry station moments before an assistant manager directs the same employee to prepare Pinocchio's Pizzas. Along the same lines, Mickey's Kitchen managers might want to verify that all of their employees are being treated equally—that fry cooks, for example, don't get longer work breaks than order takers.

The behavioral approach to management suggests that Mickey's Kitchen managers should consider the people working for them and evaluate the impact of their feelings and relationships on the productivity of the new restaurants. Managers at Disney's restaurants could, for example, try to make the work more enjoyable, perhaps by allowing their employees to work at different stations (grill, beverage, french fry, cash register, etc.) each day. Managers might also consider creating opportunities for employees to become better acquainted with each other, perhaps through a Mickey's Kitchen employee picnic. In essence, the behavioral approach to management stresses that Mickey's Kitchen managers should recognize the human variable in their restaurants and strive to maximize its positive effects.

THE MANAGEMENT SCIENCE APPROACH

Churchman, Ackoff, and Arnoff define the management science, or operations research (OR), approach as (1) an application for the scientific method to problems arising in the operation of a system and (2) the solving of these problems by the solving of mathematical equations representing the system.[22] The **management science approach** suggests that managers can best improve their organizations by using the scientific method and mathematical techniques to solve operational problems.

> The **management science approach** is a management approach that emphasizes the use of the scientific method and quantitative techniques to increase organizational success.

The Beginning of the Management Science Approach

The management science, or operations research, approach can be traced to World War II. During this era, leading scientists were asked to help solve complex operational problems that existed in the military.[23] The scientists were organized into teams that eventually became known as operations research (OR) groups. One OR group was asked to determine which gunsights would best stop German attacks on the British mainland.

These early OR groups typically included physicists and other "hard" scientists, who used the problem-solving method with which they had the most experience: the scientific method. The **scientific method** dictates that scientists:

1. Systematically *observe* the system whose behavior must be explained to solve the problem.

> The **scientific method** is a method of problem-solving that involves the following sequential steps:
>
> 1. Observing.

2. Constructing a model.

3. Deducing.

4. Testing the model.

2. Use these specific observations to *construct* a generalized framework (a model) that is consistent with the specific observations and from which consequences of changing the system can be predicted.

3. Use the model to *deduce* how the system will behave under conditions that have not been observed but could be observed if the changes were made.

4. Finally, *test* the model by performing an experiment on the actual system to see if the effects of changes predicted using the model actually occur when the changes are made.[24]

The OR groups were very successful in using the scientific method to solve their operational problems.

Management Science Today

After World War II, the world again became interested in manufacturing and selling products. The success of the OR groups had been so obvious in the military that managers were anxious to try management science techniques in an industrial environment. After all, managers also had complicated operational problems.

By 1955, the management science approach to solving industrial problems had proven very effective. Many people found this approach valuable and saw great promise in refining its techniques and analytical tools. Managers and universities alike anxiously began these refinement attempts.

By 1965, the management science approach was being used in many companies and applied to many diverse management problems, such as production scheduling, plant location, and product packaging.[25]

In the 1980s, surveys of firms using management science techniques indicate that these techniques are used extensively in very large, complex organizations. The benefit of using these techniques in smaller organizations has not yet been fully realized. Finding new and beneficial ways of applying management science techniques to smaller organizations is undoubtedly a worthwhile challenge facing managers in the 1990s and beyond.[26]

Characteristics of Management Science Applications

Four primary characteristics usually are present in situations in which management science techniques are applied.[27] First, the management problems studied are so complicated that managers need help in analyzing a large number of variables. Management science techniques increase the effectiveness of the managers' decision making. Second, a management science application generally uses economic implications as guidelines for making a particular decision. Perhaps this is because management science techniques are best suited for analyzing quantifiable factors, such as sales, expenses, and units of production. Third, the use of mathematical models to investigate the decision situation is typical in management science applications. Models are constructed to represent reality and then used to determine how the real world situation might be improved. The fourth characteristic of a management science application is the use of computers. The great complexity of managerial problems and the sophisticated mathematical analysis required of problem-related information are two factors that make computers very valuable to the management science analyst.

Quality Highlight: Baldrige Award Exemplifies Quality

The application of scientific management to quality standards is the basis for the prestigious Baldrige Award, as explained in the following "Quality Highlight."

Since it was established in 1987, the Malcolm Baldrige National Quality Award has become the sought-after award for quality standard for U.S. businesses. It is to corporate America what the Oscars are to the motion-picture industry or the Grammys are to the music industry.

The award does not just emphasize quality. Guidelines for award application provide a detailed plan for improving quality in all areas of a company's business.

"The guidelines are outstanding," says James Houghton, chairman and chief executive officer of Corning Glass, which has competed for the award. "We have passed out the guidelines for our divisions and just said, 'If you want to know what quality is all about, take a look at this.' " Corning estimates that staffers spent 14,000 hours competing for the award.

Six prizes are offered each year, two each for manufacturing and service companies and two for small businesses with fewer than 500 employees. Award winners include: Motorola, Westinghouse, Globe Metallurgical, Milliken & Co., Xerox, IBM Rochester, Federal Express, Cadillac and Wallace Co.

The award is administered by the National Institute of Standards and Technology. To apply, a large company must pay a fee of $2,500 and submit answers to 133 questions on a 75-page questionnaire. A small company pays $1,000 and answers a 50-page questionnaire.

Applications are scored by volunteer examiners, largely from industry. A perfect score is 1,000 points. Companies that score more than 601 points enter the second phase of the competition, which includes a visit by four to six examiners who verify information in the application.

Finally, application scores and examiners' reports are given to a panel of nine judges who submit their choices to the U.S. Secretary of Commerce.

Because the process is so detailed, just applying for the Baldrige award forces a company to review its entire operation to discover weaknesses in quality. Applicants also receive reports from the examiners highlighting strengths and weaknesses.

Former Xerox Chairman David Kearns says that 90 percent of the value of applying for the award is in that examiners' report.

Adds David Luther, Corning Glass' vice president for quality: "It's the cheapest consulting you can ever get."

Information that the Milliken Co. received from examiners in 1988 helped the company win the award in 1989. Examiners told Milliken the company's objectives were not tough enough. They also pointed out that Milliken's top executives did not thoroughly understand statistical process controls, which were critical to its textile manufacturing business. Before competing a second time, Milliken executives took a four-day review course.

Today, managers are using such management science tools as inventory control models, network models, and probability models as aids in the decision-making process. Later parts of this text will outline some of these models in more detail and illustrate their applications to management decision making. Because management science thought is still evolving, more and more sophisticated analytical techniques can be expected.

THE CONTINGENCY APPROACH

The **contingency approach to management** is a management approach that emphasizes that what managers do in practice depends on a given set of circumstances—a situation.

In simple terms, the **contingency approach to management** emphasizes that what managers do in practice depends on, or is contingent upon, a given set of circumstances—a situation.[28] In essence, this approach emphasizes "if-then" relationships. "If" this situational variable exists, "then" this is the action a manager probably would take. As an example, if a manager has a group of inexperienced subordinates, then the contingency approach would recommend that he or she lead in a different fashion than if he or she had an experienced group.

In general, the contingency approach attempts to outline the conditions or situations in which various management methods have the best chance of success.[29] This approach is based on the premise that, although there is probably no one best way to solve a management problem in all organizations, there probably is one best way to solve any given management problem in any one organization. Perhaps the main challenges of using the contingency approach are (1) perceiving organizational situations as they actually exist, (2) choosing the management tactics best suited to those situations, and (3) competently implementing those tactics.

Although the notion of a contingency approach to management is not new,[30] the use of the term itself is relatively new. In addition, the contingency approach has become a popular discussion topic for contemporary management writers. The general consensus of their writings seems to indicate that if managers are to apply management concepts, principles, and techniques successfully, they must consider the realities of the specific organizational circumstances they face.[31]

ℰthics Highlight: Charles Schwab Protects Clients During Disaster

Stockbrokers take care of their clients' financial affairs. These clients entrust records of their financial transactions to their brokers. Charles Schwab, a large discount stock brokerage with a branch in San Francisco, determined that it owed its clients a duty to make contingency plans in case of a physical disaster. The plans were deemed necessary not only for the good of the company but for the benefit of the company's many clients. If a physical disaster hit and the financial records of clients were destroyed, they would undoubtedly suffer both financially and emotionally.

These contingency plans paid off when, in October of 1989, many parts of the San Francisco Bay area lost electrical power following an earthquake. The company's backup battery system went into operation immediately following the earthquake, and prevented the shutdown of the firm's mainframe computer. Thirty minutes later, a diesel generator took over the task of providing electric power to the computer.

Without prior contingency plans to deal with a lack of electrical power to the mainframe computer, the company could have suffered a severe information loss that would have harmed clients and the company for an extended period of time. Not all companies in the Bay area had such contingency plans. Charles Schwab's ethical concern for its clients resulted in necessary protection for its clients and the company.

THE SYSTEM APPROACH

The **system approach to management** is based on general system theory. Ludwig von Bertalanffy, a scientist who worked mainly in the areas of physics and biology, is recognized as the founder of general system theory.[32] The main premise of the theory is that to understand fully the operation of an entity, the entity must be viewed as a system. A **system** is a number of interdependent parts functioning as a whole for some purpose. For example, according to general system theory, to fully understand the operations of the human body, one must understand the workings of its interdependent parts (ears, eyes, brain, etc.). General system theory integrates the knowledge of various specialized fields so that the system as a whole can be better understood.

Types of Systems

According to von Bertalanffy, these are two basic types of systems: closed and open. **Closed systems** are not influenced by and do not interact with their environments. They are mostly mechanical and have necessary predetermined motions or activities that must be performed regardless of the environment. A clock is an example of a closed system. Regardless of its environment, a clock's wheels, gears, and so forth must function in a predetermined way if the clock as a whole is to exist and serve its purpose. The second type of system, the **open system,** is constantly interacting with its environment. A plant is an example of an open system. Constant interaction with the environment influences the plant's state of existence and its future. In fact, the environment determines whether or not the plant will live.

Systems and "Wholeness"

The concept "wholeness" is very important in general system analysis. The system must be viewed as a whole and modified only through changes in its parts. A thorough knowledge of how each part functions and of the interrelationships among the parts must be present before modifications of the parts can be made for the overall benefit of the system. L. Thomas Hopkins suggested six guidelines for system wholeness that should be remembered during system analysis.[33]

1. The whole should be the main focus of analysis, with the parts receiving secondary attention.

2. Integration is the key variable in wholeness analysis. It is defined as the interrelatedness of the many parts within the whole.

3. Possible modifications in each part should be weighed in relation to possible effects on every other part.

The **system approach to management** is a management approach based on general system theory—the theory that to understand fully the operation of an entity, the entity must be viewed as a system. This requires understanding the interdependence of its parts.

A **system** is a number of interdependent parts functioning as a whole for some purpose.

A **closed system** is a system that is not influenced by and does not interact with its environment.

An **open system** is a system that is influenced by and is constantly interacting with its environment.

4. Each part has some role to perform so that the whole can accomplish its purpose.

5. The nature of the part and its function is determined by its position in the whole.

6. All analysis starts with the existence of the whole. The parts and their interrelationships should then evolve to best suit the purpose of the whole.

Since the system approach to management is based on general system theory, analysis of the management situation as a system is stressed. The following sections present the parts of the management system and recommend information that can be used to analyze the system.

The Management System

The **management system** is an open system whose major parts are organizational input, organizational process, and organizational output.

As with all systems, the **management system** is composed of a number of parts that function on an interdependent basis to achieve a purpose. The main parts of the management system are organizational input, organizational process, and organizational output. As discussed in chapter 1, these parts consist of organizational resources, the production process, and finished goods, respectively. The parts represent a combination that exists to achieve organizational objectives, whatever they may be.

The management system is an open system, one that interacts with its environment (see Figure 2.2). Environmental factors with which the management system interacts include the government, suppliers, customers, and competitors. Each of these represents a potential environmental influence that could significantly change the future of a management system.

Environmental impact on management cannot be overemphasized. As an example, the federal government, through its Occupational Safety and Health Act (OSHA) of 1970, encourages management to take costly steps to safeguard workers. Many managers are frustrated because they believe the safeguards are not only too expensive but also unnecessary.

The critical importance of managers' knowing and understanding various components of the environments of their organizations is perhaps best illustrated by the constant struggle of supermarket managers to know and understand their

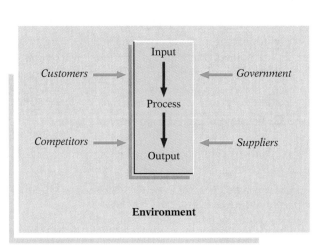

FIGURE 2.2
The open management system

customers. Supermarket managers fight for the business of a national population that is growing by less than 1 percent per year. Survival requires that supermarket managers know their customers better than the competition does. Many food retailers are conducting and using market research to uncover customer attitudes about different kinds of foods and stores. Armed with a thorough understanding of their customers, supermarket managers conducting market research hope to win business from competitors who are not benefiting from insights gained through such research.[34]

Information for Management System Analysis

As noted earlier, to better understand a system, general system theory allows for the use of information from many specialized disciplines. This certainly holds true for the management system. Information from any discipline can increase the understanding of management system operations and thereby enhance the success of the system. A broad, sweeping statement such as this, however, presents a problem. Where do managers go to get this information?

The information used to discuss the management system in the remainder of this text comes from three primary sources: (1) the classical approach to management, (2) the behavioral approach to management, and (3) the management science approach to management. The use of these three sources of information to analyze the management system is referred to as **triangular management.** Figure 2.3 presents the triangular management model. The three sources of information in the model are not meant to represent all the information that can be used to analyze the management system. Rather, they are the three bodies of

Triangular management is a management approach that emphasizes using information from the classical, behavioral, and management science schools of thought to manage the open management system.

FIGURE 2.3
Triangular management model

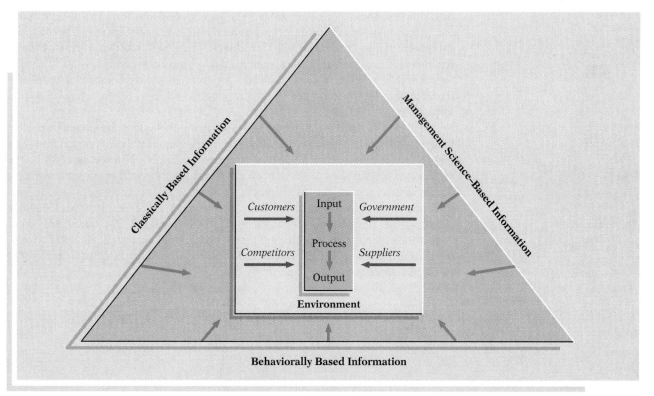

management-related information that probably would be most useful to managers analyzing the management system.

A synthesis of classically based information, behaviorally based information, and management science based information is critical to effectively managing the management system. This information is integrated and presented in this text in the five remaining parts of the book. These parts discuss management systems and planning (chapters 4–8), organizing (chapters 9–12), influencing (chapters 13–16), controlling (chapters 17–19), and topics for special emphasis (chapters 20–21).[35] In addition, some information in these parts is presented from a contingency viewpoint to give added emphasis to the practical application of management principles.

ack to the Case

Mickey's Kitchen managers could use the management science approach to solve any operational problems that arose. According to the scientific method, Mickey's Kitchen managers would first spend some time observing what takes place in their restaurants. Next, they would use these observations to outline exactly how the restaurants operate as a whole. Third, they would apply this understanding of Mickey's Kitchen operations by predicting how various changes might help or hinder the restaurants as a whole. Before implementing possible changes, they would test them on a small scale to see whether they actually affected the restaurants as desired.

If Mickey's Kitchen managers were to follow the contingency approach to management, their actions as managers would depend on the situation. For example, if some customers hadn't been served within a reasonable period because the equipment needed to make PB&J Handwiches had broken down, then a Mickey's Kitchen manager probably would not hold employees responsible. But if the manager knew that Handwich equipment had broken down because of employee mistreatment or neglect, then the management's reaction to the situation would likely be very different.

Mickey's Kitchen managers could also apply the system approach and view their restaurants as a system, a number of interdependent parts that function as a whole to reach restaurant objectives. Naturally, Mickey's Kitchen would be seen as an open system—a system that exists in and is influenced by its environment. Major factors within the environment of Mickey's Kitchen would include customers, suppliers, competitors, and the government. For example, if McDonald's, a competitor, significantly lowered its price for hamburgers to a point well below what Mickey's Kitchen was charging for a hamburger, Mickey's Kitchen management might be forced to consider modifying different parts of their restaurant system in order to meet or beat that price.

Action Summary

Circle:

Reread the learning objectives that follow. Each objective is followed by questions. Answering these questions accurately will help you retain the most important concepts discussed in this chapter. After answering each question, check your answer with the answer key at the end of this chapter. (*Hint:* If you have doubt regarding the correct response, consult the page whose number follows the answer.)

From studying this chapter, I will attempt to acquire:

1. An understanding of the classical approach to management.

T, F
    a. The classical management approach established what it considered the "one best way" to manage.

a, b, c, d, e
    b. The process of finding the one best way to perform a task is called: (a) comprehensive analysis of management; (b) the concept of wholeness; (c) the Hawthorne studies; (d) the management science approach; (e) scientific management.

2. An appreciation for the work of Frederick W. Taylor, Frank and Lillian Gilbreth, Henry L. Gantt, and Henri Fayol.

a, b, c, d, e
    a. Fayol defines fourteen principles of management. Which of the following is *not* one of those principles: (a) scalar chain of authority; (b) esprit de corps; (c) centralization; (d) unity of command; (e) directedness of command.

a, b, c, d, e
    b. Which of the following theorists assumed that any worker's job could be reduced to a science: (a) Gilbreth; (b) Gantt; (c) Mayo; (d) Fayol; (e) Taylor.

T, F
    c. Gantt increased worker efficiency by setting standards according to top management's opinion of what maximum performance should be.

3. An understanding of the behavioral approach to management.

T, F
    a. The behavioral approach to management emphasizes striving to increase production through an understanding of the organization itself.

a, b, c, d, e
    b. The behavioral approach began with: (a) the Hawthorne studies; (b) the mental revolution; (c) the Industrial Revolution; (d) motion studies; (e) the Bethlehem Steel studies.

4. An understanding of the studies at the Hawthorne Works of the Western Electric Company.

T, F
    a. The Hawthorne studies showed a direct relationship between lighting and efficiency.

T, F
    b. The Hawthorne experimenters found that people were more concerned with preserving the work group than with maximizing their pay.

5. An understanding of the management science approach to management.

a, b, c, d, e
    a. Which of the following is not one of the philosophies of the management science approach: (a) managers can improve the organization by using scientific methods; (b) mathematical techniques can solve organizational problems; (c) models should be used to represent the system; (d) individual work is better than teamwork; (e) observation of the system must take place.

T, F
    b. In the management science theory, models are used to represent reality and then to determine how the real world situation might be improved.

6. An understanding of how the management science approach has evolved.

a, b, c, d, e
    a. The management science approach emerged after: (a) World War I; (b) the Civil War; (c) the Korean War; (d) World War II; (e) the 1930 depression.

T, F
    b. Although management science was first applied to military problems, it is now applied by companies to diverse management problems.

7. An understanding of the system approach to management.

a, b, c, d, e
    a. An organization that interacts with external forces is: (a) a closed system; (b) a model; (c) an independent entity; (d) an open system; (e) a contingency.

a, b, c, d, e
    b. Which of the following is *not* one of the guidelines proposed by Hopkins in the concept of wholeness: (a) the whole should be the main focus of analysis; (b) all analysis starts with the existence of the whole; (c) the nature of the part is determined by its position in the whole; (d) each part has some role to perform so that the whole can accomplish its purpose; (e) modifications should be made as they occur.

8. An understanding of how triangular management and the contingency approach to management are related.

a, b, c, d, e
    a. The contingency approach emphasizes the viewpoint that what managers do in practice depends over all on: (a) the worker; (b) the situation; (c) the task; (d) the environment; (e) the manager's personality.

a, b, c, d, e
    b. The three sources of information in triangular management are: (a) input, process, and output; (b) management science, classically and behaviorally based; (c) mathematics, psychology, and sociology; (d) managers, directors, and stockholders; (e) executives, administrators, and supervisors.

Introductory Case Wrap-Up: Mickey's Kitchen at The Disney Store

"Mickey's Kitchen at The Disney Store" (p. 34) and its related back-to-the-case sections were written to help you better understand the management concepts contained in this chapter. Answer the following questions about this introductory case to further enrich your understanding of the chapter content:

1. What are three problems that you think the managers of The Disney Store's Mickey's Kitchen will have to solve?

2. What action(s) do you think the managers will have to take to solve these problems?

3. From what you know about fast food restaurants, how easy would it be to manage Mickey's Kitchen? Why?

Issues for Review and Discussion

1. List the five approaches to managing.

2. Define the classical approach to management.

3. Compare and contrast the contributions to the classical approach made by Frederick W. Taylor, Frank and Lillian Gilbreth, and Henry L. Gantt.

4. How does Henri Fayol's contribution to the classical approach differ from those of Taylor, the Gilbreths, and Gantt?

5. What is scientific management?

6. Describe motion study as used by the Gilbreths.

7. Describe Gantt's innovation in the area of worker bonuses.

8. List and define Fayol's general principles of management.

9. What is the primary limitation to the classical approach to management?

10. Define the behavioral approach to management.

11. What is the significance of the studies at the Hawthorne Works of the Western Electric Company?

12. What is the management science approach to management?

13. What are the steps in the scientific method of problem solving?

14. List and explain three characteristics of situations in which management science applications usually are made.

15. Define the contingency approach to management.

16. What is a system?

17. What is the difference between a closed system and an open system?

18. Explain the relationship between system analysis and "wholeness."

19. What are the parts of the management system?

20. What is triangular management?

Building on What You Know

Directions

Review the Highlight feature indicated in the next paragraph and answer its corresponding questions. Questions in this section focus on relating a Highlight example appearing in this chapter to management concepts that you have learned in a previous chapter.

Review the Global Highlight: Delta Faucet Company on page 37. In chapter 1, "An Introduction to Management," you studied the concept of management skills. In developing and implementing an automated work process like the one at Delta, are technical skills, human skills, or conceptual skills more important to the manager? Explain.

Action Summary Answer Key

1. a. T, p. 35
   b. e, p. 36

2. a. e, pp. 41–42
   b. e, pp. 36–37
   c. F, p. 40

3. a. F, p. 43
   b. a, p. 43

4. a. F, pp. 43–44
   b. T, p. 44

5. a. d, pp. 45–46
   b. T, p. 46

6. a. d, p. 46
   b. T, p. 46

7. a. d, p. 49
   b. e, pp. 49–50

8. a. b, p. 48
   b. b, p. 51

Case Study

Scientific Management at the Watertown Arsenal

by Peter B. Petersen, The Johns Hopkins University

An early application of Frederick Taylor's principles of scientific management took place in the U.S. Army prior to World War I. General William Crozier was the Army Chief of Ordnance (weapons and other military supplies) from 1901 to 1918. Crozier was aware of Taylor's work; Taylor's principles of scientific management had been used in private industry since the mid-nineteenth century, and Crozier had observed them being used by companies manufacturing munitions.

General Crozier was in charge of the Watertown Arsenal in Boston, Massachusetts, where the Army manufactured and stored weapons. Beginning in 1909, Crozier employed consultants to introduce Taylor's scientific management techniques at the arsenal. Crozier and his subordinates identified 24 reasons for inefficiency and poor performance at the arsenal. These reasons included frequent changes in management, lack of a proper supply system, lack of coordination of work done in different shops, lack of sufficient and appropriate tools, loss of time due to breakages and subsequent repairs, delays in procuring materials, added transport costs between shops, and failure to take full advantage of the machines and tools that had been provided. Crozier employed Carl Barth, a follower of Taylor, to conduct a study at the Watertown Arsenal. The study took two years and was based on Taylor's principles of analyzing existing practices, looking for ways to improve these practices, and standardizing the improvements. In 1911, Barth began to introduce the new Taylor principles at the arsenal, including making productivity-related premium payments to workers and implementing new methods of working based on the results of time study of jobs.

Initially, the changes in management were favorably received by the workers, who appeared interested and who enjoyed the premium payments they received. Crozier concluded that great economy, as well as substantial benefits to the workers, had been achieved. After two or three months of using the new system, Crozier attempted to extend its use to the foundry also—but the foundry workers saw the new management techniques as a threat to their jobs, and they went out on strike.

Organized labor became involved; they perceived Taylor's principles as a dangerous attempt to introduce restrictions to the freedom of individual workers and eventually to reduce overall wages. Congressional hearings were held, to air testimony by organized labor as well as by Crozier and other proponents of Taylor's management methods. General Crozier testified that employees at the Watertown Arsenal working under the Taylor system had increased their wages by about 25 percent, while the government had realized overall cost savings. The cost of producing a plug for a hydraulic gun carriage, for example, was reduced from 25 cents to 7 cents.

In Crozier's Report of the Chief of Ordnance in 1912, he announced annual savings of $240,000 at the Watertown Arsenal. The cost of production for 12-inch mortar carriages was reduced from $1,536.73 to $988.36, a savings of more than 35 percent. However, despite these clear savings, the Congressional inquiry continued, fueled by the objections of organized labor.

Taylor died in 1915, and by then, his methods had gained wide acceptance in American industry. Crozier continued his efforts to introduce principles of scientific management into Army munitions production. In 1914, war had broken out in Europe, and demand for American armaments increased. American productivity in arms manufacture became increasingly important. By the time that the United States entered World War I in 1917, Taylor's principles were accepted practice both in private industry and in the Army.

Crozier's attempt to introduce scientific management at the Watertown Arsenal has been criticized for having been conducted too quickly and without sufficient communication with the workers whose jobs were affected by the new methods. Today, however, Crozier is credited with having created an effective Ordnance Department that helped prepare the United States for participation in the First World War, and with having had the persistence and vision to continue his crusade for efficiency in the face of much opposition and criticism.

Discussion Questions

1. What is the basic premise behind Taylor's principles of scientific management? How was that premise applied at the Watertown Arsenal?

2. What two factors were the keys to increased productivity at the Watertown Arsenal?

3. What key variable did General Crozier apparently ignore in his application of Taylor's scientific management principles?

4. Why was the introduction of scientific management at the Watertown Arsenal important?

A Born Entrepreneur:
Fred DeLuca of Subway Sandwiches

A thorough study of management practices cannot account for the rise of every successful entrepreneur; a businessperson like Fred DeLuca of Subway Sandwiches is a "natural." In 1965, at the age of 17, DeLuca approached Peter Buck, a family friend, for advice on financing his college career. He emerged from their discussion a full partner in "Pete's Super Submarine Sandwiches," an idea that would eventually make him a millionaire.

Although DeLuca has never studied management techniques formally, his ability to influence others is uncanny. This skill is particularly important when franchisees come into play. In order to realize their ten-year goal of 32 restaurants, in 1974, DeLuca and Buck began to sell franchises of what they renamed "Subway Sandwiches." Their franchising system is unusual in the fast food industry. The franchise fee itself is extremely low relative to competitors'; it is even lower for existing franchisees seeking to open an additional store. Restaurant start-up costs are also kept intentionally low, often less than ten percent the cost of competing franchises if equipment is leased directly from Subway Sandwiches. If the franchisee purchases equipment, he or she can do so at Subway Sandwiches' cost.

DeLuca's support does not fade away after the shop has opened, either. Subway Sandwiches headquarters staffs a toll-free information line for its franchisees. Multiple copies of newsletters are available to help the individual owners with an exchange of information and assistance. New franchisees are even regular guests at the DeLuca home. "It's critical to this kind of business to keep the lines of communication open," says DeLuca.

In exchange for low start-up expenses and extensive support structures offered by Subway Sandwiches, the corporate royalty fee that franchises pay to the corporation is higher than usual in the fast food business. Also, new franchises may find themselves in direct competition with established Subway Sandwiches shops nearby; it is a corporate policy not to protect franchise territory. In fact, DeLuca sees Subway Sandwiches' saturation of a market not only as a positive gain to the corporation, but also to individual franchisees because independent sandwich shops often cannot compete successfully in a market dominated by Subway Sandwiches shops.

When Fred DeLuca and Peter Buck went into partnership in 1965, they wanted 32 shops in ten years. They expanded that goal to 5,000 by 1994. At the end of 1990, the total had already topped 5,100. "The most important thing we can do is teach people the concepts of business. . . . A lot of people get into the business with the idea of 'Okay, I'm going to open a store,' but they don't always know all the approaches that are available to them so they can maximize their results in the business. So what you want to do is make sure that you have your skills together if you want to build and sell stores."

In 1989, DeLuca bought a stake in a small chain of chicken restaurants, Cajun Joe's. Franchises are selling briskly, many of them to Subway Sandwiches franchisees: "Cajun Joe's provides them the opportunity to grow," says DeLuca. Teaching business skills and providing opportunity for growth is not only good for the franchisee, however; it has made Fred DeLuca the success he is today.

Video Case Questions

1. What management approach did Peter Buck use in setting up his original partnership with Fred DeLuca?
2. Opening a second shop in order to "create an illusion of success" exploited one major input factor in an open system. What is that factor?
3. List three ways in which management science applications might be used to help Subway Sandwiches shops increase in efficiency.
4. How does DeLuca take advantage of Fayol's principle of esprit de corps?

Video Case Activities

1. As if you were Fred DeLuca, explain to new franchisees how Fayol's general principles of unity of direction and subordination of individual interest to general interests will serve to strengthen their individual Subway Sandwiches franchises.
2. Do a time–motion study like the one you see in Table 2.2 for the action of preparing a sandwich at Subway Sandwiches. Include at least four motions.

Chapter 3

Student Learning Objectives

From studying this chapter, I will attempt to acquire:

1. An understanding of the term *corporate social responsibility*.

2. An appreciation for the arguments both for and against business assuming social responsibilities.

3. Useful strategies for increasing the social responsiveness of an organization.

4. Insights on the planning, organizing, influencing, and controlling of social responsibility activities.

5. A practical plan for how society can help business meet its social obligations.

6. An understanding of the definition and importance of business ethics.

7. An understanding of how ethics can be incorporated into management practice.

Corporate Social Responsibility and Business Ethics

hapter Outline

THE REEBOK PUMP AND SOCIETY

When Reebok International recently unveiled its new sneaker, The Pump, company officials hailed it as a technological breakthrough. By pushing a button on the tongue, the wearer pumps air into the shoe's collar. That's not all that's inflating. At about $170, The Pump and its Nike counterpart, the Air Pressure, are the most expensive mass-market athletic shoes in the United States.

Athletic-shoe sales continue to leap, propelled in large part by the lucrative market among inner-city kids. Shoemakers will peddle more than 400 million pairs this year, up from 349 million in 1987. According to Converse, kids under 18 years old account for 58 percent of revenues. But with companies pitching such pricey models as The Pump and the $110 Nike Air Jordan, a number of critics are asking [whether] sneaker makers aren't exploiting the inner-city kids.

> A number of critics are asking [whether] sneaker makers aren't exploiting the inner-city kids.

Such questions weren't raised when sneakers were just gym shoes. Today, however, sneakers are fashionable and being chicly shod is imperative—regardless of the price. At Boston sporting-goods store Mickey Finn, many inner-city kids buy new pairs of sneakers every three weeks. Those same [youths] set the trends that entice buyers elsewhere, marketing experts say.

Is there anything wrong with making lots of money off kids, especially inner-city youth? Georgette Watson, head of a Boston community program, blames the desire for status symbols like high-priced sneakers for luring kids into the drug trade. That's the only way, she says, kids can make the money to "keep them in the image they want." Police officer William Jones, who works in Los Angeles's anti-gang unit, says, "Here, the only way to be a big kid on the block is to dress flashy. And the shoe manufacturers are just cashing in."

Paul Fireman, the Reebok International Limited chief executive, is very familiar with the controversy. He is also familiar with other recent happenings within the industry. Wholesale annual sales of branded footware to retailers were recently reported at $5.5 billion, a 19.6 percent increase from the $4.6 billion of the previous year. Fireman also knows that Nike Inc. has recently overtaken Reebok as the top seller in the marketplace. Fireman's challenge seems clear—to regain the top-seller spot.

From Todd Barrett, Rita Pyrillis, and Lynn Davenport, "Has Sneaker Madness Gone Too Far?" *Newsweek.* December 18, 1989, 51. © 1989, Newsweek, Inc. All rights reserved. Reprinted by permission. It is also from Brian Bagot, "Brand Report: Shoeboom!" *Marketing & Media Decisions* (June 1990), 61–65; and Laura Jereski, "Can Paul Put Bounce Back in Reebok?" *Business Week.* June 18, 1990, 181–82.

The introductory case ends with Paul Fireman of Reebok facing the challenge of overtaking Nike as the industry's top-selling company while facing public criticism that its shoe sales are luring young customers into the drug market. This chapter presents material that a manager like Fireman needs to analyze and deal with the dilemma of reaching company objectives while protecting or improving the welfare of society. Specifically, the chapter discusses (1) fundamentals of social responsibility, (2) social responsiveness, (3) social responsibility activities and management functions, (4) how society can help business meet social obligations, and (5) business ethics.

FUNDAMENTALS OF SOCIAL RESPONSIBILITY

The term *social responsibility* means different things to different people.[1] For purposes of this chapter, however, **corporate social responsibility** is the managerial obligation to take action that protects and improves the welfare of society as a whole and organizational interests as well.[2] According to the concept of corporate social responsibility, a manager must strive to achieve both organizational and societal goals.

The amount of attention given to the area of social responsibility by both management and society has increased in recent years and probably will continue to increase in the future.[3] The following sections present the fundamentals of social responsibility of businesses by discussing (1) the Davis model of corporate social responsibility, (2) areas of corporate social responsibility, and (3) varying opinions on social responsibility.

The Davis Model of Corporate Social Responsibility

A generally accepted model of corporate social responsibility was developed by Keith Davis.[4] Stated simply, Davis's model is a list of five propositions that describe why and how business should adhere to the obligation to take action that protects and improves the welfare of society and the organization:

Proposition 1: Social responsibility arises from social power. This proposition is built on the premise that business has a significant amount of influence on, or power over, such critical social issues as minority employment and environmental pollution. In essence, the collective action of all businesses in the country determines to a major degree the proportion of minorities employed and the prevailing condition of the environment in which all citizens must live.

Building on this premise, Davis reasons that since business has this power over society, society can and must hold business responsible for social conditions that result from exercising this power.[5] Davis explains that society's legal system does not expect more of business than it does of each individual citizen exercising personal power.

Corporate social responsibility is the managerial obligation to take action that protects and improves both the welfare of society as a whole and the interests of the organization.

Proposition 2: Business shall operate as a two-way open system, with open receipt of inputs from society and open disclosure of its operation to the public. According to this proposition, business must be willing to listen to society's representatives in regard to what must be done to sustain or improve societal welfare. In turn, society must be willing to listen to the reports of business on what it is doing to meet its social responsibilities. Davis suggests that ongoing honest and open communications between business and society's representatives must exist if the overall welfare of society is to be maintained or improved.

Proposition 3: The social costs and benefits of an activity, product, or service shall be thoroughly calculated and considered in deciding whether to proceed with it. This proposition stresses that technical feasibility and economic profitability are not the only factors that should influence business decision making. Business also should consider both the long- and short-term societal consequences of all business activities before such activities are undertaken.

Proposition 4: Social costs related to each activity, product, or service shall be passed on to the consumer. This proposition states that business cannot be expected to finance completely activities that may be socially advantageous but economically disadvantageous. The cost of maintaining socially desirable activities within business should be passed on to consumers through higher prices for the goods or services related to the socially desirable activities.

Proposition 5: Business institutions, as citizens, have the responsibility to become involved in certain social problems that are outside their normal areas of operation. This last proposition makes the point that if a business possesses the expertise to solve a social problem with which it may not be directly associated, it should be held responsible for helping society solve that problem. Davis reasons that because business eventually will share increased profit from a generally improved society, business should share in the responsibility of all citizenry to generally improve society.

Quality Highlight: Xerox Corporation Provides Social Service

The Xerox Corporation developed a program that reflects the Davis model of corporate responsibility. Xerox Corporation has found that following the strategy of maintaining a serious commitment to community improvement helps the company to reach its goal of high quality products. Xerox implements this strategy through its Social Service Leave Program, which provides Xerox employees with a paid leave in order to pursue a community service project. The employees themselves develop the ideas for useful projects to be performed within the community.

The program reflects both Xerox's high regard for the community and its regard for the self-development of its employees. The company recognizes that its respect for employee initiative and social concerns fosters a more effective and positive work force and work environment, which inevitably leads to improved product quality.

According to Marian Whipple, Xerox's Community and Employee Programs manager, employees in good standing at Xerox who have been with the company for at least three years can apply for the leave program. About sixty employees apply each year to a committee that judges the merits of the community projects and awards the leaves. Xerox spends about $300,000 per year on the program, which focuses on such projects as combating homelessness, child abuse, and drug abuse.

 ## ack to the Case

Corporate social responsibility is the obligation of a business manager to take action that protects and improves the welfare of society along with the interests of the organization. Paul Fireman, the chief executive officer of Reebok, presently faces the issue of the social responsibility that he and his company may have toward inner-city youngsters. Following the logic of the Davis corporate social responsibility model, if the desire to own Reebok shoes actually does tempt young inner-city customers to become involved with drugs, Fireman might face the need to curb the sale of Reebok's products to such customers as a way of helping society handle its inner-city drug problem. The real challenge in this situation is to determine whether the sale of Reebok products indeed unduly causes its young customers to become involved with drugs. Should Reebok hold itself responsible for contributing to the delinquency of minors merely because such customers buy Reebok products with money gained through involvement with drugs? Fireman must carefully weigh the social costs, and the social benefits, as well, of providing society with such shoes, and then proceed with the course of action that will best benefit society and Reebok.

The information presented thus far implies that Fireman should listen seriously to society's concerns about Reebok's products and not simply discount those concerns as having no merit. Perhaps the best response is for Fireman to improve the technical process used to make these shoes so that they can be produced at a lower price and be more affordable to customers.

As a result of handling this situation, Fireman possibly may acquire special expertise in developing products conducive to the discouragement of drug involvement by young inner-city customers. This expertise could benefit society if Fireman shared it with business people in other areas. For example, Fireman might be able to help the president of another company make designer clothes more affordable and therefore less apt to encourage drug involvement by young inner-city customers.

Areas of Corporate Social Responsibility

The areas in which business can become involved to protect and improve the welfare of society are numerous and diverse (see Table 3.1 on pages 66 and 67). Perhaps the most publicized of these areas are urban affairs, consumer affairs, and environmental affairs.[6]

Varying Opinions on Social Responsibility

Although numerous businesses are involved in and will continue to be involved in social responsibility activities, much controversy persists about whether such involvement is necessary or appropriate. The following two sections present some arguments for and against businesses performing social responsibility activities.[7]

TABLE 3.1 Major social responsibility areas in which business can become involved

Categories of Social Responsibility Issues

Product Line

Internal standards for product
- Quality (e.g., does it last?)
- Safety (e.g., can it harm users or children finding it?)
- Disposal (e.g., is it biodegradable?)
- Design (e.g., will its use or even "easy" misuse cause pain, injury, or death?)

Average product life comparisons versus
- Competition
- Substitute products
- Internal standards or state-of-the-art regular built-in obsolescence

Product performance
- Efficacy (e.g., does it do what it is supposed to do?)
- Guarantees/warranties (e.g., are guarantees sufficient, reasonable?)
- Service policy
- Service availability
- Service pricing
- Utility

Packaging
- Environmental impact (degree of disposability; recyclability)
- Comparisons with competition (type and extent of packaging)

Marketing Practices

Sales practices
- Legal standards
- "Undue" pressure (a qualitative judgment)

Credit practices against legal standards

Accuracy of advertising claims—specific government complaints

Nondiscriminatory portrayal of women and minorities in advertising

Consumer complaints about marketing practices
- Clear explanation of credit terms
- Clear explanation of purchase price
- Complaint answering policy
  —Answered at all
  —Investigated carefully
  —Grievances redressed (and cost)
  —Remedial action to prevent future occurrences

Adequate consumer information on
- Product use (e.g., dosage, duration of use, etc.)
- Product misuse

Fair pricing
- Between countries
- Between states
- Between locations

Packaging

Employee Education, Training, and Support

Policy on leaves of absence for
- Full-time schooling
- Courses given during working hours

Dollars spent on training
- Formal vocational training
- Training for disadvantaged worker
- OJT (very difficult to isolate)
- Tuition (job-related versus non–job-related)
- Special upgrading and career development programs
- Compare versus competition

Special training program results (systematic evaluations)
- Number trained in each program per year
- Cost per trainee (less subsidy)
- Number or percent workers still with company

Plans for future programs

Career training and counseling

Failure rates

Extend personnel understanding
- Jobs
- Skills required later
- Incentive system now available
- Specific actions for promotion
- Provision of daycare resources

Corporate Philanthropy

Contribution performance
- By category, for example:
  —Art
  —Education
  —Poverty
  —Health
  —Community development
  —Public service advertising
- Dollars (plus materials and work hours, if available)
  —As a percent of pretax earnings
  —Compared to competition

Selection criteria for contributions

Procedures for performance tracking of recipient institutions or groups

Programs for permitting and encouraging employee involvement in social projects
- On company time
- After hours only
- Use of company facilities and equipment
- Reimbursement of operating units for replaceable "lost" time
- Human resource support
  —Number of people
  —Work hours

Extent of employee involvement in philanthropy decision making

Environmental Control

Measurable pollution resulting from
- Acquisition of raw materials
- Production processes
- Products
- Transportation of intermediate and finished products

Violations of government (federal, state, and local) standards

Cost estimates to correct current deficiencies

Extent to which various plants exceed current legal standards (e.g., particulate matter discharged)

Resources devoted to pollution control
- Capital expenditures (absolute and percent)
- R & D investments
- Personnel involved fulltime, parttime
- Organizational "strength" of personnel involved

Competitive company performance (e.g., capital expenditures)

Effort to monitor new standards as proposed

Programs to keep employees alert to spills and other pollution-related accidents

Procedures for evaluating environmental impact of new packages or products

External Relations

Community Development

Support of minority and community enterprises through
- Purchasing
- Subcontracting

Investment practices
- Ensuring equal opportunity before locating new facilities
- Identifying opportunities to serve community needs through business expansion (e.g., housing rehabilitation or teaching machines)
- Funds in minority banks

TABLE 3.1 continued

Government Relations

Specific input to public policy through research and analysis

Participation and development of business/government programs

Political contributions

Disclosure of Information/Communications

Extent of public disclosure of performance by activity category

Measure of employee understanding of programs such as:
- Pay and benefits
- Equal opportunity policies and programs
- Position on major economic or political issues (as appropriate)

Relations/communications with constituencies such as stockholders, fund managers, major customers, and so on

International

Comparisons of policy and performance between countries and versus local standards

Employee Relations, Benefits, and Satisfaction with Work

Comparisons with competition (and/or national averages)
- Salary and wage levels
- Retirement plans
- Turnover and retention by level
- Profit sharing
- Day care and maternity
- Transportation
- Insurance, health programs, and other fringes
- Participation in ownership of business through stock purchases

Comparisons of operating units on promotions, terminations, hires against breakdowns by
- Age
- Sex
- Race
- Education level

Performance review system and procedures for communication with employees whose performance is below average

Promotion policy—equitable and understood

Transfer policy

Termination policy (i.e., how early is "notice" given)

General working environment and conditions
- Physical surroundings
  —Heat
  —Ventilation
  —Space/person
  —Lighting
  —Air conditioning
  —Noise
- Leisure, recreation, cultural opportunities

Fringe benefits as a percent of salary for various salary levels

Evaluation of employee benefit preferences (questions can be posed as choices)

Evaluation of employee understanding of current fringe benefits

Union/industrial relations
- Grievances
- Strikes

Confidentiality and security of personnel data

Minority and Women Employment and Advancement

Current hiring policies in relation to the requirements of all affirmative action programs

Specific program of accountability for performance

Company versus local, industry, and national performance
- Number and percent minority and women employees hired in various job classifications over last five years
- Number and percent of new minority and women employees in last two or three years by job classification
- Minority and women and nonminority turnover
- Indictments for discriminatory hiring practices

Percent minority and women employment in major facilities relative to minority labor force available locally

Number of minority group and women members in positions of high responsibility

Promotion performance of minority groups and women

Specific hiring and job upgrading goals established for minority groups and women
- Basic personnel strategy
- Nature and cost of special recruiting efforts
- Risks taken in hiring minority groups and women

Programs to ease integration of minority groups and women into company operations (e.g., awareness efforts)

Specialized minority and women career counseling

Special recruiting efforts for minority groups and women

Opportunities for the physically handicapped
- Specific programs
- Numbers employed

Employee Safety and Health

Work environment measures
- OSHA requirements (and extent of compliance)
- Other measures of working conditions

Safety performance
- Accident severity—work hours lost per million worked
- Accident frequency (number of lost time accidents per million hours)
- Disabling injuries
- Fatalities

Services provided (and cost of programs and human resources) for
- Addictive treatment (alcohol, narcotics)
- Mental health

Spending for safety equipment
- Required by law/regulation
- Not required

Special safety programs (including safety instruction)

Comparisons of health and safety performance with competition and industry in general

Developments/innovations in health and safety

Employee health measures (e.g., sick days, examinations)

Food facilities
- Cost/serving to employee, to company
- Nutritional evaluation

Arguments FOR Business Performing Social Responsibility Activities

The best-known argument supporting the performance of social responsibility activities by business was alluded to earlier in this chapter. This argument begins with the premise that business as a whole is a subset of society and exerts a significant impact on the way in which society exists. The argument continues that, since business is such an influential member of society, it has the responsibility to help maintain and improve the overall welfare of society. After all, since society asks no more and no less of any of its members, why should business be exempt from such responsibility?

In addition, some make the argument that business should perform social responsibility activities because profitability and growth go hand in hand with responsible treatment of employees, customers, and the community. In essence, this argument implies that performing social responsibility activities is a means of earning greater organizational profit.[8]

However, later empirical studies have not demonstrated any clear relationship between corporate social responsibility and profitability. In fact, several companies that were acknowledged as leaders in social commitment during the 1960s and '70s, including Control Data Corporation, Atlantic Richfield, Dayton-Hudson, Levi Strauss, and Polaroid, experienced serious financial difficulties during the 1980s.[9] (No relationship between corporate social responsibility activities and these financial difficulties was shown, however.)

Arguments AGAINST Business Performing Social Responsibility Activities

The best-known argument against business performing social responsibility activities is advanced by Milton Friedman, one of America's most distinguished economists. Friedman argues that to make business managers simultaneously responsible to business owners for reaching profit objectives and to society for enhancing societal welfare represents a conflict of interest that has the potential to cause the demise of business as it is known today.[10] According to Friedman, this demise almost certainly will occur if business continually is forced to perform socially responsible behavior that is in direct conflict with private organizational objectives.[11]

Friedman also argues that to require business managers to pursue socially responsible objectives may in fact be unethical, since it requires managers to spend money that really belongs to other individuals:

> In a free enterprise, private property system, a corporate executive is an employee of the owners of the business. He has direct responsibility to his employers. That responsibility is to conduct the business in accordance with their desires, which generally will be to make as much money as possible while conforming to the basic rules of society, both those embodied in law and those embodied in ethical custom. . . . Insofar as his actions reduce returns to stockholders, he is spending their money. Insofar as his actions raise the price to customers, he is spending the customers' money.[12]

An example that Friedman could use to illustrate his argument is the Control Data Corporation. Former chairman William Norris involved Control Data in many socially responsible programs that cost the company millions of dollars—

from building plants in the inner city and employing a minority work force to researching farming on the Alaskan tundra. When Control Data began to incur net losses of millions of dollars in the mid-1980s, critics blamed Norris's "do-gooder" mentality. Eventually, a new chairman was installed to restructure the company and return it to profitability.[13]

Many more arguments for and against business performing social responsibility activities are presented in Table 3.2.

TABLE 3.2 Major arguments for and against business performing social responsibility activities

Major Arguments for Social Responsibility

1. It is in the best interest of the business to promote and improve the communities where it does business.
2. Social actions can be profitable.
3. It is the ethical thing to do.
4. It improves the public image of the firm.
5. It increases the viability of the business system. Business exists because it gives society benefits. Society can amend or take away its charter. This is the "iron law of responsibility."
6. It is necessary to avoid government regulation.
7. Sociocultural norms require it.
8. Laws cannot be passed for all circumstances. Thus, business must assume responsibility to maintain an orderly, legal society.
9. It is in the stockholders' best interest. It will improve the price of stock in the long run because the stock market will view the company as less risky and less open to public attack and therefore award it a higher price-earnings ratio.
10. Society should give business a chance to solve social problems that government has failed to solve.
11. Business, by some groups, is considered to be the institution with the financial and human resources to solve social problems.
12. Prevention of problems is better than cures—so let business solve problems before they become too great.

Major Arguments Against Social Responsibility

1. It might be illegal.
2. Business plus government equals a monolith.
3. Social actions cannot be measured.
4. It violates profit maximization.
5. Cost of social responsibility is too great and would increase prices too much.
6. Business lacks social skills to solve societal problems.
7. It would dilute business's primary purposes.
8. It would weaken U.S. balance of payments because price of goods has to go up to pay for social programs.
9. Business already has too much power. Such involvement would make business too powerful.
10. Business lacks accountability to the public. Thus, the public would have no control over its social involvement.
11. Such business involvement lacks broad public support.

$\mathcal{B}$ ack to the Case

Table 3.2 indicates that there are many different social responsibility areas in which Paul Fireman and Reebok could become involved. The situation with The Pump, however, can best be categorized under the headings of "product line and marketing practices," since society's criticism focus on the undue fashion emphasis of the shoe as well as advertisements that seem to focus primarily on inner-city youths.

No doubt that whatever Fireman did to ease this situation with The Pump would result in a short-run decrease in The Pump sales and even cost additional money while Fireman looked for and invested in better ways to manufacture the product. At first glance such actions might seem unbusinesslike, but performing these social responsibility acts could significantly improve the public image of Reebok and be instrumental in Reebok overtaking Nike as the industry's leading seller.

Conclusions About Business Performing Social Responsibility Activities

The preceding two sections presented several major arguments for and against businesses performing social responsibility activities. Regardless of which argument or combination of arguments particular managers might support, they generally should make a concerted effort to (1) perform all legally required social responsibility activities, (2) consider voluntarily performing social responsibility activities beyond those legally required, and (3) inform all relevant individuals of the extent to which their organization will become involved in performing social responsibility activities.

Performing Required Social Responsibility Activities. Federal legislation requires that businesses perform certain social responsibility activities. In fact, several government agencies have been established and are maintained to develop such business-related legislation and to make sure the laws are followed (see Table 3.3). The Environmental Protection Agency does indeed have the authority to require businesses to adhere to certain socially responsible environmental standards. Examples of specific legislation that require the performance of corporate social responsibility activities are (1) the Equal Pay Act of 1963, (2) the Equal Employment Opportunity Act of 1972, (3) the Highway Safety Act of 1978, and (4) the Clean Air Act Amendments of 1990. The following highlight discusses DuPont's involvement with a clean air issue.

Voluntarily Performing Social Responsibility Activities. Adherence to legislated social responsibilities represents the minimum standard of social responsibility performance that business managers must achieve. Managers must ask themselves, however, how far beyond the minimum they should attempt to go.

The process of determining how far to go is simple to describe yet difficult and complicated to implement. It entails assessing the positive and negative outcomes of performing social responsibility activities over both the short and long term and then performing only the social responsibility activities that maximize management system success while making some desirable contribution to maintaining or improving the welfare of society.

TABLE 3.3 Primary functions of several federal agencies involved with social responsibility legislation

Federal Agency	Primary Agency Activities
Equal Employment Opportunity Commission	Investigates and conciliates employment discrimination complaints that are based on race, sex, or creed
Office of Federal Contract Compliance Programs	Ensures that employers holding federal contracts grant equal employment opportunity to people regardless of race or sex
Environmental Protection Agency	Formulates and enforces environmental standards in such areas as water, air, and noise pollution
Consumer Product Safety Commission	Strives to reduce consumer inquiries related to product design, labeling, etc., by promoting clarity of these messages
Occupational Safety and Health Administration	Regulates safety and health conditions in non-government workplaces
National Highway Traffic Safety Administration	Attempts to reduce traffic accidents through the regulation of transportation-related manufacturers and products
Mining Enforcement and Safety Administration	Attempts to improve safety conditions for mine workers by enforcing all mine safety and equipment standards

Global Highlight: DuPont Protects the Environment

E.I. DuPont de Nemours and Company, a producer of chemical products, exemplifies a company whose actions affect the environment at both national and international levels. When scientists in the early 1970s began to theorize that certain types of gases—gases related to some of DuPont's products—could be contributing to the breakdown of the ozone layer, DuPont encouraged further research and began looking for alternative products. As more conclusive evidence of ozone depletion caused by these gases became available, the company stepped up research efforts in order to make informed decisions about its products and their impact on the environment. As a company that conducts business in many countries, DuPont wished to assure its customers and concerned citizens throughout the world that it was sensitive to the ozone issue and that it was acting in a socially responsible manner to ensure that its products would not contribute to further deterioration of the ozone layer.

Critics, however, could argue that DuPont is merely reacting to pressure from stakeholders and/or outside pressures from environmentalists instead of proactively seeking solutions to global environmental problems.

Sandra Holmes asked top executives in 560 of the major firms in such areas as commercial banking, life insurance, transportation, and utilities to indicate the possible negative and positive outcomes their firms could expect to experience from performing social responsibility activities.[14] Table 3.4 lists the outcomes and indicates the percentage of executives questioned who expected to experience them. Although this information furnishes managers with general insights on how involved their organizations should become in social responsibility activities, it does not and cannot furnish them with a clear-cut statement about what to do. Managers can determine the appropriate level of social responsibility involvement for a specific organization only by examining and reacting to specific factors related to that organization.

Communicating the Degree of Social Responsibility Involvement. Determining the extent to which a business should perform social responsibility activities beyond legal requirements is a subjective process. Despite this subjectivity, however, managers should have a well-defined position in this vital management

TABLE 3.4 Outcomes of social responsibility involvement expected by executives and the percent who expected them

	Percent Expecting
Positive Outcomes	
Enhanced corporate reputation and goodwill	97.4
Strengthening of the social system in which the corporation functions	89.0
Strengthening of the economic system in which the corporation functions	74.3
Greater job satisfaction among all employees	72.3
Avoidance of government regulation	63.7
Greater job satisfaction among executives	62.8
Increased chances for survival of the firm	60.7
Ability to attract better managerial talent	55.5
Increased long-term profitability	52.9
Strengthening of the pluralistic nature of American society	40.3
Maintaining or gaining customers	38.2
Investor preference for socially responsible firms	36.6
Increased short-term profitability	15.2
Negative Outcomes	
Decreased short-term profitability	59.7
Conflict of economic or financial and social goals	53.9
Increased prices for consumers	41.4
Conflict in criteria for assessing managerial performance	27.2
Disaffection of stockholders	24.1
Decreased productivity	18.8
Decreased long-term profitability	13.1
Increased government regulation	11.0
Weakening of the economic system in which the corporation functions	7.9
Weakening of the social system in which the corporation functions	3.7

area and should inform all organization members of the position. Taking these steps will ensure that managers and organization members behave consistently to support the position and that societal expectations of what a particular organization can achieve in this area are realistic.

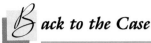

ack to the Case

Some social responsibility activities are legislated and therefore must be performed by business. Most of the legislated activities, however, are aimed at larger companies. Even though Reebok is a relatively large company, there probably is no existing legislation that would require Fireman to change The Pump.

Because Fireman is not required by law to modify The Pump for the benefit of society, whatever modifications he decides to make would be strictly voluntary. In making his decision, Fireman should assess the positive and negative outcomes of modifying his shoes over both the long and short term and then make whatever modifications, if any, that would maximize the success of Reebok as well as offer some desirable contribution to society. Fireman should tell organization members and the public what he believes to be the best action regarding The Pump and his reasons for that decision.

SOCIAL RESPONSIVENESS

The previous section discussed social responsibility as a business's obligation to take action that protects and improves the welfare of society along with the business's own interests. This section defines and discusses **social responsiveness** as the degree of effectiveness and efficiency an organization displays in pursuing its social responsibilities.[15] The greater the degree of effectiveness and efficiency, the more socially responsive the organization is said to be. The two sections that follow discuss (1) social responsiveness and decision making and (2) approaches to meeting social responsibilities.

> **Social responsiveness** is the degree of effectiveness and efficiency an organization displays in pursuing its social responsibilities.

Social Responsiveness and Decision Making

The socially responsive organization that is both effective and efficient meets its social responsibilities and does not waste organizational resources in the process. Determining exactly which social responsibilities an organization should pursue and then deciding how to pursue them are perhaps the two most critical decision-making aspects of maintaining a high level of social responsiveness within an organization.

Figure 3.1 on page 74 is a flowchart that managers can use as a general guideline for making social responsibility decisions that enhance the social responsiveness of their organization. This figure implies that for managers to achieve and maintain a high level of social responsiveness within an organization, they must pursue only the social responsibilities that their organization actually possesses and has a right to undertake. Furthermore, once managers decide to meet a specific social responsibility, they must decide the best way to undertake activities related to meeting this obligation. That is, managers must decide whether their organization should undertake the activities on its own or acquire the help of outsiders with more expertise in the area.

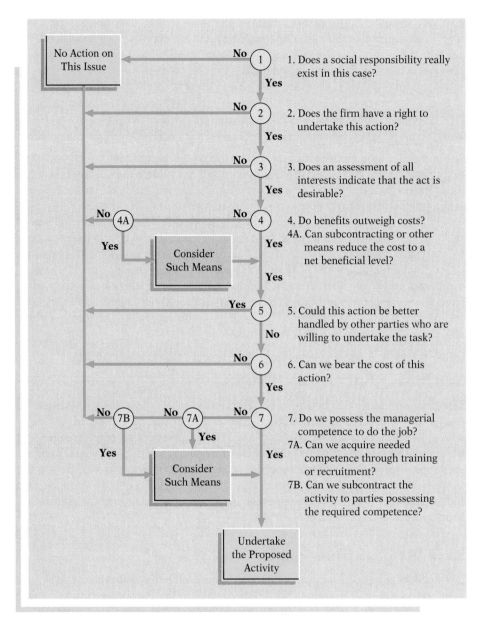

FIGURE 3.1

Flowchart of social responsibility decision making that generally will enhance the social responsiveness of an organization

Approaches to Meeting Social Responsibilities

In addition to decision making, various managerial approaches to meeting social
obligations are another determinant of an organization's level of social responsiveness. According to Lipson, a desirable and socially responsive approach to
meeting social obligations (1) incorporates social goals into the annual planning
process; (2) seeks comparative industry norms for social programs; (3) presents

reports to organization members, the board of directors, and stockholders on social responsibility progress; (4) experiments with different approaches for measuring social performance; and (5) attempts to measure the cost of social programs as well as the return on social program investments.[16]

S. Prakash Sethi presents three management approaches to meeting social obligations: (1) the social obligation approach, (2) the social responsibility approach, and (3) the social responsiveness approach.[17] Each of these approaches and the types of behavior typical of them on several dimensions are presented in Table 3.5.

TABLE 3.5 Three approaches to social responsibility and the types of behavior associated with each

Dimensions of Behavior	Approach 1: Social Obligation Prescriptive	Approach 2: Social Responsibility Prescriptive	Approach 3: Social Responsiveness Anticipatory and Preventive
Search for legitimacy	Confines legitimacy to legal and economic criteria only; does not violate laws; equates profitable operations with fulfilling social expectations	Accepts the reality of limited relevance of legal and market criteria of legitimacy in actual practice; willing to consider and accept broader extralegal and extramarket criteria for measuring corporate performance and social role	Accepts its role as defined by the social system and therefore subject to change; recognizes importance of profitable operations but includes other criteria
Ethical norms	Considers business value-neutral; managers expected to behave according to their own ethical standards	Defines norms in community-related terms: e.g., good corporate citizen; avoids taking moral stand on issues that may harm its economic interests or go against prevailing social norms (majority views)	Takes definite stand on issues of public concern; advocates institutional ethical norms even though they may be detrimental to its immediate economic interest or prevailing social norms
Social accountability for corporate actions	Construes narrowly as limited to stockholders; jealously guards its prerogatives against outsiders	Construes narrowly for legal purposes, but broadened to include groups affected by its actions; management more outward looking	Willing to account for its actions to other groups, even those not directly affected by its actions
Operating strategy	Exploitative and defensive adaptation; maximum externalization of costs	Reactive adaptation; where identifiable, internalizes previously external costs; maintains current standards of physical and social environment; compensates victims of pollution and other corporate-related activities even in the absence of clearly established legal grounds; develops industrywide standards	Proactive adaptation; takes lead in developing and adapting new technology for environmental protectors; evaluates side effects of corporate actions and eliminates them prior to the action's being taken; anticipates future social changes and develops internal structures to cope with them

TABLE 3.5 continued

Dimensions of Behavior	Approach 1: Social Obligation Prescriptive	Approach 2: Social Responsibility Prescriptive	Approach 3: Social Responsiveness Anticipatory and Preventive
Response to social pressures	Maintains low public profile, but if attacked, uses PR methods to upgrade its public image; denies any deficiencies; blames public dissatisfaction on ignorance or failure to understand corporate functions; discloses information only where legally required	Accepts responsibility for solving current problems; will admit deficiencies in former practices and attempt to persuade public that its current practices meet social norms; attitude toward critics conciliatory; freer information disclosures than in approach 1	Willingly discusses activities with outside groups; makes information freely available to public; accepts formal and informal inputs from outside groups in decision making; is willing to be publicly evaluated for its various activities
Activities pertaining to government actions	Strongly resists any regulation of its activities except when it needs help to protect its market position; avoids contact; resists any demands for information beyond that legally required	Preserves management discretion in corporate decisions, but cooperates with government in research to improve industrywide standards; participates in political processes and encourages employees to do likewise	Openly communicates with government; assists in enforcing existing laws and developing evaluations of business practices; objects publicly to government activities that it feels are detrimental to the public's good
Legislative and political activities	Seeks to maintain status quo; actively opposes laws that would internalize any previously externalized costs; seeks to keep lobbying activities secret	Willing to work with outside groups for good environmental laws; concedes need for change in some status quo laws; less secrecy in lobbying than in approach 1	Avoids meddling in politics and does not pursue special-interest laws; assists legislative bodies in developing better laws where relevant; promotes honesty and openness in government and in its own lobbying activities
Philanthropy	Contributes only when direct benefit to it clearly shown; otherwise, views contributions as responsibility of individual employees	Contributes to noncontroversial and established causes; matches employee contributions	Activities of approach 2 *plus* support and contributions to new, controversial groups whose needs it sees as unfulfilled and increasingly important

The **social obligation approach** is an approach to meeting social obligations that considers business to have primarily economic purposes and confines social responsibility activity mainly to conformance to existing legislation.

As the table indicates, each of Sethi's three approaches contains behavior that reflects a somewhat different attitude with regard to business performing social responsibility activities. The **social obligation approach,** for example, considers business as having primarily economic purposes and confines social responsibility activity mainly to conformance to existing legislation. The **social responsibility approach** sees business as having both economic and societal goals. The **social responsiveness approach** considers business as having both societal and economic goals as well as the obligation to anticipate upcoming social problems and to work actively toward preventing their appearance.

Organizations characterized by attitudes and behaviors consistent with the social responsiveness approach generally are more socially responsive than organizations characterized by attitudes and behaviors consistent with either the social responsibility approach or the social obligation approach. Also, organizations characterized by the social responsibility approach generally achieve higher levels of social responsiveness than organizations characterized by the social obligation approach. As one moves from the social obligation approach to the social responsiveness approach, management becomes more proactive. Proactive managers will do what is prudent from a business viewpoint to reduce liabilities whether an action is required by law or not.[18]

The **social responsibility approach** is an approach to meeting social obligations that considers business as having both societal and economic goals.

The **social responsiveness approach** is an approach to meeting social obligations that considers business to have societal and economic goals as well as the obligation to anticipate upcoming social problems and to work actively toward preventing their appearance.

ack to the Case

Fireman should strive to maintain a relatively high level of social responsiveness in pursuing issues such as the one involving The Pump. To do this, he should make decisions appropriate to this social responsibility area.

In terms of The Pump, Fireman must first decide if Reebok has a social responsibility to fight society's inner-city drug problem through the design and marketing of its products. If Fireman decides that Reebok has such a responsibility, he must then determine exactly how to accomplish the activities necessary to meet the responsibility. For example, can the people presently employed by Reebok develop and implement a more efficient production process for The Pump (one that would lower the price of The Pump), or should Fireman instead donate a percentage of the company's profits to drug rehabilitation and education programs? Making appropriate decisions will help Reebok meet social obligations effectively and efficiently.

In an approach that will increase Reebok's social responsiveness, Fireman should view his organization as having both societal and economic goals. He should attempt to anticipate the emergence of social problems such as the problem created by intense demand for a product in markets that cannot afford to purchase it. He should work actively to satisfy that demand with a less expensive product.

SOCIAL RESPONSIBILITY ACTIVITIES AND MANAGEMENT FUNCTIONS

This section discusses social responsibility as a major organizational activity. As such, it should be subjected to the same management techniques used for other major organizational activities, such as production, personnel, finance, and marketing activities. Managers have known for some time that to achieve desirable results in these areas, managers must be effective in planning, organizing, influencing, and controlling. Achieving social responsibility results is not any different. The following sections discuss planning, organizing, influencing, and controlling social responsibility activities.

Planning Social Responsibility Activities

Planning was defined in chapter 1 as the process of determining how the organization will achieve its objectives, or get where it wants to go. Planning social responsibility activities therefore involves determining how the organization will achieve its social responsibility objectives, or get where it wants to go in the area of social responsibility. The following sections discuss how the planning of social responsibility activities is related to the overall planning process of the organization and how the social responsibility policy of the organization can be converted into action.

The Overall Planning Process

The model shown in Figure 3.2 below depicts how social responsibility activities can be handled as part of the overall planning process of the organization. According to this figure, social trends forecasts should be performed within the organizational environment along with the more typically performed economic, political, and technological trends forecasts. Examples of social trends are prevailing and future societal attitudes toward water pollution and safe working conditions. Each of the forecasts would influence the development of the long-run plans, or plans for the more distant future, and short-run plans, or plans for the relatively near future.

Converting Organizational Policies on Social Responsibility into Action

A *policy* is a management tool that furnishes broad guidelines for channeling management thinking in specific directions. Managers should establish organizational policies in the social responsibility area just as they do in some of the more generally accepted areas, such as hiring, promotion, and absenteeism.

To be effective, social responsibility policies must be converted into appropriate action. According to Figure 3.3, this conversion involves three distinct and generally sequential phases.

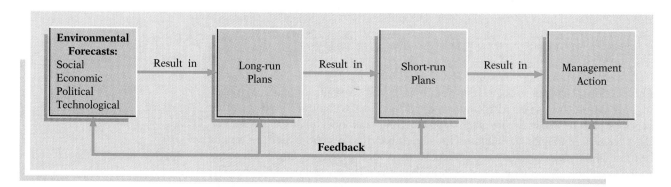

FIGURE 3.2

Integration of social responsibility activities and planning activities

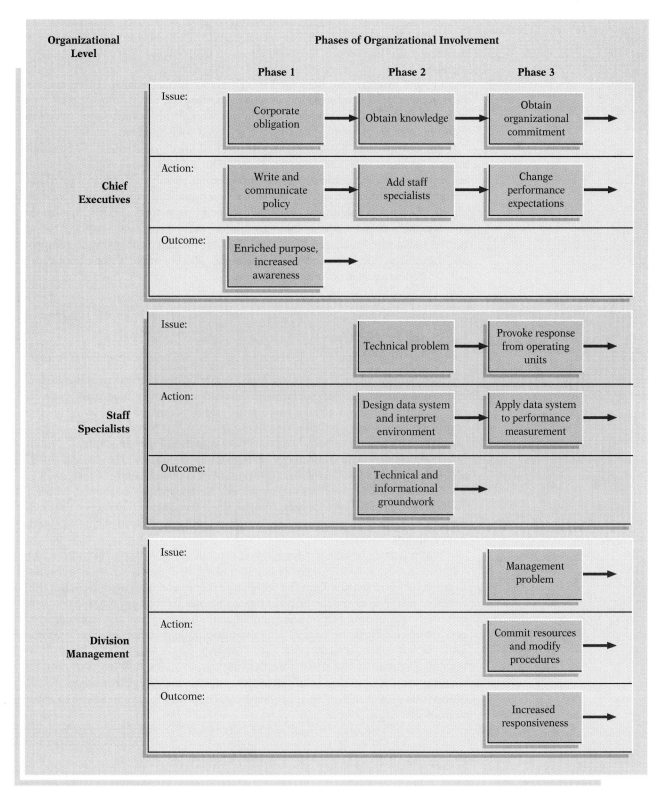

FIGURE 3.3

Conversion of social responsibility policy into action

Phase 1 consists of top management recognizing that its organization possesses some social obligation. Top management then must formulate and communicate some policy about the acceptance of this obligation to all organization members.

Phase 2 involves staff personnel as well as top management. In this phase, top management gathers information related to meeting the social obligation accepted in phase 1. Staff personnel generally are involved at this point to give advice on technical matters related to meeting the accepted social obligation.

Phase 3 involves division management in addition to organization personnel already involved from the first two phases. During this phase, top management strives to obtain the commitment of organization members to live up to the accepted social obligation and attempts to create realistic expectations about the effects of such a commitment on organizational productivity. Staff specialists encourage the responses within the organization that are necessary to meet the accepted social obligation properly. And division management commits resources and modifies existing procedures so appropriate socially oriented activities can and will be performed within the organization.

 ack to the Case

Fireman should know that pursuing social responsibility objectives could be a major management activity at Reebok. Therefore, Fireman must plan, organize, influence, and control Reebok's social responsibility activities if the company is to be successful in reaching those objectives.

In terms of planning social responsibility activities, Fireman should determine how Reebok can achieve its social responsibility objectives. He can do this by incorporating social responsibility planning into his overall planning process. That is, Fireman can make social trends forecasts along with his economic, political, and technological trends forecasts. In turn, these forecasts will influence the development of plans and, ultimately, the action taken by Reebok in the area of social responsibility.

Fireman must be able to turn Reebok's social responsibility policy into action. Fireman may want to follow the policy of making Reebok's shoes more affordable to customers and thereby limit the company's role in encouraging inner-city youth to resort to crime in order to obtain money to buy Reebok products. To convert this policy into action, Fireman first should communicate the policy to all organization members. Next, he should obtain additional knowledge of exactly how to generate lower product costs that can ultimately be passed on to the customers. Finally, Fireman should make sure that all people at Reebok are committed to meeting this social responsibility objective and that lower-level managers are allocating funds and establishing appropriate opportunities for organization members to implement this policy.

Organizing Social Responsibility Activities

Organizing was discussed in chapter 1 as the process of establishing orderly uses for all resources within the organization. These uses, of course, emphasize the attainment of management system objectives and flow naturally from management system plans. Correspondingly, organizing for social responsibility activities entails establishing for all organizational resources logical uses that emphasize the attainment of the organization's social objectives and that are consistent with the organization's social responsibility plans.

Figure 3.4 shows how Standard Oil Company of Indiana decided to organize for the performance of its social responsibility activities. The vice president for law and public affairs holds the primary responsibility in the area of societal affairs within this company and is responsible for overseeing the related activities of numerous individuals. This chart, of course, is intended only as an illustration of

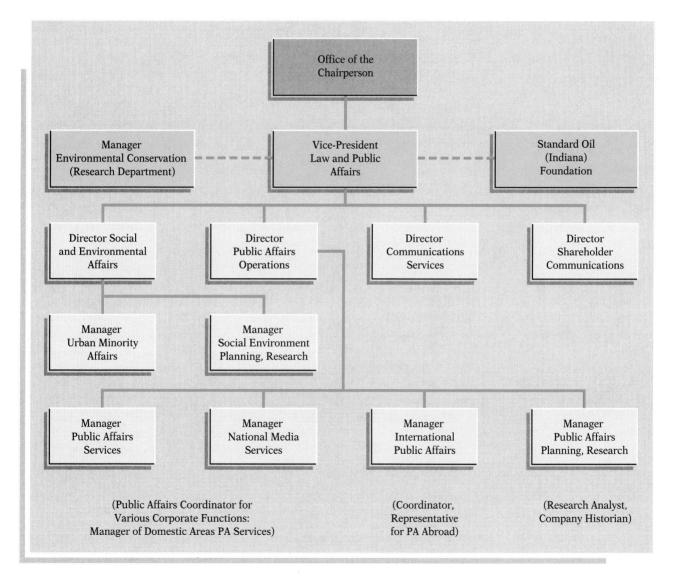

FIGURE 3.4

How Standard Oil Company of Indiana includes social responsibility in its organization chart

how a company might include its social responsibility area on its organization chart. The specific organizing in this area always should be tailored to the unique needs of each company.

Influencing Individuals Performing Social Responsibility Activities

Influencing was defined in chapter 1 as the management process of guiding the activities of organization members in directions that enhance the attainment of organizational objectives. As applied to the social responsibility area, influencing is simply the process of guiding the activities of organization members in directions that will enhance the attainment of the organization's social responsibility objectives. More specifically, to influence appropriately in this area, managers must lead, communicate, motivate, and work with groups in ways that result in the attainment of existing social responsibility objectives.

Controlling Social Responsibility Activities

Controlling, as discussed in chapter 1, is making things happen as they were planned to happen. To control, managers assess or measure what is occurring in the organization and, if necessary, change these occurrences in some way to make them conform to plans. Controlling in the area of social responsibility entails the same two major tasks. The following sections discuss various areas in which social responsibility measurement takes place and examine the social audit, a tool for determining and reporting progress in the attainment of social responsibility objectives.

Areas of Measurement

To be consistent, measurements to gauge organizational progress in reaching social responsibility objectives could be taken in any of the areas listed in Table 3.1. The specific areas in which individual companies actually take such measurements vary, of course, depending on the specific social responsibility objectives of the companies. All companies, however, probably should take such social responsibility measurements in at least the following four major areas:[19]

1. *The economic function area.* A measurement should be made of whether the organization is performing such activities as producing goods and services that people need, creating jobs for society, paying fair wages, and ensuring worker safety. This measurement gives some indication of the economic contribution the organization is making to society.

2. *The quality-of-life area.* The measurement of quality of life should focus on whether the organization is improving or degrading the general quality of life in society. Producing high-quality goods, dealing fairly with employees and customers, and making an effort to preserve the natural environment are all indicators that the organization is upholding or improving the general quality of life in society. As an example of not upholding the quality of life, some people believe that cigarette companies, because they produce goods that actually can harm the health of society over all, are socially irresponsible.[20]

3. *The social investment area.* The measurement of social investment deals with the degree to which the organization is investing both money and human resources to solve community social problems. Here, the organization could be involved in assisting community organizations involved in education, charities, and the arts.

4. *The problem-solving area.* The measurement of problem solving should focus on the degree to which the organization deals with social problems. Such activities as participating in long-range community planning and conducting studies to pinpoint social problems generally could be considered dealing with social problems.

The Social Audit: A Progress Report

A **social audit** is the process of taking measurements of social responsibility to assess organizational performance in the social responsibility area. The basic steps in conducting a social audit are monitoring, measuring, and appraising all aspects of an organization's social responsibility performance. Although companies like General Electric that pioneered concepts of social reporting are still continuing their efforts, few new companies are joining their ranks.[21]

Table 3.6 on page 84 is an example of a social audit that would be prepared by a bank. This table does not illustrate any type of standard format used for writing up the results of a social audit. In fact, probably no two organizations conduct and present the results of a social audit in exactly the same way.[22]

A **social audit** is the process of measuring the social responsibility activities of an organization. It monitors, measures, and appraises social responsibility performance.

 ack to the Case

In addition to planning social responsibility activities at Reebok, Fireman must organize, influence, and control them. To organize social responsibility activities, Fireman must establish orderly use of all resources at Reebok to carry out the company's social responsibility plans. Developing an organization chart that shows the social responsibility area at Reebok along with corresponding job descriptions, responsibilities, and specifications for the positions on this chart would be an appropriate step for Fireman to take.

To influence social responsibility activities, Fireman must guide the activities of organization members in directions that will enhance the attainment of Reebok's social responsibility objectives. He must lead, communicate, motivate, and work with groups in ways appropriate to meet those objectives.

To control, Fireman must make sure that social responsibility activities at Reebok are happening as planned. If they are not, he should make changes to ensure that they will be handled properly in the near future. One tool Fireman can use to check Reebok's progress in meeting social responsibilities is the social audit. With the audit, he can check and assess management system performance in such areas as economic functions, quality of life, social investment, and problem solving.

TABLE 3.6 Portion of sample social audit report

Social Performance Report Part 1—Mainstream Issues

Priority—Consumer Issues

Issue—Discrimination in Credit—Minorities

Potential	New legislation pending in Congress, which should be enacted within two years. Growing public awareness due to increased press coverage. Class actions a possibility.
Progress	New guidelines instituted for small loans (under $5,000), credit cards. Race no longer part of the application, emphasis on employment and credit history. No automatic restrictions.
Problems	No progress in increasing applications from minorities.
Position	Keeping pace with the competition. Better advertising of new policies would help generate new business.

Issue—Complaints and Errors

Potential	Most stated reason for customer choosing another bank is errors. A 3% reduction in closed accounts would be the equivalent of increased profits of $320,000. This could be dramatically increased if complaints were handled more quickly.
Progress	Instituted toll-free line to handle complaints. Feedback has been positive. Cost: $50,000. New manager hired in checking. Instituted a system whereby all checks are double-processed. Errors down 18%. Cost: $80,000.
Problems	No progress in ridding checking and savings account statements of errors.
Position	Perception in the marketplace regarding our service is improved. Substantial reduction in closed accounts (7%).

Priority—Employee Development

Issue—Affirmative Action

Potential	Continued close monitoring by government. Potential liability by class actions now $1 million to $10 million. Program to upgrade underutilized talent in bank (especially women) could significantly increase productivity, as well as decrease recruitment costs. Growing number of qualified minorities in area increase pool of qualified candidates.
Progress	Strong minority program instituted during the year with goals, timetables, and mechanisms for enforcement. The recent record is good: 1988, 18.3% of employees minority; 1989, 19.9%; 1990, 23.7%; 1992 goal is parity.
Problems	Minorities and women still concentrated in the lower ranks:

Percent of Bank Officers Who Are:	1986	1988	1990	1992 Goal
Minority	5.8%	7.1%	9.2%	10.8%
Women	19.7%	22.0%	26.7%	35.0%

	To reach 1992 goals, we must concentrate on developing programs to identify and train potential candidates for promotion.
Position	The above effort is largely required. It will offer no competitive advantage or disadvantage, since it is mandated industrywide.

HOW SOCIETY CAN HELP BUSINESS MEET SOCIAL OBLIGATIONS

Although the point has been made that there must be an open and honest involvement of both business and society for business to meet desirable social obligations, the bulk of this chapter has focused on what business should do in the area of social responsibility. This section emphasizes action that society should take to help business accomplish its social responsibility objectives.

Jerry McAfee, chairman of the board and chief executive officer of Gulf Oil Corporation, says that although business has some responsibilities to society, society also has the following responsibilities to business.[23]

1. *Set rules that are clear and consistent.* This is one of the fundamental things that society, through government, ought to do. Although it may come as a surprise to some, I believe that industry actually needs an appropriate measure of regulation. By this I mean that the people of the nation, through their government, should set the bounds within which they want industry to operate.

    But the rules have got to be clear. Society must spell out clearly what it is it wants the corporations to do. The rules can't be vague and imprecise. Making the rules straight and understandable is really what government is all about. One of my colleagues described his confusion when he read a section of a regulation that a federal regulatory representative had cited as the reason for a certain decision that had been made. "You're right," the official responded, "that's what the regulation says, but that's not what it means."

2. *Keep the rules technically feasible.* Business cannot be expected to do the impossible. Yet the plain truth is that many of today's regulations are unworkable. Environmental standards have on occasion exceeded those of Mother Nature. For example, the Rio Blanco shale-oil development in Colorado was delayed by the fact that the air-quality standards, as originally proposed, required a higher quality of air than existed in the natural setting.

3. *Make sure the rules are economically feasible.* Society cannot impose a rule that society is not prepared to pay for because, ultimately, it is the people who must pay, either through higher prices or higher taxes, or both. Furthermore, the costs involved include not only those funds constructively spent to solve problems, but also the increasingly substantial expenditures needed just to comply with the red-tape requirements. Although the total cost of government regulation of business is difficult to compute, it is enormous. To cite an example, the Commission on Federal Paperwork estimated the energy industry's annual cost of complying with federal energy-reporting requirements at possibly $335 million per year.

4. *Make the rules prospective, not retroactive.* Nowadays, there is an alarming, distressing trend toward retroactivity, toward trying to force retribution for the past. Certain patterns of taxation and some of the regulations and applications of the law are indications of this trend.

    A case in point is the "Notices of Proposed Disallowance" issued by the Federal Energy Administration (now the Department of Energy) in 1977 against Gulf Oil for alleged overcharges on imported crude oil during the 1973–74 oil embargo. The fact is that during those difficult months we were struggling to supply the nation's energy needs, and increasing imports with the government's support.

    We were doing our level best to follow the existing regulations on pricing imports. The charges against us, as well as many other issues raised by the

DOE, were the result of retroactive applications of vague, poorly written and confusing regulations.

It is counterproductive to make today's rules apply retroactively to yesterday's ball game.

5. *Make the rules goal-setting, not procedure-prescribing.* The proper way for the people of the nation, through their government, to tell their industries how to operate is to set the goals, set the fences, set the criteria, set the atmosphere, but don't tell us how to do it. Tell us what you want made, but don't tell us how to make it. Tell us the destination we're seeking, but don't tell us how to get there. Leave it to the ingenuity of American industry to devise the best, the most economical, the most efficient way to get there, for industry's track record in this regard has been pretty good.

BUSINESS ETHICS

The study of ethics in management can be approached from many different viewpoints. Perhaps the most practical approach is to view ethics as a catalyst causing managers to take socially responsible actions. The movement toward including the study of ethics as a critical part of management education began in the 1970s, grew significantly in the '80s, and is expected to continue growing throughout the '90s. John Shad was the chairman of the Securities and Exchange Commission during the 1980s when Wall Street became involved in a number of insider trading scandals. He recently pledged a $20 million trust fund to the Harvard Business School to create a curriculum in business ethics for MBA students. And television producer Norman Lear gave $1 million to underwrite the Business Enterprise Trust, which will give national awards to companies and "whistleblowers . . . who demonstrate courage, creativity, and social vision in the business world."[24]

The following sections present business ethics as a critical part of management by defining ethics, explaining why ethical considerations are a vital part of management practices, discussing a code of ethics, and giving some suggestions on how to create an ethical workplace.

A Definition of Ethics

Ethics is our concern for good behavior; our obligation to consider not only our own personal well-being but also that of other human beings.

Business ethics involve the capacity to reflect on values in the corporate decision-making process, to determine how these values and decisions affect the various stakeholder groups, and to establish how managers can use these observations in day-to-day company management.

Famous humanitarian Dr. Albert Schweitzer defined ethics as "our concern for good behavior. We feel an obligation to consider not only our own personal well-being, but also that of other human beings." This is similar to the precept of the Golden Rule: Do unto others as you would have them do unto you.

In business, **ethics** can be defined as the capacity to reflect on values in the corporate decision-making process, to determine how these values and decisions affect the various stakeholder groups, and to establish how managers can use these observations in day-to-day company management. Ethical managers strive for success within the confines of sound management practices that are characterized by fairness and justice.[25]

Why Ethics Is a Vital Part of Management Practices

John F. Akers, chairman of the board of IBM, recently said that it makes good business sense for managers to be ethical. Without being ethical, he believes, companies cannot be competitive at either the national or international levels. According to Akers,

> Ethics and competitiveness are inseparable. We compete as a society. No society anywhere will compete very long or successfully with people stabbing each other in the back; with people trying to steal from one another; with everything requiring notarized confirmation because you can't trust the other person; with every little squabble ending in litigation; and with government writing reams of regulatory legislation, tying business hand and foot to keep it honest.[26]

While ethical management practices may not necessarily be linked to specific indicators of financial profitability, there is no inevitable conflict between ethical practices and a firm's emphasis on making a profit.[27] As Akers's statement suggests, our system of competition presumes underlying values of truthfulness and fair dealing.

The employment of ethical business practices can enhance overall corporate health in three important areas. The first area is productivity. The employees of a corporation are stakeholders who are affected by management practices. When management employs a consideration of ethics in its actions toward stakeholders, employees can be positively affected. For example, a corporation may decide that business ethics requires a special effort to ensure the health and welfare of employees. Many corporations have established Employee Advisory Programs (EAPs), to help employees with family, work, financial, or legal problems, or with mental illness or chemical dependency. These programs can even be a source of enhanced productivity for a corporation. Control Data Corporation found that its program reduced health costs and sick-leave usage significantly.[28]

A second area in which ethical management practices can enhance corporate health is by positively affecting "outside" stakeholders, such as suppliers and customers. A positive public image can attract customers who view such an image as desirable. For example, Johnson & Johnson, manufacturer of baby products, carefully guards its public image as a company that puts customer health and well-being ahead of corporate profits, as exemplified in its code of ethics in Table 3.7 on page 88. James E. Burke, the chairman of Johnson & Johnson, is one of the directors of Norman Lear's new Business Enterprise Trust, which will support and encourage ethical business management.

*E*thics Highlight: *A&P Feeds the Needy*

A&P is another example of a company that took direct action to aid its community and has received a wealth of positive publicity in return. For A&P, the national supermarket chain, business ethics involves corporate social responsibility, and it has received much positive publicity for its efforts in providing food for the needy. The program was started in 1988 by Linda Reichert, an employee of A&P, in Montvale, New Jersey. The supermarket chain began donating food to the Community Food Bank of New Jersey, which—through its affiliation with Second Harvest, a national chain for food donations—provides food to the needy throughout the nation. A&P donates damaged goods rather than discarding them, after ensuring that the damage has not rendered the food harmful.

The food donation program has become so important to A&P that the company recently named Reichert its new food donation coordinator. This position was created in direct response to the success of Reichert's efforts. Company officials say that the primary motivation for its program is to develop an ethical or humanitarian focus within the company, although the positive publicity A&P has received may have attracted new customers as well. A&P now plans to set up food donation centers in all twenty-five states in which it operates.

The third area in which ethical management practices can enhance corporate health is in minimizing regulation from government agencies. Where companies are believed to be acting unethically, the public is more likely to put pressure on legislators and other government officials to regulate those businesses or to enforce existing regulations. For example, in 1990 hearings were held on the rise in gaso-

TABLE 3.7 The Johnson & Johnson code of ethics

We believe our first responsibility is to the doctors, nurses, and patients, to mothers and all others who use our products and services.
In meeting their needs everything we do must be of high quality.
We must constantly strive to reduce our costs in order to maintain reasonable prices.
Customers' orders must be serviced promptly and accurately.
Our suppliers and distributors must have an opportunity to make a fair profit.

We are responsible to our employees, the men and women who work with us throughout the world.
Everyone must be considered as an individual.
We must respect their dignity and recognize their merit.
They must have a sense of security in their jobs.
Compensation must be fair and adequate, and working conditions clean, orderly and safe.
Employees must feel free to make suggestions and complaints.
There must be equal opportunity for employment, development, and advancement for those qualified.
We must provide competent management, and their actions must be just and ethical.

We are responsible to the communities in which we live and work and to the world community as well.
We must be good citizens—support good works and charities and bear our fair share of taxes.
We must encourage civic improvements and better health and education.
We must maintain in good order the property we are privileged to use, protecting the environment and natural resources.

Our final responsibility is to our stockholders.
Business must make a sound profit.
We must experiment with new ideas.
Research must be carried on, innovative programs developed and mistakes paid for.
New equipment must be purchased, new facilities provided, and new products launched.
Reserves must be created to provide for adverse times.
When we operate according to these principles, the stockholders should realize a fair return.

line and home heating oil prices following Iraq's invasion of Kuwait, in part due to the public perception that oil companies were not behaving ethically.

A Code of Ethics

A code of ethics is a formal statement that acts as a guide for how people within a particular organization should act and make decisions in an ethical fashion. Ninety percent of the Fortune 500 firms, and almost half of all other firms, have ethical codes.[29] Codes of ethics commonly address issues like conflict of interest, competitors, privacy of information, gift giving, and giving and receiving political contributions or business. According to a recent survey, the development and distribution of a code of ethics within an organization is perceived as an effective and efficient means of encouraging ethical practices within organizations.[30] The code of ethics that Johnson & Johnson developed to guide company business practices (Table 3.7) is distributed in its annual report.

Managers cannot assume that merely because they have developed and distributed a code of ethics within a company the organization members have all the guidelines necessary to determine what is ethical and to act accordingly. There is no way that all ethical and unethical conduct within an organization can be written into one code.[31] Codes of ethics must be monitored continually to determine that they are comprehensive and usable guidelines for making ethical business decisions. Managers should view codes of ethics as tools that periodically must be evaluated and refined in order to more efficiently and effectively encourage ethical practices within organizations.

> **A code of ethics** is a formal statement that acts as a guide for making decisions and acting within an organization.

Creating an Ethical Workplace

Managers in most organizations commonly strive to encourage ethical practices, not only to be morally correct but to gain whatever business advantage there may be in having potential consumers and employees regard the company as ethical. The cartoon illustrates a manager who is attempting to discourage ethical practices

"I'm sensing confidence, boldness and moral sensibility. You're not going to turn out to be a whistle-blower are you?"

Wall Street Journal, November 27, 1989.
Reprinted by permission of Cartoon Features Syndicate.

TABLE 3.8 Martin Marietta's corporate ethics office

To ensure continuing attention to matters of ethics and standards on the part of all Martin Marietta employees, the Corporation has established the Corporate Ethics Office. The Director of Corporate Ethics is charged with responsibility for monitoring performance under this Code of Ethics and for resolving concerns presented to the Ethics Office.

Martin Marietta calls on every employee to report any violation or apparent violation of the Code. The Corporation strongly encourages employees to work with their supervisors in making such reports and, in addition, provides to employees the right to report violations directly to the Corporate Ethics Office. Prompt reporting of violations is considered to be in the best interest of all.

Employee reports will be handled in absolute confidence. No employee will suffer indignity or retaliation because of a report he or she makes to the Ethics Office. . . .

The Chairman of the Corporate Ethics Committee will be the President of the Corporation. The Committee will consist of five other employees of the Corporation including representatives of the Corporation's operating elements, each of whom will be appointed by the Chairman of the Committee subject to the approval of the Audit and Ethics Committee of the Corporation's Board of Directors.

The Chairman of the Corporate Ethics Committee reports to the Audit and Ethics Committee of the Martin Marietta Corporation Board of Directors.

in an organization. Creating, distributing, and continually improving a company's code of ethics is one usual step managers take to establish an ethical workplace.

Another step managers can take to create an ethical workplace is to create a special office or department with the responsibility of ensuring ethical practices within the organization. For example, management at Martin Marietta, a major supplier of missile systems and aircraft components, has established a corporate ethics office. This ethics office is a tangible sign to all employees that management is serious about encouraging ethical practices within the company (see Table 3.8).

Another way to promote ethics in the workplace is to furnish organization members with appropriate training. General Dynamics, McDonnell Douglas, Chemical Bank, and American Can Company are examples of corporations that conduct training programs aimed at encouraging ethical practices within their organizations.[32] Such programs do not attempt to teach managers what is moral or ethical but, rather, give managers criteria they can use to help determine how ethical a certain action might be. Managers can feel confident that a potential action will be considered ethical by the general public if it is consistent with one or more of the following standards:[33]

1. *The golden rule.* Act in a way you would expect others to act toward you.

2. *The utilitarian principle.* Act in a way that results in the greatest good for the greatest number.

3. *Kant's categorical imperative.* Act in such a way that the action taken under the circumstances could be a universal law, or rule, of behavior.

4. *The professional ethic.* Take actions that would be viewed as proper by a disinterested panel of professional peers.

5. *The TV test.* Managers should always ask, "Would I feel comfortable explaining to a national TV audience why I took this action?"

6. *The legal test.*[34] Is the proposed action or decision legal? Established laws are generally considered minimum standards for ethics.

7. *The four-way test.*[35] Managers can feel confident that a decision is ethical if they can answer "yes" to the following questions as they relate to the decision: Is the decision truthful? Is it fair to all concerned? Will it build goodwill and better friendships? Will it be beneficial to all concerned?

Finally, managers can take responsibility for creating and sustaining conditions in which people are likely to behave ethically and for minimizing conditions in which people might be tempted to behave unethically.[36] Two practices that commonly inspire unethical behavior in organizations are to give unusually high rewards for good performance and unusually severe punishments for poor performance. By eliminating such factors, managers can reduce much of the pressure that people feel to perform unethically in organizations.

 ack to the Case

Legislation does not exist that would require Fireman to modify The Pump to more specifically address the inner-city drug problem. If such legislation were being developed, legislators could take certain steps to help Fireman meet social responsibilities in this area. Clear, consistent, and technically feasible laws could ensure that Fireman understands what action is expected of him and of Reebok.

Laws that are written should be economically feasible, emphasize the future, and allow flexibility. Fireman should be given the flexibility to follow these laws to the best advantage of Reebok, rather than having to conform to laws by following specific steps, and he should not be penalized for what has happened in the past.

Assuming that Fireman is an ethical manager, he would be inclined to consider the well-being of other people. He would be likely to consider seriously any reasonable action to aid customers such as those in the inner city. However, if Fireman limited the enticement that his products had for customers to an extent that significantly limited the profitability and success of his company, he could be accused of being unethical in regard to his employees or anyone else who had a genuine interest in his organization's success.

Action Summary

Circle:

Reread the learning objectives that follow. Each objective is followed by questions. Answering these questions accurately will help you retain the most important concepts discussed in this chapter. After answering each question, check your answer with the answer key at the end of this chapter (*Hint:* If you have doubt regarding the correct response, consult the page whose number follows the answer.)

From studying this chapter, I will attempt to acquire:

1. An understanding of the term *corporate social responsibility.*

T, F
    a. According to Davis, since business has certain power over society, society can and must hold business responsible for social conditions that result from the exercise of this power.

a, b, c, d, e
    b. Major social responsibility areas in which business can become involved include all of the following except: (a) urban affairs; (b) consumer affairs; (c) pollution control; (d) natural resource conservation; (e) all of the above are areas of potential involvement.

2. An appreciation for the arguments both for and against business assuming social responsibilities.

T, F
    a. Some argue that since business is an influential member of society, it has the responsibility to help maintain and improve the overall welfare of society.

a, b, c, d, e
    b. Milton Friedman argues that business cannot be held responsible for performing social responsibility activities. He does not argue that: (a) doing so has the potential to cause the demise of American business as we know it today; (b) doing so is in direct conflict with the organizational objectives of business firms; (c) doing so would cause the nation to creep toward socialism, which is inconsistent with American business philosophy; (d) doing so is unethical because it requires business managers to spend money that rightfully belongs to the firm's investors; (e) doing so ultimately would either reduce returns to the firm's investors or raise prices charged to consumers.

3. Useful strategies for increasing the social responsiveness of an organization.

a, b, c, d, e
    a. When using the flowchart approach in social responsibility decision making, which of the following questions is out of appropriate sequential order: (a) Can we afford this action? (b) Does a social responsibility actually exist? (c) Does the firm have a right to undertake this action? (d) Does an assessment of all interests indicate that the act is desirable? (e) Do benefits outweigh costs?

T, F
    b. The social obligation approach to performing social responsibility activities is concerned primarily with complying with existing legislation on the topic.

4. Insights on the planning, organizing, influencing, and controlling of social responsibility activities.

T, F
    a. Organizational policies should be established for social responsibility matters in the same manner as, for example, for personnel relations problems.

a, b, c, d, e
    b. Companies should take social responsibility measurements in all of the following areas except: (a) economic utility area; (b) economic function area; (c) quality-of-life area; (d) social investment area; (e) problem-solving area.

5. A practical plan for how society can help business meet its social obligations.

   a. Ultimately, the citizens in a society must pay for the social responsibility activities of business by paying higher prices or higher taxes or both.   T, F

   b. Which of the following is *not* one of the responsibilities that society has to business, as listed by Jerry McAfee: (a) setting rules that are clear and concise; (b) making rules prospective, not retroactive; (c) making rules goal-setting, not procedure-prescribing; (d) making rules that are subjective, not objective; (e) making sure the rules are economically feasible.   a, b, c, d, e

6. An understanding of the relationship between ethics and management.

   a. The utilitarian principle suggests that managers should act in such a way that the action taken under the circumstances could be a universal law, or rule, of behavior.   T, F

   b. Management might strive to encourage ethical behavior in organizations in order to: (a) be morally correct; (b) gain a business advantage by having employees perceive their company as ethical; (c) gain a business advantage by having customers perceive the company as ethical; (d) avoid possible costly legal fees; (e) all of the above.   a, b, c, d, e

   c. Once developed, a company's code of ethics generally does not have to be monitored or revised for at least two years.   T, F

   d. Some managers create a special "office of ethics" to show employees the critical importance of ethics.   T, F

Introductory Case Wrap-Up: Reebok

"The Reebok Pump and Society" and its related back-to-the-case sections were written to help you better understand the management concepts contained in this chapter. Answer the following discussion questions about this introductory case to further enrich your understanding of chapter content:

1. Do you think that Fireman has a responsibility to respond in some way to a situation in which inner-city youths become involved in drugs so that they can earn money necessary to buy the Reebok Pump? Explain.

2. Assuming that Fireman has such a responsibility, under what conditions would it be relatively easy for him to commit the company to assume that responsibility?

3. Assuming that Fireman has such a responsibility, when would it be relatively difficult for him to live up to it?

Issues for Review and Discussion

1. Define *corporate social responsibility*.
2. Explain three of the major propositions in the Davis model of corporate social responsibility.
3. Summarize three arguments that support business pursuing social responsibility objectives.
4. Summarize Milton Friedman's arguments against business pursuing social responsibility objectives.
5. What is meant by the phrase *performing required social responsibility activities*?

6. What is meant by the phrase *voluntarily performing social responsibility activities?*

7. List five positive and five negative outcomes a business could experience as a result of performing social responsibility activities.

8. What is the difference between social responsibility and social responsiveness?

9. Discuss the decision-making process that can help managers increase the social responsiveness of a business.

10. In your own words, explain the main differences among Sethi's three approaches to meeting social responsibilities.

11. Which of Sethi's approaches has the most potential for increasing the social responsiveness of a management system? Explain.

12. What is the overall relationship between the four main management functions and performing social responsibility activities?

13. What suggestions does this chapter make about planning social responsibility activities?

14. Describe the process of turning social responsibility policy into action.

15. How do organizing and influencing social responsibility activities relate to planning social responsibility activities?

16. List and define four main areas in which any management system can take measurements to control for social responsibility activities.

17. What is a social audit? How should the results of a social audit be used by management?

18. How can society help business meet its social responsibilities?

19. What is the relationship between ethics and social responsibility?

20. Explain how managers can try to judge if a particular action is ethical.

21. What steps can managers take to make their organizations more ethical workplaces?

Building on What You Know

Directions

Review the Highlight feature as indicated below and answer its corresponding questions. Questions in this section focus on relating a Highlight example appearing in this chapter to management concepts that you have learned in a previous chapter.

Review the Ethics Highlight: A&P on page 87. In chapter 1, "An Introduction to Management," you studied the concept of managerial efficiency. Is having a source of damaged goods to donate to the poor a sign of A&P's inefficiency? Explain. Would you be concerned if you were part of top management at A&P? Why?

Action Summary Answer Key

1. a. T, p. 63
   b. e, pp. 66, 67
2. a. T, pp. 68, 69
   b. c, pp. 68, 69
3. a. a, p. 74
   b. T, p. 76
4. a. T, p. 78
   b. a, pp. 82, 83
5. a. T, p. 85
   b. d, pp. 85, 86
6. a. F, p. 90
   b. e, pp. 86–89
   c. F, p. 89
   d. T, p. 90

Volvo's Deception: Image Is Everything

by Charles B. Shrader, Iowa State University

AB Volvo of Sweden is one of the premier automobile and truck manufacturers in the world. It employs approximately 80,000 people worldwide and does approximately $15 billion in U.S. sales annually. The company's innovative management techniques, which include semi-autonomous teams of workers, modern factories, and employee incentives, are well known in the auto industry. The company's major strength, however, is its product image.

Volvo's cars are known for their durability and safety. In the past, the Volvo 240 has been selected as the safest car in its class by the National Highway Traffic Safety Administration (NHTSA). Volvos were among the first cars to be equipped with shoulder safety belts, orthopedically designed seats, laminated windshields, and front disc brakes. The company has also received numerous NHTSA awards for safety research efforts. Volvo spends approximately ten percent of its gross profits on research and development and on safety-related programs.

Volvo takes advantage of this safety image in its advertising. Many ads describe Volvos that have served their owners for hundreds of thousands of miles. Other ads compare Volvo to auto makers such as Mercedes Benz, the products of which are renowned for safety and longevity. The Volvo crash test ads showing safety researchers running cars into retaining walls are so well known that Subaru has copied the classic Volvo ads to tout the safety of its own cars. Overall, Volvos symbolize safety, reliability, and integrity.

Thus, it came as no surprise when Volvo introduced a print and television ad in 1990 which showed a Volvo 240 station wagon as the lone survivor among a row of cars, the only one able to resist the crushing impact of "Bearfoot," a highly modified monster pickup truck with oversized tires. The ad, filmed in Austin, Texas, depicted the Bearfoot crushing all the cars in the line except the Volvo, and the print caption stated, "We couldn't ask for a better endorsement."

Unfortunately for Volvo, however, this dramatic endorsement had been faked. Scali, McCabe, Sloves—the advertising agency hired by Volvo—had staged the whole thing. They blatantly reinforced the Volvo 240 by welding steel posts to the body and frame in the presence of 400 spectators before driving the truck over the row of cars. The Volvo clearly had an unfair advantage.

An angry group of spectators complained, prompting an investigation. By November, 1990, Texas Attorney General Jim Mattox forced Volvo to retract the ads and to pay over $300,000 in investigation costs. Mattox summed up the experience by saying, "Although Volvo repeatedly touts that 'Volvo is a car you can believe in,' the same cannot be said of its advertising. The . . . representation is false, misleading, and deceptive, and the car-crushing exhibition was a hoax and a sham." Volvo was also directed to apologize for the misleading ads. Their response read, "It was unfortunate that we did not label this advertisement as a dramatization. It would be even more unfortunate, however, if our agreement to withdraw the advertisement at this time created any doubt about the real-world safety of Volvo cars" (*U.S. News and World Report,* November 19, 1990, p. 19).

The aftermath spelled trouble for Volvo. Following disclosure of the faked ad, several unaltered, standard Volvos were trampled by a Bearfoot, and, as might be expected, the Volvos did, in fact, fare well, resisting its crushing impact. Nonetheless, Volvo sales began to nose-dive as more consumers became aware of the issue. Sales declined thirty-one percent in October and thirty-eight percent in November of 1990; by early 1991, inventories had swollen and the company was forced to lay off numerous employees. Volvo discounted the effect of negative publicity on sales by attributing the slump to an overall decline in the world auto market.

Another result of the false ad was that Scali, McCabe, Sloves "resigned" their $40 million account with Volvo. Volvo had to hire a consulting firm to find a new agency for their sizeable advertising account. Neither Scali, McCabe, Sloves nor Volvo ever formally accepted responsibility for faking the ad. Worse still, on November 19, 1990, *The Wall Street Journal* ran an article dealing with truth in advertising issues wherein Volvo was cited as rigging previous ads. Apparently, one series of ads from the 1970s, showing Volvo cars with large trucks resting on their hoods, was also rigged: The suspensions of these Volvos had been modified to hold the heavy loads, and jacks were used to keep the car tires from being flattened. A standard Volvo car would have sagged under such a load, and the tires would have exploded. None of the modifications were visible in the ads, but Volvo defended their use, stating that they were selling safety and not suspensions. From Volvo's point of view, reinforcing the suspension was not deceptive.

The corporate image Volvo attempts to convey focuses on their concern for employees, for product safety, and for integrity in product design. The irony is that this state-of-the-art auto manufacturer was so concerned with maintaining its good image that it lost track of the truth and may have badly damaged its image in the process.

Discussion Questions

1. To what extent is Volvo responsible for the actions of the ad agency? To whom is it responsible? What principles of ethical management are involved in this case?
2. What is your assessment of Volvo's apology? As a manager, how might your response be different?
3. What do you think were the ad agency's reasons for faking the ad in the first place? What was it trying to sell? Was the Volvo ad truly deceptive? Were Volvo's prior ads, with rigged suspensions and jacks, deceptive advertising?
4. What do you think will be the long-term effects of the faked ad on Volvo's image and sales? Has Volvo's image been permanently damaged?

Eugene Lang: Corporate Director, REFAC Technology Development Corporation

Eugene Lang is a classic example of a corporate director whose sense of social responsibility is not only corporate but also very personal. Lang's actions have not only served his organization, but also improved society as a whole. He holds an honored place in the world of corporate giving.

Lang's major philanthropic effort began in 1981, when he was asked to deliver the sixth-grade commencement address at his alma mater, P.S. 121 in Harlem, New York. Wanting to offer the black and Hispanic children he found there more than words, Lang spontaneously offered to pay for the college education of any student in the room who would graduate from high school. Over the subsequent nine years, Lang's scholarship program expanded to include other sponsors who now provide college educations to 9,000 children in thirty cities.

Lang started the REFAC Technology Development Corporation with only $3,000 in 1952, to market an industrial fastening he had invented. When he tried to get licensing for production abroad, he encountered difficulties and realized that independent inventors universally had difficulty in obtaining foreign licenses. Seeing this obstacle as an opportunity, he made himself an expert in foreign licensing and technology transfer, and he built REFAC by investing in and licensing for foreign production the products of other businesses.

Ever-sympathetic to the underdog, Lang soon saw that many inventors could not afford to bring their inventions to market without both financial and practical support. In desperation, they often sold their inventions to large corporations for a flat (and often minimal) fee, giving away future royalty payments and resale rights. Lang decided to offer inventors an alternative. He arranged for the production and marketing of their inventions in exchange for a ten percent royalty on sales. The inventors retained all rights to their inventions. "Large corporations know that individuals or small companies don't have a million dollars to spend to sue for patent infringement," says Lang, so REFAC set out to advocate on behalf of these inventors.

Lang achieved early public notice by pressing claims against major corporations such as Ford Motor Company and Motorola to get back the patent rights for Gordon Gould, one of the inventors Lang had discovered. Gould had invented the gas-discharge laser, and REFAC spent twelve years fighting to win back the patent rights for him. Since then, REFAC has sued numerous corporations on patent infringement claims, winning licensing rights for many other inventors. REFAC sued more than thirty companies for patent rights for digital time displays. In 1985, REFAC filed suit against thirty-nine companies involved in manufacturing, selling, and using automatic bank teller machines. The company is currently pursuing patent rights for blister packaging, credit card verification systems, and compact laser-disc technology.

Despite these impressive achievements and laudable advocacy efforts, Lang is not famous for his company's amazing growth or for winning Robin Hood suits against corporate giants. The public knows Lang through his philanthropic activities, which have won him many awards, including the prestigious Horatio Alger Award in 1987.

What sets Lang's philanthropy apart from that of his generous peers? His program attracts attention because it works. Lang does more than promise money to those he calls "my children"; he makes sure they get the support and encouragement they need to make it to college. He personally meets with his kids on a regular basis, and he offers a wide range of academic, cultural, and recreational activities to them and their families to keep college dreams alive. His efforts have paid off; of the sixty-one children in Lang's pilot group, thirty-four attended college, and nine others came directly to Lang for jobs.

Perhaps the greatest result of Lang's philanthropy is that his project is now a model for many others. The I Have a Dream Foundation has helped other corporate sponsors to "adopt a classroom" for $300,000. As a result, thousands of children have attended college who would not otherwise have had the opportunity.

Lang's imaginative approach to philanthropy mirrors his innovative approach to business: Both have their roots in personal advocacy. How has this advocacy paid off for Lang? Lang owns thirty-four percent of REFAC stock and claims a personal worth of $50 million. Lang says, "The easiest thing to do when you have money is to write a check. I don't believe in accepting responsibility on the basis of the easiest thing to do. I think that it is right that I do it." This philosophy of imagining a right way to do the right thing for those in need has brought extraordinary success to Eugene Lang.

Video Case Questions

1. What positive outcomes has the I Have a Dream Foundation brought to REFAC Technology? What are potential negative outcomes?

2. Into what categories of social responsibility does Lang's philanthropic activity fall? See Table 4.3.

3. Did Lang skip any recommended steps in launching the I Have a Dream Foundation? If so, what were they?

4. Discuss the ethics regarding a corporation's use of philanthropic efforts in order to achieve good publicity.

Video Case Activities

1. Divide into two groups. One group advocates for Gordon Gould and his claim to rights for his gas-discharge laser invention. The second group advocates for IBM, on the opposite side of the issue. Use the seven standards for determining ethical behavior outlined in the text on page 89 to evaluate and support your arguments.

2. The I Have a Dream Foundation activities clearly fall within the category of corporate philanthropy. Design an alternative social responsibility plan for REFAC Technology, which does not rely on philanthropic education support. How would the particular strengths of REFAC be especially useful or applicable to your plan?

PART 1

INTEGRATIVE CASE

Arthur Andersen's Ethics Program

by Robert E. Kemper, Northern Arizona University

The Arthur Andersen Worldwide Organization comprises two strategic business units: Arthur Andersen, which markets accounting, auditing, and tax services, and Andersen Consulting, an information consulting service. Over 54,000 employees operate through member firms in 54 countries, offering their professional services at 243 locations.

Andersen Consulting, an offshoot of the original Arthur Andersen program, employs between 18,000 and 19,000 consultants and serves clients through 157 offices in 45 countries. Andersen Consulting may be small relative to its big brother, but its business is large for the field, and it is an industry leader in information technology consulting. Andersen employees work with client organizations to apply available technologies and achieve the most effective business advantages.

Andersen Consulting particularly prides itself on training its employees to combine general business skills with an understanding of relevant technology in a vast number of differing industries, to help their clients manage the changes required to reach the top and stay there. Employees begin by working in a team, to gain exposure to a variety of client organizations. Thus, they have the opportunity to develop a range of business and technical skills. As their experience grows, they are then encouraged to refine their knowledge in an industry area of particular interest to them.

The partners of the Arthur Andersen Worldwide Organization are known not only for investing in the training and education of their employees around the world, but also in the continuing education of both business students and educators in the United States. In 1989, Andersen committed 7.9 percent, or $269 million, of annual revenues toward continuing education of its employees. The year before, they had announced a five-year, $5 million commitment to assist and encourage the teaching of business ethics in undergraduate and graduate business programs throughout the country. This program came in the wake of charges that only a small fraction of the millions of college and university students who go into business are exposed to any type of formal education in business ethics.

Andersen's ethics education goal was to assist undergraduate and graduate business students to understand and use the moral reasoning skills necessary for success in today's business environment. Ethical decisions rarely devolve into a choice between two black-and-white alternatives; Andersen's program would focus on providing budding executives with the tools to make sound decisions in gray areas.

The Andersen partners initiated the program because they believed the public interest can be best served by fostering ethical business practices grounded in trust and in moral choice. Through Andersen's commitment, business students would learn to respond to the complexities and demands of the ever-changing business world in which they would, presumably, spend their working lives.

As an initial step in designing the program, the Arthur Andersen Advisory Council on Ethics was created, composed of noted educators and business executives. Among other findings and suggestions, the council recommended that business school faculties be provided with teaching materials that could be integrated easily into the existing curricula.

It was determined that the program would feature a practical and intensive approach to business education. Materials were designed to focus on ethical dilemmas that professionals might expect to face early in their careers.

Faculty members received case studies, videotapes, and other resources specifically created for use in teaching business ethics. Andersen provided a two-day training program to enable faculty members to (1) apply basic ethics principles and problem-solving models to realistic situations, (2) recognize the complexity of moral reasoning skills, (3) facilitate discussions containing moral issues, (4) use a variety of teaching techniques to integrate ethical issues into functional courses, and (5) effectively use the case studies and videotapes provided for their functional business coursework.

In fact, however, the high-flying rhetoric of a national program on ethics education does not always conform to the company's ethical practices. For example, women executives have historically been very rare among the ranks of Andersen's leadership, and company representatives do not offer information on how many may have reached the ranks of Andersen partners. In addition, some members of the United States Senate have recently accused Andersen auditors of giving "unqualified" approval to the audits of a number of now-defunct savings and loan associations. Andersen's chief executive, Lawrence A. Weinbach, responded to questions regarding the future for partners involved in the savings and loan crisis by saying that "the liability system for professionals needs to be rethought." Perhaps their business ethics education may need to be rethought as well.

Discussion Questions

1. Consider the question of an ethics education program in the light of the four basic management functions. Which function(s) do you think a corporate ethics program should affect most? Why?

2. Why should students learning business ethics with examples drawn from a specific field—such as energy technology—be able to learn to apply those lessons effectively to a totally different field—such as insurance sales management? (*Hint:* Consider Andersen Consulting and the functions its employees perform for their clients.)

3. Review Fayol's general principles of management listed in Chapter 2. Discuss three of these principles in terms of what might be gained by introducing an ethical management program at a company that had not previously articulated its ethical policy.

4. Do you think Weinbach's response to congressional questions about the responsibility of Andersen partners in the bankruptcy of savings and loans reflects an appropriate ethical position? Why or why not?

5. How should an executive's business education in ethics be reflected in a document that the executive writes, which outlines company policy on social responsibility?

Cadillac Motor Car Division won the Malcolm Baldrige award in 1990 in the manufacturing division. Cadillac was recommended for its overall quality of operations and attention to manufacturing detail.

Planning

The purpose of this section is to provide a thorough explanation of planning. Planning is the first management function covered in this text because most management theorists agree that planning is the fundamental management function, the function on which all other functions should build.

Planning begins with a discussion of organizational objectives. Topics covered include the relationship between management and organizational objectives, individual versus organizational objectives, operational objectives, and management by objectives. Planning is further emphasized through extended discussion of topics like strategic planning, the decision-making process, and the various plans and planning tools available to managers. In more specific terms, the section offers the following planning fundamentals: a definition of *planning*, the steps of the planning process, the relationship between planning and the chief executive, the qualifications and duties of planners, and the evaluation of planners. The material on decision making emphasizes the definition of *decision*, important elements of the decision situation, and the use of probability theory and decision trees as tools for making decisions involving risk. The strategic planning material discusses environmental analysis establishing organizational direction, strategy formulation, strategy implementation, and strategic control. It also includes information about the tools that managers can use to develop organizational strategy: critical question analysis, SWOT, the BCG Growth-Share Matrix, the GE Portfolio Matrix, and Porter's Model for Industry Analysis. Plans and planning tool sections cover such topics as the dimensions of a plan, why plans fail, plant facilities planning, human resource planning, forecasting, and scheduling.

As with the previous section, the material here is challenging. As you study this section, think about how planning concepts relate to the material you read about in part 1. Remember, also, that an understanding of this new information is important to the comprehension of the material in the remaining sections of the text.

Chapter 4

Student Learning Objectives

From studying this chapter, I will attempt to acquire:

1. An understanding of organizational objectives.

2. An appreciation for the importance of organizational objectives.

3. An ability to tell the difference between organizational objectives and individual objectives.

4. A knowledge of the areas in which managers should set organizational objectives.

5. An understanding of the development of organizational objectives.

6. Some facility in writing good objectives.

7. An awareness of how managers use organizational objectives and help others to attain the objectives.

8. An appreciation for the potential of a management by objectives (MBO) program.

Organizational Objectives

hapter Outline

THE GROWTH OBJECTIVE CAUSES PROBLEMS AT TRANS WORLD MUSIC

Since starting Trans World Music Corporation 17 years ago, Robert Higgins has pursued success with extraordinary grit. He returned to work the day after jaw surgery and spoke at meetings through clenched teeth.

While such determination has served Higgins well—his 68% stake in Trans World is worth $128 million and his annual pay exceeds $1 million—he now needs as much grit as he can muster. In five years, Trans World has grown from 64 stores, most of them in New York, to 437 outlets in 30 states. Net income soared 11-fold, to $13.5 million, on a seven-fold increase in sales, to $268 million. Few, if any, of its competitors have grown as fast.

Yet even Trans World's investors weren't prepared for Higgins's pace.

A few other chains—The Musicland Group in Minneapolis and North Canton, Ohio-based Camelot Enterprises, among them—also have rapidly added stores. Yet even Trans World's investors weren't prepared for Higgins's pace. In 1986, the company told prospective buyers of its stock it planned to expand by 20 stores annually. In the following three years, it grew five times that fast.

Mr. Higgins formed Trans World in 1972, but the company didn't start its rapid growth until its founder noted a trend: consumers' growing demand for service and selection. So in 1982, he sold Trans World's wholesale business and accelerated the opening or acquisition of retail music stores, most of them in shopping malls.

But recently, Mr. Higgins's company has shown signs of excessive growth. The company, based in Albany, has been criticized for paying too much to rent space and to buy companies and for failing to stock a broad-enough selection of music. More worrisome is Trans World's unprecedented drop in comparable-store sales, a key retailing indicator applied to stores . . . in a crowded retail-music market.

Alarming recent news was Trans World's 6% drop during the second quarter in comparable-store sales. Mr. Higgins blames the downturn on a recent combination of a dearth of hot-selling releases and a summer full of blockbuster movies that siphoned off business from music stores. But analysts say problems digesting fast growth contributed to the decline of sales.

Finally, there is the danger that Trans World and other fast-growing retailers will glut the market. Last year, according to the Recording Industry Association of America, recorded-music sales increased 12%, to $6.25 billion. According to a survey by Billboard, over a comparable period the number of music stores nationally grew at nearly twice that rate.

Despite his company's problems, Higgins is charging ahead. "Music," he says, "is part of almost everyone's life."

From Michael Selz, "Music Retailer's Woes Mirror Dangers of Fast Growth," *Wall Street Journal* (September 12, 1989), B2. Reprinted by permission of *Wall Street Journal,* © 1989 Dow Jones & Company, Inc. All rights reserved worldwide.

Managers like Robert Higgins, the chief executive officer of Trans World Music, must recognize that a preoccupation with one organizational objective such as growth can cause serious problems for an organization. This chapter can help a manager gain a broad appreciation of how objectives can be used to guide organizations appropriately to success. This chapter discusses (1) the general nature of organizational objectives, (2) different types of organizational objectives, (3) various areas in which organizational objectives should be set, (4) how managers actually work with organizational objectives, and (5) management by objectives (MBO).

GENERAL NATURE OF ORGANIZATIONAL OBJECTIVES

Definition of Organizational Objectives

Organizational objectives are the targets toward which the open management system is directed. Organizational input, process, and output, discussed in chapter 2, all exist to reach organizational objectives (see Figure 4.1). Properly developed organizational objectives reflect the purpose of the organization; that is, they flow naturally from the organizational purpose. The **organizational purpose** is what the organization exists to do, given a particular group of customers and customer

Organizational objectives are the targets toward which the open management system is directed. They flow from organizational purpose or mission.

The **organizational purpose** is what the organization exists to do, given a particular group of customers and customer needs.

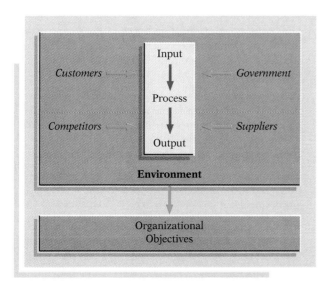

FIGURE 4.1

Existence of open management system to reach organizational objectives

needs. Table 4.1 contains several statements of organizational purpose, or mission, as developed by actual companies. If an organization is accomplishing its objectives, it is simultaneously accomplishing its purpose and thereby justifying its reason for existence.

Organizations exist for various purposes and thus have various types of objectives. A hospital, for example, may have the primary purpose of providing high-quality medical services to the community. Therefore, its primary objective is furnishing this assistance. The primary purpose of a business organization, in contrast, usually is to make a profit. The primary objective of the business organization, therefore, is to concentrate on making that profit. To illustrate, the primary organizational objective of the Lincoln Electric Company is profit oriented and has been stated as follows:

> The goal of the organization must be this—to make a better and better product to be sold at a lower and lower price. Profit cannot be the goal. Profit must be a by-product. This is a state of mind and a philosophy. Actually, an organization doing this job as it can be done will make large profits which must be properly divided between user, worker, and stockholder. This takes ability and character.[1]

In a classic article, John F. Mee has suggested that organizational objectives for businesses can be summarized in three points:

1. Profit is the motivating force for managers.
2. Service to customers by the provision of desired economic values (goods and services) justifies the existence of the business.

TABLE 4.1 Examples of statements of organizational purpose

Organization Name	Organizational Purpose (Mission)
DuPont	DuPont is a multinational high-technology company that manufactures and markets chemically related products. It services a diversified group of markets in which proprietary technology provides the competing edge.
Polaroid	Polaroid manufactures and sells photographic products based on its inventions in the field of one-step instant photography and light-polarizing products. Utilizing its inventions in the field of polarized light, the company considers itself to be engaged in one line of business.
Central Soya	The basic mission of Central Soya is to be a leading producer and merchandiser of products for the worldwide agribusiness and food industry.
General Portland Cement	It has long been a business philosophy of General Portland that "we manufacture and sell cement, but we market concrete." The company sees its job as manufacturing top-quality cement and working with customers to develop new applications for concrete while expanding current uses.

3. Social responsibilities do exist for managers in accordance with ethical and moral codes established by the society in which the industry resides.[2]

One of the most important actions managers take is to decide on the objectives for an organization. Unrealistically high objectives are frustrating for employees, and objectives that are too low do not push employees to maximize their potential. Managers should establish performance objectives that they know from experience are within reach for employees, but not within *easy* reach.[3]

Importance of Organizational Objectives

Marshall E. Dimock stresses that "fixing your objective is like identifying the North Star—you sight your compass on it and then use it as the means of getting back on track when you tend to stray."[4] Organizational objectives give managers and all other organization members important guidelines for action in such areas as decision making, organizational efficiency, organizational consistency, and performance evaluation.

Guide for Decision Making

A significant portion of managerial responsibility involves making decisions that inevitably influence the everyday operation and existence of the organization and of organization members. Once managers have a clear understanding of organizational objectives, they know the direction in which the organization must move. It then becomes their responsibility to make decisions that move the organization toward the achievement of its objectives.

Guide for Organizational Efficiency

Because inefficiency results in a costly waste of human effort and resources, managers strive to increase organizational efficiency whenever possible. Efficiency is defined in terms of the total amount of human effort and resources that an organization uses to achieve organizational aims. Therefore, before organizational efficiency can improve, managers must have a clear understanding of organizational goals. Only then are they able to use the limited resources at their disposal as efficiently as possible.

Guide for Organizational Consistency

Organization members often need work-related directives. If organizational objectives are used as the basis for these directives, the objectives serve as a guide to consistent encouragement of such things as productive activity, quality decision making, and effective planning.

Guide for Performance Evaluation

Periodically, the performance of all organization members is evaluated to assess individual productivity and to determine what might be done to increase it. Organizational goals are the guidelines or criteria that should be used as the basis for these evaluations. The individuals who contribute most to the attainment of organizational goals should be considered the most productive. Specific recommendations for increasing productivity should include suggestions about what individuals can do to help the organization move toward goal attainment.

Back to the Case

The discussion of organizational objectives gives managers like Higgins, the chief executive officer of Trans World Music, useful insights on how a company can be put on the right track and kept there. The introductory case revealed that Higgins has focused over the last several years on the objective of company growth. Based on case information, Higgins has used the objective of growth appropriately as a guide for decision making and organizational consistency. Higgins also must have evaluated the performance of organization members appropriately based on the extent to which they contributed to company growth. Merely in terms of establishing his growth objective and then managing in order to achieve that objective, Higgins should probably be complimented.

TYPES OF OBJECTIVES IN ORGANIZATIONS

Objectives can be separated into two categories: organizational and individual. Recognizing the two categories and reacting appropriately to each is a challenge for all modern managers.

Organizational Objectives

Organizational objectives are the formal targets of the organization and are set to help the organization accomplish its purpose. They concern such areas as organizational efficiency, productivity, and profit maximization.

Y.K. Shetty conducted a study to determine the nature and pattern of corporate objectives as they actually exist in organizations. Shetty analyzed 193 companies in four basic industrial groups: (1) chemicals and drugs, (2) packaging materials, (3) electricity and electronics, and (4) food processing.[5] The results of his study indicate that the most common organizational objectives relate to profitability, growth, and market share. Social responsibility and employee welfare objectives are also common and probably reflect a change in managerial attitude over a period of years. Still important but less commonly used objectives, according to the Shetty study, relate to efficiency, research and development, and financial stability.

Global Highlight: Gillette Plans Global Sales Strategy

Gillette is an excellent example of how companies focus on specific objectives. Objectives at The Gillette Company, a worldwide manufacturer of products for personal care or use, include increased growth and profitability. Some of this growth must be achieved by expanding into new markets and particularly into international markets.

In looking for ways to implement its objectives, Gillette discovered that only 8 percent of Mexican men who shave use shaving cream. The rest simply soften their beards with soapy or plain water before shaving.

Sensing an opportunity, the company introduced a new product in Guadala-jara: plastic tubs of shaving cream that sell for about half the price of Gillette's aerosol. Within about a year, 13 percent of the Guadalajaran men were using shaving cream. On the basis of this information, Gillette has developed strategies for selling its new product in the rest of Mexico, in Colombia, and in Brazil. According to Rodney Mills, retired executive vice president for Gillette's international business, the market for men's shaving products is stagnant in developed countries; new opportunities for growth will be found in underdeveloped countries. According to company information, a high proportion of the population in these countries is under fifteen years old; therefore, there is a large number of young men who will soon be shaving. Based on this information, the company will probably continue to seek growth by expanding into new international markets.

Individual Objectives

Individual objectives, which also exist within organizations, are the personal goals each organization member would like to reach through activity within the organization. These objectives might include high salary, personal growth and development, peer recognition, and societal recognition.

A management problem arises when organizational objectives and individual objectives are not compatible.[6] For example, a professor may have an individual goal of working at a university primarily to gain peer recognition. Perhaps she pursues this recognition primarily by channeling most of her energies into research. This professor's individual objective could make a significant contribution to the attainment of organizational objectives if she were at a university whose organizational objectives emphasized research. Her individual objective might contribute little or nothing to organizational goal attainment, however, if she were employed at a teaching-oriented university. Rather than improving her general teaching ability and the quality of her courses, as the university goals would suggest, she would be secluded in the library writing research articles.

One alternative managers have in situations of this type is to structure the organization so that individuals have the opportunity to accomplish individual objectives while contributing to organizational goal attainment. For example, the teaching-oriented university could take steps to ensure that good teachers received peer recognition—for example, by offering an "excellence in teaching" award. In this way, professors could strive for their personal peer recognition goal while also contributing to the university's organizational objective of good teaching.

An objective, or goal, integration model can assist managers trying to understand and solve problems related to conflict between organizational and individual objectives. Jon Barrett's model, presented in Figure 4.2 on page 112, depicts a situation in which the objectives in area C are the only individual ones (area A) compatible with organizational ones (area B). Area C represents the extent of **goal integration.**

Individual objectives are personal goals that each organization member would like to reach as a result of personal activity in the organization.

Goal integration is compatibility between individual and organizational objectives. It occurs when organizational and individual objectives are the same.

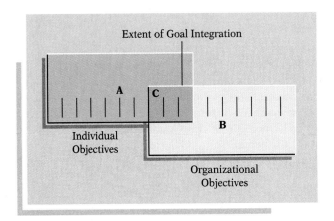

FIGURE 4.2

Goal integration model

Managers should keep two things in mind about the situation depicted in this figure: The individual will tend to work for goals in area C without much managerial encouragement, because the attainment of these goals will result in some type of reward the individual considers valuable. And the individual will usually not work for goals outside area A without some significant type of managerial encouragement, because the attainment of these goals holds little promise of any reward the individual considers valuable. Barrett suggests that "significant types of managerial encouragement" could be (1) modifications to existing pay schedules, (2) considerate treatment from superiors, and (3) additional opportunities to engage in informal social relationships with peers.

Back to the Case

Finding a common ground between organizational objectives and individual objectives often is no easy task, and conflict between these two types of objectives can spell trouble for an organization. Perhaps part of the success that Higgins has had in accomplishing growth at Trans World Music is the compatibility between organizational and individual objectives. For example, key managers at Trans World could have individual objectives of national visibility and recognition within the music industry. Assuming that they believe that company growth can contribute to the satisfaction of these two individual needs, they will normally do all they can to help Higgins achieve the organizational goal of company growth. In this type of situation, a significant degree of goal integration should help Higgins achieve company growth.

AREAS FOR ORGANIZATIONAL OBJECTIVES

Peter F. Drucker, one of the most influential management writers of modern times, indicates that the very survival of a management system may be endangered if managers emphasize only a profit objective. This single-objective emphasis encourages managers to take action that will make money today with little regard for how a profit will be made tomorrow.[7]

In practice, managers should strive to develop and attain a variety of objectives in all management system areas where activity is critical to the operation and success of the system. Following are the eight key areas in which Drucker advises managers to set management system objectives:

1. *Market standing*. Management should set objectives indicating where it would like to be in relation to its competitors.

2. *Innovation*. Management should set objectives outlining its commitment to the development of new methods of operation.

3. *Productivity*. Management should set objectives outlining the target levels of production.

4. *Physical and financial resources*. Management should set objectives with regard to the use, acquisition, and maintenance of capital and monetary resources.

5. *Profitability*. Management should set objectives that specify the profit the company would like to generate.

6. *Managerial performance and development*. Management should set objectives that specify rates and levels of managerial productivity and growth.

7. *Worker performance and attitude*. Management should set objectives that specify rates of worker productivity as well as the attitudes workers possess.

8. *Public responsibility*. Management should set objectives that indicate the company's responsibilities to its customers and society and the extent to which the company intends to live up to those responsibilities. An example of public or social responsibility objectives can be seen in the following "Ethics Highlight."

Ethics Highlight: IBM France Fights AIDS

In France, IBM has set clearly focused objectives of social responsibility. According to Patrick Vienot, the health and safety manager for IBM France, employers have a responsibility to help preserve the general health of society. Vienot feels that companies can help to enhance the health of society by fighting the spread of acquired immune deficiency syndrome (AIDS) through educating employees and their families.

Worldwide, IBM openly and publicly discusses AIDS to educate its employees and the general public about preventing and coping with the illness. IBM tries to protect its 400,000 employees worldwide by providing leaflets about the disease, and by providing small kits for traveling employees. These kits include needles and syringes in case employees need medical treatment in countries where contaminated medical equipment is a serious risk. IBM has stated publicly that it will not ostracize employees who have AIDS.

According to Drucker, since the first five goal areas relate to tangible, impersonal characteristics of organizational operation, most managers would not dispute their designation as key areas. Designating the last three as key areas could arouse some managerial opposition, however, since these areas are more personal and subjective. Regardless of potential opposition, an organization should have objectives in all eight areas to maximize its probability of success.

WORKING WITH ORGANIZATIONAL OBJECTIVES

Short-term objectives are targets to be achieved in one year or less.

Intermediate-term objectives are targets to be achieved within one to five years.

Long-term objectives are targets to be achieved within five to seven years.

The **principle of the objective** is a management guideline that recommends that before managers initiate any action, organizational objectives should be clearly determined, understood, and stated.

Appropriate objectives are fundamental to the success of any organization. Theodore Levitt states that some leading industries may be on the verge of facing the same financial disaster as did the railroads, because their objectives are inappropriate for their organizations.[8] Managers, therefore, should approach the development, use, and modification of organizational objectives with utmost seriousness. In general, an organization should have (1) **short-term objectives** (targets to be achieved in one year or less), (2) **intermediate-term objectives** (targets to be achieved in one to five years), and (3) **long-term objectives** (targets to be achieved in five to seven years).

The necessity of predetermining appropriate organizational objectives has led to the development of what is called the **principle of the objective.** The principle is that before managers initiate any action, organizational objectives should be clearly determined, understood, and stated.[9]

Establishing Organizational Objectives

Setting objectives increasingly is becoming a required and important part of a manager's job. Managers commonly are being asked to establish objectives for themselves, their departments, and their employees.[10] The three main steps that managers must take to develop a set of working organizational objectives are (1) determine the existence of any environmental trends that could significantly influence the operation of the organization, (2) develop a set of objectives for the organization as a whole, and (3) develop a hierarchy of organizational objectives. These three steps are interrelated and usually require input from several people at different levels and operational sections of the organization. Each step is further developed in the paragraphs that follow.

Analyzing Trends

The first step in setting organizational objectives is to list major trends that have existed in the organizational environment over the past five years and to determine if these trends have had a noticeable impact on organizational success. Conceivably, the trends could include such factors as marketing innovations of competitors, government controls, and social trends such as decreasing family size. Management should then decide which present and future trends are likely to affect organizational success over the next five years. This decision will determine what kinds of objectives are set at various levels of the organization.

Developing Objectives for the Organization as a Whole

After analyzing environmental trends, management should develop objectives that reflect this analysis for the organization as a whole. For example, the analysis may show that a major competitor has been continually improving its products over the past five years and, as a result, is gaining an increasingly larger share of the market. In reaction to this trend, management should set a product improvement objective in an effort to keep up with competitors. This objective would result directly from identification of a trend within the organizational environment and from the organizational purpose of profit. The paragraphs that follow illustrate how management might set financial objectives, product-market mix objectives, and functional objectives for the organization as a whole.

Establishing Financial Objectives. Financial objectives are organizational targets relating to monetary issues. In some organizations, government regulations guide management's setting of these objectives. Managers of public utility organizations, for example, have definite guidelines for the types of financial objectives they are allowed to set. In organizations free from government constraints, the setting of financial objectives is influenced mainly by return on investment and financial comparisons with competitors.

Return on investment (ROI) is the amount of money an organization earns in relation to the amount of money invested to keep the organization in operation.[11] Figure 4.3 shows how to use earnings of $50,000 and an investment of $500,000 to calculate a return on investment. If the calculated return is too low, managers can set an overall objective to improve the organization's rate of return.

Information on organizational competition is available through published indexes, such as Dun & Bradstreet's *Ratios for Selected Industries*. These ratios reflect industry averages for key financial areas. Comparing company figures with the industrial averages should tell management about the areas in which new financial objectives probably should be set or the ways in which existing objectives should be modified.[12]

Establishing Product-Market Mix Objectives. Product-market mix objectives outline which products—and the relative number or mix of these products—

> **Financial objectives** are organizational targets relating to monetary issues. They are influenced by return on investment and financial comparison with competitors.

> **Product-market mix objectives** are objectives that outline which products and the relative number or mix of these products the organization will attempt to sell.

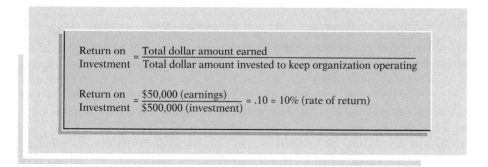

$$\text{Return on Investment} = \frac{\text{Total dollar amount earned}}{\text{Total dollar amount invested to keep organization operating}}$$

$$\text{Return on Investment} = \frac{\$50,000 \ (\text{earnings})}{\$500,000 \ (\text{investment})} = .10 = 10\% \ (\text{rate of return})$$

FIGURE 4.3

Calculations for return on investment

the organization will attempt to sell. Granger suggests the following five steps in formulating product-market mix objectives:[13]

1. Examination of key trends in the business environments of the product-market areas.

2. Examination of growth trends (both market and volume) and profit trends (for the industry and for the company) in the individual product-mix areas.

3. Separation of product-market areas into those that are going to pull ahead and those that are going to drag. For promising areas, these questions need to be asked: How can these areas be made to flourish? Should additional injections of capital, marketing effort, technology, management talent, or the like be used? For the less promising areas, these questions are pertinent: Why is the product lagging? How can this be corrected? If it cannot be corrected, should the product be milked for whatever can be regained, or should it be withdrawn from the market?

4. Consideration of the need or desirability of adding new products or market areas to the mix. In this regard, management should ask these questions: Is there a profit gap to be filled? Based on the criteria of profit opportunity, compatibility, and feasibility of entry, what are possible new areas of interest in order of priority? What sort of programs (acquisitions or internal development) does the company need to develop the desired level of business in these areas?

5. Derivation of an optimum yet realistic product-market mix profile based on the conclusions reached in steps 1–4. This profile embodies the product-market mix objectives, which should be consistent with the organization's financial objectives. Interaction while setting these two kinds of objectives is advisable.

Functional objectives are targets relating to key organizational functions. They should be consistent with financial and product-market mix objectives.

Establishing Functional Objectives. **Functional objectives** are targets relating to key organizational functions, including marketing, accounting, production, and personnel. Functional objectives that are consistent with the financial and product-market mix objectives should be developed for these areas. People in the organization should perform their functions in a way that helps the organization attain its other objectives.[14]

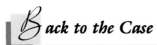 ack to the Case

The information just presented implies that managers such as Higgins should set objectives in addition to growth objectives. These other objectives should be set in such areas as profitability, market standing, innovation, productivity, physical and financial resources, managerial performance and development, worker performance and attitude, and public responsibility. Naturally, objectives should be set for the short, intermediate, and long term.

Before developing such objectives, Higgins should pinpoint any environmental trends that could influence Trans World Music operations. Objectives that reflect the environmental trends could then be set for the organization as a whole. They normally would include financial, product-market mix, and functional objectives.

Developing a Hierarchy of Objectives

In practice, an organizational objective must be broken down into subobjectives so that individuals of different levels and sections of the organization know what they must do to help reach the overall organizational objective.[15] An organizational objective is attained only after the subobjectives have been reached.

A **hierarchy of objectives** are the overall organizational objectives and the subobjectives assigned to the various people or units of the organization.

The overall organizational objective and the subobjectives assigned to the various people or units of the organization are referred to as a **hierarchy of objectives.** Figure 4.4 presents a sample hierarchy of objectives for a medium-sized company.

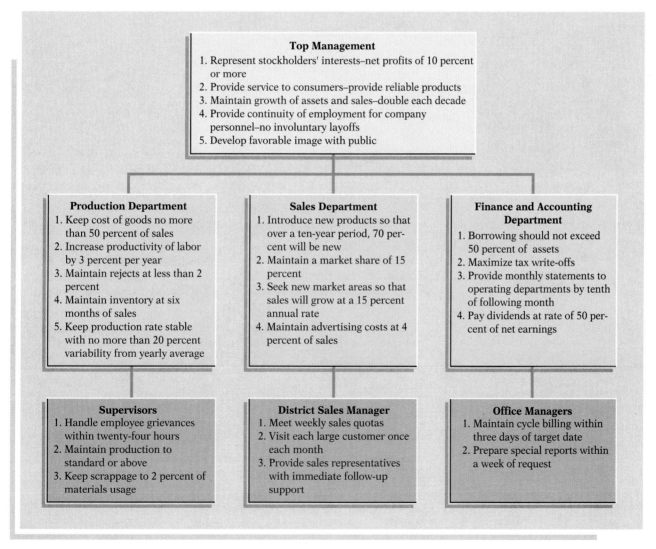

Top Management
1. Represent stockholders' interests–net profits of 10 percent or more
2. Provide service to consumers–provide reliable products
3. Maintain growth of assets and sales–double each decade
4. Provide continuity of employment for company personnel–no involuntary layoffs
5. Develop favorable image with public

Production Department
1. Keep cost of goods no more than 50 percent of sales
2. Increase productivity of labor by 3 percent per year
3. Maintain rejects at less than 2 percent
4. Maintain inventory at six months of sales
5. Keep production rate stable with no more than 20 percent variability from yearly average

Sales Department
1. Introduce new products so that over a ten-year period, 70 percent will be new
2. Maintain a market share of 15 percent
3. Seek new market areas so that sales will grow at a 15 percent annual rate
4. Maintain advertising costs at 4 percent of sales

Finance and Accounting Department
1. Borrowing should not exceed 50 percent of assets
2. Maximize tax write-offs
3. Provide monthly statements to operating departments by tenth of following month
4. Pay dividends at rate of 50 percent of net earnings

Supervisors
1. Handle employee grievances within twenty-four hours
2. Maintain production to standard or above
3. Keep scrappage to 2 percent of materials usage

District Sales Manager
1. Meet weekly sales quotas
2. Visit each large customer once each month
3. Provide sales representatives with immediate follow-up support

Office Managers
1. Maintain cycle billing within three days of target date
2. Prepare special reports within a week of request

FIGURE 4.4

Hierarchy of objectives for a medium-sized organization

Suboptimization is a condition wherein organizational subobjectives are conflicting or not directly aimed at accomplishing overall organizational objectives.

Suboptimization exists when subobjectives are conflicting or not directly aimed at accomplishing the overall organizational objective. Figure 4.4 shows that suboptimization could exist within this company between the first subobjective for the finance and accounting department and the second subobjective for the supervisors. Suboptimization would result if supervisors needed new equipment to maintain production and the finance and accounting department couldn't approve the loan without the company's borrowing surpassing 50 percent of company assets. In this situation, established subobjectives would be aimed in different directions. A manager would have to choose which subobjective would best contribute to obtaining overall objectives and should therefore take precedence.

Controlling suboptimization in organizations is part of a manager's job. Suboptimization can be minimized by developing a thorough understanding of how various parts of the organization relate to one another and by making sure that subobjectives properly reflect these relations.

Guidelines for Establishing Quality Objectives

As with all humanly developed commodities, the quality of goal statements can vary drastically. Managers can increase the quality of their objectives, however, by following some general guidelines:

1. *Managers should let the people responsible for attaining the objectives have a voice in setting them.* Often, the people responsible for attaining the objectives know their job situation better than the managers do and can help to make the objectives more realistic. (They will also be better motivated to achieve them.) Work-related problems that these people face should be thoroughly considered when meaningful objectives are being developed.

2. *Managers should state objectives as specifically as possible.* Precise statements minimize confusion and misunderstanding and ensure that employees have explicit directions for what they should do. Research shows that when objectives are not specific, the productivity of individuals attempting to reach those objectives tends to fluctuate significantly over time.[16]

3. *Managers should relate objectives to specific actions whenever necessary.* In this way, employees do not have to infer what they should do to accomplish their goals.

4. *Managers should pinpoint expected results.* Employees should know exactly how managers will determine whether or not an objective has been reached.

5. *Managers should set goals high enough that employees will have to strive to meet them but not so high that employees give up trying to meet them.* Managers want employees to work hard but not to be frustrated.

6. *Managers should specify when goals are expected to be achieved.* Employees must know the time frame for accomplishing their objectives. They then can be somewhat flexible and pace themselves accordingly.

7. *Managers should set objectives only in relation to other organizational objectives.* In this way, conflicting objectives and suboptimization can be kept to a minimum.

8. *Managers should state objectives clearly and simply.* The written or spoken word should not get in the way of communicating a goal to organization members.

Guidelines for Making Objectives Operational

Objectives must be stated in operational terms. That is, if an organization has **operational objectives,** managers should be able to tell if the objectives are being attained by comparing the actual results with the goal statements.[17]

For example, assume that a physical education instructor has set the following objectives for his students:

1. Each student will strive to develop a sense of balance.

2. Each student will attempt to become flexible.

3. Each student will try to become agile.

4. Each student will try to become strong.

5. Each student will work on becoming powerful.

6. Each student will strive to become durable.

These objectives are not operational because the activities and operations a student must perform to attain them are not specified. Additional information, however, could easily make the objectives operational. For example, the fifth physical education objective could be replaced with: Each student will strive to develop the power to do standing broad jumps the distance of his or her height plus one foot. Table 4.2 lists four basically nonoperational objectives and then shows how each can be made operational.

 B *ack to the Case*

Once managers have set overall objectives for their organization, their next step is to develop a company hierarchy of objectives. The development of this hierarchy entails breaking down the organization's overall objectives into subobjectives so that all organization members know what they must do to help the company reach its overall objectives. At Trans World Music, although a hierarchy of objectives

Operational objectives are objectives that are stated in observable or measurable terms. They specify the activities or operations needed to attain them.

TABLE 4.2 Nonoperational objectives versus operational objectives

Nonoperational Objectives	*Operational Objectives*
1. Improve product quality	1. Reduce quality rejects to 2 percent
2. Improve communications	2. Hold weekly staff meetings and initiate a newsletter to improve communications
3. Improve social responsibility	3. Hire fifty hard-core unemployed each year
4. Issue monthly accounting reports on a more timely basis	4. Issue monthly accounting reports so they are received three days following the close of the accounting period

may have existed, it probably did not include a wide array of objectives. Most employees no doubt understood that the company placed a serious emphasis on opening and maintaining retail outlets and knew what their particular roles were regarding this emphasis. Although other objectives might have existed for Trans World Music, we are led to believe that the company's hierarchy of objectives was weak in areas like social responsibility, employee welfare, and diversification.

In establishing a hierarchy of objectives, managers must be careful not to suboptimize, or establish subobjectives that conflict with one another. Suboptimization is probably not a serious problem at Trans World Music because there seems to have been an absence of different kinds of objectives. In most organizations, confusion about issues, such as not knowing what organizational objectives and subobjectives actually exist, make it difficult for managers to recognize when subobjectives are in conflict.

Other guidelines for establishing quality objectives include making the objectives clear, consistent, challenging, and specific. Perhaps most important of all, organizational objectives should be operational. These are certainly good guidelines for Higgins to follow in formulating objectives for Trans World Music. In addition, if Higgins allows workers to participate in establishing organizational objectives, he can ensure that company objectives are realistic and that organization members are committed to reaching them.

Attainment of Objectives

The attainment of organizational objectives is the obvious goal of all conscientious managers. Managers quickly discover, however, that moving the organization toward goal attainment requires taking appropriate actions within the organization to reach the desired ends. This process is called means–ends analysis.

Means–ends analysis is the process of outlining the means by which various objectives, or ends, in the organization can be achieved.

Basically, **means–ends analysis** entails "(1) starting with the general goal to be achieved; (2) discovering a set of means, very generally specified, for accomplishing this goal; and (3) taking each of these means, in turn, as a new subgoal and discovering a more detailed means for achieving it."[18]

Table 4.3 illustrates means–ends analysis for three sample goals for a hotel: increased market share, financial stability, and owner satisfaction. The goal of increased market share includes two means: good service, and employee morale/loyalty. These two means are subgoals that the hotel manager must focus on attaining in order to reach the goal of increased market share. The last column of the table lists the measures that can be taken to operationalize the subgoals.

Effective managers are aware of the importance not only of setting organizational objectives but also clearly outlining the means by which these objectives can be attained. They know that means–ends analysis is important for guiding their own activities as well as those of their subordinates. The better everyone within the organization understands the means by which goals are to be attained, the greater the probability that the goals actually will be reached.

How to Use Objectives

As stated previously, organizational objectives flow naturally from organizational purpose and reflect the organization's environment. Managers must have a firm understanding of the influences that mold organizational objectives, because as

TABLE 4.3 Sample goals, means, and measures for a hotel

Goals	Means	Measures
Increased market share	Good service	Ratio of repeat business Occupancy Informal feedback
	Employee morale and loyalty	Turnover Absenteeism Informal feedback
Financial stability	Image in financial markets	Price-earnings ratio Share price
	Profitability	Earnings per share Gross operating profit Cost trends Cash flow
	Strength of management team	Turnover Divisional profit Rate of promotion Informal feedback
Owner satisfaction	Adequate cash flow	Occupancy Sales Gross operating profit Departmental profit

these influences change, the objectives themselves must change. Objectives are not unchangeable directives. In fact, a significant managerial responsibility is to help the organization change objectives when necessary.

MANAGEMENT BY OBJECTIVES (MBO)

Some managers find organizational objectives such an important and fundamental part of management that they use a management approach based exclusively on them. This management approach, called **management by objectives (MBO),** has been popularized mainly through the writings of Peter Drucker.[19] Although mostly discussed as a valuable tool for managers of profit oriented companies, MBO should also be considered a valuable management tool for managers of nonprofit organizations like libraries or community clubs.[20] The MBO strategy has three basic parts:

Management by objectives (MBO) is a management approach that uses organizational objectives as the primary means by which to manage organizations.

1. All individuals within an organization are assigned a specialized set of objectives that they try to reach during a normal operating period. These objectives are mutually set and agreed upon by individuals and their managers.

2. Performance reviews are conducted periodically to determine how close individuals are to attaining their objectives.

3. Rewards are given to individuals on the basis of how close they come to reaching their goals.[21]

The MBO process contains five steps (see Figure 4.5):

1. *Review organizational objectives.* The manager gains a clear understanding of the organization's overall objectives.

2. *Set worker objectives.* The manager and worker meet to agree on worker objectives to be reached by the end of the normal operating period.

3. *Monitor progress.* At intervals during the normal operating period, the manager and worker check to see if the objectives are being reached.

4. *Evaluate performance.* At the end of the normal operating period, the worker's performance is judged on the extent to which the worker reached the objectives.

5. *Give rewards.* Rewards are given to the worker on the basis of the extent to which the objectives were reached.

Factors Necessary for a Successful MBO Program

Certain key factors are necessary for an MBO program to be successful. First, appropriate goals must be set by top managers of the organization. All individual MBO goals are based on these overall objectives. If overall objectives are inappropriate, individual MBO objectives also are inappropriate; and the related individual work activity is nonproductive. Second, managers and subordinates together must develop and agree on each individual's goals. Both managers and subordinates must feel that the individual objectives are just and appropriate if each party is to use them seriously as a guide for action. Third, employee performance should be conscientiously evaluated on the basis of established objectives.[22] This evaluation helps determine whether the objectives are fair and if appropriate means are being used to attain them. Fourth, management must follow through on the employee performance evaluations and reward employees accordingly.[23]

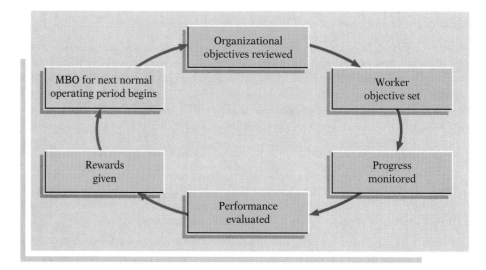

FIGURE 4.5
The MBO Process.

If employees are to continue to strive to reach their MBO program objectives, managers must reward those employees who reach or surpass their objectives more than those who perform short of their objectives. Managers must be careful, however, not to conclude that employees have produced at an acceptable level merely because they have reached their objectives. The objectives set for the employees may have been too low in the first place, and managers failed to recognize it at the time.[24]

MBO Programs: Advantages and Disadvantages

Experienced MBO managers say that there are two advantages to the MBO approach. First, MBO programs continually emphasize what should be done in an organization to achieve organizational goals. Second, the MBO process secures employee commitment to attaining organizational goals. Because managers and subordinates have developed objectives together, both parties are more interested in working to reach those goals.

Managers also admit that MBO programs have disadvantages.[25] One disadvantage is that, because organization members develop objectives together, they actually have less time in which to do their work.[26] Also, elaborate written goals, careful communication of goals, and detailed performance evaluations naturally increase the volume of paperwork in an organization.

Most managers seem to think, however, that MBO's advantages outweigh its disadvantages. Overall, they find MBO programs beneficial.[27] The following events at Boehringer Mannheim Company illustrate how a company can benefit from an MBO program.

Quality Highlight: Boehringer Mannheim Corporation

For Boehringer Mannheim Corporation, a health care company in Indianapolis, Indiana, increases in individual employee productivity and creative problem solving and in teamwork have enhanced the quality of the services they provide. Their corporate MBO program has significantly contributed to their success in these areas. The program was certainly carefully designed and implemented. In this company, all key employees were asked to set objectives, in dollar terms, regarding how much they would contribute over the next year to the company's profits. The program resulted in added focus by all employees on company profits and led to substantial profit gains for the company.

The company began implementing its MBO program in 1985 with training sessions that were attended by company management at all levels, in order to clearly demonstrate to all employees the extent of company involvement and commitment to the program. Over the years, to emphasize that MBO was not a one-shot program, performance appraisal and reward systems were modified to make them consistent with and supportive of the MBO program.

The MBO activities at Boehringer Mannheim Corporation are evidence that an effective MBO program can produce quality improvements that contribute to organizational success. In addition, these activities indicate that building such a program requires substantial support and effort by management.

$\mathcal{B}$ack to the Case

In addition to making sure that an appropriate set of objectives has been developed for an organization, management must also clearly outline for employees the means by which these objectives can be attained. Although Higgins probably did this for the objective of growth, he may not have followed guidelines for objectives related to areas like resource conservation, product quality, or the training and development of managers.

Higgins might want to consider clarifying company objectives for employees through a management by objectives program. If he does so, each employee would develop with his or her manager a set of objectives mutually agreed on. Performance reviews would give employees feedback on their progress in reaching their objectives, and rewards would be given to the employees who made the most progress.

Action Summary

Circle:

Reread the learning objectives that follow. Each objective is followed by questions. Answering these questions accurately will help you retain the most important concepts discussed in this chapter. After answering each question, check your answer with the answer key at the end of this chapter. (*Hint:* If you have doubt regarding the correct response, consult the page whose number follows the answer.)

From studying this chapter, I will attempt to acquire:

1. **An understanding of organizational objectives.**

T, F
a. Organizational objectives should reflect the organization's purpose.

a, b, c, d, e
b. The targets toward which an open management system is directed are referred to as: (a) functional objectives; (b) organizational objectives; (c) operational objectives; (d) courses of action; (e) individual objectives.

2. **An appreciation for the importance of organizational objectives.**

a, b, c, d, e
a. Organizational objectives serve important functions in all of the following areas except: (a) making performance evaluations useful; (b) establishing consistency; (c) increasing efficiency; (d) improving wages; (e) decision making that influences everyday operations.

T, F
b. Implied within organizational objectives are hints on how to define the most productive workers in the organization.

3. **An ability to tell the difference between organizational objectives and individual objectives.**

a, b, c, d, e
a. Which of the following is considered to be an individual objective: (a) peer recognition; (b) financial security; (c) personal growth; (d) b and c; (e) all of the above.

a, b, c, d, e
b. When goal integration exists: (a) there is a positive situation, desired by management; (b) managers will not see conflict between organizational and

personal objectives; (c) the individual will work for goals without much managerial encouragement; (d) additional opportunities to engage in informal social relationships with peers will not be necessary to encourage the individual; (e) all of the above.

4. **A knowledge of the areas in which managers should set organizational objectives.**

   a. The eight key areas in which Peter F. Drucker advises managers to set objectives include all of the following except: (a) market standing; (b) productivity; (c) public responsibility; (d) inventory control; (e) manager performance and development.

   a, b, c, d, e

   b. Long-term objectives are defined as targets to be achieved in one to five years.

   T, F

5. **An understanding of the development of organizational objectives.**

   a. Which of the following factors would not be considered in analyzing trends: (a) marketing innovations of competitors; (b) projections for society; (c) government controls; (d) known existing and projected future events; (e) product-market mix.

   a, b, c, d, e

   b. Which of the following factors would not be considered in the "developing objectives for the organization as a whole" stage of setting organizational objectives: (a) establishing a hierarchy of objectives; (b) establishing product-market mix objectives; (c) establishing financial objectives; (d) establishing return-on-investment objectives; (e) establishing functional objectives.

   a, b, c, d, e

6. **Some facility in writing good objectives.**

   a. Which of the following is an objective stated in nonoperational terms: (a) reduce customer complaints by 9 percent; (b) make great progress in new product development; (c) develop a new customer; (d) increase profit before taxes by 10 percent; (e) reduce quality rejects by 2 percent.

   a, b, c, d, e

   b. An example of a good operational objective is: "Each student in this class will try to learn how to manage."

   T, F

7. **An awareness of how managers use organizational objectives and help others to attain the objectives.**

   a. Means–ends analysis implies that the manager is results-oriented and discovers a set of means for accomplishing a goal.

   T, F

   b. Which of the following guidelines should managers use in changing objectives: (a) objectives should not be changed; (b) adapt objectives when the organization's environmental influences change; (c) change objectives to create suboptimization as needed; (d) adapt objectives so that they are nonoperational; (e) all of the above are valid guidelines.

   a, b, c, d, e

8. **An appreciation for the potential of a management by objectives (MBO) program.**

   a. Both performance evaluations and employee rewards should be tied to objectives assigned to individuals when the firm is using MBO.

   T, F

   b. A method under which a manager is given specific objectives to achieve and is evaluated according to the accomplishment of these objectives is: (a) means–ends analysis; (b) operational objectives; (c) individual objectives; (d) management by objectives; (e) management by exception.

   a, b, c, d, e

Introductory Case Wrap-Up: Trans World Music

"The Growth Objective Causes Problems at Trans World Music" (p. 106) and its related back-to-the-case sections were written to help you better understand the management concepts discussed in this chapter. Answer the following discussion questions about this introductory case to further enrich your understanding of the chapter content:

1. Do you believe that Higgins should have developed and emphasized objectives other than the growth objective at Trans World Music? Why?

2. Explain fully how Higgins's preoccupation with company growth could have caused problems like spending too much on rent, paying too much to buy companies, and experiencing declining sales. What kinds of objectives could Higgins develop for Trans World Music to eliminate these problems in the future?

3. As a manager, what strengths does Higgins appear to have? What weaknesses does he appear to have?

Issues for Review and Discussion

1. What are organizational objectives and how do they relate to organizational purpose?

2. Explain why objectives are important to an organization.

3. List four areas in which organizational objectives can act as important guidelines for performance.

4. Explain the difference between organizational objectives and individual objectives.

5. What is meant by goal integration?

6. List and define eight key areas in which organizational objectives should be set.

7. How do environmental trends affect the process of establishing organizational objectives?

8. How does return on investment relate to setting financial objectives?

9. Define *product-market mix objectives*. What process should a manager go through to establish them?

10. What are functional objectives?

11. What is a hierarchy of objectives?

12. Explain the purpose of a hierarchy of objectives.

13. How does suboptimization relate to a hierarchy of objectives?

14. List eight guidelines a manager should follow to establish quality organizational objectives.

15. How does a manager make objectives operational?

16. Explain the concept of means–ends analysis.

17. Should a manager ever modify or change existing organizational objectives? If no, why? If yes, when?

18. Define *MBO* and describe its main characteristics.

19. List and describe the factors necessary for an MBO program to be successful.

20. Discuss the advantages and the disadvantages of MBO.

Building on What You Know

Directions

Review the Highlight feature as indicated on page 127 and answer its corresponding question(s). Questions in this section focus on relating a Highlight appearing in this chapter to management concepts that you have learned in a previous chapter.

Review the Ethics Highlight: IBM France on page 113. In chapter 3, "Corporate Social Responsibility and Business Ethics," you studied several standards that can be used to try to determine if a particular management action is ethical. Which of these standards can be used to argue that IBM's actions in France are ethical? Explain. In your opinion, can any of these standards be used to argue that the actions are unethical? Explain.

Action Summary Answer Key

1. a. T, p. 107
   b. b, p. 107
2. a. d, pp. 109–110
   b. T, pp. 109–110

3. a. e, pp. 110–111
   b. e, pp. 111–112
4. a. d, p. 113
   b. F, p. 114

5. a. e, p. 114
   b. a, pp. 115–116
6. a. b, p. 119
   b. F, p. 119

7. a. T, p. 120
   b. b, pp. 120–121
8. a. T, p. 121
   b. d, p. 122

Case Study

Over-Organizing at Winnebago Industries

by Robert E. Kemper, Northern Arizona University

In 1986, after seventeen years as a fast-track vice president for Control Data Corporation in Minneapolis, Gerald Gilbert moved to Forest City, Iowa, for some tranquil country life. The 4,300 residents of Forest City prized simple, family pleasures; life moved to the rhythm of the changing seasons and the factory whistle. "The opportunity was just unbelievable," Gilbert said of his new position as chief executive officer of Winnebago Industries. He could hardly wait to show that modern management techniques could revolutionize this low-tech industry and could help Winnebago to dominate the industry.

Winnebago Industries was founded by John K. Hanson, who, at the age of seventy-five, remained as chairman of the board. During the fourteen years prior to hiring Gilbert, Winnebago had run through five chief executives under Hanson's leadership, but Gilbert did not plan to be merely number six.

At that time, Winnebago's primary business was manufacturing motor homes and self-contained recreational vehicles, as well as travel trailers, van conversions, and cargo/passenger compartments for small trucks. Gilbert and his chief assistant, Richard Berreth, saw themselves leading Winnebago to dominate this low-tech, cottage industry by reducing production costs and streamlining operations. The factory was as advanced as any, but Gilbert and Berreth had numerous new ideas. They would implement several procedures to streamline production of Winnebago's freeway yachts, such as "statistical process control," "mixed model production," and "work cells." They didn't consult Hanson, the plant's management, or the workers about the advisability of these procedures, because they knew the procedures had proved highly effective elsewhere.

A motor home is essentially a studio apartment on wheels. Only 60,000 sell industrywide each year, so mass production is a relative notion. A Winnebago starts life as a Chevrolet-powered truck chassis, stretched a bit, with outriggers added to hold storage bins, wiring, and plumbing. On the assembly line, it gets floor and carpet, lower cabinets and walls, a roof and doors.

Berreth set to work, immediately cutting inventory costs by demanding that the most heavily used components be unloaded directly from trucks to the assembly line. He made employee teams ("work cells") responsible for the quality of particular assembly jobs from start to finish. Eager to get the products to market, he cut the total time of manufacture of the motor home's first section. He believed that if more products got to market more quickly, Winnebago could increase its share of the market.

Next, he sought a way to jettison the time-honored method of installing interior equipment after the walls were up. Berreth saw this as a waste of time and personnel; furthermore, the equipment and interior surfaces were constantly getting dings and dents. Following the 1987 stock market crash, Gilbert and

128

Berreth seized the opportunity of a slowdown in sales to make a major MBO move: merging three assembly lines into two. This cleared space for an ambitious subassembly operation, where workers would preattach appliances and cabinets to the interior walls before hoisting them onto the assembly line.

While the plant was still reeling from the revolutionary merger of assembly lines, another MBO change got underway: switching from batch production—50 of these, 100 of those—to a mixed-run ("mixed-model") system in which any of 58 models could be next down the line. Workers literally had no idea what they might be expected to do next. In the previous operation of the plant, workers' bodies and hands and minds could settle into a comfortable rhythm of actions for each batch before having to shift into a new rhythm for the next one. Clearly, these city guys had a different and more frenetic pace in mind for the factory.

That was the situation when orders increased dramatically in April, 1988. As production picked up, the two remaining assembly lines became jammed with workers. Overtime, including Saturdays, was mandatory. Pastoral pacing was gone forever.

Though the production of existing models was far from smooth, new models were rushed into production and further complicated the byzantine production process. The workers saw only the bitter irony when they read, "Quality is chief on this reservation" on the signs above the line. Holes in the parts did not line up, so fasteners could not be inserted. Parts were not ready. A parking lot soon filled with not-quite-finished motor homes as a summer heat wave seared the Midwest. With no air conditioning in the factory and temperatures near 100 degrees, the crowded assembly lines became unbearable. Tempers flared, morale plummeted, and epithets were scrawled on plant walls. Some long-standing employees quit.

Reenter John Hanson, enraged about what was happening to his employees. "This work force would not tolerate what Gerald and Richard did. Ten hours a day, six days a week in hot weather? They were pooped out." He was also angry about what had happened to his products, and his dealers were furious. Gerald Gilbert—number six—and his sidekick, Richard Berreth, would have to go.

The sales and earnings at Winnebago were slower to respond, but their statements were harsher than Hanson's words. In 1986, Gerald Gilbert's first year at Winnebago, sales had been just over $380 million, with earnings of 0.77 per share. Earnings and sales rose in 1987, and sales rose again in 1988, although earnings per share (EPS) began to drop. By the time EPS fell into negative numbers, Gilbert and Berreth were long gone from Winnebago. With sales continuing to fall, Hanson was once again looking for a new CEO—one who would understand that Winnebago's objectives were not limited solely to high production quotas.

Discussion Questions

1. Based on the information presented, do you see differences between John Hanson's individual objectives and Winnebago's organizational objectives? Explain.

2. List the organizational objectives for Winnebago Industries, as you would imagine that John Hanson might perceive them.

3. From the material presented, list the organizational objectives for Winnebago Industries as interpreted by Gerald Gilbert and Richard Berreth.

4. What mistakes do you believe Gerald Gilbert made as CEO of Winnebago?

Edward Lewis: The Essence of Essence Communications

Edward Lewis, the chairman, founder, and guiding light of Essence Communications, built his company from a $130,000 stake into a $38 million operation in little more than twenty years. Lewis's primary objective has been to provide a print voice for black women in America through *Essence* magazine. In addition, Essence has branched into other media, including mail order catalogue sales, sewing patterns, an eyewear line, and even television. Essence is now one of the top twenty black-owned businesses in the United States.

When Lewis and his partner Clarence Smith founded Essence Communications, they saw an opportunity to fill a niche, as there were no other magazines addressing the needs of black women. Filling this niche led to their mission: to focus on and deal with a trilogy of needs—jobs, housing, and education—from a black woman's perspective. "I think that's how we survive," Lewis says, "because we deal with real issues. At the same time, we take into consideration [that] she has to work, she's also beautiful, she's also intelligent, she wants to look good and we try to make her feel good through the pages of *Essence*." Of course, *Essence*'s broader mission is to achieve all of this while being profitable.

The development of *Essence*'s profitability is revealed by the growth in its advertising income. The first issue, in May 1970, included 13 pages of ads; the twentieth anniversary issue carried 124 pages of ads. With this many advertisers, and with a monthly circulation of 850,000 readers, the magazine is making money.

Essence's success has given Ed Lewis the opportunity to attain personal goals through business achievement. His generous *Essence* salary enables him to live comfortably and support a household in New York City. He enjoys national recognition and is occasionally seen hobnobing with Jesse Jackson.

Lewis has not always been successful, though. Despite receiving an alumnus award from his alma mater, the University of New Mexico, academic success was out of reach early in his career. In fact, he acknowledges that academic failures have goaded him on to succeed in business: "It was very difficult because, not having failed before [after failing law school], I began to realize that in life you have your ups and downs and you've got to pick yourself up."

Ed Lewis picked himself up more than twenty years ago and began to define his personal goals: "to speak loud against injustices and really never stop talking, from the standpoint of doing what's right." Lewis sees *Essence* as representative of and as giving voice to the black community in general, as well as to black women in particular. Further, *Essence* offers an innovative product of unquestionable value, combining serious cultural and life-style issues with a sales approach more typical of women's beauty magazines.

Essence Communications provides an excellent example of how an entrepreneur can combine individual and organizational objectives to emerge successful.

The growing circulation of *Essence,* the annual *Essence* awards, and the financial growth and diversification of Essence Communications all show that—whether personally or in his business—Ed Lewis continually moves forward.

Video Case Questions

1. What is the organizational purpose of *Essence* magazine?
2. Based on the video material, how do you think organizational objectives of *Essence* influence decisions regarding advertising?
3. How do the organizational purpose and organizational objectives of Essence Communications differ? What about Ed Lewis's individual objectives?
4. The text lists eight key areas that Drucker recommends emphasizing as areas for organizational objectives. Which of these does Lewis seem most concerned with, and why?

Video Case Activities

1. Consult Table 4.3. Given the goals of increased market share and advertising growth, suggest sample means and measures for *Essence* magazine operations.
2. Imagine you are an advertising department manager and must prepare an MBO performance evaluation for Jane Doe. Jane has been soliciting ads for *Essence* for twelve months; during the first six months, she was a trainee. Recently, her sales volume has been above average, with major sales to baby food companies, jewelry companies (including diamonds mined in South Africa), and companies selling desktop computer systems. What factors would you note in her evaluation?

Chapter 5

 tudent Learning Objectives

From studying this chapter, I will attempt to acquire:

1. A definition of planning and an understanding of the purposes of planning.
2. A knowledge of the advantages and potential disadvantages of planning.
3. Insights on how the major steps of the planning process are related.
4. An understanding of the planning subsystem.
5. A knowledge of how the chief executive relates to the planning process.
6. An understanding of the qualifications and duties of planners and how planners are evaluated.
7. Guidelines on how to get the greatest return from the planning process.

Fundamentals
of Planning

hapter Outline

$\mathcal{I}$ntroductory Case

POOR PLANNING AT WEYERHAEUSER KILLS A GOOD PRODUCT

At Wegmans Food Markets, musical videos showed happy babies cooing because a new diaper called UltraSofts kept them dry while it saved their parents money.

Samples and discount coupons were mailed to 50,000 shoppers near the Rochester, N.Y., chain. The hype "was unprecedented," recalls Mary Ellen Burris, Wegmans' consumer affairs director.

Wegmans introduced the product with a huge promotion and advertising campaign last winter. With the $1-off coupon mailed to homes, the bag of 32 large-sized diapers sold for $8.39, or about $1.60 less than the leading brands.

We've got about 20 problems in the manufacturing process. Many are simple. Some need significant work.

And consumers liked the product. Juanita Gerringer has tried all three national brands but chose UltraSofts for her three-year-old granddaughter, Tina. The toddler is more comfortable in UltraSofts, she says, and they cost at least 10% less. "I wouldn't change over to anything else," says the Honeoye, N.Y., consumer.

Such testimonials made the company optimistic.

But problems were brewing at its Bowling Green, Ky., plant. The system that sprayed the superabsorbent material into the pad didn't work very well. Too much of the material missed the diaper and got into the production line's electronic parts, causing them to corrode.

Transformers on the line overheated. The pulp-grinding process, when operated at high speeds, began to burn. "We've got about 20 problems in the manufacturing process," Mr. Abraham said a few weeks ago. "Many are simple. Some need significant work."

In addition, Weyerhaeuser couldn't offer suppliers long-term contracts when buying materials needed for the diapers. Without those agreements, the suppliers, who had been manufacturing on a pilot scale wouldn't expand production of key items like the diaper lining.

In turn, production slowed on the UltraSofts line. Instead of full-time production, the Bowling Green plant was making the diapers only once or twice a month, supplying just enough for Wegmans.

Making matters worse, Weyerhaeuser increased UltraSofts' price to retailers 22% to cover the expense of its manufacturing problems. Wegmans says it kept the retail price at $9.39 a bag but couldn't offer nearly as many promotions. The retailer's profits on the diaper have declined because of the price increase, although they won't say by how much.

But, 10 months later, UltraSofts is just about dead. Manufacturing problems—including fires and breakdowns on the plant floor that snarled production and triggered a sharp price increase to retailers—have killed Weyerhaeuser Co.'s dream of taking the diaper nationwide. "It's been a disappointment," says Bobby Abraham, president of Weyerhaeuser's personal care products division.

The UltraSofts case shows how even the best product innovation can die from poor planning and unexpected problems.

From Alecia Swasy, "Diaper's Failure Shows How Poor Plans, Unexpected Woes Can Kill New Products," *Wall Street Journal* (October 9, 1990), B1, B4. Reprinted by permission of *Wall Street Journal*, © 1990 Dow Jones & Company, Inc. All Rights Reserved Worldwide.

WHAT'S AHEAD

The introductory case discusses the introduction of a new product, UltraSofts baby diapers, by the Weyerhaeuser Company. The case suggests that poor planning can cause the introduction of a new and good product to fail. Concepts in this chapter will help managers such as those at Weyerhaeuser to understand why planning is so important, not only for a new-product-introduction situation, but also for carrying out virtually any other organizational activity. This chapter describes the fundamentals of planning: (1) the general characteristics of planning, (2) steps in the planning process, (3) the planning subsystem, (4) the relationship between planning and the chief executive, (5) the qualifications and duties of planners and how planners are evaluated, and (6) how to maximize the effectiveness of the planning process.

GENERAL CHARACTERISTICS OF PLANNING

Defining Planning

Planning is the process of determining how the organization can get where it wants to go. Chapter 4 emphasized the importance of organizational objectives and explained how to develop them. Planning is the process of determining exactly what the organization will do to accomplish its objectives. In more formal terms, planning is "the systematic development of action programs aimed at reaching agreed business objectives by the process of analyzing, evaluating, and selecting among the opportunities which are foreseen."[1]

Planning is a critical management activity regardless of the type of organization being managed. Modern managers face the challenge of sound planning in small and relatively simple organizations as well as large, more complex organizations.[2] In addition, planning challenges confront managers of nonprofit organizations such as libraries[3] as much as they do managers of organizations such as General Motors.

Purposes of Planning

Over the years, management writers have presented several different purposes of planning. For example, C. W. Roney indicates that organizational planning has two purposes: protective and affirmative. The protective purpose of planning is to minimize risk by reducing the uncertainties surrounding business conditions and clarifying the consequences of related management action. The affirmative purpose is to increase the degree of organizational success.[4] Still another purpose of planning is to establish a coordinated effort within the organization. An absence of planning is usually accompanied by an absence of coordination and, therefore, usually contributes to organizational inefficiency.

The fundamental purpose of planning, however, is to help the organization reach its objectives. As stated by Koontz and O'Donnell, the primary purpose of

Planning is the process of determining how the management system will achieve its objectives. In other words, it determines how the organization can get where it wants to go.

135

planning is to "facilitate the accomplishment of enterprise and objectives."[5] All other purposes of planning are simply spin-offs of this fundamental purpose.

Planning: Advantages and Potential Disadvantages

A vigorous planning program has many benefits. One is that it helps managers to be future oriented. They are forced to look beyond their normal everyday problems to project what may confront them in the future. Decision coordination is a second advantage of a sound planning program. No decision should be made today without some idea of how it will affect a decision that might have to be made tomorrow. The planning function helps managers coordinate their decisions. A third advantage to planning is that it emphasizes organizational objectives. Since organizational objectives are the starting points for planning, managers are constantly reminded of exactly what their organization is trying to accomplish.

Overall, planning is very advantageous to an organization. According to a recent survey, as many as 65 percent of all newly started businesses are not around to celebrate a fifth anniversary. This high failure rate seems primarily caused by inadequate planning within the new businesses. Successful businesses have an established plan, a formal statement that outlines the objectives the organization is attempting to achieve. Planning does not eliminate risk, but it can help managers identify and eliminate organizational problems before they arise.[6]

If the planning function is not well executed within the organization, planning can have several disadvantages. For example, an overemphasized planning program can take up too much managerial time. Managers must strike an appropriate balance between time spent on planning and time spent on organizing, influencing, and controlling. If they don't, some activities that are extremely important to the success of the organization may be neglected. Usually, the disadvantages of planning result from the planning function's being used incorrectly. Overall, the advantages of planning definitely outweigh the disadvantages.

Quality Highlight: L.L. Bean Reschedules to Improve Service

Management at L.L. Bean, a retailer of outdoor clothing and equipment, recently faced the challenge of improving the quality of its customer service through improvements in the scheduling of its phone agents. L.L. Bean does much of its business through mail order catalogs; customers often place their orders by telephone. The company employs approximately 350 employees to provide phone service on both a part-time and a full-time basis.

Management at L.L. Bean needed a reliable method for forecasting the workload for the telemarketing center on an hourly basis. These forecasts are then translated into the number of phone operators needed, and this information is used to generate weekly schedules for the part-time and full-time workers.

To meet this scheduling challenge, management at L.L. Bean developed a staffing evaluation model (SEM). This model is based on management science techniques that include observing an organization and using those observations to construct a framework or model that reflects how the organization works. A model can help managers to understand better how the organization functions and, as a result, to more ably make decisions that improve operations.

L.L. Bean's model was based on historical data of actual operator workloads, forecasts of demands for new as well as established products, and issues that were raised by selected members of the organization who had dealt with scheduling challenges in the past. The model has helped L.L. Bean management understand the operation of its telephone sales division and has enabled management to improve the quality of its customer service.

Primacy of Planning

Planning is the primary management function—the function that precedes and is the foundation for the organizing, influencing, and controlling functions of managers. Only after managers have developed their plans can they determine how they want to structure their organization, place their people, and establish organizational controls. As discussed in chapter 1, planning, organizing, influencing, and controlling are interrelated. Planning is the foundation function and the first function to be performed. Organizing, influencing, and controlling are based on the results of planning. Figure 5.1 shows this interrelationship.

 ## *ack to the Case*

From the facts presented in the introductory case, one may conclude that Weyerhaeuser managers did not plan adequately for the introduction of its new UltraSofts baby diaper product. The process used to determine what Weyerhaeuser should do in fields such as manufacturing and building supplier relations in order to reach its objective of introducing UltraSofts was obviously deficient.

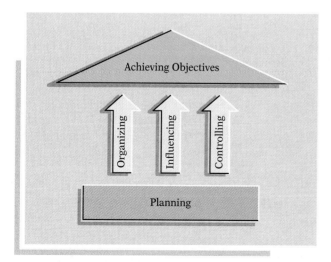

FIGURE 5.1

Planning as the foundation for organizing, influencing, and controlling

Because of the many related benefits of planning, Weyerhaeuser managers should make certain that the planning process for its next new product introduction is much more thorough and comprehensive. One particularly notable benefit is the probability of increased profits. To gain the benefits of planning, however, Weyerhaeuser managers must be careful that the planning function is well executed and not overemphasized.

Weyerhaeuser management should also keep in mind that planning is the primary management function. Thus, as managers, they should not begin to organize, influence, or control when introducing a new product like UltraSofts until the planning process is complete. Planning is the foundation management function on which all other functions at Weyerhaeuser should base.

STEPS IN THE PLANNING PROCESS

The planning process contains the following six steps:

1. *State organizational objectives.* A clear statement of organizational objectives is necessary for planning to begin, since planning focuses on how the management system will reach those objectives.[7] In essence, objectives stipulate those areas in which organizational planning must occur.[8] Chapter 4 discusses how the objectives themselves are developed.

2. *List alternative ways of reaching objectives.* Once organizational objectives have been clearly stated, a manager should list as many available alternatives as possible for reaching those objectives.

3. *Develop premises on which to base each alternative.* To a large extent, the feasibility of using any one alternative to reach organizational objectives is determined by the **premises,** or assumptions, on which the alternative is based. For example, two alternatives a manager could generate to reach the organizational objective of increasing profit might be: (a) increase the sale of products presently being produced, or (b) produce and sell a completely new product. Alternative a would base on the premise that the organization could get a larger share of an existing market. Alternative b would base on the premise that a new product would capture a significant portion of a new market. A manager should list all of the premises for each alternative.

4. *Choose the best alternative for reaching objectives.* An evaluation of alternatives must include an evaluation of the premises on which the alternatives are based. A manager usually finds that the premises on which some of the alternatives are based are unreasonable and can therefore be excluded from further consideration. This elimination process helps determine which alternative would be best to accomplish organizational objectives. The decision making required for this step is discussed more fully in chapter 6.

5. *Develop plans to pursue the chosen alternative.* After an alternative has been chosen, a manager begins to develop strategic (long-range) and tactical (short-range) plans.[9] More information about strategic and tactical planning is presented in chapter 6.

6. *Put the plans into action.* Once plans have been developed, they are ready to be put into action. The plans should furnish the organization with both long-range and short-range direction for activity. Obviously, the organization does not directly benefit from the planning process until this step is performed.

Figure 5.2 shows how the six steps of the planning process relate to one another.

Premises are assumptions on which alternative ways of accomplishing objectives are based.

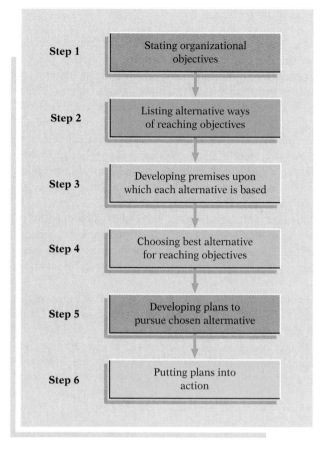

Step 1	Stating organizational objectives
Step 2	Listing alternative ways of reaching objectives
Step 3	Developing premises upon which each alternative is based
Step 4	Choosing best alternative for reaching objectives
Step 5	Developing plans to pursue chosen alternative
Step 6	Putting plans into action

FIGURE 5.2

Elements of the planning process

Certo Management: Figure 5.2

Global Highlight: Tower Records' International Expansion

Tower Records, a U.S. company, chose expansion into Japan as its best way to reach its objective of company growth. The company has been cashing in on the Japanese love of foreign popular music for the last ten years. Tower Records is the only completely foreign-owned record retailer in Japan. Its wide range of music is perhaps the company's biggest customer appeal. Keith Cahoon, the Far East managing director at Tower, says that before Tower, imports of records and tapes were a small business in Japan, but now the demand is growing and substantial.

Japanese law requires that music products made within the country be sold at fixed prices. Because Tower's music products are not made in Japan, they are not covered by the Japanese law and historically have offered lower prices than the Japanese-made competing products. Now, however, Japanese rivals such as Wave and Disc Music are beginning to challenge Tower's prices. Tower may have to look to other international markets in the future in order to meet its objective of company growth.

THE PLANNING SUBSYSTEM

Once managers understand the basics of planning, they can take steps to implement the planning process in their organization. This implementation is the key to a successful planning process. Even though managers might be experts on facts related to planning and the planning process, if they cannot transform this understanding into appropriate action, they are not able to generate useful organizational plans.

One way of approaching this implementation is to view planning activities as an organizational subsystem. A **subsystem** is a system created as part of the process of the overall management system. Figure 5.3 illustrates this relationship between the overall management system and a subsystem. Subsystems help managers organize the overall system and enhance its success.

Figure 5.4 presents the elements of the planning subsystem. The purpose of this subsystem is to increase the effectiveness of the overall management system through more effective planning. The planning subsystem helps managers to identify planning activities within the overall system and to guide and direct these activities.

Obviously, only a portion of organizational resources is used as input in the planning subsystem. This input is allocated to the planning subsystem and transformed into output through the steps of the planning process.

How planning subsystems are organized in the industrial world can be exemplified by the rather informal planning subsystem at the Quaker Oats Company and the more formal planning subsystem at the Sun Oil Company.[10]

Quaker Oats Company

At Quaker Oats, speculations about the future are conducted, for the most part, on an informal basis. To help anticipate particular social changes, the company has opened communication lines with various groups believed to be the harbingers of change. To spearhead this activity, the company has organized a "non-committee" whose members represent a diversity of orientations. They listen to what is going on—monitor social changes—and thus augment the company's

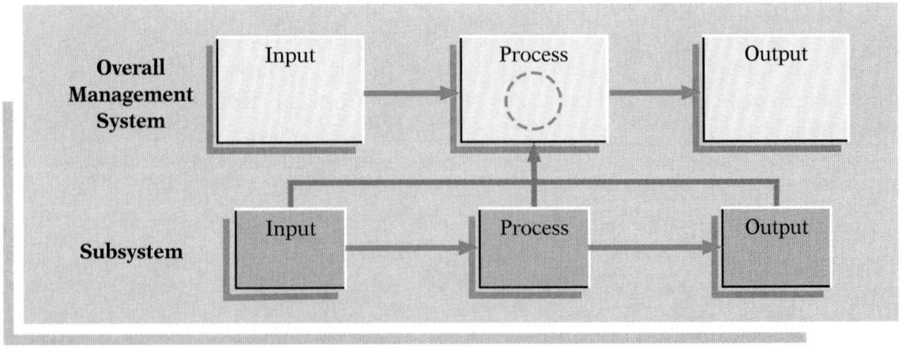

A **subsystem** is a system created as part of the process of the overall management system. The planning subsystem increases the effectiveness of the overall management system.

FIGURE 5.3

Relationship between overall management system and subsystem

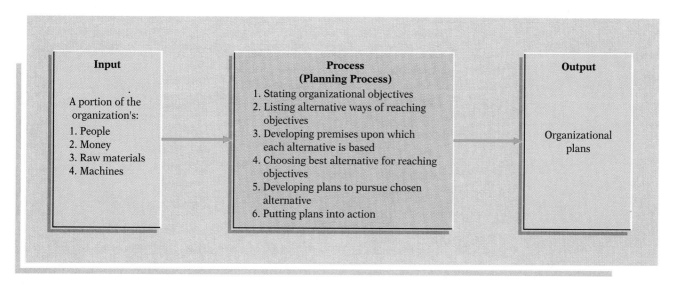

FIGURE 5.4

The planning subsystem

understanding of social change. Many companies throughout the world plan in an informal way like Quaker Oats does.[11]

Sun Oil Company

Several groups within Sun Oil Company are engaged in formal business planning and forecasting. Operational planning with a five-year horizon is done annually. The planning activity with the longest time horizon exists within the Sun Oil Company of Pennsylvania, the corporation's refining, transportation, and marketing arm. A centralized planning group, reporting to the vice president of development and planning, is responsible for helping top management set the company's long-term objectives, develop plans to achieve these objectives, and identify likely consumer needs and market developments of the future that might indicate business areas for diversification. Current efforts focus on discussions of a series of long-range issues with the executive committee, a planning process designed to generate a restatement of long-term objectives.

ack to the Case

For the next new product introduction at Weyerhaeuser, management should design and implement a more useful plan. The process of developing this plan should consist of six steps, beginning with a statement of an organizational objective to successfully introduce the new product and ending with guidelines for putting organizational plans into action.

To implement a planning process at Weyerhaeuser appropriately, management should view planning as a subsystem that is part of the process of the overall management system. They should use a portion of all the organizational resources available at Weyerhaeuser for the purpose of organizational planning. Following our new-product-introduction example, the output of this subsystem would be the actual plans to be used to introduce a new product. Topics such as refining a manufacturing process for the new product and ensuring that supplies can furnish needed components of the product would be emphasized. Naturally, a comprehensive planning effort at Weyerhaeuser would focus on many other organizational areas, besides new product introduction, such as obtaining needed funds and fighting competitors for established products.

PLANNING AND THE CHIEF EXECUTIVE

Henry Mintzberg has pointed out that the top managers—the chief executives—of organizations have many different roles to perform.[12] As organizational figureheads, they must represent their organizations in a variety of social, legal, and ceremonial matters. As leaders, they must ensure that organization members are properly guided in relation to organizational goals. As liaisons, they must establish themselves as links between their organizations and factors outside their organizations. As monitors, they must assess organizational progress. As disturbance handlers, they must settle disputes between organization members. And as resource allocators, they must determine where resources will be placed to benefit their organizations best.

In addition to these many and varied roles, chief executives have the final responsibility for organizational planning. As the scope of planning broadens to include a larger portion of the management system, it becomes increasingly important for chief executives to become more involved in the planning process.

As planners, chief executives seek answers to the following broad questions:

1. In what direction should the organization be going?

2. In what direction is the organization going now?

3. Should something be done to change this direction?

4. Is the organization continuing in an appropriate direction?[13]

Keeping informed about social, political, and scientific trends is of utmost importance in helping chief executives to answer these questions.

Given the importance of top management's participating in organizational planning and performing other time-consuming roles, more and more top managers obtain planning assistance by establishing a position for an organization planner.[14] Just as managers can ask others for help and advice in making decisions, they can involve others in formulating organizational plans.[15]

Chief executives of most substantial organizations need help to plan.[16] The remainder of this chapter, therefore, assumes that the organization planner is an individual who is not the chief executive of the organization. The planner is presented as a manager inside the organization who is responsible for giving assistance to the chief executive on organizational planning issues.[17] If, by chance, the planner and the chief executive are the same person in a particular organization, the following discussion relating to the planner can be modified slightly to apply also to the chief executive.

THE PLANNER

Perhaps the most important input in the planning subsystem is the planner. This individual combines all other input and influences the subsystem process so that effective organizational plans become subsystem output. The planner is responsible not only for the plans that are developed but also for advising management about what action should be taken in relation to those plans. Regardless of who actually does the planning or of the organization in which the planning is being done, the qualifications and duties of planners and how planners are evaluated are very important considerations in increasing the effectiveness of the planning subsystem.

Qualifications of Planners

Planners should have four primary qualifications. First, they should have considerable practical experience within their organization. Preferably, they should have been executives in one or more of the organization's major departments. This experience will help them develop plans that are both practical and tailormade for the organization.

Second, planners should be able to replace any narrow view of the organization (probably acquired while holding other organizational positions) with an understanding of the organization as a whole. They must know how all parts of the organization function and interrelate. In other words, they must possess an abundance of the conceptual skills mentioned in chapter 1.

Third, planners should have some knowledge of and interest in the social, political, technical, and economic trends that could affect the future of the organization. They must be skillful in defining these trends and have the expertise to determine how the organization should react to the trends to maximize success. This particular qualification cannot be overemphasized.

The fourth and last qualification is that planners should be able to work well with others. They inevitably will work closely with several key members of the organization and should possess personal characteristics that are helpful in collaborating and advising effectively. The ability to communicate clearly, both orally and in writing, is one of the most important of these characteristics.[18]

Duties of Planners

Organizational planners have at least three general duties to perform: (1) overseeing the planning process, (2) evaluating developed plans, and (3) solving planning problems.[19]

Overseeing the Planning Process

First, and perhaps foremost, planners must see that planning gets done. To this end, they establish rules, guidelines, and planning objectives that apply to themselves and others involved in the planning process. In essence, planners must develop a plan for planning.

Simply described, a **plan for planning** is a listing of all of the steps that must be taken to plan for an organization. It generally includes such activities as evaluating an organization's present planning process in an effort to improve it, determining how much benefit an organization can gain as a result of planning, and developing a planning timetable to ensure that all of the steps necessary to plan for a particular organization are performed by some specified date.

A **plan for planning** is a listing of all steps that must be taken to plan for an organization. It ensures that planning gets done.

Evaluating Developed Plans

The second general duty of planners is to evaluate plans that have been developed. Planners must decide if plans are sufficiently challenging for the organization, if they are complete, and if they are consistent with organizational objectives. If the developed plans do not fulfill these three requirements, they should be modified appropriately.

Ethics Highlight: Chrysler's Quality Assurance Clashes with Ethics

Managers commonly face situations in which they must evaluate plans to ensure that the plans are challenging, complete, and consistent with organizational objectives. Recent events at Chrysler suggest that within such situations, managers should also take the time to evaluate plans to ensure that they are ethical. If Chrysler had evaluated some of its recent quality assurance plans from an ethical perspective, perhaps the company could have avoided significant embarrassment.

Chrysler was indicted recently for mail and wire fraud and conspiracy. Car odometers were disconnected on new automobiles so that managers could take the cars home at night. These cars, as many as 48,000 of them, were later sold as new. Chrysler planned the managers' use of the cars so that managers could personally test product quality.

Chairman Lee Iacocca headed a public relations campaign in both print and television advertisements promising adjustments for buyers of the predriven cars. In the legal arena, however, Chrysler's reaction has been different. The company has fought the government in legal proceedings and caused many unnecessary legal delays. Although most citizens would probably disagree, it seems to others that the Chrysler management has not fully accepted the notion that taking cars for unmetered test drives is unethical.

Solving Planning Problems

Planners also have the duty to gather information that will help solve planning problems. Sometimes, they may find it necessary to conduct special studies within the organization to obtain this information. They can then recommend what the organization should do in the future to deal with planning problems and forecast how the organization might benefit from related opportunities.

For example, a planner may observe that production objectives set by the organization are not being met. This is a symptom of a planning problem. The problem causing this symptom might be that objectives are unrealistically high or that plans developed to achieve production objectives are inappropriate. The planner must gather information pertinent to the problem and suggest to management how the organization can solve its problem and become more successful.

Other symptoms that could signify planning problems are weakness in dealing with competition, declining sales volume, inventory levels that are either too high or too low, high operating expenses, and too much capital being invested in equipment.[20]

King and Cleland have presented the relationships among problems, symptoms, and opportunities in Figure 5.5.

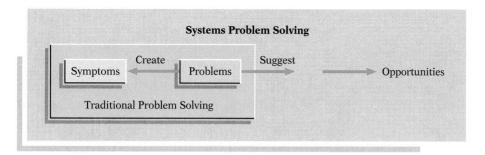

FIGURE 5.5

Relationships among symptoms, problems, and opportunities that face the planner

The three duties of planners just discussed—overseeing the planning process, evaluating developed plans, and solving planning problems—are general comments on planners' activities. Table 5.1 lists the specific responsibilities of an organization planner at a large manufacturing company. As this list implies, the main focus of the planner's activities is to advise management on what should be done in the future. The planner helps management not only determine appropriate future action but ensure that the timing of that action is appropriate. In the end, the possibility always exists that the manager may not accept the planner's recommendations.

TABLE 5.1 Responsibilities of an organization planner

The planner has the responsibility to—

1. Provide information to help management formulate long- and short-range goals and plans of the company. Also assist in the updating of these goals and generally monitor their progress toward attainment.

2. Coordinate activities and prepare special studies centering on acquisitions, disposals, joint endeavors, manufacturing rights, and patents.

3. Serve as resource for determining the acquisition, disposal, and movement of physical properties.

4. Encourage the stimulation of ideas from management toward broadening company operations. Extract these ideas and follow up on possibilities.

5. Develop, recommend, and obtain management approval of plans, procedures, and policies to be followed in implementing a diversification program.

6. Perform basic research on diversification, using such sources as the American Management Association, National Industrial Conference Board, Research Institute of America, and others.

7. Perform internal and external economic studies to secure necessary information for overall planning.

8. Utilize staff service personnel plus line and committee persons in accumulating and evaluating data.

9. Analyze the company's physical properties and personnel capabilities to determine production spans.

10. In conjunction with staff services, periodically survey performance capabilities of sales, engineering, manufacturing, and service components of the company.

11. Conduct an initial survey of the manufacturing organization's physical properties (facilities, equipment, and tools) and keep information current.

12. Investigate and determine possibilities of other significant use for basic products.

13. Assist in communicating and implementing the diversification decisions of management during transition periods.

14. Prepare necessary reports to keep management informed.

Evaluation of Planners

As with all other organization members, it is very important that the performance of planners is evaluated against the contribution they make toward helping the organization achieve its objectives.[21] The quality and appropriateness of the system for planning and the plans that the planners develop for the organization should be the primary considerations in this evaluation. Because the organizing, influencing, and controlling functions of the manager are based on the fundamental planning function, the evaluation of planners becomes critically important.

Although the assessment of planners is somewhat subjective, a number of objective indicators do exist. For example, the use of appropriate techniques is one objective indicator. If a planner is using appropriate techniques, it is probable that the planner is doing an acceptable job. The degree of objectivity displayed by the planner is another indicator. To a great extent, the planner's advice should be based on a rational analysis of appropriate information.[22] This is not to say that subjectivity and judgment should be excluded by the planner. Typically, however, opinions should be based on specific and appropriate information.

Malik suggests that objective evidence that a planner is doing a reputable job exists if—

1. The organizational plan is in writing.

2. The plan is the result of all elements of the management team working together.

3. The plan defines present and possible future business of the organization.

4. The plan specifically mentions organizational objectives.

5. The plan includes future opportunities and suggestions on how to take advantage of them.

6. The plan emphasizes both internal and external environments.

7. The plan describes the attainment of objectives in operational terms when possible.

8. The plan includes both long- and short-term recommendations.[23]

These eight conditions furnish managers with some objective guidelines for evaluating the performance of planners. This evaluation, however, should never be completely objective. More subjective considerations include how well planners get along with key members of the organization, the amount of organizational loyalty they display, and their perceived potential.

$\mathcal{B}$ ack to the Case

Technically, the chief executive officer (CEO) at Weyerhaeuser is responsible for planning for the organization as a whole and for performing such related time-consuming functions as keeping abreast of internal and external trends that could affect the future of the company. Because planning requires so much time, and because the chief executive officer of Weyerhaeuser has many other responsibilities within the company, the CEO might want to consider appointing a director of planning.

The director of planning at Weyerhaeuser would need certain qualities. Ideally, the planner should have some experience at Weyerhaeuser, be able to see the company as an entire organization, have some ability to gauge and react to major trends that probably will affect the company's future, and be able to work well with others. The planner must oversee the planning process, evaluate developed plans, and solve planning problems. An evaluation of Weyerhaeuser's organization planner would be based on both objective and subjective appraisals of his performance. Perhaps the first problem a company planner at Weyerhaeuser should address is the historically poor planning for the introduction of new products like UltraSofts.

MAXIMIZING THE EFFECTIVENESS OF THE PLANNING PROCESS

Success in implementing a planning subsystem is not easily attainable. As the size of the organization increases, the planning task becomes more complicated, requiring more people, more information, and more complicated decisions.[24] Several safeguards, however, can ensure the success of an organizational planning effort. These safeguards include (1) top management support, (2) an effective and efficient planning organization, (3) an implementation-focused planning orientation, and (4) inclusion of the right people.

Top Management Support

Top management in an organization must support the planning effort, or other organization members may not take the planning effort seriously.[25] Whenever possible, top management should actively help to guide and participate in planning activities. Furnishing the planner with whatever resources are needed to structure the planning organization, encouraging planning as a continuing process (not as a once-a-year activity), and preparing people for the changes that usually result from planning are clear signs that top management is solidly behind the planning effort. The chief executive must give continual and obvious attention to the planning process if it is to be successful.[26] He or she must not be so concerned about other matters that planning is not given the emphasis it deserves.[27]

An Effective and Efficient Planning Organization

A well-designed planning organization is the primary vehicle by which planning is accomplished and planning effectiveness is determined. The planner must take the time to design a planning organization as efficient and effective as possible.

The planning organization should have three built-in characteristics. First, it should be designed to use established management systems within the company. As expressed by Paul J. Stonich:

> Many organizations separate formal planning systems from the rest of the management systems that include organization, communication, reporting, evaluating, and performance review. These systems must not be viewed as separate from formal planning systems. Complex organizations need a comprehensive and coordinated set of management systems, including formal planning systems to help them toward their goals.[28]

Second, the planning organization should be simple, yet complex enough to ensure a coordinated effort of all planning participants. Planning can be a complicated process requiring a somewhat large planning organization. The planner should strive to simplify the planning organization and make its complex facets as clearly understood as possible.

Last, the planning organization should be flexible and adaptable. Planning conditions are constantly changing, and the planning organization must be able to respond to these changing conditions.

An Implementation-Focused Planning Orientation

Because the end result of the planning process is some type of action that will help achieve stated organizational objectives, planning should be aimed at implementation.[29] As Peter Drucker points out, a plan is effective only if its implementation helps attain organizational objectives.[30] Plans should be developed and scrutinized after the planner has looked ahead to when they are to be implemented.[31] Ease of implementation is a positive feature of a plan that should be built in whenever possible.

The marketing plan for the Edsel automobile introduced by Ford in the 1950s is an example of how a sound plan can become unsuccessful simply because of ineffective implementation.[32] The rationale behind the Edsel was complete, logical, and defensible. Three consumer trends at that time solidly justified the automobile's introduction: (1) a trend toward the purchase of higher priced cars, (2) a general income increase that resulted in all income groups purchasing higher priced cars, and (3) owners of lower priced Fords trading them in on Buicks, Oldsmobiles, or Pontiacs after they became more affluent. Conceptually, these trends were so significant that Ford's plan to introduce the larger and more expensive Edsel appeared virtually risk free.

Two factors in the implementation of this plan, however, turned the entire Edsel situation into a financial disaster. First, the network of controllers, dealers, marketing managers, and industrial relations managers created within Ford to get the Edsel to the consumer became very complicated and inefficient. Second, because Ford pushed as many Edsels as possible onto the road immediately after introduction, the quality of the Edsel suffered, and consumers were buying poorly manufactured products. Although the plan to make and market the Edsel was defensible, the long-run influence of the organization and manufacturing processes created to implement the plan doomed it to failure.

Inclusion of the Right People

Planning must include the right people. Whenever possible, planners should obtain input from the managers of the functional areas for which they are planning.

These managers are close to the everyday activity of their segments of the organization and can provide planners with invaluable information. They probably also will be involved in implementing whatever plan develops and will be able to furnish the planner with feedback on how easily various plans are being implemented. In general, managers who are to be involved in implementing plans should also be involved in developing the plans.[33]

Input from individuals who will be directly affected by the plans also can be helpful to planners. The individuals who do the work in the organization can give opinions on how various plans will influence work flow. Although it is extremely important that planners involve others in the planning process, not all organization members can or should be involved. Stonich offers the following advice on the involvement of organization members in the planning process:

> In many corporations, the wrong sets of people participate in particular planning activities. Planning requires not only generation of information for making decisions, but decision making itself. The kinds of decisions and types of data needed should dictate the choice of who is involved in what aspects of planning within an organization.[34]

Back to the Case

Regardless of who actually ends up having primary responsibility for planning at Weyerhaeuser, a number of safeguards can be taken to ensure that the planning efforts of this person will be successful. First, top executives should actively encourage planning activities and show support for the planning process. Second, the planning organization designed to implement the planning process should use established systems at Weyerhaeuser, be simple yet complex, and be flexible and adaptable. Third, the entire planning process at Weyerhaeuser should be oriented toward easing the implementation of generated plans. Finally, all key people at Weyerhaeuser should be included in the planning process. These safeguards should help Weyerhaeuser management ensure that there will be sound planning for future new-product introductions as well as for all other organizational areas.

Action Summary

Reread the learning objectives that follow. Each objective is followed by questions. Answering these questions accurately will help you retain the most important concepts discussed in this chapter. After answering each question, check your answer with the answer key at the end of this chapter. (*Hint:* If you have doubt regarding the correct response, consult the page whose number follows the answer.)

Circle:

From studying this chapter, I will attempt to acquire:

1. **A definition of planning and an understanding of the purposes of planning.**

   a. The affirmative purpose of planning is to increase the degree of organizational success.

   T, F

   b. Which of the following is not one of the purposes of planning: (a) systematic; (b) protective; (c) affirmative; (d) coordination; (e) fundamental.

   a, b, c, d, e

2. A knowledge of the advantages and potential disadvantages of planning.

a, b, c, d, e

    a. The advantages of planning include all of the following except: (a) helping managers to be future oriented; (b) helping coordinate decisions; (c) requiring proper time allocation; (d) emphasizing organizational objectives; (e) all of the above are advantages of planning.

a, b, c, d, e

    b. The following is a potential disadvantage of planning: (a) too much time may be spent on planning; (b) an inappropriate balance between planning and other managerial functions may occur; (c) some important activities may be neglected; (d) incorrect use of the planning function could work to the detriment of the organization; (e) all of the above.

3. Insights on how the major steps of the planning process are related.

a, b, c, d, e

    a. The first major step in the planning process, according to the text, is: (a) developing premises; (b) listing alternative ways of reaching organizational objectives; (c) stating organizational objectives; (d) developing plans to pursue chosen alternatives; (e) putting plans into action.

a, b, c, d, e

    b. The assumptions on which alternatives are based are usually referred to as: (a) objectives; (b) premises; (c) tactics; (d) strategies; (e) probabilities.

4. An understanding of the planning subsystem.

T, F

    a. A subsystem is a system created as part of the process of the overall management system.

a, b, c, d, e

    b. The purpose of the planning subsystem is to increase the effectiveness of the overall management system through which of the following: (a) systematizing the planning function; (b) more effective planning; (c) formalizing the planning process; (d) integrating the planning process; (e) none of the above.

5. A knowledge of how the chief executive relates to the planning process.

T, F

    a. The responsibility for organizational planning rests with middle management.

a, b, c, d, e

    b. The final responsibility for organizational planning rests with: (a) the planning department; (b) the chief executive; (c) departmental supervisors; (d) the organizational planner; (e) the entire organization.

6. An understanding of the qualifications and duties of planners and how planners are evaluated.

T, F

    a. The performance of planners should be evaluated with respect to the contribution they make toward helping the organization achieve its objectives.

a, b, c, d, e

    b. The organizational planner's full responsibilities are: (a) developing plans only; (b) advising about action that should be taken relative to the plans that the chief executive developed; (c) advising about action that should be taken relative to the plans of the board of directors; (d) selecting the person who will oversee the planning process; (e) none of the above.

7. Guidelines on how to get the greatest return from the planning process.

T, F

    a. Top management should encourage planning as an annual activity.

a, b, c, d, e

    b. Which of the following is not a built-in characteristic of an effective and efficient planning organization: (a) it should be designed to use established systems within a company; (b) it should be simple, yet complex enough to ensure coordinated effort; (c) it should cover an operating cycle of not more than one year; (d) it should be flexible and adaptive; (e) all of the above are characteristics of an effective and efficient planning organization.

ntroductory Case Wrap-Up: Weyerhaeuser

"Poor Planning at Weyerhaeuser Kills a Good Product" and its related back-to-the-case sections were written to help you better understand the management concepts contained in this chapter. Answer the following questions about this introductory case to further enrich your understanding of chapter content:

1. What evidence do you see that Weyerhaeuser's planning needs to improve? Explain.

2. What problems will Weyerhaeuser managers face in trying to make the company stronger in the planning function?

3. Based upon information in the case, who do you think was excluded but should not have been absent from the planning for the introduction of Ultra-Softs? Explain.

Issues for Review and Discussion

1. What is planning?
2. What is the main purpose of planning?
3. List and explain the advantages of planning.
4. Why are the disadvantages of planning called *potential* disadvantages?
5. Explain the phrase *primacy of planning*.
6. List the six steps in the planning process.
7. Outline the relationships between the six steps in the planning process.
8. What is an organizational subsystem?
9. List the elements of the planning subsystem.
10. How do the many roles of a chief executive relate to his or her role as organization planner?
11. Explain the basic qualifications of an organization planner.
12. Give a detailed description of the general duties an organization planner must perform.
13. How would you evaluate the performance of an organization planner?
14. How can top management show its support of the planning process?
15. Describe the characteristics of an effective and efficient planning organization.
16. Why should the planning process emphasize the implementation of organizational plans?
17. Explain why the Edsel automobile failed to generate consumer acceptance.
18. Which people in an organization typically should be included in the planning process? Why?

Building on What You Know

Directions

Review the information on the Borden Company on page 152 and answer the corresponding questions. Questions in this section focus on relating the following example to management concepts that you have learned in a previous chapter. In chapter 4, "Organizational Objectives," you studied the concept of setting and reaching organizational targets. List three trends that Borden's management may have uncovered to make "decreasing its reliance on the dairy business" an advisable objective to set and pursue. Explain why each trend would be significant in the eyes of Borden's management.

The preceding information implies that management must face the situation of implementing plans once they are developed. The following information discusses Borden management's involvement in facing a planning implementation situation.

An interesting example of a manager implementing plans involves Rome J. Ventres, the chairman and chief executive officer at Borden Inc. In response to a recent company plan to reduce Borden's dependence on the highly competitive dairy business, Ventres quietly engineered 78 different acquisitions for Borden. The Ventres acquisitions focused mainly on purchasing companies in the packaged foods business.

The immediate result of these acquisitions was to make Borden a food giant and to broaden its previous dairy focus. From an historical viewpoint, one of Borden's most successful products has been Creamette, an additive for coffee. As a result of the acquisitions, one of the company's focuses for the future will be to become a leader in the pasta business. Implementation of Borden's plan to become less dependent on the dairy business finds Ventres in the process of selling or closing 20 dairy facilities. These sales will eliminate Borden as a major competitor in dairy markets throughout the Southeast and the Midwest.

Action Summary Answer Key

1. a. T, p. 135
   b. a, p. 135
2. a. c, p. 136
   b. e, p. 136
3. a. c, p. 138
   b. b, p. 138
4. a. T, p. 140
   b. b, p. 140
5. a. F, p. 142
   b. b, p. 142
6. a. T, p. 146
   b. e, pp. 143–146
7. a. F, p. 147
   b. c, pp. 147, 148

Case Study

Planning at Pizza Hut

by Leslie Toombs, University of Texas at Tyler, and Leslie Brunetta

Pizza Hut is the number one chain of pizza restaurants in the world. The company has grown by leaps and bounds since PepsiCo acquired it in 1977. PepsiCo is more than just the world's second largest maker of soft drinks (ranking behind only archrival Coca-Cola), it is also the world's largest producer of salty snacks, marketed under PepsiCo's Frito-Lay brand names. Also, PepsiCo's ownership of the Taco Bell, Kentucky Fried Chicken, and Pizza Hut companies makes it the world's largest restaurant corporation, too.

Clearly, PepsiCo abides by the rule that bigger is better. Its corporate objectives are to increase sales, market shares, and profits annually in each division. The objectives for Pizza Hut are no exception.

Pizza Hut executives pride themselves on consistently anticipating changes in the marketplace. When they realized that more and more Americans had become accustomed to eating dinner out, they lured them into Pizza Hut at lunchtime by offering personal-sized pan pizzas. As more women took jobs outside the home and found themselves with less time to spend preparing meals, Pizza Hut introduced meal delivery service. This increased profits in two ways. First, by getting in on the fast-growing restaurant delivery market early, Pizza Hut not only made sales to families who might not have bothered going out for pizza, but also established a sense of customer loyalty before competition became fiercer. Second, by setting up a number of delivery-only Pizza Huts, which cost considerably less to build and run than full-service restaurants, Pizza Hut was able to establish new customer bases without incurring major costs.

Pizza Hut's expansion strategy differs from that of many other restaurant chains. Rather than open new outlets in an area where other pizza restaurants already exist, diluting the customer base, Pizza Hut often buys up existing small restaurant chains and converts them into Pizza Huts. Also, whereas most restaurant chain companies own fewer than one third of their restaurants, selling the rest to franchisees, Pizza Hut owns more than half. Pizza Hut executives say that ownership allows them closer oversight of experiments such as new product launches and the introduction of new inventory, staffing, and kitchen procedures.

Pizza Hut's success in the United States has been phenomenal, but Pizza Hut and PepsiCo executives believe that even greater opportunities for growth exist outside the United States. Several obstacles lie in the way of foreign expansion, however. The concept of restaurant chains is unfamiliar to most of the world's population. Moreover, pizza is also unfamiliar, and may seem a luxury rather than a staple food item. An additional problem hinders development of Asian markets: One of the main ingredients of pizza—cheese—would be unwelcome in Asia. Most Asians have grown up without eating dairy products, and therefore have not developed digestive tolerances for them.

Executives at Pizza Hut have taken steps in their planning to account for these obstacles. For instance, in Thailand, William Heinecke opened the first Thai Pizza Hut about 20 years ago. At the time, few people in Thailand even knew what a pizza was, and few Thais had disposable income to spend on what they considered to be luxury foods. Nonetheless, Heinecke believed that a Westernized middle class was growing, so he opened his first Pizza Hut. He opened it in a resort town where foreign tourists were familiar with the idea of pizza and could keep him in business. As Heinecke had hoped, Thais belonging to the new middle class—who had increased exposure to American popular culture and to foreign foods, and who had developed a tolerance to dairy products—began stopping in for pizzas. Today, there are more than 15 Pizza Huts in Thailand; and more than four million Thai customers now eat at Pizza Hut every year. It is the country's largest restaurant chain.

Pizza Hut executives knew they would face similar obstacles, as well as political complications, trying to crack the USSR and People's Republic of China markets. PepsiCo already had experience in the USSR, where it had been selling Pepsi since the 1970s. It had figured out a way to deal with a huge stumbling block: The ruble, the currency of the USSR, is not convertible into currencies such as the U.S. dollar. Selling Pepsi to Soviet citizens for rubles was like giving it away free. So PepsiCo executed an agreement whereby it buys Stolichnaya vodka from the Soviets for dollars, and sells it in the United States. Soviet suppliers then use those dollars to buy Pepsi-Cola, which they sell at home for rubles.

Pizza Hut arranged a similar deal, but with a twist. First, they entered a partnership with a Soviet firm. The partners opened two Pizza Huts in Moscow, where there are many tourists and foreign residents. One Pizza Hut sells its products for convertible currencies such as U.S. dollars, German marks, and Japanese yen. The Soviet partners use a share of these profits to import ingredients needed to supply both restaurants. The second, ruble-accepting Pizza Hut uses its income to pay the local bills for both restaurants. Lines of customers have formed outside both restaurants since their opening.

In China, Pizza Hut followed the same strategy, opening in Beijing. Pizza Hut expects tourists and foreign residents, as well as members of Beijing's large bureaucratic elite, to keep the restaurant profitable until more Chinese people have the income and the desire to become regular customers. This venture has created tremendous worldwide publicity.

On the opposite side of the globe, in late 1990, PepsiCo announced plans to open at least 100 new Pizza Huts in Brazil. Pizza Hut executives expect the Brazilian expansion to lead to a greater presence across South America. They hope that by the end of this century, foreign Pizza Huts will outnumber the more than 7,000 restaurants already open in the United States.

Discussion Questions

1. What are Pizza Hut's organizational objectives?
2. What are two alternatives that you believe Pizza Hut executives listed to reach these objectives? Explain the premises on which these alternatives are based.

3. How important do you think coordination of management teams is to Pizza Hut's plans? Why?

4. Based on the evidence presented in this case, list possible long- and short-term recommendations by Pizza Hut planners.

Edward Finkelstein: Chairman, R. H. Macy, Inc.

Ed Finkelstein is chairman and chief executive officer of R. H. Macy, Inc., one of the world's largest retail chains. When Finkelstein became CEO of Macy's in 1979, the firm was a $2 billion, publicly held company. Today, their worth exceeds $7 billion and is still expanding. This is because Finkelstein plans what he wants to see happen, and his plans work.

In the face of the poor economy of the late 1980s and early 1990s, Finkelstein and his management team have avoided bankruptcy by increasing Macy's assets and curbing its debt, while watching many other large department store chains go broke around them. Increasingly, Macy's has chosen to compete on local levels with smaller specialty stores rather than on a national basis with the struggling, larger chains.

In 1986, Finkelstein and 350 Macy's managers decided to buy out the company for $3.6 billion. The team determined that Macy's would fare better as a privately held company and would be less subject to the takeovers and bankruptcies plaguing many of its counterparts. They planned their leveraged buyout carefully, to keep the level of debt serviceable so that they did not drive themselves into bankruptcy while trying to avoid being bankrupted by others.

Two years later, a privately held Macy's competed against Canadian retailer Robert Campeau in a bid for the Federated Department Stores. Although Macy's lost the Federated stores to Campeau, as a part of the negotiated deal, Macy's bought the Bullock's-Wilshire and the I. Magnin stores in southern California. Finkelstein wanted these properties to take advantage of that region's lucrative market. He knew that to develop stores in that market from scratch would take a decade or longer, but by taking on Bullock's and I. Magnin, Macy's gained an immediate, strong presence in southern California.

Just as these deals were being finalized, consumer economy weakened—so much so that Campeau's empire went bankrupt soon after. Macy's had also been affected. Finkelstein had long-range plans to accommodate the huge debt ($4.8 billion in early 1990) incurred from the leveraged buyout and the subsequent acquisitions in the Federated deal, but he needed immediate cash flow to service that debt. He decided that Macy's must move out inventory, even if it meant taking a loss.

Another part of Finkelstein's long-range plan debt-reduction plan was to reduce operating expenses by $80 million annually. He achieved this by reorganizing into four corporate divisions, each of which would be responsible for reducing intradivision operating expenses: (1) Atlanta stores, plus the Bullock's in Los Angeles and Macy's in Texas and Florida; (2) the remaining I. Magnin and Bullock's-Wilshire stores; (3) the other California stores; and (4) New York, along with the New Jersey stores. A third key to Finkelstein's plan was to sell Macy's real estate holdings, including many shopping centers acquired with I. Magnin and Bullock's; the store properties themselves were leased back from the buyers. The equity could be used to pay off other debts, and the mortgages could be removed from their list of debts.

Macy's has lost money since purchasing its southern California properties, but Ed Finkelstein is not seriously concerned. With solid backers such as General Electric (20%) and Larry Tisch and Michael Price (12.5% each), and with Macy's huge real assets, Finkelstein is sure that it won't be long before things are on a forward roll once again. As he points out, Macy's wasn't doing well in the 1970s, but it recovered under his leadership. He believes he can do it again.

Video Case Questions

1. One of Ed Finkelstein's objectives as CEO of Macy's was to capture a large share of the southern California market. What alternatives were available to accomplish this objective? What premises did he base his choice on?

2. In your opinion, was the "protective purpose of planning" a factor in Ed Finkelstein's decision to take Macy's private?

3. Planning subsystems exist within most corporations to forecast change and to prepare the company for it. Give an example of how a planning subsystem failure might have been responsible for leaving Macy's with too much inventory on hand following their Christmas season.

4. If you were a planner working with Finkelstein following the acquisition of Bullock's and I. Magnin, would you have recommended selling the real estate held by those stores? Why do you think Macy's made this move?

Video Case Activity

1. Assume you are the chief planner for Macy's at the time of acquiring I. Magnin and Bullock's-Wilshire. Prepare a list of the people you would meet with prior to developing a plan to reorganize Macy's new Atlanta division. List why each of these people should be involved.

Chapter 6

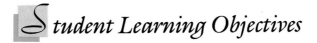
Student Learning Objectives

From studying this chapter, I will attempt to acquire:

1. A fundamental understanding of the term *decision*.

2. An understanding of each element of the decision situation.

3. An ability to use the decision-making process.

4. An appreciation for the various situations in which decisions are made.

5. An understanding of probability theory and decision trees as decision-making tools.

Making Decisions

Chapter Outline

IACOCCA MAKES A WRONG DECISION AT CHRYSLER?

When R.S. Miller, Jr., vice chairman of Chrysler Corp., addressed a dinner meeting of company managers a couple of years ago, he concluded by inviting questions from the floor. The first to raise a hand was Mr. Miller's wife, Maggie, who had accompanied him to the event. Would Mr. Miller run Chrysler differently, she asked, if he were chairman instead of Lee Iacocca?

The question startled Mr. Miller, but he quickly recovered. His first move, he replied, would be to bar

spouses from corporate meetings. The group broke up in laughter.

Nowadays, though, the question isn't so funny. Lots of people, both inside and outside Chrysler, wonder how the company would be doing without Mr. Iacocca. That's because Chrysler is doing so badly *with* him.

Mr. Iacocca vows to stay the course and lead Chrysler out of its problems. But with remarkable candor, he concedes that he is to blame for many of the company's woes. "I'm confessing my sins here," declares Mr. Iacocca, who turns 66 next month.

His big sin, Mr. Iacocca says, was trying to diversify. His decision put the company into the aerospace and defense businesses but siphoned management attention and money from the crucial task of producing new vehicles. Now Chrysler has sold, or is trying to sell, those businesses. Meanwhile, it hasn't brought to market a single new car whose development was begun after Mr. Iacocca arrived in 1978. Chrysler's current lineup still derives from the decade-old K-car.

> "If I made a mistake it was following other companies. And maybe those were grandiose schemes."

In fairness to Mr. Iacocca, say his admirers, his wish to diversify was understandable. Chrysler is being sorely pressed by Japanese competition, which notably doesn't exist in the aerospace and defense businesses. General Motors Corp. and Ford Motor Co. made similar moves. Ford, like Chrysler, is selling those businesses, though GM is sticking with them.

"If I made a mistake it was following other companies. And maybe those were grandiose schemes," says Mr. Iacocca.

From Paul Ingrassia and Bradley A. Stertz, "With Chrysler Ailing Lee Iacocca Concedes Mistakes in Managing," *Wall Street Journal* (September 17, 1990), A1, A8. Reprinted by permission of *Wall Street Journal,* © 1990 Dow Jones & Company, Inc. All Rights Reserved Worldwide.

FUNDAMENTALS OF DECISIONS

Definition of a Decision

A **decision** is a choice made between two or more available alternatives. Choosing the best alternative for reaching objectives—the fourth step of the planning process (presented in chapter 5)—is, strictly speaking, making a decision. Although decision making is covered in the planning section of this text, a manager also must make decisions when performing the other three managerial functions: organizing, controlling, and influencing.

Everyone is faced with decision situations each day. A decision situation may involve simply choosing among studying, swimming, or golfing as ways of spending the day. It does not matter which alternative is chosen, only that a choice is actually made.[1]

On a daily basis, managers are concerned with making decisions and communicating them to other organization members.[2] Not all of the decisions are of equal significance to the organization. Some affect a large number of organization members, cost much money to carry out, or have a long-term effect on the organization. These significant decisions can have a major impact not only on the management system itself but on the career of the manager. Other decisions are fairly insignificant, affecting only a small number of organization members, costing little to carry out, and having only a short-term effect on the organization.

> A **decision** is a choice made between two or more available alternatives.

Types of Decisions

Decisions can be categorized by how much time a manager must spend in making them, what proportion of the organization must be involved in making them, and the organizational functions on which they focus.[3] Probably the most generally accepted method of categorizing decisions, however, is based on computer language and divides the decisions into two basic types: programmed and nonprogrammed.[4]

Programmed decisions are routine and repetitive, and the organization typically develops specific ways to handle them. A programmed decision might involve determining how products will be arranged on the shelves of a supermarket. This

> **Programmed decisions** are decisions that are routine and repetitive, and that typically require specific handling methods.

Nonprogrammed decisions are decisions that typically are one-shot occurrences and usually are less structured than programmed decisions.

is a routine and repetitive problem for the organization, and standard arrangement decisions typically are made according to established management guidelines.

Nonprogrammed decisions, in contrast, typically are one-shot occurrences and are usually less structured than programmed decisions. One example of a nonprogrammed decision that many managers have had to make in recent years is whether to close a plant.[5] Another example would be a decision focusing on whether a supermarket should carry an additional type of bread. In making this decision, the manager must consider whether the new bread will stabilize bread sales by competing with existing bread carried in the store or increase bread sales by offering a choice of breads to customers who have never before bought bread in the store. These types of issues must be dealt with before the manager can finally decide whether to offer the new bread. Table 6.1 shows traditional and modern ways of handling programmed and nonprogrammed decisions.

Programmed and nonprogrammed decisions should be thought of as being at opposite ends of a programming continuum, as shown in Figure 6.1. The continuum also indicates that some decisions clearly may not be either programmed or nonprogrammed but some combination of the two.

The Responsibility for Making Organizational Decisions

Many different kinds of decisions must be made within an organization—such as how to manufacture a product, how to maintain machines, how to ensure product quality, and how to establish advantageous relationships with customers. With varied decisions of this sort, some type of rationale must be developed to stipulate who within the organization has the responsibility for making which decisions.

TABLE 6.1 Traditional and modern ways of handling programmed and nonprogrammed decisions

	Decision-Making Techniques	
Types of Decisions	*Traditional*	*Modern*
Programmed:		
Routine, repetitive decisions Organization develops specific processes for handling them	1. Habit 2. Clerical routine: Standard operating procedures 3. Organization structure: Common expectations A system of subgoals Well-defined information channels	1. Operations research: Mathematical analysis Models Computer simulation 2. Electronic data processing
Nonprogrammed:		
One-shot, ill-structured, novel policy decisions Handled by general problem-solving processes	1. Judgment, intuition, and creativity 2. Rules of thumb 3. Selection and training of executives	Heuristic problem-solving techniques applied to: Training human decision makers Constructing heuristic computer programs

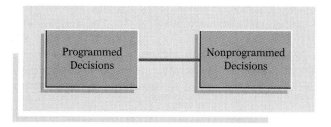

FIGURE 6.1

Continuum of extent of decision programming

One such rationale is based primarily on two factors: the scope of the decision to be made and the levels of management. The **scope of the decision** is the proportion of the total management system that the decision will affect. The greater this proportion, the broader the scope of the decision is said to be. *Levels of management* are simply lower level management, middle level management, and upper level management. The rationale for designating who makes which decisions is this: The broader the scope of a decision, the higher the level of the manager responsible for making that decision. Figure 6.2 illustrates this rationale.

The **scope of the decision** is the proportion of the total management system that a particular decision will affect. The broader the scope of a decision, the higher the level of the manager responsible for making that decision.

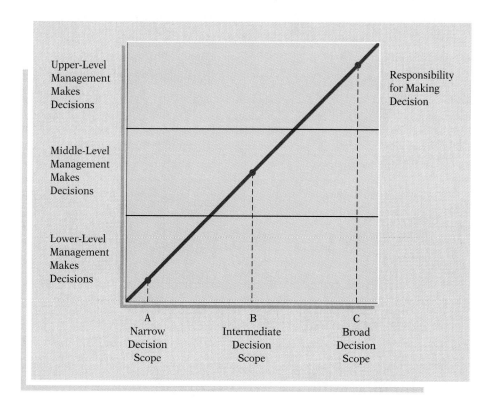

FIGURE 6.2

Level of managers responsible for making decisions as decision scope increases from *A* to *B* to *C*

One example of this decision-making rationale is the manner in which E.I. DuPont de Nemours and Company handles decisions related to the research-and-development function.[6] As Figure 6.3 shows, this organization makes relatively narrow-scope research-and-development decisions, such as "which markets to test" (made by lower level managers), and relatively broad-scope research-and-development decisions, such as "authorize full-scale plant construction" (made by upper level managers).

Even the manager who has the responsibility for making a particular decision can ask the advice of other managers or subordinates. In fact, some managers advise having groups make certain decisions.

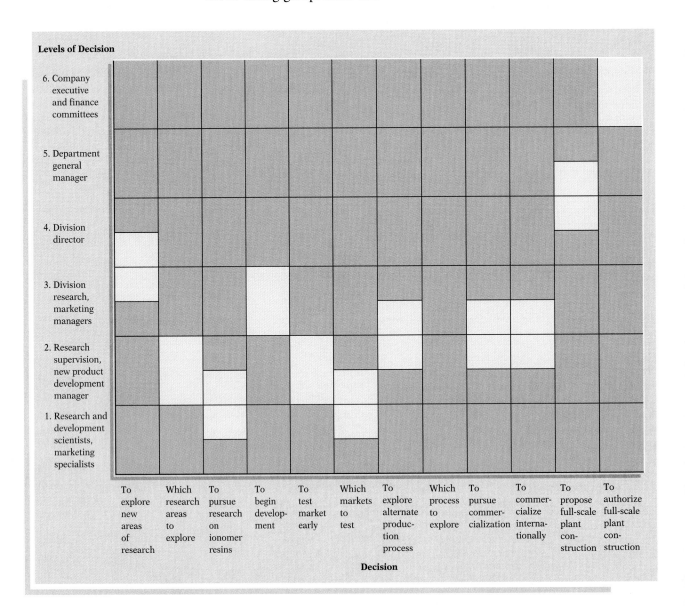

FIGURE 6.3

How scope of decision affects management level making decision at DuPont

Consensus is one method a manager can use in getting a group to arrive at a particular decision.[7] **Consensus** is agreement on a decision by all the individuals involved in making the decision. It usually occurs after lengthy deliberation and discussion by members of the decision group, who may be either all managers or a mixture of managers and subordinates.

Although asking individuals to arrive at a consensus decision is an option available to a manager, the manager must keep in mind that some individuals simply may not be able to arrive at such a decision. Lack of technical skill or poor interpersonal relations within a group may be barriers to arriving at a consensus decision. As the following cartoon lightheartedly implies, when individuals arrive at a stalemate in making a decision together, it's probably time for managers to offer assistance in making the decision or simply to make the decision themselves.

Decisions through consensus have both advantages and disadvantages. One advantage is that managers can focus "several heads" on the decision. Another is that individuals in the decision group are more likely to be committed to implementing a decision if they helped make it. The main disadvantage to decisions through consensus is that discussions relating to the decisions tend to be lengthy and therefore costly.

Consensus is agreement on a decision by all individuals involved in making the decision.

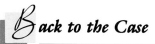

Back to the Case

If Lee Iacocca, the top manager at Chrysler, were forced to confront an issue such as how to design and manufacture automobiles that would have fewer Japanese competitors than the ones he was producing, he would definitely be faced with a formal decision situation, one requiring that he decide upon one of a number of

VIETOR'S FUNNY BUSINESS

"Need any help deciding?"

USA Today (August 27, 1990), 2B. Copyright, USA Today.
Reprinted with permission.

possible solutions. Iacocca would need to scrutinize his decision carefully because of its significance to the organization and to him. Technically, this decision would be nonprogrammed in nature and therefore would be characterized more by judgment than by simple quantitative data.

As the top manager at Chrysler, Iacocca would probably have the ultimate responsibility for making such a broad-scope decision. This does not mean, however, that Iacocca would have to make the decision by himself. He could ask for advice from other Chrysler employees and perhaps even appoint a group of managers/employees to arrive at a consensus on which of the decision alternatives he should implement.

ELEMENTS OF THE DECISION SITUATION

Wilson and Alexis isolate six basic elements in the decision situation.[8] These elements and their definitions follow.

State of Nature

State of nature refers to the aspects of the decision maker's environment that can affect the choice. Robert B. Duncan conducted a study in which he attempted to identify the environmental characteristics that influenced decision makers. He grouped the characteristics into two categories: the internal environment and the external environment (see Table 6.2).[9]

The Decision Makers

Decision makers are the individuals or groups who actually make the choice among alternatives. According to Dale, weak decision makers can have four different orientations: receptive, exploitation, hoarding, and marketing.[10]

Decision makers who have a receptive orientation believe that the source of all good is outside themselves, and therefore they rely heavily on suggestions from other organization members. Basically, they want others to make their decisions for them.

Decision makers with an exploitation orientation also believe that good is outside themselves, and they are willing to take ethical or unethical steps to steal ideas necessary to make good decisions. They build their organization on the ideas of others and typically extend little or no credit for the ideas to anyone but themselves.

The hoarding orientation is characterized by decision makers who preserve the status quo as much as possible. They accept little outside help, isolate themselves from others, and are extremely self-reliant. These decision makers emphasize maintaining their present existence.

Marketing-oriented decision makers consider themselves commodities that are only as valuable as the decisions they make. They try to make decisions that will enhance their value and are therefore conscious of what others think of their decisions.

The ideal decision-making orientation is one that emphasizes trying to realize the potential of the organization as well as of the decision maker. Ideal decision

TABLE 6.2 Environmental factors that can influence managerial decision making

Internal Environment	External Environment

1. Organizational personnel component
  a. Educational and technological background and skills
  b. Previous technological and managerial skill
  c. Individual member's involvement and commitment to attaining system's goals
  d. Interpersonal behavior styles
  e. Availability of human resources for utilization within the system
	4. Customer component
	  a. Distributors of product or service
	  b. Actual users of product or service

	5. Supplier component
	  a. New materials suppliers
	  b. Equipment suppliers
	  c. Product parts suppliers
	  d. Labor supply

2. Organizational functional and staff units component
  a. Technological characteristics of organizational units
  b. Interdependence of organizational units in carrying out their objectives
  c. Intraunit conflict among organizational functional and staff units
  d. Interunit conflict among organizational functional and staff units
	6. Competitor component
	  a. Competitors for suppliers
	  b. Competitors for customers

	7. Sociopolitical component
	  a. Government regulatory control over the industry
	  b. Public political attitude toward industry and its particular product
	  c. Relationship with trade unions with jurisdiction in the organization

3. Organizational level component
  a. Organizational objectives and goals
  b. Integrative process integrating individuals and groups into contributing maximally to attaining organizational goals
  c. Nature of the organization's product service
	8. Technological component
	  a. Meeting new technological requirements of own industry and related industries in production of product or service
	  b. Improving and developing new products by implementing new technological advances in the industry

makers try to use all of their talents and are influenced mainly by reason and sound judgment. They do not possess the qualities of the four undesirable decision-making orientations just described.

Goals to Be Served

The goals that decision makers seek to attain are another element of the decision situation. In the case of managers, these goals should most often be organizational objectives. (Chapter 4 discusses specifics about organizational objectives.)

Relevant Alternatives

The decision situation is usually composed of at least two relevant alternatives. A **relevant alternative** is one that is considered feasible for implementation and for solving an existing problem. Alternatives that cannot be implemented or will not solve an existing problem are irrelevant alternatives and should be excluded from the decision-making situation.

Relevant alternatives are alternatives that are considered feasible for implementation and for solving an existing problem.

Ordering of Alternatives

The decision situation must have a process or mechanism that ranks alternatives from most desirable to least desirable. The process can be subjective, objective, or some combination of the two. Past experience of the decision maker is an example of a subjective process, and the rate of output per machine is an example of an objective process.

Choice of Alternatives

The last element of the decision situation is an actual choice between available alternatives. This choice establishes the fact that a decision is made. Typically, managers choose the alternative that maximizes long-term return for the organization.

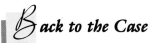
Back to the Case

As Iacocca was making his decision about whether to diversify into aerospace and defense businesses, he would need to be aware of all the elements in the decision situation. Both the internal and external environments of Chrysler would be one focus of Iacocca's analysis. For example: Does Chrysler have the internal financial resources and expertise to diversify into these areas? Externally, is there a market for aerospace and defense products that Chrysler would offer? Reason and sound judgment must characterize Iacocca's orientation as a decision maker. Iacocca would have to keep Chrysler's organizational objectives in mind and list relevant alternatives in addition to aerospace or defense businesses. For example, other relevant alternatives might be to design and manufacture earth-moving equipment or farm machinery. In addition, Iacocca would need to list relevant alternatives in some order of desirability before choosing an alternative objective to implement. According to the case, Iacocca admitted that the alternative he chose in this decision situation was inappropriate. The case does not tell us which other alternatives he may have had or why he chose the one that he did.

THE DECISION-MAKING PROCESS

The **decision-making process** is the steps a decision maker takes to make a decision.

A decision is a choice of one alternative from a set of available alternatives. The **decision-making process** is the steps the decision maker takes to choose an alternative. The process that a manager uses to make decisions has significant impact on the quality of decisions made. If managers use an organized and systematic process, the probability that their decisions will be sound is higher than if the process is more disorganized and unsystematic.[11]

A model of the decision-making process that is recommended for managerial use is presented in Figure 6.4. In order of occurrence, the decision-making steps this model depicts are (1) identify an existing problem, (2) list possible alternatives to solve the problem, (3) select the most beneficial of these alternatives, (4) put the selected alternative into action, and (5) gather feedback to find out if the implemented alternative is solving the identified problem. The paragraphs that follow elaborate upon each of these steps and explain their interrelationships.[12]

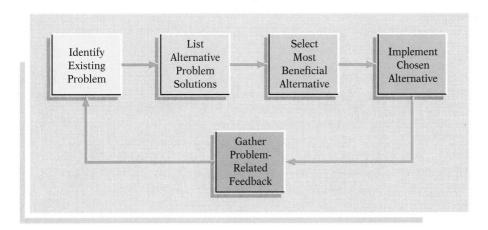

FIGURE 6.4
Model of the decision-making process

This model of the decision-making process is based on three primary assumptions.[13] First, the model assumes that humans are economic beings with the objective of maximizing satisfaction or return. Second, it assumes that within the decision-making situation all alternatives and their possible consequences are known. The last assumption is that decision makers have some priority system that allows them to rank the desirability of each alternative. If each of these assumptions is met in the decision-making situation, decision makers probably will make the best possible decision for the organization. In reality, one or more of the assumptions often are not met, and related decisions, therefore, are usually something less than the best possible ones for the organization.

Identifying an Existing Problem

Decision making is essentially a problem-solving process that involves eliminating barriers to organizational goal attainment. Naturally, the first step in this elimination process is identifying exactly what the problems or barriers are. Only after the barriers have been adequately identified can management take steps to eliminate them. Chester Barnard has stated that organizational problems are brought to the attention of managers mainly through (1) orders issued by managers' supervisors, (2) situations relayed to managers by their subordinates, and (3) the normal activity of the managers themselves.[14]

Listing Alternative Problem Solutions

Once a problem has been identified, managers should list the various possible solutions. Very few organizational problems can be solved in only one way. Managers must search out the many alternative solutions that exist for most organizational problems.

Before searching for solutions, managers must be aware of five limitations on the number of problem-solving alternatives available: (1) authority factors (for example, a manager's superior may have told the manager that the alternative was feasible); (2) biological or human factors (for example, human factors within the organization may be inappropriate for implementing the alternatives); (3) physical factors (for example, the physical facilities of the organization may be inappropriate for certain alternatives to be seriously considered); (4) technological factors (for example, the level of organizational technology may be inadequate for certain alternatives); and (5) economic factors (for example, certain alternatives may be too costly for the organization).[15]

Figure 6.5 presents additional factors that can limit managers' decision alternatives. This diagram uses the term *discretionary area* to designate feasible alternatives available to managers. Factors that limit this area are legal restrictions, moral and ethical norms, formal policies and rules, and unofficial social norms.[16]

Ethics Highlight: Pharmacy Industry Sells Cigarettes?

Disagreement about what ethical norms actually exist in a decision situation can cause significant differences in the way different managers react to the same decision situation. Pharmacy managers face the dilemma of determining what ethical norms exist in decisions about whether to sell tobacco products to the public. A recent survey of pharmacy managers regarding this issue uncovered ethical foundations both for selling and for curtailing sales, and there appeared to be no consensus. Only 35 percent of those surveyed decided NOT to sell the products. However, 9 out of 10 pharmacy managers surveyed said that they would not sell tobacco products to minors and would ask for proof of age when in doubt. Most of the pharmacy managers who made the decision to sell cigarettes think that adults should have the right to decide if they wish to consume tobacco products at risk to their health. Pharmacy managers choosing NOT to sell the products believe that a pharmacy manager has an ethical responsibility to protect society from products harmful to it. In this situation, because pharmacy managers have interpreted ethical norms regarding the sale of cigarettes much differently, they have made different decisions regarding whether to sell tobacco products.

Selecting the Most Beneficial Alternative

Decision makers can select the most beneficial solution only after they have evaluated each alternative very carefully. This evaluation should consist of three steps. First, decision makers should list, as accurately as possible, the potential effects of each alternative as if the alternative had already been chosen and implemented. Second, a probability factor should be assigned to each of the potential effects. This would indicate how probable the occurrence of the effect would be if the alternative were implemented. Third, keeping organizational goals in mind, decision makers should compare each alternative's expected effects and their respective probabilities.[17] The alternative that seems to be most advantageous to the organization should be chosen for implementation.

Global Highlight: Expansion Hindered by China's Politics

Making managerial decisions includes assessing the benefits that an alternative will bring. Although this sounds like a clear and straightforward procedure, in an actual decision-making situation, assessing the benefits of an alternative can be a very difficult task.

Consider a manager faced with a decision of how best to expand a business. Assume that the manager pinpoints expanding into China as one of his or her business-expansion alternatives. After this alternative has been identified, the manager must determine the benefits of expanding into China. In other times, many modern managers believed that expanding into China should be considered a growth-oriented alternative that would almost certainly result in success. More recently, however, the Chinese government's violent and bloody crackdown on its citizens who were demonstrating in Tiananmen Square for a democratic government has left managers throughout the world somewhat suspicious and hesitant to initiate business operations in China. The Chinese government says that in terms of business relationships, the situation has not changed and China is still an excellent location for foreign businesses to expand.

Many managers throughout Europe and the United States, however, are now much more reluctant to expand into China. Their uncertainty about the role of the Chinese government has made it very difficult to assess accurately the benefits of expanding into that country. As a result, more and more managers now reject expansion into China as a viable way of expanding their businesses.

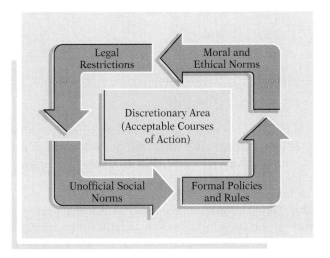

FIGURE 6.5

Additional factors that limit a manager's number of acceptable alternatives

Implementing the Chosen Alternative

The next step is to put the chosen alternative literally into action. Decisions must be supported by appropriate action if they are to have a chance of being successful.

Gathering Problem-Related Feedback

After the chosen alternative has been implemented, decision makers must gather feedback to determine the effect of the implemented alternative on the identified problem. If the identified problem is not being solved, managers need to search out and implement some other alternative.

*B*ack to the Case

Assume that Lee Iacocca is facing a decision to increase product safety. He first would need to identify the problem. He would need to find out if customer injury resulted from faulty parts, inadequate safety devices, or poor operating instructions. Once he identified the problem, he would have to list all possible problem solutions; for example: Can the quality of parts be improved? Would better operating instructions reduce the risk of injury? Can additional safety devices be invented?

After eliminating nonfeasible solutions, Iacocca would have to evaluate all remaining solutions, select one, and implement it. If operating instructions were unreliable because of customer error, or if better quality parts were too expensive to manufacture, the best alternative might be to create new safety devices for Chrysler products. Iacocca would then have to initiate appropriate action within the company so that such devices could be designed and manufactured. Problem-related feedback would be extremely important once the safety devices were added. Iacocca would need to find out if the new devices in fact did reduce customer injury. If they did not, he would need to decide what additional action should be taken to improve product safety.

DECISION-MAKING CONDITIONS

In most instances, it is impossible for decision makers to be sure of exactly what the future consequences of an implemented alternative will be. The word *future* is the key in discussing decision-making conditions. For all practical purposes, because organizations and their environments are constantly changing, future consequences of implemented decisions are not perfectly predictable.

In general, there are three different conditions under which decisions are made. Each of these conditions is based on the degree to which the future outcome of a decision alternative is predictable. These conditions are (1) complete certainty, (2) complete uncertainty, and (3) risk.[18] Figure 6.6 shows these three conditions on a continuum of predictability of the organizational environment, with complete certainty at one end and complete uncertainty at the other.

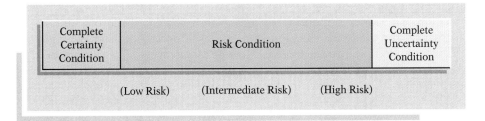

FIGURE 6.6
Continuum of decision-making conditions

Complete Certainty Condition

The **complete certainty condition** exists when decision makers know exactly what the results of an implemented alternative will be. In this condition, managers have complete knowledge about a decision. All they have to do is list outcomes for alternatives and then choose the outcome with the highest payoff for the organization. For example, the outcome of an investment alternative based on buying government bonds is, for all practical purposes, completely predictable because of established government interest rates. Deciding to implement this alternative essentially would be making a decision in a complete certainty situation. Unfortunately, most organizational decisions are made outside the complete certainty situation.

The **complete certainty condition** is the decision-making situation in which the decision maker knows exactly what the results of an implemented alternative will be.

Complete Uncertainty Condition

The **complete uncertainty condition** exists when decision makers have absolutely no idea what the results of an implemented alternative will be. The complete uncertainty condition would exist, for example, if there were no historical data on which to base a decision. Not knowing what happened in the past makes it difficult to predict what will happen in the future. In this situation, decision makers usually find that sound decisions are merely a matter of chance. An example of a decision made in a complete uncertainty situation would be choosing to pull the candy machine lever labeled "Surprise of the Day" rather than the lever that would deliver a candy bar that is familiar. It is fortunate that few organizational decisions need to be made in the complete uncertainty condition.

The **complete uncertainty condition** is the decision-making situation in which the decision maker has absolutely no idea what the results of an implemented alternative will be.

Risk Condition

The primary characteristic of the **risk condition** is that decision makers have only enough information about the outcome of each alternative to estimate how probable the outcome will be if the alternative is implemented. Obviously, the risk condition is somewhere between complete certainty and complete uncertainty. The manager who hires two extra salespeople to increase annual organizational sales is deciding in a risk situation. He may believe that the probability is high that these two new salespeople will increase total sales, but it is impossible for him to know for sure. Some risk is associated with this decision.

The **risk condition** is the decision-making situation in which the decision maker has only enough information to estimate how probable the outcome of implemented alternatives will be.

In reality, *degrees* of risk can be associated with decisions made in the risk situation. The lower the quality of information related to the outcome of an alternative, the closer the situation is to complete uncertainty and the higher is the risk of choosing that alternative. Most decisions made in organizations have some amount of risk associated with them. The following highlight illustrates PepsiCo's highly effective system for handling risk in decision making.

Quality Highlight: PepsiCo Teaches Risk Taking

PepsiCo feels that making risky decisions well is a very important part of maintaining a desirable level of product quality—so important, in fact, that teaching managers how to take risks is a critical component of PepsiCo's management training program.

PepsiCo has the most sophisticated and comprehensive U.S. system for turning bright young people into strong managers. The company's chief executive officer, Wayne Calloway, describes the process as taking eagles and teaching them to fly in formation. In a recent survey, PepsiCo ranks first in attracting and developing talented people. As part of their training, managers are encouraged to make decisions on their own, to make them fast, and to get used to taking risks related to their decisions. Calloway indicates that wrong decisions are more likely to be tolerated if the person who made the decision calculated the risk carefully and accurately. PepsiCo teaches its managers that the best time to make relatively more risky decisions is when the company is being successful; the time for more conservative and less risky decisions is when competition is strong and the business seems somewhat less successful.

Back to the Case

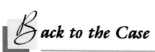

The introductory case reveals that Lee Iacocca faces a decision regarding how to handle increased competition, especially from the Japanese. Iacocca's decision-making condition for such a situation is somewhere between complete certainty and complete uncertainty about the outcome of his alternatives. He could decide, for example, to lower Chrysler's prices or to increase advertising to fight off the competition, but he has no guarantee that such measures would produce the desired results. He *does* know, however, what has worked in the past to stop competitors, and thus he is not dealing with a complete unknown. Therefore, any decision that Iacocca would make about handling increased competition would be made under the risk condition. In other words, Iacocca would have to determine the outcome probability for each of his alternatives and base his decision on the alternative that looked most advantageous.

DECISION-MAKING TOOLS

Most managers develop intuition about what decisions to make. This intuition is a mostly subjective feeling, developed from years of experience in a particular organization or industry, that gives managers insights about making a decision.[19] Although intuition can be an important part of making a decision, most managers tend to emphasize more objective decision-making tools, such as linear programming, queuing or waiting-line methods, and game theory.[20] Perhaps the two most widely used of the objective decision-making tools are probability theory and decision trees.

Probability Theory

Probability theory is a decision-making tool used in risk situations—situations wherein decision makers are not completely sure of the outcome of an implemented alternative. Probability refers to the likelihood that an event or outcome will actually occur and allows decision makers to calculate an expected value for each alternative. The **expected value (EV)** for an alternative is the income (I) it would produce multiplied by its probability of making that income (P). In formula form, EV = I × P. Decision makers generally choose and implement the alternative with the highest expected value.[21]

An example will clarify the relationship of probability, income, and expected value. A manager is trying to decide where to open a store that specializes in renting surfboards. She is considering three possible locations (A, B, and C), all of which seem feasible. For the first year of operation, the manager has projected that, under ideal conditions, she would earn $90,000 in Location A, $75,000 in Location B, and $60,000 in Location C. After studying historical weather patterns, however, she has determined that there is only a 20 percent chance, or a .2 probability, of ideal conditions during the first year of operation in Location A. Locations B and C have a .4 and a .8 probability, respectively, for ideal conditions during the first year. Expected values for each of these locations are as follows: Location A—$18,000; Location B—$30,000; Location C—$48,000. Figure 6.7

Probability theory is a decision-making tool used in risk situations—situations in which the decision maker is not completely sure of the outcome of an implemented alternative.

Expected value (EV) is the measurement of the anticipated value of some event, determined by multiplying the income an event would produce by its probability of making that income (EV = I × P).

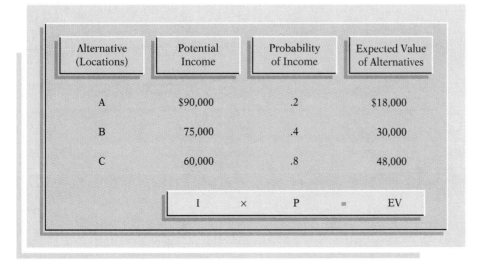

Alternative (Locations)	Potential Income	Probability of Income	Expected Value of Alternatives
A	$90,000	.2	$18,000
B	75,000	.4	30,000
C	60,000	.8	48,000
	I ×	P =	EV

FIGURE 6.7

Expected values for locating surfboard rental store in each of three possible locations

shows the situation this decision maker faces. According to her probability analysis, she should open a store in Location C, the alternative with the highest expected value.

Decision Trees

In the previous section, probability theory was applied to a relatively simple decision situation. Some decisions, however, are more complicated and involve a series of steps. These steps are interdependent; that is, each step is influenced by the step that precedes it. A **decision tree** is a graphic decision-making tool typically used to evaluate decisions containing a series of steps.[22]

A **decision tree** is a graphic decision-making tool typically used to evaluate decisions containing a series of steps.

John F. Magee has developed a classic illustration that outlines how decision trees can be applied to a production decision.[23] In his illustration (see Figure 6.8),

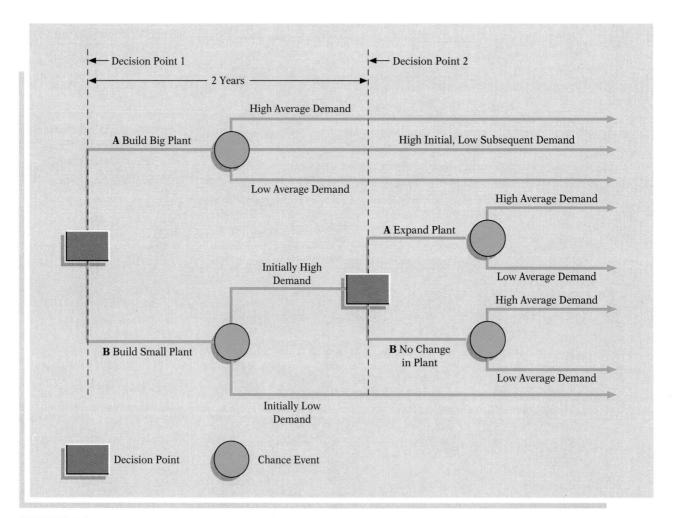

FIGURE 6.8

A basic decision tree illustrating the decision facing Stygian management

the Stygian Chemical Company must decide whether to build a small or a large plant to manufacture a new product with an expected life of ten years. This figure clearly shows that management must decide whether to build a small plant or a large one (Decision Point 1). If the choice is to build a large plant, the company could face high or low average product demand or high initial and then low demand. If, however, the choice is to build a small plant, the company could face either initially high or initially low product demand. If the small plant is built and high product demand exists during an initial two-year period, management could then choose whether to expand the plant (Decision Point 2). Whether the decision is made to expand or not to expand, management could then face either high or low product demand.

Now that various possible alternatives related to this decision have been outlined, the financial consequence of each different course of action must be compared. To adequately compare these consequences, management must (1) study estimates of investment amounts necessary for building a large plant, for building a small plant, and for expanding a small plant; (2) weigh the probabilities of facing different product demand levels for various decision alternatives; and (3) consider projected income yields for each decision alternative.

Analysis of the expected values and net expected gain for each decision alternative helps management to decide on an appropriate choice. *Net expected gain* is defined in this situation as the expected value of an alternative minus the investment cost. For example, if building a large plant yields the highest net expected gain, Stygian management should decide to build the large plant.

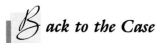

ack to the Case

Lee Iacocca has two tools available to make better decisions at Chrysler. First, he can use probability theory to obtain an expected value for various decision alternatives and then implement the alternative with the highest expected value. For example, in determining a tactic for meeting Japanese competition, Iacocca may need to decide whether to devote more of the company's resources to making higher quality automobiles or initiating more effective advertising for his present products. This decision would depend on such factors as manufacturing costs of quality improvements and expected impact of new advertising.

Second, in making a decision about choices that involves a series of steps related to each alternative, Iacocca could use a decision tree to help him picture and evaluate each alternative. For example, to meet the Japanese competition he could choose to design an entirely new solar-powered automobile or devote more resources to the improvement of existing automobiles. Either of these alternatives would indicate different decision-making steps.

Iacocca must remember that business judgment is an essential adjunct to the effective use of any decision-making tool. The purpose of the tool is to improve the quality of the judgment, not to replace it. Iacocca not only must choose alternatives with the help of probability theory and a decision tree, but he must use his own good judgment in deciding what is best for Chrysler.

Action Summary

Circle:

Reread the learning objectives that follow. Each objective is followed by questions. Answering those questions accurately will help you retain the most important concepts discussed in this chapter. After answering each question, check your answer with the answer key at the end of this chapter. (*Hint:* If you have doubt regarding the correct response, consult the page whose number follows the answer.)

From studying this chapter, I will attempt to acquire:

1. **A fundamental understanding of the term** *decision.*

T, F
    a. A decision is a choice made between two or more alternatives.

a, b, c, d, e
    b. Decision making is involved in which of the following functions: (a) planning; (b) organizing; (c) controlling; (d) influencing; (e) all of the above.

2. **An understanding of each element of the decision situation.**

a, b, c, d, e
    a. Which type of decision-making orientation involves the belief that the source of all good is outside oneself and that, therefore, one must rely heavily on suggestions from other organizational members: (a) exploitation; (b) hoarding; (c) marketing; (d) natural; (e) receptive.

a, b, c, d, e
    b. According to Wilson and Alexis, all of the following are elements of the decision situation except: (a) the state or nature of the decision environment; (b) the decision makers; (c) the goals to be served; (d) the timeliness of the decision; (e) the relevant alternatives.

3. **An ability to use the decision-making process.**

a, b, c, d, e
    a. After identifying an existing problem, the next major step in the decision-making process is: (a) defining the terminology in the problem statement; (b) listing possible alternatives to solve the problem; (c) investigating possible alternatives to determine their effect on the problem; (d) determining what parties will participate in the problem-solving process; (e) identifying sources of alternatives to solve the problem.

a, b, c, d, e
    b. After going through the decision-making process, if the identified problem is not being solved as a result of the implemented alternative, the manager should: (a) attempt to redefine the problem; (b) turn attention to another problem; (c) search out and implement some other alternative; (d) attempt to implement the alternative until the problem is solved; (e) accept the fact that the problem cannot be solved.

4. **An appreciation for the various situations in which decisions are made.**

T, F
    a. The risk condition exists when decision makers have absolutely no idea of what the results of an implemented alternative will be.

T, F
    b. When operating under the complete uncertainty condition, decision makers usually find that sound decisions are a matter of chance.

5. **An understanding of probability theory and decision trees as decision-making tools.**

a, b, c, d, e
    a. Expected value is determined by using the formula: (a) $EV = I \times P$; (b) $EV = I/P$; (c) $EV = I + P$; (d) $EV = P - I$; (e) $EV = 2P \times I$.

b. In the case of the Stygian Chemical Company, the problem was solved   a, b, c, d, e
through the use of: (a) executive experience; (b) decision tree technique;
(c) queuing theory; (d) linear programming; (e) demand probability.

 ntroductory Case Wrap-Up: Chrysler

"Iacocca Makes a Wrong Decision at Chrysler?" (p. 160) and its related back-to-the-case sections were written to help you better understand the management concepts contained in this chapter. Answer the following discussion questions about this introductory case to further enrich your understanding of chapter content:

1. List three alternatives that Iacocca might have considered in meeting Japanese competition before

making a decision to diversify into aerospace and defense businesses.

2. What information would Iacocca need to evaluate these three alternatives?

3. Do you think that you would enjoy making the kinds of decisions at Chrysler that Iacocca must make? Explain.

Issues for Review and Discussion

1. What is a decision?

2. Describe the difference between a significant decision and an insignificant decision. Which would you rather make? Why?

3. List three programmed and three nonprogrammed decisions that the manager of a nightclub would probably have to make.

4. Explain the rationale for determining which managers in the organization are responsible for making which decisions.

5. What is the consensus method of making decisions? When would you use it?

6. List and define the six basic elements of the decision-making situation.

7. How does the receptive orientation for decision making differ from the ideal orientation for decision making?

8. List as many undesirable traits of a decision maker as possible. (They are implied within the explanations of the receptive, exploitation, hoarding, and marketing orientations to decision making.)

9. What is a relevant alternative? An irrelevant alternative?

10. Draw and describe in words the decision-making process presented in this chapter.

11. What is meant by the term *discretionary area*?

12. List the three assumptions on which the decision-making process presented in this chapter is based.

13. Explain the difference between the complete certainty and complete uncertainty decision-making situations.

14. What is the risk decision-making situation?

15. Are there degrees of risk associated with various decisions? Why?

16. How do decision makers use probability theory? Be sure to discuss expected value in your answer.

17. What is a decision tree?

18. Under what conditions are decision trees usually used as decision-making tools?

Building on What You Know

Directions

Review the Highlight feature indicated in the accompanying paragraph and answer its corresponding questions. Questions in this section focus on relating a Highlight appearing in this chapter to management concepts that you have learned in a previous chapter.

Review the Global Highlight: China on page 171. In chapter 5, "Fundamentals of Planning," you studied the steps of the planning process. If a manager chose to expand into China, would he or she follow different steps in planning for the organization? Why or why not? Which step would become the most important to ensure successful planning? Explain.

Action Summary Answer Key

1. a. T, p. 161
   b. e, p. 161
2. a. e, p. 166
   b. d, pp. 166–168

3. a. b, p. 169
   b. c, p. 172
4. a. F, p. 173
   b. T, p. 173

5. a. a, p. 175
   b. b, pp. 176–177

Case Study

Lawrence Rawl and the Exxon *Valdez*

by Michael Bowen, University of Notre Dame

On March 23, 1989, no one was particularly worried about the Exxon *Valdez* or any of the other supertankers slowly filling with rich North Slope Alaskan crude oil in Valdez harbor. Shipping operations at the port of Valdez, located at the mouth of Alaska's Prince William Sound, were business as usual that evening. Not even the free-floating icebergs were unusual, as they drifted through the waters of the Sound, forcing tanker captains to steer out of their assigned traffic lanes to avoid them.

For the top-level managers of the Exxon Corporation, that Thursday night also seemed quiet. Exxon chairman Lawrence Rawl spent the evening at home, with no reason to think about anything that was happening at Valdez, one of his company's many oil terminals around the world.

Just after midnight, however, on what was now March 24, the third mate on the Exxon *Valdez* sensed that the ship had somehow gone significantly off course and was in imminent danger of running aground on Bligh Reef, about 23 miles from port and in the middle of the Sound. Telephoning the ship's captain, who had left the bridge to do paperwork in his cabin about twelve minutes earlier, he said, "I think we are in serious trouble." Suddenly, at about four minutes past midnight, the crew felt a jolt, and the huge ship began to shudder; for about ten seconds, the fully loaded supertanker seemed to be riding over the top of something. In what turned out to be a classic understatement, the ship's captain, Joseph Hazelwood, said later in recalling this moment, "I knew we'd struck something; something major had happened to the vessel." That was indeed the case: The grounding of the Exxon *Valdez* resulted in the biggest oil spill ever in United States history.

Four and a half hours later, at 8:30 A.M. EST, as Lawrence Rawl was having breakfast, his kitchen phone rang in his home in Westchester County, New York. The *Valdez* had been punctured ("holed") in Prince William Sound. He asked the caller how it had happened—Had a rudder broken? Had the ship lost its engine? "At that point, I didn't even know what it hit. All I knew was it hit something, and it was holed pretty badly," Rawl recounted later. "When you have a large ship on the rocks, and they tell you it's leaking oil, you know it's going to be bad, bad, bad."

To deal most directly with the developing crisis, Rawl decided not to waste time driving to his New York City office and began setting up conference calls from his home. He knew that in moments of crisis, it is essential to make well-informed, careful decisions as soon as possible after the problem arises, and he wanted to begin immediately sorting out the situation and directing appropriate responses. As events unfolded during the day, Rawl directed his energies toward corporate policy issues related to the disaster. Among the critical issues to be faced was the question of Exxon's official stance on the grounding: Should the company assume responsibility for the accident? Should he, as Exxon's chief executive, go to Alaska to take charge of recovery efforts and to demonstrate corporate concern for the resulting spill?

Rawl quickly decided that Exxon would indeed accept full blame for the accident, as well as full responsibility for cleaning up the damage that had occurred and would continue to do so until the *Valdez* was drained and removed from Bligh Reef. It was apparent to Rawl and to other top-level Exxon managers that the company was in fact responsible, in the broad sense, for the crash and the cleanup. The company owned the ship and its cargo and, indirectly through the Exxon Shipping Company, also employed the crew. There was little question in their minds that they should openly acknowledge responsibility.

Rawl still faced the decision about whether to leave immediately for Alaska. His initial inclination was to go. In that way, he could take charge of the crisis management there, see that Exxon's internal investigation of the spill got off to a quick and effective start, and show both his personal and Exxon's corporate concern for what had happened.

His fellow Exxon executives disagreed, though. Their rationale was simple: He would probably be in the way of people better equipped to deal with the situation, and he could serve the company's interests better from his own office in New York. Rawl acknowledged the pros and cons of each option and eventually was convinced that he could be more effective if he stayed out of the way of those employees who had been trained to deal with this sort of emergency. It was a decision that, in light of subsequent intense criticism in the press and from shareholders, he would later regret. "I wake up in the night questioning the decision to stay home."

Discussion Questions

1. Was Rawl's dilemma about whether to go to Alaska a programmed or a nonprogrammed decision? In your opinion, did Rawl use elements of traditional or modern decision making in determining his choice?

2. Create a model of the decision-making process as shown in Figure 6.4 to illustrate Rawl's decision not to go to Alaska.

3. Which of Dale's decision-making orientations do you believe Rawl demonstrated in this case?

4. Refer to Table 6.2. Which factors in Exxon's internal environment do you think were important to Rawl's decision?

John Georges of International Paper

As chief executive officer of the largest paper company in the world, John Georges has weathered some challenging times and has made some difficult decisions. He's used his decision-making skills to survive an industrywide depression and a brutal labor strike, and he's come out on top in both situations.

International Paper (IP) produces lumber, grocery bags, juice cartons, and all sorts of products created from wood, in addition to paper. It is a $9.5 billion enterprise, and John Georges has made it one of the thirty blue-chip companies on the Dow-Jones Industrial Average.

Nonetheless, money is not all that matters to Georges; he has a very personal attitude toward being CEO. He believes in working with each employee according to his or her skills and abilities, and he works with each one differently. He treats each employee according to individual needs, desires, and talents.

When Georges became IP's president in 1981, the company's mills were not doing well. The economy was in a recession, and the paper industry was hard hit. Earnings were poor, and the short-term outlook throughout the industry was bleak. Mills were shutting down, and workers were being laid off. In the face of this, Georges and his management team decided to spend $7 billion to modernize their operations.

Their decision was not made lightly. Georges and his managers discussed at length whether it was appropriate, in light of the paper industry's troubles, to reinvest in IP's old plants, or whether they should move on to new products and new challenges. However, they kept coming back to the same decision: to do what they knew how to do and build up their base business. If they could succeed, then at some point in the future, they would have the luxury to expand into new areas as well. The decision was the right one. IP experienced ten percent growth per year in the decade from 1979 to 1989, in the face of industry losses. In 1988 alone, IP showed an eighty-two percent increase.

To gain as they did, Georges and his team had to make other tough decisions when it came to labor problems. Union management saw the opportunity to combine workers from many mills in a strike that would bring potentially crippling pressure to bear on IP, thereby gaining a major bargaining advantage in contract negotiations. IP management locked out over 2,000 workers at one of the mills in response to the strike and hired replacements for them. When three other mills struck, they hired replacement workers there, too. Over 2,000 people lost permanent jobs as a result of that strike, but IP prevailed.

In addition, John Georges's long-term decisions on behalf of IP must reflect a concern for environmental issues. Trees, the prime ingredient of IP's products, are only a renewable resource if properly managed. For each tree IP cuts, five new ones are planted. The new trees are hybrids created through IP's genetic research programs. They have increased pest and disease resistance, as well as generally faster growth rates than naturally occurring trees. As a result, the replacement trees are more likely to survive and thrive and can usually be harvested at an earlier age than natural forests.

IP's policy also forbids harvesting trees along roadsides, rivers, and lakeshores. There is an obvious public relations profit in not exposing the public to the devastating appearance of raw cutting, but there is a more important gain for IP in the long run. To cut in these sites would expose reforestation areas and natural water supplies to environmental stresses that would eventually cause a reduction of future harvests. Thus, simple conservation techniques such as saving forested belts along a lakeshore benefit IP twice: a short-term public relations gain and a long-term financial gain. These benefits are balanced against the one-time benefit of harvesting the existing trees in those protected areas—Georges clearly made another right decision.

John Georges's attitude toward problems is to meet them squarely. He harvests as much information and advice as he can and then makes a decision. In the end, as he says, you've got to get on with the job.

Video Case Questions

1. Give an example of a nonprogrammed decision made by John Georges and the IP management team.
2. Plot the steps in the decision-making process that led to IP's choice of plant modernization.
3. Describe the scope of the decisions Georges and his team made regarding modernization at IP, and also regarding labor problems that they confronted.
4. According to the text, what style of decision-making process was used in choosing the modernization plan?

Video Case Activities _____

1. Figure 6.6 shows a continuum of decision-making conditions relative to risk. Design a continuum chart showing alternatives for modernization at International Paper.

2. Use the information in this case study to prepare a decision tree for a management decision confronting International Paper.

Chapter 7

Student Learning Objectives

From studying this chapter, I will attempt to acquire:

1. Definitions of both strategic planning and strategy.

2. An understanding of the strategy management process.

3. A knowledge of the impact of environmental analysis on strategy formulation.

4. Insights on how to use critical question analysis and SWOT analysis to formulate strategy.

5. An understanding of how to use business portfolio analysis and industry analysis to formulate strategy.

6. Insights on what tactical planning is and on how strategic and tactical planning should be coordinated.

Strategic Planning

Chapter Outline

ℐntroductory Case

STRATEGIC PLANNING AND CELLULAR PHONES AT BELL ATLANTIC

In the back of a gray Dodge minivan, Joseph Karatka sits in a swivel seat gathering intelligence. Pointing a transmitter into the air, he listens and waits. A computer screen starts flashing tangerine-colored graphics, which he quickly deciphers.

"The competition has turned on their extra spectrum," Mr. Karatka exclaims. "That wasn't there last week."

Mr. Karatka pilots the snoop van for Bell Atlantic Corp.'s Mobile Systems unit. In the high-tech vehicle, equipped with three antennae, two powerful computers, three cellular telephones, a facsimile machine, and a printer, his daily mission is to find out how archrival Metrophone's cellular system compares with Bell Atlantic's.

"Once, I drove down the Pennsylvania Turnpike measuring their service quality against ours," says Mr. Karatka. "It took me the entire day. But we got a lot of good information."

Competition for cellular phone service has become so intense that companies are resorting to more clandestine tactics and bolder marketing ploys to keep an

edge. Some cellular companies dispatch spies to check on rival's merchandise and promotions. All of them enlist department stores, electronics retailers, and auto supply shops to sell their cellular phone service along with their equipment. In return, they offer commissions of $200 to $300 for each customer contract, up from only about $50 a few years ago.

> Companies are resorting to more clandestine tactics and bolder marketing ploys to keep an edge.

The stakes are high for dominance in the cellular market. In 1989, Americans spent nearly $2 billion on cellular calls. [In 1990,] revenue [reached] $3.2 billion. Some locations, such as Los Angeles and New York, are straining to accommodate the current volume of calls, but with digital technology facilitating the industry's growth, revenue could reach $15 billion by 1995, experts say.

Cellular phone usage is soaring even though basic rates aren't dropping. Since cellular phone service was first offered in 1984, the number of mobile phone customers in the U.S. has surged to 3.5 million. Yet the cost of a cellular call during peak hours hasn't varied much from current rates of about 37 cents to 50 cents a minute. (For the average subscriber, that translates into a monthly bill of about $100.) By 1998, the number of cellular subscribers will grow more than sevenfold to 26 million, according to Donaldson, Lufkin & Jenrette Securities Corp.

"Growth is phenomenal," says Michael E. Kalgoris, chief executive officer of Metrophone, a joint venture of McCaw Cellular Communications Inc. and Metromedia Inc. "That's why it's so fiercely competitive."

Metrophone offers customers free long-distance calling on weekends. Nynex Mobile Communications is offering free "voice mail"—a phone message service. Until recently, Chicago-based Ameritech gave away cellular telephones to any customer who signed a one-year service contract.

From Julie Amparano Lopez, "Marketers Spy and Entice to Get an Edge," *Wall Street Journal*, May 14, 1990, B1, B7. Reprinted by permission of *Wall Street Journal*, © 1990 Dow Jones & Company, Inc. All Rights Reserved Worldwide.

STRATEGIC PLANNING

For managers to be successful strategic planners, they must understand the fundamentals of strategic planning and how to formulate strategic plans.

Fundamentals of Strategic Planning

Defining Strategic Planning

Strategic planning is long-range planning that focuses on the organization as a whole.[1] Managers consider the organization as a total unit and ask themselves what must be done in the long term to attain organizational goals. *Long range* is usually defined as a period of time extending about three to five years into the future. Hence, in strategic planning, managers try to determine what their organization should do to be successful at some point three to five years in the future. The most successful managers tend to be those who are able to encourage innovative strategic thinking within their organizations.[2]

Managers may have a problem trying to decide exactly how far into the future they should extend their strategic planning. As a general rule, they should follow the **commitment principle,** which states that managers should commit funds for planning only if they can anticipate, in the foreseeable future, a return on planning expenses as a result of the long-range planning analysis. Realistically, planning costs are an investment and therefore should not be incurred unless a reasonable return on that investment is anticipated.

Defining Strategy

Strategy is defined as a broad and general plan developed to reach long-term objectives. Organizational strategy can, and generally does, focus on many different organizational areas, such as marketing, finance, production, research and development, personnel,[3] and public relations.[4]

Actually, strategy is the end result of strategic planning. Although larger organizations tend to be more precise in their development of organizational strategy than smaller organizations,[5] every organization should have a strategy of some sort.[6] For a strategy to be worthwhile, however, it must be consistent with organizational objectives, which in turn must be consistent with organizational purpose.

Strategic planning is long-term planning that focuses on the organization as a whole.

The **commitment principle** is a management guideline that advises managers to commit funds for planning only if they can anticipate, in the foreseeable future, a return on planning expenses as a result of the long-range planning analysis.

Strategy is a broad and general plan developed to reach long-term organizational objectives; it is the end result of strategic planning.

Table 7.1 illustrates this relationship between organizational objectives and strategy by presenting sample organizational objectives and strategies for three well-known business organizations.

Strategy Management

Strategy management is the process of ensuring that an organization possesses and benefits from the use of an appropriate organizational strategy. Within this definition, an appropriate strategy is a strategy best suited to the needs of an organization at a particular time.

The strategy management process is generally thought to consist of five sequential and continuing steps: (1) environmental analysis, (2) establishing organizational direction, (3) strategy formulation, (4) strategy implementation, and (5) strategic control.[7] The relationships among these steps are illustrated in Figure 7.1.

> **Strategy management** is the process of ensuring that an organization possesses and benefits from the use of an appropriate organization strategy.

ack to the Case

In developing a plan to compete with other sellers of cellular phones, management at Bell Atlantic should begin by thinking strategically. That is, management should determine what can be done to ensure that Bell Atlantic will be successful with its cellular phone operations at some point three to five years in the future. Although developing a cellular phone that is best for the marketplace is part of this thinking,

TABLE 7.1 Examples of organizational objectives and related strategies for three organizations in different business areas

Company	Type of Business	Sample Organization Objectives	Strategy to Accomplish Objectives
	Automobile manufacturing	1. Regain market share recently lost to General Motors 2. Regain quality reputation that was damaged because of Pinto gas tank explosions	1. Resize and down-size present models 2. Continue to produce sub-compact, intermediate, standard, and luxury cars 3. Emphasize use of programmed combustion engines instead of diesel engines
	Fast food	Increase productivity	1. Increase people efficiency 2. Increase machine efficiency
	Transportation	1. Continue company growth 2. Continue company profits	1. Modernize 2. Develop valuable real estate holdings 3. Complete an appropriate railroad merger

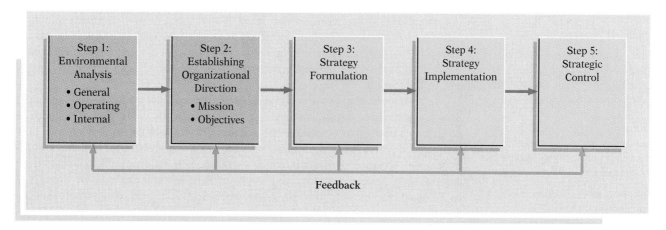

FIGURE 7.1

Steps of the Strategy Management Process

Bell Atlantic management must be careful to spend funds on strategic planning only if they can anticipate a return on these expenses in the foreseeable future.

The end result of Bell Atlantic's strategic planning will be a strategy—a broad plan that outlines what must be done to reach long-range objectives and carry out the organizational purpose of the company. This strategy will focus on many organizational areas, one of which will be how to compete with other cellular phone sellers. Once the strategy has been formulated using the results of an environmental analysis, Bell Atlantic management must conscientiously carry out the remaining steps of the strategy management process: strategy implementation and strategic control.

Environmental Analysis

The first step of the strategy management process is environmental analysis. Chapter 2 presented organizations as open management systems that are constantly interacting with their environment. In essence, an organization can be successful only if it is appropriately matched to its environment. **Environmental analysis** is the study of the organizational environment to pinpoint environmental factors that can significantly influence organizational operations. Managers commonly perform environmental analyses to help them understand what is happening both inside and outside their organization and to increase the probability that the organizational strategies they develop will appropriately reflect the organizational environment.

In order to perform an environmental analysis efficiently and effectively, a manager must thoroughly understand how organizational environments are structured.[8] For purposes of environmental analysis, the environment of an organization is generally divided into three distinct levels: the general environment, the operating environment, and the internal environment.[9] Figure 7.2 illustrates the relative positions of these levels to one another and to the organization; it also shows the important components of each level. Overall, managers must be aware of these three environmental levels, understand how each level affects organizational performance, and then formulate organizational strategies in response to this understanding.

Environmental analysis is the study of the organizational environment to pinpoint environmental factors that can significantly influence organizational operations.

The **general environment** is the level of an organization's external environment that contains components normally having broad long-term implications for managing the organization; its components are economic, social, political, legal, and technological.

Economics is the science that focuses on understanding how people of a particular community or nation produce, distribute, and use various goods and services.

The General Environment. The level of an organization's external environment that contains components normally having broad long-term implications for managing the organization is the **general environment.** The components normally considered part of the general environment are economic, social, political, legal, and technological.

The *economic component* is the part of the general environment that indicates how resources are being distributed and used within the environment. This component is based on **economics,** the science that focuses on understanding how people of a particular community or nation produce, distribute, and use various goods and services. Important issues considered in an economic analysis of an environment generally include the wages paid to labor, inflation, the taxes paid by labor and businesses, the cost of materials used during the production process, and the prices at which produced goods and services are sold to customers.[10]

Economic issues such as these can significantly influence the environment in which a company operates and the ease or difficulty the organization experiences in attempting to reach its objectives. For example, it should be somewhat easier

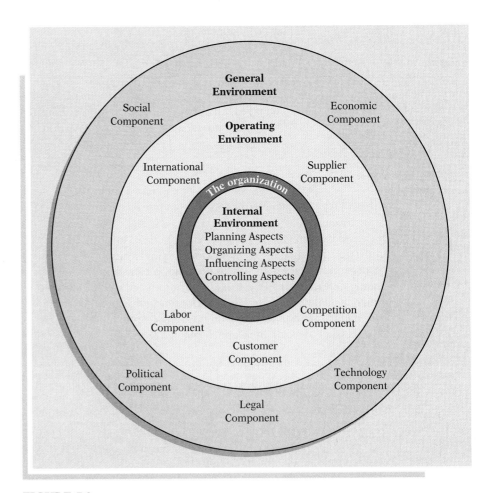

FIGURE 7.2

The organization, the levels of its environment, and the components of those levels

for an organization to sell its products at higher prices if potential consumers in the environment are earning relatively high wages and paying relatively low taxes than if these same potential customers are earning relatively low wages and have significantly fewer after-tax dollars to spend.

Naturally, organizational strategy should reflect the economic issues in the organization's environment. To build on the preceding example, if the total amount of after-tax income that potential customers earn has significantly declined, an appropriate organizational strategy might be to lower the price of goods or services to make them more affordable. Such a strategy should be evaluated carefully, however, because it could have a serious impact on organizational profits.

The *social component* is the part of the general environment that describes the characteristics of the society in which the organization exists. Two important features of a society commonly studied during environmental analysis are demographics and social values.[11]

Demographics are the statistical characteristics of a population. The characteristics include changes in number of people and income distribution among various population segments. These changes can influence the reception of goods and services within the organization's environment and thus should be reflected in organizational strategy.

For example, the demand for retirement housing probably would increase dramatically if both the number and the income of retirees in a particular market area doubled. Effective organizational strategy would include a mechanism for dealing with such a probable increase in demand within the organization's environment.

An understanding of demographics also can be helpful in developing a strategy aimed at recruiting new employees to fill certain positions within an organization. Knowing that only a small number of people have a certain type of educational background, for example, would indicate to an organization that it should compete more intensely to attract these people. To formulate a recruitment strategy, managers need a clear understanding of the demographics of the groups from which employees eventually will be hired.

Social values are the relative degrees of worth that society places on the ways in which it exists and functions. Over time, social values can change dramatically, causing obvious changes in the way people live. Table 7.2 offers several brief examples of how changes in social values can cause changes in the way people live.

Demographics are the statistical characteristics of a population. Organizational strategy should reflect demographics.

Social values are the relative degrees of worth society places on the manner in which it exists and functions.

TABLE 7.2 Examples of how social values can affect strategy

- For many years, people were opposed to gambling. This has changed in some places, such as Las Vegas and Atlantic City. A number of states have legalized state-run lotteries. But legalized gambling was voted down in Miami, Florida. The social value that gambling is immoral has special relevance for such firms as Resorts International and Holiday Inns.
- At one time, it was thought that families should have two to four children. Today, not all accept this norm, and the new standards have a big impact on P&G (Pampers), Gerber (baby food), builders (houses versus condominiums), Mattel (toys), and others.
- It used to be common for retired people, single people, widows, and widowers to live with relatives. Now there is a trend toward living alone, and this has a big impact on builders, appliance manufacturers, food packers, magazine publishers, and others.

TABLE 7.2 Continued

- For years, most married women stayed home. Now, most work. This has caused problems for firms that sold door-to-door (Avon and Fuller Brush) and has increased business for a variety of firms, such as nursery schools, prepared food firms, restaurants (two-employee families eat out more frequently), and home security systems, to name a few.
- At one time, people lived in one place all their lives. Now, there are thousands of people who are nomads. They live in campers and motor homes and move from place to place as jobs open up or as the spirit moves them. This provides opportunities for and threats to firms.
- Increased education has led to new attitudes on the part of employees about how many hours they wish to work, the quality of life they expect at work, and the kind of supervisory style they expect, which can affect how strategies are developed and implemented. New benefits programs are also needed for new lifestyles.
- After the Three Mile Island nuclear plant incident, when an accident at the plant caused a release of radiation, more people started to question the safety of nuclear power. New plant construction and uranium mining in Canada, the United States, and Australia have been cut drastically, while coal operators are seeing new opportunities.

These changes alter the organizational environment and, as a result, have an impact on organizational strategy. It is important for managers to remember that although changes in the values of a particular society may come either slowly or quickly, they are inevitable.[12] The following Ethics Highlight shows how Quaker Oats responded to changing societal values.

Ethics Highlight: Quaker Oats Cashes in on Fitness Fad

As values of our society have shifted toward exercising and maintaining better physical health, Quaker Oats intensified its marketing of Gatorade, a drink touted as an after-exercise refreshment that effectively and efficiently replaces body nutrients lost through exercise. Recently, however, Quaker Oats has come under some attack. Scientific analyses have shown that Gatorade is really no more effective than water in replenishing body fluids. Some might say that it is unethical for Quaker Oats to present Gatorade as a worthwhile product. The company could argue, however, that as with other image products, merely consuming the drink gives a person a special athletic self-image that makes him or her feel better.

Gatorade has locked up the so-called sports drink market in the United States and is Quaker Oats' biggest brand, growing roughly 30 percent a year for the past six years. Competitors estimate Gatorade now spends about $100 million a year on marketing the drink. Many companies have tried to win market share from Gatorade, but none have been very successful.

The *political component* is the part of the general environment that contains the elements related to government affairs. Examples include the type of government in existence, the government's attitude toward various industries, lobbying efforts by interest groups, progress on the passage of laws, and political party platforms and candidates. Recent events such as the reunification of the Federal Republic of Germany and the German Democratic Republic and the shift from a Marxist-Socialist government in the Soviet Union illustrate how the political component of an organization's general environment can change at the international level.

The *legal component* is the part of the general environment that contains passed legislation. Simply stated, this component is the rules or laws that society's members must follow. Some examples of legislation specifically aimed at the operation of organizations are the Clean Air Act of 1963 (most recently amended in 1990) that focuses on minimizing air pollution, the Occupational Safety and Health Act of 1970 (most recently amended in 1984) that aims at maintaining a safe workplace, the Comprehensive Environmental Response, Compensation, and Liability Act of 1980 (most recently amended in 1988) that emphasizes controlling hazardous waste sites, and the Consumer Products Safety Act of 1972 (most recently amended in 1988) that upholds the notion that businesses must provide safe products for consumers. Naturally, over time, new laws are passed and some old ones are eliminated.

The *technology component* is the part of the general environment that includes new approaches to producing goods and services. These approaches can include new procedures as well as new equipment. The trend toward exploiting robots to improve productivity is an example of the technology component. The increasing use of robots in the next decade should vastly improve the efficiency of U.S. industry.

The Operating Environment. The level of an organization's external environment that contains components normally having relatively specific and more immediate implications for managing the organization is the **operating environment.** As Figure 7.2 shows, major components of this environmental level are generally thought to include customers, competition, labor, suppliers, and international issues.

The *customer component* is the operating environment segment that is composed of factors relating to those who buy goods and services provided by the organization. Profiles—detailed descriptions—of those who buy organizational products are commonly created by businesses. Developing such profiles helps management generate ideas for improving customer acceptance of organizational goods and services.

The *competition component* is the operating environment segment that is composed of those with whom an organization must battle in order to obtain resources. Overall, strategy involves the search for a plan of action that will give one organization an advantage over its competitors.[13] Because understanding competitors is a key factor in developing effective strategy, understanding the competitive environment is a fundamental challenge to management. Basically, the purpose of competitive analysis is to help management understand the strengths, weaknesses, capabilities, and likely strategies of existing and potential competitors.[14]

The **operating environment** is the level of the organization's external environment that contains components normally having relatively specific and immediate implications for managing the organization.

The *labor component* is the operating environment segment that is composed of factors influencing the supply of workers available to perform needed organizational tasks. Issues such as skill levels, trainability, desired wage rates, and average age of potential workers are important to the operation of the organization. Another important but often overlooked issue is the potential workers' desire to work for a particular organization.

The *supplier component* is the operating environment segment that entails all variables related to the individuals or agencies that provide organizations with resources needed to produce goods or services. The individuals or agencies are called **suppliers.** Issues such as how many suppliers offer specified resources for sale, the relative quality of the materials offered by suppliers, the reliability of supplier deliveries, and the credit terms offered by suppliers all become important in managing an organization effectively and efficiently.

Suppliers are individuals or agencies that provide organizations with resources needed to produce organizational goods and services.

Global Highlight: The Limited, Inc. Plans Global Manufacturing

The Limited Inc. is one of the largest purchasers of women's clothing in the world. More than 50 percent of its merchandise is manufactured overseas. Vital to the company's success is its international supplier network. Managing such a complex network and integrating them into their vast retailing operation requires tremendous planning.

Limited Chairman Leslie Wexner took control of that network in 1978, when he purchased Mast Industries, Limited Inc.'s major supplier. Today, Mast coordinates production with more than 300 manufacturers, and more than 6,000 suppliers. Most are in the Far East. The network allows production at the lowest possible cost, both because labor in these countries is cheaper than in the United States and because Limited Inc. orders in such large volume.

One drawback to the existing system is that it can be difficult to control quality. Because the company orders in such large volume, one supplier often cannot fill the entire order. One style of shorts, for instance, can be manufactured in three or four countries, with varying levels of quality.

"Great-quality factories don't grow on trees," says Martin Trust, Mast's president. "If I could, I'd make everything in one country."

On evaluating the situation, Mast developed a strategic plan to take more control of production quality: Mast has formed joint ventures with manufacturers. With Limited Inc.'s financial backing, these manufacturers build and operate factories in countries that are not subject to U.S. apparel import restrictions.

The *international component* is the operating environment segment that is composed of all the factors relating to the international implications of organizational operations. Although not all organizations must deal with international issues, the number is increasing dramatically and continually. Significant factors in the international component include other countries' laws, culture, economics, and politics.[15] Important variables within each of these four categories are presented in Table 7.3.

TABLE 7.3 Important aspects of the international component of the organization's operating environment

Legal Environment	Cultural Environment
Legal tradition	Customs, norms, values, beliefs
Effectiveness of legal system	Language
Treaties with foreign nations	Attitudes
Patent and trademark laws	Motivations
Laws affecting business firms	Social institutions
	Status symbols
Economic Environment	Religious beliefs
Level of economic development	
Population	**Political System**
Gross national product	Form of government
Per capita income	Political ideology
Literacy level	Stability of government
Social infrastructure	Strength of opposition parties and
Natural resources	groups
Climate	Social unrest
Membership in regional economic blocks	Political strife and insurgency
(EEC, LAFTA, etc.)	Government attitude toward foreign
Monetary and fiscal policies	firms
Nature of competition	Foreign policy
Currency convertibility	
Inflation	
Taxation system	
Interest rates	
Wage and salary levels	

The Internal Environment. The level of an organization's environment that exists inside the organization and normally has immediate and specific implications for managing the organization is the **internal environment.** In broad terms, the internal environment includes marketing, finance, and accounting. From a more specifically management viewpoint, it includes planning, organizing, influencing, and controlling within the organization. Table 7.4 contains these more management-specific factors in the internal environment and sample questions that managers can ask in exploring them.

The **internal environment** is the level of an organization's environment that exists inside the organization and normally has immediate and specific implications for managing the organization.

Back to the Case

As part of the strategy development process, Bell Atlantic management should spend time analyzing the environment in which the organization exists. Naturally, managers should focus on Bell Atlantic's general, operating, and internal environments. Environmental data important for them to consider as they pursue strategic planning include the number of competitive sellers of cellular phones in the marketplace and estimates whether this number will be increasing or decreasing. Other factors should include the strengths and weakness of their cellular phones when

TABLE 7.4 Several management-specific aspects of an organization's internal environment and questions related to exploring them

Planning Aspects
- Are organizational plans clearly linked to organizational goals?
- Is the sequencing for the performance of specific tasks appropriate?
- Are plans developed for both the short term and the long term?

Organizing Aspects
- Are tasks assigned to the right people?
- Do organizing efforts put plans into action?
- Are tasks appropriately assigned to either individuals or groups?

Influencing Aspects
- Do the rewards offered employees actually motivate them?
- Are organization members encouraged to do work that actually contributes to organizational goal attainment?
- Is communication within the organization effective and efficient?

Controlling Aspects
- Is information gathered to measure recent performance?
- Is present performance compared to preestablished standards?
- Are organizational characteristics modified when necessary to ensure that preestablished standards are met?

compared to competitive products, the purposes for which cellular phones are used, and the methods competitors are using to promote their products to their customers. Information in the case indicates that through the use of its "snoop van" Bell Atlantic management is gathering important environmental information about how competitive communication systems are structured and used. Obtaining information about environmental issues such as these will increase the probability that any strategy developed for Bell Atlantic will be appropriate for the environment in which the company operates and will assure that the company is successful in the long term.

Establishing Organizational Direction

The second step of the strategy management process is establishing organizational direction. Through an interpretation of information gathered during environmental analysis, managers can determine the direction in which an organization should move. Two important ingredients of organizational direction are organizational mission and organizational objectives.

The **organizational mission** is the purpose for which or the reason why an organization exists.

Determining Organizational Mission. The most commonly taken initial act in establishing organizational direction is to determine an organizational mission. **Organizational mission** is the purpose for which—the reason why—an organization exists. In general, the firm's organizational mission reflects such information as what types of products or services the organization produces, who its customers tend to be, and what important values it holds. Organizational mission is a very broad statement of organizational direction and is based upon a thorough analysis of information generated through environmental analysis.

Developing a Mission Statement. A **mission statement** is a written document developed by management, normally based or input by managers as well as nonmanagers, that describes and explains what the mission of an organization actually is. Normally, the mission is expressed in writing to ensure that all organization members have easy access to it and thoroughly understand exactly what the organization is trying to accomplish. Sample mission statements for three different organizations are contained in Table 7.5.

The Importance of Organizational Mission. An organizational mission is normally very important to an organization because it usually helps management to increase the probability that an organization will be successful. This probability is increased for several reasons. First, the existence of an organizational mission helps management to focus human effort in a common direction. The mission makes explicit the major targets the organization is trying to reach and helps managers keep these targets in mind as they make decisions. Second, the existence of an organizational mission helps managers because it serves as a sound rationale for allocating resources. A properly developed mission statement gives managers

A **mission statement** is a written document developed by management, normally based upon input by managers as well as nonmanagers, that describes and explains what the mission of an organization actually is.

TABLE 7.5 Mission statements for three different organizations

The Crummer School[1]

The mission of the Crummer School is to improve general management through formal education programs stressing an administrative point of view, research and publication involving new knowledge and teaching materials, and relationships with businesses and the community. In fulfilling this mission the School is committed to programs that emphasize high quality, innovation, problem solving, and the application of management theory.

The emphasis of the Crummer School is on the full-time MBA program. The primary target market for this core business is the national pool of applicants, with or without an academic background in business, but including those who have business experience.

IBM[2]

IBM Corporation is in the business of applying advanced information technology to help solve the problems of business, government, science, space exploration, defense, education, medicine, and other areas of human activity. IBM offers customers solutions that incorporate information processing systems, software, communications systems, and other products and services to address specific needs. These solutions are provided by IBM's worldwide marketing organizations, as well as through the company's business partners, including authorized dealers and remarketers.

Federal Express[3]

Federal Express is committed to our People-Service-Profit philosophy. We will produce outstanding financial returns by providing totally reliable, competitively superior, global air-ground transportation of high-priority goods and documents that require rapid, time-certain delivery. Equally important, positive control of each package will be maintained utilizing real time electronic tracking and tracing systems. A complete record of each shipment and delivery will be presented with our request for payment. We will be helpful, courteous, and professional to each other and the public. We will strive to have a completely satisfied customer at the end of each transaction.

general but useful guidelines about how resources should be used to best accomplish organizational purpose. Third, the existence of a mission statement can help managers because it pinpoints broad but important job areas within an organization. A well-developed mission generally helps management define critical jobs that must be accomplished.

The Relationship Between Mission and Objectives. Organizational objectives were defined in chapter 4 as the targets toward which the open management system is directed. Sound organizational objectives reflect and flow naturally from the purpose of the organization. The purpose of an organization is contained in its mission statement. As a result, useful organizational objectives must reflect and flow naturally from an organizational mission that, in turn, was designed to reflect and flow naturally from the results of an environmental analysis.

Strategy Formulation

After managers involved in the strategic management process have analyzed the environment and determined organizational direction through the development of a mission statement and organizational objectives, they are ready to formulate strategy. **Strategy formulation** is the process of determining appropriate courses of action for achieving organizational objectives and thereby accomplishing organizational purpose.

Tools for Developing Organizational Strategies. Managers formulate strategies that reflect environmental analysis, lead to the fulfillment of organizational mission, and result in the reaching of organizational objectives. Special tools that managers can use for assistance in formulating strategies include (1) critical question analysis, (2) SWOT analysis, (3) business portfolio analysis, and (4) Porter's Model for Industry Analysis.

The four strategy development tools are related but distinct. Managers should use which one tool or combination of tools seems most appropriate for them and their organizations.

1. *Critical Question Analysis.* A synthesis of the ideas of several contemporary management writers suggests that formulating appropriate organizational strategy is a process of **critical question analysis**—answering the following four basic questions.[16]

   What are the purposes and objectives of the organization? The answer to this question states where the organization wants to go. As indicated earlier, appropriate strategy reflects organizational purpose and objectives. By answering this question during strategy formulation, managers are likely to remember this important point and thereby minimize inconsistencies among purposes, objectives, and strategies.

   Where is the organization presently going? The answer to this question can tell managers if an organization is achieving organizational goals and, if so, whether the level of such progress is satisfactory. Whereas the first question focuses on where the organization wants to go, this one focuses on where the organization is actually going.

   In what kind of environment does the organization now exist? Both internal and external environments—factors both inside and outside the organization—are

A **strategy formulation** is the process of determining appropriate courses of action for achieving organizational objectives and thereby accomplishing organizational purpose.

Strategy development tools include critical question analysis, SWOT analysis, business portfolio analysis, and Porter's Model for Industry Analysis.

**Critical question analysis** is a strategy development tool composed mainly of four questions:

What are the purposes and objectives of the organization?

Where is the organization presently going?

In what kind of environment does the organization exist?

covered in this question. For example, assume that a poorly trained middle-management team and a sudden influx of competitors in a market are factors that exist respectively in the internal and external environments of an organization. Any strategy formulated, if it is to be appropriate, probably should deal with these factors.

What can be done to better achieve organizational objectives in the future? The answer to this question actually results in the strategy of the organization. The question should be answered, however, only after managers have had adequate opportunity to reflect on the answers to the previous three questions. Managers can develop appropriate organizational strategy only if they have a clear understanding of where the organization wants to go, where the organization *is* going, and in what environment the organization exists.

> What can be done to better achieve organizational objectives in the future?

2. *SWOT Analysis.* **SWOT analysis** is a strategic planning tool that matches internal organizational strengths and weaknesses with external opportunities and threats.[17] (SWOT is an acronym for a firm's Strengths and Weaknesses and its environmental Opportunities and Threats.) SWOT analysis is based on the assumption that if managers carefully review such strengths, weaknesses, opportunities, and threats, a useful strategy for ensuring organizational success will become evident. Table 7.6 contains several key considerations that managers should cover in performing a SWOT analysis.

> **SWOT analysis** is a strategy-development tool that matches internal organizational strengths and weaknesses with external opportunities and threats.

TABLE 7.6 Important considerations for SWOT analysis

Internal		External	
Strengths	*Weaknesses*	*Opportunities*	*Threats*
A distinctive competence?	No clear strategic direction?	Enter new markets or segments?	Likely entry of new competitors?
Adequate financial resources?	A deteriorating competitive position?	Add to product line?	Rising sales of substitute products?
Good competitive skills?	Obsolete facilities?	Diversify into related products?	Slower market growth?
Well thought of by buyers?	Subpar profitability because . . .?	Add complementary products?	Adverse government policies?
Quality of product/service?	Lack of quality product/service?	Integrate vertically?	Growing competitive pressures?
An acknowledged market leader?	Lack of managerial depth and talent?	Integrate horizontally?	Vulnerability to business cycles?
Well-conceived functional area strategies?	Missing key skills or competencies?	Able to move to better strategic group?	Growing bargaining power of customers or suppliers?
Access to economies of scale?	Poor track record in implementing strategy?	Complacency among rival firms?	Changing buyer needs and tastes?
Insulated (at least somewhat) from strong competitive pressures?	Plagued with internal operating problems?	Faster market growth?	Adverse demographic changes?
Proprietary technology?	Vulnerable to competitive pressures?	Other?	Other?
Cost advantages?	Falling behind in R&D?		
Competitive advantages?	Too narrow a product line?		
Product innovation abilities?	Weak market image?		
Proven management?	Competitive disadvantages?		
Other?	Below-average marketing skills?		
	Inability to finance needed changes in strategy?		
	Other?		

$\mathcal{Q}$uality Highlight: Harley-Davidson Strives for High Quality

As a result of analyzing their market strategy, management at Harley-Davidson, the last U.S. motorcycle maker, realized that in order to survive it must follow a strategy of producing a high-quality product. Only through a high-quality product could Harley-Davidson draw customers away from Japanese motorcycle manufacturers. Pursuing this strategy involved teaching workers what high-quality work was, training managers in how to encourage workers to strive for high quality in their work, and helping suppliers to develop high-quality parts that eventually end up as components of a Harley-Davidson motorcycle.

Company efforts to improve product quality have paid off. Customers believe that the quality of Harley-Davidson motorcycles has recently risen significantly. Market research indicates that the company has made major progress by capturing nearly 50 percent of the super-heavyweight motorcycle market.

Business portfolio analysis is the development of business-related strategy that is based primarily on the market share of businesses and the growth of markets in which businesses exist.

3. *Business Portfolio Analysis.* Business portfolio analysis is another strategy development tool that has gained wide acceptance.[18] **Business portfolio analysis** is an organizational strategy formulation technique that is based on the philosophy that organizations should develop strategy much as they handle investment portfolios. Just as sound financial investments should be supported and unsound ones should be discarded, sound organizational activities should be emphasized and unsound ones deemphasized. Two business portfolio tools are the BCG Growth-Share Matrix and the GE Multifactor Portfolio Matrix.

   The BCG Growth-Share Matrix. The Boston Consulting Group (BCG), a leading manufacturing consulting firm, developed and popularized a portfolio analysis tool that helps managers develop organizational strategy based upon market share of businesses and the growth of markets in which businesses exist.[19]

"Good evening, cash flow fans."

USA Today, August 30, 1990, 2B. Copyright 1990, *USA Today.* Reprinted with permission

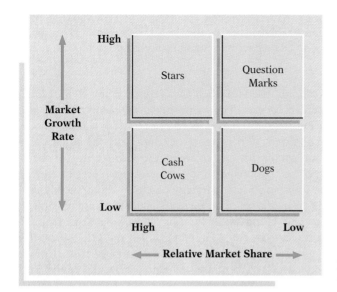

FIGURE 7.3

The BCG Growth-Share Matrix

The first step in using the BCG Growth-Share Matrix is identifying strategic business units (SBUs) that exist within an organization. **A strategic business unit** is a significant organization segment that is analyzed to develop organizational strategy aimed at generating future business or revenue. Exactly what constitutes an SBU varies from organization to organization. In larger organizations, an SBU could be a company division, a single product, or a complete product line. In smaller organizations, it might be the entire company. Although SBUs vary drastically in form, each has the characteristics of (a) being a single business or collection of related businesses, (b) having its own competitors, (c) having a manager who is accountable for its operation, and (d) being an area that can be independently planned for within the organization.[20]

After SBUs have been identified for a particular organization, the next step in using the BCG Matrix is to categorize them as being within one of the following four matrix quadrants (see Figure 7.3):

1. *Stars.* SBUs that are "stars" have a high share of a high-growth market and typically need large amounts of cash to support their rapid and significant growth. Stars also generate large amounts of cash for the organization and are usually areas in which management can make additional investments and earn attractive returns.

2. *Cash cows.* SBUs that are "cash cows" have a large share of a market that is growing only slightly. Naturally, these SBUs provide the organization with large amounts of cash. Since the market is not growing significantly, however, the cash is generally used to meet the financial demands of the organization in other areas, such as in the expansion of a star SBU. The cartoon on page 202 humorously makes the point that managers typically find "cash cows" very desirable. Perhaps the main reason for this desirability is the financial flexibility that a "cash cow" provides a manager.

3. *Question marks.* SBUs that are "question marks" have a small share of a high-growth market. They are called "question marks" because it is uncertain whether management should invest more cash in them to get a larger share of the market or should deemphasize or eliminate them because such an investment would be ineffective. Naturally, through further investment, management attempts to turn question marks into stars.

A **strategic business unit (SBU)** is, in business portfolio analysis, a significant organizational segment that is analyzed to develop organizational strategy aimed at generating future business or revenue. SBUs vary in form but have four common characteristics.

4. *Dogs*. SBUs that are "dogs" have a relatively small share of a low-growth market. They may barely support themselves, or they may even drain cash resources that other SBUs have generated. Examples of dogs are buggy whips and slide rules.

Companies such as Westinghouse and Shell Oil have used the BCG Matrix in their strategy management processes. There are, however, some possible pitfalls in this technique. For example, the matrix does not consider such factors as (a) various types of risk associated with product development, (b) threats that inflation and other economic conditions can create in the future, and (c) social, political, and ecological pressures.[21] Managers must remember to weigh such factors carefully when designing organizational strategy based on the BCG Matrix.

The GE Multifactor Portfolio Matrix. The General Electric Company (GE), with the help of McKinsey and Company, a leading consulting firm, has also developed a popular portfolio analysis tool. This tool, called the GE Multifactor Portfolio Matrix, helps managers develop organizational strategy that is based primarily on market attractiveness and business strengths. The GE Multifactor Portfolio Matrix was designed to be more complete than the BCG Growth-Share Matrix.

The basic use of the GE Multifactor Portfolio Matrix is illustrated in Figure 7.4. Each of the organization's businesses or SBUs is plotted in a matrix on two dimensions, industry attractiveness and business strengths. Each of these two dimensions is actually a composite of a variety of factors that each firm must determine for itself given its own unique situation. As examples, industry attractiveness might be determined by factors such as the number of competitors in an industry, the rate of industry growth, and the weakness of competitors within an industry. Business strengths might be determined by factors such as a company's

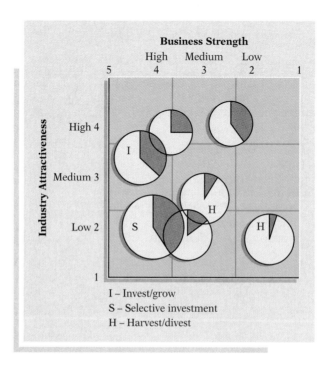

FIGURE 7.4
GE's Multifactor Portfolio Matrix

financially solid position, its good bargaining position over suppliers, and its high level of technology use.

Several circles appear on the GE Multifactor Portfolio Matrix: Each circle represents a company line of business or SBU. Circle size indicates the relative market size for each line of business. The shaded portion of a circle represents the proportion of the total SBU market that a company has captured.

Specific strategies for a company are implied by where their businesses (represented by circles) fall on the matrix. Businesses falling in the cells that form a diagonal from lower left to upper right are medium-strength businesses that should be invested in only selectively. Businesses above and to the left of this diagonal are the strongest and the ones that the company should invest in and help to grow. Businesses in the cells below and to the right of the diagonal are low in overall strength and are serious candidates for divestiture.

Overall, portfolio models provide graphic frameworks for analyzing relationships among the businesses of an organization, and they can provide useful strategy recommendations. However, no such model yet devised provides a universally accepted approach for dealing with these issues. Portfolio models should never be applied in a mechanistic fashion, and any conclusions they suggest must be carefully considered in the light of sound managerial judgment and experience.

4. *Porter's Model for Industry Analysis.* Perhaps the most well known tool for formulating strategy is a model developed by Michael E. Porter, an internationally acclaimed strategic-management expert.[22] Essentially, Porter's model outlines the primary forces that determine competitiveness within an industry and illustrates how the forces are related. Porter's model suggests that in order to develop effective organizational strategies, managers must understand and react to forces within an industry that determine an organization's level of competitiveness within that industry.

Porter's model is presented within Figure 7.5 on page 206. According to the model, competitiveness within an industry is determined by the following: new entrants or new companies within the industry; products that might act as a substitute for goods or services that companies within the industry produce; the ability of suppliers to control issues like costs of materials that industry companies use to manufacture their products; the bargaining power that buyers possess within the industry; and the general level of rivalry or competition among firms within the industry. According to the model, buyers, product substitutes, suppliers, and potential new companies within an industry all contribute to the level of rivalry among industry firms.

Understanding the forces that determine competitiveness within an industry should help managers develop strategies that will tend to make individual companies within the industry more competitive. Porter has developed three generic strategies to illustrate those that managers might develop to make organizations more competitive:

Differentiation. **Differentiation** is a strategy that focuses on making an organization more competitive by developing a product(s) that customers perceive as being different from products offered by competitors. Products might be offered to customers as different because of uniqueness in areas like product quality, design, or level of service after a sale. Examples of products that customers commonly purchase because they are perceived as being different include Nike's Air Jordan shoes, because of their high-technology "air" construction, and Honda automobiles, because of their high reliability.

Differentiation is a strategy that focuses on making an organization more competitive by developing a product(s) that customers perceive as being different from products offered by competitors.

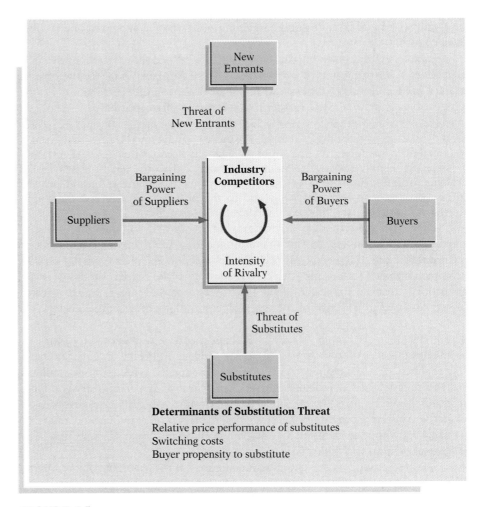

New
Entrants

Threat of
New Entrants

**Industry
Competitors**

Bargaining
Power
of Suppliers

Suppliers

Bargaining
Power
of Buyers

Buyers

Intensity
of Rivalry

Threat of
Substitutes

Substitutes

Determinants of Substitution Threat
Relative price performance of substitutes
Switching costs
Buyer propensity to substitute

FIGURE 7.5

Porter's model of factors that determine competitiveness within an industry

Cost leadership is a strategy that focuses on making an organization more competitive by producing its products more cheaply than competitors can.

Cost Leadership. **Cost leadership** is a strategy that focuses on making an organization more competitive by producing its products more cheaply than competitors can. According to the logic behind this strategy, by producing products more cheaply than competitors, organizations can offer products to customers at lower prices than the competitors', and thereby hope to increase market share. Examples of tactics managers might use to gain cost leadership include obtaining lower prices for product parts purchased from suppliers and using technology like robots to increase organizational productivity.

Focus is a strategy that emphasizes making an organization more competitive by targeting a particular customer.

Focus. **Focus** is a strategy that emphasizes making an organization more competitive by targeting a particular customer. Magazine publishers commonly use a focus strategy in offering their products to specific customers. *Working Woman* and *Ebony* are examples of magazines that are aimed respectively at the target markets of employed women and African Americans.

Sample Organizational Strategies. Analyzing the organizational environment and applying one or more of the strategy tools—critical question analysis,

SWOT analysis, business portfolio analysis, and Porter's model—give managers a foundation on which to formulate an organizational strategy. Four of the organizational strategies that can evolve are growth, stability, retrenchment, and divestiture. The following discussion of sample organizational strategies features business portfolio analysis as the tool used to arrive at the strategy, but the same strategies could also result from critical question analysis, SWOT analysis, or Porter's model.

Growth. **Growth** is a strategy adopted by management to increase the amount of business that an SBU is currently generating. The growth strategy is generally applied to star SBUs or question mark SBUs that hold the potential of becoming stars. Management generally invests substantial amounts of money to implement this strategy and may even sacrifice short-term profit to build long-term gain.[23]

Managers can also encourage growth by purchasing an SBU from another organization. For example, Black & Decker, not satisfied with being an international power in power tools, purchased General Electric's small-appliance business. Through this purchase, Black & Decker hoped that the amount of business it did would grow significantly over the long term.[24]

Stability. **Stability** is a strategy adopted by management to maintain or slightly improve the amount of business that an SBU is generating. This strategy is generally applied to cash cows, since these SBUs are already in an advantageous position. Management must be careful, however, that the strategy doesn't turn cash cows into dogs.

Retrenchment. In this section, *retrench* is used in the military sense: to defend or fortify. Through **retrenchment** strategy, management attempts to strengthen or protect the amount of business an SBU is generating. The strategy is generally applied to cash cows or stars that begin to lose market share.

Douglas D. Danforth, the chief executive of Westinghouse, is convinced that retrenchment is an important strategy for his company. According to Danforth, bigger profits at Westinghouse depend not only on fast-growing new products but also on the revitalization of Westinghouse's traditional businesses of manufacturing motors and gears.[25]

Divestiture. **Divestiture** is a strategy generally adopted to eliminate an SBU that is not generating a satisfactory amount of business and that has little hope of doing so in the near future. In essence, the organization sells or closes down the SBU in question. This strategy is generally applied to SBUs that are dogs or question marks that have failed to increase market share but still require significant amounts of cash. The cartoon illustrates that divestiture means discarding or getting rid of something.

Strategy Implementation

Strategy implementation, the fourth step of the strategy management process, is putting formulated strategies into action. Without success in strategy implementation, valuable and worthwhile strategies that managers have developed are virtually worthless.

The successful implementation of strategy requires four basic skills[26]:

Interacting skill is the ability to manage people during implementation. Managers who have the ability to understand the fears and frustrations that others feel during the implementation of a new strategy tend to be the best implementers. These managers are also able to show empathy for organization members and bargain for the best way to put a strategy into action.

Growth is a strategy adopted by management to increase the amount of business that a strategic business unit is currently generating.

Stability is a strategy adopted by management to maintain or slightly improve the amount of business a strategic business unit is generating.

Retrenchment is a strategy adopted by management to strengthen or protect the amount of business a strategic business unit is currently generating.

Divestiture is a strategy adopted to eliminate a strategic business unit that is not generating a satisfactory amount of business and has little hope of doing so in the future.

Strategy implementation is the fourth step of the strategy management process, putting formulated strategy into action.

Allocating skill is the ability to provide organizational resources necessary to implement a strategy. Successful implementers have talent to schedule jobs, budget time and money, and allocate other resources that are critical for implementation.

Monitoring skill is the ability to use information to determine whether a problem has arisen that is blocking implementation. Good strategy implementers set up feedback systems that constantly give them information about the status of strategy implementation.

Organizing skill is the ability to create throughout the organization a network of people who can help to solve implementation problems when they occur. Good implementers customize this network to include those people who can solve the special types of problems that will characterize the implementation of a particular strategy.

Overall, the successful implementation of a strategy requires a focus on handling people appropriately, allocating resources necessary for implementation, monitoring implementation progress, and solving implementation problems when they occur. Perhaps the most important requirements are to know which people can solve specific implementation problems and to be able to involve them when those problems arise.

Strategic Control

Strategic control is the last step of the strategy management process, monitoring and evaluating the strategy management process as a whole in order to make sure that it is operating properly.

Strategic control, the last step of the strategy-management process, is monitoring and evaluating the strategy-management process as a whole in order to make sure that it is operating properly.[27] Strategic control focuses on the activities involved in environmental analysis, organizational direction, strategy formulation, strategy implementation, and strategic control itself—ensuring that all steps of the strategy management process are appropriate, compatible, and functioning properly. Strategic control is a special type of organizational control. Organizational control is featured in chapters 17, 18, and 19.

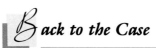

Back to the Case

Based on our information about Bell Atlantic, we understand that the company has performed its environmental analysis. Using that data, the managers must determine the direction in which the organization will move regarding its cellular phone business. To develop a mission statement with related objectives would clearly signal all organization members which role the cellular phone will play in the organization's future.

Bell Atlantic management has several tools available to help in formulating strategy. If managers are to be effective in this area, however, they must use the tools in conjunction with environmental analysis. One of the tools, critical question analysis, would require management to analyze the purpose of Bell Atlantic, the direction in which the organization is going, the environment in which it exists, and how the goals might be better achieved.

SWOT analysis, another strategy development tool, would require management to generate information regarding the internal strengths and weaknesses of Bell Atlantic and the opportunities and threats that exist within the organization's environment. Management could classify the products of competitors like Metrophone as environmental threats and significant factors to be considered in its strategy development process.

Business portfolio analysis would require Bell Atlantic management to classify each SBU as a star, cash cow, question mark, or dog, depending on the growth rate of the market in which the SBU exists and the SBU's market share. Management could decide, for example, to consider cellular phones and each of its other products as an SBU and categorize them according to the four classifications. As a result of this categorizing, managers could develop, perhaps for each different product that they offer, strategies for growth, stability, retrenchment, or divestiture. Bell Atlantic management should use whichever strategy development tools would be most useful to achieve the objective of developing an appropriate strategy for Bell Atlantic's cellular phones.

To be successful at using the strategy it has developed, management at Bell Atlantic must apply its interacting, allocating, monitoring, and organizing skills. In addition, management must have the ability to improve the strategy management process when necessary.

TACTICAL PLANNING

Tactical planning is short-range planning that emphasizes the current operations of various parts of the organization. *Short range* is defined as a period of time extending only about one year or less into the future. Managers use tactical planning to outline what the various parts of the organization must do for the organization to be successful at some point one year or less into the future.[28] Tactical plans usually are developed for organizations in the areas of production, marketing, personnel, finance, and plant facilities.

Tactical planning is short-range planning that emphasizes current operations of various parts of the organization.

COMPARING AND COORDINATING STRATEGIC AND TACTICAL PLANNING

In striving to implement successful planning systems within organizations, managers must remember several basic differences between strategic planning and tactical planning. First, because upper-level managers generally have a better understanding of the organization as a whole than do lower-level managers, and since lower-level managers generally have a better understanding of the day-to-day organizational operations than do upper-level managers, strategic plans usually are developed by upper-level management and tactical plans by lower-level management. Second, because strategic planning emphasizes analyzing the future and tactical planning emphasizes analyzing the everyday functioning of the organization, facts on which to base strategic plans are usually more difficult to gather than are facts on which to base tactical plans.

A third difference between strategic and tactical planning involves the amount of detail in the final plans. Because strategic plans are based primarily on a prediction of the future and tactical plans on known circumstances that exist within the organization, strategic plans generally are less detailed than tactical plans. Last, because strategic planning focuses on the long term and tactical planning on the short term, strategic plans cover a relatively long period of time whereas tactical plans cover a relatively short period of time. All of these major differences between strategic and tactical planning are summarized in Table 7.7 on page 210.

TABLE 7.7 Major differences between strategic and tactical planning

Area of Difference	Strategic Planning	Tactical Planning
Individuals involved	Developed mainly by upper-level management	Developed mainly by lower-level management
Facts on which to base planning	Facts are relatively difficult to gather	Facts are relatively easy to gather
Amount of detail in plans	Plans contain relatively little detail	Plans contain substantial amounts of detail
Length of time plans cover	Plans cover long periods of time	Plans cover short periods of time

In spite of their differences, tactical and strategic planning are integrally related. As Russell L. Ackoff states:

> In general, strategic planning is concerned with the longest period worth considering; tactical planning is concerned with the shortest period worth considering. Both types of planning are necessary. They complement each other. They are like the head and tail of a coin. We can look at them separately, even discuss them separately, but we cannot separate them in fact.[29]

In other words, managers need both tactical and strategic planning programs, but these programs must be closely related to be successful. Tactical planning should focus on what to do in the short term to help the organization achieve the long-term objectives determined by strategic planning.

PLANNING AND LEVELS OF MANAGEMENT

Top management of an organization has the primary responsibility for seeing that the planning function is carried out. Although all levels of management typically are involved in the planning process, upper-level managers usually spend more time planning than do lower-level managers. Lower-level managers are highly involved with the everyday operations of the organization and therefore normally have less time to contribute to planning than does top management. Middle-level managers usually spend more time planning than lower-level managers but less time than upper-level managers. Figure 7.6 shows the increase in planning time spent as managers move from lower-level to upper-level management positions. In small as well as large organizations, deciding on the amount and nature of the work that managers should personally handle is extremely important.[30]

The type of planning managers do also changes as the managers move up in the organization. Typically, lower-level managers plan for the short term, middle-level managers plan for a somewhat longer term, and upper-level managers plan for an even longer term. The expertise of lower-level managers in everyday operations makes them the best planners for what can be done in the short term to reach organizational objectives—in other words, tactical planning. Upper-level managers usually have the best understanding of the organizational situation as a whole and are therefore better equipped to plan for the long term—or to develop

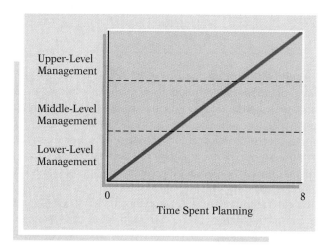

FIGURE 7.6

Increase in planning time as manager moves from lower-level to upper-level management positions

strategic plans. Figure 7.7 shows that as managers move from lower to upper management, they spend more time on strategic planning and less time on tactical planning. The total amount of time spent on strategic planning by lower-level managers, however, has been increasing.[31]

	Today	One Week Ahead	One Month Ahead	Three to Six Months Ahead	One Year Ahead	Two Years Ahead	Three to Four Years Ahead	Five to Ten Years Ahead
President	1%	2%	5%	17%	15%	25%	30%	5%
Vice-President	2%	4%	10%	29%	20%	20%	13%	2%
Works Manager	4%	8%	15%	38%	20%	10%	5%	
Superintendent	6%	10%	20%	43%	10%	9%	2%	
Department Manager	10%	10%	25%	39%	10%	5%	1%	
Section Supervisor	15%	20%	25%	37%	3%			
Group Supervisor	38%	40%	15%	5%	2%			

FIGURE 7.7

Movement of planning activities from a short-range to a long-range emphasis as a manager moves from a lower-level to an upper-level management position

ℬack to the Case

In addition to developing strategy plans for its organization, Bell Atlantic management should consider tactical, or short-range, plans that would complement its strategic plans. Tactical plans for Bell Atlantic should emphasize what can be done within approximately the next year to reach the organization's three- to five-year objectives and to stem competition from other cellular phone sellers. For example, Bell Atlantic could devote more resources to aggressive, short-range marketing campaigns, or it could increase its systems capability in order to provide its customers with the shortest wait time for placing calls.

In addition, Bell Atlantic management must closely coordinate strategic and tactical planning within the company. Managers must keep in mind that strategic planning and tactical planning are different types of activities that may involve different people within the organization and result in plans with different degrees of detail. Yet they must also remember that these two types of plans are interrelated. Whereas lower-level managers would be mostly responsible for developing tactical plans, upper-level managers would mainly spend time on long-range planning and developing strategic plans that reflect company goals.

Action Summary

Circle:

Reread the learning objectives that follow. Each objective is followed by questions. Answering these questions accurately will help you retain the most important concepts discussed in this chapter. After answering each question, check your answer with the answer key at the end of this chapter. (*Hint:* If you have doubt regarding the correct response, consult the page whose number follows the answer.)

From studying this chapter, I will attempt to acquire:

1. Definitions of both strategic planning and strategy.

T, F

   a. Strategic planning is long-range planning that focuses on the organization as a whole.

a, b, c, d, e

   b. Strategy (a) is a specific, narrow plan designed to achieve tactical planning; (b) is designed to be the end result of tactical planning; (c) is a plan designed to reach long-range objectives; (d) is timeless, and the same strategy can meet organizational needs anytime; (e) is independent of organizational objectives and therefore need not be consistent with them.

2. An understanding of the strategy-management process.

a, b, c, d, e

   a. Which of the following is not one of the steps in strategy management: (a) strategy formulation; (b) strategy implementation; (c) strategy control; (d) environmental analysis; (e) all of the above are steps.

T, F

   b. The steps of the strategy management process are sequential but usually not continuing.

3. A knowledge of the impact of environmental analysis on strategy formulation.

T, F

   a. Environmental analysis is the strategy used to change an organization's environment to satisfy the needs of the organization.

    b. All of the following are factors to be considered in environmental analysis except: (a) suppliers; (b) economic issues; (c) demographics; (d) social values; (e) none of the above.   a, b, c, d, e

4. Insights on how to use critical question analysis and SWOT analysis to formulate strategy.

    a. Which of the following is *not* one of the four basic questions used in critical question analysis: (a) Where has the organization been? (b) Where is the organization presently going? (c) What are the purposes and objectives of the organization? (d) In what kind of environment does the organization now exist? (e) What can be done to better achieve organizational objectives in the future?   a, b, c, d, e

    b. SWOT is an acronym for "Strengths and Weaknesses, Objectives and Tactics."   T, F

5. An understanding of how to use business portfolio analysis to formulate strategy.

    a. Use of the BCG Matrix considers which of the following factors: (a) types of risk associated with product development; (b) threats that economic conditions can create in the future; (c) social factors; (d) market shares and growth of markets in which products are selling; (e) political pressures.   a, b, c, d, e

    b. When using the BCG Matrix, products that capture a high share of a rapidly growing market are sometimes known as: (a) cash cows; (b) milk products; (c) sweepstakes products; (d) stars; (e) dog products.   a, b, c, d, e

    c. Use of the GE Multifactor Portfolio Matrix considers total market size for an SBU but generally does not consider the amount of that market that the SBU has won.   T, F

6. Insights on what tactical planning is and on how strategic and tactical planning should be coordinated.

    a. Tactical plans generally are developed for one year or less and usually contain fewer details than strategic plans.   T, F

    b. Which of the following best describes strategic planning: (a) facts are difficult to gather, and plans cover short periods of time; (b) facts are difficult to gather, and plans cover long periods of time; (c) facts are difficult to gather, and plans are developed mainly by lower-level managers; (d) facts are easy to gather, and plans are developed mainly by upper-level managers; (e) facts are easy to gather, and plans are developed mainly by lower-level managers.   a, b, c, d, e

Introductory Case Wrap-Up

"Strategic Planning and Cellular Phones at Bell Atlantic" and its related back-to-the-case sections were written to help you better understand the management concepts discussed in this chapter. Answer the following discussion questions about this introductory case to

further enrich your understanding of chapter content:

1. Is Bell Atlantic management's response to its cellular telephone competitors a function of strategic management? Explain.

2. Give three factors in Bell Atlantic's internal environment that management should be assessing in determining the company's organizational direction. Why are these factors important?

3. Using the business portfolio matrix, categorize cellular phones at Bell Atlantic as dogs, question marks, stars, or cash cows. From a strategic planning viewpoint, what do you recommend that Atlantic Bell management do as a result of this categorization? Why?

Issues for Review and Discussion

1. What is strategic planning?
2. How does the commitment principle relate to strategic planning?
3. Define *strategy* and discuss its relationship with organizational objectives.
4. What are the major steps in the strategy management process? Discuss each step fully.
5. Why is environmental analysis an important part of strategy formulation?
6. List one major factor from each environmental level that could have significant impact on specific strategies developed for an organization. How could the specific strategies be affected by each factor?
7. Discuss the significance of the questions answered during critical question analysis.
8. Explain in detail how SWOT analysis can be used to formulate strategy.
9. What is business portfolio analysis?
10. Discuss the philosophy on which business portfolio analysis is based.
11. What is an SBU?
12. Draw and explain the BCG Growth-Share Matrix.
13. What potential pitfalls must managers avoid in using this matrix?
14. Explain three major differences in using the GE Multifactor Portfolio Matrix to develop organizational strategy as opposed to the BCG Matrix.
15. Draw and explain Porter's model of factors that determine competitiveness within an industry. What is the significance of this model in regard to developing organizational strategy?
16. List and define four sample strategies that can be developed for organizations.
17. What is tactical planning?
18. How do strategic and tactical planning differ?
19. What is the relationship between strategic and tactical planning?
20. How do time spent planning and scope of planning vary as management level varies?

Building on What You Know

Directions

Review the Highlight feature as indicated below and answer its corresponding questions. Questions in this section focus on relating a Highlight appearing in this chapter to management concepts that you have learned in a previous chapter.

Review the Quality Highlight: Harley-Davidson Strives for High Quality, the Highlight feature on page 202. In chapter 6, "Making Decisions," you studied the various conditions under which managers typically make decisions and learned that probability theory and decision trees are two decision-making tools available to managers. Did Harley-Davidson management decide upon its product quality strategy under the condition of complete certainty, complete uncertainty, or risk? Explain. Discuss how probability analysis and decision trees could have been used to help Harley Davidson management choose its product quality strategy.

Action Summary Answer Key

1. a. T, p. 189
   b. c, p. 189
2. a. e, p. 190
   b. F, p. 190

3. a. F, p. 191
   b. e, pp. 192–196
4. a. a, pp. 200–201
   b. F, p. 201

5. a. d, p. 202
   b. d, p. 203
   c. F, pp. 204–205

6. a. F, p. 209
   b. b, p. 209

Case Study

EPI Products

by Leslie Toombs, University of Texas at Tyler, and Leslie Brunetta

In 1988, it looked as though the Krok sisters had it made. Within two years of founding EPI Products, Inc., they'd hit the $100 million sales mark on the strength of their original product alone. With the introduction of a new range of EPI products, they predicted they would triple that figure in 1989. Instead, they filed for bankruptcy. What went wrong? Industry analysts say the Kroks' catastrophic failure was due to a fatal lack of planning by these business world beginners.

The story had started happily enough. Solomon Krok, a South African pharmaceutical company owner, bought United States marketing rights to an Israeli hair-removal product called "Epilady." Epilady works by somewhat comfortably pulling hairs out by their roots; this offers women who shave their legs an opportunity to throw away their razors—and to stop nicking themselves. Solomon gave the Epilady marketing rights and start-up money to three of his daughters. The sisters established EPI Products in California, with Arlene as President, Loren as head of East Coast operations, and Sharon as head of advertising.

In July, 1987, the Kroks launched Epilady in some of the country's most prestigious department stores, including Bloomingdale's and Marshall Field. Things went better than they had imagined. Within five months, Epilady was the top-selling department store item of any kind.

However, Remington Products, Inc., which is one of the nation's leading manufacturers of shaving products and which had originally turned down the opportunity to purchase the rights to Epilady, soon posed a daunting challenge to the Kroks: It announced the impending introduction of Smooth & Silky, a product that would do the same job as Epilady but would be available in more stores for less money. So the Kroks came up with a plan: They would market a deluxe edition of the original Epilady, packaged with luxury accessories, to be sold at top-dollar prices in high-end department stores. Then, about six months later, they would start selling the original Epilady model, with no deluxe packaging or accessories, at sharply discounted prices in the same mass-market stores Remington had targeted. This way, they could maintain the high profit margins they garnered at the top stores while competing in the mass market with Remington.

Meanwhile, the Kroks decided it was time to start trading on the now familiar EPI name. They introduced EpiSauna, a facial sauna, and EpiPed, a foot whirlpool massager, as well as a brush with retractable bristles, a tooth whitener, and about 20 additional grooming products, all to be sold in high-end department stores.

When the Kroks had first announced plans to move the original Epilady to the mass-market, many of the more exclusive store executives had been furious. They worried that the strategy would detract from Epilady's prestige and thereby slow sales in their stores. Despite these fears, EPI product sales at these department stores were strong during the 1988 Christmas season—traditionally the peak sales time for personal grooming appliances—and the executives backed down.

During 1989, Epilady seemed to be working faster and smoother for the Kroks than they or the industry analysts had ever anticipated. That year, EPI Products racked up $200 million in sales. However, in the spring of 1990, the Kroks' glittering new company began to fall apart quickly. Profits from EPI product sales couldn't keep up with the pace at which the Kroks were spending money to keep their company expanding. By autumn, EPI Products, Inc., had filed for Chapter 11 bankruptcy.

Industry analysts who had once marveled at the Kroks' success began to conduct the EPI Products autopsy. Sales of second-generation products such as the EpiSauna had fallen off steeply after the initial rush. Analysts said the Kroks should have expected this: None was as original a concept—or considered by many women to be as necessary—as the Epilady. EPI Products was too new a company to expect that the *Epi* prefix alone could sell just any product, they said. Analysts also called the Kroks' advertising strategy unsophisticated and not worthy of a company of EPI's size. Rather than advertising all the EPI products together, some analysts said, the products should have been advertised separately, and the benefits of each product for potential customers should have been emphasized.

Also, the Kroks' original strategy to outwit Remington, which had been hailed by many as brilliant when it seemed to be working, was a drastic mistake, analysts added. Customers were bound to figure out that they could buy essentially the same product sold in top-drawer department stores for less money in mass-market stores. This both sliced into EPI's profit margins and cheapened its image.

By the end of 1990, the Kroks had hired professional managers to try to pull EPI Products out of bankruptcy, but many analysts predicted that it was too late to turn the company around.

Discussion Questions

1. In considering the general environment within which EPI Products functions, how do you think social values affected Epilady sales, and how should these have been taken into account in planning future sales strategies?

2. In considering the operating environment, understanding competition is essential to good strategic planning. What major competitive advantage did Remington's Soft and Silky have over Epilady? What major advantage did Epilady have?

3. Write a brief (under 50 words) mission statement for EPI Products. How might a clear mission statement have helped the Krok sisters to clarify their planning and avoid bankruptcy?

4. As a small business unit (SBU) of EPI Products, Epilady should be characterized as which of the following—a star? a cash cow?

5. Do you think the Kroks engaged in strong strategic planning? In strong tactical planning? Why or why not?

Carnival Cruise Lines: Micky Arison's Fun Vacations

Micky Arison sells fun for a living. As chief executive officer of Carnival Cruise Lines, he sees his mission as bringing affordable, fun vacations to the 800,000 passengers who travel on his ships each year. Carnival now holds a 20 percent share of the $5 billion cruise market worldwide; for the past decade, it has maintained an annual growth rate of about 30 percent. It looks as though Arison and Carnival are fulfilling their mission.

The strategy Arison has used to achieve success is based on the "fun" mission. The Carnival line has a reputation as a "magic kingdom for adults." Arison labels his vessels "funships." Whatever you would like to do on a Carnival cruise, Arison would like you to be able to do—watch a revue, dance all night, gain weight eating great food, lose weight exercising in the sun—Arison wants his guests to have a good time.

In addition to more exotic and expensive travel options, Carnival offers 3- or 4-day funship cruises that are not very costly. These are designed to appeal to consumers of a wide age and income range, many of whom are experimenting with cruise vacations for the first time. All Carnival cruises are priced based on the assumption that the ships will be completely full on every cruise—and this assumption is usually right. Most other lines base their assumptions on filling 80 percent of passenger space, and price accordingly, so Carnival's cost to the consumer is at least 20 percent lower than competitors'. This strategy has been very effective over the past several years, and Arison plans to continue to charge less than the competition.

However, Arison's growth strategy is tied to more than giving good value. He believes that as the message about fun vacations for a reasonable price gets out, more people will choose to experience cruising. Carnival's repeat customers will then become increasingly sophisticated in their cruising desires. This is a major reason that Arison bought Holland America, an established, upscale, luxury line, in 1989. With Arison's business and promotion experience overlaid on Holland America's reputation for excellence, the first year he owned Holland America was also the most profitable year in its 117-year history.

Micky Arison's father Ted founded Carnival Cruise Lines in 1972 and handed over the helm to his son eight years later. During those years, Micky Arison had worked as a ship's steward, in reservations, in sales, and at other jobs throughout the business. Six months after starting, he knew he wanted to cruise for the rest of his work life.

Carnival hasn't always had smooth sailing, though, When Carnival was first started, it encountered some very rough weather. When Carnival bought the *Mardi Gras* in 1972, they did not have the money to refurbish her completely. She ran aground on her very first cruise. The rest of the year was no better, and Micky Arison feared that Carnival, too, would be grounded. Nonetheless, his father had faith and patience, and Carnival became a successful line.

In 1979, Micky Arison became CEO of Carnival, which then had three ships. Construction on the *Fantasy,* the first of three planned superliners for the line, had just begun. By 1989, there were 15 ships, with *Fantasy,* Carnival's new flagship, only a few feet shorter than the world's largest cruise vessel.

Video Case Questions

1. Write a mission statement for Carnival Cruise Lines.
2. One reason Arison purchased Holland America was to expand Carnival Cruises into the Pacific. Give three examples of tactical (short-term) plans that might help support a long-term strategy of developing business in the Pacific.
3. Examine the four organizational strategies of growth, stability, retrenchment, and divestiture in light of Carnival's current business and future expectations.
4. How do demographics play a significant role in Arison's strategic planning for Carnival?
5. Using what you have read about environmental analysis, consider the impacts of the following components for Carnival Cruise Lines: competition, labor, and international.

Video Case Activities

1. Consider Table 7.1 on page 190, which gives examples of organizational objectives and related strategies. Expand the table by adding sample objectives and strategies for Carnival Cruise Lines.
2. Construct a SWOT Analysis table for Carnival Cruise Lines, based on the format of Table 7.6 on page 201. List at least two entries in each category.

Chapter 8

Student Learning Objectives

From studying this chapter, I will attempt to acquire:

1. A complete definition of a plan.

2. Insights regarding various dimensions of plans.

3. An understanding of various types of plans.

4. Insights on why plans fail.

5. A knowledge of various planning areas within an organization.

6. A definition of forecasting.

7. An ability to see the advantages and disadvantages of various methods of sales forecasting.

8. A definition of scheduling.

9. An understanding of Gantt charts and PERT.

Plans and Planning Tools

Chapter Outline

Introductory Case: Fiat Plans
Car Production

Plans
Plans: A Definition
Dimensions of Plans
Types of Plans

☐ Ethics Highlight: Exxon

☐ Global Highlight: Japanese Auto
Manufacturers

Why Plans Fail
Planning Areas: Input Planning

☐ Quality Highlight: Toyota Motor
Corporation

Planning Tools
Forecasting
Scheduling

Case Study: Carol Kirby of
Baskin-Robbins: Planning a New Image

CNN Video Case: James Kinnear:
A Lucky Star

Introductory Case

FIAT PLANS CAR PRODUCTION

Automobile group Fiat, shrugging off the slowdown in European car demand, plans to build a major car plant in Basilicata, southern Italy, and expand and remodel an existing parts factory at Avellino, near Naples.

The decision involves investments totaling five trillion lire ($4.5 billion) over the next three years, with work due to be completed by late 1993 or early 1994.

The Basilicata car plant will produce 1,800 cars a day and employ 7,000 workers, while the Avellino parts plant will be transformed into a factory producing 3,600 engines a day and employing 1,300 people.

The company is going ahead with the plan despite having cut back production in recent weeks because of slack European demand. [Recently,] Fiat doubled the number of workers temporarily laid off to 70,000 as part of a program of plant closures that cut planned output by about 90,000 cars. As a result, Fiat expects to produce about 2,150,000 cars this year worldwide, down from 2,250,000 in 1989.

> "The move is a little bit surprising, given that they have announced production cutbacks."

Susanne Oliver, European automotive analyst at London brokerage firm Hoare Govett, said the move was unexpected in the current depressed state of the market. "The move is a little bit surprising, given that they have announced production cutbacks. And that in the medium term there is no sign of an upswing in demand," she said.

"Obviously, it takes some years to bring the plants on stream . . . , nevertheless, capacity is being underutilized," she added. The Basilicata plant will have a theoretical capacity of almost 400,000 cars a year, working an average 220 days a year. Avellino could produce 790,000 engines a year.

Fiat will be eligible for hefty state aid on both plants. The company declined to put a figure on the subsidies, but a [spokesperson] said, "We have asked the government for the maximum the law allows—nothing special, but the maximum."

An official of the ministry dealing with Italy's depressed South, the Mezzogiorno, said state grants of 15% were available on large productive investments of this type. On this calculation, Fiat could receive a subsidy of about 750 billion lire, though not all funds invested may be eligible.

In addition, soft loans, at 60% of prime rate, are available to cover 30% of the investment cost, and reductions will also be given on social security payments for workers. Extra subsidies may also be available because the plants are in zones that sustained earthquake damage in 1980.

Fiat, which already has ambitious production plans in Poland, is calculating that European car demand will sustain a further increase in capacity. "We think Europe will continue to absorb cars—maybe not at the record level of the past two to three years, but the market is healthy," a [spokesperson] said.

The introductory case describes Fiat's plans to build one new plant and to increase the capacity of another. This chapter emphasizes several fundamental issues about plans that should be useful to managers like those at Fiat who are involved in planning. This chapter describes what plans are and discusses several valuable tools that can be used in actually developing plans.

PLANS

The first half of the chapter covers the basic facts about plans. It (1) defines what a plan is, (2) outlines the dimensions of a plan, (3) lists various types of plans, (4) discusses why plans fail, and (5) explains two major organizational areas in which planning usually takes place.

Plans: A Definition

A **plan** is a specific action proposed to help the organization achieve its objectives. A critical part of the management of any organization is developing logical plans and then taking necessary steps to put the plans into action.[1] Regardless of how important experience-related intuition may be to managers, successful management actions and strategies typically are based on reason. Rational managers are extremely important to the development of an organizational plan.[2]

A **plan** is a specific action proposed to help the organization achieve its objectives.

Dimensions of Plans

Kast and Rosenzweig identify a plan's four major dimensions: (1) repetitiveness, (2) time, (3) scope, and (4) level.[3] Each dimension is an independent characteristic of a plan and should be considered during plan development.[4]

The **repetitiveness dimension** describes the extent to which a plan is used time after time. Some plans are specially designed for one situation that is relatively short term in nature. Plans of this sort are essentially nonrepetitive. Other plans, however, are designed to be used time after time for situations that continue to occur over the long term. These plans are basically repetitive in nature.

The **time dimension** of a plan is the length of the time period the plan covers. In chapter 7, strategic planning was defined as being long term in nature, and tactical planning was defined as being short term. It follows, then, that strategic plans cover relatively long periods of time and tactical plans cover relatively short periods of time.

The **scope dimension** describes the portion of the total management system at which the plan is aimed. Some plans are designed to cover the entire open management system: the organizational environment, inputs, process, and outputs. A plan for the management system as a whole is often referred to as a master plan. Other plans, however, are developed to cover only a portion of the

In planning, managers should consider:

the **repetitiveness dimension,** the extent to which the plan is to be used over and over again;

the **time dimension,** the length of time the plan covers;

the **scope dimension,** the portion of the total management system at which the plans are aimed;

and the **level dimension,** the level of the organization at which the plan is aimed.

management system. An example would be a plan developed to cover the recruitment of new workers—a portion of the organizational input segment of the management system. The greater the portion of the management system that a plan covers, the broader the scope of the plan is said to be.

The **level dimension** of a plan indicates the level of the organization at which the plan is aimed. Top-level plans are those designed for the top-management level of the organization, whereas middle-level and lower-level plans are designed for middle-level and lower-level management, respectively. Because all parts of the management system are interdependent, however, plans for any level of the organization have some effect on all other levels.

Figure 8.1 illustrates the four dimensions of an organizational plan. This figure stresses that when managers develop a plan, they should consider the degree to which it will be used over and over again, the period of time it will cover, the parts of the management system on which it focuses, and the organizational level at which it is aimed.

Back to the Case

In developing plans for a company like Fiat, management is actually developing recommendations for future actions. As such, plans should be action oriented. Plans should state precisely what Fiat is going to do in order to achieve its goals.

In developing the plans, managers like those at Fiat should consider how often the plans will be used and the length of time they will cover. Will a plan be implemented only once or be used on a long-term basis to handle an ongoing issue such as maintaining product quality? Obviously, a plan to build a new factory would not be used very often by most companies and would be designed to cover a specific amount of time.

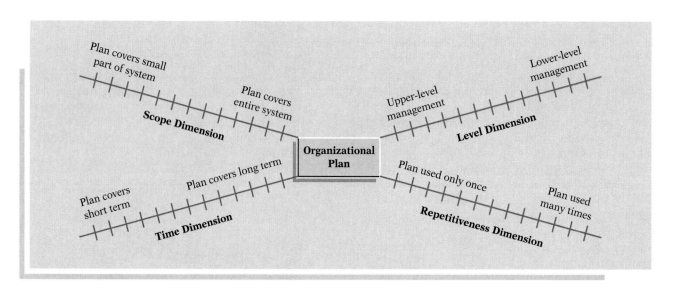

FIGURE 8.1

Four major dimensions to consider when developing a plan

Managers like those at Fiat should consider at which part of the organization to aim the plans that they develop and on which level the plans will focus. For example, a plan to cut costs may encompass all Fiat operations, whereas a plan to improve product quality may affect only one part of the production process. Similarly, a plan to cut costs may be aimed at top-level management, whereas a product quality plan may be aimed toward lower-level management and the auto assemblers themselves. Of course, managers like those at Fiat must realize that because management systems are interdependent, any plans they implement will affect the system as a whole.

Types of Plans

With the repetitiveness dimension as a guide, organizational plans usually are divided into two types: standing and single-use. **Standing plans** are used over and over again because they focus on organizational situations that occur repeatedly. **Single-use plans** are used only once or several times, because they focus on relatively unique situations within the organization. Figure 8.2 illustrates that standing plans can be subdivided into policies, procedures, and rules and that single-use plans can be subdivided into programs and budgets.

Standing Plans: Policies, Procedures, and Rules

A **policy** is a standing plan that furnishes broad, general guidelines for channeling management thinking toward taking action consistent with reaching organizational objectives. For example, an organizational policy relating to personnel might be worded as follows: "Our organization will strive to recruit only the most talented employees." This policy statement is very broad, giving managers only a general idea of what to do in the area of employment. The policy is intended to display the extreme importance management has attached to hiring competent employees and to guiding action accordingly.

Standing plans are plans that are used over and over because they focus on organizational situations that occur repeatedly.

Single-use plans are plans that are used only once or several times because they focus on organizational situations that do not occur repeatedly.

A **policy** is a standing plan that furnishes broad guidelines for channeling management thinking in specified directions.

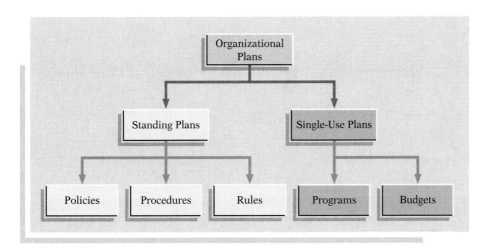

FIGURE 8.2

Standing plans and single-use plans

A **procedure** is a standing plan that outlines a series of related actions that must be taken to accomplish a particular task.

A **rule** is a standing plan that designates specific required action.

A **procedure** is a standing plan that outlines a series of related actions that must be taken to accomplish a particular task. In general, procedures outline more specific actions than do policies. Organizations usually have many different sets of procedures covering the various tasks to be accomplished. The sample procedure in Table 8.1 lists the series of steps that recruiters take to interview prospective academic employees at Indiana State University.

A **rule** is a standing plan that designates specific required action. In essence, a rule indicates what an organization member should or should not do and allows no room for interpretation. An example of a rule that many companies are now establishing is No Smoking.[5] The concept of rules may become clearer if one thinks about the purpose and nature of rules in such games as Scrabble and Monopoly.

Ethics Highlight: Exxon's Lax Rules Cost Millions

As an example of a situation in which management did not establish and enforce rules, one can consider Exxon's recent monumental oil spill in Alaska. Because of Exxon's improper operation of an oil tanker, the company has faced monumental charges. The company already has paid more than $180 million in damage compensation to 13,000 fishers and other claimants and has spent over $2 billion in cleanup costs. Environmentalists, fishers, and others are battling Exxon in more than 180 lawsuits. These people claim that Exxon owes them at least $400 million in lost income and other damages. In addition, Alaskan officials are seeking claims against Exxon as a result of damages to natural resources.

Exxon probably could have avoided this entire situation if it had better planned for proper operation of its tankers. A more effective establishment and enforcement of company rules regarding maritime safety in the operation of oil tankers would have been one step in this direction. Such rules and their enforcement might have saved the company from appearing to be unethical or socially irresponsible.

Although policies, procedures, and rules are all standing plans, they are different from one another and have different purposes within the organization. As Figure 8.3 on page 228 illustrates, however, for the standing plans of an organization to be effective, policies, procedures, and rules must be consistent and mutually supportive.

Single-Use Plans: Programs and Budgets

A **program** is a single-use plan designed to carry out a special project in an organization. Programs aid success indirectly.

A **program** is a single-use plan designed to carry out a special project within an organization. The project itself typically is not intended to be in existence over the entire life of the organization. However, the program exists to achieve some purpose that, if accomplished, will contribute to the organization's long-term success.

A common example is the management development program found in many organizations. This program exists to raise the skill levels of managers in regard to one or more of the skills mentioned in chapter 1: technical skills, conceptual skills, or human skills. Increasing the skill levels, however, is not an end in itself.

TABLE 8.1 Procedure for interviewing prospective academic employees at Indiana State University

1. Any candidate brought to campus for an interview should be a best prospect of at least three qualified persons whose credentials have been examined. Personnel supply in an academic field may reduce the number of possible candidates.

2. Before an invitation is extended to a candidate who must travel a distance greater than 500 miles to reach Terre Haute, the department chairperson should:

   a. ascertain the existence of the vacancy or authorization by a call to the assistant vice president for academic affairs.
   b. forward to the dean and assistant vice president credentials that should include, if possible, parts d, e, f, and g, Item 6, below.

3. Any administrative person who is scheduled to interview a candidate should be forwarded credentials for the candidate prior to the interview.

4. Interviews with administrative personnel should be scheduled as follows:
   A candidate whose probable academic rank will be instructor or assistant professor should talk with the dean prior to the assistant vice president. A candidate whose academic rank should probably be associate professor should be scheduled for an interview with the vice president for academic affairs in addition to the dean and assistant vice president. In addition to the above, a candidate for appointment as professor or department chairperson should also be scheduled for a meeting with the president.

5. Although courtesy to the candidate may demand that the interview schedule be maintained, the vice president, at his or her discretion or in agreement with the suggestion by the chairperson, dean, or assistant vice president, may cancel the interview for the candidate with the president.

6. A recommendation for appointment should contain the following:

   a. a letter from the department chairperson (or dean) setting forth the recommendation and proposing the academic rank and salary.
   b. a statement from the dean if the recommendation letter is prepared by the department chairperson.
   c. the completed university resume form. This can be completed by the candidate when on campus or returned to the chairperson by mail later, but must be included.
   d. vitae information.
   e. placement papers.
   f. official transcripts (especially important if placement papers are not current or were prepared by a university bureau).
   g. as many as three letters of recommendation, one or two of these reflecting the candidate's current assignment. These letters are necessary if the placement materials have not been updated to contain current recommendations.
   h. a written report on any telephone conversations concerning the candidate made by the department chairperson.

7. Because of the difficulty in arranging interviews on Saturday, campus visits should occur during the week.

8. Whenever possible, accommodations at the Hulman Center should be limited to one overnight. The university cannot accept any charge for hotel accommodations other than at the Hulman Center. "Hotel accommodations" are defined to be lodging only, and not food, telephone, or other personal services.

9. Travel can be reimbursed in one of the following ways:

   a. a candidate traveling in-state will have mileage paid, at the rate of 25 cents per mile. The official Indiana map is used to compute mileage rather than a speedometer reading.
   b. a candidate traveling from out-of-state can claim the cost of airfare (tourist class) or train fare (coach class).
   c. a candidate who may choose to drive from out of state cannot be paid a mileage cost. Instead, airfare and train-fare amounts are determined and the lesser of the two is paid as an automobile mileage reimbursement.

The purpose of the program is to produce competent managers who are equipped to help the organization be successful over the long term. Once managerial skills have been raised to a desired level, the management development program can be deemphasized. Areas on which modern management development programs commonly focus include understanding and using the computer as a management

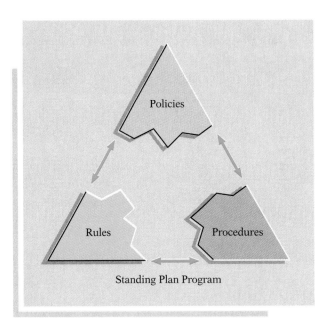

FIGURE 8.3

A successful standing plan program with mutually supportive policies, procedures, and rules

tool, handling international competition, and planning for a major labor shortage by the year 2000.[6]

A **budget** is a control tool that outlines how funds in a given period will be spent, as well as how they will be obtained.

A **budget** is a single-use financial plan that covers a specified length of time. It details how funds will be spent on labor, raw materials, capital goods, information systems, marketing, and so on, as well as how the funds will be obtained.[7] Although budgets are planning devices, they are also strategies for organizational control. They are covered in more detail in chapter 18.

Global Highlight: Japanese Auto Manufacturers Budget to Increase American Sales

Managers commonly encounter the need to establish a budget to outline how an organization plans to use its resources to achieve specified objectives. Recently, many Japanese automakers are facing this situation to achieve a very important objective through their budget allocations: How to become more competitive in the U.S. marketplace.

Although the automakers seem to have the same objective, they vary significantly on the way they choose to allocate their financial resources to achieve this objective. The Toyota Motor Corporation, for example, has sold more vehicles than any other Japanese manufacturers in recent years. Robert B. McCurry, Toyota's vice president for marketing, reports that his company's budget focuses on gaining a competitive edge through training organization members in areas such as business management and used car sales. The American Honda Motor Company, on the other hand, has a budget focus of remaining competitive by raising its advertising expenditure of about $138 million per year to an estimated $185 million. The Nissan Motor Company budgets to remain competitive in yet a different way. The Nissan professional auto-racing team has recently become very successful, and Nissan hopes to protect or improve its market share by increasing its budget to promote even greater racing success and thereby attract the attention of automobile enthusiasts in that unique way.

Why Plans Fail

If managers know why plans fail, they can take steps to eliminate the factors that cause failure and thereby increase the probability that their plans will be successful. A study by K.A. Ringbakk determined that plans fail when:[8]

1. Corporate planning is not integrated into the total management system.
2. There is a lack of understanding of the different steps of the planning process.
3. Management at different levels in the organization has not properly engaged in or contributed to planning activities.[9]
4. Responsibility for planning is wrongly vested solely in the planning department.
5. Management expects that plans developed will be realized with little effort.
6. In starting formal planning, too much is attempted at once.
7. Management fails to operate by the plan.
8. Financial projections are confused with planning.
9. Inadequate inputs are used in planning.
10. Management fails to see the overall planning process.

Planning Areas: Input Planning

As discussed earlier, organizational inputs, process, outputs, and environment are major factors in determining how successful a management system will be. Naturally, a comprehensive organizational plan should focus on each of these factors. The following two sections cover planning in two areas normally associated with the input factor: plant facilities planning and human resource planning. Planning in areas such as these normally is called **input planning**—the development of proposed action that will furnish sufficient and appropriate organizational resources for reaching established organizational objectives.

Plant Facilities Planning

Plant facilities planning involves determining the type of buildings and equipment an organization needs to reach its objectives. A major part of this determination is called **site selection**—deciding where a plant facility should be located.

Input planning is the development of proposed action that will furnish sufficient and appropriate organizational resources for reaching established organizational objectives.

Plant facilities planning is input planning that involves developing the type of work facility an organization will need to reach its objectives. One facet of plant facilities planning is site selection.

Site selection is determining where a plant facility should be located. It may involve a weighting process to compare site differences.

Table 8.2 shows several major areas to be considered in plant site selection, and it gives sample questions that can be asked when these areas are to be explored. Naturally, the specifics of site selection vary from organization to organization.[10]

One factor that can significantly influence site selection is whether a site is being selected in a foreign country. In a foreign country, management may face such issues as foreign governments taking different amounts of time to approve site purchases and political pressures slowing down or preventing the purchase of a site.

Many organizations use a weighting process to compare site differences among foreign countries. Basically, this process involves (1) deciding on a set of variables that are critical to obtaining an appropriate site; (2) assigning each of these variables a weight, or rank, of relative importance; and (3) ranking alternative sites, depending on how they reflect these different variables.

As an example, Table 8.3 shows the results of such a weighting process for seven site variables and six countries. In this table, "living conditions" are worth 100 points and are the most important variable; "effect on company reputation" is worth 35 points and is the least important variable. Also in this table, various countries are given a number of points for each variable, depending on the impor-

---

TABLE 8.2 Major areas of consideration when selecting a plant site and sample exploratory questions

Major Areas for Consideration in Site Selection	Sample Question to Begin Exploring Major Areas
Profit	
Market location	Where are our customers in relation to the site?
Competition	What competitive situation exists at the site?
Operating costs	
Suppliers	Are materials available near the site at reasonable cost?
Utilities	What are utility rates at the site? Are utilities available in sufficient amounts?
Wages	What wage rates are paid in comparable organizations near the site?
Taxes	What are tax rates on income, sales, property, and so on for the site?
Investment costs	
Land/development	How expensive is land and construction at the site?
Others	
Transportation	Are airlines, railroads, highways, and so on available to the site?
Laws	What laws exist related to zoning, pollution, and so on that influence operations if the site is chosen?
Labor	Does an adequate labor supply exist around the site?
Unionization	What degree of unionization exists in the site area?
Living conditions	Are housing, schools, and so on appropriate around the site?
Community relations	Is the community supportive of the organization moving into the area?

TABLE 8.3 Results of weighting seven site variables for six countries

Criteria	Maximum Value Assigned	Sites					
		Japan	Chile	Jamaica	Australia	Mexico	France
Living conditions	100	70	40	45	50	60	60
Accessibility	75	55	35	20	60	70	70
Industrialization	60	40	50	55	35	35	30
Labor availability	35	30	10	10	30	35	35
Economics	35	15	15	15	15	25	25
Community capability and attitude	30	25	20	10	15	25	15
Effect on company reputation	35	25	20	10	15	25	15
Total	370	260	190	165	220	275	250

tance of the variable and how it exists within the country. The illustration shows that given the established set of weighted criteria, Japan, Mexico, and France received more points and therefore are more desirable sites than Chile, Jamaica, and Australia.

Quality Highlight: Toyota Motor Corporation Plans a Smooth Move

When Toyota considered locating its Camry automobile plant in Georgetown, Kentucky many factors were used to decide whether sake and sour mash would mix well. The nonunion, abundant labor force was one consideration. Others were Kentucky's central location, which makes shipping easier, the success of other Japanese car manufacturers that had located in Kentucky, and the availability of land in neighboring states for Japanese suppliers who made the move with Toyota. State officials also offered a $125 million incentive package.

Early in the selection process, Toyota began meeting regularly with Georgetown Mayor Tom Prather to hear community concerns about the proposed plant overburdening local services, including the school system. In addition, some townspeople frankly expressed fear of the Japanese because they were unfamiliar.

To stem anxiety, Toyota invested in the local community, giving Georgetown $1 million for a community center, roughly $8.5 million to the local school district, and $1 million to the University of Kentucky Library. Also, many of the company's Japanese managers participated in community events, joining the local Chamber of Commerce, Rotary Club, and United Way. Although it could not eliminate all the anti-Japanese, antidevelopment feelings in Georgetown, Toyota's early recognition of problems, thorough planning, and substantial financial investment in the region won over much of the community.

Toyota's move to Georgetown has shown relatively smooth progress from ground-breaking to an efficiently run plant. The positive feelings of the community and the high morale of the workers ensure the production of high-quality automobiles.

Back to the Case

Managers such as those at Fiat would normally use both standing plans and single-use plans in a company. Standing plans include policies, procedures, and rules, and should be developed for situations that occur repeatedly. One such policy Fiat management could develop might focus on the degree of product quality the managers want to emphasize with employees.

Single-use plans include programs and budgets and should be developed to help manage situations that occur less often. The Fiat example implies that Fiat management has worked on a budget that allows it to renovate an existing plant in Avellino, Italy. In developing such plans, managers like those at Fiat should thoroughly understand the reasons why plans can fail and take steps to avoid those pitfalls.

Planning plant facilities and human resource planning are two types of planning that managers commonly perform. In Fiat's case, planning plant facilities entails designing the types of factories that the company needs to reach its objectives. The company developed plans to build a new plant in Basilicata and to expand and remodel an existing parts factory near Avellino. An influential part of the decision to develop these plans most certainly was the financial support package offered the company by the government.

Human resource planning involves obtaining or developing the personnel an organization needs to reach its objectives. Fiat management certainly must have considered the numbers and kinds of employees needed to run the new and renovated factories. Such discussion inevitably had to have focused on issues such as when such employees would be needed, how they would be obtained, and how they would be trained appropriately after joining the Fiat company.

Human Resource Planning

Human resources are another area of concern to input planners. Organizational objectives cannot be attained without appropriate personnel. Future needs for human resources are influenced mainly by employee turnover, the nature of the present work force, and the rate of growth of the organization.[11]

Personnel planners should try to answer such questions as: (1) What types of people does the organization need to reach its objectives? (2) How many of each type are needed? (3) What steps for the recruitment and selection of these people should the organization take? (4) Can present employees be further trained to fill future needed positions? (5) At what rate are employees lost to other organizations? These are not the only questions personnel planners should ask, but they are representative.

Figure 8.4 shows the human resource planning process developed by Bruce Coleman. According to his model, **human resource planning** involves reflecting on organizational objectives to determine overall human resource needs, comparing these needs to the existing human resource inventory to determine net human resource needs, and, finally, seeking appropriate organization members to meet the net human resource needs.

Human resource planning is input planning that involves obtaining the human resources necessary for the organization to achieve its objectives.

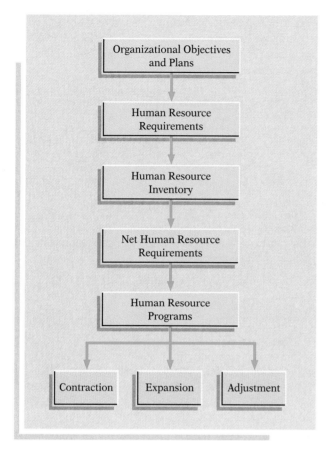

FIGURE 8.4
The human resource planning process

PLANNING TOOLS

Planning tools are techniques managers can use to help develop plans. The remainder of this chapter discusses forecasting and scheduling, two of the most important of these tools.

Planning tools are techniques managers can use to help develop plans.

Forecasting

Forecasting is the process of predicting future environmental happenings that will influence the operation of the organization. Although sophisticated forecasting techniques have been developed only rather recently, the concept of forecasting can be traced at least as far back in the management literature as Fayol.[12] The importance of forecasting lies in its ability to help managers understand the future makeup of the organizational environment, which in turn helps them formulate more effective plans.

Forecasting is a planning tool used to predict future environmental happenings that will influence the operation of the organization.

William C. House, in describing the Insect Control Services Company, has developed an excellent illustration of how forecasting works. Table 8.4 lists the primary factors the company attempts to measure in developing its forecast. In general, Insect Control Services forecasts by attempting to:[13]

1. Establish relationships between industry sales and national economic and social indicators.

2. Determine the impact of government restrictions concerning the use of chemical pesticides on the growth of chemical, biological, and electromagnetic energy pest control markets.

3. Evaluate sales growth potential, profitability, resources required, and risks involved in each of its market areas (commercial, industrial, institutional, governmental, and residential).

4. Evaluate the potential for expansion of marketing efforts in geographical areas of the United States as well as foreign countries.

5. Determine the likelihood of technological breakthroughs that would make existing product lines obsolete.

TABLE 8.4 Primary factors measured during Insect Control Services' forecasting process

Gross National Product

Measure of total dollars available for industrial, commercial, institutional, and residential purchases of insect control units.

Personal Consumption Expenditures

Measure of dollars available for consumer purchases of:

1. *Services*—affect potential contract insect control services.
2. *Durables*—affect market potential for residential units.
3. *Nondurables*—affect sales of food, drugs, and other products that influence expansion of industrial and commercial users of insect control equipment.

Governmental Purchases of Goods, Services

Measure of spending for hospitals, government food services, other institutions that purchase insect control equipment.

Gross Private Domestic Investment in New Plant and Equipment

A measure of business expansion that indicates the size and nature of market potential for industrial and commercial purchases of insect control units in new or expanded existing establishments.

Industrial Production for Selected Industries

Measure of expansion of industrial output for industries that are users, potential users of insect control units, or

materials suppliers for insect control services. Such expansion (or contraction) of output will likely affect:

1. Industrial and commercial purchases of insect control units.
2. Availability of materials used to manufacture insect control units.

Employment and Unemployment Levels

Indicates availability or scarcity of human resources available to augment Insect Control Services' human resources pool.

Consumer, Wholesale Prices

Measure of ability, willingness of homeowners to purchase residential units, and availability and cost of raw materials and component parts.

Corporate Profits

Indicates how trends in prices, unit labor costs, and productivity affect corporate profits. Size of total corporate profits indicates profit margins in present and potential markets and funds available for expansion.

Business Borrowings, Interest Rates

Measures of the availability and cost of borrowed funds needed to finance working capital needs and plant and equipment expansion.

In addition to the more general process of organizational forecasting illustrated by Insect Control Services are specialized types of forecasting, such as economic forecasting, technological forecasting, social trends forecasting, and sales forecasting. Although a complete organizational forecasting process can and usually should include all of these types of forecasting, sales forecasting is typically cited as the key organizational forecast. A *sales forecast* is a prediction of how high or how low sales will be over the period of time under consideration. It is the key forecast because it serves as the fundamental guideline for planning within the organization. Once the sales forecast has been completed, managers can decide, for example, if more salespeople should be hired, if more money for plant expansion must be borrowed, or if layoffs are upcoming and cutbacks in certain areas are necessary. The following section describes various methods of sales forecasting.

Methods of Sales Forecasting

Jury of Executive Opinion Method. The **jury of executive opinion method** of sales forecasting is straightforward. A group of managers within the organization assemble to discuss their opinions on what will happen to sales in the future. Since these discussion sessions usually revolve around the hunches or experienced guesses of each of the managers, the resulting forecast is a blend of expressed opinions.

> The **jury of executive opinion method** is a method of predicting future sales levels primarily by asking appropriate managers to give their opinions on what will happen to sales in the future.

A more recently developed forecasting method, similar to the jury of executive opinion method, is called the *delphi method*.[14] This method also gathers, evaluates, and summarizes expert opinions as the basis for a forecast.[15] The basic delphi method employs the following steps:

Step 1: Various experts are asked to answer independently, in writing, a series of questions about the future of sales or whatever other area is being forecasted.

Step 2: A summary of all the answers is then prepared. No expert knows how any other expert answered the questions.

Step 3: Copies of the summary are given to the individual experts with the request that they modify their original answers if they think they should.

Step 4: Another summary is made of these modifications, and copies again are distributed to the experts. This time, however, expert opinions that deviate significantly from the norm must be justified in writing.

Step 5: A third summary is made of the opinions and justifications, and copies are distributed to the experts. Justification for all answers is now required in writing.

Step 6: The forecast is generated from all of the opinions and justifications that arise from step 5.

Sales Force Estimation Method. The **sales force estimation method** is a sales forecasting technique that predicts future sales by analyzing the opinions of salespeople. Salespeople interact with customers and use this interaction as the basis for predicting future sales. As with the jury of executive opinion method, the resulting forecast normally is a blend of the views of the salespeople as a group.

> The **sales force estimation method** is a method of predicting future sales levels primarily by asking appropriate salespeople for their opinions of what will happen to sales in the future.

The sales force estimation method is generally considered a very valuable management tool and is commonly used in business and industry throughout the world. Although the accuracy of sales forecasts using this method are mostly satisfactory, managers have found that accuracy can be improved by such simple steps as providing salespeople with sufficient time to forecast and offering incentives for accurate forecasts. Some companies even offer special training to help salespeople become better forecasters by helping them to better interpret their interactions with customers.[16]

The **time series analysis method** is a method of predicting future sales levels by analyzing the historical relationship in an organization between sales and time.

Times Series Analysis Method. The **time series analysis method** predicts future sales by analyzing the historical relationship between sales and time. Information showing the relationship between sales and time typically is presented on a graph, as in Figure 8.5. This presentation clearly displays past trends, which can be used to predict future sales.

The actual number of years included in a time series analysis will vary from company to company. As a general rule, managers should include as many years as necessary to make sure that important sales trends do not go undetected. At the Coca-Cola Company, for example, management believes that in order to validly predict the annual sales of any one year, it must chart annual sales in each of the ten successive previous years.[17]

A **product life cycle** is the five stages through which most new products and services pass: introduction, growth, maturity, saturation, and decline.

The time series analysis in Figure 8.5 indicates steadily increasing sales over time. However, since, in the long term, products generally go through what is called a product life cycle, the predicted increase probably is overly optimistic. A **product life cycle** is the five stages through which most new products and services pass. The stages are introduction, growth, maturity, saturation, and decline.

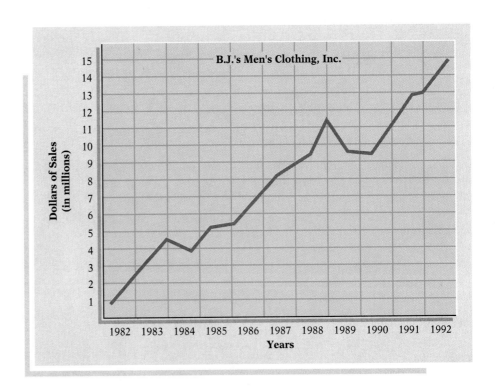

FIGURE 8.5

Time series analysis method

Figure 8.6 shows how these five stages are related to product sales over a period of time. In the introduction stage, a product is brand new, and sales are just beginning to build. In the growth stage, because the product has been in the marketplace for some time and is now becoming more accepted, product sales continue to climb. During the maturity stage, competitors enter the market; and while sales are still climbing, they normally climb at a slower rate than in the growth stage. After the maturity stage comes the saturation stage, when nearly everyone who wanted the product has it. Sales during the saturation stage typically are due to replacements of a worn-out product or to population growth. The last product life cycle stage—decline—finds the product being replaced by a competing product.

Managers may be able to keep some products out of the decline stage through improvements in product quality, or innovations. Other products, such as scissors, may never reach this last stage because of the lack of competing products.

Evaluating Sales Forecasting Methods

The sales forecasting methods just described are not the only ones available to managers. Other more complex methods include the statistical correlation method and the computer simulation method.[18] The methods just discussed, however, do provide a basic foundation for understanding sales forecasting.

In practice, managers find that each sales forecasting method has advantages and disadvantages, as shown in Table 8.5. Before deciding to use a particular sales forecasting method, a manager must carefully weigh the advantages and disadvantages as they relate to a particular organization. The decision may be to use a combination of methods rather than just one. Whatever method is finally adopted, the framework should be logical, fit the needs of the organization, and be capable of adaptation to changes in the environment.[19]

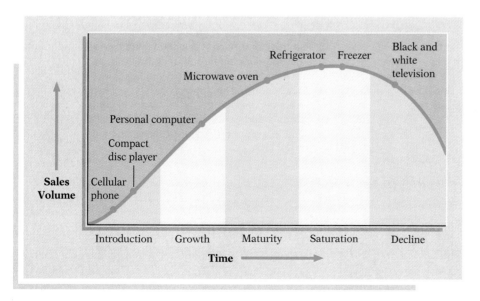

FIGURE 8.6

Stages of the product life cycle

TABLE 8.5 Advantages and disadvantages of three methods of sales forecasting

Sales Forecasting Method	Advantages	Disadvantages
Jury of executive opinion	1. Can provide forecasts easily and quickly 2. May not require the preparation of elaborate statistics 3. Pools a variety of specialized viewpoints for experience and judgment 4. May be the only feasible means of forecasting, especially in the absence of adequate data	1. Is inferior to a more factual basis of forecasting, since it is based so heavily on opinion 2. Requires costly executive time 3. Is not necessarily more accurate, because opinion is averaged 4. Disperses responsibility for accurate forecasting 5. Presents difficulties in making breakdowns by products, time intervals, or markets for operating purposes
Sales force estimation	1. Uses specialized knowledge of people closest to the market 2. Places responsibility for the forecast in the hands of those who must produce the results 3. Gives sales force greater confidence in quotas developed from forecasts 4. Tends to give results greater stability because of the magnitude of the sample 5. Lends itself to the easy development of product, territory, customer, or sales representatives' breakdowns	1. Sales representatives of some firms may be poor estimators, being either more optimistic or more pessimistic than conditions warrant 2. If estimates are used as a basis for setting quotas, sales representatives are inclined to understate the demand to make the goal easier to achieve 3. Sales representatives are often unaware of the broad economic patterns shaping future sales and are thus incapable of forecasting trends for extended periods 4. Since sales forecasting is a subsidiary function of the sales force, sufficient time may not be made available for it 5. Requires an extensive expenditure of time by executives and sales force 6. Elaborate schemes are sometimes necessary to keep estimates realistic and free from bias
Time series analysis	1. Forces the forecaster to consider the underlying trend, cycle, and seasonal elements in the sales series 2. Takes into account the particular repetitive or continuing patterns exhibited by the sales in the past 3. Provides a systematic means of making quantitative projections	1. Assumes the continuation of historical patterns of change in sales components without considering outside influences that may affect sales in the forecast period 2. Is often unsatisfactory for short-term forecasting, since, for example, the pinpointing of cyclical turning points by mechanical projections is seldom possible 3. May be difficult to apply in cases where erratic, irregular forces disrupt or hide the regularity of component patterns within a sales series 4. Requires technical skill, experience, and judgment

Back to the Case

One of the planning tools available to Fiat management is forecasting, which involves predicting future environmental events that could influence the operation of the company. Although various specific types of forecasting—such as economic, technological, and social trends forecasting—are available to it, Fiat management would probably use sales forecasting as its key forecast since that method will predict for managers how high or low their sales will be during the time period they are considering. According to the information we have, Fiat managers made a sales forecast, and the results of this forecast were used to help make the decision to construct a new factory and expand an existing one.

In order to forecast sales, managers like those at Fiat could follow the jury of executive opinion method by having Fiat executives discuss their opinions of future sales. This method would be quick and easy to use, and assuming that Fiat executives have a good feel for product demand, might be as valid as any other method that the company might use.

Fiat management could also ask its auto retailers (sales force) for opinions on predicted sales. Although the opinions of car dealers may not be completely reliable, these salespeople are closest to the market and must ultimately make the sales.

Finally, Fiat management could use the time series analysis method and analyze the relationship between sales and time. Although this method takes into account the cyclical patterns and past history of sales, it also assumes the continuation of these patterns in the future without considering outside influences, such as economic downturns, that could cause the patterns to change.

Because each sales forecasting method has both advantages and disadvantages, managers at Fiat should carefully analyze each of the methods before deciding which method alone or in combination should be used in their company.

Scheduling

Scheduling is the process of formulating a detailed listing of activities that must be accomplished to attain an objective. This listing is an integral part of an organizational plan. Two scheduling techniques are Gantt charts and the program evaluation and review technique (PERT).

Gantt Charts

The **Gantt chart,** a scheduling device developed by Henry L. Gantt, is essentially a bar graph with time on the horizontal axis and the resource to be scheduled on the vertical axis. Possible resources to be scheduled include management system inputs, such as human resources and machines.

Figure 8.7 shows a completed Gantt chart for a work period entitled "Workweek 28." The resources scheduled over the five workdays on this chart were

Scheduling is the process of formulating detailed listings of activities that must be performed to accomplish a task, allocating resources necessary to complete the task, and setting up and following timetables for completing the task.

The **Gantt chart** is a scheduling tool composed essentially of a bar chart with time on the horizontal axis and the resource to be scheduled on the vertical axis. The Gantt chart is used for scheduling resources.

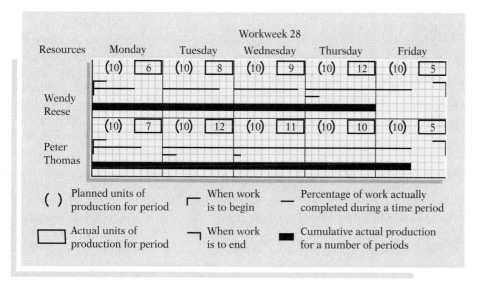

FIGURE 8.7

Completed Gantt chart

human resources: Wendy Reese and Peter Thomas. During this workweek, both Reese and Thomas were scheduled to produce ten units a day for five days. Actual units produced, however, show a deviation from this planned production. There were days when each of the two workers produced more than ten units, as well as days when each produced fewer than ten units. Cumulative production on the chart shows that Reese produced forty units and Thomas produced forty-five units over the five days.

Although the Gantt chart may seem quite simple, it has many valuable uses for managers. First, managers can use the chart as a summary overview of how organizational resources are being used. From this summary, they can detect such facts as which resources are consistently contributing to productivity. Second, managers can use the Gantt chart to help coordinate organizational resources. The chart can show which resources are not being used during specific periods, thereby allowing the resources to be scheduled for work on other production efforts. Third, the chart can be used to establish realistic worker output standards. For example, if workers are completing scheduled work too quickly, output standards may need to be raised so that workers are scheduled for more work per time period.

Program Evaluation and Review Technique (PERT)

The main weakness of the Gantt chart is that it does not contain any information about the interrelationship of tasks to be performed. All tasks to be performed are listed on the chart, but there is no way of telling if one task must be performed before another can be completed. The program evaluation and review technique (PERT), a technique that evolved in part from the Gantt chart, is a scheduling tool designed to emphasize the interrelationship of tasks.

The **program evaluation and review technique (PERT)** is a scheduling tool that is essentially a network of project activities showing estimates of time necessary to complete each activity and the sequential relationship of activities that must be followed to complete the project.

Activities and events are the primary elements of a PERT network. **Activities** are specified sets of behavior within a project. **Events** are completions of major project tasks.

Defining PERT. **PERT** is a network of project activities showing both the estimates of time necessary to complete each activity within the project and the sequential relationships among activities that must be followed to complete the project. PERT was developed in 1958 for use in designing the Polaris submarine weapon system.[20] The individuals involved in managing this project found Gantt charts and other existing scheduling tools of little use because of the complicated nature of the Polaris project and the interdependence of its tasks.[21]

The PERT network contains two primary elements: activities and events. **Activities** are specified sets of behavior within a project, and **events** are the completions of major project tasks. Within the PERT network, each event is assigned corresponding activities that must be performed before the event can materialize.[22]

A sample PERT network designed for the building of a house is presented in Figure 8.8. In this figure, events are symbolized by circles and activities are symbolized by arrows. To illustrate, the figure indicates that after the event "Foundation Complete" (represented by a circle) has materialized, certain activities (represented by an arrow) must be performed before the event "Frame Complete" (represented by another circle) can materialize.

Two other features of the network shown here also should be emphasized. First, the left-to-right presentation of events shows how the events interrelate or the sequence in which they should be performed. Second, the numbers in parentheses above each arrow indicate the units of time necessary to complete each activity. These two features should help managers ensure that only necessary work is being done on a project and that no project activities are taking too long.

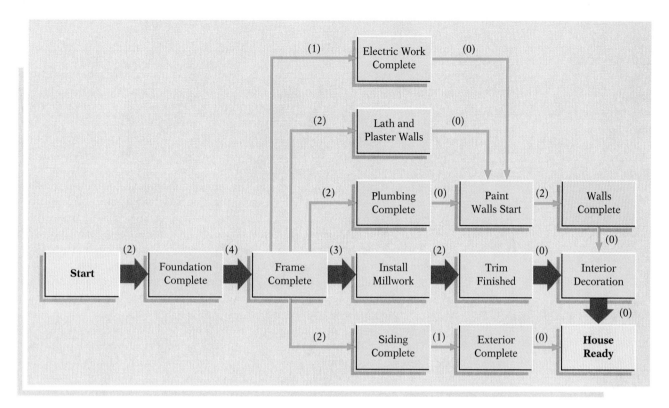

FIGURE 8.8

PERT network designed for building a house

Critical Path. Close attention should be paid to the **critical path** of a PERT network—the sequence of events and activities requiring the longest period of time to complete. The path is called the critical path because a delay in the time necessary to complete this sequence results in a delay for the completion of the entire project. The critical path in Figure 8.8 is indicated by thick arrows; all other paths are indicated by thin arrows. Managers try to control a project by keeping it within the time designated by the critical path. The critical path can help managers predict which features of a schedule will become unrealistic. It can provide insights concerning how the issues might be eliminated.[23]

> A **critical path** is the sequence of events and activities within a program evaluation and review technique (PERT) network that requires the longest period of time to complete.

Steps in Designing a PERT Network. When designing a PERT network, managers should follow four primary steps:[24]

Step 1: List all the activities/events that must be accomplished for the project and the sequence in which these activities/events should be performed.

Step 2: Determine how much time will be needed to complete each activity/event.

Step 3: Design a PERT network that reflects all of the information contained in steps 1 and 2.

Step 4: Identify the critical path.

$\mathcal{B}$ack to the Case

Scheduling is another planning tool available to Fiat management. It involves the detailed listing of activities that must be accomplished to reach an objective. For example, if Fiat's goal is to have all of its employees working proficiently on updated equipment in its planned renovated factory within two years, management needs to schedule activities such as installing the equipment, training the employees, and establishing new output standards.

Two scheduling techniques available to Fiat management are Gantt charts and PERT. To schedule employee production output, Fiat managers might want to use Gantt charts—bar graphs with time on the horizontal axis and the resources to be scheduled on the vertical axis. Managers also might find these charts helpful for evaluating workers' performance and setting new production standards.

If Fiat managers want to see the relationships among tasks, they can use PERT to develop a flowchart showing activities, events, and the amount of time necessary to complete each task. For example, a PERT network would be helpful in scheduling the installation of new machines, because this type of schedule would indicate which equipment needed to be installed first, the amount of time each installation would require, and how other activities in renovating an existing factory would be affected before the installation was completed. PERT also would demonstrate to Fiat the critical path managers must follow for successful installation. This path represents the sequence of activities and events requiring the longest amount of time to complete, and it determines the total time the project will need to finish. If, for example, new welding machinery takes longer to install than other types of equipment, Fiat management should target the completion of the entire equipment installation on the basis of this component's installation time.

Action Summary

Circle:

Reread the learning objectives that follow. Each objective is followed by questions. Answering these questions accurately will help you retain the most important concepts discussed in this chapter. After answering each question, check your answer with the answer key at the end of this chapter. (*Hint:* If you have doubt regarding the correct response, consult the page whose number follows the answer.)

From studying this chapter, I will attempt to acquire:

1. **A complete definition of a plan.**

a, b, c, d, e
   a. A plan is: (a) the company's buildings and fixtures; (b) a specific action proposed to help the company achieve its objectives; (c) a policy meeting; (d) a projection of future sales; (e) an experiment to determine the optimal distribution system.

a, b, c, d, e
   b. Which of the following is generally *not* an important component of a plan: (a) the evaluation of relevant information; (b) the assessment of probable future developments; (c) a statement of a recommended course of action; (d) a statement of manager intuition; (e) strategy based on reason or rationality.

2. **Insights regarding various dimensions of plans.**
   a. Most plans affect top management only.   T, F
   b. Which of the following is one of the four major dimensions of a plan: a, b, c, d, e
   (a) repetitiveness; (b) organization; (c) time; (d) a and c; (e) b and c.

3. **An understanding of various types of plans.**
   a. Standing plans that furnish broad guidelines for channeling management   a, b, c, d, e
   thinking in specified directions are called: (a) procedures; (b) programs;
   (c) single-use plans; (d) policies; (e) rules.
   b. Programs and budgets are examples of: (a) single-use plans; (b) standing   a, b, c, d, e
   rules; (c) procedures; (d) Gantt chart components; (e) critical paths.

4. **Insights on why plans fail.**
   a. Which of the following is a reason that plans fail: (a) adequate inputs   a, b, c, d, e
   are used in planning; (b) corporate planning is integrated into the total
   management system; (c) management expects that plans developed will be
   realized with little effort; (d) management operates by the plan; (e) responsibility for planning is vested in more than just the planning department.
   b. The confusion of planning with financial projections will have no effect on   T, F
   the success of the plans.

5. **A knowledge of various planning areas within an organization.**
   a. Input planning includes only site selection planning.   T, F
   b. Personnel planners who reflect on organizational objectives to determine   a, b, c, d, e
   overall human resource needs and compare needs to existing human re-
   source inventory are engaging in a type of planning called: (a) process
   layout; (b) plant facilities; (c) input; (d) life cycle; (e) delphi.

6. **A definition of forecasting.**
   a. Forecasting is the process of setting objectives and scheduling activities.   T, F
   b. According to the text, which of the following products is in the growth   a, b, c, d, e
   stage of the product life cycle: (a) microwave oven; (b) cellular phone;
   (c) black and white television; (d) personal computer; (e) refrigerator.

7. **An ability to see the advantages and disadvantages of various methods of
   sales forecasting.**
   a. The sales forecasting technique that utilizes specialized knowledge based on   a, b, c, d, e
   interaction with customers is: (a) jury of executive opinion; (b) sales force
   estimation; (c) time series analysis; (d) a and b; (e) b and c.
   b. One of the advantages of the jury of executive opinion method of forecast-   T, F
   ing sales is that it may be the only feasible means of forecasting, especially
   in the absence of adequate data.

8. **A definition of scheduling.**
   a. Scheduling can best be described as: (a) the evaluation of alternative courses   a, b, c, d, e
   of action; (b) the process of formulating goals and objectives; (c) the process
   of formulating a detailed listing of activities; (d) the calculation of the
   breakeven point; (e) the process of defining policies.
   b. Scheduling is the process of predicting future environmental happenings   T, F
   that will influence the operations of the organization.

9. An understanding of Gantt charts and PERT.

a, b, c, d, e   **a.** Which of the following is not an acceptable use of a Gantt chart: (a) as a summary overview of how organizational resources are being used; (b) to help coordinate organizational resources; (c) to establish realistic worker output standards; (d) to determine which resources are consistently contributing to productivity; (e) none of the above (all are acceptable uses of Gantt charts).

a, b, c, d, e   **b.** In a PERT network, the sequence of events and activities requiring the longest period of time to complete is: (a) called the network; (b) indicated by thin arrows; (c) the path that managers avoid; (d) the critical path; (e) eliminated from the rest of the project so the project will not take too long.

Introductory Case Wrap-Up

"Fiat Plans Car Production" and its related back-to-the-case sections were written to help you better understand the management concepts contained in this chapter. Answer the following discussion questions about this introductory case to further enrich your understanding of chapter content:

1. Should Fiat's plant facilities planning be related to its human resource planning? Explain.

2. Explain this statement: "The quality of Fiat's decision to build another factory and to expand and renovate another is largely determined by the validity of the company's sales forecast."

3. What sales forecasting method(s) do you think Fiat management should have used as the basis for making its plant facilities decision? Explain.

Issues for Review and Discussion

1. What is a plan?
2. List and describe the basic dimensions of a plan.
3. What is the difference between standing plans and single-use plans?
4. Compare and contrast policies, procedures, and rules.
5. What are the two main types of single-use plans?
6. Why do organizations have programs?
7. Of what use is a budget to managers?
8. Summarize the ten factors that cause plans to fail.
9. What is input planning?
10. Evaluate the importance of plant facilities planning to the organization.
11. What major factors should be involved in site selection?
12. Describe the human resource planning process.
13. What is a planning tool?
14. Describe the measurements usually employed in forecasting. Why are they taken?
15. Draw and explain the product life cycle.
16. Discuss the advantages and disadvantages of three methods of sales forecasting.
17. Elaborate on the statement that all managers should spend some time scheduling.
18. What is a Gantt chart? Draw a simple chart to assist you in your explanation.
19. How can information related to the Gantt chart be used by managers?
20. How is PERT a scheduling tool?
21. How is the critical path related to PERT?
22. List the steps necessary to design a PERT network.

Building on What You Know

Directions

Review the Highlight feature as indicated below and answer its corresponding questions. Questions in this section focus on relating a Highlight feature appearing in this chapter to management concepts that you have learned in a previous chapter.

Review the Quality Highlight: Toyota Motor Corporation on page 231. In chapter 7 you studied the strategic management process. How does the issue of choosing a plant site relate to Toyota's strategic planning process? How can the techniques of SWOT analysis, critical question analysis, and Porter's model be related to the process of Toyota's choosing its plant site location?

Action Summary Answer Key

1. a. b, p. 223
   b. d, p. 223
2. a. F, p. 224
   b. d, pp. 223–224
3. a. d, p. 225
   b. a, p. 225
4. a. c, p. 229
   b. F, p. 229
5. a. F, p. 229
   b. c, p. 232
6. a. F, p. 233
   b. d, p. 237
7. a. b, pp. 235–236
   b. T, p. 238
8. a. c, p. 239
   b. F, p. 239
9. a. e, pp. 239–240
   b. d, p. 241

Case Study

Carol Kirby of Baskin-Robbins: Planning a New Image

by Samuel C. Certo, Rollins College

Irvine Robbins and Burton Baskin first set up their ice cream business in 1946. They developed and manufactured ice cream products, operated retail stores, and granted franchises. They designed a carnival-like atmosphere for their stores and introduced the concept of a variety of ice cream flavors beyond the usual vanilla, chocolate, and strawberry. Baskin-Robbins became well known for its ice cream "flavor-of-the-month." The company was able to compete successfully against established ice cream chains such as Friendly's and Carvel and, by 1984, Baskin-Robbins had 3,300 retail operations and a second-place standing in ice cream sales, trailing only Dairy Queen.

Carol Kirby was first invited to Baskin-Robbins in 1984 as a marketing consultant to conduct a strategic study of the famous ice cream firm. Although a 1984 survey found Baskin-Robbins the favorite fast-food chain for the second consecutive year and profits continued to grow at a steady pace, management realized that there was a lot of change taking place in the ice cream industry and that they could ill afford to sit back and watch it all happen. They knew they should be able to capitalize on their excellent product awareness and product preference (almost everyone knew about and liked Baskin-Robbins and their famous 31 flavors) but realized that they would need a plan to compete against the many new entries in the ice cream market. Yuppie tastes for the new super premium ice creams plus a growing trend toward health-conscious eating habits seemed likely to start to erode Baskin-Robbins' profits.

Indeed, in her study, Kirby found that many adults tended to think of Baskin-Robbins as a place they used to go, or as a place where they would go only for children's birthday parties. Although the famous and off-beat Baskin-Robbins flavors like "Bubble Gum" and "Lunar Cheesecake" might keep the young customers happy and coming back, they would no longer be enough to attract adults as well. It was clear that a plan to change the company's image was necessary.

After the initial study ended, Kirby was invited to stay on as marketing chief. She knew that planning an updated company image would be her biggest task and that, in order to successfully create such a plan, more research would be needed. Kirby conducted focus groups, telephone interviews, and direct mail surveys to determine potential customers' perceptions of the company. She found out that many people perceived Baskin-Robbins as being out of step with the times. Young men and women watching their weight and people of all ages who were concerned about cholesterol intake wanted a healthier alternative to ice cream. Kirby decided not to tamper with the recipe for their already premium ice cream product in order to try to compete with the new super-rich premium ice creams like Häagen Dazs and Frusen-Gladje. Also, the "31 Flavors" was what set Baskin-

Robbins apart from all the others so she realized that they should not abandon that concept. Instead, Kirby felt that Baskin-Robbins should expand into the niche of the market neglected by the super premiums—lighter desserts. Kirby proposed an array of new products for health-conscious consumers that would be introduced gradually. Baskin-Robbins introduced their frozen yogurt in 1988, sugar-free ice cream in 1989, and low-fat ice cream in 1990. In each case, the trademark of Baskin-Robbins—a variety of interesting flavors—was offered. Convincing store owners to embrace the plan was not easy, since it required them to invest in costly new equipment. But Kirby presented her plan as a challenge rather than a threat and was able to win them over.

To help customers recognize the change in the Baskin-Robbins product line, a whole new look was needed for their retail stores. Kirby initiated a softer, more "upscale" store decor with a more adult atmosphere to replace the old pink and brown carnival stripes. Natural wood furniture replaced the school desks that so many adults found so uncomfortable, and sleek new store signs promoting Baskin-Robbins Ice Cream and Frozen Yogurt were added.

When the whole package was in place, it was time to advertise the changes. A series of television spots featuring Brian Bonsall, the child actor from the popular television series "Family Ties," focused on the new health-oriented products. The new tag line "Now there's more to love us for," summarized the new image.

The planned, new image seems to have taken hold. "The market was calling out for lower-calorie, lower-fat desserts," says Kirby. "Now 25 percent of our sales come from those products, products we didn't even have four years ago."

Discussion Questions:

1. Evaluate Kirby's plan for Baskin-Robbins' new image in terms of repetitiveness, time, scope, and level.

2. What specific steps did Kirby take to ensure that the plan would not fail?

3. Which of the sales forecasting options described in the chapter would be most useful to Kirby in forecasting ice cream and frozen yogurt sales?

4. Prepare a PERT chart to plan and implement the image changes Kirby formulated for Baskin-Robbins.

James Kinnear: A Lucky Star

Generations of Americans have grown up hearing that they can trust their cars to the man who wears the Texaco star. In the 1960s James Kinnear, then a budding Texaco executive, had a vision of Texaco's future: "I was of the view, with the way the modern motorist goes down the interstate highways, we wanted a simple, identifiable symbol, that he would know that there was a Texaco service station. And so more and more, rather than using the printed word, we decided to concentrate on the star."

To become the chief executive officer of one of America's oldest and largest oil companies requires a clear understanding of both personal and corporate objectives, but in his marketing acumen, as in other areas, Kinnear exemplifies a more important attribute—the ability to forecast change. He could imagine automobile travel growing, speeds increasing, and interstate highway systems expanding, and by imagining these changes, he knew that in the future, Texaco would need a symbol that could be identified quickly, easily, from a distance.

Marketing was one area of many Kinnear experienced at Texaco in his rise through the corporate ranks. He began pumping gas and washing cars in 1954, a trainee just home from the Korean War. His training led him to the oilfields of Texas and then, in 1959, to the new state of Hawaii to start operations in a new territory for Texaco.

Kinnear considers himself fortunate in his progression at Texaco: He's never been bored or unhappy at his job. Nonetheless, he must have had some doubts when, in January of 1987, he took the reins as CEO of a company in turmoil. In 1985, Texaco had lost a historic legal judgment to a small wildcatting oil company, Pennzoil; Pennzoil claimed that Texaco's 1984 purchase of Getty Oil had breached a prior purchase agreement between Pennzoil and Getty. The courts ordered Texaco to pay $10.5 billion to Getty, and Texaco faced insolvency.

On April 12, 1987, Kinnear announced that Texaco had been forced to file for reorganization under Chapter 11. "We can answer to our shareholders and our employees," Kinnear stated. "And that answer is that today's action had to be taken to safeguard tomorrow's future."

As CEO of a company in reorganization, Kinnear still faced a tremendous challenge, but with one advantage. The protection offered by the terms of Chapter 11 of the Internal Revenue Code enabled Texaco to design a plan for the future without fear of immediate suffocation at the hands of creditors. Kinnear's new plans were soon threatened from another side, though.

During the 1980s, Carl Icahn had become known for a series of flamboyant and generally successful takeover bids against publicly held companies. Within a year of Texaco's filing, Icahn began buying Texaco stock. He soon became Texaco's largest shareholder—and although Kinnear had achieved some degree of safety from creditor actions, he and his management team were still ultimately responsible to their shareholders.

Texaco's objective under reorganization was not only to become profitable once again, but also to use this opportunity to reorder and streamline its operations from top to bottom. Corporate raiders—takeover experts such as Icahn—frequently have a more short-range view. Long-term profitability is often seen as secondary to an immediate opportunity to realize profits and sell off assets. Kinnear wanted to preserve Texaco, but to hold off Icahn's takeover bid, he knew he would have to move quickly to increase dividends and restore profits. He succeeded; in June of 1989, Icahn withdrew from contention for Texaco. Dividends were up; stock prices were up; and company morale was once again high. On January 29, 1990, Texaco emerged from Chapter 11.

James Kinnear credits Texaco's management team with the successful reorganization. While he held off the takeover bid, just as he had fended off the press in April of 1987, his team created a leaner structure for the entire company. "We had a plan," says Kinnear; "we had our objectives, and we proceeded toward that plan. And the fact that it's worked out so well for us and, I must say, for our stockholders certainly makes me very, very proud. And I'm really proud of the people in this company that, through the organizational structure that we have, enabled them to continue to run the business while we fought the wars."

Video Case Questions

1. How do the four dimensions of repetitiveness, time, scope, and level relate to James Kinnear's plans for the reorganization of Texaco while it was under Chapter 11 bankruptcy?
2. Review the list of reasons for plan failure in the text. Which, if any, of these do you think was responsible for Texaco's loss to Pennzoil? Why?
3. When Kinnear was a trainee with Texaco, oil consumption per capita was increasing in the United States. During the 1970s, when oil became more expensive, consumption dropped. Suggest special projects for which Kinnear might have designed single-use plans in each situation.
4. When James Kinnear forecasts the future for Texaco's oil interests, what factors will he be looking at? List one possible consideration in each of the following categories: economic, technological, social trends, sales.

Video Case Activities

1. Draw a graph illustrating the time-series analysis method of sales forecasting as applied to Texaco for the period 1953 to the present. Include the "gas crisis" of the early 1970s, the environmental movement, the advent of nuclear energy sources, and technological advances making cars and home heating units more fuel efficient.
2. Imagine that you are planning to build Texaco's new Pacific headquarters, and you must choose the site. Based on Table 8.2, assign relative values on a scale of 1 to 10 for each of the criteria. Which do you think is most important, and why? Which is least important, and why?

PART 2

INTEGRATIVE CASE

Eighty Years of Planning for McDonnell Douglas

by Robert E. Kemper, Northern Arizona University

Based on 1988 financial data, McDonnell Douglas is the twenty-fifth largest industrial corporation in the United States and is the nation's largest defense contractor. However, in 1908, when Donald Douglas visited the Wright Brothers' exhibition, his idea of a company to manufacture airplanes was only a dream. Only after World War I, when the public imagination was captured by the notion of a war fought in the skies, would Douglas find support to make his dream a reality. In 1920, David R. Davis agreed to underwrite the expense of developing the "Cloudster."

By 1921, Douglas had sold a torpedo plane to the U.S. Navy and was working on plans for the Douglas Dolphin, a commercial "flying boat" to be introduced in 1928. The Douglas Company's (DC) next major breakthrough came in 1932, when Trans World Airlines commissioned a passenger aircraft, the DC-1, followed by the DC-2 in 1933. A new revenue source opened up for budding commercial airlines when airmail legislation was passed in 1934. In 1936, Douglas introduced the DC-3, the first aircraft to make a profit based on carrying passengers.

Despite these successes, Douglas did not lose sight of a potentially far greater profit center. From the drawing board, the DC-3 had been designed not only for commercial applications but also for military use. During World War II, over 10,000 D-18 bombers and C-47 transports, both variants of the DC-3, were sold. Military contracts represented the major part of Douglas's business from 1935, with the introduction of the B-18 bomber, through the 1940s and into the 1950s.

In 1950, the Douglas Company entered a new business—missiles. Delivery began in 1954 with the A-4 Skyhawk, which was followed by updated models

and, in 1956, the first surface-to-air missiles, the NIKE HAAX.

Later in that decade, the boom in defense contracts had occasioned a slowdown in production of commercial airliners, which would plague Douglas. Development of the DC-8 was delayed in 1958, just as Boeing's 707 approached readiness. Douglas's contracts with American Airlines were lost to Boeing, and ongoing production backlogs caused the loss of many smaller orders, as well. Introduction of the DC-9 in 1965 was overshadowed by remaining DC-8 cost overruns, and by 1966, banks were withholding their financial support.

The Douglas Company was sold in 1967 to McDonnell Aircraft, a company with a reputation for effective and innovative management. The new company was called "McDonnell Douglas" (MD). Manufacture of a fighter jet, the F-15, began in 1970, and soon MD declared that fighters were to be the company's strategic manufacturing priority.

Major changes hit MD in the late 1970s, led by new personnel policies resulting from charges made by the U.S. Civil Rights Commission, regarding discriminatory hiring and promotional practices. Earnings increased, however, and the McDonnell Douglas Research Laboratory, a $7 million facility, was built. MD diversified once again, purchasing Microdata Corporation, a producer of small business computers, in 1979. The decade ended badly, though, when the FAA suspended all DC-10 flights for five weeks following a fatal crash in Chicago.

MD returned in 1980 to its tried-and-true strategy of upgrading existing products, introducing the MD-80, an advanced version of the DC-9, and the

KC-10, a military derivative of the DC-10. However, the combination of the FAA suspension, deregulation, an air traffic controller strike, and worldwide recession were devastating to the airline industry. Military contracts—the KC-10, Tomahawk missiles, and anti-ship missile development—carried the company. New chief executives were appointed at Douglas Aircraft, McDonnell Aircraft, Microdata, and McDonnell Douglas Automation Company (MC Auto).

New management strategies included scuttling development of proposed MD-90 and MD-100 jets, to concentrate commercial resources on the MD-80. This plan paid off, and MD-80 orders topped 100 in 1984, 1985, 1986, and 1987; meanwhile, a smaller version, the MD-87, entered the product line in 1984. Once again, commercial contracts achieved economic importance.

Another old strategy, diversification, recurred, with the purchase in 1983 of Hughes Helicopter, and in 1984 of Tymshare Incorporated and Computer Sharing Services. Hughes Helicopter, renamed MCD Helicopter Company, relocated to Arizona and delivered the first production Apache helicopters to the Army in 1985.

That same year, the C17 advanced transport plane entered development for the Air Force, and MD won a $331 million contract to develop technology basic to the Strategic Defense Initiative. SDI missile interceptor design and testing contracts followed in 1986. Research and development were contracted by the armed forces for a new hypersonic aircraft. In 1987, MD was chosen to design and build a major part of NASA's proposed space station. Production continued on Tomahawk and advanced cruise missiles. The Navy awarded a joint contract to MD and General Dynamics to develop a new tactical aircraft. With MD-80 sales declining and no new commercial aircraft ready for delivery, MD once more found itself heavily reliant on defense contracts—and global political changes threatened the defense industry.

In 1988, John F. McDonnell was appointed CEO of McDonnell Douglas. A new mission statement was announced in 1989, which reads as follows.

> McDonnell Douglas is a synergistic blend of 123,000 men and women, backed by extensive financial resources and modern laboratory, office, and manufacturing facilities throughout the United States, Canada, and abroad. McDonnell Douglas is a company structured around Total Management Systems and fueled by continuous improvement in its work force—improvement that emerges as elevated expectations for its people, its suppliers, its communities, and its customers. Its products cover a spectrum of programs in aviation, space, missiles, training, electronics, and integrated systems, as well as services in lease finance, travel, and real estate. Sales are approximately 2/3 government and 1/3 commercial. World Headquarters is in St. Louis, Missouri.

Discussion Questions

1. Create a SWOT analysis for McDonnell Douglas as it enters the 1990s. List at least 3 items in each category.

2. Give two examples of situations in which MD's management modified product life cycles to maximize sales. In your opinion, does this extension of life cycles represent strategy or tactics?

3. Consider the decision-making process defined in Chapter 6. How does MD's experience with Hughes Helicopter from 1983 to 1985 correlate to that process?

4. In your opinion, what are MD's corporate objectives? How do its corporate strategies of the 1980s reflect those objectives? As a planner, what would your suggestions be for changing those strategies in the 1990s?

5. How is planning used as a tool against risk at MD?

The Federal Express Corporation won the Malcolm Baldrige award in 1990 in the service company division. Federal Express was recognized for its strong management philosophy that emphasizes people – service – profit, in that order.

Organizing

This section discusses the second major management function—organizing. Organizing naturally follows planning, discussed in the previous section, because it is the primary mechanism by which managers put plans into action.

In general, the section covers the fundamentals of organizing, responsibility, authority, and delegation, managing human resources, and organizational change and stress. More specifically, it covers several organizing fundamentals, including the definition of *organizing,* the five main steps involved in organizing, and the classical principles that influence the organizing process.

The material will focus on responsibility as a fundamental ingredient in the organizing process and will indicate that delegating authority is an important component of organizing. In addition, the point will be made that an organization can be centralized or decentralized, depending on the amount of authority its management delegates. The discussion of managing human resources will emphasize the tasks of furnishing the organization with people who will make desirable contributions toward the attainment of organizational objectives and the tasks of utilizing the processes of recruitment, selection, training, and performance evaluation. Finally, the section will explain that organizational change is often necessary in order to increase organizational effectiveness and that the success of a particular change is based on the collective influence of such issues as how and what type of changes are made. This discussion also will address the relationship between stress and organizational change and will emphasize the importance of studying and managing stress.

One important point to remember is that organizing naturally follows planning. Organizing concepts discussed here will be challenging and relate to concepts discussed in previous sections. Understanding organizing is important to understanding the remainder of the text.

Chapter 9

Student Learning Objectives

From studying this chapter, I will attempt to acquire:

1. An understanding of the organizing function.

2. An appreciation for the complications of determining appropriate organizational structure.

3. Insights on the advantages and disadvantages of division of labor.

4. A working knowledge of the relationship between division of labor and coordination.

5. An understanding of span of management and the factors that influence its appropriateness.

6. An understanding of scalar relationships.

Fundamentals
of Organizing

hapter Outline

$\mathcal{L}$ *ntroductory Case*

MCI COMMUNICATIONS ORGANIZES TO BE MORE COMPETITIVE

MCI Communications Corporation, headquartered in Washington, D.C., provides a wide spectrum of domestic and international voice and data communication services. For residential customers, the company offers long distance opportunities like PrimeTime and SuperSaver. For business customers, communication opportunities provided by MCI enable businesspeople

The streamlining is intended to allow managers to react more swiftly to competition.

to strengthen relationships between customers and suppliers and to eliminate the traditional communications barriers of time and distance. MCI is the only telecommunications services company offering a full spectrum of voice, data messaging, and fax services with international capability. MCI, facing vigorous competition and a sluggish economy, recently announced that it is restructuring operations and may lay off 1,500 employees nationwide over the next six months.

The long-distance company is revamping operations along commercial and residential lines, setting up a Business Markets unit and a Consumer Markets unit. The business unit will have four divisions, pared down from seven. In addition, a Network Services organization is being set up to meet new demands of both the business and consumer units.

The streamlining, which gives MCI a structure more like AT&T's, is intended to allow managers to react more swiftly to competition and position the company for growth. The previous structure, with seven regions corresponding to the seven regional Bell companies, has proven unwieldy as AT&T has sharpened efforts to stem further erosion of its market share. That share has dropped to around 70 percent of the $50 billion to $55 billion long-distance market.

Bert C. Roberts, Jr., MCI president, said the reorganization is being driven by "our recognition of the

changing conditions that most businesses are experiencing" and the demands of a more competitive marketplace. He said that MCI expects to grow more rapidly than the overall market for long-distance service.

From Mary Lu Carnevale, "MCI to Revamp Units, May Cut 1,500 Staffers," *Wall Street Journal.* November 16, 1990, A3. Reprinted by permission of *Wall Street Journal,* © 1990 Dow Jones & Company, Inc. All Rights Reserved Worldwide.

The introductory case describes, in general, how MCI is being organized in order to be more competitive. Information in this chapter would be useful to a manager like Bert. C. Roberts, Jr. in contemplating organizing issues. This chapter emphasizes both a definition of organizing and principles of classical organizing theory that can be useful in actually organizing a company.

A DEFINITION OF ORGANIZING

Organizing is the process of establishing orderly uses for all resources within the management system. These uses emphasize the attainment of management system objectives and assist managers not only in making objectives apparent but also in clarifying which resources will be used to attain them.[1] A primary focus of organizing includes determining both what individuals will do in an organization and how their individual efforts should best be combined to contribute to the attainment of organizational objectives.[2] *Organization* refers to the result of the organizing process.

In essence, each organizational resource represents an investment from which the management system must get a return. Appropriate organization of these resources increases the efficiency and effectiveness of their use. Henri Fayol developed sixteen general guidelines for organizing resources:[3]

1. Judiciously prepare and execute the operating plan.
2. Organize the human and material facets so that they are consistent with objectives, resources, and requirements of the concern.
3. Establish a single competent, energetic guiding authority (formal management structure).
4. Coordinate all activities and efforts.
5. Formulate clear, distinct, and precise decisions.
6. Arrange for efficient selection so that each department is headed by a competent, energetic manager and all employees are placed where they can render the greatest service.
7. Define duties.
8. Encourage initiative and responsibility.
9. Offer fair and suitable rewards for services rendered.
10. Make use of sanctions against faults and errors.
11. Maintain discipline.
12. Ensure that individual interests are consistent with the general interests of the organization.
13. Recognize the unity of command.

Organizing is the process of establishing orderly uses for all resources in the organization.

14. Promote both material and human coordination.

15. Institute and effect controls.

16. Avoid regulations, red tape, and paperwork.

The Importance of Organizing

The organizing function is extremely important to the management system, because it is the primary mechanism with which managers activate plans. Organizing creates and maintains relationships between all organizational resources by indicating which resources are to be used for specified activities and when, where, and how they are to be used. A thorough organizing effort helps managers to minimize costly weaknesses, such as duplication of effort and idle organizational resources.

Some management theorists consider the organizing function so important that they advocate the creation of an organizing department within the management system. Typical responsibilities of this department would include developing (1) reorganization plans that make the management system more effective and efficient, (2) plans to improve managerial skills to fit current management system needs, and (3) an advantageous organizational climate within the management system.[4]

The Organizing Process

The five main steps of the organizing process, as presented in Figure 9.1, are (1) reflecting on plans and objectives,[5] (2) establishing major tasks, (3) dividing major tasks into subtasks, (4) allocating resources and directives for subtasks, and (5) evaluating the results of implemented organizing strategy. As the figure implies, managers should continually repeat these steps. Through repetition they obtain feedback that will help them improve the existing organization.

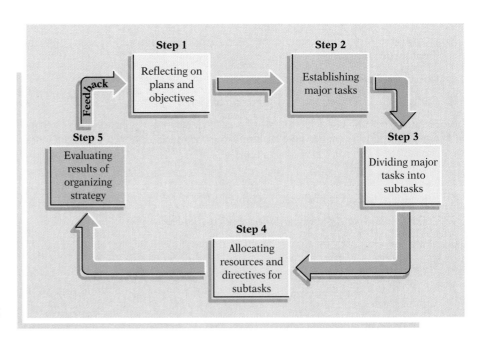

FIGURE 9.1

Five main steps of the organizing process

The management of a restaurant can illustrate how the organizing process might work. The first step the manager would take to initiate the organizing process would be to reflect on the restaurant's plans and objectives. Because planning involves determining how the restaurant will attain its objectives, and organizing involves determining how the restaurant's resources will be used to activate plans, the restaurant manager must start to organize by understanding planning.

The second and third steps of the organizing process focus on tasks to be performed within the management system. The manager must designate major tasks or jobs to be performed within the restaurant. Two such tasks might be serving customers and cooking food. Then the tasks must be divided into subtasks. For example, the manager might decide that serving customers includes the subtasks of taking orders and clearing tables.

The fourth organizing step is determining who will take orders, who will clear the tables, and what the details of the relationship between these individuals will be. The size of tables and how the tables are to be set also are factors to be considered at this point.

In the fifth step, evaluating the results of a particular organizing strategy, the manager gathers feedback on how well the implemented organizing strategy is working. This feedback should furnish information that can be used to improve the existing organization. For example, the manager may find that a particular type of table is not large enough and that larger ones must be purchased if the restaurant is to attain its goals.

The Organizing Subsystem

The organizing function, like the planning function, can be visualized as a subsystem of the overall management system (see Figure 9.2). The primary purpose of

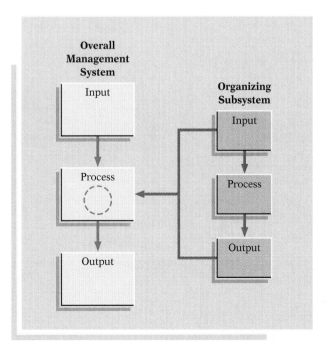

FIGURE 9.2

Relationships between overall management system and organizing subsystem the organizing subsystem is to enhance the goal attainment of the general management system by providing a rational approach for using organizational resources. Figure 9.3 presents the specific ingredients of the organizing subsystem. The input is a portion of the total resources of the organization, the process is the steps involved in the organizing function, and the output is organization.

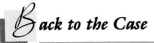

Back to the Case

In contemplating how MCI should be organized, Bert C. Roberts can focus on answering several important questions. These questions should be aimed at establishing an orderly use of MCI's organizational resources. Because these resources represent an investment on which he must get a return, Roberts's questions should be geared toward gaining information that will be used to maximize this return. Overall, such questions should focus on determining the use of MCI's resources that will best accomplish its goals. Some preliminary questions might be as follows:

1. What organizational objectives exist at MCI? For example, does MCI want to focus on international markets as well as domestic markets? Does MCI want to grow or to maintain its present size?

2. What plans does MCI have to accomplish these objectives? Is MCI going to open more offices abroad? Are additional training programs being added to enable employees to understand how best to work abroad?

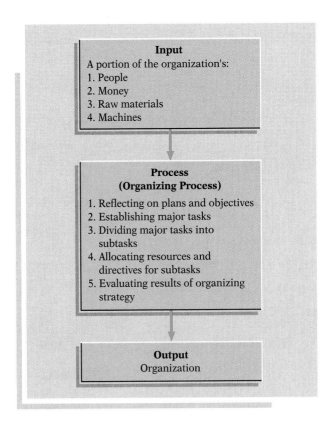

FIGURE 9.3
Organizing subsystem

3. What are the major tasks MCI must go through to offer message and voice products? For example, how many steps are involved in developing needed fax equipment and making it available to appropriate customers?

4. What resources does MCI have to run its operations? Answers to this question focus on such issues as the number of employees, financial resources available, equipment being used, and so on.

Roberts also should begin thinking of some mechanism for evaluating the organizing strategy he develops. Once the strategy is implemented, Roberts must be able to get feedback on how all of MCI's resources are functioning so he can improve his organizing efforts. For example, Roberts may find that in order for MCI to become more competitive he needs greater voice-messaging capability in one country than in another and more employees in the Consumer Markets unit. With appropriate feedback, Roberts can continually improve MCI's existing organizational system.

CLASSICAL ORGANIZING THEORY

Classical organizing theory is the cumulative insights of early management writers on how organizational resources can best be used to enhance goal attainment. The writer who probably had the most profound influence on classical organizing theory was Max Weber.[6] According to Weber, the main components of an organizing effort are detailed procedures and rules, a clearly outlined organizational hierarchy, and, mainly, impersonal relationships among organization members.

Weber used the term **bureaucracy** to label the management system that contains these components. Although Weber firmly believed in the bureaucratic approach to organizing, he became concerned when managers seemed to overemphasize the merits of a bureaucracy.[7] He cautioned that a bureaucracy is not an end in itself but a means to the end of management system goal attainment. The main criticism of Weber's bureaucracy, as well as the concepts of other classical organizing theorists, is the obvious lack of concern for the human variable within the organization.[8] Considerable discussion on this variable is presented in chapters 13 through 16.

The rest of this chapter summarizes four main considerations of classical organizing theory that all modern managers should include in their organizing efforts. They are (1) structure, (2) division of labor, (3) span of management, and (4) scalar relationships.

Structure

In any organizing effort, managers must choose an appropriate structure.[9] **Structure** refers to designated relationships among resources of the management system. Its purpose is to facilitate the use of each resource, individually and collectively, as the management system attempts to attain its objectives.[10]

Organization structure is represented primarily by means of a graphic illustration called an **organization chart.** Traditionally, an organization chart is constructed in pyramid form, with individuals toward the top of the pyramid having more authority and responsibility than individuals toward the bottom.[11] The relative positioning of individuals within boxes on the chart indicates broad working relationships, and lines between boxes designate formal lines of communication between individuals.

Classical organizing theory is the cumulative insights of early management writers on how organizational resources can best be used to enhance goal attainment. Max Weber used the term **bureaucracy** to describe a management system with detailed procedures and rules, a clearly outlined organizational hierarchy, and, mainly, impersonal relationships among organization members.

Structure is designated relationships among resources of the management.

An **organization chart** is a graphic representation of organizational structure.

Figure 9.4 is an example of an organization chart. Its dotted line is not part of the organization chart but has been added to illustrate the pyramid shape of the chart. The positions close to the restaurant manager's involve more authority and responsibility; the positions farther away involve less authority and responsibility. The locations of positions also indicate broad working relationships. For example, the positioning of the head chef over the three other chefs indicates that the head chef has authority over them and is responsible for their productivity. The lines between the individual chefs and the restaurant manager indicate that formal communication from chef 1 to the restaurant manager must go through the head chef.

Historically speaking, pyramidal organization structures are probably modeled on the structure of military command; in the western world, the structure of organized religion has also been hierarchical, with authority derived from the top. Some researchers have found that women are not comfortable with this type of hierarchical structure. As more and more women enter the management field, a new model may need to be created. In *The Female Advantage: Women's Ways of Leadership,* author Sally Helgesen postulates that women create networks or "webs" of authority and that women's leadership styles are relational rather than hierarchical and authoritarian.[12] Management writer Tom Peters suggests that, in the 1990s, these styles will be inherently better suited to new kinds of organizational structures, required for a competitive global environment, that will feature teamwork and participative management.[13]

Formal and Informal Structure

Formal structure is defined as the relationships among organizational resources as outlined by management.

In reality, two basic types of structure exist within management systems: formal and informal. **Formal structure** is defined as the relationships among organizational resources as outlined by management. It is represented primarily by the organization chart.

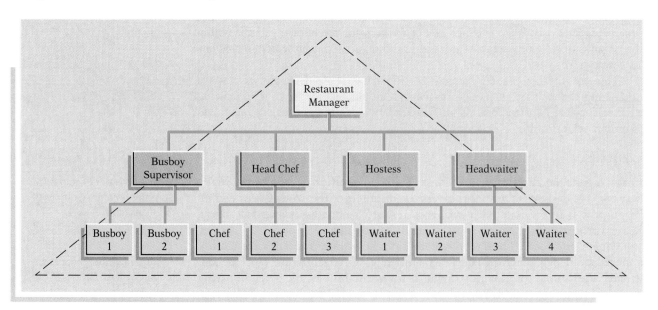

FIGURE 9.4

Sample organization chart for a small restaurant

Informal structure is defined as the patterns of relationships that develop because of the informal activities of organization members. It evolves naturally and tends to be molded by individual norms, values, or social relationships. In essence, informal structure is a system or network of interpersonal relationships that exists within, but is not usually identical to, an organization's formal structure.[14] The primary focus of this chapter is formal structure. More details on informal structure are presented in chapter 16.

> **Informal structure** is defined as the patterns of relationships that develop because of the informal activities of organization members.

Departmentalization and Formal Structure: A Contingency Viewpoint

The most common method of instituting formal relationships among resources is by establishing departments. Basically, a **department** is a unique group of resources established by management to perform some organizational task. The process of establishing departments within the management system is called **departmentalization.** These departments typically are based on, or contingent on, such situational factors as the work functions being performed, the product being assembled, the territory being covered, the customer being targeted, and the process designed for manufacturing the product. (For a quick review of the contingency approach to management, see p. 48.)

> **A department** is a unique group of resources established by management to perform some organizational task.
>
> **Departmentalization** is the process of establishing departments in the management system.

Perhaps the most widely used base for establishing departments within the formal structure is the type of *work functions* (activities) being performed within the management system.[15] The major categories into which the functions typically are divided are marketing, production, and finance. Figure 9.5 is an organization chart showing structure based primarily on function for a hypothetical organization, Greene Furniture Company.

Organization structure based primarily on *product* departmentalizes resources according to the products being manufactured. As more and more products are manufactured, it becomes increasingly difficult to coordinate activities across them. Organizing according to product allows managers to logically group the resources necessary to produce each product. Figure 9.6 is a Greene Furniture Company organization chart showing structure based primarily on product.

Structure based primarily on *territory* departmentalizes according to the place

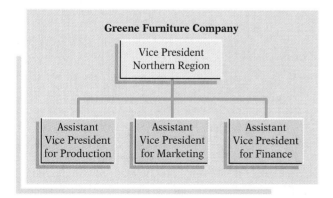

FIGURE 9.5

Organization structure based primarily on function

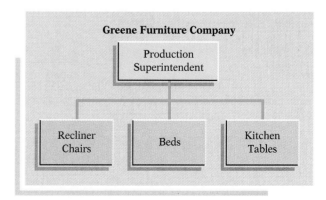

FIGURE 9.6

Organization structure based primarily on product

where the work is being done or the geographic market area on which the management system is focusing. As market areas and work locations expand, the physical distance between places can make the management task extremely cumbersome. The distances can range from a relatively short span between two points in the same city to a relatively long span between two points in the same state, in different states, or even in different countries.[16] To minimize the effects of distances, resources can be departmentalized according to territory. Figure 9.7 is a Greene Furniture Company organization chart based primarily on territory.

Structure based primarily on the *customer* establishes departments in response to the organization's major customers. This structure, of course, assumes that major customers can be identified and divided into logical categories. Figure 9.8 is a Greene Furniture Company organization chart based primarily on customers. Greene Furniture obviously can clearly identify its customers and divide them into logical categories.

Structure based primarily on *manufacturing process* departmentalizes according to the major phases of the process used to manufacture products. In the case of Greene Furniture Company, the major phases are woodcutting, sanding, glueing, and painting. Figure 9.9 is the organization chart that reflects these phases.

If the situation warrants it, individual organization charts can be combined to show all five of these factors. Figure 9.10 shows how all the factors are included on the same organization chart for Greene Furniture Company.

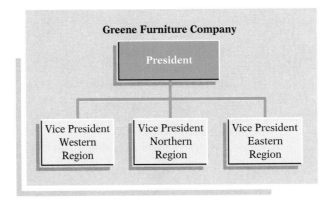

FIGURE 9.7

Organization structure based primarily on territory

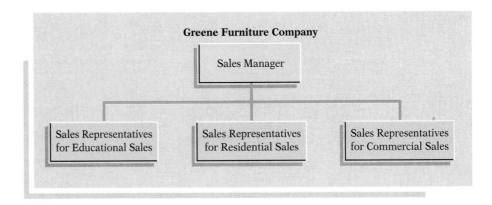

FIGURE 9.8

Organization structure based primarily on customers

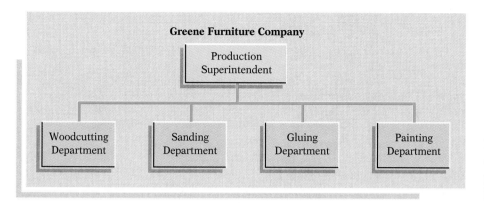

FIGURE 9.9
Organization structure based primarily on manufacturing process

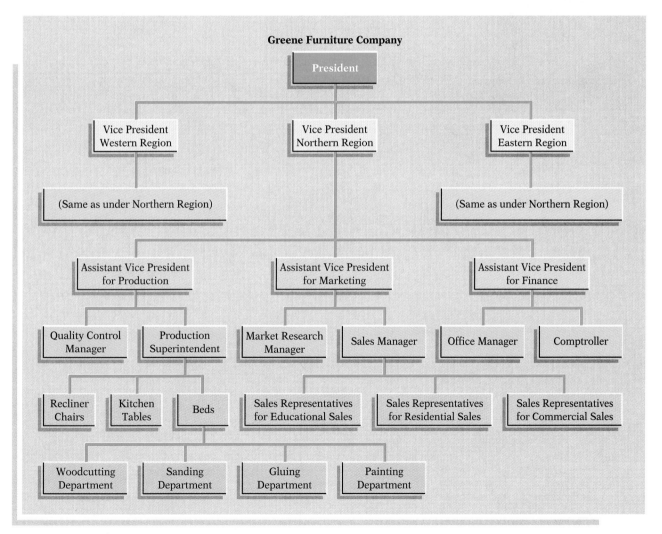

FIGURE 9.10
Organization structure based primarily on function, product, territory, customers, and manufacturing process

Ethics Highlight: Gerber Products Company's Structure Fails to Perform

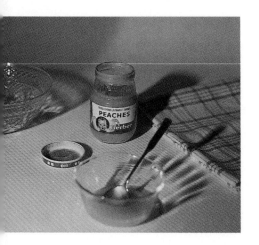

Recent happenings at the Gerber Products Company indicate that managers should also study and communicate about the manufacturing process from a more nontraditional, socially responsible viewpoint. When a woman found a chip of ceramic in some Gerber baby food and reported it to the firm, it was considered a routine consumer complaint and the company spent no time reflecting on the manufacturing process used to produce the food. After the media found out about the chip, however, Gerber's social responsibility focus was quickly questioned. The general public was outraged that such an event had occurred. The situation escalated into a crisis as executives fought a barrage of complaints that translated into consumer pressure for a total recall of the product.

The situation didn't have to become a crisis. Gerber's tightlipped, noncooperative responses about its manufacturing process greatly alarmed the general public. In today's business environment, managers must realize that society is very interested in manufacturing processes used to produce the goods that it buys and consumes. As a result of the way Gerber handled this situation, the company's image was tarnished in the eyes of consumers and in society as a whole, which almost inevitably would have a negative impact on an organization's profits.

Forces Influencing Formal Structure

According to Shetty and Carlisle, the formal structure of a management system is continually evolving. Four primary forces influence this evolution: (1) forces in the manager, (2) forces in the task, (3) forces in the environment, and (4) forces in the subordinates.[17] The evolution of a particular organization is actually the result of a complex and dynamic interaction among these forces, as Figure 9.11 illustrates.

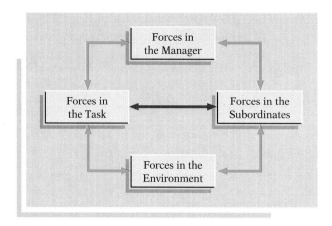

FIGURE 9.11
Forces influencing the evolution of organization structure

Forces in the manager are the unique way in which a manager perceives organizational problems. Naturally, background, knowledge, experience, and values influence the manager's perception of how formal structure should exist or be changed. Forces in the task include the degree of technology involved in the task and the complexity of the task. As task activities change, a force is created to change the existing organization. Forces in the environment include the customers and suppliers of the management system, along with existing political and social structures. Forces in the subordinates include the needs and skill levels of subordinates. Obviously, as the environment and subordinates vary, forces are created simultaneously to change the organization.

Back to the Case

In order to develop a sound organizing effort, a manager should take classical organizing theory into consideration. Of the four major elements of classical organizing theory, the first to be considered here is structure. Roberts's considerations regarding the structure of MCI would be aimed at creating working relationships among all MCI employees. In order to develop an effective organizational structure, Roberts must analyze situational factors in the company, such as functions, products, geographic locations, customers, and processes involved in offering its products to customers.

Information within the case suggests that Roberts's new organization structure for MCI is based primarily on customers. For example, the case informs us that the long distance company is revamping its operations along commercial and residential lines; the company is setting up a Business Markets unit (business customers) and a Consumer Markets unit (residential customers). According to Roberts's concept, the Business Markets unit will have four different divisions. In addition, Roberts's organizing strategy includes a Network Services unit that will be set up to meet the new demands of both the Business Markets and the Consumer Markets units.

A manager like Roberts typically uses an organization chart to represent organization structure. Such a chart would not only allow Roberts to see the lines of authority and responsibility at MCI, but also to understand the broad working relationships among his employees.

Division of Labor

The second main consideration of any organizing effort is how to divide labor. The **division of labor** is the assignment of various portions of a particular task among a number of organization members. Rather than one individual's doing the entire job, several individuals perform different parts of it. Production is divided into a number of steps, with the responsibility for completion of various steps assigned to specific individuals.[18] In essence, individuals specialize in doing part of the task rather than the entire task.

A commonly used illustration of division of labor is the automobile production line. Rather than one individual assembling an entire car, specific portions of the car are assembled by various individuals. The following sections discuss the advantages and disadvantages of division of labor and the relationship between division of labor and coordination.

Division of labor is the assignment of various portions of a particular task among a number of organization members. Division of labor calls for specialization.

Advantages and Disadvantages of Division of Labor

Several generally accepted explanations have been offered for why division of labor should be employed. First, because workers specialize in a particular task, their skill for performing that task tends to increase. Second, workers do not lose valuable time in moving from one task to another. Because they typically have one job and one place in which to do it, time is not lost changing tools or locations. Third, because workers concentrate on performing only one job, they naturally try to make the job easier and more efficient. Last, division of labor creates a situation in which workers need only to know how to perform their part of the work task rather than the process for the entire product. The task of understanding their work, therefore, typically does not become too much of a burden.

Arguments also have been presented to discourage the use of extreme division of labor.[19] Overall, these arguments stress that the advantages of division of labor focus solely on efficiency and economic benefit and overlook the human variable. Work that is extremely specialized tends to be boring and therefore usually causes production rates to go down. Clearly, some type of balance is needed between specialization and human motivation. How to arrive at this balance is discussed further in chapter 15.

Division of Labor and Coordination

In a division of labor situation with different individuals doing portions of a task, the importance of effective coordination becomes obvious. Mooney has defined **coordination** as "the orderly arrangement of group effort to provide unity of action in the pursuit of a common purpose."[20] Coordination involves encouraging the completion of individual portions of a task in a synchronized order that is appropriate for the overall task. Groups cannot maintain their productivity without coordination.[21] Part of the synchronized order for assembling an automobile entails installing seats only after the floor has been installed; adhering to this order of installation is an example of coordination.

Establishing and maintaining coordination may, but does not always, involve close supervision of employees. Managers can also establish and maintain coordination through bargaining, formulating a common purpose, or improving on specific problem solutions.[22] Each of these efforts is considered a specific management tool. Managers should try to break away from the idea that coordination is achieved only through close employee supervision.

Mary Parker Follett has furnished concerned managers with valuable advice on how to establish and maintain coordination within the organization. First, Follett says that coordination can be attained with the least difficulty through direct horizontal relationships and personal communications. When a coordination problem arises, speaking with peer workers may be the best way to solve it. Second, Follett suggests that coordination be a discussion topic throughout the planning process. In essence, managers should plan for coordination. Third, maintaining coordination is a continuing process and should be treated as such. Managers cannot assume that because their management system shows coordination today it will show coordination tomorrow. Follett also notes that managers should not leave the existence of coordination to chance. Coordination can be achieved only through purposeful management action. Last, according to Follett, the importance of the human element and the communication process should be consid-

Coordination is the orderly arrangement of group effort to provide unity of action in the pursuit of a common purpose. It involves encouraging the completion of individual portions of a task in an appropriate, synchronized order.

ered in any attempt to encourage coordination. Employee skill levels and motivation levels are primary considerations, as is the effectiveness of the human communication process used during coordination activities.[23]

Quality Highlight: Nike Coordinates to Capitalize on Trend

Lack of effective coordination among Nike's departments had affected the quality of Nike products, and they had begun to lose ground to Reebok, Nike's primary competitor. Philip Knight, the chief executive officer at Nike, found the source of the problem and decided to take action to improve the coordination within company departments and divisions.

In the early 1980s, Nike was run primarily by former athletes, some of whom tended to change jobs often. Such turnover in key positions contributed to the poor coordination among design, marketing, and production departments at Nike. Recognizing the relationship between key individuals leaving the company and a lack of coordination within company departments, Knight took steps to reduce executive turnover.

Knight's actions proved effective, which enabled Nike to notice that customer tastes were changing. After several years of preferring the stylish look of shoes such as Reebok, buyers were beginning to appreciate the high-performance quality of Nike's shoes. With more effective coordination, Nike could take advantage of this trend and could maximize the performance quality of their shoes. This coordinated strategy has proven so effective that Nike has tripled its profits to $101.7 million in the past few years. Nike is quite pleased with the bold actions of its Knight.

Back to the Case

In developing the most appropriate way to organize MCI employees, Roberts can reflect on the second major element in classical organizing theory: division of labor. Roberts could decide, for example, that instead of having one person do all the work involved in servicing a business customer, the labor could be divided so that, for each business customer, one person would make the initial contact, one person would assess communication needs of the organization, and yet another person would explore various alternative MCI ways of meeting those needs. In this way, employees could work more quickly and could specialize in one area of business customer relations, such as assessing business needs or meeting needs of business customers.

In considering the appropriateness of division of labor at MCI, Roberts could also consider a mechanism for enhancing coordination. In order to develop such a mechanism, Roberts must have a thorough understanding of how various MCI business processes occur so he can split up various tasks and maintain coordination within the various MCI divisions. In addition, Roberts must stress communication as a prerequisite for coordination. Without having MCI employees continually communicate with one another, coordination will be virtually impossible. In taking action aimed at enhancing organizational coordination, Roberts must also plan for and take action toward maintaining such coordination.

Span of Management

The **span of management** is the number of individuals a manager supervises.

The third main consideration of any organizing effort is **span of management**—the number of individuals a manager supervises. The more individuals a manager supervises, the greater the span of management. Conversely, the fewer individuals a manager supervises, the smaller the span of management. The span of management has a significant effect on how well managers can carry out their responsibilities.[24] Span of management is also called span of control, span of authority, span of supervision, and span of responsibility.

The central concern of span of management is a determination of how many individuals a manager can supervise effectively.[25] To use human resources effectively, managers should supervise as many individuals as they can best guide toward production quotas. If they are supervising too few individuals, they are wasting a portion of their productive capacity. If they are supervising too many, they lose part of their effectiveness.

Designing Span of Management: A Contingency Viewpoint

As reported by Harold Koontz, several important situational factors influence the appropriateness of the size of an individual's span of management.[26]

Similarity of Functions. The degree to which activities performed by supervised individuals are similar or dissimilar. As the similarity of subordinates' activities increases, the span of management appropriate for the situation becomes wider. The converse is also generally accurate.

Geographic Contiguity. The degree to which subordinates are physically separated. In general, the closer subordinates are physically, the more of them managers can supervise effectively.

Complexity of Functions. The degree to which workers' activities are difficult and involved. The more difficult and involved the activities are, the more difficult it is to manage a large number of individuals effectively.

Coordination. The amount of time managers must spend to synchronize the activities of their subordinates with the activities of other workers. The greater the amount of time managers must spend on coordination, the smaller their span of management should be.

Planning. The amount of time managers must spend developing management system objectives and plans and integrating them with the activities of their subordinates. The more time managers must spend on planning activities, the fewer individuals they can manage effectively.

Table 9.1 summarizes the factors that tend to increase and decrease span of management.

Graicunas and Span of Management

Perhaps the best-known contribution to span of management literature was made by V.A. Graicunas, a management consultant.[27] His contribution was the development of a formula for determining the number of *possible* relationships between a

TABLE 9.1 Major factors that influence the span of management

Factor	Factor Has Tendency to Increase Span of Management When—	Factor Has Tendency to Decrease Span of Management When—
1. Similarity of functions	1. Subordinates have similar functions	1. Subordinates have different functions
2. Geographic contiguity	2. Subordinates are physically close	2. Subordinates are physically distant
3. Complexity of functions	3. Subordinates have simple tasks	3. Subordinates have complex tasks
4. Coordination	4. Work of subordinates needs little coordination	4. Work of subordinates needs much coordination
5. Planning	5. Manager spends little time planning	5. Manager spends much time planning

manager and subordinates when the number of subordinates is known. **Graicunas's formula** is as follows:

$$C = n\left(\frac{2^n}{2} + n - 1\right)$$

C is the total number of possible relationships between manager and subordinates, and *n* is the known number of subordinates. Table 9.2 shows what happens to the total possible number of manager-subordinate relationships as the number of subordinates increases from 1 to 18. As the number of subordinates increases arithmetically, the number of possible relationships between the manager and those subordinates increases geometrically. Figure 9.12 (p. 272) illustrates the six possible relationships between a manager and two subordinates.

A number of criticisms have been leveled at Graicunas's work. Arguments that Graicunas did not take into account a manager's relationships outside the organization and that he considered only potential relationships rather than actual

Graicunas's formula is a formula that makes the span of management point that as the number of a manager's subordinates increases arithmetically, the number of possible relationships between the manager and the subordinates increases geometrically.

TABLE 9.2 Geometric increase of possible manager-subordinate relationships

Number of Subordinates	Number of Relationships
1	1
2	6
3	18
4	44
5	100
6	222
7	490
8	1,080
9	2,376
10	5,210
11	11,374
12	24,708
18	2,359,602

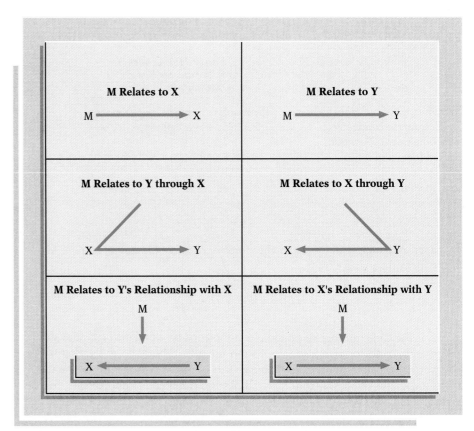

FIGURE 9.12

Six possible relationships between manager M and two subordinates, X and Y

relationships have some validity. The real significance of Graicunas's work, however, does not lie within the realm of these criticisms. His main contribution was pointing out that span of management is an important consideration that can have a far-reaching organizational impact.[28]

Height of Organization Chart

A definite relationship exists between span of management and the height of an organization chart. Normally, the greater the height of the organization chart, the smaller the span of management. It also follows that the lower the height of the organization chart, the greater the span of management. Organization charts with little height are usually referred to as **flat;** those with much height are usually referred to as **tall.**

A **flat organization chart** is an organization chart characterized by few levels and relatively large spans of management; a **tall organization chart** is an organization chart characterized by many levels and relatively small spans of management. A broad span of management indicates a flat organization chart; a narrow span indicates a tall organization chart.

Figure 9.13 is a simple example of the relationship between organization chart height and span of management. Organization chart A has a span of management of six, and organization chart B has a span of management of two. As a result, chart A is flatter than chart B. Both charts have the same number of individuals at the lowest level. The larger span of management in A is reduced in B merely by adding a level to B's organization chart.

An organization's structure should be built from top to bottom to ensure that appropriate spans of management are achieved at all levels. Increasing spans of management merely to eliminate certain management positions and thereby reduce

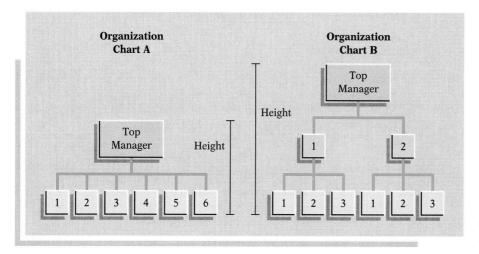

FIGURE 9.13
Relationship between
organization chart height and
span of management

salary expenses may be very shortsighted.[29] Increasing spans of management for objectives such as increasing the speed of organizational decision making or building a more flexible organization seems more appropriate for helping the organization achieve success in the longer run.[30]

Global Highlight: Reebok International Reorganizes to Better Respond

There can be several sound reasons for flattening the structure of an organization involved in international business. Paul B. Fireman, the chief executive officer at Reebok International, hopes that flattening his organization's structure will help organization members regain a spirit of worldwide entrepreneurship. According to Fireman, his predecessor, C. Joseph LaBonte, buried this spirit under several layers of management.

Fireman has other hopes for the flattening of Reebok's organization structure. For one, he hopes that his flatter organization structure will enable the company to be more responsive to the varying needs of consumers as well as its retailers throughout the world.

Fireman also hopes that fewer managers will mean that decisions can be made and implemented faster—that Reebok's leaner organization structure will help it to be more flexible, to move more quickly, and to be more competitive in the international business arena.

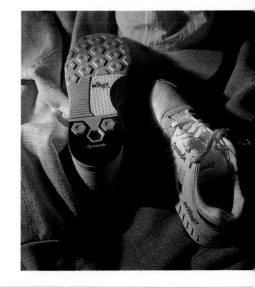

Scalar Relationships

The fourth main consideration of any organizing effort is **scalar relationships**—the chain of command. Organization is built on the premise that the individual at the top possesses the most authority and that other individuals' authority is scaled downward according to their relative position on the organization chart. The lower an individual's position on the organization chart, the less authority possessed.

Scalar relationships refer to the chain of command positioning of individuals on an organization chart.

Unity of command is a management principle that recommends that an individual have only one boss.

The scalar relationship, or chain of command, is related to the unity of command. **Unity of command** means that an individual should have only one boss. If too many bosses give orders, the probable result is confusion, contradiction, and frustration, a situation that usually results in ineffectiveness and inefficiency. Although the unity of command principle first appeared in more modern management literature well over seventy-five years ago, it is still discussed today as a critical ingredient of successful, contemporary organizations.[31]

Fayol has indicated that strict adherence to the chain of command is not always advisable.[32] Figure 9.14 serves to explain Fayol's rationale. If individual F needs information from individual G and follows the concept of chain of command, F has to go through individuals D, B, A, C, and E before reaching G. The information would get back to F only by going from G through E, C, A, B, and D. Obviously, this long and involved process can be very expensive for the organization in terms of time spent getting the information.

A **gangplank** is a communication channel extending from one organizational division to another but not shown in the lines of communication outlined on an organization chart. Use of Fayol's gangplank may be quicker, but it could be costly in the long run.

To decrease this expense, Fayol has recommended that in some situations a bridge, or **gangplank,** be used to allow F to go directly to G for information. This bridge is represented in Figure 9.14 by the dotted line that goes directly from F to G. Managers should use these organizational bridges with great care, however, because although F might get the information from G more quickly and cheaply, individuals D, B, A, C, and E are left out of the communication channel. The lack of information caused by Fayol's bridge might be more costly in the long run than would going through the established chain of command. If managers do use an organizational bridge, they must be extremely careful to inform all other appropriate individuals within the organization of the information they received.

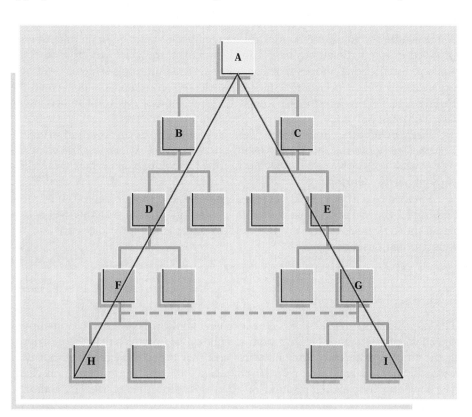

FIGURE 9.14

Sample organization chart showing that to always adhere to the chain of command is not advisable

Back to the Case

The last two major elements in classical organizing theory that a manager could reflect on are span of management and scalar relationships. For Roberts, span of management focuses on the number of subordinates that managers in various roles at MCI can successfully supervise. In thinking about span of management, Roberts might explore several important situational factors, such as similarities among various MCI activities, the extent to which MCI workers being managed are physically separated, and the complexity of various MCI work activities.

For example, Roberts should consider that merely signing up a business customer as a long-distance user is fairly simple and that installing a special equipment network within a company is much more difficult. Therefore, the span of management for workers doing the signing up should generally be larger than the span of management for workers doing the installation. Two other important factors Roberts should consider in determining spans of management for various MCI managers are the amount of time managers must spend coordinating workers' activities and the amount of time managers spend planning. With all of this information, Roberts should be quite capable of determining appropriate spans of management for MCI managers.

Action Summary

Reread the learning objectives that follow. Each objective is followed by questions. Answering these questions accurately will help you retain the most important concepts discussed in this chapter. After answering each question, check your answer with the answer key at the end of this chapter. (*Hint:* If you have doubt regarding the correct response, consult the page whose number follows the answer.)

Circle:

From studying this chapter, I will attempt to acquire:

1. **An understanding of the organizing function.**

   a. Of the five steps in the organizing process, which of the following is grossly out of order: (a) reflect on plans and objectives; (b) establish major tasks; (c) allocate resources and directives for subtasks; (d) divide major tasks into subtasks; (e) evaluate results of the implemented organizational strategy.

   a, b, c, d, e

   b. Proper execution of the organizing function normally results in minimal duplication of effort.

   T, F

2. **An appreciation for the complications of determining appropriate organizational structure.**

   a. The XYZ Corporation is organized as follows: it has (1) a president, (2) a vice president in charge of finance, (3) a vice president in charge of marketing, and (4) a vice president in charge of human resources management. This firm is organized on the: (a) functional basis; (b) manufacturing process basis; (c) customer basis; (d) territorial basis; (e) production basis.

   a, b, c, d, e

   b. All of the following forces are influences on the evolution of formal structure except: (a) forces in the manager; (b) forces in subordinates; (c) forces in the environment; (d) forces in the division of labor; (e) forces in the task.

   a, b, c, d, e

3. Insights on the advantages and disadvantages of division of labor.

a, b, c, d, e

    a. Extreme division of labor tends to result in: (a) human motivation; (b) boring jobs; (c) nonspecialized work; (d) decreased work skill; (e) all of the above.

a, b, c, d, e

    b. Which of the following is *not* a generally accepted advantage of division of labor within an organization: (a) workers' skills in performing their jobs tend to increase; (b) workers need to know only how to perform their specific work tasks; (c) workers do not waste time in moving from one task to another; (d) workers naturally tend to try to make their individual tasks easier and more efficient; (e) none of the above (all are advantages of the division of labor).

4. A working knowledge of the relationship between division of labor and coordination.

T, F

    a. Effective coordination is best achieved through close employee supervision.

T, F

    b. Mary Parker Follett has contended that managers should plan for coordination.

5. An understanding of span of management and the factors that influence its appropriateness.

a, b, c, d, e

    a. Of the factors listed, which one would have a tendency to increase (expand) the span of management: (a) subordinates are physically distant; (b) subordinates have similar functions; (c) subordinates have complex tasks; (d) subordinates' work needs close coordination; (e) manager spends much time in planning.

a, b, c, d, e

    b. The concept of span of management concerns: (a) seeing that managers at the same level have equal numbers of subordinates; (b) employee skill and motivation levels; (c) supervision of one less than the known number of subordinates; (d) a determination of the number of individuals a manager can effectively supervise; (e) a and d.

6. An understanding of scalar relationships.

a, b, c, d, e

    a. The management concept that recommends that employees should have one and only one boss is termed: (a) departmentalization; (b) function; (c) unity of command; (d) scalar relationship; (e) none of the above.

T, F

    b. According to Fayol, under no circumstances should a gangplank be used in organizations.

Introductory Case Wrap-Up: MCI

"MCI Communications Organizes to Be More Competitive" and its related back-to-the-case sections were written to help you better understand the management concepts contained in this chapter. Answer the following discussion questions about this introductory case to further enrich your understanding of the chapter content:

1. Does it seem reasonable that Roberts is attempting to better organize MCI in order to remain more competitive? Explain.

2. List all the questions you can think of that Roberts should ask himself in exploring how to best organize MCI.

3. Explain why it would be important for Roberts to ask each of the questions you listed.

Issues for Review and Discussion

1. What is organizing?

2. Explain the significance of organizing to the management system.

3. List the steps in the organizing process. Why should managers continually repeat these steps?

4. Can the organizing function be thought of as a subsystem? Explain.

5. Fully describe what Max Weber meant by the term *bureaucracy*.

6. Compare and contrast formal structure with informal structure.

7. List and explain three factors that management structure is based on, or contingent on. Draw three sample portions of organization charts that illustrate the factors you listed.

8. Describe the forces that influence formal structure. How do these forces collectively influence structure?

9. What is division of labor?

10. What are the advantages and disadvantages of employing division of labor within a management system?

11. Define *coordination*.

12. Does division of labor increase the need for coordination? Explain.

13. Summarize Mary Parker Follett's thoughts on how to establish and maintain coordination.

14. Is span of management an important management concept? Explain.

15. Do you think that similarity of functions, geographic contiguity, complexity of functions, coordination, and planning influence appropriate span of control in all management systems? Explain.

16. Summarize and evaluate Graicunas's contribution to span of management literature.

17. What is the relationship between span of management and *flat* and *tall* organizations?

18. What are scalar relationships?

19. Explain the rationale behind Fayol's position that always adhering to the chain of command is not necessarily advisable.

20. What caution should managers exercise when they use the gangplank Fayol described?

Building on What You Know

Directions

Review the Highlight feature below and answer its corresponding questions. Questions in this section focus on relating a Highlight appearing in this chapter to management concepts that you have learned in a previous chapter.

Review the Quality Highlight: Nike on page 269. In chapter 8 you studied various types of scheduling techniques available to managers. Could Gantt charts and PERT be useful to Nike managers in attempting to enhance coordination among design, marketing, and production departments? Be sure to include critical path analysis. Be as specific as possible in your responses.

Action Summary Answer Key

1. a. c, p. 258
   b. T, p. 258
2. a. a, p. 263
   b. d, pp. 266–267
3. a. b, p. 268
   b. e, p. 268
4. a. F, pp. 268–269
   b. T, pp. 268–269
5. a. b, p. 270
   b. d, p. 270
6. a. c, p. 274
   b. F, p. 274

Case Study

Organizing the Sedona Fire Department

by Robert E. Kemper

Less than an hour south of Flagstaff on U.S. 89A is Oak Creek Canyon, one of the most beautiful landmarks in Arizona, and at the south entrance of Oak Creek lies the picture-postcard town of Sedona. Combining the best of frontier style and contemporary materials, Sedona is a testament to an active, concerned community. In this land of eroded red-rock mesas and pillars, the town is in harmony with its setting.

Through the center of town runs a county line, so the community is represented by two separate fire districts: the Sedona–Red Rock Fire District in Yavapai County and the Sedona–Oak Creek Fire District in Coconino County. These districts functioned separately from their inception until July 1, 1985, when they signed an intergovernmental agreement to form the Sedona Fire Department (SFD). Although their activities are now combined, Arizona law prevents total merger with respect to tax dollars, land, buildings, and fire protection vehicles.

The SFD serves a region of 120 square miles, including the city of Sedona (incorporated in 1988) and some outlying areas. Eight fire stations, four in each district, protect the region. Volunteer members of the SFD are assigned to the station nearest their individual residences.

Members from both original districts govern the Sedona Fire Department. Each district has a five-member board that votes not only on district matters but also on matters concerning the SFD. Together, the boards hire a fire chief, who serves as the executive officer of the SFD and is responsible for general management and day-to-day operations.

The SFD is a volunteer-oriented organization, consisting of 121 volunteers and 24 full-time employees. An organizational chart located in the fire chief's office shows eleven divisions: (1) fire chief/deputy chief, (2) administrative, (3) fire marshall, (4) personnel, (5) repair and maintenance, (6) communications, (7) resources, (8) suppression, (9) emergency medical services (EMS), (10) nondivisional, and (11) finance. All division heads report to the fire chief. However, chapter 1 of the SFD "Organization and Rules and Regulations" describes only two divisions, the Fire Division and the EMS Division. These are in turn supported by six subcenters: administrative services section, communications division, fire prevention, repair and maintenance division, public information section, and resource division.

The Fire Division is responsible for suppressing and assisting in the prevention of hostile fires and hazardous situations within the SFD's operating boundaries. EMS provides emergency medical patient care, rescue, and transportation within those boundaries. The six subcenters are charged with providing appropriate support for those two primary functions.

The mission of the SFD is to save lives, protect property, and reduce human suffering within the scope and capabilities of the Fire and EMS Divisions. Department members acknowledge a loyalty and commitment to the ideals of public service and pledge always to act in the best interest of the Sedona community.

Job descriptions exist for some of the volunteer and paid employee positions, but not for some key full-time positions and certain volunteer jobs. The job descriptions in use are generally outdated and may either not describe actual duties performed or not encompass other legitimate duties belonging to the job.

Full-time employees receive performance evaluations. The form, however, is generic; employees are evaluated on major strengths and weaknesses but not on specifics of job performance. Furthermore, if an employee does not agree with his or her evaluation, there is little recourse. The only existing grievance procedures deal with disciplinary actions and terminations.

In fact, no SFD employee has ever received a bad performance evaluation. The previous fire chief's attitude toward personnel was more than benign; pay raises and promotions were automatic. As a result, some employees are filling posts for which they are not qualified; equipment purchases by individuals have been uncontrolled; some volunteers respond to emergency calls only after determining which full-time supervisor is on duty. Morale, of course, is low.

The new fire chief wants to modernize job descriptions, performance evaluations, and grievance procedures; up to $20,000 has been allocated for this project. He has asked the personnel director, who had no prior experience or formal training in human resource management, to prepare bid specifications. Her specifications identify the following needs: (1) updated performance evaluation forms designed to match each job description and to evaluate the actual work required; (2) grievance procedures for performance evaluations, disciplinary actions, and terminations; (3) personnel guidelines on how to document, evaluate, and discipline employees; (4) a program to train the personnel manager and supervisors on use of personnel guidelines; and (5) a systematic program to assist the personnel manager to create an updated personnel handbook.

Discussion Questions

1. Based on the bid specifications prepared by the personnel manager, evaluate her understanding of the five steps in the organizing process. How does she plan to organize personnel management for the Sedona Fire Department?

2. On the basis of material provided in the case, evaluate the organization structure of the Sedona Fire Department.

3. Clearly the organizational structure of the SFD is based primarily on work functions. Is it based on territory in any way? How?

4. How do the concepts of division of labor and span of management relate to the problems described at SFD?

Organization of a Family Business at Alixandre Furs

The businesslike organization of a company can, as a general rule, be successfully achieved by adhering to the basic principles outlined in the text for this chapter. A structure is chosen, and a graphic representation can be made as an organizational chart. Tasks and portions of tasks are assigned to different members of the management and production teams. Their efforts are coordinated to create a rational progression toward completion of the assigned tasks. The span of management—responsibility for completion of tasks and authority over the individuals and teams who complete them—is determined according to the factors that influence any one manager's or executive's reasonable ability to provide solid control. Finally, a chain of command emerges, which, like the structure and span, can then be represented graphically.

How does this logical system of organizing apply to a family business? How might informal family relationships and internal stresses affect the organization as a whole?

In 1927, at the brink of the Depression, Russian immigrant Samuel Shulman founded a company in his adopted home town of New York—Alixandre Furs. From the beginning, his company targeted a clientele that demanded high quality, and that clientele has carried Alixandre Furs through the Depression and through good times, through "Republican cloth coats" and through antifur activism. Samuel Shulman determined that his company would always buy the best-quality pelts and would sew to the specifications of the best fur designers—and Alixandre Furs dominates the quality fur market now as it did 50 years ago.

Stanley Shulman joined the family business in 1952 after completing a master's program in finance at Columbia University. He had planned to go to work on Wall Street, but his father told him that was unacceptable, so Stanley Shulman, like everyone else in his family, obeyed his father. Now he is president of the most successful furrier in the United States.

It was not easy for Stanley Shulman to abandon his dream of becoming a Wall Street wizard, and he harbored great resentment: "My brother Edwin and I—who had preceded me in the business—both worked in the factory at first. And we used to look in the showroom and I used to kick him and say, 'We'll never get in the showroom. . . ' and he used to kick me and say, 'Keep quiet, put your head down, work. We'll get there someday.' And the someday happened." Stanley Shulman is now king of the most glamorous showroom in the fur industry.

Edwin Shulman, vice president and treasurer of Alixandre Furs, is in charge of what he calls "the dirty end" of the business. He manages production, from the purchasing and preparation of pelts through sewing the designer labels into finished garments. Over almost forty years in business together, he and his brother have become good partners. "We both understand each other and we respect each other, and we have different facets of the business which we are now bringing third generation in[to], to teach."

However, Stanley and Edwin Shulman's children have not been coerced into their fathers' business as their fathers were before them. They have been exposed to Alixandre all their lives and have been taught that it is a business and must be nurtured as a business by a devoted team. Having chosen to join the team, three sons are now learning that business from the inside out.

"It's extremely important that much thought be given to the relationships among the principals of the firm and the children," says Stanley Shulman. "We run this business very much as if it were a team and that third generation is like . . . the junior varsity, and during these years they fill these niches and find out where they're comfortable also. It isn't something that comes down from on top. It's done mutually." Shulman is particularly proud of what he has learned from his son Brett through working together. When Stanley Shulman and his father disagreed, they didn't communicate; when Brett Shulman and his father disagree, they concentrate on resolving the business issue rather than on their relationship—"and it saves so much anguish and pain and wasted time that it's tremendous."

Together, Stanley and Edwin Shulman control the most glamorous, and the largest, furrier in the United States, with contracts overseas as well. Their mutual respect and their solid professional relationship has been key to ensuring Alixandre Fur's continued domination of the high-end fur market. They learned how to manage a fur business from their father, but they have learned to manage a family business by considering the needs of the business separately from the needs of the family. "There were ways of doing things," Stanley Shulman learned, "and if you couldn't do it in the best possible way, you shouldn't do it; you should get out and do something else."

Video Case Questions

1. How do environmental forces of family relationships affect management at Alixandre Furs in this generation? How did they affect management in the past?

2. Consider Figures 9.5 through 9.8 on pp. 263–264. Which of these department formulas applies to Alixandre Furs?

3. The text states that a primary focus of organizing human resources is not merely assigning jobs, but also determining how each person's efforts can best be combined with the efforts of others to reach organizational objectives. Based on the case material, how does Stanley Shulman support this statement?

4. Based on the information in this case, does use of Fayol's "gangplank" concept to bypass time lost communicating up and down the chain of command seem to be a good idea for Alixandre Furs?

5. Give two examples of ways in which problems with coordination of labor might cause tremendous difficulties at Alixandre Furs.

Video Case Activities

1. Draw the organizational chart for Alixandre Furs, based on material in the video.

2. Consideration of organizational objectives and plans is the first step in the organizing process. List what you believe to be the organizational objectives at Alixandre Furs.

Chapter 10

tudent Learning Objectives

From studying this chapter, I will attempt to acquire:

1. An understanding of the relationship of responsibility, authority, and delegation.

2. Information on how to divide and clarify job activities of individuals within an organization.

3. Knowledge of the differences among line authority, staff authority, and functional authority.

4. An appreciation for the issues that can cause conflict in line and staff relationships.

5. Insights on the value of accountability to the organization.

6. An understanding of how to delegate.

7. A strategy for eliminating various barriers to delegation.

8. A working knowledge of when and how an organization should be decentralized.

Responsibility, Authority, and Delegation

Chapter Outline

"FAMOUS" AMOS: THE ORGANIZING CHALLENGE

Wally "Famous" Amos, a pioneer of the now burgeoning $450-million-a-year gourmet cookie industry, . . . is an entrepreneur who is famous not only for his delicious chocolate chip cookies but [also] for his upbeat take on life in general. This former William Morris Talent Agency employee, the first [African American] ever hired by the agency to be a talent agent, founded his company in 1975 with $24,000 (in exchange for 25 percent of stock) lent by celebrity friends Helen Reddy, her husband Jeff Wald, and singer Marvin Gaye. Amos had been baking cookies since he was a teenager (his Aunt Della got him started) and he regularly used them as a "hook" to charm the producers and other Hollywood executives he met during his 14 years as an agent. People kept telling Amos he should sell his cookies, but it wasn't until he took a downturn as an agent that he decided he wanted a more stable business of his own to run.

> He traded in his tailored suits for Hawaiian-style shirts, baggy pants, and a panama hat.

Amos opened his first store, which an artist friend designed, on Sunset Boulevard. He traded in his tailored suits for Hawaiian-style shirts, baggy pants, and a panama hat. Then he had himself photographed and put on each package of Famous Amos cookies. For the opening, he sent out 2,500 invitations to the press, and, as a band played, poured champagne and dispensed cookies to his willing publicity pawns. By the next morning, lines formed outside his door as people tried to purchase part of L.A.'s latest media event.

The Famous Amos Chocolate Chip Cookie Company quickly grew to [include] stores in Santa Monica and Hawaii. The company grossed $300,000 in its first year, $4 million in 1979, and $10 million in 1987. Today, there are 27 "fresh-baked" retail outlets across the country, and Famous Amos cookies line the shelves of thousands of grocery stores and supermarkets worldwide.

Recently, Amos sold his company to Denver real estate investors and entrepreneurs Jeffrey and Ronald Baer. Wally Amos remains a director and a shareholder of the company that he has sold. The outstanding initial success of "Famous" Amos Cookies is primarily based upon the ability of Amos to see a market and to sell his vision. One of the most pressing challenges that the company must now meet is how to professionally manage the company that has evolved. Meeting ever present management challenges like how to best organize the efforts of employees throughout the company will be a prerequisite to company success in the future.

From CNN Cable News Network "Pinnacle" interview, September 24, 1988 and Dennis P. Kimbro, "Dreamers: Black Sales Heros and Their Secrets," *Success* 37 (May 1990), 40–41.

WHAT'S AHEAD

The introductory case describes how Wally Amos initiated and built his "Famous" Amos Cookie Company, which he eventually sold to Jeffrey and Ronald Baer. The case ends with the implication that the company has gone beyond an initial fledgling phase and must now focus more on meeting normal management challenges if the company is to maintain its existence. The case indicates that one such challenge is how best to organize the efforts of employees throughout the company. The information in this chapter, organizing the job activities of individuals within an organization, should be of great value to managers like Amos and the Baers. Three major elements of organizing—(1) responsibility, (2) authority, and (3) delegation—are presented.

Chapter 9 has discussed how to apply principles of organizational structure, division of labor, span of management, and scalar relationships to establish an orderly use of resources within the management system. Productivity within any management system, however, results from specific activities performed by individuals within that organization. An effective organizing effort therefore includes not only a rationale for the orderly use of management system resources but also three other elements of organizing that specifically channel the activities of organization members. These three elements are responsibility, authority, and delegation.

RESPONSIBILITY

Perhaps the most fundamental method of channeling the activity of individuals within an organization, **responsibility** is the obligation to perform assigned activities. It is the self-assumed commitment to handle a job to the best of one's ability. The source of responsibility lies within the individual. A person who accepts a job agrees to carry out a series of duties or activities or to see that someone else carries them out.[1] The act of accepting the job means that the person is obligated to a superior to see that job activities are successfully completed. Because responsibility is an obligation that a person *accepts*, there is no way it can be delegated or passed on to a subordinate.

A summary of an individual's job activities within an organization is usually in a formal statement called a **job description**—a listing of specific activities that must be performed by whoever holds the position. Unclear job descriptions can confuse employees and may cause them to lose interest in their jobs.[2] When properly designed, job descriptions communicate job content to employees, establish performance levels that employees must maintain, and act as a guide that employees can follow to help the organization reach its objectives.[3]

Job activities are delegated by management to enhance the accomplishment of management system objectives. Management analyzes its objectives and assigns specific duties that will lead to reaching those objectives. A sound organizing strategy includes specific job activities for each individual within the organization. As objectives and other conditions within the management system change, however, individual job activities within the organization may have to be changed.

Responsibility is the obligation to perform assigned activities.

A job description is a listing of specific activities that must be performed to accomplish some task or job.

Three areas related to responsibility are (1) dividing job activities, (2) clarifying job activities of managers, and (3) being responsible. Each of these topics is discussed in the sections that follow.

Dividing Job Activities

Because many individuals work within a given management system, organizing necessarily involves dividing job activities among a number of people. One individual cannot be obligated or responsible for performing all of the activities within an organization. Some method of distributing job activities and thereby channeling the activities of several individuals is needed.

The phrase *functional similarity* refers to what many management theorists believe to be the most basic method of dividing job activities. Stated simply, the **functional similarity method** suggests that management should take four basic interrelated steps to divide job activities. These steps, in the sequence in which they should be taken, are (1) management examines management system objectives, (2) management designates appropriate activities that must be performed to reach those objectives, (3) management designs specific jobs by grouping similar activities, and (4) management makes specific individuals responsible for performing those jobs. Figure 10.1 illustrates the sequence of activities suggested by the functional similarity method.

At least three additional guides can be used to supplement the functional similarity method.[4] The first of these supplemental guides suggests that overlapping responsibility should be avoided in making job activity divisions. **Overlapping responsibility** exists when more than one individual is responsible for the same activity. Generally speaking, only one individual should be responsible for completing any one activity. When two or more employees are unclear about who should do a job because of overlapping responsibility, it usually leads to conflict and poor working relationships among the employees.[5] Often, neither employee will do the job, each assuming the other will do it. The second supplemental guide is to avoid responsibility gaps. A **responsibility gap** exists when certain tasks are not included in the responsibility area of any individual. In essence, a responsibility gap creates a situation in which nobody within the organization is obligated to perform certain necessary activities. The third supplemental guide is to avoid creat-

The **functional similarity method** is a method for dividing job activities in the organization.

Overlapping responsibility is the situation in which more than one individual is responsible for the same activity.

Responsibility gap is the situation in which certain organizational tasks are not included in the responsibility area of any individual organization member.

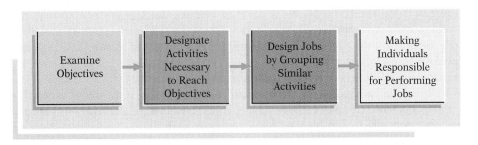

FIGURE 10.1

Sequence of activities for the functional similarity method of dividing responsibility

ing job activities for accomplishing tasks that do not enhance goal attainment. Organization members should be obligated to perform only those activities that lead to goal attainment.

When job responsibilities are distributed inappropriately, both responsibility gaps and overlapping responsibilities result. The effects of responsibility gaps on product quality are obvious, but overlapping responsibilities also impair product quality. When two (or more) employees are uncertain as to who is responsible for a task, four outcomes are possible:

1. One of the two may perform the job; the other may either forget to or choose not to do the job—neither of which are desirable outcomes for product quality control.

2. Both employees may perform the job; at the least, this results in duplicated effort, which dampens employee morale, and at the worst, one employee may actually diminish the value of the other employee's work, resulting in a decrement in product quality.

3. Neither employee may perform the job, each expecting the other to have done it.

4. The employees may spend valuable time negotiating each aspect and phase of each job, to carefully intermesh their job responsibilities, thus minimizing both duplication of effort and responsibility gaps. Though time consuming, this is actually the most desirable option in terms of product quality.

Each of these outcomes clearly affects both product quality and overall productivity.

Quality Highlight: Motorola Streamlines Responsibility

The managers at Motorola realized that they needed to streamline their organizational structure, to minimize overlapping responsibilities, as well as responsibility gaps. An additional objective of this effort was to lower their labor costs while performing the same amount of work, in order to become more competitive in their markets. Management became committed to the tasks of eliminating unneeded positions.

The first step in Motorola's process was to ask each division manager to draw a more productive organization chart showing relationships from their level all the way down to the worker level. The drawing of this new organization chart caused managers to make judgments about whether the number of levels of management and spans of control that existed were appropriate for the organization. Organization charts for all divisions were combined to develop Motorola's new organization structure.

Motorola's streamlining efforts resulted in higher product quality as well as a more productive organization. A major reason why organizational productivity increased was that management became aware of and eliminated overlapping responsibilities within the company. Jobs that had two or more people responsible for accomplishing them were redesigned so that only one person was performing them. Management estimated that the new organization structure resulted in a savings of over $4.3 million.

$\mathcal{B}$ack to the Case

Amos (and later the Baers), managers in the introductory case, face the challenge of organizing required activities of various individuals within the "Famous" Amos Cookie Company. Organizing such activity should help the company ensure its success if the managers derive the activities directly from company objectives. Amos and the Baers' specific steps to organize these should include analysis of company objectives, outlining specific company activities that must be performed to reach those objectives, designing company jobs by the grouping of similar activities, and assigning these jobs to company personnel. To supplement these steps, Amos and the Baers must be careful not to create overlapping responsibilities, responsibility gaps, or responsibilities for activities that do not lead directly to goal attainment.

Clarifying Job Activities of Managers

Clarification of the job activities of managers is as important as, if not more important than, dividing the job activities of nonmanagers, because managers affect greater portions of resources within the management system. Hence, such factors as responsibility gaps usually have a more significant impact on the management system when they relate to managers as opposed to nonmanagers.

One process used to clarify management job activities "enables each manager to actively participate with his or her superiors, peers, and subordinates in systematically describing the managerial job to be done and then clarifying the role each manager plays in relationship to his or her work group and to the organization."[6] The purpose of this interaction is to assure that no overlaps or gaps in perceived management responsibilities exist and that managers are performing only the activities that lead to the attainment of management system objectives. Although this process typically has been used to clarify the responsibilities of managers, it may also be effective in clarifying the responsibilities of nonmanagers.

A **management responsibility guide** is a tool that can be used to clarify the responsibilities of various managers in the organization.

A specific tool developed to implement this interaction process is the **management responsibility guide**.[7] This guide, some version of which is used in most organizations, assists organization members in describing the various responsibility relationships that exist in their organization and summarizing how the responsibilities of various managers within their organization relate to one another.

The seven main organizational responsibility relationships described by this tool are listed in Table 10.1. Once organization members decide which of these relationships exist within their organization, they define the relationships between these responsibilities.

Being Responsible

Managers can be described as responsible if they perform the activities they are obligated to perform.[8] Because managers typically have more impact on an organization than nonmanagers, responsible managers are a prerequisite for management system success. Several studies have shown that responsible management behavior is highly valued by top executives, because the responsible manager guides many other individuals within the organization in performing their duties appropriately.

TABLE 10.1 Seven responsibility relationships among managers, as used in the management responsibility guide

1. *General Responsibility*—The individual guides and directs the execution of the function through the person accepting operating responsibility.
2. *Operating Responsibility*—The individual is directly responsible for the execution of the function.
3. *Specific Responsibility*—The individual is responsible for executing a specific or limited portion of the function.
4. *Must Be Consulted*—The individual, if the decision affects his or her area, must be called on before any decision is made or approval is granted, to render advice or relate information, but not to make the decision or grant approval.
5. *May Be Consulted*—The individual may be called on to relate information, render advice, or make recommendations.
6. *Must Be Notified*—The individual must be notified of action that has been taken.
7. *Must Approve*—The individual (other than persons holding general and operating responsibility) must approve or disapprove.

The degree of responsibility that managers possess can be determined by analysis of managers' (1) attitude toward and conduct with subordinates, (2) behavior with upper management, (3) behavior with other groups, and (4) personal attitudes and values. Table 10.2 summarizes what each of these dimensions includes for the responsible manager.

 ack to the Case

In organizing the activities of employees, Amos (and the Baers) must recognize, for example, that a department manager's job activities within the company, as well as those of his or her subordinates, are a major factor in company success.

TABLE 10.2 Four key dimensions of responsible management behavior

Behavior with Subordinates	Behavior with Upper Management	Behavior with Other Groups	Personal Attitudes and Values
Responsible managers— 1. Take complete charge of their work groups 2. Pass praise and credit along to subordinates 3. Stay close to problems and activities 4. Take action to maintain productivity and are willing to terminate poor performers if necessary	Responsible managers— 1. Accept criticism for mistakes and buffer their groups from excessive criticism 2. Ensure that their groups meet management expectations and objectives	Responsible managers make sure that any gaps between their areas and those of other managers are securely filled	Responsible managers— 1. Identify with the group 2. Put organizational goals ahead of personal desires or activities 3. Perform tasks for which there is no immediate reward but that help subordinates, the company, or both 4. Conserve corporate resources as if the resources were their own

Because actions of department managers have an impact on all personnel within the department, a department manager's job activities must be well defined. From the viewpoint of company divisions, one department manager's job activities should be coordinated with the activities of other departments. Amos and the Baers might choose to use the management responsibility guide process to achieve this coordination of responsibilities.

Over all, for managers within the Famous Amos Cookie Company to be responsible managers, they must perform the activities that they are obligated to perform. They must also respond appropriately to their subordinates, their superiors in the company, and their peers in other departments in the division.

AUTHORITY

Individuals are assigned job activities to channel their behavior appropriately. Once they have been given the assignments they must be given a commensurate amount of authority to perform the obligations.

Authority is the right to perform or command.

Authority is the right to perform or command. It allows its holders to act in certain designated ways and to directly influence the actions of others through orders. It also allows its holder to allocate the organization's resources in order to achieve the objectives of the organization.[9]

The following example illustrates the relationship between job activities and authority. Two primary tasks for which a particular service station manager is responsible are pumping gasoline and repairing automobiles. The manager has the complete authority necessary to perform either of these tasks. If he or she chooses, however, the activity of automobile repair can be delegated to the assistant manager. Along with the activity of repairing, however, the assistant also should be delegated the authority to order parts, to command certain attendants to help, and to do anything else necessary to perform the repair jobs. Without this authority, the assistant manager may find it impossible to complete the delegated job activities.

Practically speaking, authority is a factor that only increases the probability that a specific command will be obeyed.[10] The following excerpt emphasizes that authority does not always exact obedience:

> People who have never exercised power have all kinds of curious ideas about it. The popular notion of top leadership is a fantasy of capricious power: the top man [*or woman*] presses a button and something remarkable happens; he [*or she*] gives an order as the whim strikes him [*or her*], and it is obeyed. Actually, the capricious use of power is relatively rare except in some large dictatorships and some small family firms. Most leaders are hedged around by constraints— tradition, constitutional limitations, the realities of the external situation, rights and privileges of followers, the requirements of team work, and most of all, the inexorable demands of large-scale organization, which does not operate on capriciousness. In short, most power is wielded circumspectly.[11]

As chapter 9 showed, the positioning of individuals on an organization chart indicates the relative amount of authority delegated to each individual. Individuals toward the top of the chart possess more authority than individuals toward the bottom. Chester Barnard writes, however, that in reality the source of authority is determined not by decree from the formal organization but by whether or not authority is accepted by those existing under it. According to Barnard, authority exists and will exact obedience only if it is accepted.

In line with this rationale, Barnard defines *authority* as the character of communication by which an order is accepted by an individual as governing the actions the individual takes within the system. Barnard maintains that authority will be accepted only if the individual (1) can understand the order being communicated, (2) believes the order is consistent with the purpose of the organization, (3) sees the order as compatible with personal interests, and (4) is mentally and physically able to comply with the order. The fewer of these four conditions that exist, the smaller the probability that authority will be accepted and that obedience will be exacted.

Barnard also offers some guidance on what action managers can take to raise the odds that their commands will be accepted and obeyed. According to Barnard, more and more of a manager's commands will be accepted over the long term if:[12]

1. Formal channels of communication are used by the manager and are familiar to all organization members.

2. Each organization member has an assigned formal communication channel through which orders are received.

3. The line of communication between manager and subordinate is as direct as possible.

4. The complete chain of command is used to issue orders.

5. Managers possess adequate communication skills.

6. Managers use formal communication lines only for organizational business.

7. A command is authenticated as coming from a manager.

 ack to the Case

Amos and the Baers must be sure that any individuals within their company who are delegated job activities also are delegated a commensurate amount of authority to give related orders and to accomplish their obligated activities. Company managers must recognize that authority must be accepted if obedience is to be exacted. To increase the probability of acceptance, care should be taken to ensure that individuals understand internal orders and see orders as being consistent with the objectives of both the department they work in as well as the company. Employees should perceive that the orders that they are given are compatible with their individual interests, and they should see themselves as being mentally and physically able to follow the orders.

Types of Authority

Three main types of authority can exist within an organization: (1) line authority, (2) staff authority, and (3) functional authority. Each type exists only to enable individuals to carry out the different types of responsibilities with which they have been charged.

Line and Staff Authority

Line authority, the most fundamental authority within an organization, reflects existing superior–subordinate relationships. It is the right to make decisions and

Line authority is the right to make decisions and to give orders concerning the production-, sales-, or finance-related behavior of subordinates.

Staff authority is the right to advise or assist those who possess line authority.

to give orders concerning the production-, sales-, or finance-related behavior of subordinates. Over all, line authority pertains to matters directly involving management system production, sales, and finance and, as a result, the attainment of objectives. Individuals directly responsible for these areas within the organization are delegated line authority to assist them in performing their obligated activities.

Whereas line authority involves giving orders concerning production activities, **staff authority** is the right to advise or assist those who possess line authority and other staff personnel. Staff authority exists to enable those responsible for improving the effectiveness of line personnel to perform their required tasks. Examples of organization members with staff authority are members of accounting and human resource departments. Obviously, line and staff personnel must work closely together to maintain the efficiency and effectiveness of the organization. To help ensure that line and staff personnel work together productively, a manager must be sure that both groups understand the organizational mission, have specific objectives to strive for, and understand how they act as partners to help the organization reach its objectives.[13]

Size is perhaps the most significant factor in determining whether or not staff personnel are used within an organization. Generally, the larger the organization, the greater the need and ability to pay for staff personnel. As an organization grows, management generally finds a greater need for more expertise in more diversified areas. Although small organizations may also need this expertise, they may find that hiring part-time consultants when a need arises may be more practical than hiring a full-time staff individual who may not always be kept busy.

Figure 10.2 shows how line-staff relationships can be presented on an organization chart. The plant manager on this chart has line authority over each imme-

FIGURE 10.2

Possible line-staff relationships in selected organizational areas

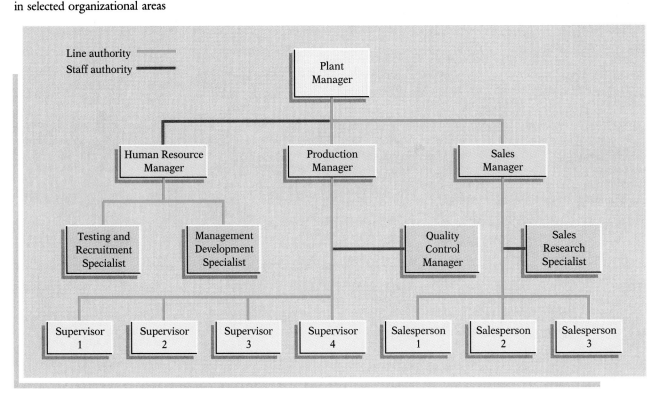

diate subordinate—human resource manager, production manager, and sales manager. The human resource manager also has staff authority in relation to the plant manager. This simply means that the human resource manager possesses the right to advise the plant manager on human resource matters. Final decisions concerning human resource matters, however, are in the hands of the plant manager, the individual holding line authority. Similar relationships exist between the sales manager and the sales research specialist, as well as between the production manager and the quality control manager. To carry the example of the human resource manager's staff authority one step further, Table 10.3 contains a detailed listing of the types of decision areas over which a human resource manager generally has jurisdiction. These decision areas are not directly related to production but could ultimately have a favorable influence on it.

Roles of Staff Personnel. Harold Stieglitz has pinpointed the following three roles that staff personnel typically perform to assist line personnel:[14]

1. *The advisory or counseling role.* The professional expertise of staff personnel in this role is aimed at solving organizational problems. The staff personnel are seen as internal consultants, with the relationship between line and staff being similar to that between a professional and a client. An example of this role

---

TABLE 10.3   Typical decision areas for a human resource director

Human resource records/reports	Employee communications/publications
Human resource research	Executive compensation administration
Insurance benefits administration	Human resource planning
Unemployment compensation administration	Safety programs/OSHA compliance
EEO compliance/affirmative action	Management development
Wage/salary/administration	Food services
Workers' compensation administration	Performance evaluation, nonmanagement
Tuition aid/scholarships	Community relations/fund drives
Job evaluation	Suggestion systems
Health/medical services	Thrift/savings plan administration
Retirement preparation programs	Security/plant protection
Preemployment testing	Organization development
Vacation/leave processing	Management appraisal/MBO
Induction/orientation	Stock plan administration
Promotion/transfer/separation processing	Skill training, nonmanagement
Counseling/employee assistance programs	Public relations
Pension/profit-sharing plan administration	Administrative services (mail, PBX, phone, messengers, fax, photocopying, etc.)
College recruiting	
Recreation/social/recognition programs	Payroll processing
Recruiting/interviewing/hiring	Travel/transportation services administration
	Library
Attitude surveys	Maintenance/janitorial services
Union/labor relations	
Complaint/disciplinary procedures	
Relocation services administration	
Supervisory training	

might be the staff quality control manager who advises the line production manager on possible technical modifications to the production process that will help maintain the quality of products produced.

2. *The service role.* Staff personnel in this role provide services that can more efficiently and effectively be provided by a single centralized staff group than by many individuals within the organization attempting to provide the services themselves. This role can probably best be understood by our viewing staff personnel as suppliers and line personnel as customers. For example, members of a human resource department recruit, employ, and train workers for all organizational departments. In essence, they are the suppliers of workers; and the various organizational departments needing workers are their customers.

3. *The control role.* In this role, staff personnel help establish a mechanism for evaluating the effectiveness of organizational plans. Staff personnel exercising this role are seen as representatives, or agents, of top management.

These three are not the only roles performed by staff personnel within organizations, but they are the main ones. In the final analysis, the role of staff personnel in any organization should be specially designed to best meet the needs inherent within that organization. It is entirely possible that to meet the needs of a particular organization, staff personnel must perform some combination of the three main roles.

Ethics Highlight: General Electric Staff Organizes Renovation

At General Electric, a social responsibility project was recently organized and managed by one of its staff personnel, Bob Hess, a marketing specialist. As part of a sales meeting, G.E. salespeople renovated San Diego's Vincent de Paul Joan Kroc urban center for the homeless. The project was part of a company program in which tired buildings used by a worthy nonprofit organization are selected and then renovated by its employees. At the beginning of the renovation day, G.E. workers formed teams, each having a captain, a safety expert, and a task expert. In about eight hours, G.E. work teams completed 95 percent of the job, renovating space for 400 beds and preparing space for 200 additional beds.

The handling of sales training at General Electric reflects a very progressive management attitude. Through staff activities, the company has been able to demonstrate a desire and ability to make a worthwhile contribution to society.

Conflict in Line-Staff Relationships. Most management practitioners readily admit that a noticeable amount of conflict usually centers around line-staff relationships.[15] From the viewpoint of line personnel, conflict is created between line and staff personnel because staff personnel tend to assume line authority, do not give sound advice, steal credit for success, do not keep line personnel informed, and do not see the whole picture. From the viewpoint of staff personnel, conflict is created between line and staff personnel because line personnel do not make proper use of staff personnel, resist new ideas, and do not give staff personnel enough authority.

To overcome these potential conflicts, staff personnel must strive to emphasize the objectives of the organization as a whole, encourage and educate line personnel in the appropriate use of staff personnel, obtain needed skill if it is not already possessed, and deal with resistance to change rather than view this resistance as an immovable barrier. Line personnel's effort in minimizing line-staff conflict should include using staff personnel wherever possible, making proper use of the abilities of staff personnel, and keeping staff personnel appropriately informed.[16]

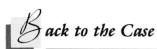
Back to the Case

Assuming that a main objective of the Famous Amos Cookie Company is to produce the highest quality cookie possible, Famous Amos personnel who are directly responsible for achieving this objective should possess line authority to perform their responsibilities. For example, individuals responsible for purchasing ingredients for cookies must be given the right to do everything necessary to obtain cookie ingredients that will result in the best possible cookies.

This organization may need one or more individuals charged with the responsibility of assisting the line through a staff position. Perhaps such individuals could be responsible for advising Famous Amos management through the results of various surveys focusing on issues such as how the consumer rates the quality of Famous Amos Cookies relative to that of a competitor (Mrs. Fields' Cookies, for example), or how employees should be trained to become more productive. Anyone responsible for advising the line should be delegated appropriate staff authority.

As in all organizations, the potential for conflict between Famous Amos Cookie Company line personnel and staff personnel probably would be significant. Company management should be aware of this potential and encourage both line and staff personnel to minimize it.

Functional Authority

Functional authority is the right to give orders within a segment of the organization in which this right is normally nonexistent. This authority usually is assigned to individuals to complement the line or staff authority they already possess. Functional authority generally covers only specific task areas and is operational only for designated amounts of time. It typically is possessed by individuals who, in order to meet their responsibilities, must be able to exercise some control over organization members in other areas.

The vice president for finance in a particular organization is an example of someone with functional authority. Among his or her basic responsibilities, this manager is obligated to monitor the financial situation within the management system. To accomplish this monitoring, however, he or she must have appropriate financial information continually flowing in from various segments of the organization. The vice president for finance usually is delegated the functional authority to order various departments to furnish the kinds and amounts of information he

Functional authority is the right to give orders within a segment of the management system in which the right is normally nonexistent.

or she needs to perform an analysis. In reality, the functional authority this manager possesses allows him or her to give orders to personnel within departments in which he or she normally cannot give orders.

From the previous discussion on line authority, staff authority, and functional authority, it is reasonable to conclude that although authority can exist within an organization in various forms, these forms should be used in a combination that will best enable individuals to carry out their assigned responsibilities and thereby best help the management system accomplish its objectives. When trying to decide what authority combination is best for a particular organization, managers must keep in mind that the use of each type of authority naturally has both advantages and disadvantages (see Table 10.4). Figure 10.3 is an organization chart that shows how the three types of authority could be combined for the overall benefit of a hospital management system.

Accountability

Accountability is the management philosophy that individuals are held liable, or accountable, for how well they use their authority or live up to their responsibility of performing predetermined activities.

Accountability is the management philosophy whereby individuals are held liable, or accountable, for how well they use their authority and live up to their responsibility of performing predetermined activities.[17] The concept of accountability implies that if predetermined activities are not performed, some type of penalty, or punishment, is justifiably forthcoming.[18] One company executive has summed up the punishment theme of accountability with the statement, "Individuals who do not perform well simply will not be around too long."[19] Also implied in the accountability concept, however, is the notion that some kind of reward follows if predetermined activities are performed well.

TABLE 10.4 Advantages and disadvantages of line authority, staff authority, and functional authority

Advantages	*Disadvantages*
Line Authority	
Maintains simplicity	Neglects specialists in planning
Makes clear division of authority	Overworks key people
Encourages speedy action	Depends on retention of a few key people
Staff Authority	
Enables specialists to give expert advice	Confuses organization if functions are not clear
Frees line executive of detailed analysis	Reduces power of experts to put recommendations into action
Affords young specialists a means of training	Tends toward centralization of organization
Functional Authority	
Relieves line executives of routine specialized decisions	Makes relationships more complex
Provides framework for applying expert knowledge	Makes limits of authority of each specialist a difficult coordination problem
Relieves pressure of need for large numbers of well-rounded executives	Tends toward centralization of organization

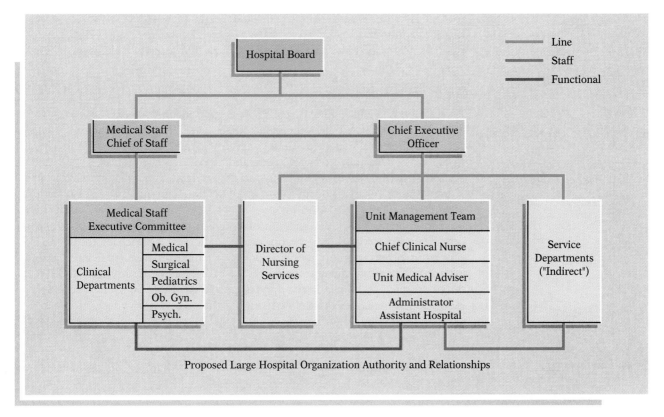

FIGURE 10.3
Proposed design for incorporating three types of authority in a hospital

ack to the Case

Functional authority and accountability are two additional factors that Amos and the Baers must consider when organizing employee activities within the Famous Amos Cookie Company. Some employee may have to be delegated functional authority to supplement the line or staff authority already possessed. For example, the accountant, a staff person who advises management on financial affairs, may need to gather financial results of various company retail outlets throughout the country. Functional authority would enable staff individuals to command that this information be channeled to them.

In organizing employee activity, Amos and the Baers should also stress the concept of accountability—that living up to assigned responsibilities brings rewards, and not living up to them has negative consequences.

DELEGATION

Previous sections of this chapter have discussed responsibility and authority as complementary factors that channel activity within the organization. **Delegation** is the actual process of assigning job activities and corresponding authority to

Delegation is the process of assigning job activities and related authority to specific individuals in the organization.

specific individuals within the organization. This section focuses on (1) steps in the delegation process, (2) obstacles to the delegation process, (3) elimination of obstacles to the delegation process, and (4) centralization and decentralization.

Steps in the Delegation Process

According to Newman and Warren, there are three steps in the delegation process, any of which may be either observable or implied.[20] The first of the three steps is assigning specific duties to the individual. In all cases, the manager must be sure that the subordinate has a clear understanding of what these duties entail. Whenever possible, the activities should be stated in operational terms so the subordinate knows exactly what action must be taken to perform the assigned duties. The second step of the delegation process involves granting appropriate authority to the subordinate. The subordinate must be given the right and power within the organization to accomplish the duties assigned. The last step of the delegation process involves creating the obligation for the subordinate to perform the duties assigned. The subordinate must be aware of the responsibility to complete the duties assigned and must accept that responsibility. Table 10.5 offers several suggestions that managers can follow to ensure the success of the delegation process.

Obstacles to the Delegation Process

Obstacles that can make delegation within an organization difficult or even impossible can be classified in three general categories: (1) obstacles related to the supervisor, (2) obstacles related to subordinates, and (3) obstacles related to organizations.

One supervisor-related obstacle to delegation is that some supervisors resist delegating their authority to subordinates because they find using their authority very satisfying. The cartoon characterizes a manager who seems to delegate simply

TABLE 10.5 Guidelines for making delegation effective

- Give employees freedom to pursue tasks in their own way.

- Establish mutually agreed-upon results and performance standards related to delegated tasks.

- Encourage an active role on the part of employees in defining, implementing, and communicating progress on tasks.

- Entrust employees with completion of whole projects or tasks whenever possible.

- Explain relevance of delegated tasks to larger projects or to department or organization goals.

- Give employees the authority necessary to accomplish tasks.

- Allow employees not ordinarily available access to information, people, and departments necessary to perform delegated task.

- Provide training and guidance necessary for employees to complete delegated tasks satisfactorily.

- When possible, delegate tasks on basis of employee interests.

Wall Street Journal. March 9, 1990, A13.

because he enjoys exercising authority. Two other such obstacles are that supervisors may be afraid that their subordinates will not do a job well or that surrendering some of their authority may be seen by others as a sign of weakness. Also, if supervisors are insecure in their job or see specific activities as being extremely important to their personal success, they may find it difficult to put the performance of these activities into the hands of others.

Even if supervisors wish to delegate to subordinates, they may encounter several subordinate-related roadblocks. First, subordinates may be reluctant to accept delegated authority for fear of failure or because of a lack of self-confidence. These two obstacles probably will be especially apparent if subordinates have not experienced the use of delegated authority previously. Other obstacles include the feeling that the supervisor will not be available for guidance once the delegation is made or that being a recipient of additional authority may complicate comfortable working relationships.

Characteristics of the organization itself also may make delegation difficult. For example, a very small organization may present the supervisor with only a minimal number of activities to be delegated. In addition, if few job activities and little authority have been delegated over the history of the organization, an attempt to initiate the delegation process could make individuals reluctant and apprehensive. In essence, the supervisor would be introducing a change in procedure that some members of the organization might resist very strongly.

Eliminating Obstacles to the Delegation Process

Delegation usually results in several organizational advantages, thus the elimination of obstacles to delegation is important to managers. Advantages of delegation include improved subordinate involvement and interest, more free time for the supervisor to accomplish tasks, and, as the organization gets larger, assistance from subordinates in completing tasks the manager simply wouldn't have time for otherwise.[21] Although delegation also has potential disadvantages, such as the possibility of the manager losing track of the progress of a task once it has been delegated,[22] the potential advantages of some degree of delegation generally outweigh the potential disadvantages.

What can managers do to eliminate obstacles to the delegation process? First of all, they must continually strive to uncover any obstacles to delegation that exist in their organization. Next, they should approach specific action to eliminate these obstacles with the understanding that the obstacles may be deeply ingrained and may therefore require long-term time and effort. Specific managerial actions usually necessary to overcome obstacles include building subordinate confidence in the use of delegated authority, minimizing the impact of delegated authority on established working relationships, and helping the delegatee with problems whenever necessary.

Koontz, O'Donnell, and Weihrich say that for managers to overcome the obstacles to delegation, they must possess certain critical characteristics. These characteristics include the willingness to consider seriously the ideas of others, the insight to allow subordinates the free rein necessary to carry out their responsibilities, trust in the abilities of subordinates, and the ability to allow people to learn from their mistakes without suffering unreasonable penalties for making them.[23]

Back to the Case

To delegate effectively within the Famous Amos Cookie Company, managers must assign specific duties to individuals, grant corresponding authority to these individuals, and create the awareness within these individuals that they are obligated to perform these activities.

In encouraging the use of delegation within their company, Amos and the Baers must be aware that obstacles to delegation may exist within managers, their subordinates, or the departments within which they work. They must be sure that managers meet the delegation challenge: discovering which delegation obstacles exist within their work environments and then taking steps to eliminate them. If Famous Amos managers are to be successful delegators, they also must be willing to consider the ideas of their subordinates, allow them the free rein necessary to perform their assigned tasks, trust them, and help them learn from their mistakes without suffering unreasonable penalties.

Centralization and Decentralization

Centralization is the situation in which a minimal number of job activities and a minimal amount of authority are delegated to subordinates.

Decentralization is the situation in which a significant number of job activities and a maximum amount of authority are delegated to subordinates.

Noticeable differences exist in the relative number of job activities and the relative amount of authority delegated to subordinates from organization to organization. In practice, it is not a case of delegation either existing or not existing within an organization. Delegation exists in most organizations but in varying degrees.

The terms **centralization** and **decentralization** describe the general degree to which delegation exists within an organization. These terms can be visualized at opposite ends of a delegation continuum (see Figure 10.4). From this figure, it is apparent that centralization implies that a minimal number of job activities and a minimal amount of authority have been delegated to subordinates by management, whereas decentralization implies the opposite.

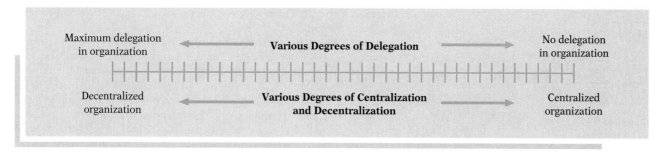

FIGURE 10.4

Centralized and decentralized organizations on delegation continuum

The problems that practicing managers usually face are determining whether to further decentralize an organization and deciding how to decentralize if that course of action is advisable. The section that follows contains practical suggestions on whether an organization should be decentralized and how decentralization should take place.

Decentralizing an Organization: A Contingency Viewpoint

The degree of decentralization that managers should employ depends on, or is contingent on, their own unique organizational situation. Specific questions to determine the amount of decentralization appropriate for a situation include:

1. *What is the present size of the organization?* As stated earlier, the larger the organization, the greater the likelihood that decentralization will be advantageous. As an organization increases in size, managers have to assume more and more responsibility and different types of tasks. Delegation is typically an effective means of helping managers keep up with this increased work load.

2. *Where are the organization's customers located?* As a general rule, the more physically separated the organization's customers are, the more viable a significant amount of decentralization is. Decentralization places appropriate management resources close to the customers and thereby allows for quick customer service. J.C. Penney, for example, decentralized its purchasing activities to give managers the ability to buy merchandise best suited to customers of their individual stores.[24]

3. *How homogeneous is the product line of the organization?* As the product line becomes more heterogeneous, or diversified, the appropriateness of decentralization generally increases. Different kinds of decisions, talents, and resources are needed to manufacture different products. Decentralization usually minimizes the potential confusion that can result from diversification by separating organizational resources by product and keeping pertinent decision making close to the manufacturing process.

4. *Where are organizational suppliers?* The location of raw materials from which the organization's products are manufactured is another important consideration. Time loss and perhaps even transportation costs associated with shipping

raw materials over great distances from supplier to manufacturer could support
the need for decentralizing certain functions.

For example, the wood necessary to manufacture a certain type of bedroom
set may be available only from tree growers in certain northern states. If the
bedroom set is an important enough product line for a furniture company and
if the costs of transporting the lumber are substantial, a sound basis for a
decision to decentralize probably exists. The effect of this decision might be
the building of a plant that produces only bedroom sets in a northern state
close to where the necessary wood is readily available. The advantages of such
a costly decision, of course, would accrue to the organization only over the
long term.

5. *Is there a need for quick decisions in the organization?* If there is a need for
speedy decision making within the organization, a considerable amount of
decentralization is probably in order. Decentralization avoids red tape and
allows the subordinate to whom authority has been delegated to make on-the-
spot decisions if necessary.[25] This delegation is advisable only if the potential
delegatees have the ability to make sound decisions. If they don't, the increased
decision-making speed via delegation has no advantage. Quick or slow, a decision cannot reap benefits for the organization if it is unsound.

6. *Is creativity a desirable feature of the organization?* If creativity is desirable, then
some decentralization probably is advisable. Decentralization allows delegatees
the freedom to find better ways of doing things. The mere existence of this
freedom can encourage the incorporation of new and more creative techniques
within the task process.[26]

*Global Highlight: The Bank of Tokyo
Decentralizes to Compete*

The number of Japanese banks in the United States has grown dramatically in the
last few years. In order to remain competitive, these banks have been forced to
reexamine and improve the technologies that they use to provide service to customers. To keep up with competing banks in the area of technology, many Japanese
banks like the Bank of Toyko New York Group delegate a significant amount of
authority to their U.S. managers. This authority allows managers of Japanese
banks in the United States to monitor the technology level of surrounding banks
and to take steps to ensure that the technology of Japanese banks is competitive.

According to Yoji Izumi, the top information executive at the Bank of Tokyo
New York Group, the trend toward greater delegation of technology decisions in
foreign banks is likely to grow in the future. Izumi believes that this is one tactic
that Japanese banks can use to ensure that their technology is competitive with
U.S. banks as well as other local foreign banks. Not all Japanese bank managers
agree with Izumi, however. For example, technology decisions for Chiba Bank's
New York branch are made in Japan by a centralized information specialist
division.

$\mathscr{B}$ack to the Case

Centralization implies that few job activities and little authority have been delegated to subordinates; decentralization implies that many job activities and much authority have been delegated. Managers within the Famous Amos Cookie Company will have to determine the best degree of delegation for their individual situations. For guidelines, Famous Amos managers can use the rules of thumb that greater degrees of delegation probably will be appropriate for the company as departments becomes larger, as retail outlets become more dispersed and diversified, and as the need for quick decision making and creativity increases.

Decentralization at Massey-Ferguson: A Classic Example

Positive decentralization is decentralization that is advantageous for the organization in which it is being implemented; negative decentralization is the opposite. One way to ascertain how an organization should be decentralized is to study a classic example of an organization with positive decentralization: Massey-Ferguson.[27]

Massey-Ferguson is a worldwide farm equipment manufacturer that has enjoyed noticeable success with decentralization over the past several years.[28] The company has three guidelines for determining the degree of decentralization of decision making that is appropriate for a situation:[29]

1. The competence to make decisions must be possessed by the person to whom authority is delegated. A derivative of this is that the superior must have confidence in the subordinate to whom authority is delegated.

2. Adequate and reliable information pertinent to the decision is required by the person making the decision. Decision-making authority therefore cannot be pushed below the point at which all information bearing on the decision is available.

3. If a decision affects more than one unit of the enterprise, the authority to make the decision must rest with the manager accountable for the most units affected by the decision.

Massey-Ferguson also encourages a definite attitude toward decentralization. The company's organization manual indicates that delegation is not delegation in name only but a frame of mind that includes both what a supervisor says to subordinates and the way the supervisor acts toward them. Managers at Massey-Ferguson are encouraged to allow subordinates to make a reasonable number of mistakes and to help subordinates learn from these mistakes.

Another feature of the positive decentralization at Massey-Ferguson is that decentralization is complemented by centralization:

> The organization plan that best serves our total requirements is a blend of centralized and decentralized elements. Marketing and manufacturing responsibilities, together with supporting service functions, are located as close as possible to local markets. Activities that determine the long-range character of the company, such as the planning and control of the product line, the planning and control of facilities and money, and the planning of the strategy to react to changes in the patterns of international trade, are highly centralized.[30]

Massey-Ferguson management recognizes that decentralization is not necessarily an either/or decision and uses the strengths of both centralization and decentralization to its advantage.

Not all activities at Massey-Ferguson, however, are eligible for decentralization consideration. Only management is allowed to follow through on the following responsibilities:[31]

1. The responsibility for determining the overall objectives of the enterprise.

2. The responsibility for formulating the policies that guide the enterprise.

3. The final responsibility for the control of the business within the total range of the objectives and policies, including control over any changes in the nature of the business.

4. The responsibility for product design where a product decision affects more than one area of accountability.

5. The responsibility for planning for the achievement of overall objectives and for measuring actual performance against those plans.

6. The final approval of corporate plans or budgets.

7. The decisions pertaining to the availability and the application of general company funds.

8. The responsibility for capital investment plans.

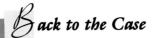

Back to the Case

The Massey-Ferguson decentralization situation could give Amos and the Baers many valuable insights on what characteristics the decentralization process within the company should assume. First, Famous Amos managers should use definite guidelines to decide whether their situation warrants added decentralization. In general, additional delegation would be warranted within the company as the competence of subordinates increases, as Famous Amos managers' confidence in their subordinates increases, and as more adequate and reliable decision-making information within the company becomes available to subordinates. For delegation to be advantageous for the Famous Amos Cookie Company, company managers must help subordinates learn from their mistakes. Depending on their situations, individual Famous Amos managers may want to consider supplementing decentralization with centralization.

Action Summary

Reread the learning objectives that follow. Each objective is followed by questions. Answering these questions accurately will help you retain the most important concepts discussed in this chapter. After answering each question, check your answer with the answer key at the end of this chapter. (*Hint:* If you have doubt regarding the correct response, consult the page whose number follows the answer.)

From studying this chapter, I will attempt to acquire: *Circle:*

1. **An understanding of the relationship of responsibility, authority, and delegation.**

   a. Responsibility is a person's self-assumed commitment to handle a job to   T, F
   the best of his or her ability.

   b. Which of the following elements is *not* an integral part of an effective or-   a, b, c, d, e
   ganizing effort: (a) rationale for the orderly use of management system
   resources; (b) responsibility; (c) authority; (d) delegation; (e) none of the
   above (they are all important).

2. **Information on how to divide and clarify job activities of individuals within an organization.**

   a. Which of the following is *not* one of the four basic steps for dividing respon-   a, b, c, d, e
   sibility by the functional similarity method: (a) designing specific jobs by
   grouping similar activities; (b) examining management system objectives;
   (c) formulating management system objectives; (d) designating appropriate
   activities that must be performed to reach objectives; (e) making specific
   individuals responsible for performing activities.

   b. A management responsibility guide can assist organization members in   a, b, c, d, e
   which of the following ways: (a) by describing the various responsibility
   relationships that exist in their organization; (b) by summarizing how the
   responsibilities of various managers within the organization relate to one
   another; (c) by identifying manager work experience; (d) a and b; (e) none
   of the above.

3. **Knowledge of the differences among line authority, staff authority, and functional authority.**

   a. The production manager has mainly: (a) functional authority; (b) staff   a, b, c, d, e
   authority; (c) line authority; (d) a and c; (e) all of the above.

   b. An example of functional authority is the vice president of finance being   T, F
   delegated the authority to order various departments to furnish him or her
   with the kinds and amounts of information needed to perform an analysis.

4. **An appreciation for the issues that can cause conflict in line and staff relationships.**

   a. From the viewpoint of staff personnel, one reason for line-staff conflict is   a, b, c, d, e
   that line personnel: (a) do not make proper use of staff personnel; (b) resist
   new ideas; (c) do not give staff personnel enough authority; (d) a and c;
   (e) all of the above.

   b. From the viewpoint of line personnel, conflicts between line and staff can   a, b, c, d, e
   occur for which of the following reasons: (a) staff may assume line author-
   ity; (b) staff may not offer sound advice; (c) staff may steal credit for success;
   (d) staff may fail to keep line informed; (e) all of the above.

5. **Insights on the value of accountability to the organization.**

   a. Accountability is how well individuals live up to their responsibility for   T, F
   performing predetermined activities.

   b. Rewarding employees for good performance is most closely related to: a, b, c, d, e
   (a) simplicity; (b) a clear division of authority; (c) centralization; (d) decentralization; (e) accountability.

6. An understanding of how to delegate.

T, F
a. The correct ordering of the steps in the delegation process is the assignment of duties, the creation of responsibility, and the granting of authority.

a, b, c, d, e
b. Which of the following are obstacles to the delegation process: (a) obstacles related to supervisors; (b) obstacles related to subordinates; (c) obstacles related to the organization; (d) all of the above; (e) none of the above.

7. A strategy for eliminating various barriers to delegation.

a, b, c, d, e
a. Eliminating obstacles to delegation usually results in which of the following advantages: (a) improved subordinate involvement and interest; (b) more free time for the supervisor; (c) assistance for the supervisor to accomplish tasks he or she wouldn't be able to do otherwise; (d) all of the above; (e) none of the above.

T, F
b. Generally, the potential advantages of some degree of delegating outweigh the disadvantages.

8. A working knowledge of when and how an organization should be decentralized.

a, b, c, d, e
a. A high degree of centralization within an organization would be most advisable under which of the following conditions: (a) the organization is relatively small; (b) the organization is relatively large; (c) creativity is important to the firm's success; (d) the delegatees have the ability to make sound decisions; (e) the product line is diversified.

T, F
b. According to the management philosophy that exists at Massey-Ferguson, the responsibility for formulating the policies that guide the organization should be highly decentralized.

Introductory Case Wrap-Up: Famous Amos

"Famous Amos: The Organizing Challenge" (p. 284) and its related back-to-the-case sections were written to help you better understand the management concepts contained in this chapter. Answer the following discussion questions about this introductory case to further enrich your understanding of the chapter content:

1. What first step would you recommend that Amos

and the Baers take in organizing the activities of individuals within their company? Why?

2. Discuss the roles of responsibility, authority, and accountability in organizing the activities of individuals within the Famous Amos company.

3. At this time, do you think that the company should be more centralized or more decentralized? Why?

Issues for Review and Discussion

1. What is responsibility, and why does it exist in organizations?

2. Explain the process a manager would go through to divide responsibility within an organization.

3. What is a management responsibility guide, and how is it used?

4. List and summarize the four main dimensions of responsible management behavior.

5. What is authority, and why does it exist in organizations?

6. Describe the relationship between responsibility and authority.

7. Explain Barnard's notion of authority and acceptance.

8. What steps can managers take to increase the probability that subordinates will accept their authority? Be sure to explain how each of these steps increases the probability.

9. Summarize the relationship that generally exists between line and staff personnel.

10. Explain three roles that staff personnel can perform in organizations.

11. List five possible causes of conflict in line-staff relationships and suggest appropriate action to minimize the effect of these causes.

12. What is functional authority?

13. Give an example of how functional authority actually works in an organization.

14. Compare the relative advantages and disadvantages of line, staff, and functional authority.

15. What is accountability?

16. Define *delegation* and list the steps of the delegation process.

17. List three obstacles to the delegation process and suggest action for eliminating them.

18. What is the relationship between delegation and decentralization?

19. What is the difference between decentralization and centralization?

Building on What You Know

Directions

Review the Highlight feature as indicated below and answer its corresponding questions. Questions in this section focus on relating a Highlight appearing in this chapter to management concepts that you have learned in a previous chapter.

Review the Global Highlight: The Bank of Tokyo Decentralizes to Compete on page 302.

In chapter 9 you studied a concept called span of management. How should the concept of span of management influence such decisions to decentralize?

Action Summary Answer Key

1. a. T, p. 285
   b. e, p. 285
2. a. c, p. 286
   b. d, pp. 288–289
3. a. c, pp. 291–292
   b. T, pp. 295–296
4. a. e, pp. 294–295
   b. e, pp. 294–295
5. a. F, p. 296
   b. e, p. 296
6. a. F, p. 298
   b. d, pp. 298–299
7. a. d, pp. 299–300
   b. T, p. 300
8. a. a, p. 301
   b. F, pp. 303–304

Case Study

Taking Charge at Value Line Incorporated

by Robert E. Kemper, Northern Arizona University

Value Line Incorporated provides financial advisory services by publishing investment information and by offering advisory services to individual, institutional, and mutual fund clients. Value Line publications have become a virtual bible of stock information for small investors. By the early 1980s, Arnold Bernhard, Value Line's strong-willed founder, had done everything for his company but choose a successor.

In the 1960s, Bernhard had brought his son, Van, into the company, but internal conflict had driven Van back out. Then Bernhard tried a succession of three non-family managers; none worked out. Finally, he brought in his daughter, Jean Buttner, in 1983. Her only experience in the securities and publishing businesses was through summer jobs at Value Line while she was a Vassar student in the 1950s, but she began with some sound new ideas. "Jean was intelligent and eager to learn," a Value Line veteran recalled. "She approved better computer systems, and she apparently urged her father to pay more attention to employees' needs." Although some analysts took delight in finding gaps in her knowledge, Buttner was made president of Value Line in 1984.

After she assumed command, Value Line grew along with the bull market until late 1987, when misfortune struck. The October stock market crash frightened investors and chilled their interest in stock services, and in December, Arnold Bernhard died. Buttner then added the corporate chair and CEO duties to her presidential role. With her family controlling over 80 percent of Value Line stock, she was undeniably in charge.

Jean Buttner walked into trouble. In her first 15 months at the helm, Value Line's earnings weakened, quarter by quarter. Circulation of the *Value Line Investment Survey,* its flagship publication, fell to 91,800 by September 1989, from an all-time high of 111,000 in 1983.

Some employees began to assail Buttner's management style. She allegedly irritated them by subjecting them to "room inspections" and requiring messy offices to be tidied; she required all employees—including executives—to sign in and out when they left during office hours; she proposed to pay research analysts on a piecework basis. Other employees, however, were convinced that she would make Value Line bigger and better than ever.

Two top managers jumped ship during Buttner's first year as CEO. Peter Lowenstein, the general counsel, quit in early 1988, apparently enraged by a request to tidy his office. He was quickly replaced. In October, Mark Tavel, the head of investment management, left after 20 years at Value Line to join Rothschild Incorporated. Norfolk Dredging Company and several other pension clients dropped Value Line's fund management service as a result.

Following Tavel's departure, some managers were required to sign noncompetition and confidentiality agreements if they wished to remain on important committees. A ban was placed on taking home notebooks without written permission, justified by Buttner "so everyone would feel comfortable discussing new ideas without seeing them walk out the door."

Prior to the turmoil of these years, Value Line had long been the epitome of a successful niche company. Its *Value Line Investment Survey,* a series of fact-filled, one page reports ranking up to 1,700 stocks, is "probably the most useful quick source of stock information around," says David Dreman, a New York money manager. A rival, Standard and Poors, concedes that Value Line is "clearly number one in the individual market." Historically, the business has been very profitable, with profit a lofty 15 to 28 percent of revenue.

Nonetheless, the company had some weaknesses, too. Operations were not computerized until 1986; pension management, mutual fund, and electronic data bases were also late to computerize; equipment was difficult to procure; and traditional pay and expense accounts for employees were low. Good analysts could double their pay in three years but were unlikely to get big raises after that—so Value Line had always been a revolving door.

Value Line reported a record $20.5 million profit for the year ending April 30, 1988, on a revenue of $74.7 million, but then profits began to slip. By fiscal year 1990, profits had fallen to $12.5 million, with revenue at only $63.5 million. It is hoped that new projects will allow profits to boom once again.

Jean Buttner plans to expand Value Line's activities outside of publishing stock research information, which still accounts for about two thirds of the company's revenue. Targeted growth areas are mutual fund management (Value Line already manages about $2.1 billion of funds) and institutional money management (now about $1.3 billion). Value Line also plans to publish a new bond newsletter. Other innovations may be less likely to succeed; plans to offer asset allocation strategies for institutional clients will pit Value Line against established competitors in a crowded field, and sales of computer disk listings of stock information are already dominated by Standard and Poors' *Compustat.*

Discussion Questions

1. Given that Value Line has a reputation as a "revolving door" for employees, do you think Jean Buttner should maintain a relatively centralized or decentralized organizational structure? Why?

2. Barnard has identified four prerequisites for the acceptance of authority: An individual must understand the order being given, believe the order to be consistent with organizational purpose, believe it compatible with personal interests, and be able to comply with the order. Based on these, how might Buttner have undermined her own authority at Value Line?

3. Sign-in sheets, noncompetition agreements, and the ban on taking home work notes all suggest that Buttner is trying to develop in Value Line's staff a greater sense of _____ .

4. Suggest a possible reason that Arnold Bernhard ran through four candidates for a successor prior to choosing his daughter Jean.

Lillian Vernon: Queen of the Catalogues

Lillian Vernon is the founder and chief executive officer of the Lillian Vernon Corporation, a $150-million-dollar catalogue sales company. Although sales are primarily within the United States, merchandise is purchased from all over the world. Items in a typical Lillian Vernon catalogue range from soap dishes to rocking horses, from taffeta clothes hangers to fishing caps with fans in the crown. The company publishes over 20 catalogues each year, and in each, there is always "something for everyone."

Lillian Vernon's first venture into mail-order sales was a far cry from the giant company that she recently took public, however. It was 1951. She was pregnant with son Fred (now the president of the Lillian Vernon Corporation), and she was bored with staying at home. In the early 1950s, though, most married women were not expected to have a career outside the home, so Lillian Vernon started her business at home with a $2,000 stake. She took out ads in the back pages of *Seventeen,* to offer accessories manufactured by her father. One small success followed another; within three years, she was ready to sell through direct-mail catalogues.

Since the 1950s, the tenor of the U.S. work force has changed, and by the 1990s, most women are employed out of the home. As a result, they have less time to spend shopping. Catalogues have proliferated, and mail-order sales have boomed. Lillian Vernon's company now processes 20,000 orders each day in New York and ships over four million packages annually from their new Virginia business center. They are riding the crest of the biggest wave to hit U.S. consumers in decades.

Vernon feels that an essential building block in her company's success is responsiveness to the consumer. "We just say 'Send it back if you don't like it. We'll give you a refund; we'll replace it.' And we feel that is how we have built loyalty in our customers and how we have built a repeat business." Being responsive and responsible to the customer is a hallmark of any successful mail-order enterprise.

Lillian Vernon asserts that good management is learned by example, and she sees herself as a responsible but driven businessperson. She hopes that her example inspires the women working for her company now. "We have a number of female vice presidents," she says. "They're very, very successful; they're very well paid. . . . Equality is really equal pay for equal jobs, and I think we've just not done that in America."

Responsibility to customers and to employees is only one aspect of good managing, however. Vernon perceives some managerial skills in terms of talent— "a buyer is like a dancer or a singer." However, regardless of innate talent, a good manager is always learning. When asked how she discovered that bossy, dictatorial relationships are no more effective at work than in a family, Vernon points out that she tried it that way, and it didn't work. By trusting employees to take authority for their areas and their actions, she has parlayed her years of hard work into major success on a national scale.

Vernon's son David is vice president of the Lillian Vernon Corporation for public affairs. As such, he is responsible for much of the outward face of the company, including areas such as customer service and catalogue distribution. Other key personnel in a mail-order sales company include the buyers, order-takers, warehouse staff and shipping clerks, financial managers, and catalogue designers. There are specialists in such disparate specialties as inventory control, import–export regulations, computer management systems, and product photography.

Lillian Vernon does not feel threatened by weak economic forecasts. "People always have enough money to spoil the baby," she says, and her catalogues always offer perfect gifts for spoiling the baby—and for everyone else. "I feel I have this innate talent for things. I'm in the thing business!"

Video Case Questions

1. In the Lillian Vernon Corporation, do you think there is mostly line authority or staff authority? Who in the organization might have functional authority?
2. What aspects of organizational management do you think should probably not be decentralized for the Lillian Vernon Corporation? Why not?
3. Assume that all organizational operations in the New Rochelle, New York, offices are related to taking orders and performing customer-service functions, and all organizational operations in the Virginia Beach, Virginia, facility are related to shipping out orders. List three possible responsibility gaps.
4. Comment on the type of power Lillian Vernon wields. Specifically, does she believe in giving orders? What does this say about her as a manager?

Video Case Activities

1. Imagine that you are employed in the purchasing department of the Lillian Vernon Corporation; you manage the buying activities for kitchenware (pots and pans, dish towels, matched sets of measuring cups, and the like). Construct a list of responsibility guidelines to clarify your job duties (*Hint:* See Table 10.1 for ideas).
2. Now imagine you are a manager in the telephone-order area. In what ways might you delegate job activities to your employees, and what sorts of decisions would you not allow them to make independently?

Chapter 11

 tudent Learning Objectives

From studying this chapter, I will attempt to acquire:

1. An overall understanding of how appropriate human resources can be provided for the organization.

2. An appreciation for the relationship among recruitment efforts, an open position, sources of human resources, and the law.

3. Insights on the use of tests and assessment centers in employee selection.

4. An understanding of how the training process operates.

5. A concept of what performance appraisals are and how they best can be conducted.

Managing Human Resources

hapter Outline

GETTING THE RIGHT PEOPLE FOR UNIVERSAL STUDIOS

The new Universal Studios Florida (Orlando) is part film production center and part tourist park. In anticipation of hiring employees for the grand opening of the tourist park section of the operation, the company ran an ad in a local paper.

Management found that some people will do almost anything to get a job at Universal Studios Florida. One job seeker paid for an airplane to tow a banner over the studio tour's office in Orlando to get attention. A man who applied for an advertising position sent a wedding-cake ornament, complete with bride and groom figurines. He said he and Universal would be a "match made in heaven." Another aspiring publicist sent a shoe box with one shoe inside. He said he wanted to get his foot in the door.

The tourist park . . . received more than 30,000 resumes for 2,500 positions.

In response to the ad and other recruiting efforts, the tourist park operation received more than 30,000 resumes for the 2,500 positions it needed to fill. Interest in Universal's jobs continues to build, and the company's human resources department recently reported that it receives about 250 applications and dozens of telephone inquiries each day.

The studio tour itself is not in the business of hiring performers and technicians who work on movies and TV shows—that's the job of film producers who lease sound stages from Universal. Universal Studios Florida is owned by MCA, Inc., which also owns Universal Studios Hollywood in Universal City, California, and Rank Organisation PLC in London.

In fact, most of the jobs at Universal Studios Florida have little to do with Hollywood. Jobs such as cooks, cashiers, parking attendants, security officers, and ride operators can be found at most other tourist attractions in Central Florida, including, of course, the Disney-MGM Studios Theme Park.

When Universal receives an application, it enters the information into its "applicant tracking system" computer and then mails postcards with E.T.'s picture, thanking applicants for their interest. In some instances, an applicant will be called in for an interview. But usually prospects are told that limited job opportunities are available.

From "Movie Theme Park Is Rehearsal for Foreign Venture," *Marketing News* 24 (July 9, 1990), 5; Adam Yeomans, "Job Seekers Go All Out at Universal," *The Orlando Sentinel* (September 27, 1989), C1, C6.

*The introductory case discusses an unusually high interest shown by people in working for the tourist park segment of Universal Studios Florida. The task of hiring not just people, but the **right** people is part of managing human resources in an organization. This chapter discusses the process of managing human resources within an organization and illustrates how hiring the right employees fits within this process. This chapter focuses on the process by first defining appropriate human resources and then examining the steps to be followed in providing them.*

The emphasis in chapter 10 has been on organizing the activity of individuals within the management system. To this end, responsibility, authority, and delegation were discussed in detail. This chapter continues to explore the relationship between individuals and organizing by discussing how appropriate human resources can be provided for the organization.

DEFINING APPROPRIATE HUMAN RESOURCES

The phrase **appropriate human resources** refers to the individuals within the organization who make a valuable contribution to management system goal attainment. This contribution, of course, is a result of productivity in the positions they hold. The phrase *inappropriate human resources* refers to organization members who do not make a valuable contribution to the attainment of management system objectives. In essence, these individuals are ineffective in their jobs.

Productivity in all organizations is determined by how human resources interact and combine to use all other management system resources. Such factors as background, age, job-related experience, and level of formal education all have some role in determining the degree of appropriateness of the individual to the organization. Although the process of providing appropriate human resources for the organization is involved and somewhat subjective, the following section offers insights on how to increase the success of this process.

Appropriate human resources are the individuals in the organization who make a valuable contribution to management system goal attainment.

STEPS IN PROVIDING APPROPRIATE HUMAN RESOURCES

To provide appropriate human resources to fill either managerial or nonmanagerial openings, managers follow four sequential steps: (1) recruitment, (2) selection, (3) training, and (4) performance appraisal. Figure 11.1 illustrates these steps.

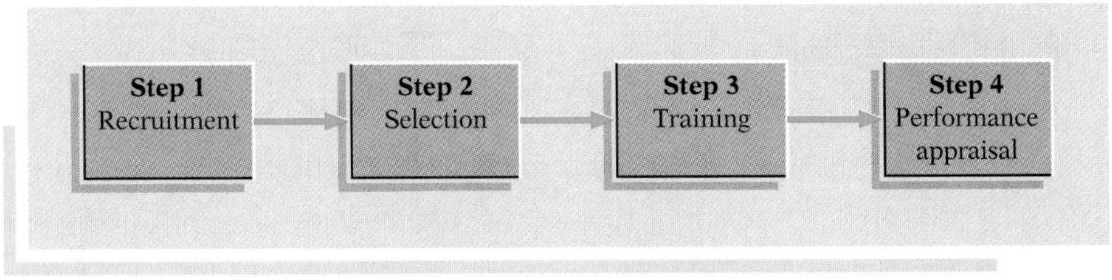

Step 1 Recruitment → **Step 2** Selection → **Step 3** Training → **Step 4** Performance appraisal

FIGURE 11.1

Four sequential steps to provide appropriate human resources for an organization

315

Recruitment

Recruitment is the initial attraction and screening of the total supply of prospective human resources available to fill a position.

Recruitment is the initial attraction and screening of the total supply of prospective human resources available to fill a position. Its purpose is to narrow a large field of prospective employees to a relatively small group of individuals from which someone eventually will be hired. To be effective, recruiters must know (1) the job they are trying to fill, (2) where potential human resources can be located, and (3) how the law influences recruiting efforts.

Knowing the Job

Recruitment activities must begin with a thorough understanding of the position to be filled so the broad range of potential employees can be narrowed intelligently. **Job analysis** is a technique commonly used to gain an understanding of a position. Basically, job analysis is aimed at determining a **job description** (the activities a job entails)[1] and a **job specification** (the characteristics of the individual who should be hired for the job). Figure 11.2 shows the relationship of job analysis to job description and job specification.

Job analysis is a technique commonly used to gain an understanding of what a task entails and the type of individual who should be hired to perform the task.

A **job description** is a list of specific activities that must be performed to accomplish some task or job.

A **job specification** is a list of characteristics of the individual who should be hired to perform a specific task or job.

The U.S. Civil Service Commission has developed a procedure for performing a job analysis (see Table 11.1).[2] As with all job analysis procedures, the Civil Service procedure uses information gathering as the primary means of determining what workers do and how and why they do it. Naturally, the quality of the job analysis depends on the accuracy of information gathered.[3] This information is used to develop both a job description and a job specification.

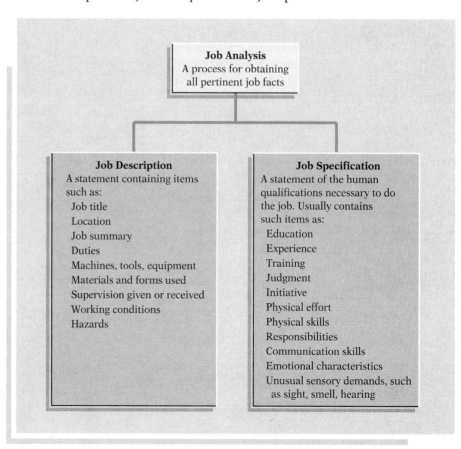

FIGURE 11.2

Relationship of job analysis, job description, and job specification

TABLE 11.1 Information to obtain when performing a job analysis

Identifying Information (such as):

Name of incumbent
Organization/unit
Title and series
Date
Interviewer

Brief Summary of Job:

(This statement will include the primary duties of the job. It may be prepared in advance from class specifications, job descriptions, or other sources. However, it should be checked for accuracy using the task statements resulting from the analysis.)

Job Tasks:

What does the worker do? How does the worker do it? Why? What output is produced?
What tools, procedures, aids are involved? How much time does it take to do the task?
How often does the worker perform the task in a day, week, month, or year?

Knowledge, Skills, and Abilities Required:

What does it take to perform each task in terms of the following?
1. Knowledge required
   a. What subject matter areas are covered by the task?
   b. What facts or principles must the worker have an acquaintance with or understand in these subject matter areas?
   c. Describe the level, degree, and breadth of knowledge required in these areas or subjects.
2. Skills required
   a. What activities must the worker perform with ease and precision?
   b. What are the manual skills required to operate machines, vehicles, equipment, or to use tools?
3. Abilities required
   a. What is the nature and level of language ability, written or oral, required of the worker on the job?
      Are there complex oral or written ideas involved in performing the task, or simple instructional materials?
   b. What mathematical ability must the worker have? Will the worker use simple arithmetic, complex algebra?
   c. What reasoning or problem-solving ability must the worker have?
   d. What instructions must the worker follow? Are they simple, detailed, involved, abstract?
   e. What interpersonal abilities are required? What supervisory or managing abilities are required?
   f. What physical abilities such as strength, coordination, and visual acuity must the worker have?

Physical Activities:

Describe the frequency and degree to which the incumbent is engaged in such activities as: pulling, pushing, throwing, carrying, kneeling, sitting, running, crawling, reaching, climbing.

TABLE 11.1 Information to obtain when performing a job analysis (*cont.*)

Environmental Conditions:

   Describe the frequency and degree to which the incumbent will encounter working under such conditions as these: cramped quarters, moving objects, vibration, inadequate ventilation.

Typical Work Incidents:

   1. Situations involving the interpretation of feelings, ideas, or facts in terms of personal viewpoint.
   2. Influencing people in their opinions, attitudes, or judgments about ideas or things.

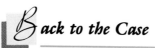

Back to the Case

In hiring new employees for an operation like Universal Studios Florida, management must be careful to emphasize hiring not just workers, but the *right* workers. For Universal Studios Florida, appropriate human resources are those people who will make a valuable contribution to the attainment of Universal's organizational objectives. In hiring cooks, cashiers, parking attendants, security officers, and ride operators, management should consider hiring only those people who will best help the organization become successful. In finding appropriate human resources, management at Universal Studios Florida has to follow four basic steps: (1) recruitment, (2) selection, (3) training, and (4) performance appraisal.

   Basically, recruitment would entail the initial screening of individuals available to fill open positions at Universal. For recruitment efforts to be successful at a company like Universal, recruiters have to know the jobs they are trying to fill, where potential human resources can be located, and how the law influences recruiting efforts.

   Recruiters could acquire an understanding of open positions at a company like Universal by performing a job analysis. The job analysis would force them to determine the job description of the open position—the activities of a cook, parking attendant, or security officer, for example—and the job specification of the position, including the type of individual who should be hired to fill that position.

Knowing Sources of Human Resources

Besides a thorough knowledge of the position the organization is trying to fill, recruiters must be able to pinpoint sources of human resources. A barrier to this pinpointing is the fact that the supply of individuals from which to choose is continually changing; there are times when finding appropriate human resources is much harder than at other times. For example, an article that appeared about twenty-five years ago indicated that organizations should prepare for a frantic scramble to obtain managers from a very low supply in the labor market.[4]

   In discussing the same managerial recruitment issue, however, a later article portrayed a situation that had changed dramatically: "For the past couple of years, a few thoughtful observers of new business trends have been warning that a glut of corporate executives is imminent. The reason, of course, is the U.S. baby boom of the late 1940s and 1950s."[5] Over all, sources of human resources available to fill a position can be categorized in two ways: (1) sources inside the organization and (2) sources outside the organization.

Sources Inside the Organization. The existing pool of employees in an organization is one source of human resources. Individuals already in an organization may be well qualified for an open position. Although existing personnel sometimes are moved laterally within an organization, most internal movements are usually promotions. Promotion from within typically has the advantages of building morale, encouraging employees to work harder in hopes of being promoted, and helping individuals decide to stay with a particular organization because of possible future promotions.[6] Companies such as Exxon and General Electric find it very rewarding to train managers themselves for upward movement within the organization.[7]

Some type of **human resource inventory** usually is helpful to a company to keep current with possibilities for filling a position from within. The inventory should indicate which individuals in the organization would be appropriate for filling a position if it became available. Walter S. Wikstrom suggested three types of records that can be combined to maintain a useful human resource inventory in an organization.[8] Although Wikstrom focused on filling managerial positions, slight modifications to his inventory forms would make his records equally applicable to nonmanagerial positions. Many organizations computerize records like the ones Wikstrom suggests in order to make a human resource inventory system as efficient and effective as possible.

The first of Wikstrom's three record-keeping forms for a human resource inventory is a **management inventory card** (see Figure 11.3 on page 320). The card in the figure has been completed for a fictional manager named Mel Murray. It indicates Murray's age, year of employment, present position and length of time it has been held, performance ratings, strengths and weaknesses, the positions to which Murray might move, when he would be ready to assume these positions, and additional training he would need to fill the positions. In short, this card is both an organizational history of Murray and an explanation of how he might be used in the future.

Figure 11.4 on page 321 shows Wikstrom's second human resource inventory form—a **position replacement form.** This form focuses on maintaining position-centered information, rather than the people-centered information on the management inventory card. The form in the figure indicates little about Murray as a person but much about individuals who could replace him. The position replacement form is helpful in determining what would happen to Murray's present position if Murray were selected to be moved within the organization or if he left the organization altogether.

Wikstrom's third human resource inventory form is called a **management manpower replacement card** (see Figure 11.5 on page 322). This chart presents a composite view of the individuals who management considers significant for human resource planning. The performance rating and promotion potential of Murray can easily be compared with those of other employees when the company is trying to determine which individual would most appropriately fill a particular position.

The management inventory card, the position replacement form, and the management manpower replacement chart are three separate record-keeping devices for a human resource inventory. Each form furnishes different data on which to

A **human resource inventory** is an accumulation of information concerning the characteristics of the organization members; this information focuses on the past performance of organization members as well as on how they might be trained and best used in the future.

The **management inventory card** is a form used in compiling a human resource inventory—containing an organizational history of an individual and an explanation of how the individual might be used in the future.

The **position replacement form** is a form used in compiling a human resource inventory—summarizing information about organization members who could fill a position should it open.

A **management manpower replacement chart** is a form used in compiling a human resource inventory—people-oriented and presenting a total composite view of individuals whom management considers significant to human resource planning.

Name Murray, Mel	Age 47	Employed 1980
Present Position Manager, Sales (House Fans Division)		On Job 6 years
Present Performance Outstanding–exceeded sales goal in spite of stiffer competition		
Strengths Good planner–motivates subordinates very well–excellent communication.		
Weaknesses Still does not always delegate as much as situation requires. Sometimes does not understand production problems.		
Efforts to Improve Has greatly improved in delegating in last two years; also has organized more effectively after taking a management course on own time and initiative.		
Could Move to Vice President, Marketing		**When** 1992
Training Needed More exposure to problems of other divisions (attend top staff conference?). Perhaps university program stressing staff role of corporate marketing versus line sales.		
Could Move to Manager, House or Industrial Fans Division		**When** 1993 1994
Training Needed Course in production management; some project working with production people; perhaps a good business game somewhere.		

FIGURE 11.3

Management inventory card

base a hiring-from-within decision. The questions these forms help answer are (1) What is the organizational history of an individual, and what potential does the person possess (management inventory card)? (2) If a position becomes vacant, who might be eligible to fill it (position replacement form)? (3) What are the relative merits of one individual filling the position as compared to another (management manpower replacement chart)? Considering the answers to these three questions collectively should help to ensure the success of hiring-from-within decisions. Computer software is available to help managers keep track of complex human resource inventories and to make resulting better decisions about how people should be best deployed and developed.[9]

Sources Outside the Organization. If a position cannot be filled by someone presently in the organization, numerous sources of prospective human resources are available outside the organization. They include:

1. *Competitors.* One commonly tapped external source of human resources is competing organizations. Since there are several advantages to luring human

Position	Manager, Sales (House Fans Division)		
Performance Outstanding	**Incumbent** Mel Murray	**Salary** $44,500	**May Move** 1 Year
Replacement 1 Earl Renfrew		**Salary** $39,500	**Age** 39
Present Position Field Sales Manager, House Fans		**Employed:** Present Job 3 years	Company 10 years
Training Needed Special assignment to study market potential for air conditioners to provide forecasting experience.		**When ready** now	
Replacement 2 Bernard Storey		**Salary** $38,500	**Age** 36
Present Position Promotion Manager, House Fans		**Employed:** Present Job 4 years	Company 7 years
Training Needed Rotation to field sales. Marketing conference in fall 1991.		**When ready** 2 years	

FIGURE 11.4

Position replacement form

resources away from competitors, this type of piracy has become a common practice. Among the advantages are (1) the individual knows the business, (2) the competitor will have paid for the individual's training up to the time of hire, (3) the competing organization will probably be weakened somewhat by the loss of the individual, and (4) once hired, the individual becomes a valuable source of information about how to best compete with the other organization.

2. *Employment agencies.* Employment agencies help people find jobs and help organizations find people. They can be either public or private. Public employment agencies do not charge fees, whereas private ones collect a fee from either the person hired or the organization, once a hiring has been finalized.

3. *Readers of certain publications.* Perhaps the most widely addressed source of potential human resources is the readership of certain publications. To tap this source, recruiters simply place an advertisement in a suitable publication. The advertisement describes the open position in detail and announces that the organization is accepting applications from qualified individuals. The type of position to be filled determines the type of publication in which the advertisement is placed. The objective is to advertise in a publication whose readers are likely to be interested in filling the position. An opening for a top-level executive might be advertised in *The Wall Street Journal,* a training director opening might be advertised in the *Journal of Training and Development,* and an educational opening might be advertised in the *Chronicle of Higher Education.*

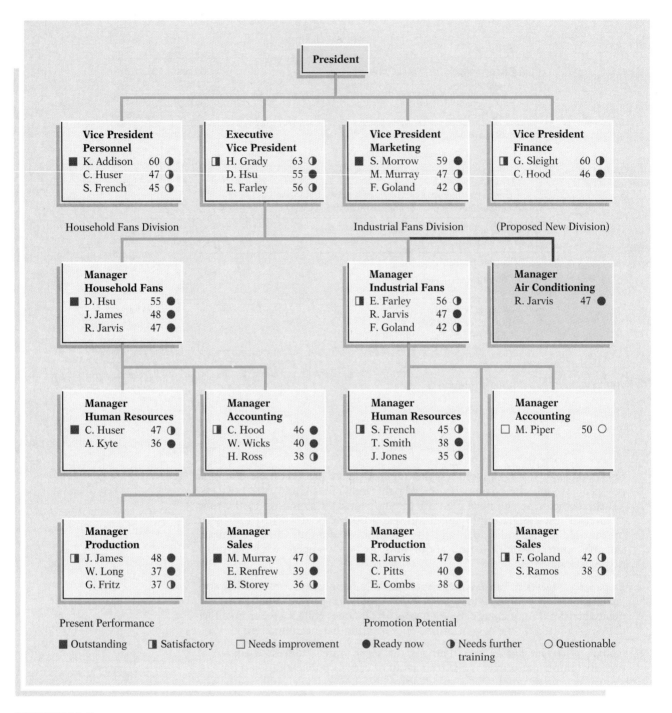

Management manpower
replacement chart

FIGURE 11.5

Management manpower
replacement chart

4. *Educational institutions.* Several recruiters go directly to schools to interview
   students close to graduation. Liberal arts schools, business schools, engineering
   schools, junior colleges, and community colleges all have somewhat different
   human resources to offer. Recruiting efforts should focus on the schools with
   the highest probability of providing human resources appropriate for the open
   position.

Knowing the Law

Modern legislation has a major impact on organizational recruitment practices, and a recruitment effort must reflect the laws that govern it. The Civil Rights Act passed in 1964 and amended in 1972 created the **Equal Employment Opportunity Commission (EEOC)** to enforce the laws established to prohibit discrimination on the basis of race, color, religion, sex, and national origin in recruitment, hiring, firing, layoffs, and all other employment practices. The EEOC report was amended in 1978 to include the Pregnancy Discrimination Act, which required employees to treat pregnancy as any other form of medical disability, as far as leave and insurance.

Equal opportunity legislation protects the right of a citizen to work and to get a fair wage based primarily on merit and performance. The EEOC seeks to maintain the existence of this right by holding labor unions, private employers, educational institutions, and government bodies responsible for its continuance. The four steps usually followed by the EEOC to hold organizations accountable are presented in Table 11.2.

In response to equal opportunity legislation, many organizations have **affirmative action programs.** Translated literally, *affirmative action* can be defined as positive movement. "In the area of equal employment opportunity, the basic purpose of positive movement or affirmative action is to eliminate barriers and increase opportunities for the purpose of increasing the utilization of underutilized and/or disadvantaged individuals."[10] The organization can judge how well it is eliminating these barriers by (1) determining how many minority and disadvantaged individuals it presently employs, (2) determining how many minority and disadvantaged individuals it should employ according to EEOC guidelines, and (3) comparing

The **Equal Employment Opportunity Commission (EEOC)** is an agency established to enforce the laws that regulate recruiting and other managerial practices.

Affirmative action programs are programs in the area of equal employment opportunity whose basic purpose is to eliminate barriers against and increase opportunities for underutilized or disadvantaged individuals.

TABLE 11.2   Four steps followed by the EEOC to uphold equal opportunity legislation

1. The EEOC receives a charge alleging employment discrimination. Such a charge can be filed by an individual, by a group on behalf of an individual, or by any of the EEOC commissioners. Primary consideration for processing the charge is given to an approved state or local employment practices agency, if one exists. This agency has 60 days in which to act on the charge (120 days if the agency has been in operation less than a year). In the absence of such an agency, the EEOC is responsible for processing the charge. If neither the local agency nor the EEOC has brought suit within 180 days of the official filing date, the charging party may request a right-to-sue letter by which to initiate private civil action.

2. The EEOC investigates the charge to gather sufficient facts to determine the precise nature of the employer or union practice. If these facts show *probable cause* to believe that discrimination exists, the EEOC initiates step 3.

3. The EEOC conciliates or attempts to persuade the employer to voluntarily eliminate the discrimination. In this regard, the EEOC will provide extensive technical aid to any employer or union in voluntary compliance with the law. If conciliation fails, the EEOC initiates step 4.

4. The EEOC files suit in federal court (or the aggrieved parties may initiate their own private civil action). Court-ordered compliance with Title VII usually results in large expenses for the employer, often exceeding the cost of voluntary affirmative action.

the numbers obtained in steps 1 and 2. If the two numbers are close to the same, employment practices within the organization probably should be maintained; if the numbers are not about the same, employment practices should be modified accordingly.

Modern management writers recommend that managers follow the guidelines of affirmative action not because they are mandated by law, but primarily because of the characteristics of today's labor supply.[11] According to these writers, more than one-half of the U.S. work force now consists of minorities, immigrants, and women. Because the overall work force is diverse in its makeup, employees in today's organizations will tend to be more diverse. Modern managers face the challenge of developing a productive work force from an increasingly diverse labor pool. This task is more formidable than simply complying with affirmative action laws.

Back to the Case

A successful recruitment effort at Universal requires recruiters to know where to locate the available human resources to fill open positions. These sources may be both within Universal and outside it. Because Universal Studios Florida is relatively new, sources within the company would be limited to other divisions already operating, such as Universal Studios Hollywood.

When making plans to open an operation like Universal Studios Florida, management had to plan for obtaining needed appropriate human resources along with other resources like equipment and real estate. To do this, management kept current on the possibilities of filling positions from within by maintaining some type of human resource inventory. This inventory helped management organize information about (1) the organizational histories and potential of various Universal employees, (2) the employees at other Universal locations who might be eligible to fill the positions needed to complete the work force in Florida, and (3) the relative abilities of various Universal employees to fill the necessary openings. Other sources of potential human resources outside Universal are competitors, public and private employment agencies, the readers of industry-related publications, and various types of educational institutions.

Universal management must also be aware of how the law influences its recruitment efforts. Basically, the law says that Universal recruitment practices cannot discriminate on the basis of race, color, religion, sex, or national origin. If recruitment practices at Universal are found to be discriminatory, the company is subject to prosecution by the Equal Employment Opportunity Commission.

Selection

Selection is choosing an individual to hire from all of those who have been recruited.

The second major step involved in managing human resources for the organization is **selection**—choosing an individual to hire from all those who have been recruited. Hence, selection is dependent on and follows recruitment. The cartoon on page 325 lightheartedly illustrates the importance of selecting the right people for an organization.

The selection process typically is represented as a series of stages through which prospective employees must pass to be hired.[12] Each stage reduces the total

THE WALL STREET JOURNAL

MIKE SHAPIRO

"How many times do I have to tell Personnel
we want a hip young crowd buying our
products, not working for us?"

group of prospective employees until, finally, one individual is hired. Figure 11.6
lists the specific stages of the selection process, indicates reasons for eliminating
prospective employees at each stage, and illustrates how the group of potential
employees is narrowed down to the individual who ultimately becomes the employee. Two tools often used in the selection process are testing and assessment
centers.

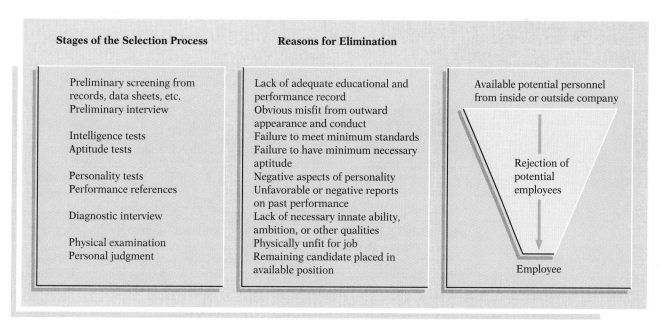

Stages of the Selection Process	Reasons for Elimination	
Preliminary screening from records, data sheets, etc.	Lack of adequate educational and performance record	Available potential personnel from inside or outside company
Preliminary interview	Obvious misfit from outward appearance and conduct	
Intelligence tests	Failure to meet minimum standards	
Aptitude tests	Failure to have minimum necessary aptitude	Rejection of potential employees
Personality tests	Negative aspects of personality	
Performance references	Unfavorable or negative reports on past performance	
Diagnostic interview	Lack of necessary innate ability, ambition, or other qualities	
Physical examination	Physically unfit for job	
Personal judgment	Remaining candidate placed in available position	Employee

FIGURE 11.6

Summary of major factors involved in the selection process

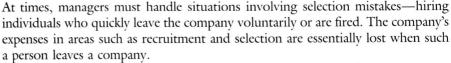

Global Highlight: Compaq Computer Company's International Selection Slipups

At times, managers must handle situations involving selection mistakes—hiring individuals who quickly leave the company voluntarily or are fired. The company's expenses in areas such as recruitment and selection are essentially lost when such a person leaves a company.

Growth at Compaq Computer Company, a computer manufacturer in Houston, Texas, has been phenomenal over recent years. The seven-year-old firm has recently had annual sales of $2.1 billion with $225 million in net profit. The company's expansion into international markets has been a significant reason for its success. Selection mistakes in this international arena are likely to be more expensive for the company than selection mistakes in the domestic arena. This expense difference exists simply because foreign assignments are usually more expensive for an American company like Compaq to set up and maintain than domestic assignments. Expenses incurred by a company with employees posted to a foreign country include salary based on the value of the U.S. dollar in that country, housing allowance, cost-of-living adjustments, transportation allowances, and tuition for children's private schools.

Testing

Testing is examining human resources for qualities relevant to performing available jobs.[13] Although many different kinds of tests are available for organizational use, they generally can be divided into four categories.[14]

1. *Aptitude tests.* Tests of aptitude measure the potential of an individual to perform a task. Some aptitude tests measure general intelligence, and others measure special abilities, such as mechanical, clerical, or visual abilities.

2. *Achievement tests.* Tests that measure the level of skill or knowledge an individual possesses in a certain area are called achievement tests. This skill or knowledge may have been acquired through various training activities or through experience in the area. The skill tests may include typing or keyboarding tests.

3. *Vocational interest tests.* Tests of vocational interest attempt to measure an individual's interest in performing various kinds of jobs and are administered on the assumption that certain people perform jobs well because the job activities are interesting to them. The basic purpose of this type of test is to help select the individuals who find certain aspects of an open position interesting.

4. *Personality tests.* Personality tests attempt to describe an individual's personality dimensions in such areas as emotional maturity, subjectivity, honesty,[15] and objectivity. Personality tests can be used advantageously if the personality characteristics needed to do well in a particular job are well defined and if individuals possessing those characteristics can be pinpointed and selected.

Several guidelines should be observed when tests are used as part of the selection process. First, care should be taken to ensure that the test being used is both valid and reliable. A test is *valid* if it measures what it is designed to measure and *reliable* if it measures similarly time after time.[16] Second, test results should not be used as the sole source of information to determine whether to hire someone. People change over time, and someone who doesn't score well on a particular test might still develop into a productive employee. Such factors as potential and desire to obtain a position should be assessed subjectively along with test scores in the final selection decision. A third guideline is that care should be taken to determine that the tests used are nondiscriminatory in nature; many tests contain language or cultural biases that may discriminate against minorities. This third guideline is especially important in that the EEOC has the authority to prosecute organizations that use discriminatory testing practices.

Assessment Centers

Another tool often used to help increase the success of employee selection is the **assessment center.** Although the assessment center concept is discussed in this chapter primarily as an aid to selection, it also has been used as an aid in such areas as human resource training and organization development. The first industrial use of the assessment center is usually credited to AT&T.[17] Since AT&T's initial efforts, the assessment center concept has been growing quickly and today is used not only as a means for identifying individuals to be hired from outside an organization, but also for identifying individuals from inside the organization who should be promoted. Corporations that have used assessment centers extensively include J.C. Penney, Standard Oil of Ohio, and IBM.[18]

An assessment center has been defined as a program, not a place, in which participants engage in a number of individual and group exercises constructed to simulate important activities at the levels to which participants aspire.[19] These exercises might include such activities as participating in leaderless discussions, giving oral presentations, or leading a group in solving some assigned problem. Individuals performing the activities are observed by managers or trained observers who evaluate both their ability and their potential.[20] In general, participants are assessed on the basis of (1) leadership, (2) organizing and planning ability, (3) decision making, (4) oral and written communication skills, (5) initiative, (6) energy, (7) analytical ability, (8) resistance to stress, (9) use of delegation, (10) behavior flexibility, (11) human relations competence, (12) originality, (13) controlling, (14) self-direction, and (15) overall potential.[21]

An **assessment center** is a program in which participants engage in and are evaluated on a number of individual and group exercises constructed to simulate important activities at the organizational levels to which these participants aspire.

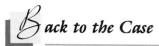 ack to the Case

After the initial screening of potential human resources, Universal Studios Florida was faced with the task of selecting the individuals to be hired from those who had been screened. Two tools that Universal could use in this selection process are testing and assessment centers. After screening potential employees for positions at Universal, management could administer aptitude tests, achievement tests, vocational interest tests, or personality tests to see which of the individuals screened had the qualities necessary to work a specific job. In using these tests, however, management had to make sure that the tests were both valid and reliable, that they were not the sole basis on which a selection decision was made, and that they were nondiscriminatory.

Universal can also use assessment centers to simulate the tasks necessary to perform jobs that workers will be performing. Individuals who performed well on these tasks would probably be more appropriate for the positions than would those who did poorly. The use of assessment centers might be particularly appropriate in evaluating applicants for positions such as ride attendant. Simulating this job would help give management an idea of how prospective attendants might interact with customers during actual rides.

Training

After recruitment and selection, the next step in providing appropriate human resources for the organization is training. **Training** is the process of developing qualities in human resources that ultimately will enable them to be more productive and thus to contribute more to organizational goal attainment. The purpose of training is to increase the productivity of individuals in their jobs by influencing their behavior. Table 11.3 provides an overview of the types and popularity of training being offered by organizations.

The training of individuals is essentially a four-step process: (1) determining training needs, (2) designing the training program, (3) administering the training program, and (4) evaluating the training program. These steps are presented in Figure 11.7. Each of these steps is described in more detail in the sections that follow.

Determining Training Needs

The first step of the training process is determining the organization's training needs.[22] **Training needs** are the information or skill areas of an individual or

TABLE 11.3 Types and popularity of training offered by organizations

Types of Training	Percentage of Surveyed Companies That Offer This Type of Training
1. Management skills and development	74.3
2. Supervisory skills	73.4
3. Technical skills/knowledge updating	72.7
4. Communication skills	66.8
5. Customer relations/services	63.8
6. Executive development	56.8
7. New methods/procedures	56.5
8. Sales skills	54.1
9. Clerical/secretarial skills	52.9
10. Personal growth	51.9
11. Computer literacy/basic computer skills	48.2
12. Employee/labor relations	44.9
13. Disease prevention/health promotion	38.9
14. Customer education	35.7
15. Remedial basic education	18.0

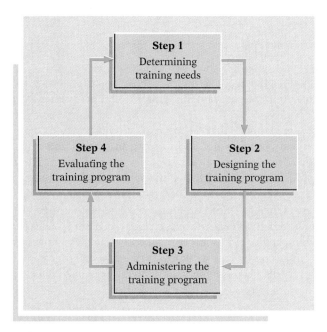

FIGURE 11.7

Steps of the training process

group that require further development to increase the organizational productivity of that individual or group. Only if training focuses on these needs can it be of some productive benefit to the organization.

The training of organization members is typically a continuing activity. Even individuals who have been with an organization for some time and who have undergone initial orientation and skills training need continued training to improve skills.

Several methods of determining which skills to focus on for more established human resources are available. The first method is evaluating the production process within the organization. Such factors as excessive rejected products, deadlines that are not met, and high labor costs are clues to existing levels of production-related expertise. Another method for determining training needs is direct feedback from employees on what they believe are the organization's training needs. Organization members may be able to verbalize clearly and accurately exactly what types of training they need to help them do a better job. A third way of determining training needs involves looking into the future. If the manufacture of new products or the use of newly purchased equipment is foreseen, some type of corresponding training almost certainly will be needed.

Designing the Training Program

Once training needs have been determined, a training program aimed at meeting those needs must be designed. Basically, designing a program entails assembling various types of facts and activities that will meet the established training needs. Obviously, as training needs vary, the facts and activities designed to meet those needs vary.

ʙ ack to the Case

After hiring, Universal Studios Florida must train new employees to be productive organization members. To train effectively, Universal must determine training needs, design a corresponding training program, and administer and evaluate the training program.

Designing a training program requires that Universal assemble facts and activities that address specific company training needs: information or skill areas that must be further developed in Universal employees in order to make them more productive. As time goes on, Universal should focus on training more established employees as well as newly hired employees.

As mentioned in the case, Universal Studios Florida is a new operation. In this situation, management should try to learn as much as possible from similar training programs that the company operates in other locations such as Universal Studios Hollywood. Knowing strengths and weaknesses of training programs at such company locations would help management at Universal Studios Florida design efficient and effective training programs for its operation.

Administering the Training Program

The next step of the training process is administering the training program, or actually training the individuals. Various techniques exist for both transmitting necessary information and developing needed skills in training programs. Several of these techniques are discussed in the sections that follow.

Techniques for Transmitting Information. Two techniques for transmitting information in training programs are lectures and programmed learning. Although it probably could be argued that these techniques develop some skills in individuals as well as transmit information to them, they are primarily devices for the dissemination of information.

1. *Lectures.* Perhaps the most widely used technique for transmitting information in training programs is the lecture. The **lecture** is a primarily one-way communication in which an instructor orally presents information to a group of listeners. The instructor typically does most of the talking in this type of training situation. Trainees participate primarily through listening and note taking.

A **lecture** is primarily a one-way communication situation in which an instructor trains by orally presenting information to an individual or group.

An advantage of the lecture is that it allows the instructor to expose trainees to a maximum amount of information within a given time period. The lecture, however, also has its disadvantages:

The lecture generally consists of a one-way communication: the instructor presents information to the group of passive listeners. Thus, little or no opportunity exists to clarify meanings, to check on whether trainees really understand the lecture material, or to handle the wide diversity of ability, attitude, and interest that may prevail among the trainees. Also, there is little or no opportunity for practice, reinforcement, knowledge of results, or overlearning. . . . Ideally, the competent lecturer should make the material meaningful and intrinsically motivating to his or her listeners. However, whether most lectures achieve this goal is a moot question. . . . These limitations, in turn, impose further limitations on the lecture's actual content. A skillful lecturer may be fairly successful in transmitting conceptual knowledge to a group of trainees who are ready to receive it; however, all the evidence available indicates that the nature of the lecture situation makes it of minimal value in promoting attitudinal or behavioral change.[23]

Quality Highlight: Aetna Life and Casualty Company Trains via TV

When Aetna Life and Casualty Company evaluated its employee training program, it found that the key problem was not the quality of the instructors, the tools and styles of program presentations, the content, or even the materials that supplement the workshops. Instead, Aetna found that the key problem in the training program was enabling large numbers of geographically distributed trainees to attend programs given at a central location and providing rooms large enough for programs at additional locations.

Aetna realized that if it wanted to provide high-quality service to its customers, it had to train more than a select few of its employees who were able to travel to the program locations. Aetna's goal was to dramatically increase the number of its employees involved in training, thereby enhancing the quality of the service they could provide to their customers. Aetna executives and training personnel brainstormed ideas for disseminating their employee training more widely and came up with a plan to offer interactive training via television.

Aetna has developed the Aetna Television Network, which links 235 field offices with the home office. The Aetna Television Network enables the company to extend the use of its training programs by making them available throughout the country to office locations that normally would be unable to take advantage of them. As an example, over the past few years 810 Aetna employees have participated in a business-writing workshop in person, whereas over 3,000 have participated in them on Aetna's television network.

Training employees via television is gaining in popularity throughout the business world. Television networks established for business training enable training programs to be extremely flexible. The same workshop can be heard by employees throughout a company at the same time or at different times as schedules allow. The trend toward using television as a vehicle for increasing the quality of training should continue to grow in the future.

---

2. *Programmed Learning.* Another commonly used technique for transmitting information in training programs is called programmed learning. **Programmed learning** is a technique for instructing without the presence or intervention of a human instructor.[24] Small parts of information that require related responses are presented to individual trainees. The trainees can determine from the accuracy of their responses whether their understanding of the obtained information is accurate. The types of responses required of trainees vary from situation to situation but usually are multiple-choice, true-false, or fill-in-the-blank. Figure 11.8 on page 332 shows a portion of a programmed learning training package that could be used to familiarize trainees with PERT (program evaluation and review technique).

Programmed learning is a technique for instructing without the presence of a human instructor—small pieces of information requiring responses are presented to individual trainees. It has advantages and disadvantages.

Frame 3²⁴

Program evaluation and review technique, PERT, is performed on a set of time-related activities and events which must be accomplished to reach an objective. The evaluation gives the expected completion time and the probability of completing the total work within that time. By means of PERT, it is possible not only to know the exact schedule, but also to control the various activities on a daily basis. Overlapping and related activities are reviewed. PERT is more practical for jobs involving a one-time effort than for repeat jobs. It is a planning-controlling medium designed to: (1) focus attention on key components, (2) reveal potential problem areas, (3) provide a prompt reporting on accomplishments, and (4) facilitate decision making.

The time-related activities and events are set forth by means of a PERT network (see figure 17). In this illustration, the circles represent events that are sequential accomplishment points; the arrows represent activities or the time-consuming elements of the program. In this type of network, an arrow always connects two activities. All of the activities and events must be accomplished before the end objective can be attained. The three numbers shown for each arrow or activity represent its estimated times, respectively, for the optimistic, most likely, and pessimistic times. The program starts with event

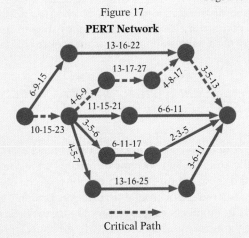

Figure 17
PERT Network

Critical Path

no.1 and ends with event no.12. From calculations for the time required for each path from no.1 to no.12, it is found that path 1-2-4-8-11-12 requires the *longest time* and, hence, is the *critical path* because it controls the time required to complete the program. Toward it, managers would direct their attention in order to: (1) ensure that no breakdowns occur in it; (2) better the current times required, if possible; and (3) trade off time from the noncritical paths to the critical path, if the net effect is to reduce total time of the critical path.

Indicate whether each of the following statements is true or false by writing "T" or "F" in the space provided.

___1. PERT centers its attention on social constraints.
___2. PERT is best applied to assembly-line operations.
___3. In PERT, the *critical path* is the path that requires the longest time.
___4. In the PERT network, circles represent events and the arrows represent activities.

Now turn to Answer Frame 3²⁴, page 146.

Answer frame 3²⁴

1. False. PERT centers its attention on *time* constraints.
2. False. PERT is more practical for jobs involving a one-time effort than for repeat jobs.
3. True. In PERT, the critical path is the path that requires the *longest* time. If this path can be shortened, the program can be completed in a shorter time period.
4. True. Circles represent events that are sequential accomplishment points, and arrows represent activities or the time-consuming elements for the program.

You have completed chapter 24. Now turn to chapter 25.

FIGURE 11.8

Portion of a programmed learning training package featuring PERT

As with the lecture method, programmed learning has both advantages and disadvantages. Among the advantages are that it can be computerized and students can learn at their own pace, know immediately if they are right or wrong, and participate actively. The primary disadvantage of this method is that no one is present to answer questions for the learner.

Techniques for Developing Skills. Techniques for developing skills in training programs can be divided into two broad categories: on-the-job and classroom. Techniques for developing skills on the job usually are referred to as **on-the-job training.** These techniques reflect a blend of job-related knowledge and experience and include coaching, position rotation, and special project committees. Coaching is direct critiquing of how well an individual is performing a job. Position rotation involves moving an individual from job to job to enable the person to obtain an understanding of the organization as a whole. Special project committees involve assigning a particular task to an individual to furnish him or her with experience in a designated area.[25]

> **On-the-job training** is a training technique that blends job related knowledge with experience in using that knowledge on the job.

Classroom techniques for developing skills also reflect a blend of job-related knowledge and experience. The skills addressed through these techniques can range from technical skills, such as computer programming, to interpersonal skills, such as leadership. Specific classroom techniques aimed at developing skills include various types of management games and role-playing activities. The most common format for management games requires small groups of trainees to make and then evaluate various management decisions. The role-playing format typically involves acting out and then reflecting on some people-oriented problem that must be solved in the organization.

Contrary to the typical one-way-communication role in the lecture situation, the skills instructor in the classroom encourages high levels of discussion and interaction among trainees, develops a climate in which trainees learn new behavior from carrying out various activities, acts as a resource person in clarifying related information, and facilitates learning through job-related knowledge and experience in applying that knowledge.[26] The difference between the instructional role used in information dissemination and the instructional role used in skill development is dramatic.[27]

Evaluating the Training Program

After the training program has been completed, management should evaluate its effectiveness. Because training programs represent a cost investment—costs include materials, trainer time, and production loss while the individuals are being trained rather than doing their jobs—a reasonable return is required.

Basically, management must evaluate the training program to determine if it meets the needs for which it was designed. Answers to questions such as the following help determine training program effectiveness:

1. Has the excessive reject rate declined?

2. Are deadlines being met more regularly?

3. Are labor costs per unit produced decreasing?

If the answer to such questions is yes, the training program is at least somewhat successful, but perhaps its effectiveness could be enhanced through certain selective changes. If the answer is no, some significant modification to the training program is warranted.

In a recent survey of business people, 50 percent of the respondents thought that there would be no change in their sales per year if training programs for experienced salespeople were halted.[28] Such feedback should be scrutinized very closely to see if the sales training as it presently exists in respondents' companies should be discontinued, modified slightly, or drastically altered in an effort to make it more valuable. Based on the results of this survey, the training will probably be changed significantly to make it valuable to experienced salespeople. This survey illustrates the importance of gathering feedback aimed at making training more effective and efficient.

Back to the Case

After training needs at Universal Studios Florida are determined and programs have been designed to meet those needs, the programs must be administered. In administering its training programs, Universal might use both the lecture technique and the programmed learning technique for transmitting information to trainees. For developing skills in trainees, Universal could use on-the-job-training methods, such as coaching, position rotation, or special project committees. For developing skills in a classroom setting, Universal could use instructional techniques such as role-playing activities. For example, waiters could be asked to handle customers who display various kinds of attitudes and have different-sized families. These situations then could be videotaped and reviewed as often as necessary from the standpoint of improving waiter-customer relationships.

Once a Universal training program has been completed, it must be evaluated to determine if it has met the training need for which it was designed. Training programs aimed at specific motor skills such as cash-register operating would be much easier to evaluate than training programs aimed at interpersonal skills such as developing customer relations. The evaluation of any training program at Universal, of course, should emphasize how to improve the program the next time it is implemented.

Performance Appraisal

Performance appraisal is the process of reviewing past productive activity to evaluate the contribution individuals have made toward attaining management system objectives.

Even after individuals have been recruited, selected, and trained, the task of making them productive within the organization is not finished. The fourth step in the process of providing appropriate human resources for the organization is **performance appraisal**—the process of reviewing individuals' past productive activity to evaluate the contribution they have made toward attaining management system objectives. As with training, performance appraisal is a continuing activity that focuses on the more established human resources within the organization as well as on the relatively new ones. A main purpose is to furnish feedback to organization members about how they can become more productive. Performance appraisal also has been called performance review and performance evaluation. Table 11.4 describes several methods of performance appraisal.

TABLE 11.4 Descriptions of several methods of performance appraisal

Name of Appraisal Method	Description
Rating scale	Individuals appraising performance use a form containing several employee qualities and characteristics to be evaluated (e.g., dependability, initiative, leadership). Each evaluated factor is rated on a continuum or scale ranging, for example, from 1 to 7 or more points.
Employee comparisons	Appraisers rank employees according to such factors as job performance and value to the organization. Only one employee can occupy a particular ranking.
Free-form essay	Appraisers simply write down their impressions of employees in paragraph form.
Critical-form essay	Appraisers write down particularly good or bad events involving employees as these events occur. Records of all documented events for any one employee are used to evaluate that person's performance.

Why Use Performance Appraisals?

Most firms in the United States use some type of performance appraisal system.[29] Douglas McGregor has suggested the following three reasons for using performance appraisals in an organization:[30]

1. They provide systematic judgments to support salary increases, promotions, transfers, and sometimes demotions or terminations.

2. They are a means of telling subordinates how they are doing and of suggesting needed changes in behavior, attitudes, skills, or job knowledge; they let subordinates know where they stand with the boss.

3. They also are being used increasingly as a basis for the coaching and counseling of individuals by superiors.

Handling Performance Appraisals

If performance appraisals are not handled well, their benefit to the organization is minimized. Several guidelines can assist in increasing the appropriateness with which the appraisals are conducted.[31] The first guideline is that performance appraisals should stress both the performance within the position the individual holds and the success with which the individual is attaining objectives. Performance and objectives should become inseparable topics of discussion during performance appraisals. The second guideline is that appraisals should emphasize the individual in the job, not the evaluator's impression of observed work habits. In other words, emphasis should be more on an objective analysis of performance than on a subjective evaluation of habits. The third guideline is that the appraisal should be acceptable to both the evaluator and the evaluatee. Both individuals should agree that the appraisal can be of some benefit to the organization and to the worker. The fourth, and last, guideline is that performance appraisals should be used as the basis for improving individuals' productivity within the organization[32] by making them better equipped to produce.[33]

Potential Weaknesses of Performance Appraisals

To maximize the potential payoff of performance appraisals to the organization, managers must avoid several potential weaknesses of the appraisal process. Some of these potential weaknesses are (1) individuals involved in performance appraisals could view them as a reward-punishment situation, (2) the emphasis of performance appraisal could be put on completing paperwork rather than on critiquing individual performance, (3) individuals being evaluated could view the process as being unfair or biased, and (4) some type of negative reaction from a subordinate could be generated when the evaluator offers any unfavorable comments.[34]

To avoid these potential weaknesses, supervisors and employees should view the performance appraisal process as an opportunity to increase the worth of the individual through constructive feedback, not as a means of rewarding or punishing individuals through positive or negative comments. Paperwork should be seen only as an aid in providing this feedback, not as an end in itself. Also, care should be taken to make appraisal feedback as tactful and objective as possible to help minimize any negative reactions of the evaluatee.[35]

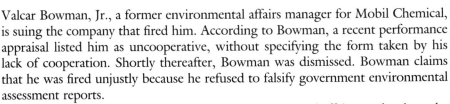

Ethics Highlight: Mobil Chemical Company
Employee Challenges Performance Appraisal

Valcar Bowman, Jr., a former environmental affairs manager for Mobil Chemical, is suing the company that fired him. According to Bowman, a recent performance appraisal listed him as uncooperative, without specifying the form taken by his lack of cooperation. Shortly thereafter, Bowman was dismissed. Bowman claims that he was fired unjustly because he refused to falsify government environmental assessment reports.

Bowman was hired to manage Mobil's environmental affairs; at the time, the company assured Bowman that it was committed to a program of environmental excellence. Bowman says that he came to believe otherwise. As one of the last significant events while Bowman was still employed by Mobil, Bowman's staff was ordered to give to a company attorney an environmental report that the staff had written concerning Mobil's Bakersfield, California, plant. Bowman believes that this action was taken to keep the report out of the hands of the government's Environmental Protection Agency.

This case emphasizes the importance of management's properly using the performance appraisal process. Had they specifically documented legitimate ways in which Bowman had been uncooperative, they would have been in a stronger legal position.

The case will be heard by a jury in the U.S. District Court in Newark, New Jersey. If the court finds that Bowman's allegations are true, he will probably be able to recover substantial damages, because improper use of the performance appraisal process could subject the company to litigation initiated by employees.

In addition, the company would probably find itself the target of additional investigations by the government regarding the validity and distribution of reports that it has generated.

*B*ack to the Case

The final step in providing appropriate human resources at Universal Studios Florida is performance appraisal. This means that the contributions that Universal employees make to the attainment of management system objectives must be evaluated. Although in the next few years all employees having their performances appraised at Universal would be relatively new employees, ultimately the performance appraisal process at Universal should focus as well on more established employees.

It would be difficult to visualize a Universal employee who could not benefit from a properly conducted performance appraisal. Such an appraisal would stress activities on the job and effectiveness in accomplishing job objectives. An objective appraisal would provide Universal employees with tactful, constructive criticism that should help to increase their productivity. Handled properly, Universal's appraisals would not be a reward or a punishment in themselves, but rather an opportunity to increase employees' value to the company and help employees become more productive over time rather than being without guidance and perhaps moving toward an inevitable outcome of dismissal.

Action Summary

Reread the learning objectives that follow. Each objective is followed by questions. Answering these questions accurately will help you retain the most important concepts discussed in this chapter. After answering each question, check your answer with the answer key at the end of this chapter. (*Hint:* If you have doubt regarding the correct response, consult the page whose number follows the answer.)

Circle:

From studying this chapter, I will attempt to acquire:

1. **An overall understanding of how appropriate human resources can be provided for the organization.**

    a. An appropriate human resource is an individual whose qualifications are matched to job specifications.

    T, F

    b. The term *appropriate human resources* refers to: (1) finding the right number of people to fill positions; (b) individuals being satisfied with their jobs; (c) individuals who help the organization achieve management system objectives; (d) individuals who are ineffective; (e) none of the above.

    a, b, c, d, e

2. An appreciation for the relationship among recruitment efforts, an open position, sources of human resources, and the law.

a, b, c, d, e

    a. The process of narrowing a large number of candidates to a smaller field is: (a) rushing; (b) recruitment; (c) selection; (d) enlistment; (e) enrollment.

a, b, c, d, e

    b. The characteristics of the individual who should be hired for the job are indicated by the: (a) job analysis; (b) job specification; (c) job description; (d) job review; (e) job identification.

3. Insights on the use of tests and assessment centers in employee selection.

a, b, c, d, e

    a. The level of skill or knowledge an individual possesses in a particular area is measured by: (a) aptitude tests; (b) achievement tests; (c) acuity tests; (d) assessment tests; (e) vocational interest tests.

a, b, c, d, e

    b. Which of the following guidelines does *not* apply when tests are being used in selecting potential employees: (a) the tests should be both valid and reliable; (b) the tests should be nondiscriminatory in nature; (c) the tests should not be the sole source of information for determining whether someone is to be hired; (d) such factors as potential and desire to obtain a position should not be assessed subjectively; (e) none of the above—all are important guidelines.

4. An understanding of how the training process operates.

a, b, c, d, e

    a. Four steps involved in training individuals are: (1) designing the training program, (2) evaluating the training program, (3) determining training needs, (4) administering the training program. The correct sequence for these steps is:
    (a) 1, 3, 2, 4
    (b) 3, 4, 1, 2
    (c) 2, 1, 3, 4
    (d) 3, 1, 4, 2
    (e) none of the above

T, F

    b. The lecture offers learners an excellent opportunity to clarify meanings and ask questions, since communication is a two-way one.

5. A concept of what performance appraisals are and how they best can be conducted.

a, b, c, d, e

    a. Performance appraisals are important in an organization because they: (a) provide systematic judgments to support promotions; (b) provide a basis for coaching; (c) provide a basis for counseling; (d) let subordinates know where they stand with the boss; (e) all of the above.

a, b, c, d, e

    b. To achieve the maximum benefit from performance evaluations, a manager should: (a) focus only on the negative aspects of performance; (b) punish the worker with negative feedback; (c) be as subjective as possible; (d) focus only on the positive aspects of performance; (e) use only constructive feedback.

Introductory Case Wrap-Up

"Getting the Right People for Universal Studios" (p. 314) and its related back-to-the-case sections were written to help you better understand the management concepts contained in this chapter. Answer the following discussion questions about this introductory case to further enrich your understanding of chapter content:

1. How important to an organization such as Universal Studios Florida is the training of employees? Explain.

2. What actions besides training must an organization such as Universal take to make employees as productive as possible? Why?

3. Based upon information in the case, what do you think will be the biggest challenge for Universal management in successfully providing appropriate human resources for the organization? Explain.

Issues for Review and Discussion

1. What is the difference between appropriate and inappropriate human resources?

2. List and define the four major steps in providing appropriate human resources for the organization.

3. What is the purpose of recruitment?

4. How are job analysis, job description, and job specification related?

5. List the advantages of promotion from within.

6. Compare and contrast the management inventory card, the position replacement form, and the management manpower replacement chart.

7. List three sources of human resources outside the organization. How can these sources be tapped?

8. Does the law influence organizational recruitment practices? If so, how?

9. Describe the role of the Equal Employment Opportunity Commission.

10. Can affirmative action programs be useful in recruitment? Explain.

11. Define *selection*.

12. What is the difference between aptitude tests and achievement tests?

13. Discuss three guidelines for using tests in the selection process.

14. What are assessment centers?

15. List and define the four main steps of the training process.

16. Explain two possible ways of determining organizational training needs.

17. What are the differences between the lecture and programmed learning as alternative methods of transmitting information in the training program?

18. On-the-job training methods include coaching, position rotation, and special project committees. Explain how each of these methods works.

19. What are performance appraisals, and why should they be used?

20. If someone asked your advice on how to conduct performance appraisals, describe in detail what you would say.

Building on What You Know

Directions

Review the Highlight feature as indicated below and answer its corresponding questions. Questions in this section focus on relating a Highlight appearing in this chapter to management concepts that you have learned in a previous chapter.

Review the Quality Highlight: Aetna Life and Casualty

Company on page 331. In chapter 10 you studied about line and staff authority. Would the jobs of individual trainers making lectures on television be line or staff positions? Discuss. Assuming that they are staff positions, list some issues that could cause conflict between the trainers and various line positions in the organization. Be sure to explain why these areas could cause conflict.

Action Summary Answer Key

1. a. F, p. 315
   b. c, p. 315

2. a. b, p. 316
   b. b, p. 316

3. a. b, p. 326
   b. d, p. 327

4. a. d, p. 328
   b. F, p. 330

5. a. e, p. 335
   b. e, p. 336

Case Study

Managing Diversity

by Mary S. Thibodeaux, University of North Texas

According to the Bureau of Labor Statistics, the annual work force growth rate in the United States will be 1.2 percent for the years from 1988 until 2000. Only 32 percent of the new entrants to the work force will be American-born white men. Women will make up about 47 percent of workers, and immigrants and members of ethnic minorities will hold 26 percent of all jobs. Although estimates differ slightly from one source to another, there is a consensus that white males will account for less than 40 percent of the American work force by the year 2010. Women and people of color will fill approximately 75 percent of the 24 million jobs that will be created during the intervening years.

In a word, the work force will be more diverse. What is diversity? *Diversity* in this sense denotes differences in age, ethnicity, gender, physical abilities or qualities, race, and sexual or affectional orientation. It may also include differences in educational background, geographic location, income, marital status, military experience, parental status, religious beliefs, and work experience.

The key phrase for recruiting, training, and promoting this new rainbow coalition of workers is "managing diversity." Demographic changes like the aforementioned demand a new way of running business. A new approach will require recognizing that burgeoning diversity is already a fact of life. To increase the probability of success in managing diversity, companies are training their managers, supervisors, and workers to be more tolerant of language and cultural differences, to identify and reject any existing racial and sexual prejudices, and to be more accommodating to "differently able" individuals. Businesses are also supporting diversity programs by establishing literacy programs in the workplace, allowing flexible work schedules, and providing day care facilities for children and elderly dependents.

A growing number of progressive companies such as Wang Laboratories, Mobil Corporation, Hewlett-Packard, DuPont, Apple Computers, Philip Morris, and Digital Equipment have taken steps to recognize the differences among workers. Not-for-profit organizations such as the United Way, the University of California, Los Angeles, and the University of North Texas have also implemented programs to address the increasing diversity among their employees and volunteers or students. By identifying and discussing stereotypes about races, national origins, and gender, these organizations are preparing their managers to deal with the relentless shift toward a work force made up more and more of minority members and women. These companies are now in the process of learning both to value the diversity of their employees and to manage them fairly. For example, Wang Laboratories has already put over 1,000 managers through its managing-diversity training program. United Way of America initiated the Project Blueprint program in 1988 to assist local United Way branches in accelerating the involvement of Asian-, African-, Hispanic-, and Native American volunteer policymakers on

United Way agency boards and committees. At Digital Equipment Corporation, seeking out diverse employees has become a major focus of recruitment efforts.

Diversity training will not change lifetime attitudes overnight. Its purpose is to make managers aware of the constellation of issues and needs involved. Although no two programs will be identical, many will involve the following components: (1) behavioral awareness, (2) acknowledgment of biases and stereotypes, (3) focus on job performance, (4) avoidance of assumptions, and (5) modification of policy and procedure manuals.

Some of the existing programs are ongoing and are set up as a part of the corporate Human Resources/Personnel function; other programs are presented in 2- or 3-day workshops. Still others rely on outside consultants to provide the direction for learning efforts. As with most major corporate programs, top management commitment of time and resources is important for the success of such programs. Other necessary factors may include increased exposure to and interaction with people of diverse backgrounds, open and frank discussion about differences, and supportive follow-up endeavors.

Why should organizations be concerned about managing diversity? First of all, it is not a fad. Diversity of the work force is here to stay. Second, organizations that do a good job of managing diversity stand to gain such advantages as (1) hiring and retaining the best qualified members of the labor pool, (2) gaining access to more innovative thinking, (3) achieving better performance among female and minority workers, and (4) gaining the opportunity to make the most of workers of nonwhite ethnic or national background.

Discussion Questions

1. Do you think corporate programs for managing diversity should be standing plans or special projects developed for single applications? Why?

2. How does managing diversity differ from affirmative action? Are affirmative action programs becoming things of the past?

3. In a company such as Digital Equipment, with an emphasis on recruiting a diverse work force, which aspect of job analysis would probably be adjusted to meet that emphasis? Why?

4. Imagine that you are a human resources manager for a large firm in Miami. Why might you actively prefer to hire a minority member?

Henry Kates:
Mutual Benefit Life Insurance Company

Mutual Benefit Life Insurance Company is the eighteenth largest company in the insurance industry. It was founded in Newark, New Jersey, in 1845. With the largest insurance company in the United States, the Prudential, also headquartered in Newark, over the years, Mutual Benefit Life has had the opportunity to see close up how diversification can strengthen and enrich a successful insurance company.

Thus, in addition to insurance, Mutual Benefit Life offers consumers other financial products such as mutual funds, annuities, and real estate, and it has investments in holdings as logically and geographically diverse as Rhode Island television stations and a chain of home center stores in Washington state.

Nonetheless, the primary business of Mutual Benefit Life for 145 years has been to offer insurance products, and its primary objective today is to provide the best quality service possible to its clients.

Henry Kates was named chief executive officer of Mutual Benefit Life in 1989. Kates began his insurance career in his father's independent agency in Colorado. Like many other sons, he found that he and his father were not compatible as business partners. In 1960, Kates signed on as a salesman with Mutual Benefit Life. He progressed quickly, becoming the company's youngest general agent ever at the age of 27. Soon after that, he was transferred to the East Coast, and subsequently into the company's executive management structure.

Despite his great success, in some respects, Henry Kates's career with Mutual Benefit Life has been a typical one. Like most other sales agents, Kates was already trained when hired by Mutual Benefit Life; it is standard for the company to hire agents from competitors rather than training new agents from scratch. Sales training is oriented around written materials describing specific company offerings.

Entry-level staff other than sales agents, on the other hand, are usually recruited from the community, either through advertising or through an incentive program. Current employees may introduce candidates for listed jobs to the company; if a candidate is hired, the sponsoring employee receives a cash reward. Evaluation of new-hire candidates may include various aptitude or skills tests, in addition to interviews and informal assessment activities.

Tests do not end once a staff member has been hired at Mutual Benefit Life. Math aptitude and personality tests are usually administered immediately, followed by an orientation program given by the human resources staff. A complete job description is also provided to each newly hired staff member. The company maintains a complete file of job descriptions for all employment positions, and the file is available to all employees.

For a time, when Henry Kates was in his 40s, he dealt not only with the pressures of his burgeoning career, but also with his wife's terminal illness. "The lucky thing was living in Providence, Rhode Island, for most of the illness. My house was 10 blocks from the office. So in the last year of her life I was able to literally work out of the house, and people came to see me rather than the other way around." That sense of fair give-and-take, of support that he received from his employer—"a very faithful and honest relationship with me and Mutual Benefit"—became a cornerstone for Kates's ideal of the relationship between employer and employee.

Under Henry Kates's leadership, support programs for employees are a major concern at Mutual Benefit Life. For example, the company has begun a program to deal with an increased rate of premature deaths among recent retirees, linked to a psychological grieving process that accompanies the abrupt changes in self-image and life-style that occur at retirement. "Those folks whose identity is so [inextricably] entwined with the business, when they retire and all of the trappings of the business are removed from them, their persona is left very thin and threadbare, and sometimes the immune system tends to shut down," says Kates. So he and his company have designed a progressive slowdown for retirees who choose to stay involved, using them as consultants or as part-time help as they adjust to their new lives.

It is not only the retirees who gain from this program, of course. Mutual Benefit Life has the luxury of paying independent contractor fees rather than salaries to its committed supporters. Frequently, those supporters provide invaluable inside tips, as well as formal on-the-job training, to their replacements.

Similarly, Mutual Benefit Life can show financial gains as a side effect of the company's employee health program, another pet project of Henry Kates's. The company fitness center is open every day after work, and employees are encouraged to take advantage of it. During the day, lunch-hour classes in aerobic exercise, weight loss, and life-style changes are offered. In 1989, the investment paid off handsomely, saving the company $100,000 in reduced absenteeism.

Now Henry Kates has trained his eye on the cultural well-being of his work force. Lunch-hour activities are no longer limited to eating or exercise: The company sponsors art lectures and concerts, too. There is a company-sponsored Christmas chorus, and members are given time off from work to practice and perform for their coworkers. "If we stop paying attention to the arts, we can get into some morale problems that will exacerbate all the other known problems, such as homelessness and AIDS and whatever." Henry Kates has learned from personal experience that the devotion a healthy, happy employee can bring to his company pays off in lower turnover, lower training expenses, lower absenteeism, lower health expenses, and a better quality of life for employee, employer, and society as well.

Video Case Questions

1. The text emphasizes three main considerations for recruitment of employees. Based on material available in this case, how do you think Mutual Benefit Life deals with these considerations?

2. Why is retaining the current work force important to Mutual Benefit Life? Give at least two reasons.

3. Review the list of types of training in Table 11.3 on page 328. With respect to a beginning sales agent such as Henry Kates in 1960, which three types of training do you think Mutual Benefit Life should emphasize? Which should be least important? Why?

4. How would programmed learning techniques be helpful to Mutual Benefit Life in training a sales agent newly recruited away from the Prudential?

5. Imagine you are a supervisor in Mutual Benefit Life's claim file area. You are preparing a performance appraisal for a clerk who does excellent work but has missed more than three weeks of work time in the past six months due to minor illnesses—mostly hangovers. How can you use the appraisal to deal with this problem?

Video Case Activities

1. Mutual Benefit Life saved $100,000 in absentee costs in 1989 alone through its fitness program. Suggest four additional employee programs that it might introduce to save even more money in recruiting and training expenses.

2. Design an assessment center exercise aimed to help in the selection of a life insurance claims investigator.

Chapter 12

tudent Learning Objectives

From studying this chapter, I will attempt to acquire:

1. A working definition of *changing an organization*.

2. An understanding of the relative importance of change and stability to an organization.

3. Some ability to know what kind of change should be made within an organization.

4. An appreciation for why individuals affected by a change should be considered when the change is being made.

5. Some facility in evaluating change.

6. An understanding of how organizational change and stress are related.

Organizational Change and Stress

 hapter Outline

Introductory Case

PEPSICO REORGANIZES PIZZA HUT AND TACO BELL

PepsiCo Inc. manufactures, sells, and distributes soft drink concentrates, syrups, and snack foods. The company also operates and develops franchise restaurants such as Pizza Hut and Taco Bell.

PepsiCo Inc., seeking to pump more expertise into its rapidly growing international restaurants, recently announced that it is combining the operations of its businesses abroad with those of its more mature domestic chains.

Under the realignment, PepsiCo turned to two executives who have propelled its restaurants above competitors amid the depressed U.S. fast-food business. Steve Reinemund, forty-two-year-old president and chief executive officer of Pizza Hut's U.S. business, and John Martin, forty-five, his counterpart at Taco Bell, now also are responsible for the overseas operations of their respective chains.

Those international divisions previously were run under a separate PepsiCo division, PepsiCo Food Service International, which also supplied PepsiCo's U.S.

and Canadian restaurants with items like straws, napkins, and cups.

The reorganization underscores the growing importance of PepsiCo's overseas restaurants, which have been quietly building sales at a 33 percent clip in recent years. Since 1980, under PepsiCo Food Service, Taco Bell and Pizza Hut have boosted annual sales overseas to more than $1 billion, while spreading to sixty-two countries from its original eighteen.

> The reorganization underscores the growing importance of PepsiCo's overseas restaurants.

"Our international restaurant business has really come of age in the last few years," said Wayne Calloway, chairman and chief executive officer of PepsiCo, in a statement. A spokesman at PepsiCo, based in Purchase, New York, wouldn't say whether the reorganization involved an increase in spending abroad.

Some industry observers said the moves may have been spurred by the slumping U.S. fast-food market even though PepsiCo's restaurants, which also include Kentucky Fried Chicken, have generally outperformed the industry. "In the current climate [in the United States] it's better to be positioned more globally," says Ron Paul, president of Technomic Inc., a food-service consulting company.

The PepsiCo spokesman said the changes had been under consideration since 1986, when PepsiCo acquired Kentucky Fried Chicken. That chain has had a structure under which the international and domestic businesses reported to one executive. And PepsiCo's other divisions—soft drinks and snack foods—have a similar structure.

PepsiCo also said that Graham Butler, fifty-one, who was president of PepsiCo Food Service, would head his reorganized division, PepsiCo Food Systems Worldwide Distribution. The division will now serve as the distribution arm of supplies for PepsiCo's global restaurants.

From Michael J. McCarthy, "PepsiCo to Consolidate Its Restaurants, Combining U.S. and Foreign Operations," *Wall Street Journal* (October 30, 1990), A4.

In essence, in the introductory case, Wayne Calloway, the PepsiCo chairman and chief executive officer, has decided to make certain changes within his company. Managers like Calloway ultimately are held accountable for making such changes successfully. As a result, Calloway and other managers undergoing the task of modifying an organization pay careful attention to the kinds of topics featured in this chapter. Topics such as the fundamental effects of changing an organization, the factors to consider when changing an organization, and stresses attending organizational changes must be faced thoughtfully and planned for carefully by managers responsible for those changes.

FUNDAMENTALS OF CHANGING AN ORGANIZATION

Thus far, discussion in this "Organizing" section of the text has centered on the fundamentals of organizing, furnishing appropriate human resources for the organization, authority, delegation, and responsibility. This chapter focuses on changing an organization.

Defining "Changing an Organization"

Changing an organization is the process of modifying an existing organization. The purpose of organizational modifications is to increase organizational effectiveness—that is, the extent to which an organization accomplishes its objectives. These modifications can involve virtually any organizational segment and typically include changing the lines of organizational authority, the levels of responsibility held by various organization members, and the established lines of organizational communication.

Most managers agree that if an organization is to be successful, it must change continually in response to significant developments, such as customer needs, technological breakthroughs, and government regulations. The study of organizational change is extremely important because all managers at all organizational levels are faced throughout their careers with the task of changing their organization. Managers who determine appropriate changes to make in organizations and then can implement such changes enable their organizations to be more flexible and innovative.[1] Because change is such a fundamental and necessary part of organizational existence, managers who can successfully implement change are very important to organizations of all kinds.[2]

Many managers consider change to be so critical to the success of the organization that they encourage employees to continually search for areas in which beneficial organizational change can be made. In a classic example, General Motors has provided employees with a "think list" to encourage them to develop ideas for organizational change and to remind them that change is important to the continued success of GM. The think list contained the following questions.[3]

Changing an organization is the process of modifying an existing organization to increase organizational effectiveness.

[See below]

350 PART THREE ORGANIZING

1. Can a machine be used to do a better or faster job?
2. Can the fixture now in use be improved?
3. Can handling of materials for the machine be improved?
4. Can a special tool be used to combine the operations?
5. Can the quality of the part being produced be improved by changing the sequence of the operation?
6. Can the material used be cut or trimmed differently for greater economy or efficiency?
7. Can the operation be made safer?
8. Can paperwork regarding this job be eliminated?
9. Can established procedures be simplified?

Change versus Stability

In addition to organizational change, some degree of stability is a prerequisite for long-term organizational success.[4] Figure 12.1 presents a model developed by Hellriegel and Slocum that shows the relative importance of change and stability to organizational survival. Although these authors use the word *adaptation* in their

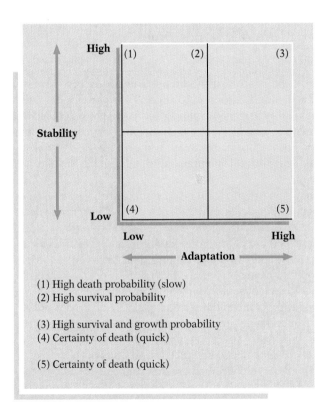

(1) High death probability (slow)
(2) High survival probability

(3) High survival and growth probability
(4) Certainty of death (quick)

(5) Certainty of death (quick)

FIGURE 12.1

Adaptation, stability, and organizational survival

model rather than *change,* the two terms are essentially synonymous. This model stresses that the greatest probability of organizational survival and growth exists when both stability and adaptation are high within the organization (number 3 on the model). The organization without stability to complement or supplement change is at a definite disadvantage. When stability is low, the probability for organizational survival and growth declines. Change after change without stability typically results in confusion and employee stress.[5]

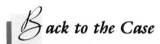ack to the Case

The foregoing information provides several insights about how Calloway should make a decision like changing PepsiCo's organization structure as it relates to Pizza Hut and Taco Bell. As an example, Calloway should evaluate such a change in relation to the degree that the changes would better enable PepsiCo to accomplish its objectives. Calloway should understand that making such changes is extremely important; if PepsiCo is to have continued success over the long run, such changes will probably have to be made a number of times. In fact, appropriate change is so important to a company like PepsiCo that Calloway may want to consider initiating some type of program that would encourage employees to submit their ideas on how to change the company in order to increase its effectiveness. When considering possible changes, however, Calloway will have to keep in mind that some level of stability is also necessary if his company is to survive and grow over the long term.

FACTORS TO CONSIDER WHEN CHANGING AN ORGANIZATION

How managers deal with the major factors to be considered when changing an organization determines to a great extent how successful an organizational change will be. These factors are (1) the change agent, (2) determining what should be changed, (3) the kind of change to make, (4) individuals affected by the change, and (5) evaluation of change. Although the following sections discuss each of these factors individually, Figure 12.2 on page 352 makes the point that their collective influence ultimately determines the success of a change.

The Change Agent

Perhaps the most important factor to be considered by managers when changing an organization is determining who will be the **change agent**—anyone inside or outside the organization who tries to effect change.[6] The change agent might be a self-designated manager within the organization or possibly an outside consultant hired because of a special expertise in a particular area. Although in reality the change agent may not be a manager, the terms *manager* and *change agent* are used synonymously throughout this chapter.

Several special skills are necessary for success as a change agent, including the ability to determine how a change should be made, to solve change-related problems, and to use behavioral science tools to influence people appropriately during

A **change agent** is an individual inside or outside the organization who tries to modify an existing organizational situation.

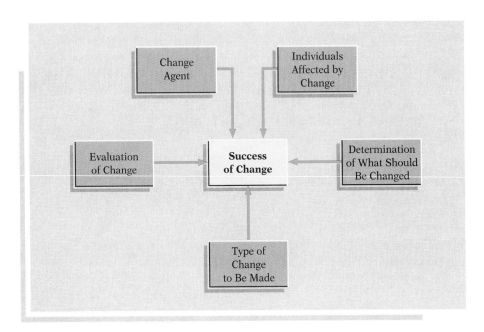

FIGURE 12.2

The collective influence of five major factors on the success of changing
an organization

the change. Perhaps the most overlooked skill of successful change agents is the
ability to determine how much change employees can withstand.[7]

Over all, managers should choose change agents who possess the most expertise in the areas suggested by the necessary special skills. A potentially beneficial
change for the organization might not result in any advantages if the wrong person
is designated to make the change.

Global Highlight: Xerox's Change Agent—the Euromanager

A manager recently appointed at Xerox, who will be an important change agent,
came from within the company. In his newly named corporate position at Xerox
in Stamford, Connecticut, Parisian Roland Magin is called a "Euromanager" because his area of responsibility primarily involves Europe. His most significant
challenges for the future are formulating and implementing organizational changes
that will enable Xerox to be more competitive at the international level.

Xerox is locked in a life-and-death struggle with its Japanese competitors for
world supremacy in photocopiers. Magin knows the kinds of changes he will have
to make because he has fought this type of battle before. Recently, six years of his
career were spent at a French subsidiary, Rank Xerox, where Magin faced a full-
scale attack from a new generation of Japanese photocopier companies. Based on
this experience, Magin believes that changes he must make at Xerox in the United
States include developing a new sense of internationalism in the Xerox work force
in the United States as well as holding individuals at lower levels of the organiza-

tion responsible for making more complex and important decisions. Over all, Magin believes that he must change Xerox in the United States so that it more closely resembles the organization structure of its Japanese competitors.

*B*ack to the Case

Because Wayne Calloway undoubtedly had the main role in deciding to make the Taco Bell/Pizza Hut change at PepsiCo as well as actually implementing the change, for this particular change Calloway is the change agent. Calloway probably designated himself change agent because of his ability to determine if and how this particular type of change within PepsiCo should be made. After all, Calloway is probably the one manager in the company best suited to evaluate the advantages and disadvantages of having a separate international restaurant division for Pizza Huts and Taco Bells, as opposed to having every restaurant in a particular chain report to a single U.S. manager regardless of the restaurant's location.

As change agent, Calloway must have the ability to use behavioral science tools to influence organization members during the implementation of the Pizza Hut/Taco Bell change. Examples: Calloway must determine how much change these PepsiCo employees can withstand. He must influence his staff so its members learn to work together in their new divisions. And he must implement his changes gradually, so that employees will not be overwhelmed. Over all, the ability to use behavioral science tools will help Calloway to be successful in implementing his Pizza Hut/Taco Bell change at PepsiCo.

Determining What Should Be Changed

Another major factor managers should consider is exactly what should be changed within the organization. In general, managers should make changes that increase organizational effectiveness.

It has been generally accepted for many years that organizational effectiveness is the result primarily of organizational activities centering around three main classes of factors: (1) people, (2) structure, and (3) technology.[8] **People factors** are attitudes, leadership skills, communication skills, and all other characteristics of the human resources within the organization. Organizational controls, such as policies and procedures, constitute **structural factors.** And **technological factors** are any types of equipment or processes that assist organization members in the performance of their jobs.

For an organization to maximize effectiveness, appropriate people must be matched with appropriate technology and appropriate structure. Thus, people factors, technological factors, and structural factors are not independent determinants of organizational effectiveness. Instead, as Figure 12.3 on page 354 shows, organizational effectiveness is determined by the relationship of these three factors.

The Kind of Change to Make

The kind of change to make is a third major factor that managers should consider when changing an organization. Although managers can choose to change an

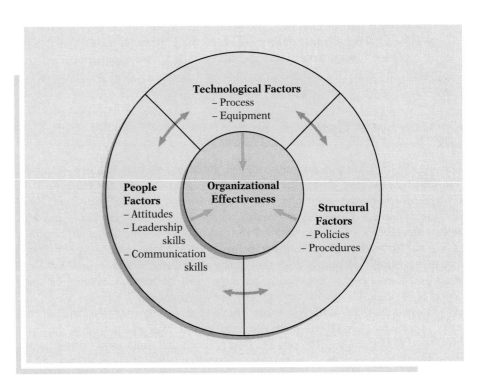

FIGURE 12.3

Determination of organizational effectiveness by the relationship of
people, technological, and structural factors

organization in many different ways, most changes can be categorized as one of
three kinds: (1) technological change, (2) structural change, or (3) people change.
These three kinds obviously correspond to the three main determinants of organizational effectiveness. Each kind of change is named for the one determinant that
the change emphasizes over the other two.

For example, **technological change** emphasizes modifying the level of technology within a management system. Because technological change often involves
outside experts and highly technical language, structural change and people change
are the two kinds discussed in more detail here.

Structural Change

Structural change emphasizes increasing organizational effectiveness by changing
controls that influence organization members during the performance of their
jobs. The following sections further describe this approach and discuss matrix
organizations (organizations modified to complete a special project) as an example
of structural change.

Describing Structural Change. **Structural change** is change aimed at increasing organizational effectiveness through modifications to the existing organizational structure. These modifications can take several forms: (1) clarifying and
defining jobs; (2) modifying organizational structure to fit the communication

Technological change is a type
of organizational change that
emphasizes modifying the level
of technology in the management system.

Structural change is a type of
organizational change that emphasizes modifying an existing
organizational structure.

needs of the organization; and (3) decentralizing the organization to reduce the cost of coordination, increase the controllability of subunits, increase motivation, and gain greater flexibility.[9] Although structural change must include some consideration of people and technology to be successful, its primary focus is obviously on changing organizational structure. In general, managers choose to make structural changes within the organization if information they have gathered indicates that the present organizational structure is the main cause of organizational ineffectiveness. The precise structural change managers make varies from situation to situation, of course. After organizational structure has been changed, management should conduct periodic reviews to make sure that the change is accomplishing its intended purpose.[10]

Quality Highlight: Union Carbide's Disaster Brings Structural Change

From the moment that poisonous gas leaked from its plant in Bhopal, India, structural changes were inevitable at the Union Carbide Corporation. The leak was the worst industrial accident in history. Union Carbide and its employees were caught in the glare of publicity. Employees were confused and depressed by the accident and by the way their company was suddenly viewed as a villain by outsiders.

Further, while Union Carbide was still reeling from the disaster, corporate raider Samuel Heyman of the GAF Corporation launched a hostile takeover bid. In the end, Union Carbide was forced to sell off its profitable consumer products businesses to pay $4.3 billion in debts incurred in repelling Heyman. The company laid off some 4,000 people, about 15 percent of the work force, and began an internal restructuring that has continued into the 1990s.

As the company progressed with its plans, it attempted to provide timely information to employees through a series of internal memos. The company stressed that the restructuring would help it function more efficiently, while reassuring managers that they would retain sufficient resources to ensure quality of company operations.

In 1986, Robert D. Kennedy became chief executive officer and worked to streamline Union Carbide's bureaucracy, asking employees for suggestions on ways to improve productivity and maintain quality in all organizational functions.

"My job," says Kennedy, "is to make people feel comfortable sticking their necks out."

Matrix Organizations. Matrix organizations provide a good illustration of structural change. According to C. J. Middleton, a **matrix organization** is a more traditional organization that is modified primarily for the purpose of completing some kind of special project.[11] In essence, a matrix organization is an organization design in which individuals from various functional departments are assigned to a project manager, who is responsible for accomplishing some specific task.[12] For

A **matrix organization** is a traditional organizational structure that is modified primarily for the purpose of completing some type of special project.

this reason, matrix organizations are also called project organizations. The project itself may be either long term or short term, with employees needed to complete the project borrowed from various organizational segments.

John F. Mee has developed a classic example showing how a more traditional organization can be changed into a matrix organization.[13] Figure 12.4 presents a portion of a traditional organizational structure divided primarily according to product line. Although this design could be generally useful, managers might learn that it makes it impossible for organization members to give adequate attention to three government projects of extreme importance to long-term organizational success.

Figure 12.5 presents one way of changing this more traditional organizational structure into a matrix organization to facilitate completion of the three government projects. A manager would be appointed for each of the three projects and allocated personnel with appropriate skills to complete the project. The three project managers would have authority over the employees assigned to them and be accountable for the performance of those people. Each of the three project managers would be placed on the chart in Figure 12.5 in one of the three boxes labeled Venus Project, Mars Project, and Saturn Project. As a result, work flow related to each project would go from right to left on the chart. After the projects were completed, the organization chart could be changed back to its original design, if that design is more advantageous.

There are several advantages and disadvantages to making structural changes such as those reflected by the matrix organization. Among the major advantages

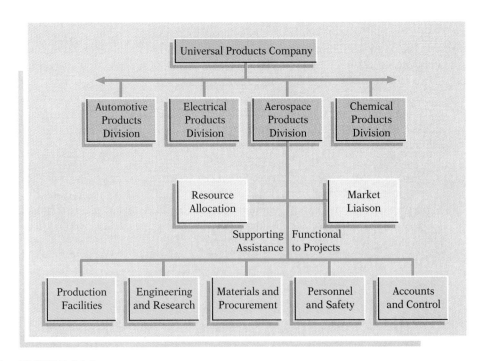

FIGURE 12.4

Portion of a traditional organizational structure based primarily on product

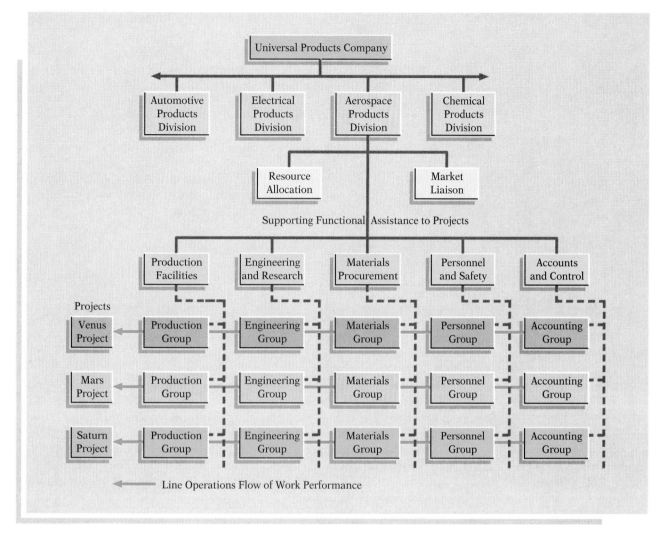

FIGURE 12.5

Traditional organization chart transformed into matrix organization

are that such structural changes generally result in better control of a project, better customer relations, shorter project development time, and lower project costs. Accompanying these advantages, however, are the disadvantages that such structural changes also generally create more complex internal operations, which commonly causes conflict, encourage inconsistency in the application of company policy, and result in a more difficult situation to manage.[14] One point, however, is clear. For a matrix organization to be effective and efficient, organization members must be willing to learn and execute somewhat different organizational roles.[15] The significance of the advantages and disadvantages relative to the success of changing a specific organization obviously varies from situation to situation.

ℬack to the Case

There are different types of changes that a manager like Wayne Calloway can make in an organization. As examples, such managers can change technological factors, people factors, and structural factors in order to increase organizational effectiveness. Calloway's change regarding Pizza Hut and Taco Bell restaurants focuses mainly on structural factors. Before the change, restaurant managers of Pizza Huts and Taco Bells in foreign countries reported to the head of a special division that existed just for them. Meanwhile, managers of Pizza Huts and Taco Bells in the United States reported to a different U.S. division head. As a result of Calloway's change, all Pizza Hut managers throughout the world will report to a designated division head, and all Taco Bell managers throughout the world will report to a different division head. Both of these new division heads will be headquartered in the United States.

People Change

Although successful people change also involves some consideration of structure and technology, the primary emphasis is on people. The following sections discuss people change and examine grid organization development, one commonly used means of attempting to change organization members.

People change is changing certain aspects of organization members to increase organizational effectiveness.

Describing People Change. **People change** emphasizes increasing organizational effectiveness by changing certain aspects of organization members. The focus of this kind of change is on such factors as employees' attitudes and leadership skills. In general, managers should attempt to make this kind of change when human resources are shown to be the main cause of organizational ineffectiveness.

Organization development (OD) is the process that emphasizes changing an organization by changing organization members and bases these changes on an overview of structure, technology, and all other organizational ingredients.

The process of people change can be referred to as **organization development (OD).** Although OD focuses mainly on changing certain aspects of people, these changes are based on an overview of structure, technology, and all other organizational ingredients.[16] Figure 12.6 demonstrates this organizational overview approach by showing both overt and covert organizational components considered during OD efforts. Overt factors are generally easily detectable and pictured as the tip of an organizational iceberg; covert factors are usually more difficult to assess and therefore are displayed as the part of the organizational iceberg that is "under water."

Grid organization development (grid OD) is a commonly used organization development technique based on a theoretical model called the managerial grid.

Grid OD. One commonly used OD technique for changing people in organizations is called **grid OD.**[17] The **managerial grid** is a basic model describing various managerial styles; it is used as the foundation for grid OD. The managerial grid is based on the premise that various managerial styles can be described by means of two primary attitudes of the manager: concern for people and concern for production. Within this model, each attitude is placed on an axis, which is scaled 1 through 9, and is used to generate five managerial styles. Figure 12.7 on page 360 shows the managerial grid, its five managerial styles, and the factors that characterize each of these styles.

A managerial grid is a theoretical model based on the premise that concern for people and concern for production are the two primary attitudes that influence management style.

The central theme of this managerial grid is that 9,9 management (as shown on the grid) is the ideal managerial style. Managers using this style have high concern for both people and production. Managers using any other style have

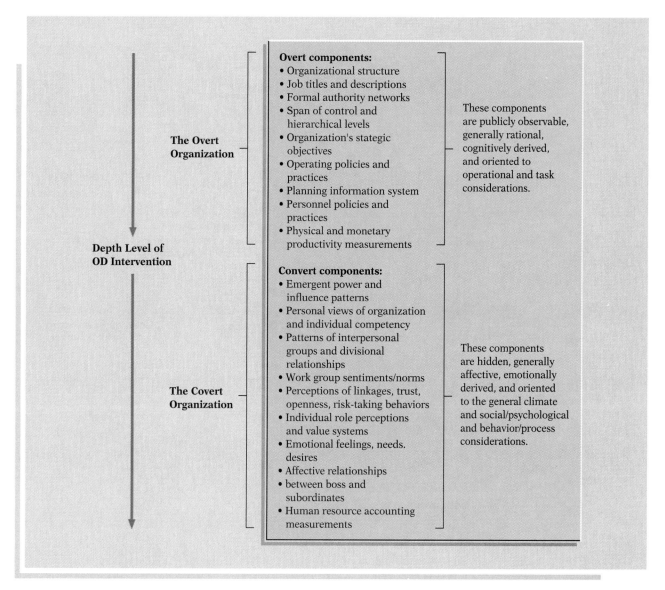

Depth Level of OD Intervention

The Overt Organization

Overt components:
- Organizational structure
- Job titles and descriptions
- Formal authority networks
- Span of control and hierarchical levels
- Organization's stategic objectives
- Operating policies and practices
- Planning information system
- Personnel policies and practices
- Physical and monetary productivity measurements

These components are publicly observable, generally rational, cognitively derived, and oriented to operational and task considerations.

The Covert Organization

Convert components:
- Emergent power and influence patterns
- Personal views of organization and individual competency
- Patterns of interpersonal groups and divisional relationships
- Work group sentiments/norms
- Perceptions of linkages, trust, openness, risk-taking behaviors
- Individual role perceptions and value systems
- Emotional feelings, needs. desires
- Affective relationships
- between boss and subordinates
- Human resource accounting measurements

These components are hidden, generally affective, emotionally derived, and oriented to the general climate and social/psychological and behavior/process considerations.

FIGURE 12.6
The organizational iceberg

lesser degrees of concern for people or production and are thought to reduce organizational success accordingly. The purpose of grid OD is to change organization managers so they will use the 9,9 management style.

How is a grid OD program conducted? The program has six main training phases for all managers within the organization. The first two phases focus on acquainting managers with the managerial grid concept and assisting them in determining which managerial style they most commonly use. The last four phases of the grid OD program concentrate on encouraging managers to adopt the 9,9 management style and showing them how to use this style within their specific job situation. Emphasis throughout the program is on developing teamwork within the organization.

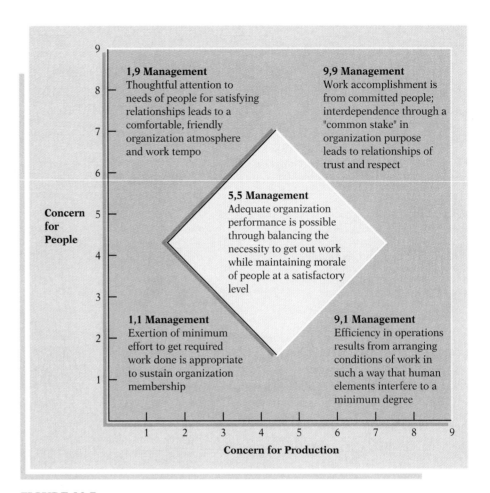

9

1,9 Management
Thoughtful attention to
needs of people for satisfying
relationships leads to a
comfortable, friendly
organization atmosphere
and work tempo

9,9 Management
Work accomplishment is
from committed people;
interdependence through a
"common stake" in
organization purpose
leads to relationships of
trust and respect

5,5 Management
Adequate organization
performance is possible
through balancing the
necessity to get out work
while maintaining morale
of people at a satisfactory
level

Concern
for
People

1,1 Management
Exertion of minimum
effort to get required
work done is appropriate
to sustain organization
membership

9,1 Management
Efficiency in operations
results from arranging
conditions of work in
such a way that human
elements interfere to a
minimum degree

Concern for Production

FIGURE 12.7
The managerial grid

Some evidence suggests that grid OD is useful because it is effective in enhancing profit, positively changing managerial behavior, and positively influencing managerial attitudes and values.[18] Grid OD probably will have to undergo more rigorous testing for an extended period of time, however, before conclusive statements about it can be made.[19]

The Status of Organization Development. If the entire OD area is taken into consideration, changes that emphasize both people and the organization as a whole seem to have inherent strength. There are, however, several commonly voiced weaknesses of OD efforts. These weaknesses indicate that (1) the effectiveness of an OD program is difficult to evaluate, (2) OD programs are generally too time consuming, (3) OD objectives are commonly too vague, (4) the total costs of an OD program are difficult to pinpoint at the time the program starts; and (5) OD programs are generally too expensive.[20]

These weaknesses, however, should not eliminate OD but should indicate areas to perfect within it. Managers can improve the quality of OD efforts by (1) systematically tailoring OD programs to meet the specific needs of the organization, (2) continually demonstrating as part of the program exactly how people should change their behavior, and (3) conscientiously changing organizational reward systems so organization members who change their behavior as suggested by the OD program are rewarded.[21]

Managers have been using OD techniques for several decades. The broad and useful applications of these techniques continue to be documented in the more recent management literature. OD techniques are being applied to business organizations as well as many other types of organizations such as religious organizations.[22]

In addition, OD applications are being documented throughout the world, with increasing use being reported in countries like Hungary, Poland, and the United Kingdom.[23]

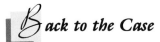

Back to the Case

Wayne Calloway's Pizza Hut/Taco Bell change would not be classified as people change. Although the people involved in the change must be considered to some extent, the main emphasis of the change is on structural change. If, however, Calloway had found that problems with human resources were the main cause of organizational ineffectiveness in foreign Pizza Huts and Taco Bells, he might have proposed organization development rather than structural change. In fact, Calloway may find at any time that he needs to use a grid OD in order to modify management styles and produce more cooperative team effort now that the proposed structural changes have been implemented.

Individuals Affected by the Change

A fourth major factor to be considered by managers when changing an organization is the people affected by the change. A good assessment of what to change and how to make the change probably will be wasted if organization members do not support the change. To increase the chances of employee support, managers should be aware of (1) the usual employee resistance to change, (2) how this resistance can be reduced, and (3) the three phases usually present when behavioral change occurs.

Resistance to Change

Resistance to change within an organization is as common as the need for change. After managers decide on making some organizational change, they typically meet with employee resistance aimed at preventing the change from occurring.[24] This resistance generally exists because organization members fear some personal loss, such as a reduction in personal prestige, a disturbance of established social and working relationships, and personal failure because of an inability to carry out new job responsibilities.

Reducing Resistance to Change

Because resistance typically accompanies proposed change, managers must be able to reduce the effects of this resistance to ensure the success of needed modifications. Resistance usually can be reduced by means of the following guidelines:[25]

1. *Avoid surprises.* People need time to evaluate a proposed change before management implements it. Elimination of time to evaluate how the change may affect individual situations usually results in automatic opposition to it. Whenever possible, individuals who will be affected by a change should be kept informed of the kind of change being considered and the probability that the change will be adopted.

2. *Promote real understanding.* When fear of personal loss related to a proposed change is reduced, opposition to the change is reduced.[26] Most managers would agree that having organization members thoroughly understand a proposed change is a major step in reducing this fear. This understanding may even generate support for the change by focusing attention on possible individual gains that could materialize as a result of it. Individuals should receive information that will help them answer the following change-related questions that invariably will be asked:

   - Will I lose my job?
   - Will my old skills become obsolete?
   - Am I capable of producing effectively under the new system?
   - Will my power and prestige decline?
   - Will I be given more responsibility than I care to assume?
   - Will I have to work longer hours?
   - Will it force me to betray or desert my good friends?[27]

3. *Set the stage for change.* Perhaps the most powerful tool for reducing resistance to change is management's positive attitude toward change. This attitude should be displayed openly by top and middle management as well as by lower management. In essence, management should demonstrate its appreciation for change as one of the basic prerequisites for a successful organization. Management also should strive to be seen as encouraging change only to increase organizational effectiveness, not just for the sake of trying something new. To emphasize this attitude toward change, some portion of organizational rewards should be earmarked for the organization members who are most instrumental in implementing constructive change.

4. *Make tentative change.* Resistance to change also can be reduced by making changes on a tentative basis. This approach establishes a trial period during which organization members spend some time working under a proposed change before voicing support or nonsupport of it. Tentative change is based on the assumption that a trial period during which organization members live under a change is the best way of reducing feared personal loss. Judson has summarized the benefits of using the tentative approach:

   - Those involved are able to test their reactions to the new situation before committing themselves irrevocably.

   - Those involved are able to acquire more facts on which to base their attitudes and behavior toward the change.

   - Those involved with strong preconceptions are in a better position to regard the change with greater objectivity. Consequently, they could review their preconceptions and perhaps modify some of them.

- Those involved are less likely to regard the change as a threat.
- Management is better able to evaluate the method of change and make any necessary modifications before carrying it out more fully.[28]

The Behavioral Side of Change

Almost any change requires that organization members modify the way in which they are accustomed to behaving or working. Therefore, managers must not only be able to decide on the best people–structure–technology relationship for the organization but also to make corresponding changes in such a way that related human behavior is changed most effectively. Positive results of any change will materialize only if organization members change their behavior as necessitated by the change.

Kurt Lewin, a German social scientist, pioneered the study of field theory. According to Lewin, behavioral change is caused by three distinct but related conditions experienced by an individual: (1) unfreezing, (2) changing, and (3) refreezing.[29]

The first condition, **unfreezing,** is the state in which individuals become ready to acquire or learn new behaviors—they experience the ineffectiveness of their present mode of behavior and are ready to attempt to learn new behavior that will make them more effective. It may be especially difficult for individuals to "thaw out" because of positive attitudes they traditionally associate with their past behavior.

Unfreezing is the state in which individuals experience a need to learn new behaviors.

Changing, the second of Lewin's conditions, is the situation in which individuals, now unfrozen, begin experimenting with new behaviors. They try the new behaviors that they hope will increase their effectiveness. According to Edgar Schein, this changing is best effected if it involves both identification and internalization.[30] *Identification* is the process in which individuals performing new behaviors pattern themselves after someone who already has expertise in those behaviors—that is, individuals model themselves after an expert. *Internalization* is the process in which individuals performing new behaviors attempt to use those behaviors as part of their normal behavioral pattern. In other words, individuals consistently try to make the new behaviors useful over an extended period of time.

Changing is the state in which individuals begin to experiment with performing new behaviors.

Refreezing, the third of Lewin's conditions, is the situation in which individuals see that the new behavior they have experimented with during "changing" is now part of themselves. They have developed attitudes consistent with performing the new behavior and see that behavior as part of their normal mode of operations. The rewards individuals receive as a result of performing the new behavior are instrumental in refreezing.

Refreezing is the state in which an individual's experimentally performed behaviors become part of the person.

For managers to increase their success as change agents, they must be able to make their changes in such a way that individuals who will be required to modify their behavior as a result of the change live through Lewin's three conditions. Here is an example: A middle-level manager named Sara Clark has gathered information indicating that Terry Lacey, a lower-level manager, must change his technique for transmitting memos. Clark knows that Lacey firmly believes he can save time and effort by writing out his intracompany memos rather than having them typed, proofread, corrected if necessary, and then sent out. Lacey also believes that an added benefit to this strategy is the fact that it frees his secretary to do other kinds of tasks.

Clark, however, has been getting several requests for help in reading Lacey's sometimes illegible handwriting and knows that some of Lacey's memos are written so poorly that words and sentences are misinterpreted. Obviously, some change is necessary. As Lacey's superior, Clark could simply mandate change by telling Lacey to write more clearly or to have his memos typed. This strategy, however, might not have enough effect to cause a lasting behavioral change and could conceivably result in the additional problem of personal friction between the two managers.

Clark could increase the probability of Lacey's changing his behavior in a more lasting way if she helps Lacey experience unfreezing, changing, and refreezing. To encourage unfreezing, Clark could direct all questions she receives about Lacey's memos back to Lacey himself and make sure that Lacey is aware of all misinterpretations and resulting mistakes. This should demonstrate to Lacey that there is some need for change.

Once Lacey recognizes the need for changing the way in which he writes his memos, he will be ready to try alternative memo-writing methods. Clark could then suggest methods to Lacey, taking special care to give him examples of what others do to write intracompany memos (identification). Over time, Clark could also help Lacey develop the method of transmitting memos that best suits his talents (internalization).

After Lacey has developed an effective method of writing memos, Clark should take steps to ensure that positive feedback about his memo writing reaches Lacey. This feedback, of course, will be instrumental in refreezing Lacey's new method. The feedback can come from Clark, from Lacey's subordinates and peers, and from Lacey's own observations.

Evaluation of Change

As with all other actions, managers should spend some time evaluating the changes they make. The purpose of this evaluation is not only to gain insights into how the change itself might be modified to further increase organizational effectiveness but also to determine whether the steps taken to make the change can be modified to increase organizational effectiveness the next time they are used.

According to Margulies and Wallace, making this evaluation may be difficult, because data from individual change programs may be unreliable.[31] Regardless of the difficulty, however, managers must do their best to evaluate change to increase the organizational benefit from the change.

Evaluation of change often involves watching for symptoms that indicate that further change is necessary. For example, if organization members continue to be oriented more to the past than to the future, if they recognize the obligations of rituals more than the challenges of current problems, or if they owe allegiance more to departmental goals than to overall company objectives, the probability is relatively high that further change is necessary.[32]

A word of caution is needed at this point. Although symptoms such as those listed in the preceding paragraph generally indicate that further change is warranted, this is not always the case. The decision to make additional changes should not be made solely on the basis of symptoms; more objective information also should be considered. In general, additional change is justified if it (1) further improves the means for satisfying someone's economic wants, (2) increases profitability, (3) promotes human work for human beings, or (4) contributes to individual satisfaction and social well-being.[33]

ack to the Case

Wayne Calloway must realize that even though he has formulated a change that would be beneficial to PepsiCo, his attempt to implement this change could prove unsuccessful if he does not appropriately consider the people affected by the change. For example, because Calloway is implementing new reporting lines to the United States for foreign Pizza Huts and Taco Bells, foreign organization members may fear that this change will diminish their control over their jobs. As a result, they may subtly resist the change.

To overcome such resistance, Calloway could use strategies like giving foreign Pizza Hut and Taco Bell employees enough time to fully evaluate and understand the change, presenting a positive attitude about the change, and, if resistance is very strong, suggesting that the proposed change will be tentative until it is fully evaluated. In addition, Calloway probably would find Lewin's unfreezing–changing–freezing theory helpful in implementing the proposed change.

Calloway's changes at PepsiCo need to be evaluated after implementation to discover whether further organizational change is necessary and whether the process used by Calloway to make the change might be improved for future use. This evaluation process could result, for example, in a suggestion that PepsiCo change back to its former organization structure, because the new structure does not allow enough independent tailoring of products to meet foreign tastes in individual countries, or that future implementations should focus more on allowing individuals affected by a change to experience unfreezing, changing, and refreezing.

CHANGE AND STRESS

This chapter focuses on changing an organization to make it more effective, efficient, and successful. When managers implement changes, they should be concerned about the stress they may be creating. Such stress could be significant enough to eliminate the improvement that was intended to be the result of the change. In fact, stress could result in the organization being less effective than it was before the change was attempted. This section defines stress and discusses the importance of studying and managing stress.

Defining Stress

The bodily strain that an individual experiences as a result of coping with some environmental factor is **stress.** Hans Selye, an early authority on this subject, said that stress is essentially the factors affecting wear and tear on the body.[34] In organizations, this wear and tear is caused primarily by the body's unconscious mobilization of energy when an individual is confronted with organizational or work demands.[35]

Stress is the bodily strain that an individual experiences as a result of coping with some environmental factor.

The Importance of Studying Stress

There are several sound reasons for studying stress.[36] First, stress can have damaging psychological and physiological effects on employees' health and on employees' contributions to the effectiveness of the organization. It can cause heart disease, and it can keep employees from being able to concentrate or to make decisions. A second important reason to study stress is that it is a major cause of employee absenteeism and turnover. Certainly, such factors severely limit the potential success of an organization. A third reason to study stress is that stress experienced by an employee can affect the safety of other workers or even the public. Another important reason for studying stress is that it represents a very significant cost to organizations. Some estimates put the cost of stress-related problems in the U.S. economy at $150 billion a year. As examples of these costs, many modern organizations spend a great deal of money treating stress-related employee problems through medical programs, and they must absorb expensive legal fees related to handling stress-related lawsuits.

Managing Stress in Organizations

Because stress is felt by virtually all employees in all organizations, insights about managing stress are valuable to all managers. This section is built on the assumption that in order to appropriately manage stress in organizations, managers must (1) understand how stress influences worker performance, (2) identify where unhealthy stress exists in organizations, and (3) help employees handle stress.

Understanding How Stress Influences Worker Performance

To deal with stress in an organization, managers must understand the relationship between the amount of stress felt by a worker and the worker's performance. This relationship is shown in Figure 12.8. According to this figure, extremely high and extremely low levels of stress tend to have negative effects on production. Additionally, increasing stress tends to increase performance up to some point (Point A in the figure). If the level of stress increases beyond this point, performance will begin to deteriorate. In sum, from a performance viewpoint, having

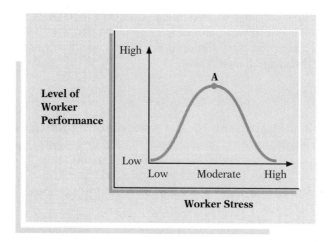

FIGURE 12.8

The relationship between worker stress and the level of worker performance

individuals experience some stress is generally considered advantageous because it tends to increase production. However, having individuals feel too much or too little stress is generally considered disadvantageous, because it tends to decrease production. The cartoon lightheartedly illustrates the profound negative effect that too much stress can have on job performance.

Identifying Unhealthy Stress in Organizations

After managers understand the impact of stress on performance, they must be able to identify where stress exists within the organization.[37] Once the existence of stress is pinpointed, the managers must determine whether the stress is at an appropriate level or if it is too high or too low. Because most stress-related organizational problems involve too much stress rather than too little, the remainder of this section focuses on undesirably high levels of stress.

It can be difficult for managers to identify the people in the organization who are experiencing detrimentally high levels of stress. Part of the difficulty is that people often respond to high stress in different ways. Another part of the difficulty is that physiological reactions to stress are hard, if not impossible, for managers to observe and monitor. Such reactions include high blood pressure, pounding heart, and gastrointestinal disorders.

Despite the difficulty, there are several observable symptoms of undesirably high stress levels that managers can recognize.[38] These symptoms are as follows:[39]

- Constant fatigue
- Low energy
- Moodiness
- Increased aggression
- Excessive use of alcohol
- Temper outbursts
- Compulsive eating
- High levels of anxiety
- Chronic worrying

Keller is a good man but totally lacking in stress-management skills.

Harvard Business Review (July/August 1987), 64.
© Lee Lorenz 1989.

Managers who observe one or more of these symptoms in employees should investigate further to determine if employees exhibiting the symptoms are indeed under too much stress. If so, the managers should attempt to help the employees reduce or handle their stress.

Helping Employees Handle Stress

A **stressor** is an environmental demand that causes people to feel stress.

A **stressor** is an environmental demand that causes people to feel stress. Stressors are common in organizational situations in which individuals are confronted by circumstances for which their usual behaviors are inappropriate or insufficient and where negative consequences are associated with their not properly dealing with the situation.[40] Organizational change is an obvious stressor, but as Figure 12.9 indicates, many other factors related to organizational policies, structure, physical conditions, and processes can also act as stressors.

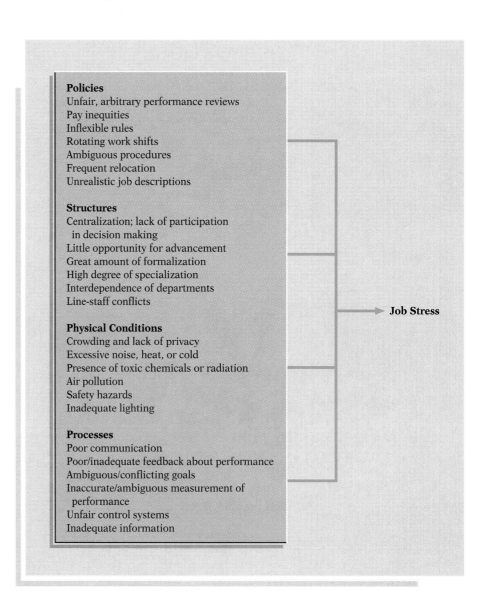

Policies
Unfair, arbitrary performance reviews
Pay inequities
Inflexible rules
Rotating work shifts
Ambiguous procedures
Frequent relocation
Unrealistic job descriptions

Structures
Centralization; lack of participation
  in decision making
Little opportunity for advancement
Great amount of formalization
High degree of specialization
Interdependence of departments
Line-staff conflicts

Physical Conditions
Crowding and lack of privacy
Excessive noise, heat, or cold
Presence of toxic chemicals or radiation
Air pollution
Safety hazards
Inadequate lighting

Processes
Poor communication
Poor/inadequate feedback about performance
Ambiguous/conflicting goals
Inaccurate/ambiguous measurement of
  performance
Unfair control systems
Inadequate information

Job Stress

FIGURE 12.9

Additional organizational stressors

In general, stress is not reduced significantly until the stressors causing it have been coped with satisfactorily or withdrawn from the environment. For example, if too much organizational change is causing undesirably high levels of stress, management may be able to reduce stress by improving organizational training that is aimed at preparing workers to deal with the job demands resulting from the change. Management might also deal with such stress by not making further organizational changes. Such action would be aimed at reducing the significance of organizational change as a stressor and thereby reducing stress levels.

In addition to working in a focused manner on organizational change and other organizational stressors after they are observed, management can adopt several strategies to help prevent the development of unwanted stressors in organizations. Three such strategies follow:[41]

1. *Create an organizational climate that is supportive of individuals.* Organizations commonly seem to evolve into large bureaucracies with formal, inflexible, impersonal climates. This setup leads to considerable job stress. Making the organizational environment less formal and more supportive of employee needs will help prevent the development of unwanted organizational stressors.

2. *Make jobs interesting.* In general, routine jobs that do not allow employees some degree of freedom often result in undesirable employee stress. Management's focus on making jobs as interesting as possible should help prevent the development of unwanted stressors related to routine, boring jobs.

3. *Design and operate career counseling programs.* Considerable stress can be generated when employees do not know what their next career step might be or when they might take it. If management can show employees what the next step will probably be and when it realistically can be achieved, the development of unwanted organizational stressors in this area can be discouraged.

IBM is an example of a company that, for many years, has focused on career planning for its employees as a vehicle for reducing employee stress.[42] IBM has a corporationwide program to encourage supervisors to conduct voluntary career planning sessions with employees on an annual basis. These sessions result in one-page career action plans. At the end of the sessions, the employees have a clear idea of where their careers are headed. The development of undesirable career-related stressors at IBM has been discouraged as a result of this program.

Ethics Highlight: Chase Manhattan Bank Plans to Avoid Possible Stressor

In the early 1970s, Chase Manhattan Bank's Employee Volunteer Program was very popular with employees; employees voluntarily signed up to assist nonprofit organizations in areas ranging from student counseling and financial management to part-time teaching. When the banking industry started to experience a profit squeeze, Chase found it necessary to deemphasize such activities.

Now Chase is bringing its volunteer program back in a way that seems to minimize its possible negative effect as an unwanted stressor because it results in job overload. First, the company is bringing back the program because the program improves corporation-community relations—employees are genuinely interested in helping their community and generally do not see the program as a barrier to their keeping up with more traditional job duties. Forcing an unwanted community-oriented program on employees or creating barriers that prevent employees from doing their everyday jobs would likely doom the program to becoming an unwanted stressor. The company is allocating full-time staff within the bank to coordinate the program. This staffing will help to minimize confusion that could eventually cause it to result in job overload and thereby become an unwanted stressor.

$\mathcal{B}$ack to the Case

Calloway should be careful not to create too much stress on other organization members as a result of his planned change. Such stress could be significant enough to eliminate any planned improvement at PepsiCo and could eventually result in such stress-related effects on employees as physical symptoms and the inability to make sound decisions.

Although some additional stress on organization members as a result of Calloway's planned change at PepsiCo could enhance productivity, too much stress could have a negative impact on production. Signs that Calloway could look for include constant fatigue, increased aggression, temper outbursts, and chronic worrying.

If Calloway determines that undesirably high levels of stress have resulted from his changes at PepsiCo, he should try to reduce the stress through training organization members to execute their new job demands resulting from the change. Or he may want to simply slow the rate of his planned change.

Naturally, it would be wise for Calloway to take action to prevent unwanted stressors from developing as a result of his planned change. Toward this end, Calloway can work to ensure that the organizational climate at PepsiCo is supportive of individual needs and that jobs resulting from the planned change are as interesting as possible.

Action Summary

Circle:

Reread the learning objectives that follow. Each objective is followed by questions. Answering these questions accurately will help you retain the most important concepts discussed in this chapter. After answering each question, check your answer with the answer key at the end of this chapter. (*Hint:* If you have doubt regarding the correct response, consult the page whose number follows the answer.)

From studying this chapter, I will attempt to acquire:

1. A working definition of *changing an organization*.

T, F
    a. The purpose of organizational modifications is to increase the extent to which an organization accomplishes its objectives.

b. Organizational modifications typically include changing: (a) overall goals and objectives; (b) established lines of organizational authority; (c) levels of responsibility held by various organization members; (d) b and c; (e) all of the above.

a, b, c, d, e

2. An understanding of the relative importance of change and stability to an organization.

a. According to the Hellriegel and Slocum model, which of the following is the most likely outcome when both adaptation and stability are high: (a) high probability of slow death; (b) high survival probability; (c) high survival and growth probability; (d) certainty of quick death; (e) possibility of slow death.

a, b, c, d, e

b. According to Hellriegel and Slocum, repeated changes in an organization without stability typically result in employees with a high degree of adaptability.

T, F

3. Some ability to know what kind of change should be made within an organization.

a. Although managers can choose to change an organization in many ways, most changes can be categorized as one of three kinds: (1) people change, (2) goal or objective change, and (3) technological change.

T, F

b. Decentralizing an organization is a structural change aimed at: (1) reducing the cost of coordination; (2) increasing the controllability of subunits; (c) increasing motivation; (d) all of the above; (e) a and b.

a, b, c, d, e

4. An appreciation for why individuals affected by a change should be considered when the change is being made.

a. Which of the following is not an example of personal loss that organization members fear as a result of change: (a) possibility of a reduction in personal prestige; (b) disturbance of established social relationships; (c) reduction in overall organizational productivity; (d) personal failure because of an inability to carry out new job responsibilities; (e) disturbance of established working relationships.

a, b, c, d, e

b. Support for a proposed change may be altered by focusing attention on possible individual gains that could materialize as a result of the change.

T, F

5. Some facility in evaluating change.

a. Symptoms indicating that further change is necessary are that organization members: (a) are oriented more to the future than to the past; (b) recognize the challenge of current problems more than the obligations of rituals; (c) owe allegiance more to overall company goals than to departmental goals; (d) none of the above; (e) a and b.

a, b, c, d, e

b. Change is an inevitable part of management and considered so important to organizational success that some managers encourage employees to suggest needed changes.

T, F

6. An understanding of how organizational change and stress are related.

a. Stress is simply the rate of wear and tear on the body.

T, F

b. From a managerial viewpoint, stress on employees can be either too high or too low.

T, F

c. Stressors are the factors within an organization that reduce employee stress.

T, F

Introductory Case Wrap-Up

"PepsiCo Reorganizes Pizza Hut and Taco Bell" and its related back-to-the-case sections were written to help you better understand the management concepts contained in this chapter. Answer the following discussion questions about this introductory case to further enrich your understanding of chapter content:

1. Would it be difficult to reorganize Pizza Hut and Taco Bell as discussed in the case? Explain your answer.

2. Do you think that certain employees will subtly resist Calloway's changes? Why or why not?

3. What elements of Calloway's plan would cause organization members to experience stress, and what could Calloway do to help alleviate this stress? Be specific.

Issues for Review and Discussion

1. What is meant in this chapter by the phrase *changing an organization?*

2. Why do organizations typically undergo various changes?

3. Does an organization need both change and stability? Explain.

4. What major factors should a manager consider when changing an organization?

5. Define *change agent* and list the skills necessary to be a successful change agent.

6. Explain the term *organizational effectiveness* and describe the major factors that determine how effective an organization will be.

7. Describe the relationship between "determining what should be changed within an organization" and "choosing a kind of change for the organization."

8. What is the difference between structural change and people change?

9. Is matrix organization an example of a structural change? Explain.

10. What is the difference between the overt and covert factors considered during organizational development?

11. Draw and explain the managerial grid.

12. Is grid OD an example of a technique used to make structural change? Explain.

13. What causes resistance to change?

14. List and explain the steps managers can take to minimize resistance to change.

15. Explain the significance of unfreezing, changing, and refreezing to changing the organization.

16. How and why should managers evaluate the changes they make?

17. Define *stress* and explain how it influences performance.

18. List three stressors that could exist within an organization. For each stressor, discuss a specific management action that could be aimed at eliminating the stressor.

19. What effect can career counseling have on employee stress? Explain.

Building on What You Know

Directions

Review the Highlight feature as indicated below and answer its corresponding questions. Questions in this section focus on relating a Highlight appearing in this chapter to management concepts that you have learned in a previous chapter.

Review the Global Highlight: Xerox on page 352. In chapter 11 you studied the relationships among job description, job analysis, and job specification. Based on information in this Highlight, what information do you think is contained in the Job Specification for the position emphasizing being a change agent? Be as specific as possible. Be sure to explain why you believe that the Job Specification contains the information you have listed.

Action Summary Answer Key

1. a. T, p. 349
   b. d, p. 349

2. a. c, pp. 350–351
   b. F, p. 351

3. a. F, p. 353
   b. d, pp. 354–355

4. a. c, p. 361
   b. T, p. 362

5. a. d, p. 364
   b. T, p. 349

6. a. T, p. 365
   b. T, pp. 366–367
   c. F, p. 368

Case Study

Change and Stress:
Kathleen A. Cote of Prime Computer

by Sylvia Keyes, Bridgewater State College

The past few years have brought a lot of changes to Massachusetts-based Prime Computer, Inc., a manufacturer of minicomputer and midrange computer systems. Kathleen Cote, as President and General Manager of Prime Service, the service division of the company, has helped both her employees and the organization as a whole to adjust to those changes.

Prior to joining Prime Computer in 1986, Kathleen Cote had experienced many changes at Wang Laboratories, another Massachusetts computer firm. A few years after coming to Wang as a senior production manager, she was asked to serve as project manager for relocating some of the manufacturing functions to a new plant. She was responsible for planning the move, scheduling the transition, plant layout, determining plant processes, and a move and setup that covered a nine-month span. A year later, she took on another plant start-up, this time from the beginning: facility design and construction, business plan, strategy planning, as well as the move, setup, and full operation in a year and a half.

Shortly after that plant was up and running, the computer industry experienced an industrywide downturn; Cote was asked to downsize and later close the facility. She said, "If I think what I am most proud of in my life, it's starting up that facility; and when I think about the thing that is most disappointing for me, it was having to close down that facility two years later. The facility, the operation, the people all had the highest quality and lowest cost production operation; we had an excellent culture, a diverse work force, and we were all very proud of what we had accomplished. So it was very, very hard to have to lay people off and close the facility."

Kathleen Cote was then asked to join Prime Computer as Vice President of Manufacturing in 1986. However, in March of 1988, big changes soon occurred when there was a hostile takeover attempt, and ten percent of the work force was laid off. In October of 1988, a so-called friendly takeover occurred; the company was restructured into five separate strategic business units, and an additional twenty percent of the work force was laid off. The new administration asked Cote if she would like to leave manufacturing and run Prime Service. She accepted because she saw that the new position would give her profit-and-loss responsibility for the first time. "It's about a $600 million business. . . . So I decided that that would be an opportunity to expand my general management experience."

In the computer industry, an economic downturn has occurred at the same time that customers' needs have changed. New technologies have led to new systems, requiring Prime to have different plant capacity, different labor needs, and a higher degree of service; competition has become fiercer. About the new computer environment, Cote says, "You do have to downsize and streamline your structure, and that is the challenge that everybody has: to do that as quickly as possible but maintain the dignity of people" where layoffs become necessary.

Of the changing business environment in the computer industry, Cote says, "The most enlightened, most successful leaders and managers are those people who are willing not only to look back, but to look each day and ask, 'Is what we're thinking about doing the right thing for today?' You cannot rely on yesterday's news, yesterday's model, or yesterday's strategy. You've got to revisit it every day. You've got to check it against what's happening with your customers, within your markets, within your industries; you've got to revise the technology and be willing to look and relook at it and reevaluate it every day."

Discussion Questions

1. Describe a situation in which Kathleen Cote might have used matrix management.

2. Proposed layoffs like those that have taken place in recent years at Prime Computer are an obvious source for stress. List four reactions that would make employees resistant to change after layoffs have occurred and they have been kept on.

3. Kathleen Cote's employees will find themselves servicing a totally different set of machines and computer applications in the near future. Suggest ways she might help them adapt to the pressures of new responsibilities.

4. How do you think building a new plant might be beneficial to employees who go to work in it? How might it be stressful?

Starting Over: I. W. Burnham of Drexel Burnham Lambert

The business of managing investments has changed dramatically for Americans during the course of this century. From a nation that saved money in mattresses as often as in banks, we have become partners in a huge industry that long ago outgrew the bounds of straightforward banking and turned Wall Street from a small, speculative businessmen's club into the core of international commerce. A new breed of businessperson was spawned along the way: investment bankers.

I. W. Burnham II was central to those changes. In 1931, fresh out of the Wharton School at the University of Pennsylvania, Burnham took off for Wall Street to make his fortune—and he did. He worked his way up in securities handling. By 1935, he was in a position to open his own firm, Burnham and Company, with a partner and two employees. Except for time spent flying for the Navy in World War II, Burnham headed his firm in the slow but steady march forward that, in 1973, allowed him to acquire the venerable Philadelphia investment firm of Drexel Firestone and, in 1976, the Lambert Group. By 1977, the firm, renamed Drexel Burnham Lambert, was headed for the top of the investment banking industry. Burnham, 67 years old, resigned from active management of the firm, although he remained its chairman.

A revolution in investment banking was underway at Drexel by the time I. W. Burnham stepped aside. The firm had begun to trade heavily in high-yield bonds. These are bonds designed to support companies embarking on major growth when more conservative means of financial backing are not forthcoming. In return for high risks, the bonds offer a significantly higher rate of return than better-rated instruments. Usually, the companies involved are already carrying a substantial load of debt, and the ventures tend to be highly speculative; the bonds are considered to be below investment grade. They are also known as "junk bonds."

In 1973, Burnham had hired the man who would eventually be called "king of the junk bonds," Michael Milken. Milken was the wizard who designed the great junk-bond offerings of the 1980s; in a matter of weeks, the offerings he engineered could raise millions in speculative investments for companies requiring immediate cash. Milken's offerings alone raised over $100 billion. Drexel Burnham Lambert led the field of junk-bond issues, with up to 46% of the total business. The firm was thriving when I. W. Burnham stepped aside as chairman in 1984.

The insider-trading scandals of the later 1980s hit Wall Street hard, but none was as hard hit as Drexel Burnham Lambert. Some analysts assert that many of the Wall Street prosecutions were entered into simply to solicit information for the eventual prosecutions of Michael Milken and Drexel. Whether or not this is true, this was the result. Drexel was left in shambles by the scandals, the lawsuits, and the collapse of the market in high-yield bonds.

From a firm with almost 11,000 employees, Wall Street's most profitable investment bank shrank drastically. In December, 1988, the firm's board of directors agreed that Drexel should plead guilty to a number of federal counts and buy its way out of further suits for $650 million. By 1989, the firm had only 5,300 employees. On February 13, 1990, Drexel Burnham Lambert filed for reorganization under the terms of U.S. Chapter 11 provisions; the proud firm was bankrupt.

I. W. Burnham, the firm's honorary chairman, heard of the bankruptcy filing indirectly and was angry and frustrated. Since retiring from the board, he had watched his firm make a number of deals that he considered foolish and a few he considered just plain wrong. "Maybe they just didn't want to call me because, had they listened, it might not have happened," he says.

I. W. Burnham is not, however, a man to let his name sink ignominiously. In September, 1989, he purchased the subsidiary Drexel Burnham Fund from Drexel Burnham Lambert. The blue-chip fund, under his management, had earned an average 18 percent annual return; now he would manage it once again. He re-named it "The Burnham Fund." Also in 1989, he founded two new mutual fund companies, Burnham Securities and Burnham Asset Management. In fact, it appears that his name will no longer be associated with Drexel Burnham Lambert; that giant firm—now down to 20 employees—will emerge from bankruptcy re-named and reoriented, as an advising firm for financially troubled companies.

I. W. Burnham still believes in high-yield bonds, though. He points to Turner Broadcasting and MCI as tremendously successful companies that would never have succeeded without junk-bond offerings. Also, although the junk-bond mar-ket dwindled to nothing in 1990, Wall Street now seems poised to follow Burn-ham's advice. RJR Nabisco has announced plans for an issue of $750 million to $1 billion in the second quarter of 1991. Analysts believe this signals a new start for the high-yield bond market.

Video Case Questions

1. Change is critical to long-term organizational success. How do you think the changes brought on by computer access to trading information and by word processors might have changed business at Drexel Burnham Lambert? What kind of changes are they?

2. How might an employee who had been with Burnham and Company for years react to the changes of the mid-1970s? How would the unfreezing condition of behavioral change apply?

3. Do you think the changes brought to Drexel by the rapidly expanding junk-bond market were too abrupt? If growth had been more gradual, would the firm have been more likely to survive? Why or why not?

4. I. W. Burnham says, "When things got busy I would stay down and work with my people. I think the key to success is being able to understand the job of everyone. . . . I don't know if that's possible now." Where do you think his management style would fall on the managerial grid shown in Figure 12.7?

Video Case Activities

1. When junk-bond issues became the major factor of business at Drexel Burnham Lambert, brokers had to learn new behaviors. Write a paragraph describing how a broker might unfreeze, change, and refreeze his behaviors to be success-ful in the new business.

2. Prepare a chart of organizational stressors that might have applied to conditions at Drexel Burnham Lambert in 1988.

PART 3

INTEGRATIVE CASE

outhwestern Bell: Change Molds an Organization

by Alice Smith, St. Louis Community College at Mettamec

On January 1, 1984, AT&T divested itself of the seven regional Bell Telephone Companies. One of these newly independent "Baby Bells," Southwestern Bell Corporation, found itself entering a period of enormous change in both technology and its regional marketplace. The corporation immediately lost 18,000 employees involved with long distance service to AT&T, dropping from 90,800 workers in 1983 to 71,854 in 1984.

Several significant change factors compounded the dramatic problem of massive reformation. First, the demand for telecommunications was growing, as more sophisticated products such as high-speed computer data lines, home personal computer lines, voice-message services, cellular telephones, cordless telephones, and fax machines entered the market. Second, the technology required to provide these services became largely automated; fewer people were needed to provide more services. Third, the economy of most of the five states of Southwestern Bell—Texas, Oklahoma, Kansas, Arkansas, and Missouri—underwent a drastic downturn as agriculture- and energy-related businesses became depressed.

These factors had a large impact as Southwestern Bell created an organizational structure to handle its new position and challenges. The regulated telephone company, the core of the organization, was reorganized into five divisions, along state lines. This decentralizes authority and responsibility. Each state division is run as a profit center, coordinated through corporate headquarters for decisions that affect all five. State divisions are generally free to accept or reject corporate recommendations.

Groups operating within the states are organized by function and then by product, consumer, or territory. Product teams with diverse members address technical, financial, and marketing questions. Teams comprise specialists working together laterally to generate new services and to price, market, and implement those services. This large number of specialized departments means that coordination among them is key to responding quickly to consumer needs.

The pressure on workers to be aware of a wide range of customer demands and of the rapid changes in telecommunications products has been handled with aggressive employee training and incentive programs. Employees are taught how to refer potential customers to sales groups, and they receive awards for sales resulting from their referrals. Workers are also rewarded, in teams and individually, for special contributions to the service and financial needs of the company. New programs to encourage employee initiative have also been established. Performance appraisals have been clarified; specific observations of worker strengths and weaknesses are now documented. Ratings are based on the individual's contributions to company objectives.

Responding to a changing market necessitated shifts in employee responsibilities and expectations; the increase in automation and the depressed Southwestern economy have brought other changes as well. Southwestern Bell wanted to avoid layoffs insofar as possible, so it instituted plans in 1986 and in 1990 to encourage management workers to consider early retirement options. Cash incentives and extra retirement benefits were offered. More than 1,100 managers retired during the 1990 plan, costing the company $45 million in incentive payments.

While downsizing its management force, Southwestern Bell also took steps to flatten its organizational structure. Several layers of managements were eliminated by combining authority levels. Span of control was increased in many departments as managers left and were not replaced. The distinction between line and staff workers was minimized; staff personnel became advisors rather than directors. Groups that serve many line departments were consolidated.

The rapid adaptation at Southwestern Bell did not come without stress to its employees. Promotion opportunities decreased as the organization became smaller and flatter, so the company instituted programs to help people derive greater satisfaction from their current jobs. Programs were established to provide ways for employees to acquire new skills through lateral moves. Career planning and development were made available through resource centers and training/retraining programs. An assistance plan provides counseling to workers experiencing problems on or off the job.

The new subsidiaries—*Publications, Telecom, Metromedia Paging, Mobile Systems,* and *Gulf Printing*—also provide job opportunities outside of the traditional telephone market and beyond the five state service region. Another subsidiary has been established to expand international holdings, including cable television franchises in Great Britain and Israel, and a controlling interest in Telmex, the Mexican national telephone company.

All of these subsidiaries have offered many positions that could be filled by existing telephone company workers.

Since 1984, Southwestern Bell has taken many steps forward as an organization. It has expanded its products and operations and now does business in such far-flung places as the Fiji Islands and New Zealand. Its employees have adapted to a customer orientation and a streamlined structure; they are encouraged to assume greater responsibility and are rewarded accordingly. The company's aim is summed up by chairman and CEO Edward E. Whitacre, Jr.: "As we head toward the next century, you'll see Southwestern Bell Corporation at the forefront of a dynamic industry, one that's been cited by industry analysts as having excellent potential for growth."

Discussion Questions

1. Southwestern Bell has only been an independent corporation since 1984; before that, it was wholly owned by AT&T. How has this magnified the organizational challenges it faced?

2. Southwestern Bell has streamlined by reducing management layers and increasing spans of control. What are the advantages and disadvantages of this structural change?

3. To reduce the size of the work force while keeping layoffs minimal, Southwestern Bell offered cash and other compensations in return for some employees' taking early retirement. Do you think this was a reasonable use of $45 million of company funds? Why?

4. Now that promotion opportunities are reduced at Southwestern Bell, the company encourages workers to get greater satisfaction from current jobs and through lateral moves. If you were an ambitious employee, would you consider this an adequate solution? If not, what alternatives would you see?

5. Of three change factors—new products/markets, technological advances, and a depressed regional economy—which do you think had the greatest effect? Why?

Motorola, Inc. won the Malcolm Baldrige award in 1988 in the manufacturing division. Motorola makes a stated goal of "total customer satisfaction" and applies itself diligently to reducing product defects through its "Six Sigma" strategy. (The Six Sigma Quality is a statistical measure of variation from a desired result with a target goal of no more than 3.4 defects per million product *s*.)

Influencing

nfluencing is the third of the four major management functions that must be performed for organizations to have long-term success. The last two sections of the text focused on how managers plan and organize resources in order to reach organizational objectives. This section discusses important people-oriented issues that managers must consider in influencing workers to become and remain productive. In general, the most important influencing tasks are communication, leadership, motivation, and groups and corporate culture.

The discussion of the fundamentals of influencing and communication defines *influencing* and presents it as a subsystem of the overall management system. The discussion also indicates that within this subsystem, communication is an important issue. It involves specific elements and processes, can be successful or unsuccessful, and can take various forms, such as verbal or nonverbal and formal or informal. The explanation of leadership will include the definition of *leadership*, specific leadership strategies that relate to decision making, the level of follower maturity, and the process of engineering situations to fit leadership styles.

This section will also include the definition of *motivation* and a discussion of several models that are used to describe it. It will describe theories that focus on human needs as an integral part of motivation theory and several strategies that managers can use to motivate organization members.

Finally, the discussion on groups and corporate culture will stress that for managers to influence organization members, they must be able to manage groups of people. This discussion will define *groups*, distinguish between formal and informal groups, and suggest ways that managers can maximize group effectiveness. Discussion also focuses on corporate culture as a variable in managing groups.

Although the material in this section will be new and challenging, learning it is crucial to a comprehension of the new topics that will be presented later. As you study this material on influencing, remember what you have learned in the previous portions of the text so you can continue to build a comprehensive understanding of the management process.

Chapter 13

Student Learning Objectives

From studying this chapter, I will attempt to acquire:

1. An understanding of influencing.
2. An understanding of interpersonal communication.
3. A knowledge of how to use feedback.
4. An appreciation for the importance of nonverbal communication.
5. Insights on formal organizational communication.
6. An appreciation for the importance of the grapevine.
7. Some hints on how to encourage organizational communication.

Fundamentals of Influencing and Communication

 hapter Outline

GENERAL MOTORS FOCUSES ON INFLUENCING PEOPLE

Corporate-management meetings tend to be filled with "yes [people]" reverentially deferring to superiors—especially at General Motors Corp., the world's largest corporate bureaucracy. "At GM, we not only shoot the messenger," the joke goes, "we bayonet the stretcher carrier."

But at a gathering of GM's top 900 executives . . . , David A. Hansen, a mid-level executive, stood up to report from Table 37. "We would really appreciate it if you could lick the temperature problem in this corner of the room," he complained.

[Former] chairman Roger B. Smith's typically imperious response: "I've got a sweater on. One of the things we've got to do in this corporation is find 15-cent solutions to million-dollar problems."

Undeterred, Mr. Hansen shot back: "Could I please borrow your sweater?"

The crowd laughed nervously, but Mr. Smith calmly climbed off the stage, walked to the back of the room, took off his brown cardigan and handed it to Mr. Hansen. He then strode back to the podium amid enthusiastic applause.

GM officials insist that the episode wasn't rehearsed, but they are seizing on it as symbolic. During much of the 1980s—Mr. Smith's tenure—the No. 1 auto maker . . . lunged from one breathtaking strategy to another, often ignoring how it [was] jarring the 750,000 employees expected to carry out the plans. . . . After watching sales and profits plunge, GM is waking up with the repentant fervor of Ebenezer Scrooge on Christmas morning. The world's largest industrial company proclaims that it has discovered the real path to corporate health: listening to, and trusting, its people.

[GM] has discovered the real path to corporate health: listening to, and trusting, its people.

It [may] take a while . . . to convince the rank and file. GM has eliminated 40,000 white-collar workers in the past three years and reduced pay and benefits. Moreover, GM has a long history of poor relations with its hourly workers. Just three years ago, amid talk of a new era of cooperation, the union found company officials planning a comprehensive revamping of factory organization without seeking worker approval or even advice.

From Jacob M. Schlesinger and Paul Ingrassia, "People Power," *Wall Street Journal* (January 12, 1989), A1, A6. For an interesting view of how Robert C. Stempel, Roger Smith's recent successor, has dealt with some of the issues that he inherited from Smith, see Joseph B. White, "Stamp of Stempel, New GM Chairman Has No-Frills Look," *Wall Street Journal* (August 2, 1990), A3.

WHAT'S AHEAD

In the introductory case, Roger B. Smith, then chairman at General Motors, was accused of building an organization that was insensitive to the needs of its employees. According to the case, Smith wanted to build GM into an organization that employees could see as one that trusted them and would listen to them. The information in this chapter emphasizes the value of transforming GM into a company that its employees could see as being more human oriented and offers a manager some insights regarding how to meet this challenge. The chapter is divided into two main parts: the fundamentals of influencing and the skill of communication.

FUNDAMENTALS OF INFLUENCING

The four basic managerial functions—planning, organizing, influencing, and controlling—were introduced in chapter 1. *Influencing* follows *planning* and *organizing*, to be the third of these basic functions covered in this text. A definition of *influencing* and a discussion of the influencing subsystem follow.

Defining "Influencing"

Influencing is the process of guiding the activities of organization members in appropriate directions. Appropriate directions, of course, are those that lead to the attainment of management system objectives. Influencing involves focusing on organization members as people and dealing with such issues as morale, arbitration of conflicts, and the development of good working relationships among individuals. Influencing is a critical part of a manager's job. The ability of a manager to influence others is a primary determinant of how successful a manager will be.[1]

The Influencing Subsystem

As with the planning and organizing functions, the influencing function can be viewed as a subsystem that is part of the overall management system process (see Figure 13.1, p. 386). The primary purpose of the influencing subsystem is to enhance the attainment of management system objectives by guiding the activities of organization members in appropriate directions.

Figure 13.2 on page 387 shows the specific ingredients of the influencing subsystem. The input of this subsystem is composed of a portion of the total resources of the overall management system, and the output is appropriate organization member behavior. The process of the influencing subsystem involves the performance of four primary management activities: (1) leading, (2) motivating, (3) considering groups, and (4) communicating. Managers transform a portion of organizational resources into appropriate organization member behavior mainly by performing these four activities.

Influencing is the process of guiding the activities of organization members in appropriate directions, involving the performance of four primary management activities: (1) leading, (2) motivating, (3) considering groups, and (4) communicating.

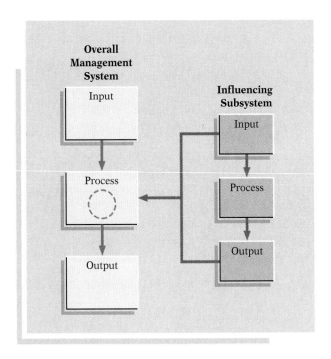

FIGURE 13.1
Relationship between overall management system and influencing
subsystem

As Figure 13.2 shows, leading, motivating, and considering groups are related
influencing activities, each of which is accomplished, to some extent, by managers
communicating with organization members. For example, managers decide what
kind of a leader they should be only after they analyze the characteristics of various
groups with which they will interact and determine how these groups can best be
motivated. Then, regardless of the strategy they adopt, their leading, motivating,
and working with groups will be accomplished, at least to some extent, by communication with other organization members.

In fact, as Figure 13.3 implies, all management activities are accomplished at
least in part through communication or communication-related endeavors.[2] Because communication is used repeatedly by managers, communication skills are
often referred to as the fundamental management skill.

Supporting the notion that communication is the fundamental management
skill are the results of a recent survey of chief executives. The results (which appear
in Table 13.1, p. 388) show communication skill as the most important skill (along
with interpersonal skills) to be taught to management students.

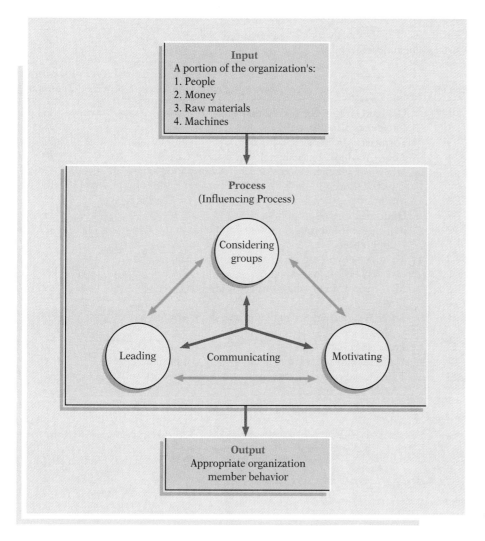

FIGURE 13.2

The influencing subsystem

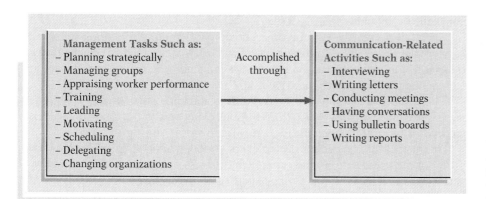

FIGURE 13.3

Management tasks and possible communication-related behavior used to help accomplish those tasks

TABLE 13.1 Chief executives rank importance of skills to be taught to
management students

Rank*	Key Learning Area	Frequency Indicated
1	Oral and written communication skills	25
1	Interpersonal skills	25
3	Financial/managerial account skills	22
4	Ability to think, be analytical, and make decisions	20
5	Strategic planning and goal setting—concern for long-term performance	13
6	Motivation and commitment to the firm—to give 110%	12
7	Understanding of economics	11
8	Management information systems and computer applications	9
8	To know all you can about your business, culture, and overall environment	9
8	Marketing concept (the customer is king) and skills	9
11	Integrity	7
11	To know yourself: Setting long- and short-term career objectives	7
13	Leadership skills	6
13	Understanding of the functional areas of the business	6
13	Time management: Setting priorities—how to work smart, not long or hard	1

*1 is most important.

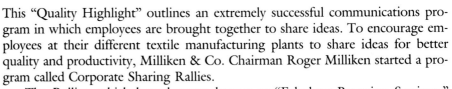

*Quality Highlight: Milliken & Co.
Motivates Employees to Excel*

This "Quality Highlight" outlines an extremely successful communications program in which employees are brought together to share ideas. To encourage employees at their different textile manufacturing plants to share ideas for better quality and productivity, Milliken & Co. Chairman Roger Milliken started a program called Corporate Sharing Rallies.

The Rallies, which have become known as "Fabulous Bragging Sessions," bring employees together to communicate with each other. Instead of being forced to listen to top management, employees are influenced by their peers in a setting that encourages them to try new methods.

The sessions are conducted every 90 days and each lasts for two days. Each one has a theme, such as cost reduction, improving quality, or boosting sales. A hundred or more teams present ideas to success stories during the sessions.

At the end of the sessions, employees choose winners, based both on the quality of the presentations and on the effectiveness of the ideas. Every employee who attends a session receives a framed participation certificate signed by company President Thomas Malone.

Since 1981, when Milliken & Co. began its Pursuit of Excellence program, of which the sessions are a part, productivity has increased by 42 percent. In 1989, the company won the Malcolm Baldrige National Quality Award.

Malone attributes the improvement to restructuring employees into teams. The teams schedule work, establish performance objectives, and create training programs. By fostering communication among employees, Milliken & Co. has been able to positively influence employee attitudes toward productivity.

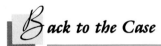

Back to the Case

One of the primary functions of GM's Roger Smith was influencing—guiding the activities of GM employees to enhance the accomplishment of organizational objectives. Smith could perform this function by motivating such individuals as division managers and corporate market research staff to do better jobs, by working well with various groups of GM employees, and by communicating successfully with GM employees.

Of all of these influencing activities, however, communication would have been especially important to Smith. Communication is the main tool through which Smith, at least to some extent, accomplished his duties as GM chairman. As an example in the introductory case, through communication Smith spread the message that GM needed "fifteen-cent solutions to million dollar problems." Almost any effect that Smith exerted on GM (planning, organizing, or controlling) required him to communicate with other GM employees.

Communication is discussed further in the rest of this chapter. Leading, motivating, and considering groups are discussed in chapters 14, 15, and 16, respectively.

COMMUNICATION

Communication is the process of sharing information with other individuals. Information, as used here, is any thought or idea that managers desire to share with other individuals. In general, communication involves one individual projecting a message to one or more others that results in all people arriving at a common meaning of a message.[3] Because communication is a commonly used management skill and is often cited as the one ability most responsible for a manager's success, prospective managers must learn how to communicate.[4]

The communication activities of managers generally involve interpersonal communication—sharing information with other organization members. The following sections feature both the general topic of interpersonal communication and the more specific topic of interpersonal communication in organizations.

Interpersonal Communication

To be a successful interpersonal communicator, a manager must understand (1) how interpersonal communication works, (2) the relationship between feedback and interpersonal communication, and (3) the importance of verbal versus nonverbal interpersonal communication.

Communication is the process of sharing information with other individuals.

How Interpersonal Communication Works

Interpersonal communication is the process of sharing information with other individuals.[5] To be complete, the process must have the following three basic elements:

The **source/encoder** is the person in the interpersonal communication situation who originates and encodes information that the person wants to share with others.

1. *The source/encoder.* The **source/encoder** is the person in the interpersonal communication situation who originates and encodes information to be shared with another person. Encoding is the process of putting information in a form that can be received and understood by another individual. Putting thoughts into a letter is an example of encoding. Until information is encoded, it cannot be shared with others. (From here on, the source/encoder will be referred to simply as the source.)

A **message** is encoded information that the source/encoder intends to share with others. The **signal** is a message that has been transmitted from one person to another.

2. *The signal.* Encoded information that the source intends to share constitutes a **message.** A message that has been transmitted from one person to another is called a **signal.**

Global Highlight: Compression Labs Sends Messages via Videoconferencing

According to Carl Marszewski of Compression Labs, Inc., the increased need to compete with other businesses on the international level has driven organizations to look for new and better ways of projecting communication signals. As with Compression Labs, a growing number of businesses are using international videoconferencing, conferences via television, as an economical yet effective way to communicate about topics like new areas for organizational research, reviewing budgets, and overall organizational problem solving. In general, organizations have met with some difficulty in providing videoconferences across national borders. Issues like a lack of coordination between the United States and other countries has made the process challenging. Given the intense competition among firms at the global level along with the effectiveness and efficiency of videoconferencing, aggressive firms will undoubtedly find ways to overcome any difficulties relating to the videoconferencing process. A rapid growth in the area of international videoconferencing is forecasted for the future.

3. The **decoder/destination** is the person or people in the interpersonal communication situation with whom the source/encoder attempts to share information.

3. *The decoder/destination.* The **decoder/destination** is the person with whom the source is attempting to share information. This individual receives the signal and decodes, or interprets, the message to determine its meaning. Decoding is the process of converting messages back into information. In all interpersonal communication situations, message meaning is a result of decoding. (From here on, decoder/destination will be referred to as the destination.)

The classic work of Wilbur Schramm helps us understand the role played by each of the three elements of the interpersonal communication process. As implied in Figure 13.4, the source determines what information to share, encodes this

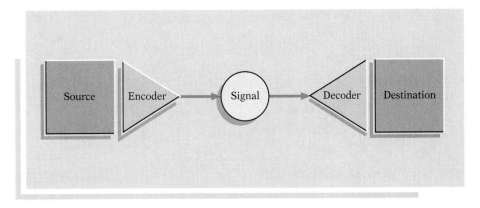

FIGURE 13.4

Role of the source, signal, and destination in the communication process

information in the form of a message, and then transmits the message as a signal to the destination. The destination decodes the transmitted message to determine its meaning and then responds accordingly.

A manager who desires to assign the performance of a certain task to a subordinate would use the communication process in the following way: First, the manager would determine exactly what task he or she wanted the subordinate to perform. Then the manager would encode and transmit a message to the subordinate that would accurately reflect this assignment. The message transmission itself could be as simple as the manager telling the subordinate what the new responsibilities include. Next, the subordinate would decode the message transmitted by the manager to ascertain its meaning and then would respond to it appropriately.

Successful and Unsuccessful Interpersonal Communication. Successful communication is an interpersonal communication situation in which the information the source intends to share with the destination and the meaning the destination derives from the transmitted message are the same. Conversely, **unsuccessful communication** is an interpersonal communication situation in which the information the source intends to share and the meaning the destination derives from the transmitted message are different.

To increase the probability that communication will be successful, the message must be encoded to ensure that the source's experience with the way a signal should be decoded is equivalent to the destination's experience of the way it should be decoded. If this situation exists, the probability is high that the destination will interpret the signal as intended by the source. Figure 13.5 on page 392 illustrates these overlapping fields of experience that ensure successful communication.

Barriers to Successful Interpersonal Communication. Factors that decrease the probability that communication will be successful commonly are called communication barriers. A clear understanding of these barriers is helpful to managers in their attempt to maximize communication success. The following sections discuss both communication macrobarriers and communication microbarriers.

Communication macrobarriers are factors that hinder successful communication in a general communication situation.[6] These factors relate primarily to the

Successful communication is an interpersonal communication situation in which the information the source/encoder intends to share with the decoder/destination and the meaning the decoder/destination derives from the transmitted message are the same.

Unsuccessful communication is an interpersonal communication situation in which the information the source/encoder intends to share with the decoder/destination and the meaning the decoder/destination derives from the transmitted message are different.

Communication macrobarriers are factors that hinder successful communication and that relate primarily to the communication environment and the larger world in which communication takes place.

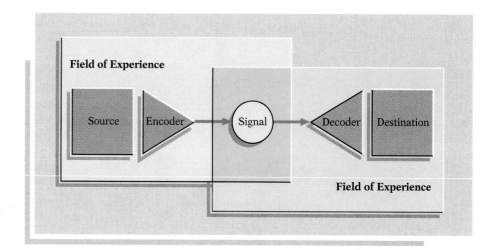

FIGURE 13.5

Overlapping fields of experience
that ensure successful
communication

communication environment and the larger world in which communication takes
place. Among the macrobarriers are the following:[7]

1. *The increasing need for information.* Because society is constantly and rapidly
   changing, individuals have a greater and greater need for information. This
   increased need tends to overload communication networks, thereby distorting
   communication. To minimize the effects of this barrier, managers should take
   steps to ensure that organization members are not overloaded with information. Only information critical to the performance of their jobs should be
   transmitted to them.

2. *The need for increasingly complex information.* With today's rapid technological
   advances, most people are faced with complex communication situations in
   their everyday lives. If managers take steps to emphasize simplicity in communication, the effects of this barrier can be lessened. Also, furnishing organization
   members with adequate training to deal with more technical areas might be
   another strategy for overcoming this barrier.

3. *The reality that individuals in the United States are increasingly coming in contact
   with individuals using languages other than English.* As business becomes international in scope and as organization members travel more, the need to know
   other languages increases. The potential communication barrier of this multi-
   language situation is obvious. Moreover, individuals who deal with foreigners
   need to be familiar not only with their languages but also with their cultures.
   Knowledge of a foreign language may be of little value if individuals don't
   know which words, phrases, and actions are culturally acceptable.

4. *The need for learning decreases time available for communication.* Many managers
   feel pressured to learn new and important concepts that they have not had to
   know in the past. Issues like learning about the intricacies of international
   business as well as computer usage continue to use significant amounts of
   managerial time. Many managers believe that because of the increased demands
   on their time called for by the need to train, less time is available for communicating with other organization members.

Communication microbarriers are factors that hinder successful communication in a specific communication situation.[8] These factors relate directly to such variables as the communication message, the source, and the destination. Among the microbarriers are the following:[9]

1. *The source's view of the destination.* The source in any communication situation has a tendency to view the destination in a specific way and to influence the messages by this view. For example, individuals tend to speak differently to people they think are informed about a subject than to those they think are uninformed. The destination can sense the source's attitudes, which often block successful communication. Managers should keep an open mind about the people with whom they communicate and should be careful not to imply any negative attitudes through their communication behavior.

2. *Message interference.* Stimuli that compete with the communication message for the attention of the destination are called **message interference,** or noise.[10] An example of message interference is a manager talking to an office worker while the worker is trying to input data into a word processor. Inputting data is message interference because it competes with the manager's communication message for the office worker's attention. Managers should attempt to communicate only when they have the total attention of the individuals with whom they wish to share information. A lighthearted example of message interference is shown in the following cartoon.

3. *The destination's view of the source.* The destination can have certain attitudes toward the source that also can hinder successful communication. If, for example, a destination believes that the source has little credibility[11] in the area about which the source is communicating, the destination may filter out much of the source's message and only slightly consider the part of the message actually received. When communicating, managers should attempt to consider the worth of messages transmitted to them independent of their personal attitudes toward the source. They may lose many valuable ideas if personal feelings toward others influence which messages they listen to carefully.

Communication microbarriers are factors that hinder successful communication and that relate primarily to such variables as the communication message, the source, and the destination.

Message interference is stimuli that compete with the communication message for the attention of the decoder/destination.

BEETLE BAILEY ®   By Mort Walker

Reprinted with special permission of King Features Syndicate, Inc.

Perception is the interpretation of a message as observed by an individual.

4. *Perception.* **Perception** is an individual's interpretation of a message. Different individuals can perceive the same message in very different ways. The two primary factors that influence the way in which a stimulus is perceived are the destination's education level and the destination's amount of experience. To minimize the negative effects of this perceptual factor on interpersonal communication, managers should try to send messages with precise meanings. Ambiguous words generally tend to magnify negative perceptions.

5. *Multimeaning words.* Because many words in the English language have several different meanings, a destination may have difficulty deciding which meaning should be attached to the words of a message. A manager should not assume that a word means the same thing to all people who use it.

   A study by Lydia Strong substantiates this point. Strong concluded that for the 500 most common words in our language, there are 4,070 different dictionary definitions. On the average, each of these words has over 18 usages. The word *run* is an example:[12]

Babe Ruth scored a *run*.
Did you ever see Jesse Owens *run*?
I have a *run* in my stocking.
There is a fine *run* of salmon this year.
Are you going to *run* this company or am I?
You have the *run* of the place.
What headline do you want to *run*?
There was a *run* on the bank today.
Did he *run* the ship aground?
I have to *run* (drive the car) downtown.
Who will *run* for president this year?
Joe flies the New York–Chicago *run* twice a week.
You know the kind of people they *run* around with.
The apples *run* large this year.
Please *run* my bath water.

When encoding information, managers should be careful to define the terms they use whenever possible and never use obscure meanings for words when designing messages.[13] They also should try to use words in the same way they see their destination using them.

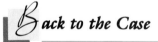

Back to the Case

In discussing Roger Smith's ability to communicate, we are actually discussing his ability to share ideas with other General Motors employees. For Smith to be a successful communicator, he had to concentrate on the three essential elements of the communication process. The first element is the source—the individual who wishes to share information with another. In this case, the source was Smith. The second element is the signal—the message transmitted by Smith. The third element is the destination—the General Motors employee with whom Smith wished to share information. Smith communicated with General Motors employees by determining what information to share, encoding that information, and then transmitting the message. The subordinates would then interpret the message and respond accordingly. Smith's communication would be successful if subordinates interpreted messages as Smith intended.

If Smith was to be a successful communicator, he had to minimize the effect of numerous communication barriers. These barriers included (1) GM employees' need to have more information and more complex information to do their jobs, (2) message interference, (3) Smith's view of the destination as well as the destination's view of Smith, (4) the perceptual process of the people involved in the communication attempt, and (5) words with multimeanings.

Feedback and Interpersonal Communication

Feedback is the destination's reaction to a message. In general, feedback can be used by the source to ensure successful communication.[14] For example, if the destination's message reaction is inappropriate, the source can conclude that communication was not successful and that another message should be transmitted. If the destination's message reaction is appropriate, the source can conclude that communication was successful. This, of course, assumes that the appropriate reaction did not happen merely by chance. Because of the potentially high value of feedback, managers should encourage feedback whenever possible and evaluate it carefully.

Feedback can be either verbal or nonverbal.[15] To gather verbal feedback, the source could simply ask the destination pertinent message-related questions. The destination's answers would probably indicate to the source whether the message was perceived as intended. To gather nonverbal feedback, the source may have to observe the destination's nonverbal response to a message. An example is a manager who has transmitted a message to a subordinate indicating new steps that must be taken in the normal performance of the subordinate's job. Assuming that no other problems exist, if the steps are not followed accurately, the manager has nonverbal feedback indicating the need for clarification of the initial message.

Robert S. Goyer has suggested other uses for feedback besides determining whether a message is perceived as intended.[16] For example, over time a source can use feedback to evaluate his or her personal communication effectiveness by determining the proportion of the destination's message reactions that he or she actually intended. A formula illustrating how this evaluation, the **communication effectiveness index**, can be calculated is shown in Figure 13.6. The higher this proportion, the greater the communication effectiveness of the source.

If managers discover that their communication effectiveness index is relatively low over an extended period of time, they should assess their situation to determine how to improve their communication skill. One problem they may discover

Feedback is, in the interpersonal communication situation, the decoder/destination's reaction to a message.

A **communication effectiveness index** is the intended message reactions divided by the total number of transmitted messages.

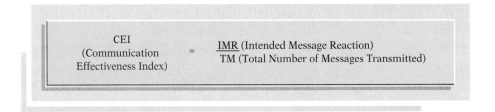

$$\text{CEI (Communication Effectiveness Index)} = \frac{\text{IMR (Intended Message Reaction)}}{\text{TM (Total Number of Messages Transmitted)}}$$

FIGURE 13.6
Calculation of communication effectiveness index

is that they are repeatedly using a vocabulary confusing to the destination. For example, a study conducted by Group Attitudes Corporation found that if managers used certain words repeatedly in communication with steelworkers, the steelworkers almost certainly would become confused.[17] Words causing confusion include accrue, contemplate, designate, detriment, magnitude, and subsequently.

Besides analyzing their vocabulary, managers should attempt to increase their communication effectiveness by following the "ten commandments of good communication" as closely as possible. These commandments are as follows:[18]

1. *Seek to clarify your ideas before communicating.* The more systematically you analyze the problem or idea to be communicated, the clearer it becomes. This is the first step toward effective communication. Many communications fail because of inadequate planning. Good planning must consider the goals and attitudes of those who will receive the communication and those who will be affected by it.

2. *Examine the true purpose of each communication.* Before you communicate, ask yourself what you really want to accomplish with your message—obtain information, initiate action, change another person's attitude? Identify your most important goal and then adapt your language, tone, and total approach to serve that specific objective. Don't try to accomplish too much with each communication. The sharper the focus of your message, the greater its chances of success.

3. *Consider the total physical and human setting whenever you communicate.* Meaning and intent are conveyed by more than words alone. Many other factors influence the overall impact of a communication, and managers must be sensitive to the total setting in which they communicate. Consider, for example, your sense of timing, that is, the circumstances under which you make an announcement or render a decision; the physical setting—whether you communicate in private or otherwise, for example; the social climate that pervades work relationships within the company or a department and sets the tone of its communications; custom and practice—the degree to which your communication conforms to, or departs from, the expectations of your audience. Be constantly aware of the total setting in which you communicate. Like all living things, communication must be capable of adapting to its environment.

4. *Consult with others, when appropriate, in planning communications.* Frequently, it is desirable or necessary to seek the participation of others in planning a communication or in developing the facts on which to base the communication. Such consultation often lends additional insight and objectivity to your message. Moreover, those who have helped you plan your communication will give it their active support.

5. *Be mindful, while you communicate, of the overtones rather than merely the basic content of your message.* Your tone of voice, your expression, your apparent receptiveness to the responses of others—all have a significant effect on those you wish to reach. Frequently overlooked, these subtleties of communication often affect a listener's reaction to a message even more than its basic content. Similarly, your choice of language—particularly your awareness of the fine shades of meaning and emotion in the words you use—predetermine in large part the reactions of your listeners.

6. *Take the opportunity, when it arises, to convey something of help or value to the receiver.* Consideration of the other person's interests and needs—trying to look at things from the other person's point of view—frequently points up opportunities to convey something of immediate benefit or long-range value to the other person. Subordinates are most responsive to managers whose messages take the subordinates' interests into account.

7. *Follow up your communication.* Your best efforts at communication may be wasted, and you may never know whether you have succeeded in expressing your true meaning and intent if you do not follow up to see how well you have put your message across. You can do this by asking questions, by encouraging the receiver to express his or her reactions, by follow-up contacts, and by subsequent review of performance. Make certain that every important communication has feedback so that complete understanding and appropriate action result.

8. *Communicate for tomorrow as well as today.* Even though communications may be aimed primarily at meeting the demands of an immediate situation, they must be planned with the past in mind if they are to maintain consistency in the receiver's view. Most important, however, communications must be consistent with long-range interests and goals. For example, it is not easy to communicate frankly on such matters as poor performance or the shortcomings of a loyal subordinate, but postponing disagreeable communications makes these matters more difficult in the long run and is actually unfair to your subordinates and your company.

9. *Be sure your actions support your communications.* In the final analysis, the most persuasive kind of communication is not what you say, but what you do. When your actions or attitudes contradict your words, others tend to discount what you have said. For every manager, this means that good supervisory practices—such as clear assignment of responsibility and authority, fair rewards for effort, and sound policy enforcement—serve to communicate more than all the gifts of oratory.

10. *Last, but by no means least: Seek not only to be understood but to understand—be a good listener.* When you start talking, you often cease to listen, at least in that larger sense of being attuned to the other person's unspoken reactions and attitudes. Even more serious is the occasional inattentiveness you may be guilty of when others are attempting to communicate with you. Listening is one of the most important, most difficult, and most neglected skills in communication. It demands that you concentrate not only on the explicit meanings another person is expressing, but also on the implicit meanings, unspoken words, and undertones that may be far more significant.

Verbal and Nonverbal Interpersonal Communication

Interpersonal communication is generally divided into two types: verbal and nonverbal. Up to this point, the chapter has emphasized **verbal communication**—communication that uses either spoken or written words to share information with others.

Nonverbal communication is sharing information without using words to encode thoughts. Factors commonly used to encode thoughts in nonverbal communication are gestures, vocal tones, and facial expressions. In most interpersonal

Verbal communication is the sharing of ideas through words.

Nonverbal communication is the sharing of ideas without the use of words.

communication, verbal and nonverbal communications are not either-or occur-rences. Instead, the destination's interpretation of a message generally is based not only on the words in the message but also on such images as the source's gestures and facial expressions.

In an interpersonal communication situation in which both verbal and nonver-bal factors are present, nonverbal factors may have more influence on the total effect of a message than verbal factors. Over two decades ago, Albert Mehrabian developed a formula that showed the relative contributions of both verbal and nonverbal factors to the total effect of a message. This formula is as follows: Total message impact = .07 words + .38 vocal tones + .55 facial expressions.[19] Of course, both vocal tones and facial expressions are nonverbal factors. Besides vocal tones and facial expressions, gestures,[20] gender,[21] and dress[22] can influence the effect of a verbal message. Given the great potential influence of nonverbal factors on the effect of a message, managers should use nonverbal message ingredients to complement verbal message ingredients whenever possible.[23]

Nonverbal messages also can be used to add new content to verbal messages. To this end, a head might be nodded or a voice might be toned to show either agreement or disagreement.

Regardless of how managers decide to combine verbal and nonverbal factors, they must be sure that the two do not present contradictory messages. For in-stance, the words of a message might express approval, whereas the nonverbal factors express disapproval. This type of situation creates message ambiguity and leaves the destination frustrated.

Back to the Case

The employees' reactions to Smith's messages could provide Smith with perhaps his most useful tool in making communication successful—feedback. When feed-back did not seem appropriate, Smith could transmit another message to clarify the meaning of his first message. A manager must be alert to both verbal and nonverbal feedback. Over time, if feedback indicated that Smith was a relatively unsuccessful communicator, he could analyze his situation carefully to improve his communication effectiveness. Smith might have found, for instance, that he was using a vocabulary that was generally inappropriate for certain employees or that he was not following one or more of the ten commandments of good communication.

In addition, a manager must remember that he can communicate to others without using words. His facial expressions, gestures, and even the tone of his voice give messages to people. In the case, most of Smith's communication situa-tions involved both verbal and nonverbal messages to General Motors employees. Because the effect of a message may be generated mostly by its nonverbal compo-nents, Smith had to be certain that his nonverbal messages complemented his verbal messages. By giving his sweater to the "corporate heckler" in the introduc-tory case, Smith nonverbally conveyed that he cared about taking care of GM employees.

Interpersonal Communication in Organizations

To be effective communicators, managers must understand not only general in-terpersonal communication concepts but also the characteristics of interpersonal communication within organizations, called **organizational communication.** Organizational communication directly relates to the goals, functions, and structure of human organizations.[24] Organizational success, to a major extent, is determined by the effectiveness of organizational communication.

Although organizational communication often was referred to by early management writers, the topic began to receive systematic study and attention only after World War II.[25] From World War II to the 1950s, organizational communication as a discipline made significant advances in such areas as mathematical communication theory and behavioral communication theory.[26] Since the 1970s emphasis on organizational communication has grown in colleges of business throughout the nation.[27] The following information focuses on three fundamental organizational communication topics: (1) formal organizational communication, (2) informal organizational communication, and (3) the encouragement of formal organizational communication.

Organizational communication is interpersonal communication within organizations.

Formal Organizational Communication

In general, organizational communication that follows the lines of the organization chart is called **formal organizational communication.**[28] As discussed in chapter 9, the organization chart depicts relationships of people and jobs and shows the formal channels of communication among them.

Formal organizational communication is organizational communication that follows the lines of the organization chart.

Types of Formal Organizational Communication. In general, there are three basic types of formal organizational communication: (1) downward, (2) upward, and (3) lateral.

Downward organizational communication is communication that flows from any point on an organization chart downward to another point on the organization chart. This type of formal organizational communication relates primarily to the direction and control of employees. Job-related information that focuses on what activities are required, when the activities should be performed, and how the activities should be coordinated with other activities within the organization must be transmitted to employees. This downward communication typically includes a statement of organizational philosophy, management system objectives, position descriptions, and other written information relating to the importance, rationale, and interrelationships of various departments.[29]

Downward organizational communication is communication that flows from any point on an organization chart downward to another point on the organization chart.

Ethics Highlight: Coopers & Lybrand Communicates Downward to Promote Volunteerism

Coopers & Lybrand (C&L), an accounting firm, recently found that downward organizational communication can be a critical means for building employee support and enthusiasm for a social responsibility program. The ninety-eight U.S. offices of C&L are focusing their funds and volunteer activity on existing local programs that help to improve the quality of secondary education in English, math, and science, and that encourage children to stay in school. C&L treats time that staff members devote to this effort as paid time. In addition, when a C&L volunteer devotes more than 150 hours annually to a preselected program, the firm donates $500 annually to that organization in the employee's name. Over two-thirds of C&L's offices are involved in a total of 156 programs in the "Supporting Youth Education" effort.

Overall, the volunteer program at C&L is an outstanding success. The content and timeliness of downward organizational communication related to the program is commonly cited as a primary reason for this success. The care and concern that management showed in making sure that C&L employees thoroughly understood the program was a significant help in building employee support, acceptance, and enthusiasm for the program.

Upward organizational communication is communication that flows from any point on an organization chart upward to another point on the organization chart.

Upward organizational communication is communication that flows from any point on an organization chart upward to another point on the organization chart. This type of organizational communication contains primarily the information managers need to evaluate the organizational area for which they are responsible and to determine if something is going wrong within the organization. Techniques that managers commonly use to encourage upward organizational communication include informal discussions with employees, attitude surveys, the development and use of grievance procedures, suggestion systems, and an "open-door" policy that invites employees to come in whenever they would like to talk to management.[30] Organizational modifications based on this feedback enable the organization to be more successful in the future.

Lateral organization communication is communication that flows from any point on an organization chart horizontally to another point on the organization chart.

Lateral organizational communication is communication that flows from any point on an organization chart horizontally to another point on the organization chart. Communication that flows across the organization usually focuses on coordinating the activities of various departments and developing new plans for future operating periods. Within the organization, all departments are related to all other departments. Only through lateral communication can these departmental relationships be coordinated well enough to enhance the attainment of management system objectives.

Patterns of Formal Organizational Communication. By nature, organizational communication creates patterns of communication among organization members. These patterns evolve from the repeated occurrence of various serial transmissions of information. According to Haney, a **serial transmission** involves passing information from one individual to another. It occurs when

A serial transmission is the passing of information from one individual through a series of individuals.

> A communicates a message to B; B then communicates A's message (or rather his or her interpretation of A's message) to C; C then communicates his or her interpretation of B's interpretation of A's message to D; and so on. The originator and the ultimate recipient of the message are separated by middle people.[31]

Of course, one of the obvious weaknesses of a serial transmission is that messages tend to become distorted as the length of the serial transmission increases. Research has shown that message details may be omitted, altered, or added in a serial transmission.[32]

As presented in a classic article by Alex Bavelas and Dermot Barrett,[33] the potential inaccuracy of transmitted messages is not the only weakness of a serial transmission. Serial transmissions can also influence morale, the emergence of a leader, the degree to which individuals involved in the transmissions are organized, and their efficiency. Three basic organizational communication pattern studies and their corresponding effects on the variables just mentioned are shown in Figure 13.7.

Back to the Case

As chair at General Motors, Roger Smith had to understand the intricacies of organizational communication—interpersonal communication as it takes place within the organization. The success of organizational communication at GM is an important factor in determining the company's level of success. Smith could communicate with his people in two basic ways: formally and informally.

In general, Smith's formal communication would have followed the lines on the organization chart. Smith could communicate downward to, for example, divisional managers or upward to, for example, GM's board of directors. Smith's

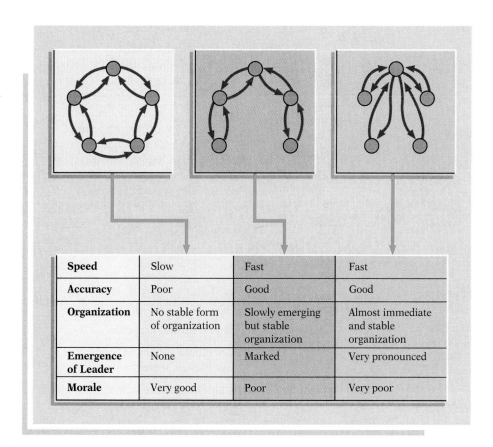

Speed	Slow	Fast	Fast
Accuracy	Poor	Good	Good
Organization	No stable form of organization	Slowly emerging but stable organization	Almost immediate and stable organization
Emergence of Leader	None	Marked	Very pronounced
Morale	Very good	Poor	Very poor

FIGURE 13.7

Relationship between three patterns of organizational communication and group characteristics of speed, accuracy, organization, emergence of leader, and morale

downward communication commonly would have focused on the activities subordinates were performing. His upward communication commonly would have illustrated how the company was performing. Because Smith was chair and had no one at the same level within the organization, he would not have communicated laterally. However, he undoubtedly took steps to ensure that lateral communication occurred at other organizational levels to enhance planning and coordination at General Motors.

Informal organizational communication is organizational communication that does not follow the lines of the organization chart.

Informal organizational communication is organizational communication that does not follow the lines of the organization chart. This type of communication typically follows the pattern of personal relationships among organization members. One friend communicates with another friend, regardless of their relative positions on the organization chart. Informal organizational communication networks generally exist because organization members have a desire for information that formal organizational communication does not furnish.

The **grapevine** is the network of informal organizational communication.

The informal organizational communication network, or **grapevine,** has three main characteristics: (1) it springs up and is used irregularly within the organization; (2) it is not controlled by top executives, who may not even be able to influence it; and (3) it is used largely to serve the self-interests of the people within it.

Understanding the grapevine is a prerequisite for a complete understanding of organizational communication. Some estimates indicate that 70 percent of all communication in organizations follows organizational grapevines.[34] Not only do grapevines carry great amounts of communication, but they carry it at very rapid speeds.[35] The company grapevine is commonly cited by employees as being the most reliable and credible source of information about company events.[36]

As with formal organizational communication, informal organizational communication uses serial transmissions. Organization members involved in these transmissions, however, are more difficult for managers to identify than are those in the formal communication network. Keith Davis's classic article that appeared in the *Harvard Business Review* has been a significant help to managers over the years in understanding how organizational grapevines exist and operate. Figure 13.8 contains the four grapevine patterns outlined by Davis that tend to exist in organizations.[37]

1. *The single-strand grapevine.* A tells B, who tells C, who tells D, and so on. This type of grapevine tends to distort messages more than any other.
2. *The gossip grapevine.* A informs everyone else on the grapevine.
3. *The probability grapevine.* A communicates randomly, for example, to F and D. F and D then continue to inform other grapevine members in the same way.
4. *The cluster grapevine.* A selects and tells C, D, and F. F selects and tells I and B, and B selects and tells J. Information in this grapevine travels only to selected individuals.

Clearly, grapevines are a factor managers must deal with because they can, and often do, generate rumors that can be detrimental to organizational success.[38] On the other hand, when employees have what they view as sufficient organizational information, it seems to build their sense of belonging to the organization

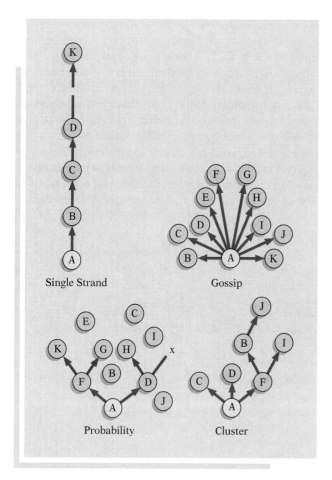

FIGURE 13.8

Four types of organizational grapevines

and their level of productivity. Grapevines could be used to help managers to maximize information flow to employees.[39] Some writers argue that managers should encourage the development of grapevines and strive to become grapevine members to gain feedback that could be very valuable in improving the organization.[40] Exactly how individual managers should deal with the grapevine, of course, depends on the specific organizational situation in which the managers find themselves.

Encouraging Formal Organizational Communication. Organizational communication often is called the nervous system of the organization. The organization acts only in the way that its nervous system, or organizational communication, directs it. Since formal organizational communication is generally the more important type of communication that takes place within the organization, managers must encourage its free flow if the organization is to be successful.

Managers can use many different strategies to encourage the flow of formal organizational communication. One strategy is listening attentively to messages that come through formal channels. Listening shows organization members that managers are interested in what subordinates have to say and encourages employees to use formal communication channels in subsequent situations. General guidelines for listening are presented in Table 13.2. Another managerial strategy is to support the flow of clear and concise statements through formal communication channels. Receiving an ambiguous message through a formal organizational communication channel can discourage members from using that channel again. A third strategy managers can use is taking care to ensure that all organization members have free access to the use of formal communication channels within the organization. Obviously, organization members cannot communicate formally within the organization if they don't have access to the formal communication network. A fourth strategy is assigning specific communication responsibilities to staff personnel who could be of enormous help to line personnel in spreading important information throughout the organization.

TABLE 13.2 Ten commandments for good listening

1. *Stop talking!*
   You cannot listen if you are talking.
   Polonius *(Hamlet):* "Give every man thine ear, but few thy voice."

2. *Put the talker at ease.*
   Help the talker feel free to talk.
   This is often called a permissive environment.

3. *Show the talker that you want to listen.*
   Look and act interested. Do not read your mail while he or she talks.
   Listen to understand rather than to oppose.

4. *Remove distractions.*
   Don't doodle, tap, or shuffle papers.
   Will it be quieter if you shut the door?

5. *Empathize with the talker.*
   Try to put yourself in the talker's place so that you can see his or her point of view.

6. *Be patient.*
   Allow plenty of time. Do not interrupt the talker.
   Don't start for the door or walk away.

7. *Hold your temper.*
   An angry person gets the wrong meaning from words.

8. *Go easy on argument and criticism.*
   This puts the talker on the defensive. He or she may "clam up" or get angry.
   Do not argue: even if you win, you *lose.*

9. *Ask questions.*
   This encourages the talker and shows you are listening.
   It helps to develop points further.

10. *Stop talking!*
    This is first and last, because all other commandments depend on it.
    You just can't do a good listening job while you are talking.

    Nature gave us two ears but only one tongue,
    which is a gentle hint that we should listen more than we talk.

*B*ack to the Case

It is virtually certain that an extensive grapevine exists at General Motors. Although the company grapevine must be dealt with, Smith may not have been able to influence it significantly. General Motors employees, as well as employees for any company, typically are involved in grapevines for self-interest and because the formal organization has not furnished them with the information they believe they need.

By developing various social relationships, Smith would conceivably have become part of the grapevine and obtained valuable feedback from it. Also, because grapevines generate rumors that could have a detrimental effect on General Motor's success, Smith would have tried to ensure that General Motors personnel were given all the information they needed to do their jobs well through formal organizational communication, thereby reducing the need for a grapevine.

Because formal organizational communication is vitally important to General Motors, Smith would have tried to encourage its flow as much as possible by listening intently to messages that came to him over formal channels, supporting the flow of clear messages through formal channels, and making sure that all GM employees had access to formal communication channels.

Action Summary

Reread the learning objectives that follow. Each objective is followed by questions. Answering these questions accurately will help you retain the most important concepts discussed in this chapter. After answering each question, check your answer with the answer key at the end of this chapter. (*Hint:* If you have doubt regarding the correct response, consult the page whose number follows the answer.)

Circle:

From studying this chapter, I will attempt to acquire:

1. **An understanding of influencing.**
   a. The influencing function can be viewed as forcing the activities of organization members in appropriate directions.   T, F
   b. Which of the following activities is *not* a major component of the influencing process: (a) motivating; (b) leading; (c) communicating; (d) correcting; (e) considering groups.   a, b, c, d, e

2. **An understanding of interpersonal communication.**
   a. Communication is best described as the process of: (a) sharing emotion; (b) sharing information; (c) sending messages; (d) feedback formulation; (e) forwarding information.   a, b, c, d, e
   b. The basic elements of interpersonal communication are: (a) source/encoder, signal, decoder/destination; (b) sender/message, encoder, receiver/decoder; (c) signal, source/sender, decoder/destination; (d) signal, source/decoder, encoder/destination; (e) source/sender, signal, receiver/destination.   a, b, c, d, e

3. A knowledge of how to use feedback.

T, F   **a.** Feedback is solely verbal.

a, b, c, d, e   **b.** Robert S. Goyer suggested using feedback: (a) as a microbarrier; (b) as a way for sources to evaluate their communication effectiveness; (c) to ensure that instructions will be carried out; (d) to evaluate the decoder; (e) all of the above.

4. An appreciation for the importance of nonverbal communication.

T, F   **a.** In interpersonal communication, nonverbal factors may play a more influential role than verbal factors.

T, F   **b.** Nonverbal messages can contradict verbal messages, which can create frustration in the destination.

5. Insights on formal organizational communication.

a, b, c, d, e   **a.** Which of the following is not upward communication: (a) cost accounting reports; (b) purchase order summary; (c) production reports; (d) corporate policy statement; (e) sales reports.

a, b, c, d, e   **b.** The primary purpose served by lateral organizational communication is: (a) coordinating; (b) organizing; (c) direction; (d) evaluation; (e) control.

6. An appreciation for the importance of the grapevine.

a, b, c, d, e   **a.** Which of the following statements concerning the grapevine is *not* correct: (a) grapevines are irregularly used in organizations; (b) a grapevine can and often does generate harmful rumors; (c) the grapevine is used largely to serve the self-interests of the people within it; (d) some managers use grapevines to their advantage; (e) in time, and with proper pressure, the grapevine can be eliminated.

T, F   **b.** The grapevine is much slower than formal communication channels.

7. Some hints on how to encourage organizational communication.

a, b, c, d, e   **a.** To encourage formal organizational communication, managers should: (a) support the flow of clear and concise statements through formal channels; (b) ensure free access to formal channels for all organization members; (c) assign specific communication responsibilities to staff personnel; (d) a and b; (e) all of the above.

T, F   **b.** Since formal organizational communication is the most important type of communication within an organization, managers must restrict its flow if the organization is to be successful.

Introductory Case Wrap-Up

"General Motors Focuses on Influencing People" (p. 384) and its related back-to-the-case sections were written to help you better understand the management concepts contained in this chapter. Answer the following discussion questions about this introductory case to further enrich your understanding of chapter content:

1. List three problems that could have been caused at General Motors if Smith had happened to have been a poor communicator.

2. Explain *how* the problems you listed in number 1 could have been caused by Smith's inability to communicate.

3. Assuming that Smith was a good communicator, discuss three ways that he positively affected General Motors as a result of this communication expertise.

Issues for Review and Discussion

1. What is influencing?
2. Describe the relationship between the overall management system and the influencing subsystem.
3. What factors make up the input, process, and output of the influencing subsystem?
4. Explain the relationship between the factors that compose the process section of the influencing subsystem.
5. What is communication?
6. How important is communication to managers?
7. Draw the communication model presented in this chapter and explain how it works.
8. How does successful communication differ from unsuccessful communication?
9. Summarize the significance of field of experience to communication.
10. List and describe three communication macrobarriers and three communication microbarriers.
11. What is feedback, and how should managers use it when communicating?
12. How is the communication effectiveness index calculated, and what is its significance?
13. Name the ten commandments of good communication.
14. What is nonverbal communication? Explain its significance.
15. How should managers use nonverbal communication?
16. What is organizational communication?
17. How do formal and informal organizational communication differ?
18. Describe three types of formal organizational communication, and explain the general purpose of each type.
19. Can serial transmissions and other formal communication patterns influence communication effectiveness and the individuals using the patterns? If so, how?
20. Draw and describe the four main types of grapevines that exist in organizations.
21. How can managers encourage the flow of formal organizational communication?

Building on What You Know

Directions

Review the Highlight feature as indicated below and answer its corresponding questions. Questions in this section focus on relating a Highlight appearing in this chapter to management concepts that you have learned in a previous chapter.

Review the Global Highlight: Compression Labs on page 390. In chapter 12, you studied about stressors and the effect that they can have on organization members. Could videoconferencing be a stressor for organization members at Compression Labs? Explain. Can videoconferencing result in unhealthy organizational stress in an organization like Compression Labs? Explain. What steps could you take to ensure that a videoconferencing program that you might introduce in your organization would not result in unhealthy organizational stress? Discuss why each of your steps is important.

Action Summary Answer Key

1. a. F, p. 385 2. a. b, p. 389 3. a. F, p. 395 4. a. T, p. 398 5. a. d, p. 400 6. a. e, p. 402 7. a. e, pp. 403–404
   b. d, p. 385   b. a, p. 390   b. b, p. 395   b. T, p. 398   b. a, p. 400   b. F, p. 402   b. F, p. 403

Case Study

The Wal-Mart Influence

by Robert E. Kemper, Northern Arizona University

Wal-Mart Stores Incorporated operates an expanding chain of modern retail outlets, marketing merchandise through discount department stores, wholesale clubs, deep-discount drugstores, supercenters, and hypermarkets. By February, 1991, these included 1,634 Wal-Mart Discount Cities, 176 Sam's Warehouse Clubs, 2 Hypermart USA's, and 15 Supercenters, and Wal-Mart plans to open at least 100 new stores every year. Stores are within a six-hour truck drive of corporate headquarters in Bentonville, Arkansas, or one of 15 regional centers.

Wal-Mart's distribution facilities are a major key to its success; it simply does distribution much better than the competition. Centers rely on laser scanners to route goods coming off company trailers along conveyor belts up to eleven miles long. The technology is standard—mechanized conveyors, bar coding, computer inventory—but no one else operates it this effectively. The average Wal-Mart distribution center ships and receives about 240,000 cases of merchandise daily. It maintains stocks of about 9,000 basic items and 2,000 seasonal items on a predetermined basis.

A Wal-Mart store is a one-stop shopping center, typically serving a community of about 150,000 people. Stores provide a wide assortment of merchandise to satisfy most of the clothing, home, recreational, and convenience needs of a family. An average store covers almost 57,000 square feet, although some are two and a half times that size. Wage costs are held at eight percent of total sales. There are 271,000 employees (associates) nationwide, and 80,000 stockholders. Insiders own forty-two percent of common stock.

Wal-Mart does everything it can to make its people feel part of a family. It hires locally, trains its people, encourages them to ask questions, and generously praises them. Sam Walton, Wal-Mart's down-home founder, prides himself on being a visible, accessible leader. Until recently, he spent the better part of each year visiting the stores personally. When the number of stores outran his ability to reach them all, riding the highways in his Wal-Mart trucks, he undertook the biggest communication task of his career.

Walton installed a six-channel satellite system that gave the remote Wal-Mart headquarters a computer-communications-complex appearance worthy of the U.S. Defense Department. Its goal is to link every location in the Wal-Mart empire by voice and video, facilitating store-to-store and store-to-home-office communications. The satellite system also gathers store data for the chain's master computers, and it reduces time and dollars spent on credit card checks, flashing back responses in four or five seconds.

One aspect of the satellite system appealed particularly to Walton. Now he can deliver an inspirational pep talk in front of a video camera in Bentonville and have it beamed live to associates huddled around television screens in hundreds of facilities scattered throughout twenty-seven states. It is the best substitute he can offer for those personal visits that he loved to make.

By satellite, Wal-Mart executives can talk to every store at the same time as often as they like, or they can direct communications to only a few. However, the biggest advantage is in sharing merchandise information. A buyer can go on video and announce, "These are the new items for Department 16. Here is how you should display them."

Wal-Mart people are motivated and productive, and high productivity lends itself to low overhead. Employees operate in an environment where ideas and change are encouraged. For example, if a store associate makes suggestions regarding merchandising ideas that would create significant sales gains for an item, or improvements to existing procedures that would result in cost savings, these ideas can be quickly disseminated by satellite. With 271,000 associates to make suggestions, this leads to substantial sales gains, cost reductions, and improved productivity.

Also, there are award programs on top of award programs for those associates: regional all-star teams, all-star departmental honor roll, VPI (volume-producing item) contests, departmental sales honor roll, the shrinkage incentive program. Names and pictures of award winners are run in the company magazine, *Wal-Mart World*.

Retail executives and consultants consider Wal-Mart the industry's leader in attention to the details that help shape shoppers' attitudes. They say the chain is particularly adept at striking that delicate balance needed to convince shoppers its prices are low but its stores are not too cheap.

Sam Walton and his 80,000 stockholders certainly wouldn't disagree. With over 1,800 outlets and sales of close to $26 billion (1990), Wal-Mart certainly seems to have a happy influence on both its associates and its clientele.

Discussion Questions

1. What effect do you think the satellite system has had on *formal* communication at Wal-Mart? Why?
2. What effect do you think the satellite system has had on *informal* communication at Wal-Mart? Why?
3. Sam Walton lives in a simple house in Bentonville, Arkansas. He drives a Chevrolet and dresses in store-bought clothes. Why do you think it might be valuable for Wal-Mart that his sales associates are aware of these things?
4. What management tasks does *Wal-Mart World* accomplish? Consult Figure 13.3.

The Art of Influence: Lester Korn of Korn/Ferry International

Lester Korn and Dick Ferry, the youngest partners of top accounting firm Peat Marwick Mitchell, decided in 1970 to strike out on their own—"to be the masters of our destinies." They did—very successfully. Within twenty years, they had built the world's largest executive search firm, with forty-two offices in sixteen countries, all devoted to locating candidates for organizations that need or want new talent in top positions. Numbered among Korn/Ferry clients are not only major corporations but also government organizations; over 100 of the Fortune 500 companies have used Korn/Ferry's services.

Lester Korn is the chairman and CEO of Korn/Ferry, running his global enterprise from Los Angeles. One of his most illustrious coups as a head-hunter benefited that city directly. In 1984, Los Angeles was home to the tremendously successful summer Olympic games. The director of those games—and subsequently the *Time* magazine Man of the Year—was Peter Ueberroth. The head-hunter who signed Peter Ueberroth onto the Olympic team was Lester Korn.

"Peter could communicate, knew the movement of people, knew the logistics. . . . It's something you find in successful people. He simply could not turn down the challenge." Lester Korn knows what makes a successful executive, and it tells something about him that the first characteristic he mentions is the ability to communicate. It is here that executive skills begin.

Korn's business requires that he, too, is an expert communicator; during his career as a head-hunter, he caught the ear of the "great communicator" himself—President Ronald Reagan. During the Reagan presidency, Korn served as a U.S. economic and social ambassador to the United Nations (U.N.). He brought a specific agenda to that diplomatic role, spending a year and a half addressing representatives of other nations singly and in large groups, including the U.N. General Assembly. His international experience and business expertise were key to introducing private-sector initiatives into the U.N. business processes, an achievement in which he takes great pride. As a result of this service—one that ran counter not only to established practices but also to the desires of some member nations—Korn was awarded U.S. State Department honors.

Communication skill may be the first characteristic that Lester Korn identifies as essential to a successful executive, but it is not the only one. Energy, logic, strategic planning skills, an orientation toward success, and in particular the desire to rise to a challenge are all factors that he seeks in candidates for his various clients. However, he has found that the most important characteristic is integrity: "When you ask the top 1,500 [U.S. business executives], as I did . . . , to rank what they think is the most important reason they are successful, they say integrity. In other words, they have avoided the quick, cheap way of what some people would think would be the road to success and have instead marched along with a great deal of integrity."

A clear signal of integrity from the top of the corporate ladder is an important force for influencing employees. Workers who are satisfied that their company is acting in accord with moral behavior that they themselves can support tend to be more willing to support their company. This means less confusion, less divisive behavior, less turnover, and more contentment with both work and workplace. As a result, leadership and motivation at all levels become simpler tasks for managers.

Respect for integrity works in both directions. Workers support a corporate leadership and corporate goals that they can trust and in which they can take pride. Similarly, management supports workers who present a clear message that they want to work hard, they want to succeed, they—in Lester Korn's words—cannot turn down a challenge. "People who run companies want to know that their people want more responsibility. The sooner you can communicate that, the better off you're going to be in your career."

So for Lester Korn, as for many top executives, integrity and responsibility are the essential message. Clear, unambiguous communication is the essential skill.

Video Case Questions

1. Peter Ueberroth ran the second largest travel agency in the United States prior to taking on the Los Angeles Olympic games. How do you think this experience assisted him in his next job?

2. In the course of Lester Korn's video interview, he is asked twice what his personal financial goal is. How does he respond? Do you think this is good communication? Why or why not?

3. If you were trying to recruit an executive for a client firm, would you approach him first personally (by phone or in person) or in writing? Why?

4. How important do you think feedback is to Lester Korn's business? How would you rate his communication effectiveness index? Why?

Video Case Activities

1. Prepare two brief résumés for John/Jane Doe, who has held summer and part-time jobs only and is about to graduate from college. One résumé is to accompany an application to GM's management training program. The other is for an application to write publicity materials for the Dance Theater of Harlem. Facts (dates, degree, etc.) should be identical. Consider how descriptions of activities and job objectives should differ for each presentation.

2. Play an adult version of "Gossip" or "Telephone." The class splits into two chains. The heads of each prepare together a 50- to 100-word written job description, including at least 5 specific responsibilities. Showing it to no one else, each head reads it to the next person in his/her chain, and it is then related orally down each chain. The last person in each chain should write down what he/she has gathered the job entails. Compare and discuss.

Chapter 14

Student Learning Objectives

From studying this chapter, I will attempt to acquire:

1. A working definition of leadership.

2. An understanding of the relationship between leading and managing.

3. An appreciation for the trait and situational approaches to leadership.

4. Insights about using leadership theories that emphasize decision-making situations.

5. Insights about using leadership theories that emphasize more general organizational situations.

6. An understanding of alternatives to leader flexibility.

7. An appreciation of both transformational leadership and trust as components of leadership theory.

Leadership

Chapter Outline

A NEW LEADER AT FIGGIE INTERNATIONAL, INC.

Harry E. Figgie, Jr., the chief executive officer of Figgie International, Inc., recently brought his son, Harry E. Figgie III into the company as his assistant. Figgie, with 1990 sales of nearly $1.4 billion, supplies fire protection and security systems and services, produces sporting goods and electronic systems, and is involved in real estate development and other activities.

The senior Figgie said from his Willoughby, Ohio, headquarters that his company has a five-year window of opportunity in which to integrate new technology into its divisions. The senior Figgie believes that there has been a technological revolution related to his company's operation. This revolution has been in the areas of machining, welding, and product assembly. According to the senior Figgie, the company that successfully uses this technology first will become the leader. The primary task of Harry E. Figgie III as a member of top management will be to speed up the adoption of this new technology within the company.

The Figgies said during a joint interview that there isn't any understanding that the move places the son, Dr. Figgie, who is thirty-seven years old, in a position to succeed his sixty-six-year-old father as the head of the company. There has been speculation for some time that the elder Figgie would keep the job in the family. Figgie Senior, however, seems to have no plans to retire in the near future. He believes that he's been waiting his whole career to experience the excitement that his company now faces.

> [Dr. Figgie] believes that he's been waiting his whole career to experience the excitement that his company now faces.

Dr. Figgie, who now is an orthopedic surgeon as well as a manufacturing executive, will phase out his medical practice over the next eighteen to thirty-six months in order to devote full time to spearhead the technology integration efforts at Figgie International. According to Dr. Figgie, he has reached a fork in the road where he must now concentrate on either business or medicine. He says that he chose business because he finds the application of new manufacturing technology exciting and challenging.

Dr. Figgie is now in a position in which he must accomplish goals primarily through the efforts of others within an organization rather than through the prowess of his own technical surgical skills. To a significant extent, Dr. Figgie's leadership abilities will be a factor in determining how successful his efforts at Figgie International will be.

From Ralph E. Winter, "Figgie Chief's Son Is Named as Vice Chairman," *Wall Street Journal* (September 28, 1990), B7.

DEFINING LEADERSHIP

Leadership is the process of directing the behavior of others toward the accomplishment of some objective. Directing, in this sense, means causing individuals to act in a certain way or to follow a particular course. Ideally, this course is perfectly consistent with such factors as established organizational policies, procedures, and job descriptions. The central theme of leadership is getting things accomplished through people. As indicated in chapter 13, leadership is one of the four main interdependent activities of the influencing subsystem and is accomplished, at least to some extent, by communicating with others. It is extremely important that managers have a thorough understanding of what leadership entails. Leadership has always been considered a prerequisite for organizational success. Given issues like the increased capability afforded by enhanced communication technology and the rise of international business, leadership is more important now than ever before.[1]

LEADER VERSUS MANAGER

Leading is not the same as managing. Many executives do not understand the difference between leading and managing, and are therefore under a misapprehension about how to carry out their organizational duties.[2] Although some managers are leaders and some leaders are managers, leading and managing are not identical activities.[3] According to Theodore Levitt, management consists of

> the rational assessment of a situation and the systematic selection of goals and purposes (what is to be done); the systematic development of strategies to achieve these goals; the marshalling of the required resources; the rational design, organization, direction, and control of the activities required to attain the selected purposes; and, finally, the motivating and rewarding of people to do the work.[4]

Leadership, as one of the four primary activities of the influencing function, is a subset of management. Managing is much broader in scope than leading and focuses on behavioral as well as nonbehavioral issues. Leading emphasizes mainly behavioral issues. Figure 14.1 makes the point that although not all managers are necessarily leaders, the most effective managers, over the long term, are leaders.

Leadership is the process of directing the behavior of others toward the accomplishment of objectives.

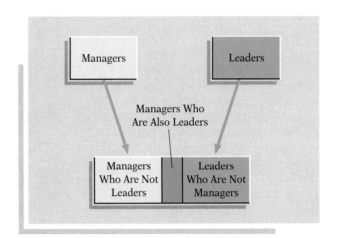

FIGURE 14.1

Most effective managers over the long term are also leaders

Merely possessing management skills is no longer sufficient for an executive to be successful in today's business world. Modern executives need a fundamental understanding of the difference between management and leading and how both activities must be combined to achieve organizational success. A manager makes sure that a job gets done and a leader cares about and focuses on the people who do the job.[5] To combine management and leadership, modern executives should demonstrate a calculated and logical focus on organizational processes (management) along with a genuine concern for workers as people (leadership).[6]

THE TRAIT APPROACH TO LEADERSHIP

The **trait approach to leader-ship** is an outdated view of leadership that sees the personal characteristics of an individual as the main determinants of how successful the individual could be as a leader.

The **trait approach to leadership** is based on early leadership research that seemed to assume that a good leader is born, not made. The mainstream of this research attempted to describe successful leaders as precisely as possible. The reasoning was that if a complete profile of the traits of a successful leader could be summarized, it would be fairly easy to pinpoint the individuals who should and should not be placed in leadership positions.

Many of the early studies that attempted to summarize the traits of successful leaders have been documented.[7] One of these summaries concludes that successful leaders tend to possess the following characteristics:[8]

1. Intelligence, including judgment and verbal ability.

2. Past achievement in scholarship and athletics.

3. Emotional maturity and stability.

4. Dependability, persistence, and a drive for continuing achievement.

5. The skill to participate socially and adapt to various groups.

6. A desire for status and socioeconomic position.

An evaluation of a number of these trait studies, however, concludes that their findings tend to be inconsistent.[9] One researcher says that fifty years of study have failed to produce one personality trait or set of qualities that can be used consistently to discriminate leaders from nonleaders.[10] It follows, then, that no trait or combination of traits guarantees that a leader will be successful. Leadership is apparently a much more complex issue.

Contemporary management writers and practitioners generally agree with the notion that leadership ability cannot be explained by an individual's traits or inherited characteristics. More popular current thought supports the notion that individuals can be trained to be good leaders. Thousands of employees each year are sent through leadership training programs in support of the idea that leaders can be and are being developed through instructional programs.[11]

$\mathcal{B}$ack to the Case

From the preceding material, a manager like Dr. Figgie, the new leader of technological change at Figgie International, should understand that his or her leadership activities are those activities within the company that involve directing the behavior of organization members so that company goals are reached. A manager like Dr. Figgie also should understand that leading and managing are not the same thing. When managing, Figgie is involved with planning, organizing, influencing, and controlling within the company. When leading, he is performing an activity that is part of the influencing function of management. To maximize his long-term success, Figgie should strive to be both a manager and a leader.

In assessing his leadership ability, Figgie should not fall into the trap of trying to increase his leadership success by changing his personal traits or attitudes to mirror those of successful leaders that he might know. Studies based on the trait approach to leadership should indicate to Figgie that merely changing his characteristics will not guarantee his success as a leader.

THE SITUATIONAL APPROACH TO LEADERSHIP: A FOCUS ON LEADER BEHAVIOR

The emphasis of leadership study has shifted from the trait approach to the situational approach. The cartoon lightheartedly makes the point that leadership style must be appropriately matched to the situation the leader faces. The more modern

"Confusing, dangerous times call for confusing, dangerous leadership!"

Wall Street Journal (October 11, 1990), a15. Reprinted by permission of *Wall Street Journal*, © 1990 Dow Jones & Company, Inc. All Rights Reserved Worldwide.

The **situational approach to leadership** is a relatively modern view of leadership that suggests that successful leadership requires a unique combination of leaders, followers, and leadership situations.

situational approach to leadership is based on the assumption that the instances of successful leadership are somewhat different and require a unique combination of leaders, followers, and leadership situations. This interaction commonly is expressed in formula form: $SL = f(L,F,S)$. In this formula, SL is *successful leadership,* f stands for *function of,* and L, F, and S are, respectively, the *leader,* the *follower,* and the *situation.*[12] A translation of this formula would be that successful leadership is a function of the leader, the follower, and the situation. In other words, the leader, the follower, and the situation must be appropriate for one another if a leadership attempt is to be successful.

Global Highlight: China's Leadership Style

One leadership challenge commonly faced by U.S. managers is how to react to their followers as well as to the particular situation appropriately when leading in a foreign country. As an example, consider the leadership challenge faced by a U.S. manager who has a position of leadership in a Chinese organization. For this leader, understanding the Chinese value system and working styles is critical. The Chinese personality and working style is presently dominated by a more traditional value system in which leaders must demonstrate strength and expertise. A leader in China is expected to build trust and personal relationships with followers. Terminating irresponsible workers is generally discouraged because such a discharged worker would lose too much "face." The Chinese are used to working at a relatively slow pace characterized by much leader patience and control. Chinese leaders commonly give employees gifts to show concern openly and offer encouragement, but they never criticize employees openly.

Leading in a Chinese organization would normally require somewhat different leadership tactics than leading in a U.S. organization. In general, U.S. managers should assess and react to situational leadership variables based on the social norms and customs of the country in which they are managing rather than on their own.

Leadership Situations and Decisions

The Tannenbaum and Schmidt Leadership Continuum

Tannenbaum and Schmidt wrote one of the first and perhaps most well-known articles on the situational approach to leadership. The authors emphasize situations in which a leader makes decisions.[13] Since one of the most important tasks of a leader is making sound decisions, practical and legitimate leadership thinking should contain some emphasis on decision making. Figure 14.2 presents Tannenbaum and Schmidt's model of leadership behavior, which contains such a decision-making emphasis.

The model presented in the figure is actually a continuum, or range, of leadership behavior available to managers in making decisions. Each type of decision-making behavior in this model has both a corresponding degree of authority used by the manager and a related amount of freedom available to subordinates.

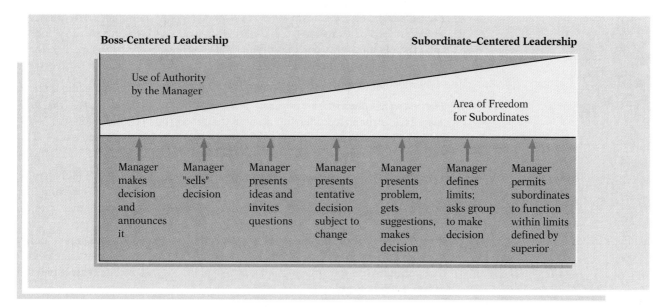

FIGURE 14.2
Continuum of leadership behavior that emphasizes decision making

Management behavior at the extreme left of the model characterizes the leader who makes decisions by maintaining high control and allowing little subordinate freedom. Behavior at the extreme right characterizes the leader who makes decisions by exercising little control and allowing much subordinate freedom and self-direction. Behavior between the extreme left and right reflects a gradual change from autocratic to democratic leadership, or vice versa. Managers displaying leadership behavior toward the right of the model are more democratic and are called subordinate-centered leaders. Managers displaying leadership behavior toward the left of the model are more autocratic and are called boss-centered leaders. Each type of leadership behavior in this model is explained in more detail in the following list:

1. *The manager makes the decision and announces it.* This behavior is characterized by the manager (a) identifying a problem, (b) analyzing various alternatives available to solve the problem, (c) choosing the alternative that will be used to solve the problem, and (d) requiring followers to implement the chosen alternative. The manager may or may not use coercion, but the followers have no opportunity to participate directly in the decision-making process.

2. *The manager "sells" the decision.* As before, the manager identifies the problem and independently arrives at a decision. Rather than announce the decision to subordinates for implementation, however, the manager tries to persuade subordinates to accept the decision.

3. *The manager presents ideas and invites questions.* Here, the manager makes the decision and attempts to gain acceptance through persuasion. One additional step is taken, however; subordinates are invited to ask questions about the decision.

4. *The manager presents a tentative decision that is subject to change.* The manager allows subordinates to have some part in the decision-making process but retains the responsibility for identifying and diagnosing the problem. The manager then arrives at a tentative decision that is subject to change on the basis of subordinate input. The final decision is made by the manager.

5. *The manager presents the problem, gets suggestions, and then makes the decision.* This is the first leadership activity described thus far that allows subordinates the opportunity to offer problem solutions before the manager does. The manager still identifies the problem in the first place.

6. *The manager defines the limits and asks the group to make a decision.* This behavior is characterized by the manager first defining the problem and setting the boundaries within which a decision must be made. The manager then sets up a partnership with subordinates to arrive at an appropriate decision. However, if the group of subordinates does not perceive the manager as genuinely desiring a serious group decision-making effort, it will tend to arrive at conclusions that reflect what the group thinks the manager wants rather than what the group actually wants.

7. *The manager permits the group to make decisions within prescribed limits.* Here the manager becomes an equal member of a problem-solving group. The entire group identifies and assesses the problem, develops possible solutions, and chooses an alternative to be implemented. Everyone within the group understands that the group's decision will be implemented.

Determining How to Make Decisions as a Leader. The true value of the model developed by Tannenbaum and Schmidt can be realized only if a leader can use it to make practical and desirable decisions. According to these authors, the three primary factors, or forces, that influence a manager's determination of which leadership behavior to use in making decisions are (1) forces in the manager, (2) forces in subordinates, and (3) forces in the leadership situation.

1. *Forces in the Manager.* Managers should be aware of four forces within themselves that influence their determination of how to make decisions as a leader. The first force is the manager's values, such as the relative importance to the manager of organizational efficiency, personal growth, the growth of subordinates, and company profits. For example, if subordinate growth is valued highly, the manager may want to give the group members the valuable experience of making a decision, even though he or she could have made the decision much more quickly and efficiently alone.

   The second influencing force within the manager is the level of confidence in subordinates. In general, the more confidence a manager has in subordinates, the more likely the style of decision making will be democratic, or subordinate-centered. The reverse is also true. The less confidence a manager has in subordinates, the more likely the style of decision making will be autocratic, or boss-centered.

   The third influencing force within the manager is personal leadership strengths. Some managers are more effective in issuing orders than in leading a group discussion, and vice versa. A manager must be able to recognize personal leadership strengths and to capitalize on them.

The fourth influencing force within the manager is tolerance for ambiguity. The move from a boss-centered style to a subordinate-centered style means some loss of certainty about how problems should be solved. If this reduction of certainty is disturbing to a manager, it may be extremely difficult for the manager to be successful as a subordinate-centered leader.

ack to the Case

The situational approach to leadership affords more insights for Dr. Figgie on how he can become a successful leader than does the trait approach. The situational approach would suggest that successful leadership for Dr. Figgie is determined by the appropriateness of a combination of three factors: (1) Dr. Figgie as a leader, (2) Figgie International employees as followers, and (3) the situation(s) within the company that Dr. Figgie will face. Each of these factors plays a significant role in determining whether Dr. Figgie is successful as a leader.

One of the most important activities Dr. Figgie performs as a leader is making decisions. He can make decisions in any number of ways, ranging from authoritarian to democratic. For example, Dr. Figgie could make the decision to use robots during the production of certain fire protection products in order to improve product quality, could announce to his employees how the robots will be used, and could require them to use the robots. Or Dr. Figgie could define the ways in which the manufacturing process of the products could be changed to improve product quality, could discuss the situation with appropriate manufacturing personnel, and could allow the staff members to come up with and implement their own methods for improving product quality. Or, for example, he could suggest to appropriate production workers that product quality needed to be improved, ask them to develop ideas for improvement, and then make the decision on the basis of his own ideas and those of the staff. In that situation, the outcome might be that using robots may not be the solution to the product quality problem that is finally decided.

2. *Forces in Subordinates.* A manager also should be aware of forces within subordinates that influence the manager's determination of how to make decisions as a leader.[14] To understand subordinates adequately, a manager should keep in mind that subordinates are both somewhat different and somewhat alike. Any cookbook approach for deciding how to lead all subordinates is therefore impossible. Generally speaking, however, a manager could increase success as a leader by allowing subordinates more freedom in making decisions when:[15]

- The subordinates have a relatively high need for independence. (People differ greatly in the amount of direction they desire.)

- They have a readiness to assume responsibility for decision making. (Some see additional responsibility as a tribute to their ability. Others see it as someone above them "passing the buck.")

- They have a relatively high tolerance for ambiguity. (Some employees prefer to have clear-cut directives given to them. Others prefer a wider area of freedom.)

- They are interested in the problem and believe it is important.

- They understand and identify with goals of the organization.
- They have the necessary knowledge and experience to deal with the problem.[16]
- They have learned to expect to share in decision making. (People who have come to expect strong leadership and then suddenly are confronted with the request to share more fully in decision making are often upset by this new experience. People who have enjoyed a considerable amount of freedom resent the boss who begins to make all the decisions alone.)

If these characteristics of subordinates do not exist in a particular situation, a manager probably should move toward a more autocratic, or boss-centered, approach to making decisions.

3. *Forces in the Situation.* The last group of forces that influence a manager's determination of how to make decisions as a leader are forces in the leadership situation. The first such situational force involves the type of organization in which the leader works. Such organizational factors as the size of working groups and their geographical distribution become especially important in deciding how to make decisions as a leader. Extremely large work groups or a wide geographic separation of work groups, for example, could make a subordinate-centered leadership style impractical.

The second situational force is the effectiveness of group members working together. To this end, a manager should evaluate such issues as the experience of the group in working together and the degree of confidence group members have in their ability to solve problems as a group. As a general rule, a manager should assign decision-making responsibilities only to effective work groups.

The third situational force is the problem to be solved. Before acting as a subordinate-centered leader, a manager should be sure that the group possesses the expertise necessary to make a decision about the existing problem. If it doesn't have the necessary expertise, the manager should move toward more boss-centered leadership.

The fourth situational force involves the time available to make a decision. As a general guideline, the less time available, the more impractical it becomes to have the decision made by a group. Typically, it takes a group more time than an individual to reach a decision.

Figure 14.3 summarizes the main forces that influence a manager's determination of how to make decisions as a leader and stresses that this determination is the result of the collective influence of all of these forces. As the situational approach to leadership implies, a manager will be successful as a decision maker only if the method used to make those decisions appropriately reflects the leader, the followers, and the situation.

Determining How to Make Decisions as a Leader: An Update. Tannenbaum and Schmidt's original article on leadership decision making was so widely accepted that the two authors were invited by *Harvard Business Review* to update their original work.[17] This update stressed that in modern organizations the relationship among forces within the manager, subordinates, and situation had become more complex and more interrelated than ever. As the relationship becomes increasingly complicated, it obviously becomes more difficult for the leader to determine how to lead.

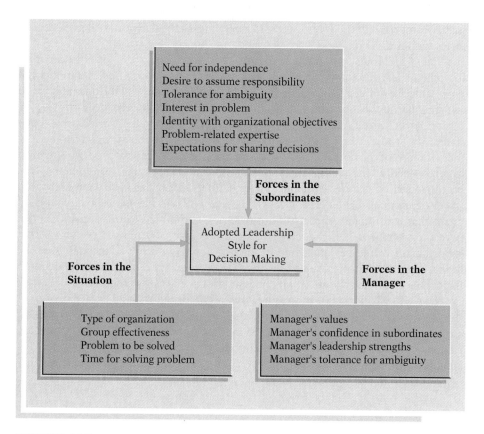

Need for independence
Desire to assume responsibility
Tolerance for ambiguity
Interest in problem
Identity with organizational objectives
Problem-related expertise
Expectations for sharing decisions

**Forces in the
Subordinates**

Adopted Leadership
Style for
Decision Making

**Forces in the
Situation**

**Forces in the
Manager**

Type of organization
Group effectiveness
Problem to be solved
Time for solving problem

Manager's values
Manager's confidence in subordinates
Manager's leadership strengths
Manager's tolerance for ambiguity

FIGURE 14.3

Collective influence of forces in the manager, the subordinates, and the
situation on the leadership style adopted for decision making

The update also stresses both societal and organizational environments as
more modern forces to consider in determining how to lead. Such societal and
organizational values as affirmative action and pollution control should have some
influence on the decision making of leaders.

The Vroom–Yetton–Jago Model

Another major decision-focused theory of leadership that has gained widespread
attention was first developed in 1973[18] and refined and expanded in 1988.[19] This
theory, which we will call the "Vroom–Yetton–Jago (VYJ) Model" after its three
major contributors, focuses on how much participation to allow subordinates in
the decision-making process. The VYJ Model is built on two important premises:
(1) organizational decisions should be of high quality (should have a beneficial
impact on organizational performance), and (2) subordinates should accept and
be committed to organizational decisions that are made.

Over all, the VYJ Model suggests that there are five different decision styles
or ways that leaders can make decisions. These decision styles range from the
leader's being autocratic (the leader makes the decision) to consultative (the leader
makes the decision after interacting with the followers) to group-focused (the

manager meets with the group, and the group makes the decision). All five decision styles within the VYJ Model are described in Figure 14.4.[20]

The VYJ Model, presented in Figure 14.5, is actually a method for determining when a leader should use which decision style. As you can see, the model is a type of decision tree.[21] In order for a leader to determine which decision style to use in a particular situation, the leader starts at the left of the decision tree by stating an organizational problem being addressed. After the problem has been stated, the leader asks a series of questions about the problem as determined by the structure of the decision tree until a decision style appropriate for the situation is determined at the far right side of the model. For example, consider the very bottom path of the decision tree. After stating an organizational problem, the leader determines that a decision related to that problem has a low-quality requirement, that it is important that subordinates are committed to the decision, and it is very uncertain that if the leader made the decision by himself or herself that subordinates would be committed to the decision. As a result of these factors, the model suggests that the leader uses the GII decision style, the leader meets with the group to discuss the situation, and the group makes the decision.

The VYJ Model seems promising. Research dealing with an earlier version of this model has yielded some evidence that decisions which managers make that are consistent with the model tend to be more successful than are decisions managers make that are inconsistent with the model.[22] The model tends to be somewhat complex, however, and therefore difficult for practicing managers to apply.

Decision Style	Definition
AI	Manager makes the decision alone.
AII	Manager asks for information from subordinates but makes the decision alone. Subordinates may or may not be informed about what the situation is.
CI	Manager shares the situation with individual subordinates and asks for information and evaluation. Subordinates do not meet as a group, and the manager alone makes the decision.
CII	Manager and subordinates meet as a group to discuss the situation, but the manager makes the decision.
GII	Manager and subordinates meet as a group to discuss the situation, and the group makes the decision.

A = autocratic; C = consultative; G = group

FIGURE 14.4

The five decision styles available to a leader according to the Vroom–Yetton–Jago Model

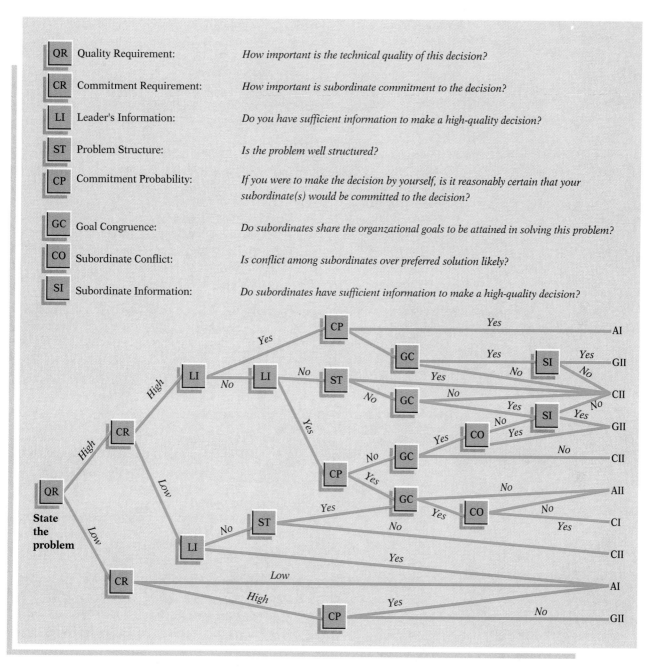

QR Quality Requirement:		*How important is the technical quality of this decision?*
CR Commitment Requirement:		*How important is subordinate commitment to the decision?*
LI Leader's Information:		*Do you have sufficient information to make a high-quality decision?*
ST Problem Structure:		*Is the problem well structured?*
CP Commitment Probability:		*If you were to make the decision by yourself, is it reasonably certain that your subordinate(s) would be committed to the decision?*
GC Goal Congruence:		*Do subordinates share the organzational goals to be attained in solving this problem?*
CO Subordinate Conflict:		*Is conflict among subordinates over preferred solution likely?*
SI Subordinate Information:		*Do subordinates have sufficient information to make a high-quality decision?*

FIGURE 14.5

The Vroom–Yetton–Jago Model

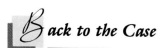

Back to the Case

In trying to decide exactly how to make his decisions as a leader, Dr. Figgie should consider forces in himself as manager, forces in his Figgie International subordinates, and forces in the specific organizational situation he faces. Forces within Dr. Figgie include his own ideas about how to lead and his level of confidence in the Figgie International employees that he is leading. If Dr. Figgie believes he is more knowledgeable about the use of new technology in the company than his staff is, he will be likely to make boss-centered decisions about what steps to take to gain a technological advantage within the company. Forces within his subordinates, such as the need for independence, the readiness to assume responsibility, and the knowledge of and interest in the issues to be decided, also affect Dr. Figgie's decisions as a leader. If his staff is relatively independent and responsible, and its members feel strongly that improved technology is important to meeting Figgie International objectives, then Dr. Figgie should be more inclined to allow his employees more freedom in deciding how to gain a technological advantage.

Forces within the company include the number of people making decisions and the problem to be solved. For example, if Dr. Figgie's staff is small, he will be more likely to use a democratic decision-making style, allowing his employees to become involved in such decisions as improving the use of technology within the company. He will also be likely to use a subordinate-centered leadership style if his staff is knowledgeable about the problem at hand.

The VYJ Model suggests that Dr. Figgie should try to make decisions in such a fashion that the quality of decisions is enhanced and followers are committed to the decisions. Dr. Figgie can try to ensure that such decisions are made by matching his decision style (autocratic, consultative, or group) to the particular situation he faces.

Leadership Situations in General

Decision-making behavior is a stream of leadership thought that focuses on leadership situations in more general terms. This stream of thought usually is said to have begun with two series of leadership studies. In one series, researchers were affiliated with the Bureau of Business Research at Ohio State University. These studies are called the OSU studies.[23] In the second series, the studies were conducted at the University of Michigan. These studies are called the Michigan Studies.

The OSU Studies

Structure behavior is leadership activity that (1) delineates the relationship between the leader and the leader's followers or (2) establishes well-defined procedures that the followers should adhere to in performing their jobs.

Consideration behavior is leadership behavior that reflects friendship, mutual trust, respect, and warmth in the relationship between the leader and the followers.

The OSU studies are a series of leadership investigations that concluded that leaders exhibit two main types of behavior. The first type, called **structure behavior,** is any leadership activity that delineates the relationship between the leader and the leader's followers or establishes well-defined procedures that followers should adhere to in performing their jobs. Over all, structure behavior limits the self-guidance of followers in the performance of their tasks. Although it would be correct to conclude that structure behavior can be, and sometimes is, relatively firm, it would be incorrect to assume that it is rude and malicious.[24]

Structure behavior can be useful to leaders as a means of minimizing follower activity that does not significantly contribute to organizational goal attainment. Leaders must be careful, however, that they do not discourage follower activity that will contribute to organizational goal attainment.

The second main type of leadership behavior described by the OSU studies, **consideration behavior,** is leadership behavior that reflects friendship, mutual trust, respect, and warmth in the relationship between the leader and the followers.

Consideration behavior generally is aimed at developing and maintaining a more human relationship between the leader and the followers.

The OSU studies resulted in a model that depicts four fundamental leadership styles. A **leadership style** is the behavior a leader exhibits while guiding organization members in appropriate directions. Each of the four leadership styles in Figure 14.6 is a different combination of structure behavior and consideration behavior. For example, the high structure/low consideration leadership style is that of a leader who emphasizes structure behavior and deemphasizes consideration behavior. The OSU studies have made a significant contribution to the understanding of leadership. The central thoughts and ideas generated by these studies still serve as the basis for modern leadership thought and research.[25]

Leadership style is the behavioral pattern a leader establishes while guiding organization members in appropriate directions.

The Michigan Studies

At about the same time that the OSU Leadership Studies were being conducted, researchers at the University of Michigan, led by Rensis Likert, were also performing a series of historically significant leadership studies.[26] Analyzing information based upon interviews of both leaders and followers or managers and subordinates, the Michigan Studies pinpointed two basic types of leader behavior: job-centered behavior and employee-centered behavior.

Job-Centered Behavior. **Job-centered behavior** is leader behavior through which the leader focuses primary attention on the work a subordinate is doing. Such behavior indicates that the leader is very interested in the work the subordinate is performing and how well the subordinate is doing the work.

Job-centered behavior is leader behavior through which the leader focuses primary attention on the work a subordinate is doing.

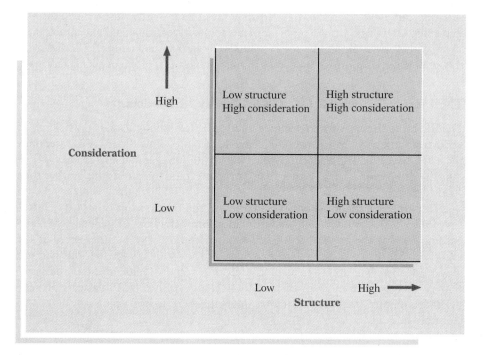

FIGURE 14.6

Four fundamental leadership styles based on structure behavior and consideration behavior

Employee-centered behavior is leader behavior through which the leader focuses primary attention on subordinates as people.

Employee-Centered Behavior. **Employee-centered behavior** is leader behavior through which the leader focuses primary attention on subordinates as people. Such behavior indicates that the leader is very attentive to the personal needs of subordinates and is interested in building cooperative work teams that are satisfying to subordinates and advantageous for the organization.

The results of the OSU studies and the Michigan Studies are very similar. Both research efforts indicated two primary dimensions of leader behavior: a work dimension (structure behavior/job-centered behavior) and a people dimension (consideration behavior/employee-centered behavior). The following section focuses, given these two primary dimensions of leader behavior, on determining the most advisable leadership style for a manager to adopt.

Effectiveness of Various Leadership Styles

An early investigation of high school superintendents concluded that desirable leadership behavior seems to be associated with high leader emphasis on both structure and consideration and that undesirable leadership behavior tends to be associated with low leader emphasis on both dimensions.[27] Similarly, the managerial grid covered in chapter 12 implies that the most effective leadership style is characterized by high consideration and high structure. Results of a more recent study indicate that high consideration is always preferred by subordinates.[28]

One should be cautious about concluding that any single leadership style is more effective than any other.[29] The leadership situation is so complex that pinpointing one leadership style as the most effective is an oversimplification. In fact, a successful leadership style for managers in one situation may be ineffective in another situation. Recognizing the need to link leadership styles to appropriate situations, in a classic article A.K. Korman says that a worthwhile contribution to leadership literature would be a rationale for systematically linking appropriate styles with various situations so as to ensure effective leadership.[30] The life cycle theory of leadership, which is covered in the next section, provides such a rationale.

The Hersey-Blanchard Life Cycle Theory of Leadership

The **life cycle theory of leadership** is a leadership concept that hypothesizes that leadership styles should reflect primarily the maturity level of the followers.

The **life cycle theory of leadership** is a rationale for linking leadership styles with various situations so as to ensure effective leadership. This theory uses essentially the same two types of leadership behavior as the OSU leadership studies, but it calls the dimensions "task" rather than "structure" and "relationships" rather than "consideration."

The life cycle theory is based primarily on the relationship of follower maturity, leader task behavior, and leader relationship behavior. In general terms, according to this theory, leadership style should reflect the maturity level of the followers. **Maturity** is defined as the ability of the followers to perform their job independently, their ability to assume additional responsibility, and their desire to achieve success. The more of each of these characteristics that followers possess, the more mature they are said to be. Maturity here is not necessarily linked to chronological age.

As used in the life cycle theory of leadership, **maturity** is an individual's ability to independently perform the job, to assume additional responsibility, and to desire success.

Figure 14.7 shows the life cycle theory of leadership model. The curved line in this model indicates the maturity level of the followers. As the maturity curve runs from right to left, the followers' maturity level increases. In more specific terms, the theory indicates that effective leadership behavior should shift from

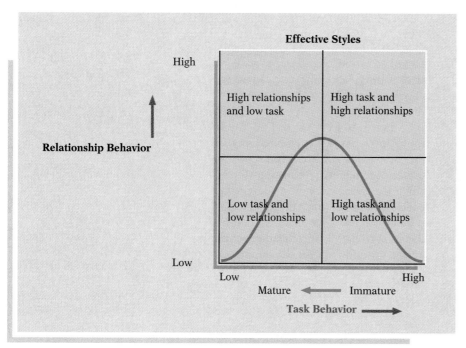

Effective Styles

FIGURE 14.7

The life cycle theory of leadership model

(1) high-task/low-relationships behavior to (2) high-task/high-relationships behavior to (3) high-relationships/low-task behavior to (4) low-task/low-relationships behavior, as one's followers progress from immaturity to maturity.[31]

The theory suggests, therefore, that a style of leadership will be effective only if it is appropriate for the maturity level of the followers. Table 14.1 describes how each of the four main leadership styles is perceived when it is both effective and ineffective, or appropriate and inappropriate, for followers' maturity levels.

TABLE 14.1 How basic leadership styles are perceived by others as effective and ineffective

Basic Styles	*Effective*	*Ineffective*
High task and low relationships	Often seen as knowing what he or she wants and imposing personal methods for accomplishing this without creating resentment	Often seen as having no confidence in others, unpleasant, and interested only in short-term output
High task and high relationships	Often seen as satisfying the needs of the group for setting goals and organizing work, but also providing high levels of socioemotional support	Often seen as initiating more structure than is needed by the group and spending more time on socioemotional support than necessary
High relationships and low task	Often seen as having implicit trust in people and as being concerned primarily with developing their talents	Often seen as interested primarily in harmony and being seen as "a good person," and being unwilling to risk disruption of a relationship to accomplish a task
Low task and low relationships	Often seen as appropriately permitting subordinates to decide how the work should be done and playing only a minor part in their social interaction	Often seen as uninvolved and passive, as a "paper shuffler" who cares little about the task at hand or the people involved

There are some exceptions to the general philosophy of the life cycle theory. For example, if there is a short-term deadline to meet, a leader may find it necessary to accelerate production through a high-task/low-relationships style, rather than a low-task/low-relationships style, even if the followers are mature. A high-task/low-relationships leadership style carried out over the long term with such followers, however, typically results in a poor working relationship of the leader and followers.

Following is an example of how the life cycle theory applies to a leadership situation: A man has just been hired as a salesperson in a men's clothing store. At first, this individual is extremely immature—that is, unable to solve task-related problems independently. According to the life cycle theory, the appropriate style for leading this salesperson at his level of maturity is high task/low relationships. The leader should tell the salesperson exactly what should be done and how it should be done. The salesperson should be shown how to make cash and charge sales and how to handle merchandise returns. The leader also should begin laying some of the groundwork for developing a personal relationship with the salesperson. Too much relationship behavior at this point, however, should be avoided, since it easily can be misinterpreted as permissiveness.

As time passes and the salesperson increases somewhat in job-related maturity, the next appropriate style for leading him is high task/high relationships. Although the salesperson's maturity has increased somewhat, the leader needs to watch him closely, because he still needs some guidance and direction at various times. The main difference between this leadership style and the first leadership style is the amount of relationship behavior displayed by the leader. Building on the groundwork laid during the period of the first leadership style, the leader is now ready to start developing an atmosphere of mutual trust, respect, and friendliness between her and the salesperson.

As more time passes, the salesperson's maturity level increases still further. The next style appropriate for leading this individual is high relationships/low task. The leader can now deemphasize task behavior, because the salesperson is now of above-average maturity in his job and usually can solve job-related problems independently. As with the previous leadership style, the leader still emphasizes the development of a human relationship with her follower.

As the salesperson's maturity level reaches its maximum, the appropriate style for leading him is low task/low relationships. Again, the leader can deemphasize task behavior, because the follower is thoroughly familiar with the job. The leader also can deemphasize relationship behavior, because she now has a good working relationship with the follower. Here, task behavior is seldom needed, and relationship behavior is used primarily to nurture the good working rapport that has developed between the leader and the follower. The salesperson, then, is left to do his job without close supervision, knowing that he has a positive working relationship with a leader who can be approached for additional guidance.

The life cycle theory of leadership has become widely accepted as a useful rationale on which to base leader behavior. The theory has served as the basis for leadership training in various organizations and has appeared in numerous management textbooks and professional journals.[32] Although at first glance it seems like a worthwhile leadership concept, some care probably should be exercised in its application because of the lack of scientific investigation verifying its worth.[33]

Quality Highlight: F. Kenneth Iverson/Nucor Corp.'s Chief Motivates Employees Through Leadership

When F. Kenneth Iverson, chief executive officer of Nucor Corporation, visits one of the company's steel mills, he wears a green hard hat like the workers instead of the traditional gold boss's helmet.

Iverson also flies coach class on business trips, carries his own bags, and eats lunch at a local delicatessen. Iverson's leadership philosophy is that if the boss wants the workers to cut costs and produce more while still maintaining quality standards, he has to set an example. "You won't find any status symbols here," he says. "The idea is to reduce any difference between management and anyone else at the company—destroy corporate hierarchy."

Nucor has only four layers of management; bonuses for managers and workers alike are based strictly on production and profit. When business is slow, both managers and workers take pay cuts. The program is called "Share the Pain," and top management's salaries are slashed by the largest percentages. In this way, Nucor is able to avoid laying off workers. The company has not had a layoff in 20 years. For Iverson, that means that in 1982, his salary dropped from $450,000 to $108,000.

Iverson sets production and quality standards for his workers, but he also rewards them appropriately. Basic hourly pay is only about $8 an hour. But production bonuses can be 100 to 150 percent above that, depending on how much additional steel is produced. Bonuses are paid each week, not at the end of the year. "If you worked real hard and you get real good performance, you get the payment for that the next week so that you can very easily relate to the fact that you worked like a dog and there's the money—not at the end of the year, but now," Iverson says.

Iverson's leadership style gets him the results he wants. The company produces 980 tons of steel a year per employee compared with an industry average of 420 tons. And Nucor's production costs are about $60 a ton, compared with $135 for the industry.

Back to the Case

The OSU leadership studies should furnish a manager like Dr. Figgie with insights on leadership behavior in general situations. According to these studies, Dr. Figgie can exhibit two general types of leadership behavior: structure and consideration. He will be using structure behavior if he tells Figgie International personnel what to do—for example, to work more quickly in adopting welding technology concepts in product manufacturing. He will be using consideration behavior if he attempts to develop a more human rapport with his employees by discussing their concerns and developing friendships with them.

Of course, depending on how Dr. Figgie emphasizes these two behaviors, his leadership style can reflect a combination of structure and consideration ranging from high structure/low consideration to low structure/high consideration. For example, if Dr. Figgie stresses giving orders to employees and deemphasizes developing relationships, he will be exhibiting high structure/low consideration. If he emphasizes a good rapport with his staff, and allows its members to function mostly independently of him, his leadership style will be termed low structure/high consideration.

Although no single leadership style is more effective than any other in all situations, the life cycle theory of leadership furnishes Dr. Figgie with a strategy for using various styles in various situations. According to this theory, Dr. Figgie should make his style consistent primarily with the maturity level of the Figgie International organization members that he is leading. As Figgie's followers progress from immaturity to maturity, his leadership style should shift systematically from (1) high-task/low-relationships behavior to (2) high-task/high-relationships behavior to (3) high-relationships/low-task behavior to (4) low-task/low-relationships behavior.

Fiedler's Contingency Theory of Leadership and Leader Flexibility

Leader flexibility is the ability of leaders to change their leadership styles.

Situational theories of leadership, such as life cycle theory, are based on the concept of **leader flexibility**—that successful leaders must change their leadership style as they encounter different situations. Can leaders be so flexible as to span all major leadership styles? The only answer to this question is that some leaders can be flexible and some cannot. After all, a leadership style may be so ingrained in a leader that it takes years to even approach flexibility. Also, some leaders may have experienced such success in a basically static situation that they believe flexibility is unnecessary. Unfortunately, there are numerous obstacles to leader flexibility.

One strategy, proposed by Fred Fiedler, for overcoming these obstacles is changing the organizational situation to fit the leader's style, rather than changing the leader's style to fit the organizational situation.[34] Relating this thought to the life cycle theory of leadership, one finds that it may be easier to shift various leaders to situations appropriate for their leadership styles than to expect leaders to change styles as situations change. It probably would take three to five years to train managers to effectively use a concept such as life cycle theory.[35] Changing the situation a particular leader faces, however, can be done in the short term simply by exercising organizational authority.

The **contingency theory of leadership** is a leadership concept that hypothesizes that, in any given leadership situation success is determined primarily by (1) the degree to which the task being performed by the followers is structured, (2) the degree of position power possessed by the leader, and (3) the type of relationship that exists between the leader and the followers.

According to Fiedler and his **contingency theory of leadership,** leader-member relations, task structure, and the position power of the leader are the three primary factors that should be used for moving leaders into situations appropriate for their leadership styles. *Leader-member relations* is the degree to which the leader feels accepted by the followers. *Task structure* is the degree to which the goals—the work to be done—and other situational factors are outlined clearly. *Position power* is determined by the extent to which the leader has control over the rewards and punishments the followers receive. How these three factors can be arranged in eight different combinations is presented in Table 14.2. Each of these eight combinations is called an octant.

Figure 14.8 shows how effective leadership varies among the eight octants. From an organizational viewpoint, this figure implies that management should attempt to match permissive, passive, and considerate leaders with situations reflecting the middle of the continuum containing the octants. The figure also implies that management should try to match a controlling, active, and structuring

TABLE 14.2 Eight combinations, or octants, of three factors: leader-member relations, task structure, and leader position power

Octant	Leader-Member Relations	Task Structure	Leader Position Power
I	Good	High	Strong
II	Good	High	Weak
III	Good	Weak	Strong
IV	Good	Weak	Weak
V	Moderately poor	High	Strong
VI	Moderately poor	High	Weak
VII	Moderately poor	Weak	Strong
VIII	Moderately poor	Weak	Weak

leader with the extremes of this continuum. Possible actions that Fiedler suggests to modify the leadership situation are as follows:[36]

1. In some organizations, we can change the individual's task assignment. We may assign to one leader very structured tasks which have implicit or explicit instructions telling him what to do and how to do it, and we may assign to another the tasks that are nebulous and vague. The former are the typical production tasks; the latter are exemplified by committee work, by the development of policy, and by tasks which require creativity.

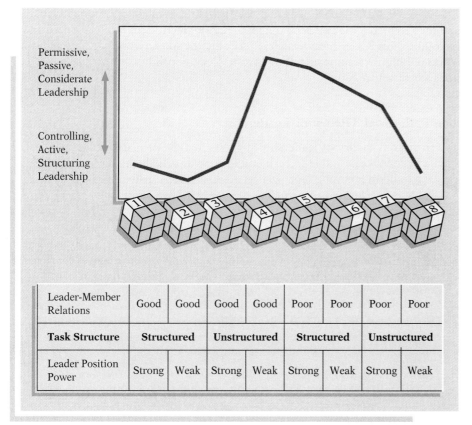

Leader-Member Relations	Good	Good	Good	Good	Poor	Poor	Poor	Poor
Task Structure	Structured		Unstructured		Structured		Unstructured	
Leader Position Power	Strong	Weak	Strong	Weak	Strong	Weak	Strong	Weak

FIGURE 14.8

How effective leadership style varies with Fiedler's eight octants

2. We can change the leader's position power. We not only can give him a higher rank and corresponding recognition, we also can modify his position power by giving him subordinates who are equal to him in rank and prestige or subordinates who are two or three ranks below him. We can give him subordinates who are experts in their specialties or subordinates who depend upon the leader for guidance and instruction. We can give the leader the final say in all decisions affecting his group, or we can require that he make decisions in consultation with his subordinates, or even that he obtain their concurrence. We can channel all directives, communications, and information about organizational plans through the leader alone, giving him expert power, or we can provide these communications concurrently to all his subordinates.

3. We can change the leader-member relations in this group. We can have the leader work with groups whose members are very similar to him in attitude, opinion, technical background, race, and cultural background. Or we can assign him subordinates with whom he differs in any one or several of these important aspects. Finally, we can assign the leader to a group in which the members have a tradition of getting along well with their supervisors or to a group that has a history and tradition of conflict.

Over all, Fiedler's work helps destroy the myths that there is one best leadership style and that leaders are born, not made. Further, Fiedler's work supports the theory that almost every manager in an organization can be a successful leader if placed in a situation appropriate for the person's leadership style. This, of course, assumes that someone in the organization has the ability to assess the characteristics of the organization's leaders and of other important organizational variables and then to match the two accordingly.[37] Although criticism of Fiedler's work can be found,[38] his leadership research is probably the most rigorous to date, and his works are highly recommended to anyone seeking insights on the challenges and how-to's of leadership.

The Path-Goal Theory of Leadership

Path-goal theory of leadership is a theory of leadership that suggests the primary activity of a leader should be to make desirable and achievable rewards available to organization members as a result of attaining organizational goals and to clarify the kinds of behavior that must be performed to earn those rewards.

The **path-goal theory of leadership** suggests that the primary activity of a leader should be to make desirable and achievable rewards available to organization members as a result of attaining organizational goals and to clarify the kinds of behavior that must be performed to earn those rewards.[39] In essence, the leader outlines the goals that followers should aim for and clarifies how (the path that followers take) to earn those goals. Over all, the path-goal theory indicates that managers can facilitate job performance by showing employees how their performance directly affects their receiving desired rewards.

According to the path-goal theory of leadership, leaders perform four primary types of behavior:

1. *Directive behavior.* Directive behavior is leader behavior aimed at telling followers what to do and how to do it. The leader indicates what performance goals exist and precisely what must be done to achieve them.

2. *Supportive behavior.* Supportive behavior is leader behavior aimed at being friendly with followers and showing interest in them as human beings. Through supportive behavior the leader shows sensitivity to the personal needs of followers.

3. *Participative behavior.* Participative behavior is leader behavior in which suggestions from the follower are sought regarding business operations with the result that followers are involved in making important organizational decisions. Consistent with this type of leader behavior, followers often help to determine the rewards that will be available to them in organizations and what must be done to earn those rewards.

4. *Achievement behavior.* Achievement behavior is leader behavior aimed at setting challenging goals for followers to reach and expressing and demonstrating confidence that followers will meet the challenge. This leader behavior focuses on making goals difficult enough so that employees find achieving them challenging but not so difficult that followers view them as impossible and therefore give up trying to achieve them.

As with other situational theories of leadership, the path-goal theory proposes that leaders can be successful if they are able to match appropriately these four types of behavior to situations that they face. For example, assuming that inexperienced followers do not have a thorough understanding of a job, a manager may appropriately use more directive behavior to develop this understanding and to ensure that serious job-related problems are avoided. For more experienced followers, assuming that they have a more complete understanding of a job, directive behavior would probably be inappropriate and might create interpersonal problems between the leader and the followers. If jobs are very structured, with little room for employee interpretation of how the work should be done, directive behavior is probably less needed than if there is much room for employees to determine how work might get done. If followers are getting much personal satisfaction and encouragement, and support from members of a work group, supportive behavior by the leader is probably not as important as when followers are getting little or no satisfaction from personal relationships in the work group.

The primary focus of the path-goal theory of leadership is on how leaders can increase employee effort and productivity by clarifying performance goals and the path to be taken to achieve those goals.[40] Over time, the path-goal theory of leadership has gained much acceptance. Research suggests that the path-goal theory holds promising potential for helping managers to enhance employee commitment to achieving organizational goals and thereby gives managers a key for increasing the probability that organizations will be successful.[41]

RECENT EMPHASIS ON LEADERSHIP

As with any academic area, the area of leadership is continually evolving. Two topics that have recently been getting more attention in the leadership literature are transformational leadership and trust. This section relates each of these topics to leadership.

Transformational Leadership

Transformational leadership is leadership that inspires organizational success by profoundly affecting followers' beliefs in what an organization should be, as well as followers' values like justice and integrity.[42] Transformational leadership creates

Transformational leadership is leadership that inspires organizational success by profoundly affecting followers' beliefs in what an organization should be, as well as followers' values like justice and integrity.

a sense of duty within an organization, encourages new ways of handling problems, and promotes learning for all organization members. Transformational leadership is closely related to concepts like charismatic leadership or inspirational leadership.

Perhaps transformational leadership is receiving more attention recently because of the dramatic changes that many organizations are going through and the critical importance of transformational leadership in "transforming" or changing organizations successfully. Lee Iacocca is often used as an example of a successful transformational leader because of his successful efforts in transforming Chrysler Corporation from a floundering company into a much more successful company that could avoid bankruptcy.

Transformational leaders perform several important tasks. Transformational leaders raise the awareness of followers concerning organizational issues and their consequences.[43] Organization members must understand the high-priority issues that exist for an organization and what will happen if the issues are not faced successfully. Transformational leaders also create a vision of what the organization should be, build commitment to that vision throughout the organization, and facilitate changes throughout the organization that support the vision.[44] In essence, transformational leadership is consistent with strategy developed through an organization's strategic management process.

Managers of the future will continue to face the challenge of significantly changing organizations. The accelerating trend toward positioning organizations to be more competitive in a global business environment will be a primary contributor to the need to change organizations significantly in the future. As a result, transformational leadership will probably get increasing attention in leadership literature. Although there is much practical appeal and interest in the topic of transformational leadership, more research is needed to develop insights about how to be a successful transformational leader.

Trust

Trust is followers' belief in and reliance on the ability and the integrity of the leader.

Perhaps the most fundamental ingredient of successful leadership is a trust that followers have for the leader. **Trust** is the followers' belief in and reliance on the ability and integrity of the leader. Without such trust in a leader, successful leadership seems difficult if not impossible.

Today there is significant concern that managers are not developing the trust with subordinates that is necessary to ensure successful leadership.[45] In general, trust that subordinates feel for organizational leaders seems to be critically low, and employee opinion polls seem to illustrate a trend indicating that this trust might decline even further in the future. For example, a recent survey of 100,000 working people conducted by Opinion Research Corporation of Princeton, New Jersey, noted a steep decline in trust and regard for top management. One reason given for this lack of trust is that managers seem to be assuming a more self-reliant and self-centered role with less and less concern being shown for subordinates.[46]

In an effort to maximize leadership success, managers should focus on reversing this trend by building trust between themselves and their followers. There are many strategies that managers can use to build trust relationships with their subordinates. One of the most popular strategies entails showing and expressing confidence in subordinates and being completely open about why important decisions are made.[47] Such actions demonstrate that a manager values his or her subordinates and will not take actions that might penalize them in any unfair way. In addition, such actions allow managers to demonstrate their competence by helping subordinates to understand how and why decisions are made. Building trust is a gradual process that requires constant management attention.[48]

ℰthics Highlight: Domino's Pizza Emphasizes Ethics

Executives who emphasize ethics tend to be seen as leaders with integrity who tend to nurture trust relationships between themselves and their subordinates. Thomas S. Monaghan, founder of Domino's Pizza, Inc., illustrates how a leader can create trust by emphasizing ethics.

Monaghan contends that his pizza empire has done well largely because his corporate philosophy follows the Golden Rule: "Do unto others as you would have them do unto you." Monaghan believes that it is natural for him to emphasize ethics in his business dealings because he has always been somewhat of a frustrated priest. He openly states that he wants to devote the rest of his life to somehow doing some good in the world. He concedes, however, that he personally often falls short of the high standards of ethical performance for which he crusades.

It is easy to argue that a manager like Monaghan who openly talks of ethics and doing good in the world would naturally be seen by his employees as an ethical leader. In fact, Domino's employees appear to trust and follow Monaghan, who they perceive as possessing integrity.

Because of the success of Domino's Pizza, Monaghan has been able to realize most of his dreams. At age 54, he owns the Detroit Tigers and has one of the largest collections of work by architect Frank Lloyd Wright. Emphasizing ethics in his business dealings has helped make Thomas S. Monaghan a successful man.

ℬack to the Case

The life cycle theory suggests that a manager should be flexible enough to behave as the situation requires. If Figgie finds it extremely difficult to be flexible, he should attempt to structure his situation so as to make it appropriate for his style. As suggested by Fiedler, if Figgie's leadership style is high task in nature, he generally will be a more successful leader in situations best described by octants 1, 2, 3, and 8 in Table 14.2 and Figure 14.8. If, however, Figgie's leadership style is more relationship oriented, he will probably be a more successful leader in situations representative of octants 4, 5, 6, and 7. Over all, Fiedler's work can provide Figgie with insights on how to engineer situations at Figgie International so they will be appropriate for his leadership style.

The path-goal theory of leadership suggests that Dr. Figgie should emphasize clarification of what rewards are available to followers in the organization, how those rewards can be earned, and elimination of barriers that could prohibit followers from earning the rewards. Dr. Figgie can use directive behavior, supportive behavior, participative behavior, and achievement behavior in implementing the path-goal theory.

Dr. Figgie should focus on being a transformational leader, a leader who inspires followers to seriously focus on achieving organizational objectives. As a transformational leader, he should strive to encourage new ideas, create a sense of duty, and encourage employees to learn and grow. As a company like Figgie International undergoes more and more significant change, the importance of its leader being a transformational leader increases. Dr. Figgie must always keep in mind that regardless of the type of leader he may be, he must earn and maintain the trust of his followers if he is to be successful in the long run.

Action Summary

Circle:

Reread the learning objectives that follow. Each objective is followed by questions. Answering these questions accurately will help you retain the most important concepts discussed in this chapter. After answering each question, check your answer with the answer key at the end of this chapter. (*Hint:* If you have doubt regarding the correct response, consult the page whose number follows the answer.)

From studying this chapter, I will attempt to acquire:

1. A working definition of leadership.

a, b, c, d, e

    a. The process of directing others toward the accomplishment of some objective is: (a) communication; (b) controlling; (c) leadership; (d) managing; (e) none of the above.

a, b, c, d, e

    b. Directing must be consistent with: (a) organizational policies; (b) procedures; (c) job descriptions; (d) none of the above; (e) all of the above.

2. An understanding of the relationship between leading and managing.

T, F

    a. Leading and managing are the same process.

a, b, c, d, e

    b. In the relationship between managers and leaders, one could say that: (a) all managers are leaders; (b) all leaders are managers; (c) some leaders are not managers; (d) managers cannot be leaders; (e) management is a subset of leadership.

3. An appreciation for the trait and situational approaches to leadership.

a, b, c, d, e

    a. Which of the following is true about the conclusions drawn from the trait approach to leadership: (a) the trait approach identifies traits that consistently separate leaders from nonleaders; (b) there are certain traits that guarantee that a leader will be successful; (c) the trait approach is based on early research that assumes that a good leader is born, not made; (d) leadership is a simple issue of describing the traits of successful leaders; (e) none of the above.

a, b, c, d, e

    b. The situational approach to leadership takes into account: (a) the leader; (b) the follower; (c) the situation; (d) a and b; (e) a, b, and c.

4. **Insights about using leadership theories that emphasize decision-making situations.**

   a. Forces in the manager that determine leadership behavior include: (a) the manager's values; (b) the manager's confidence in subordinates; (c) the manager's strengths; (d) the manager's tolerance for ambiguity; (e) all of the above.

   a, b, c, d, e

   b. Limiting the self-guidance of the follower and specifically defining procedures for the follower's task performance is called: (a) initiating behavior; (b) structure behavior; (c) maturity behavior; (d) consideration behavior; (e) relationship behavior.

   a, b, c, d, e

   c. The VYJ model suggests that a leader should match one of five decision-making styles to the particular situation that the leader faces.

   T, F

5. **Insights about using leadership theories that emphasize more general organizational situations.**

   a. The ability of followers to perform their jobs independently and to assume additional responsibility in their desire to achieve success is called: (a) maturity; (b) authority; (c) aggressiveness; (d) assertiveness; (e) consideration.

   a, b, c, d, e

   b. Usually upon entrance into an organization, an individual is unable to solve task-related problems independently. According to the life cycle theory, the appropriate style of leadership for this person is: (a) high task/low relationships; (b) high task/high relationships; (c) high relationships/low task; (d) low task/low relationships; (e) none of the above.

   a, b, c, d, e

   c. According to the path-goal theory of leadership, a leader should carefully inform followers of the rewards that are available to them in the organization and then allow them to pick their own methods of earning the rewards.

   T, F

6. **An understanding of alternatives to leader flexibility.**

   a. According to Fiedler, the three primary factors that should be used as a basis for moving leaders into more appropriate situations are: (a) task behavior, consideration behavior, maturity; (b) maturity, job knowledge, responsibility; (c) the worker, the leader, the situation; (d) leader-member relations, task structure, position power; (e) task structure, leadership style, maturity.

   a, b, c, d, e

   b. Fiedler's studies have proven true the myths that leaders are born, not made, and that there is one best leadership style.

   T, F

7. **An appreciation of both transformational leadership and trust as components of leadership theory.**

   a. Transformational leaders modify organizations by precisely carrying out strategic plans and emphasizing only slightly the values that followers may have.

   T, F

   b. Transformational leadership might be called charismatic or inspirational leadership.

   T, F

   c. From a leadership viewpoint, a subordinate's trust in a leader includes a belief in, but not necessarily a reliance on, the ability of the leader.

   T, F

   d. It is generally challenging for leaders to develop trust relationships with subordinates because building trust is a gradual process that takes constant attention.

   T, F

Introductory Case Wrap-Up

"A New Leader at Figgie International, Inc." and its related back-to-the-case sections were written to help you better understand the management concepts contained in this chapter. Answer the following discussion questions about this introductory case to further enrich your understanding of chapter content:

1. Will being the son of Figgie Senior present any spe-

cial leadership problems for Dr. Figgie? If so, list the problem(s) you see. If none, why?

2. Will Dr. Figgie's background as a physician present any special challenges for him as a leader at Figgie International? If so, what challenge(s) do you see? If none, why?

Issues for Review and Discussion

1. What is leadership?

2. How does leadership differ from management?

3. Explain the trait approach to leadership.

4. What relationship exists between successful leadership and leadership traits?

5. Explain the situational approach to leadership.

6. Draw and explain Tannenbaum and Schmidt's leadership model.

7. List the forces in the manager, the subordinates, and the situation that ultimately determine how a manager should make decisions as a leader.

8. How is the VYJ Model similar to the Tannenbaum and Schmidt Model? How is it different?

9. What contribution did the OSU studies make to leadership theory?

10. Can any one of the major leadership styles resulting from the OSU studies be called more effective than the others? Explain.

11. Compare the results of the OSU studies with the results of the Michigan Studies.

12. What is meant by *maturity* as it is used in the life cycle theory of leadership?

13. Draw and explain the life cycle theory of leadership model.

14. What is meant by *leader flexibility*?

15. Describe some obstacles to leader flexibility.

16. In general, how might obstacles to leader flexibility be overcome?

17. In specific terms, how does Fiedler suggest that obstacles to leader flexibility be overcome?

18. Based upon the path-goal theory of leadership, how would you advise a friend to lead?

19. Describe three challenges that a transformational leader must face.

20. Discuss tactics that can be used by a leader to develop a trust relationship with subordinates. Why do you think that the tactics will work?

Building on What You Know

Directions

Review the Highlight feature as indicated below and answer its corresponding questions. Questions in this section focus on relating a Highlight appearing in this chapter to management concepts that you have learned in a previous chapter.

Review the Global Highlight: China on page 418. In Chapter 13 you studied about both interpersonal and organizational communication. What special *interpersonal* communication difficulties could arise for the U.S. manager in China? Be sure to reflect on all parts of the interpersonal communication process. Might there also be special *organizational* communication difficulties for the U.S. manager? If so, what steps would you take to overcome these difficulties?

Action Summary Answer Key

1. a. c, p. 415
   b. e, p. 415
2. a. F, p. 415
   b. c, p. 415

3. a. c, p. 416
   b. e, p. 418

4. a. e, pp. 420–423
   b. b, p. 426
   c. T, pp. 423–424

5. a. a, p. 428
   b. a, p. 430
   c. F, p. 434

6. a. d, p. 432
   b. F, p. 434

7. a. F, pp. 435–436
   b. T, p. 436
   c. F, p. 436
   d. T, pp. 436–437

Case Study

Roger Smith of General Motors: What (If Anything) Was Wrong with Roger?

by Michael Bowen, University of Notre Dame

When Roger Smith took over as chair and CEO of the General Motors (GM) Corporation in 1981, few—if any—company and auto industry observers expected him to introduce any significant changes to the stodgy, heavily bureaucratized auto giant. Smith, a GM lifer, was known throughout the company as a short, bland, colorless financial wizard who was so cautious "that he wore a seat belt in his chauffeured limousine." It came as a great surprise when he took immediate action to transform GM into an entirely new company.

Smith perceived that a new corporate culture emphasizing diversity, innovation, and risk taking was essential to GM's future. He saw a high-tech response as the best weapon to combat the import invasion from Japanese automakers. Smith invested heavily in numerous automation systems so that new ideas and methods would touch virtually everything that the company did.

Smith also ordered a total restructuring of GM's business organization. He reorganized the five former car divisions—Chevrolet, Buick, Oldsmobile, Pontiac, and Cadillac—into two groups, and he created two new car companies—the Saturn and Jupiter projects—based on entirely new ways of thinking about and creating automobiles. He also built or completely refurbished 40 factories, and initiated joint ventures with Japanese carmakers.

These early moves, along with higher profits in the mid-1980s, won him the praise of many auto-industry observers. For example, Maryann Keller, a longtime industry analyst, stated, "Roger is the first person to run the company with a vision of the future of the industry. All the things that are happening are his idea." Smith played down his personal importance in shaping the new GM, however, saying "I've heard people say 'Oh, [former GM chairman] Mr. Sloan would be spinning in his grave if he knew what you were doing.' I say that's nuts. He'd be doing exactly what I'm doing. I really believe that."

Although early results of the new programs were promising, prompting managers throughout the company to discount evidence of impending trouble, it soon became apparent that the changes Smith had introduced would not be enough to restore significant profitability to GM in the long term. Not all of the advanced manufacturing techniques that Smith had purchased and counted could, in fact, be relied on to deliver what their manufacturers had promised. Productivity was dropping companywide. GM began to suffer financially relative to its major competitors, and it began to lose market share.

As Smith's plans seemed to falter, criticism of his leadership style grew. Having received several "Man of the Year" awards and having been characterized in the business press as an innovative master manager, Smith was now accused of being inept at people skills. Critics pointed out that Smith had angered the unionized work force by blaming the company's hard times on exorbitant labor costs while he boosted executive bonuses. He ordered middle managers to work harder, then cut their bonuses and laid off twenty-five percent of them.

One of Smith's chief detractors was H. Ross Perot, founder and chair of Electronic Data Systems Corporation (EDS), which Smith had purchased for GM to revitalize data processing systems. Smith had anticipated that some of EDS's aggressive, entrepreneurial spirit would rub off on GM; instead, there was a major clash of corporate cultures. Great bitterness arose between Smith and Perot, and between the employees of the two companies. Perot, newly elected as a GM board member, publicly chided GM for being a bureaucratic nightmare where decisions took too long to make and money was wasted on senseless perquisites for executives. He gloated that EDS had grown and earned substantially higher profits since the acquisition, in spite of GM's worsening performance. However, many GM insiders disputed and resented those claims. They complained that Perot's "stormtroopers" had barged into the GM organization, charging as much as three times the fees that GM would have paid to independent contractors for the same data-processing work.

To help end the vicious turf wars raging inside GM, Smith eventually purchased the ownership interest held by Perot and many of his top managers for $700 million. Nonetheless, criticism of Smith continued. Both dealers and shareholders complained about the high cost of the buyout, particularly in a time of unsold inventories and weak earnings. A successful 1989 motion picture, *Roger and Me,* depicted Smith as totally insensitive to the human side of business. Albert Lee, a former Smith speechwriter, called Smith's tenure a tragic era for GM. In his 1988 bestseller *Call Me Roger,* he wrote that no prior chair "has disrupted as many lives without commensurate rewards, has spent as much money without returns, or has alienated so many along the way."

In 1988, Roger Smith announced plans to retire from GM on his upcoming 65th birthday, in line with company policy. One of his final acts as chair, shrouded in secrecy, as Saturn executives feared negative association of their company with GM, was to drive the first Saturn production car off the assembly line at the revolutionary new plant in Spring Hill, Tennessee.

Discussion Questions

1. Based on the information given in this case, do you think that Roger Smith was more a "leader" or a "manager" at GM? Why?

2. How would you interpret your answer to Question 1 in terms of the OSU studies (Figure 14.6) and the life-cycle theory of leadership (Figure 14.7)?

3. Using Fiedler's contingency theory of leadership as a guide, was Smith's leadership style appropriate for GM in this case?

4. Based on the information provided in the case, would you characterize H. Ross Perot's leadership behavior at EDS to be more job-centered or more employee-centered than Roger Smith's at GM?

William Olsten of the Olsten Corporation: A People Person

"You want to call me a common person? Do that. That would be flattery." This is the heart of William Olsten, chair of the Olsten Corporation, founder and leader of the third largest temporary personnel agency in the world.

Olsten was a foot soldier in World War II, discharged in 1946 to a nation and a home—New York City—transformed by the war. A quiet revolution had begun in his absence. For the first time, women had entered the U.S. work force in large numbers, from Rosie the Riveter to Army nurses, and from secretaries to salespeople. Some, such as Olsten's wife Mim, worked for the government in civil service professions. One thing was certain: They were not all ready to give up working when their husbands and brothers and sons returned home.

William Olsten had finished high school and a commercial business school before going to war, and when he came home, he felt the lack of a college education. He attended night school while working during the days, but he never finished his degree. Then came the Korean War; once again, men were drafted out of the work force, and Olsten saw his opportunity. With leaflets, small advertisements, and door-to-door solicitation, he built an army of temporary and part-time office workers, bringing women back into the work force. Olsten's corporation now staffs more than 300,000 jobs a year in the United States and Canada, with men and women in various types of work.

One key to Olsten's success is his belief in people. He trusts his workers to perform the jobs they are sent out to do in a way that will reflect well not only on themselves but also on the Olsten Corporation. His trust is clearly repaid by his employees: Olsten workers are relied upon by 90% of the Fortune 500 companies to fill temporary positions.

It is not enough to display confidence in employees, however. Olsten's workers are paid according to what their skills would bring on the open market. They are trained in special skills when necessary for a particular client—skills that increase their value if they choose to move on to new employers. Like permanent staff members, they receive paid vacation benefits. Workers at the Olsten Corporation may represent a commodity for clients, but they are Olsten team members.

Newly hired workers are screened through a series of evaluations—Olsten has dropped the use of the word *tests* in this context, as being too stressful and, perhaps, demeaning. A simple change of a word such as this reflects William Olsten's employee orientation. He cares about his people, and he identifies with them. When Olsten executives attend seminars to learn better people skills, they may find William Olsten attending along with them. The advice he offers to his staff and to his children demonstrates his commitment, too: "Don't be complacent, because life is not a complacent place to be. . . . You can't just be a vegetable. You can't live off the fat of the land without putting something back into that land, and to the business, and to your life."

Olsten's way of putting something back into the business is by offering a corporate literacy program. As early as 1951, Olsten had identified illiteracy as a problem among people who wanted to work. Over the following forty years, he has seen the demands of the workplace change drastically as business becomes increasingly service oriented and as automation replaces production line workers. Literacy is more important than ever before, and the Olsten Corporation has long-standing programs to advance the reading and writing skills of employees who need help. William Olsten wants to make life better for his people.

Video Case Questions

1. Do you think William Olsten is more a "leader" or a "manager"? Why?

2. Does William Olsten's leadership as head of the Olsten Corporation better illustrate the trait approach theory or the situational approach theory to leadership?

3. The Ohio State University studies of leaders identify two types of leadership behavior: structure behavior and consideration behavior. How does William Olsten exhibit either or both types of behavior?

4. Is William Olsten a transformational leader? Why or why not?

Video Case Activities

1. Consider the Hersey–Blanchard life-cycle theory of leadership for linking leadership styles with various situations. Outline a leadership style for dealing with temporary workers and one for working with permanent workers. What are the similarities and differences between the two?

2. Imagine that you are a manager for an Olsten client, a textbook publishing company. Two temporary workers have joined your clerical staff to help process book orders during the rush season before school semesters start. What leadership style should you use to deal with these temporary employees? Why?

Chapter 15

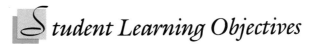

S tudent Learning Objectives

From studying this chapter, I will attempt to acquire:

1. A basic understanding of human motivation.

2. Insights on various human needs.

3. An appreciation for the importance of motivating organization members.

4. An understanding of various motivation strategies.

Motivation

hapter Outline

EMPLOYEE INCENTIVES AT HALF PRICE BOOKS

Ken Gjemre's bookstore in Houston looks more like a flea market than a mecca for bibliophiles. It's crammed with books stacked haphazardly on unfinished wooden shelves. Some of its most popular volumes have been off The Best Sellers list for years. And its advertising sometimes sounds more typical of a fabric shop than a bookstore; for those whose library could use a more studious look, it touts "Books by the Yard." And why not? "It's a hell of a lot better than throwing them in a landfill," says Gjemre.

Waldenbooks it's not. But Half Price Books, the largest used-book chain in America, is cashing in on a niche largely overlooked by the giants: used books,

magazines, records and "remainders"—new books left over from publishers and warehouses. At a time when slow mall growth has kept the major chains from expanding, HPB is in the midst of a boom. The chain has 300 employees in 33 stores and a sales volume that matches that of many regional new-book sellers. Half Price also has one distinct advantage over a Waldenbooks or a B. Dalton: low overhead. Says Bernie Rath, executive director of the American Booksellers Association: "When you buy a book for 50 cents and sell it for $5, you do a whole lot better than when you buy a book for $3 and sell it for $5."

A native of rural Indiana, Gjemre now locates most of his stores not in large cities, but in midsize towns. He has targeted 150 such venues that he considers ideal locations for his business. ("Portland, New Haven, Rochester, Syracuse, Albany. You don't even have to touch the crazy places . . . like Manhattan," he says.) The 69-year-old entrepreneur says his business philosophy meshes with his Depression-era upbringing and a lifelong interest in the environment: "We never threw anything away on the farm. Recycling books was in my blood."

> "We never threw anything away on the farm. Recycling books was in my blood."

Perhaps the most effective feature of the organization that Gjemre has built is the incentive program that he has designed for his employees. To entice employees to sell every last piece of merchandise, Gjemre returns to employees, to divide among themselves, 30 percent of the monthly net income of the store in which they work. This incentive system seems very generous, and Gjemre can afford the generosity. In the past two years his annual revenues have doubled, from $10 million to $20 million, and he plans to add six stores in the next year.

THE MOTIVATION PROCESS

To be successful in working with other people, managers first need a thorough understanding of the motivation process. To this end, a definition of **motivation,** various motivation models, and descriptions of people's needs are the main topics of discussion in this section of the chapter.

Motivation is the inner state that causes an individual to behave in a way that ensures the accomplishment of some goal.

Defining Motivation

Motivation is the inner state that causes an individual to behave in a way that ensures the accomplishment of some goal.[1] In other words, motivation explains why people behave the way they do. The more managers understand organization members' behavior, the better able they should be to influence that behavior and make it more consistent with the accomplishment of organizational objectives. Since productivity is a result of the behavior of organization members, influencing this behavior is a manager's key to increasing productivity.

Over the years, several different theories about motivation have been proposed. In general, these theories have been categorized into two basic types: process theories and content theories. **Process theories of motivation** are explanations of motivation that emphasize how individuals are motivated. In essence, the process theories focus on the steps that occur when an individual is motivated. **Content theories of motivation** are explanations of motivation that emphasize internal characteristics of people. The main focus of the content theories is understanding the needs that people possess and how they can be satisfied. The following sections discuss both important process and content theories of motivation and establish a relationship between them that can be useful to managers in motivating organization members.

Process theories of motivation are explanations of motivation that emphasize how individuals are motivated.

Content theories of motivation are explanations of motivation that emphasize internal characteristics of people.

Process Theories of Motivation

Four important theories that describe how motivation occurs are (1) the needs-goal theory, (2) the Vroom expectancy theory, (3) the equity theory, and (4) the Porter-Lawler theory. These theories build on one another to furnish a description of the motivation process that begins at a relatively simple and easily understood level and culminates at a somewhat more intricate and realistic level.

The Needs-Goal Theory of Motivation

The **needs-goal theory** is a motivation model that hypothesizes that felt needs cause human behavior.

The **needs-goal theory** of motivation (see Figure 15.1) is the most fundamental of the motivation theories discussed in this chapter. As the figure indicates, motivation begins with an individual feeling a need. This need is then transformed into behavior directed at supporting, or allowing, the performance of goal behavior to reduce the felt need. Theoretically, a goal-supportive behavior and goal behavior continue until the felt need has been reduced significantly.

For example, when an individual feels hunger (a need), this need typically is transformed first into behavior directed at supporting the performance of the goal behavior of eating. This supportive behavior could include such activities as buying, cooking, and serving the food to be eaten. The goal-supportive behaviors and the goal behavior itself—eating—typically continue until the individual's hunger substantially subsides. Once the individual experiences the hunger again, however, the entire cycle is repeated.

If managers are to have any success in motivating employees, they must understand the personal needs that employees possess. When managers offer rewards to employees that are not relevant to the personal needs of employees, the employees will not be motivated. For example, if a top executive is already in the highest income tax bracket, more money is not likely to be an effective motivator. Instead, a more meaningful incentive—perhaps a higher-level title or offer of partnership in the firm—would be a more effective motivator. Managers must be familiar with needs that employees possess and offer rewards to employees that can satisfy these needs.[2]

The Vroom Expectancy Theory of Motivation

The **Vroom expectancy theory** is a motivation theory that hypothesizes that felt needs cause human behavior and that motivation strength depends on an individual's degree of desire to perform a behavior.

Motivation strength is an individual's degree of desire to perform a behavior.

In reality, the motivation process is more complex than is depicted by the needs-goal theory. The **Vroom expectancy theory** of motivation handles some of the additional complexities.[3] As with the needs-goal theory, the Vroom expectancy theory is based on the premise that felt needs cause human behavior. In addition, however, the Vroom theory addresses the issue of **motivation strength**—an indi-

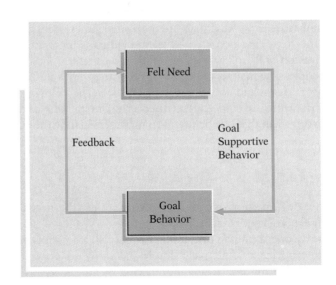

FIGURE 15.1

The needs-goal theory of motivation

vidual's degree of desire to perform a behavior. As this desire increases or decreases, motivation strength is said to fluctuate correspondingly.

Vroom's expectancy theory is shown in equation form in Figure 15.2. According to this theory, motivation strength is determined by the perceived value of the result of performing a behavior and the perceived probability that the behavior performed will cause the result to materialize. As both of these factors increase, the motivation strength, or the desire to perform the behavior, increases. In general, individuals tend to perform the behaviors that maximize personal rewards over the long term.

An illustration of how Vroom's theory applies to human behavior could be a college student who has been offered the summer job of painting three houses at the rate of $200 a house. Assuming that the student has a need for money, her motivation strength, or desire, to paint the houses is determined by two major factors: her perceived value of $600 and the perceived probability that she actually can paint the houses satisfactorily and, thus, receive the $600. As the perceived value of the $600 reward and the probability that the houses can be painted satisfactorily increase, the student's motivation strength to paint the houses increases.

Equity Theory of Motivation

The work of J. Stacy Adams, **equity theory,** looks at an individual's perceived fairness of an employment situation and finds that perceived inequities can lead to changes in behavior. When individuals believe that they have been treated unfairly compared with coworkers, Adams found that they will react in one of the following ways to attempt to bring the inequity into balance:[4]

Equity theory of motivation is an explanation of motivation that emphasizes an individual's perceived fairness of an employment situation and how perceived inequities can cause certain behaviors.

1. Some will try to change their work inputs to better match the rewards they are receiving. If they believe they are being paid too little, workers may tend to work less hard. On the other hand, if they believe that they are being paid more than their co-workers, they will increase their work outputs to match their rewards.

2. Some will try to change the compensation they receive for their work by asking for a raise or through legal action.

3. Some will try to change the perception of an inequality if attempts to change the actual inequality are unsuccessful. This can be accomplished by attempting to distort the status of certain jobs or by rationalizing that the inequity does not really exist.

Motivation strength	=	Perceived value of result of performing behavior	×	Perceived probability that result will materialize

FIGURE 15.2

Vroom's expectancy theory of motivation in equation form

4. Some will leave the situation rather than try to change it. People who feel they are being treated unfairly may decide to quit rather than to face the inequitable situation.

Perceptions of inequities can arise in any number of management situations such as work assignments, promotions, ratings reports, and office assignments, but they occur most often in terms of money. They are emotionally charged issues that deal with human beings, and even a minor inequity in the mind of a manager can be important in the minds of those affected. Effective managers attempt to keep equity issues in balance because the steps that a worker will take to try to balance the scales are not always the best for the organization.

The Porter-Lawler Theory of Motivation

The **Porter-Lawler theory** is a motivation theory that hypothesizes that felt needs cause human behavior and that motivation strength is determined primarily by the perceived value of the result of performing the behavior and the perceived probability that the behavior performed will cause the result to materialize.

Porter and Lawler developed a motivation theory that presents a more complete description of the motivation process than either the needs-goal theory or the Vroom expectancy theory.[5] The **Porter-Lawler theory** of motivation (see Figure 15.3) is consistent with the prior theories in that it accepts the premises that felt needs cause human behavior and that effort expended to accomplish a task is determined by the perceived value of rewards that will result from the task and the probability that the rewards will materialize. In addition, however, the Porter-Lawler motivation theory stresses three other characteristics of the motivation process:

1. The perceived value of a reward is determined by both intrinsic and extrinsic rewards that result in need satisfaction when a task is accomplished. **Intrinsic**

FIGURE 15.3

The Porter-Lawler theory of motivation

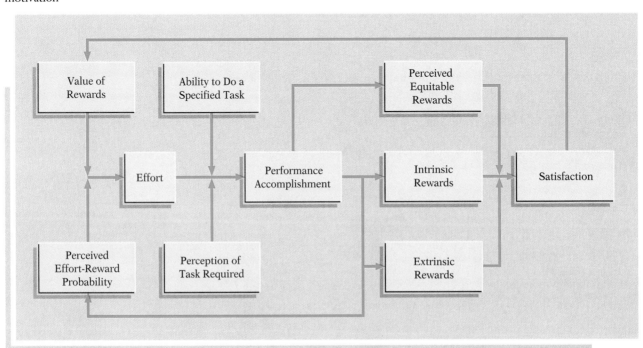

rewards come directly from performing a task, and **extrinsic rewards** are extraneous to the task. For example, when a manager counsels a subordinate about a personal problem, the manager may get some intrinsic reward in the form of personal satisfaction simply from helping another individual. In addition to this intrinsic reward, however, the manager also would receive an extrinsic reward in the form of the overall salary the manager is paid.[6]

2. The extent to which an individual effectively accomplishes a task is determined primarily by two variables: the individual's perception of what is required to perform the task and the individual's ability to perform the task. Naturally, the effectiveness at accomplishing a task increases as the perception of what is required to perform the task becomes more accurate and as the ability to perform the task increases.

3. The perceived fairness of rewards influences the amount of satisfaction produced by those rewards. In general, the more equitable an individual perceives the rewards to be, the greater the satisfaction the individual will experience as a result of receiving them.

Intrinsic rewards are rewards that come directly from performing a task.
Extrinsic rewards are rewards that are extraneous to the task accomplished.

Back to the Case

Motivation is an inner state that causes individuals to act in certain ways that ensure the accomplishment of some goal. Ken Gjemre in the introductory case seems to have an accurate understanding of the motivation process in that he is able to influence the behavior of his employees to make it consistent with the objectives of Half Price Books. That is, he seems able to encourage employees throughout his stores to maintain high sales and profit levels. The incentive program that Gjemre designed is undoubtedly a valuable tool in making this encouragement effective.

To motivate employees, Gjemre must keep five specific principles of human motivation clearly in mind: (1) felt needs cause behavior aimed at reducing those needs, (2) the degree of desire to perform a particular behavior is determined by an individual's perceived value of the result of performing the behavior and the perceived probability that the behavior will cause the result to materialize, (3) the perceived value of a reward for a particular behavior is determined by both intrinsic and extrinsic rewards that result in need satisfaction when the behavior is accomplished, (4) individuals can effectively accomplish a task only if they understand what the task requires and have the ability to perform the task, and (5) the perceived fairness of a reward influences the degree of satisfaction generated when the reward is received.

Content Theories of Motivation: Human Needs

The motivation theories discussed thus far imply that an understanding of motivation is based on an understanding of human needs. There is some evidence that people in general possess strong needs for self-respect, respect from others, promotion, and psychological growth.[7] Although pinpointing all human needs is impossible, several theories have been developed to help managers better understand these needs: (1) Maslow's hierarchy of needs, (2) Alderfer's ERG theory, (3) Argyris's maturity-immaturity continuum, and (4) McClelland's acquired needs theory.

Maslow's Hierarchy of Needs

Perhaps the most widely accepted description of human needs is the hierarchy of needs concept developed by Abraham Maslow.[8] Maslow states that human beings possess five basic needs: (1) physiological needs, (2) security needs, (3) social needs, (4) esteem needs, and (5) self-actualization needs. He theorizes that these five basic needs can be arranged in a hierarchy of importance—the order in which individuals generally strive to satisfy them. The needs and their relative positions in the hierarchy of importance are shown in Figure 15.4.

Physiological needs are Maslow's first set of human needs—for the normal functioning of the body—including the desires for water, food, rest, sex, and air.

Security, or safety, needs are Maslow's second set of human needs—reflecting the human desires to keep free from physical harm.

Physiological needs relate to the normal functioning of the body. They include the needs for water, rest, sex, and air. Until these needs are met, a significant portion of an individual's behavior is aimed at satisfying them. Once the needs are satisfied, behavior is aimed at satisfying the security needs on the next level of Maslow's hierarchy.

Security, or safety, needs are the needs individuals feel to keep themselves free from harm, including both bodily and economic disaster. Traditionally, management has probably best helped employees satisfy their physiological and security needs through adequate employee wages or salaries. It is with these salaries that employees purchase such things as food and housing in order to satisfy basic human needs.

A relatively new issue regarding employee safety needs is the threat of terrorism. The possibility of terrorism has placed executives working in international settings and in certain jobs or industries within the United States in uncomfortable situations. As a result of this threat to employee safety, many companies are developing special security and safety programs for their employees in international settings.[9]

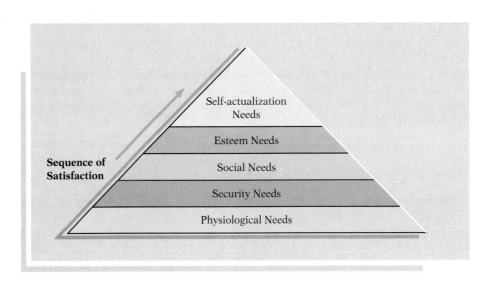

FIGURE 15.4

Maslow's hierarchy of needs

Security is a basic human need. According to Maslow's hierarchy, as security needs are satisfied, behavior tends to be aimed at satisfying social needs.

Social needs include the desire for love, companionship, and friendship. These needs reflect a person's desire to be accepted by others. As the needs are satisfied, behavior shifts to satisfying esteem needs.

Esteem needs are the desire for respect. They generally are divided into two categories: self-respect and respect for others. Once esteem needs are satisfied, the individual emphasizes satisfying self-actualization needs.

Self-actualization needs are the desire to maximize whatever potential an individual possesses. For example, in the nonprofit public setting of a high school, a principal who seeks to satisfy self-actualization needs would strive to become the best principal possible. Self-actualization needs are the highest level of Maslow's hierarchy.

Although many management theorists admit that Maslow's hierarchy can be useful in understanding human needs, they have also expressed concern about the hierarchy. Maslow himself has said:

> I of all people should know just how shaky this foundation for the theory is as a final foundation. My work on motivation came from the clinic, from a study of neurotic people. The carryover of this theory to the industrial situation has some support from industrial studies, but certainly I would like to see a lot more studies of this kind before feeling finally convinced that this carryover from the study of neurosis to the study of labor in factories is legitimate. The same thing is true of my studies of self-actualizing people—there is only this one study of mine available. There were many things wrong with the sampling, so many in fact that it must be considered to be, in the classical sense anyway, a bad or poor or inadequate experiment. I am quite willing to concede this—because I'm a little worried about this stuff which I consider to be tentative being swallowed whole by all sorts of enthusiastic people who really should be a little more tentative in the way that I am.[10]

Traditionally there have been concerns related to Maslow's hierarchy that are based on its lack of a research base,[11] a questioning of whether Maslow has accurately pinpointed five basic human needs,[12] and some doubt as to whether human needs actually are arranged in a hierarchy.[13] Despite such concerns, Maslow's hierarchy is probably the most popular conceptualization of human needs to date, and it continues to be positively discussed in the management literature.[14] The concerns do, however, indicate that Maslow's hierarchy should be considered more a subjective statement than an objective description of human needs.

Social needs are Maslow's third set of human needs—reflecting the human desires to belong, including the desire for friendship, companionship, and love.

Esteem needs are Maslow's fourth set of human needs—including the desires for self-respect and respect from others.

Self-actualization needs are Maslow's fifth set of human needs—reflecting the human desire to maximize potential.

Global Highlight: Manpower Scandinavia Manages via Maslow's Heirarchy

A recent experience at Manpower Scandinavia, an employment agency in Oslo, Norway, illustrates that behavioral concepts can be applied in different countries. The company used Maslow's hierarchy of needs as its starting point to design and implement a project aimed at better defining and satisfying the human needs of its employees. Basically, company management used Maslow's hierarchy, not simply in a theoretical fashion to define human needs, but also in a practical fashion by determining tactics managers can use to help employees satisfy these needs. As a result of this project, management modified its organization and jobs so that

employees could be paid well and recognized for outstanding performance, and thereby satisfy human needs at the lower end of Maslow's hierarchy as well as at the upper end. To ensure that managers at all levels would continually be concerned about satisfying employee's personal needs, the company published a set of values that management should possess and strive to uphold. These values emphasize that people can be trusted, that people work in order to fulfill personal needs, and that management's purpose is to see that every organization member succeeds both in being productive and in fulfilling personal needs.

Alderfer's ERG Theory

Alderfer's ERG Theory is an explanation of human needs that divides them into three basic types: existence needs, relatedness needs, and growth needs.

Clayton Alderfer responded to some of the criticism's of Maslow's work with his own study of human needs.[15] He identified three basic categories of needs: (1) existence needs—the need for physical well-being, (2) relatedness needs—the need for satisfying interpersonal relationships, and (3) growth needs—the need for continuing personal growth and development. The first letters of these needs form the acronym ERG by which the theory is now known.

Alderfer's ERG theory is similar to Maslow's theory except for three major respects: He identified only three orders of human needs, compared to Maslow's five orders of needs. In contrast to Maslow, Alderfer found that workers may sometimes activate their higher-level needs before they have completely satisfied all of the lower-level needs. Alderfer also found that movement in his hierarchy in satisfying human needs is not always upward. He found, reflected in his frustration-regression principle, that a worker frustrated by failing to satisfy an upper-level need might regress by trying to fulfill an already satisfied lower-level need. Alderfer's work, in conjunction with Maslow's work, has implications for management. Job-enrichment strategies can help an individual to meet the higher-order needs. If an employee is frustrated by work that fails to provide the opportunity for growth or development on the job, he or she might spend more energy trying to make more money, thus regressing to a lower level.

Argyris's Maturity-Immaturity Continuum

Argyris's maturity-immaturity continuum is a concept that furnishes insights on human needs by focusing on an individual's natural growth progress from immaturity to maturity.

Argyris's maturity-immaturity continuum also furnishes insights on human needs.[16] This continuum concept focuses on the personal and natural development of people to explain how needs exist.[17] According to Argyris, as people naturally progress from immaturity to maturity, they move:

1. From a state of passivity as an infant to a state of increasing activity as an adult.

2. From a state of dependence on others as an infant to a state of relative independence as an adult.

3. From being capable of behaving only in a few ways as an infant to being capable of behaving in many different ways as an adult.

4. From having erratic, casual, shallow, and quickly dropped interests as an infant to having deeper interests as an adult.

5. From having a short time perspective as an infant to having a much longer time perspective as an adult.

6. From being in a subordinate position as an infant to aspiring to occupy an equal or superordinate position as an adult.

7. From a lack of awareness of self as an infant to awareness and control over self as an adult.

Thus, according to Argyris's continuum, as individuals mature, they have increasing needs for more activity, enjoy a state of relative independence, behave in many different ways, have deeper interests, consider a relatively long time perspective, occupy an equal position with other mature individuals, and have more awareness of themselves and control over their own destiny. Unlike Maslow's needs, Argyris's needs are not arranged in a hierarchy. Like Maslow's hierarchy, however, Argyris's continuum represents primarily a subjective position on the existence of human needs.

McClelland's Acquired-Needs Theory

Another theory about human needs, called **McClelland's acquired-needs theory,** focuses on the needs that people develop through their life experiences—acquired needs. This theory, formulated by David C. McClelland in the 1960s, focuses on three of the many needs humans develop in their lifetimes: (1) the need for achievement (*nAch*)—the desire to do something better or more efficiently than it ever has been done before; (2) the need for power (*nPower*)—the desire to control, influence, or be responsible for others; and (3) the need for affiliation (*nAff*)—the desire to maintain close, friendly, personal relationships. A person's early life experiences determine which of these needs will be highly developed and therefore dominate the personality. McClelland's studies of these acquired human needs have significant implications for management.

McClelland claims that, in some business people, the need to achieve is so strong that it is more motivating than a quest for profits.[18] To maximize their satisfaction, individuals with high achievement needs tend to set goals for themselves that are challenging yet achievable.[19] Although these individuals do not avoid risk completely, they assess it very carefully. Individuals motivated by the need to achieve do not want to fail and will avoid tasks that involve too much risk. Individuals with a low need for achievement generally avoid challenges, responsibilities, and risk.

People with a high need for power are highly motivated to try to influence other people and to be responsible for subordinate behavior. They are likely to seek advancement and to assume increasingly responsible work activities. Power-oriented managers are comfortable in competitive situations and with their decision-making roles. Managers with a high need for affiliation, on the other hand, tend to have a cooperative, team-centered style of management in which a task is completed through team efforts. However, a high need for affiliation could also sacrifice a manager's effectiveness when the need for social approval and friendship interferes with the manager's ability to make managerial decisions.[20]

McClelland's Acquired-Needs Theory is an explanation of human needs that focuses on desires for achievement, power, and affiliation as needs that people develop as a result of their life experiences.

Back to the Case

Gjemre undoubtedly understands the basic motivation principle that felt needs cause behavior. Before managers like Gjemre can have maximum impact on motivating their organization members, however, they must also meet the more complex challenge of being thoroughly familiar with various individual human needs of their employees.

According to Maslow, people generally possess physiologic needs, security needs, social needs, esteem needs, and self-actualization needs arranged in a hierarchy of importance. Alderfer suggests that people generally possess existence needs, relatedness needs, and growth needs. Argyris suggests that as people mature, they have increasing needs for activity, independence, flexibility, deeper interests, analyses of longer time perspectives, a position of equality with other mature individuals, and control over personal destiny. McClelland believes that the need for achievement—the desire to do something better or more efficiently than it has ever been done before—is a strong human need.

Perhaps the financial rewards of Gjemre's incentive system are aimed at satisfying employee physiologic and safety needs. Other programs like management-development training, sales contests, or programs for outstanding performance like "employee of the month" can further motivate Gjemre's employees by attempting to satisfy other needs that they might have.

MOTIVATING ORGANIZATION MEMBERS

People are motivated to perform behavior to satisfy personal needs. Therefore, from a managerial viewpoint, motivation is the process of furnishing organization members with the opportunity to satisfy their needs by performing productive behavior within the organization. As discussed in chapter 13, motivation is one of the four primary interrelated activities of the influencing function performed by managers to guide the behavior of organization members toward attainment of organizational objectives. The following sections discuss the importance of and strategies for motivating organization members.

The Importance of Motivating Organization Members

Figure 15.5 makes the point that unsatisfied needs of organization members can lead to either appropriate or inappropriate member behavior. Managers who are successful at motivating organization members minimize inappropriate behavior and maximize appropriate behavior. Correspondingly, these managers raise the probability that productivity will increase and lower the probability that productivity will decrease.

Strategies for Motivating Organization Members

Managers have various strategies for motivating organization members. Each strategy is aimed at satisfying people's needs (consistent with those described by Maslow's hierarchy of needs, Alderfer's ERG theory, Argyris's maturity-immaturity continuum, and McClelland's acquired needs theory) through appropriate organi-

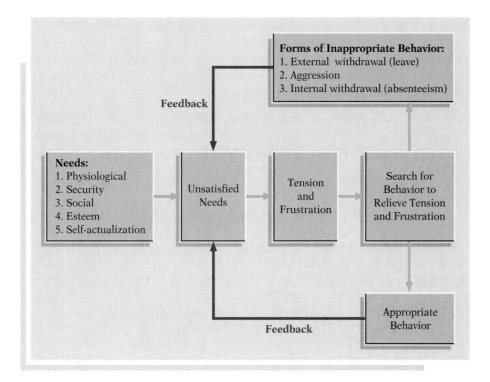

FIGURE 15.5

Unsatisfied needs of organization members resulting in either appropriate
or inappropriate behavior

zational behavior.[21] These managerial motivation strategies are (1) managerial
communication, (2) Theory X–Theory Y, (3) job design, (4) behavior modification, (5) Likert's management systems, (6) monetary incentives, and (7) nonmonetary incentives. The strategies are discussed in the sections that follow.

It is important to remember that no single strategy will necessarily always be
more effective for a manager than any other. In fact, a manager may find that some
combination of these strategies is the most effective strategy in the organizational
situation.

Managerial Communication

Perhaps the most basic motivation strategy for managers is simply to communicate
well with organization members. This manager-subordinate communication can
satisfy such basic human needs as recognition, a sense of belonging, and security.[22]
For example, such a simple action as a manager's attempting to become better
acquainted with subordinates could contribute substantially to the satisfaction of
each of these three needs. As another example, a message from a manager to a
subordinate that praises the subordinate for a job well done can help satisfy the
subordinate's recognition and security needs. As a general rule, managers should
strive to communicate often with other organization members, not only because

communication is the primary means of conducting organizational activities but also because it is a basic tool for satisfying the human needs of organization members.

Theory X—Theory Y

Theory X is a set of essentially negative assumptions about the nature of people.

Theory Y is a set of essentially positive assumptions about the nature of people.

Theory Z is the effectiveness dimension that implies that managers who use either Theory X or Theory Y assumptions when dealing with people can be successful, depending on their situation.

Another motivation strategy involves managers' assumptions about the nature of people. Douglas McGregor identified two sets of assumptions: **Theory X** involves negative assumptions about people that McGregor believes managers often use as the basis for dealing with people. **Theory Y** represents positive assumptions that McGregor believes managers should strive to use.[23] Theory X and Theory Y assumptions are presented in Table 15.1.

McGregor implies that managers who use Theory X assumptions are "bad" and that those who use Theory Y assumptions are "good." Reddin, however, argues that production might be increased by using either Theory X or Theory Y assumptions, depending on the situation the manager faces: "Is there not a strong argument for the position that any theory may have desirable outcomes if appropriately used? The difficulty is that McGregor had considered only the ineffective application of Theory X and the effective application of Theory Y."[24]

Reddin proposes a **Theory Z**—an effectiveness dimension that implies that managers who use either Theory X or Theory Y assumptions when dealing with people can be successful, depending on their situation. Figure 15.6 shows Z as an effectiveness dimension relating to Theory X and Theory Y.

TABLE 15.1 McGregor's Theory X–Theory Y assumptions about the nature of people

Theory X Assumptions	*Theory Y Assumptions*
The average person has an inherent dislike for work and will avoid it if he or she can.	The expenditure of physical and mental effort in work is as natural as play or rest.
Because of this human characteristic of dislike of work, most people must be coerced, controlled, directed, and threatened with punishment to get them to put forth adequate effort toward the achievement of organizational objectives.	People will exercise self-direction and self-control in the service of objectives to which they are committed.
The average person prefers to be directed, wishes to avoid responsibility, has relatively little ambition, and wants security above all.	Commitment to objectives is a function of the rewards associated with achievement.
	The average person learns, under proper conditions, not only to accept but to seek responsibility.
	The capacity to exercise a relatively high degree of imagination, ingenuity, and creativity in the solution of organizational problems is widely, not narrowly, distributed in the population.

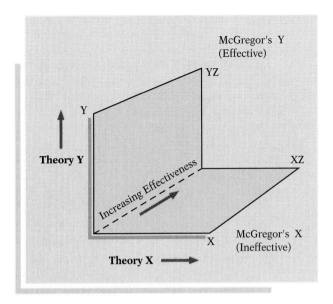

FIGURE 15.6
Theory X, Theory Y, and the effectiveness dimension Z

The basic rationale for using Theory Y rather than Theory X in most situations is that managerial activities that reflect Theory Y assumptions generally are more successful in satisfying the human needs of most organization members than are managerial activities that reflect Theory X assumptions. Therefore, the activities based on Theory Y assumptions generally are more successful in motivating organization members than are the activities based on Theory X assumptions.

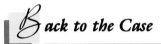 ack to the Case

Once a manager like Gjemre understands that felt needs cause behavior and is aware of people's different types of needs, he is ready to apply this information to motivating his work force. From Gjemre's viewpoint, motivating employees means furnishing them with the opportunity to satisfy their human needs by performing their jobs. This is a very important notion because successful motivation tends to increase employee productivity. If Gjemre does not furnish his employees with an opportunity to satisfy their human needs while working, low morale within the company will probably eventually develop. Signs of this low morale might be that only a few employees initiate new ideas, people avoid the confrontation of tough situations, and employees resist innovation.

What does the above information recommend that Gjemre actually do to further motivate the workers at Half Price Books? One strategy he might follow is merely taking time to communicate with his employees. Manager-employee communication can help satisfy employee needs for recognition, belonging, and security. Another of Gjemre's strategies might be based on McGregor's Theory X–Theory Y concept. In following this concept when dealing with employees,

Gjemre should assume that work is as natural as play, that employees can be self-directed in goal accomplishment, that the granting of rewards encourages the achievement of objectives at Half Price Books, that employees seek and accept responsibility, and that most employees are creative, ingenious, and imaginative. The adoption of such assumptions by Gjemre can lead to the satisfaction of many of the needs defined by Maslow, Alderfer, Argyris, and McClelland.

Job Design

A third strategy managers can use to motivate organization members involves the design of jobs that organization members perform. The following two sections discuss earlier and more recent job design strategies.

Earlier Job Design Strategies. A movement has existed in American business to make jobs simpler and more specialized so as to increase worker productivity. Theoretically, this movement is aimed at making workers more productive by enabling them to be more efficient. Perhaps the best example of this movement is the development of the automobile assembly line. A negative result of work simplification and specialization, however, is job boredom. As work becomes simpler and more specialized, it typically becomes more boring and less satisfying to the individuals performing the jobs. As a result, productivity suffers.

Perhaps the earliest major attempt to overcome job boredom was **job rotation**—moving individuals from job to job and not requiring individuals to perform merely one simple and specialized job over the long term. For example, a gardener would do more than just mow lawns; he might also trim bushes, rake grass, and sweep sidewalks. Although job rotation programs have been known to increase organizational profitability, they typically are ineffective, because, over time, individuals become bored with all the jobs they are rotated into.[25] Job rotation programs, however, usually are more effective in achieving other objectives, such as training, by providing individuals with an overview of how the various units of the organization function.

Job enlargement is another strategy developed to overcome the boredom of more simple and specialized jobs. **Job enlargement** means increasing the number of operations an individual performs and, in theory, thereby increasing the individual's satisfaction in work. According to the job enlargement concept, the gardener's job would become more satisfying as such activities as trimming bushes, raking grass, and sweeping sidewalks were added to the gardener's initial activity of mowing grass. Some research supports[26] the theory that job enlargement makes jobs more satisfying, and some does not.[27] Job enlargement programs, however, generally have been more successful in increasing job satisfaction than have job rotation programs.

More Recent Job Design Strategies. A number of other job design strategies have evolved since the development of job rotation and job enlargement programs. Two of these more recent strategies are job enrichment and flextime.

1. *Job Enrichment.* Frederick Herzberg has concluded from his research that the degrees of satisfaction and dissatisfaction that organization members feel as a

Job rotation is the process of moving individuals from one job to another and not requiring individuals to perform only one job over the long term.

Job enlargement is the process of increasing the number of operations an individual performs in a job.

result of performing a job are two different variables determined by two different sets of items.[28] The items that influence the degree of job dissatisfaction are called **hygiene**, or **maintenance, factors**. The items that influence the degree of job satisfaction are called **motivating factors,** or motivators. Hygiene factors relate to the work environment, and motivating factors relate to the work itself. The items that make up Herzberg's hygiene and motivating factors are presented in Table 15.2.

Herzberg has indicated that if hygiene factors are undesirable in a particular job situation, organization members will become dissatisfied. Making these factors more desirable by, for example, increasing salary generally will not motivate people to do a better job, but it will keep them from becoming dissatisfied. In contrast, if motivating factors are high in a particular job situation, organization members generally are motivated to do a better job. In general, people tend to be more motivated and productive as more motivators are built into their job situation.

The process of incorporating motivators into a job situation is called **job enrichment.** Earlier reports indicated that such companies as Texas Instruments[29] and Volvo[30] had notable success in motivating organization members through job enrichment programs, more recent reports continue to support the value of job enrichment,[31] and experience indicates that for a job enrichment program to be successful, it must be carefully designed and administered.[32] An outline of a successful job enrichment program is presented in Table 15.3.

Herzberg's overall findings indicate that the most productive organization members are involved in work situations characterized by desirable hygiene factors and motivating factors. The needs on Maslow's hierarchy of needs that desirable hygiene factors and motivating factors generally satisfy are shown in Figure 15.7. Esteem needs can be satisfied by both types of factors. An example of esteem needs satisfied by a hygiene factor could be a private parking space—a status symbol and a working condition evidencing the importance of the organization member. An example of esteem needs satisfied by a motivating factor could be an award received for outstanding performance—a display of importance through recognition of a job well done.

Hygiene, or **maintenance, factors** are items that influence the degree of job satisfaction.

Motivating factors are items that influence the degree of job satisfaction.

Job enrichment is the process of incorporating motivators into a job situation.

TABLE 15.2 Herzberg's hygiene factors and motivators

Dissatisfaction: Hygiene or Maintenance Factors	*Satisfaction: Motivating Factors*
1. Company policy and administration	1. Opportunity for achievement
2. Supervision	2. Opportunity for recognition
3. Relationship with supervisor	3. Work itself
4. Relationship with peers	4. Responsibility
5. Working conditions	5. Advancement
6. Salary	6. Personal growth
7. Relationship with subordinates	

TABLE 15.3 Outline of successful job enrichment program

Specific Changes Aimed at Enriching Jobs	*"Motivators"—These Changes Are Aimed at Increasing:*
1. Removing some controls while retaining accountability	Responsibility and personal achievement
2. Increasing the accountability of individuals for own work	Responsibility and recognition
3. Giving a person a complete natural unit of work (module, division, area, and so on)	Responsibility, achievement, and recognition
4. Granting additional authority to an employee in his or her activity; job freedom	Responsibility, achievement, and recognition
5. Making periodic reports directly available to the worker rather than to the supervisor	Internal recognition
6. Introducing new and more difficult tasks not previously handled	Growth and learning
7. Assigning individuals specific or specialized tasks, enabling them to become expert	Responsibility, growth, and advancement

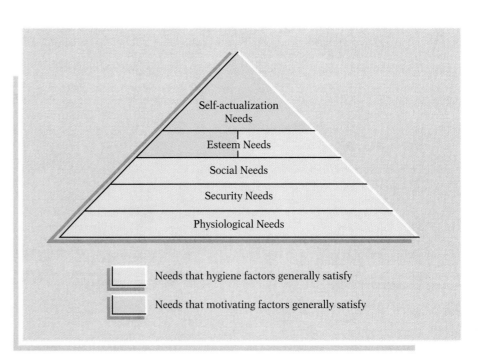

FIGURE 15.7

Needs on Maslow's hierarchy that desirable hygiene factors and motivating factors generally satisfy

Quality Highlight: Apple Computer's Job
Enrichment Excels

Apple Computer has attempted to provide both hygiene factors and motivating factors for its employees. Apple executives firmly believe that highly motivated, satisfied employees produce high-quality products. Apple's job enrichment program serves as a good example of how management can take steps to enrich a work environment.

Creating the right work environment—pleasant but challenging—is a key to encouraging people to be productive at Apple. For example, management at Apple strives to incorporate award systems for employees, such as recognition for jobs well done and opportunities for growth and advancement. In addition to these motivators, hygiene factors have been made acceptable to employees, and Apple management takes pride in providing sufficiently generous salaries to valued employees.

As one example of the recognition programs at Apple, the company announces new products and projects through the employees who developed them instead of through a public relations office. This announcement process gives recognition to hardworking employees and makes them feel as though they are making valuable contributions to the company. At Apple, rewards and recognition are an ongoing and constant part of company life. Such aspects of corporate life should help management ensure the quality of its products, such as the Macintosh and Apple computers.

2. *Flextime.* Another more recent job design strategy for motivating organization members is based on a concept called flextime. Perhaps the most common traditional characteristic of work in the United States is that jobs are performed within a fixed eight-hour workday. Recently, however, this tradition has been challenged. Faced with motivation problems and absenteeism, many managers have turned to scheduling innovations as a possible solution.[33]

The main purpose of these scheduling innovations is not to reduce the total number of work hours but to provide workers with greater flexibility in the exact hours during which they must perform their jobs. The main thrust of **flextime,** or flexible working hours programs, is that it allows workers to complete their jobs within a workweek (of a normal number of hours) that they arrange themselves.[34] The choices of starting and finishing times can be as flexible as the organizational situation allows. To ensure that flexibility does not become counterproductive within the organization, many flextime programs include a core period during which all employees must be on the job.

Various kinds of organizational studies have indicated that flextime programs have some positive organizational effects. Douglas Fleuter, for example, has reported that flextime contributes to greater job satisfaction, which typically results in greater productivity.[35] Other research concludes that flextime programs can result in higher motivation levels of workers.[36] Because organization members generally find flextime programs to be desirable, such programs can help management to better compete with other organizations in recruiting qualified new employees.[37] (A listing of the advantages and disadvantages of

Flextime is a program that allows workers to complete their jobs within a workweek of a normal number of hours that they schedule themselves.

flextime programs appears in Table 15.4.) Although many well-known companies, such as Scott Paper, Sun Oil, and Samsonite, have adopted flextime programs,[38] more research must be conducted to conclusively assess its true worth.

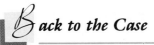

ack to the Case

Gjemre could use two major job design strategies to motivate his employees at Half Price Books. With job enrichment, Gjemre can incorporate into employee jobs such motivating factors as opportunities for achievement, recognition, and personal growth. However, for maximum success, hygiene factors at Half Price Books—company policy and administration, supervision, salary, and working conditions, for example—also should be perceived as desirable by employees.

The second major job design strategy that Gjemre can use to motivate his employees is flextime. With flextime, the employees would have some freedom in scheduling the beginning and ending of workdays. Of course, this freedom would be somewhat limited by such organizational factors as seasonal demand or peak selling seasons.

Behavior Modification

A fourth strategy that managers can use in motivating organization members is based primarily on a concept known as behavior modification. As stated by B.F. Skinner, the Harvard psychologist considered by many to be the "father" of behavioral psychology, **behavior modification** focuses on encouraging appropriate behavior as a result of the consequences of that behavior.[39] According to the law of effect,[40] behavior that is rewarded tends to be repeated, and behavior that is pun-

Behavior modification is a program that focuses on managing human activity by controlling the consequences of performing that activity.

TABLE 15.4 Advantages and disadvantages of using flextime programs

Advantages	Disadvantages
Improved employee attitude and morale	Lack of supervision during some hours of work
Accommodation of working parents	
Decreased tardiness	Key people unavailable at certain times
Fewer traffic problems—workers can avoid congested streets and highways	Understaffing at times
Accommodation of those who wish to arrive at work before interruptions begin	Problem of accommodating employees whose output is the input for other employees
Increased production	Employee abuse of flextime program
Facilitation of employee scheduling of medical, dental, and other types of appointments	Difficulty in planning work schedules
	Problem of keeping track of hours worked or accumulated
Accommodation of leisure-time activities of employees	Inability to schedule meetings at convenient times
Decreased absenteeism	Inability to coordinate projects
Decreased turnover	

ished tends to be eliminated. Although behavior modification programs typically involve the administration of both rewards and punishments, rewards generally are emphasized, because they are more effective than punishments in influencing behavior. Obviously, the main theme of behavior modification is not new.

Behavior modification theory asserts that if managers want to modify subordinates' behavior, they must ensure that appropriate consequences occur as a result of that behavior.[41] **Positive reinforcement** is a desirable consequence of a behavior, and **negative reinforcement** is the elimination of an undesirable consequence of a behavior. If a worker's arriving on time is positively reinforced, or rewarded, the probability increases that the worker will arrive on time more often. In addition, if the worker experiences some undesirable outcome on arriving late for work, such as a verbal reprimand, the worker is negatively reinforced when this outcome is eliminated by on-time arrival. According to behavior modification theory, positive reinforcement and negative reinforcement are both rewards that increase the likelihood that behavior will continue.

Punishment is the presentation of an undesirable behavioral consequence or the removal of a desirable behavioral consequence that decreases the likelihood of the behavior continuing.[42] Extending the earlier example, managers could punish employees for arriving late for work by exposing them to some undesirable consequence, such as a verbal reprimand, or by removing a desirable consequence, such as their wages for the amount of time they are late.[43] Although this punishment probably would quickly cause workers to come to work on time, it might be accompanied by undesirable side effects, such as high levels of absenteeism and turnover, if it were emphasized over the long term.

Behavior modification programs have been applied both successfully and unsuccessfully in a number of organizations.[44] The behavior modification efforts of Emery Air Freight Company, now called Emery Worldwide, resulted in the finding that the establishment and use of an effective feedback system is important in making a behavior modification program successful.[45] This feedback should be aimed at keeping employees informed of the relationship between various behaviors and their consequences. Other ingredients that successful behavior modification programs include are (1) giving different levels of rewards to different workers depending on the quality of their performances, (2) telling workers what they are doing wrong, (3) punishing workers privately in order not to embarrass them in front of others, and (4) always giving rewards and punishments when earned to emphasize that management is serious about behavior modification efforts.[46]

Positive reinforcement is a reward that is a desirable consequence of behavior.

Negative reinforcement is a reward that is the elimination of an undesirable consequence of behavior.

Punishment is the presentation of an undesirable behavioral consequence or the removal of a desirable one that decreases the likelihood of the behavior continuing.

Ethics Highlight: Government's Ethical Expectations?

Behavior is likely to be modified if it is appropriately encouraged through positive reinforcement, negative reinforcement, and punishment. The lack of ethical behavior in government, for example, may be the result of a perception by government employees that acting ethically will not result in any meaningful consequences.

The federal government's ethical standards are stated clearly in the Ethics in Government Act and in established criminal laws. However, it is questionable whether there is a clearly defined reward system tied to established ethical standards. In addition, because there are very few official violators of ethical standards who have been legally prosecuted and an even smaller number of severe penalties or punishments for violations, it is not surprising that ethical violations in government continue to occur. The lack of negative reinforcement and of punishment allows unethical behavior in government to continue without significant discouraging. According to the behavior modification concept, it seems somewhat unrealistic to expect government leaders to follow a set of ethical guidelines without a system of positive reinforcement, negative reinforcement, and punishment to encourage their following the guidelines.

Likert's Management Systems

Another strategy that managers can use for motivating organization members is based on the work of Rensis Likert, a noted management scholar.[47] As a result of studying several types and sizes of organizations, Likert has concluded that management styles in organizations can be categorized into the following systems:[48]

System 1. This style of management involves having no confidence or trust in subordinates. Subordinates do not feel free to discuss their jobs with superiors and are motivated by fear, threats, punishments, and occasional rewards. Information flow is directed primarily downward, and upward communication is viewed with great suspicion. The bulk of all decision making is at the top of the organization. The cartoon below illustrates how negative feelings of an employee toward a manager can build over time when the employee works for a system 1 manager.

System 2. This style of management involves condescending confidence and trust (such as master to servant) in subordinates. Subordinates do not feel very free to discuss their jobs with superiors and are motivated by rewards and some actual or potential punishment. Information flows mostly downward, and upward communication may or may not be viewed with suspicion. Although policies

"The reason I didn't laugh at your joke, Mr. Walters, is because it wasn't funny, it was in bad taste, and I'm retiring tomorrow."

are made primarily at the top of the organization, decisions within a prescribed framework are made at lower levels.

System 3. This style of management involves having substantial, but not complete, confidence in subordinates. Subordinates feel fairly free to discuss their jobs with superiors and are motivated by rewards, occasional punishment, and some involvement. Information flows both upward and downward. Upward communication is often accepted but at times may be viewed with suspicion. Although broad policies and general decisions are made at the top of the organization, more specific decisions are made at lower levels.

System 4. This style of management involves having complete trust and confidence in subordinates. Subordinates feel completely free to discuss their jobs with superiors and are motivated by such factors as economic rewards based on a compensation system developed through participation and involvement in goal setting. Information flows upward, downward, and horizontally. Upward communication is generally accepted. However, if it is not, related questions are asked candidly. Decision making is spread widely throughout the organization and is well coordinated.

Likert has suggested that as the management style moves from system 1 to system 4, the human needs of individuals within the organization tend to be more effectively satisfied over the long term. Thus, as the organization moves toward system 4, it tends to become more productive over the long term.

Figure 15.8 illustrates the comparative long- and short-term effects of both

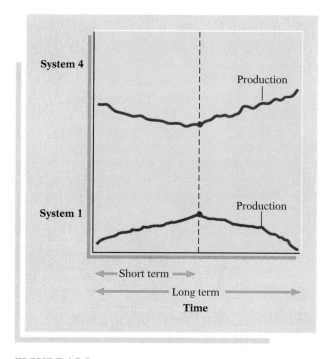

FIGURE 15.8

Comparative long-term and short-term effects of system 1
and system 4 on organizational production

system 1 and system 4 on organizational production. Managers may increase production in the short term by using a system 1 management style, because motivation by fear, threat, and punishment is generally effective in the short term. Over the long term, however, this style usually causes production to decrease, primarily because of the long-term nonsatisfaction of organization members' needs and the poor working relationships between managers and subordinates.

Conversely, managers who initiate a system 4 management style probably face some decline in production initially, but an increase in production over the long term. The short-term decline occurs because managers must implement a new system to which organization members must adapt. The production increase over the long term materializes as a result of organization members' adjustment to the new management system, greater satisfaction of the human needs of organization members, and the good working relationships that tend to develop between managers and subordinates. This long-term production increase can also be related to decision making under the two management systems. Because decisions reached in system 4 are more likely to be thoroughly understood by organization members than decisions reached in system 1, decision implementation is more likely to be efficient and effective in system 4 than in system 1.[49]

Likert has offered his **principle of supportive relationships** as the basis for management activity aimed at developing a system 4 management style. This principle states:

> The leadership and other processes of the organization must be such as to ensure a maximum probability that in all interactions and in all relationships within the organization, each member in light of his or her background, values, desires, and expectations will view the experience as supportive and one which builds and maintains his or her sense of personal worth and importance.[50]

The **principle of supportive relationships** is a management guideline that indicates that all human interaction with an organization should build and maintain the sense of personal worth and the importance of those involved in the interaction.

Monetary Incentives

A number of firms make a wide range of money-based compensation programs available to their employees as a form of motivation. For instance, employee stock ownership plans (ESOPs) motivate the employee to boost production by offering shares of company stock as a benefit. Other incentive plans include lump-sum bonuses—one-time cash payments and gain-sharing—a plan by which members of a team receive a bonus when that team exceeds an expectation. All of these plans link the amount of pay closely to performance. By putting more of the employees' pay at risk, firms are able to keep more of the wages as a percentage of sales and therefore controllable in a downturn.[51]

Nonmonetary Incentives

A firm also has the opportunity to keep employees committed and motivated by other, nonmonetary means. For instance, some companies have a policy of promoting from within. They go through an elaborate process of advertising jobs within before going to the outside to fill vacancies. Another example is to emphasize quality. It is hard to be happy in a job when you know that the work produces a shoddy product.[52]

_B_ack to the _Case_

Gjemre can apply behavior modification to his situation at Half Price Books by rewarding appropriate employee behavior and punishing inappropriate employee behavior. Punishment has to be used very carefully, however. If used continually, the working relationship between Gjemre and his employees can be destroyed. For the behavior modification program to be successful, Gjemre has to furnish employees with feedback on which behaviors are appropriate and inappropriate, to give workers different rewards depending on the quality of their performance, to tell workers what they were doing wrong, to punish workers privately, and to consistently give rewards and punishments when earned.

To use Likert's system 4 management style to motivate employees over the long term, Gjemre has to demonstrate complete confidence in his workers and to encourage workers to feel completely free to discuss problems with him. In addition, communication at Half Price Books has to flow freely in all directions within the organization structure, with upward communication generally discussed candidly. Gjemre's decision-making process under system 4 has to involve many employees. Gjemre can use the principle of supportive relationships as the basis for his system 4 management style. No single strategy mentioned in this chapter for motivating organization members would necessarily be more valuable to managers such as Gjemre than any other of the strategies. In reality, Gjemre will probably find that some combination of all of these strategies is most useful in motivating the work force at Half Price Books.

Action Summary

Reread the learning objectives that follow. Each objective is followed by questions. Answering these questions accurately will help you retain the most important concepts discussed in this chapter. After answering each question, check your answer with the answer key at the end of this chapter. (*Hint:* If you have doubt regarding the correct response, consult the page whose number follows the answer.)

Circle:

From studying this chapter, I will attempt to acquire:

1. **A basic understanding of human motivation.**
   a. An individual's inner state that causes him or her to behave in such a way as to ensure accomplishment of a goal is: (a) ambition; (b) drive; (c) motivation; (d) need; (e) leadership.

   a, b, c, d, e

   b. According to the needs-goal theory of motivation, a fulfilled need is a motivator.

   T, F

   c. Which of the following most comprehensively describes how motivation takes place: (a) the Vroom expectancy theory; (b) the needs-goal theory; (c) the Porter-Lawler theory; (d) all of the above; (e) none of the above.

   a, b, c, d, e

2. Insights on various human needs.

a, b, c, d, e
    a. Which of the following is a rank-ordered listing of Maslow's hierarchy of needs from lowest to highest: (a) self-actualization, social, security, physiologic, esteem; (b) social, security, physiologic, self-actualization; (c) esteem, self-actualization, security, social, physiologic; (d) physiologic, security, social, esteem, self-actualization; (e) physiologic, social, esteem, security, self-actualization.

a, b, c, d, e
    b. According to Argyris, as individuals mature, they have an increasing need for: (a) greater dependence; (b) a shorter-term perspective; (c) more inactivity; (d) deeper interests; (e) youth.

a, b, c, d, e
    c. The desire to do something better or more efficiently than it has ever been done before is known as the need for: (a) acceleration; (b) achievement; (c) acclamation; (d) actualization; (e) none of the above.

3. An appreciation for the importance of motivating organization members.

T, F
    a. From a managerial viewpoint, motivation is the process of furnishing organization members with the opportunity to satisfy their needs by performing productive behavior within the organization.

T, F
    b. The concepts of motivation and appropriate behavior are closely related.

4. An understanding of various motivation strategies.

a, b, c, d, e
    a. Which of the following is a Theory Y assumption: (a) the average person prefers to be directed; (b) most people must be threatened and coerced before they will put forth adequate effort; (c) commitment to objectives is a function of the rewards associated with achievement; (d) the average person seeks no responsibility; (e) all of the above.

a, b, c, d, e
    b. The process of incorporating motivators into the job situation is called: (a) job enlargement; (b) flextime; (c) satisfying; (d) job enrichment; (e) Theory X.

a, b, c, d, e
    c. Successful behavior modification programs can include: (a) giving rewards and punishments when earned; (b) giving rewards according to performance quality; (c) telling workers what they are doing wrong; (d) punishing workers privately; (e) all of the above.

Introductory Case Wrap-Up

"Employee Incentives at Half Price Books" (p. 448), and its related back-to-the-case sections were written to help you better understand the management concepts contained in this chapter. Answer the following discussion questions about this introductory case to further enrich your understanding of chapter content:

1. Do you think it would be unusual for a manager like Gjemre to spend a significant portion of his time motivating his work force? Explain.

2. Which ones of the needs on Maslow's hierarchy of needs would the incentive system at Half Price Books probably help satisfy? Why? If you have not mentioned some of the needs, explain why the incentive system probably would not satisfy those needs.

3. Assume that Gjemre has the objective of enriching the presently boring jobs of his store managers. What steps could he take to accomplish this objective, and why?

Issues for Review and Discussion

1. Define *motivation* and explain why managers should understand it.

2. Describe the difference between process and content theories of motivation.

3. Draw and explain a model that illustrates the needs-goal theory of motivation.

4. Explain Vroom's expectancy theory of motivation.

5. List and explain three characteristics of the motivation process contained in the Porter-Lawler motivation theory that are not contained in either the needs-goal or Vroom's expectancy theories.

6. What is the main theme of the equity theory of motivation?

7. What does Maslow's hierarchy of needs tell us about people's needs?

8. What concerns have been expressed about Maslow's hierarchy of needs?

9. What are the similarities and differences between Maslow's hierarchy of needs and Alderfer's ERG theory?

10. Explain Argyris's maturity-immaturity continuum.

11. What is the need for achievement?

12. Summarize the characteristics of individuals who have high needs for achievement.

13. Explain "motivating organization members."

14. Is the process of motivating organization members important to managers? Explain.

15. How can managerial communication be used to motivate organization members?

16. What are Theory X, Theory Y, and Theory Z? What does each of these theories tell us about motivating organization members?

17. What is the difference between job enlargement and job rotation?

18. Describe the relationship of hygiene factors, motivating factors, and job enrichment.

19. Define *flextime;* define *behavior modification.*

20. What basic ingredients are necessary to make a behavior modification program successful?

21. In your own words, summarize Likert's four management systems.

22. What effect do Likert's systems 1 and 4 generally have on organizational production in both the short and long terms? Why do these effects occur?

23. List three nonmonetary incentives that you personally would find desirable as an employee within an organization. Why would these incentives be desirable to you?

Building on What You Know

Directions

Review the Highlight feature as indicated below and answer its corresponding questions. Questions in this section focus on relating a Highlight appearing in this chapter to management concepts that you have learned in a previous chapter.

Review the Quality Highlight: Apple Computer on page 465. In chapter 14 you studied various types of leadership styles that managers can use. Considering the situation presented in this Highlight, would Tannenbaum and Schmidt's boss-centered or subordinate-centered leadership style be more appropriate for leaders attempting to help their followers satisfy recognition and personal growth needs? Explain. Which of the Life Cycle Theory of Leadership styles would be *least* appropriate? *Most* appropriate? Be sure to give the rationale behind your choices.

Action Summary Answer Key

1. a. c, p. 449
   b. F, p. 450
   c. c, pp. 452–453

2. a. d, pp. 454–455
   b. d, pp. 456–457
   c. b, p. 457

3. a. T, p. 458
   b. T, pp. 458–459

4. a. c, p. 460
   b. d, p. 463
   c. e, pp. 466–467

Case Study

Motivation at America West Airlines

by Samuel C. Certo, Rollins College

When the airline industry was deregulated in the United States in 1978, Edward Beauvais and Michael Conway began to amass the capital to create their own low-cost yet high-quality airline. In 1983, taking the respective roles of CEO and president, they initiated service of America West Airlines (AWA) with three aircraft and 280 employees. Today, the airline employs over 11,800 people and dominates service through Arizona with 182 daily departures from its Phoenix hub. The airline consistently ranks first in on-time performance and high in customer satisfaction. At the root of AWA's success, say Beauvais and Conway, is its focus on its number one asset—its employees.

When Beauvais and Conway established AWA, they set out to create an atmosphere that would foster strong morale and a high degree of involvement among employees. They were convinced that a highly motivated work force would be the key to successful operation, so they implemented an employee ownership program that would spur motivation. In the first year of employment, all employees are required to purchase (at a discount) shares of company stock equal to twenty percent of that year's salary, making each employee a part owner of the firm with a real interest in its well-being. Owner–pilots tend to baby their aircraft, and all owner–employees are on the lookout to save money and improve service.

Another spur to motivation that Beauvais and Conway identified is an atmosphere of respect. "Work should be more than just putting in time," says Conway. "There is a special joy in employing your full intellectual capacities, in improving yourself. Work should be pleasurable, and it is my belief that this is the secret to the high morale of the America West workforce." To foster this environment, AWA has one predominant rule: "No Rules." Everyone is treated as an individual, and employees are responsible for performing jobs their own way, without having to seek management approval. By delegating authority, management has given the ultimate compliment to their workers—They are trusted to solve problems capably. Managers are available to coach employees, to help them shape ideas, and to encourage them to develop and to try new solutions along the way.

Beauvais and Conway are convinced that AWA's open-door policy and open system of communications are also factors contributing to a highly motivated work force. Employee advisory boards representing pilots, technicians, customer service representatives, and several other work groups meet regularly with all levels of management to discuss work-related issues and to share ideas for cutting costs or improving operations. Beauvais spends about a quarter of his 50- to 70-hour workweek in visits with employees. He asks sharp questions, is a good listener, and really cares about the employees. AWA's open-door policy dictates that any employee can have access to anyone at any level of the corporate structure without fear of reprisals. In fact, managers are advised to say "yes" to any employee who needs help with a problem, if it is at all possible to do so.

The AWA work environment is also designed to allow maximum productivity on the job. An attractive package of benefits includes on-site childcare, eldercare, maternity leave, on-site medical care, and an employee assistance program that offers confidential counseling on issues ranging from personal financial management to substance abuse difficulties to interpersonal relationship problems. AWA also offers employees the opportunity to share jobs or, in some cases, to work at home. All this helps to free workers from day-to-day worries so they can concentrate on doing the best job they can.

America West also has a system of rewards and special bonuses in place, to keep workers enthusiastic about the company. Guest passes and heavily discounted tickets to special events are offered to employees with perfect attendance. Managers asking "What is perfect?" are told to give as many passes as they can justify. "Don't look at the five percent who abuse the system," they are advised; "look at the 95 percent of the people who are motivated by it." Another reward is the anniversary prepayment plan available every four years: An employee can draw a quarter of his or her annual salary in advance, allowing the employee to take a special trip or make a major purchase or perhaps simply to earn extra interest by investing the money.

Beauvais and Conway are in the airline business for the long haul. Their goal is to stay as enthusiastic about America West's twentieth year as they were about the first. By managing employees in the way they would choose to be managed themselves, these executives are continually creating and re-creating the kind of high-energy, motivated work force that is essential to success.

Discussion Questions

1. Maslow's hierarchy of needs suggests a sequence of satisfactions. How do Beauvais and Conway seek to meet employee needs?
2. Would you characterize Beauvais and Conway as Theory X, Theory Y, or Theory Z managers?
3. According to Rensis Likert, management styles can be characterized as System 1, 2, 3, or 4. How would Likert characterize the management system at AWA? Why do you think so?
4. Why do you think Beauvais and Conway feel AWA's management style is so important?

Bjorn Ahlstrom: Changes at Volvo North America

Bjorn Ahlstrom, president and chief executive officer of Volvo North America from 1972 to 1990, headed the division of Volvo that distributes the Swedish-made cars and trucks throughout North America. During Ahlstrom's tenure, the division prospered; sales mushroomed from $100 million per annum to almost $4 billion. Ahlstrom credits the steady increases in sales to Volvo's commitment to workers and to his ability to motivate people.

Volvo began redesigning its factory workers' jobs in the 1970s and has come a long way since the first formal assembly line in manufacturing—credited to Henry Ford, a pioneer of the automobile industry in the early twentieth century. Ford's idea was to pass an automobile-in-production through a series of areas; in each area, workers would build or add on a part and, at the end of the line, a completed automobile would emerge. Each worker would be responsible only for his or her own specific function in a specific area, thus reducing both the risk of error and the level of employee training needed.

The disadvantage of the assembly line, however, was that with such a level of standardization, workers felt unfulfilled. They coined a saying that you "left your head outside the factory fence" when you went to work. Therefore, Volvo changed the way their workers manufacture cars, giving them a larger picture and a wider responsibility. Now whole sections of the car are built by integrated teams of workers. Each worker in the team learns all aspects of the team's assignment, and the team members rotate through the different tasks. The philosophy is centered on maximizing the best efforts each team has to offer. By giving a worker the opportunity to do more than install window cranks for the best part of his or her working life—or perhaps to advance to assembling drive shafts—Volvo demonstrates its commitment to its workers' fulfillment.

On a more basic level, Volvo executives also committed funds to creating better work surroundings. They declared their intention to "demolish the myth that offices have a far better work environment than factories." Reengineering the factories has reduced the background noise level; this makes both production-related and social communication possible within work teams. Factory workers no longer feel isolated or punished by their environment.

However, what is good for the worker is not necessarily good for the company. Reengineering factories and retraining workers is, in the short term, a costly proposition. Further, in 1990, in an effort to strengthen its long-term position, Volvo committed itself to an intra-European project that endangered its immediate financial well-being. Volvo and Renault finalized a trade with the net effect that Volvo acquired a significant stake in the French automaker's car and truck divisions. Volvo took out large loans to finance the deal. At the same time, Renault had to undertake the considerable expense of restructuring its operations. By the end of 1990—a year that was already unprofitable for most automakers because of worldwide financial uncertainty—Volvo posted a loss for the first time in 60 years.

According to many analysts, the losses were almost entirely due to the expenses of the Renault deal. Christer Zetterberg, Volvo's CEO in Gothenburg, Sweden, characterized the January operations as "catastrophic," and stated that subsequent months merely restored "normal recession conditions." Other analysts, on the other hand, blamed the losses on an unfortunate series of misleading Volvo advertisements. (Refer to the case study in Chapter 3 for more information on these advertisements.)

The Volvo reorganization in response to these difficulties stripped Ahlstrom of many of his former responsibilities. This made the position no longer acceptable to him, so in December of 1990, after nearly twenty years heading Volvo North America, Bjorn Ahlstrom announced his resignation as CEO, although he continues to support the Renault–Volvo alliance and will continue to serve on various Volvo boards.

Industry analysts now are wondering about the impact of Ahlstrom's resignation on Volvo North America. It remains to be seen whether his successor, Albert R. Dowden, will be able to reclaim the tradition of successes that Ahlstrom had enjoyed at Volvo.

Video Case Questions

1. Volvo's stated commitment to increasing workers' sense of fulfillment and self-worth is characteristic of whose strategy for motivating organization workers? Explain.
2. What needs, according to Maslow's hierarchy, were fulfilled by Volvo's re-engineering factories to reduce noise levels? Explain.
3. Which of the motivational theories could explain why Ahlstrom chose to resign from Volvo after so many years as CEO?

Video Case Activities

1. Volvo uses job-design strategies to motivate factory workers. These include attempts to alleviate boredom through job rotation and job enlargement. List four other job-design strategies that you think would be effective motivators for Volvo factory workers.
2. Prepare positions, pro and con, for continuing changes at the Volvo factory.

Chapter 16

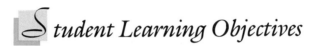
Student Learning Objectives

From studying this chapter, I will attempt to acquire:

1. A definition of the term *group* as used within the context of management.

2. A thorough understanding of the difference between formal and informal groups.

3. Knowledge of the types of formal groups that exist in organizations.

4. An understanding of how managers can determine which groups exist in an organization.

5. An appreciation for how managers must evaluate formal and informal groups simultaneously to maximize work group effectiveness.

6. Insights about managing corporate culture to enhance organizational success.

Groups and
Corporate Culture

 *hapter Outline*

HISPANICS FORM AN INFORMAL GROUP AT AT&T

The Hispanic Association of AT&T Employees was formed in 1984 in New Jersey. The group's main focus is to develop a common interest group for the purpose of furthering the professional growth and development of AT&T minority employees. Since its beginning, the organization has grown substantially and has developed into a national organization comprising twenty-two chapters in eighteen cities with membership of over 2,200. Members include both management and non-management employees, largely concentrated in the nonmanagement ranks.

Recently, AT&T Chairman and Chief Executive Officer Robert Allen addressed the Hispanic Association for the first time. At its 1990 annual meeting, about 1,000 members of the group heard Allen pledge his support to the company's Hispanic and minority

employees. Allen stated that making sure that Hispanics and other minorities had opportunities to succeed at AT&T was in the company's best interests.

Allen indicated that acquiring human resources for the future growth of AT&T is critical. Only 15 percent of the company's future staff growth is expected to come from white males. Thirty million Hispanics are expected to make up 15 percent of the U.S. population by the year 2000. Such size makes Hispanics a vital source of labor in the future. The presence of Hispanics and other minority groups are a reminder of AT&T's need to understand cultural diversity in its organization.

> Allen stated that making sure that Hispanics and other minorities had opportunities to succeed at AT&T was in the company's best interests.

As within virtually any organization, all cultural and ethnic groups must work well together at AT&T if the organization is to survive. All people within the production department at AT&T must work well together if the production department is to make a worthwhile contribution to attaining company goals, and they must work well with other groups in departments like marketing or human resources if AT&T is to survive. Designing and managing work groups that take advantage of diverse types of human resources within AT&T or any other organization is a special challenge for its managers.

This case is based upon AT&T company documents and Oscar Suris, "Hispanic Group Meets with Chief Executive," *The Orlando Sentinel* (August 11, 1990), c1, c6.

WHAT'S AHEAD

The introductory case implies that managing work groups is an important challenge for AT&T managers and that appropriately including Hispanics and other minorities as members of such work groups is part of that challenge. The material in this chapter should help a manager like Robert Allen, AT&T's chairman and chief executive officer, to gain some insight into work group management. This chapter (1) defines groups, (2) discusses the kinds of groups that exist in organizations, (3) explains what steps managers should take to manage groups appropriately, and (4) discusses the role of corporate culture in managing groups.

The previous chapters in this section have dealt with three primary activities of the influencing function: (1) communication, (2) leadership, and (3) motivation. This chapter focuses on managing groups, the last major influencing activity to be discussed in this text. As with the other three activities, managing work groups requires guiding the behavior of organization members in order to increase the probability of reaching organizational objectives.

DEFINING GROUPS

To deal with groups appropriately, managers must have a thorough understanding of the nature of groups in organizations.[1] As used in management-related discussions, a **group** is not simply a gathering of people. Rather it is "any number of people who (1) interact with one another, (2) are psychologically aware of one another, and (3) perceive themselves to be a group."[2] Groups are characterized by their members' communicating with one another over time and being small enough that each member is able to communicate with all other members on a face-to-face basis.[3] As a result of this communication, each group member influences and is influenced by all other group members.[4]

The study of groups is important to managers, because the most common ingredient of all organizations is people and the most common technique for accomplishing work through these people is dividing them into work groups. Cartwright and Lippitt list four additional reasons for studying groups:[5]

1. Groups exist in all kinds of organizations.

2. Groups inevitably form in all facets of organizational existence.

3. Groups can cause either desirable or undesirable consequences within the organization.

4. An understanding of groups can help managers increase the probability that the groups with which they work will cause desirable consequences within the organization.

A **group** is any number of people who (1) interact with one another, (2) are psychologically aware of one another, and (3) perceive themselves to be a group.

Quality Highlight: Eastman Kodak Emphasizes Work Group Management

Eastman Kodak's executives recognized that efficient and effective work groups were essential to their objective of producing high-quality products and services. They recognized the challenge managers face when trying to gain and maintain efficient work groups, so they decided to help Kodak managers by providing training specifically tailored to the work-group concept. They hired Mosaic Management Consulting Group Limited, a management training company, to design and implement a series of management training programs centered on the work-group theme, particularly focusing on ways to bolster the strengths and minimize the weaknesses of work groups.

The work-group theme for the training program continues to be invaluable for enhancing the day-to-day efficiency of work groups. In addition, the program trains managers to handle special situations where the organization structure, the jobs being performed, or some other organizational characteristic must be changed in order to improve the organization. Managers are taught to identify work groups affected by such changes and to focus on gaining their support in order to ensure that such changes are implemented successfully. Managers are trained to view organization members as individuals who must be understood and properly managed if an organization is to be successful. Additionally, Eastman Kodak managers are trained to view organization members as individuals who may need special assistance, guidance, or treatment because of the characteristics of the work groups to which they belong.

KINDS OF GROUPS IN ORGANIZATIONS

Groups that exist in organizations typically are divided into two basic types: formal and informal.

Formal Groups

A **formal group** is a group that exists in an organization by virtue of management decree to perform tasks that enhance the attainment of organizational objectives.

A **formal group** is a group that exists within an organization, by virtue of management decree, to perform tasks that enhance the attainment of organizational objectives.[6] Figure 16.1 is an organization chart showing a formal group. The placement of organization members in such areas as marketing departments, personnel departments, or production departments involves establishing formal groups.

Organizations actually are made up of a number of formal groups that exist at various organizational levels. The coordination of and communication among these groups is the responsibility of managers, or supervisors, commonly called "linking pins." Figure 16.2 shows the various formal groups that can exist within an organization and the linking pins associated with those groups. The linking pins are organization members who belong to two formal groups.

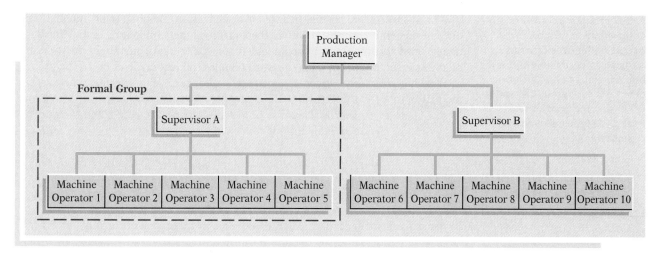

FIGURE 16.1

A formal group

Formal groups are clearly defined and structured. The following sections discuss (1) the basic kinds of formal groups, (2) examples of formal groups as they exist in organizations, and (3) the four stages of formal group development.

Kinds of Formal Groups

Formal groups commonly are divided into command groups and task groups.[7] **Command groups** are formal groups that are outlined on the chain of command on an organization chart. They typically handle the more routine organizational activities.

A **command group** is a formal group that is outlined in the chain of command on an organization chart. Command groups handle routine activities.

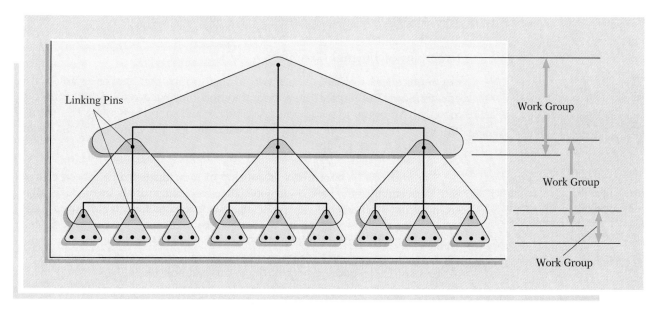

FIGURE 16.2

Formal groups and related linking pins

A **task group** is a formal group of organization members who interact with one another to accomplish mostly nonroutine organizational tasks. (Members of any one task group can and often do come from various levels and segments of an organization.)

Task groups are formal groups of organization members who interact with one another to accomplish most of the organization's nonroutine tasks. Although task groups commonly are considered to be made up of members on the same organizational level, they can consist of people from different levels of the organizational hierarchy. For example, a manager could establish a task group to consider the feasibility of manufacturing some new product. Representatives from various levels of such organizational areas as production, market research, and sales probably would be included as members.

*B*ack to the Case

In order for a manager like Allen to be able to manage work groups at AT&T, he needs to understand the definition of the term *group* and understand that there are several types of groups that exist in organizations. A *group* at AT&T or any other organization is any number of people who interact, are psychologically aware of each other, and who perceive themselves as a group. A company like AT&T is made up of formal groups, the groups that appear on the company's organization charts, such as the marketing department. Managers of groups act as the "linking pins" among departments. The ability of managers at AT&T to coordinate and communicate with these groups, as well as their success in dealing with their own departments, are certainly important to the future success of AT&T as a whole.

At times, managers at AT&T can form new groups to handle some of the less routine challenges. For example, management can form a task group—that is, they can choose two people from several different departments and get them together to develop a new and more efficient system for improving company procedures. Then, of course, AT&T, as with virtually any other organization, has informal groups (those that do not appear on the organization chart) to be considered also. More discussion on informal groups will follow later.

Examples of Formal Groups

Committees and work teams are two formal groups that can be established in organizations. Committees are a more traditional formal group. Work teams only recently have begun to gain popular acceptance and support. Because the organizing section of this text emphasized command groups, the examples in this section will emphasize task groups.

A **committee** is a task group that is charged with performing some type of specific activity. Committees are established for specific reasons.

Committees. A **committee** is a group of individuals that has been charged with performing some type of activity. Therefore, it usually is classified as a task group. From a managerial viewpoint, the major reasons for establishing committees are (1) to allow organization members to exchange ideas, (2) to generate suggestions and recommendations that can be offered to other organizational units, (3) to develop new ideas for solving existing organizational problems, and (4) to assist in the development of organizational policies.[8]

Committees typically exist within all organizations and at all organizational levels. As Figure 16.3 suggests, the larger the organization, the greater the probability that committees will be used within that organization on a regular basis. The following two sections discuss why managers should use committees and what makes committees successful.

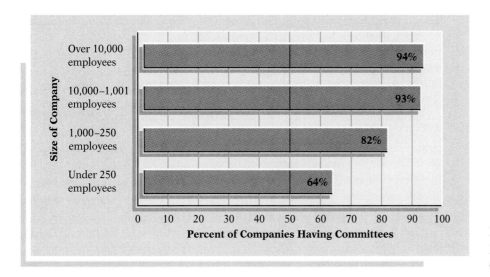

FIGURE 16.3

Percent of companies having
committees by size of company

thics Highlight: Calvary Hospital Forms
Ethics Committees

Results of a survey conducted at Calvary Hospital in the Bronx, New York, indicate that managers are commonly using committees in hospitals to help make ethical decisions. Health care professionals today are faced with many different and significant ethical dilemmas. As an example, should patients be denied treatment because they cannot afford to pay for it or they do not have appropriate medical insurance? As another example, which patients should receive transplant organs first from donors? In order to better handle such ethical dilemmas, hospital administrators are commonly establishing and seeking input from hospital ethics committees. In order to get worthwhile views from these committees, representatives from many different areas of health care are being asked to serve. Not only physicians, but nurses are being included on the committees; nurses are heavily involved in patient care, and their input in making ethical decisions can be extremely valuable. Naturally, the primary purpose of these committees is to help managers (hospital administrators and other health care professionals) to ensure that appropriate decisions are made in response to ethical dilemmas being faced. Organization members seem willing to participate in ethics committees because this participation allows them to express to management various ethical concerns they may have about the work situation.

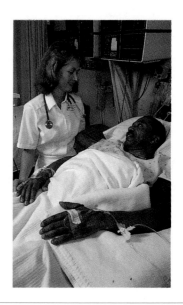

1. *Why Managers Should Use Committees.* Managers generally agree that committees have several uses in organizations. One is that committees can improve the quality of decision making.[9] As more people become involved in making a decision, the strengths and weaknesses of that decision tend to be discussed in more detail, and the quality of the decision tends to increase.

Another reason for committees is that they encourage honest opinions. Committee members feel protected because the group output of a committee logically cannot be totally associated with any one member of that group.

Committees also tend to increase organization member participation in decision making and thereby enhance support of committee decisions. Also, as a result of this increased participation, committee work creates the opportunity for committee members to satisfy their social or esteem needs.

Finally, committees ensure the representation of important groups in the decision-making process. Managers must choose committee members wisely, however, to achieve this representation. The following cartoon makes the point that when a committee does not appropriately represent various interest groups, a committee's decision quite possibly will exclude the interests of other important organizational groups.

Executives vary somewhat in their opinions about using committees in organizations. A study reported by McLeod and Jones indicates that most executives favor using committees in organizations.[10] According to this study, executives claim to get significantly more information from organizational sources other than committees. However, they find that the information from committees is more valuable to them than the information from any other source (see Figure 16.4). However, some top executives show only qualified acceptance of committees as work groups, and others express negative feelings. In general, the executives who are negative about using committees are fewer in number than those who are positive about them or who display qualified acceptance of them.

2. *What Makes Committees Successful.* Although committees have become a commonly accepted management tool, managerial action taken to establish and run

VIETOR'S   FUNNY BUSINESS

"It's unanimous then — we fat cats will get even fatter."

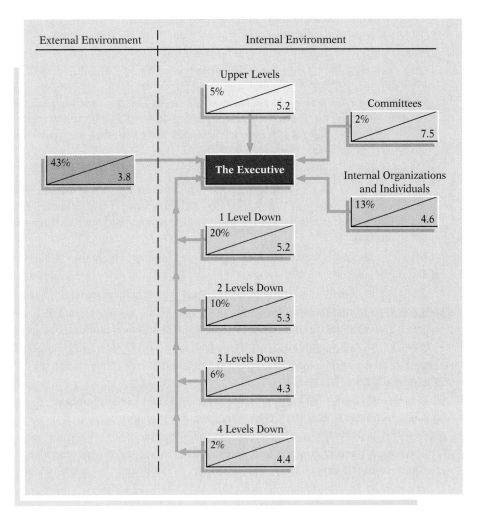

FIGURE 16.4

Comparing volume and value of information to executives from several organizational sources. *In each rectangle, the number* above *the diagonal is the percentage of overall volume for that source. The number* below *the diagonal is the average value, from 0 (no value) to 10 (maximum value), assigned the transaction. Amounts may not total 100 percent because of rounding.*

committees is a major variable in determining their degree of success. Procedural steps that can be taken to increase the probability that a committee will be successful are the following:[11]

a. The committee's goals should be clearly defined, preferably in writing. This focuses the committee's activities and reduces the time devoted to discussing what the committee is supposed to do.

b. The committee's authority should be specified. Can the committee merely investigate, advise, and recommend, or is it authorized to implement decisions?

c. The optimum size of the committee should be determined. With fewer than five members, the advantages of group work may be diminished. With more than ten or fifteen members, the committee may become unwieldly. Although size varies with the circumstances, the ideal number of committee members for many tasks seems to range from five to ten.

d. A chairperson should be selected on the basis of the ability to run an efficient meeting—that is, the ability to keep the participation of all committee members from getting bogged down in irrelevancies and to see that the necessary paperwork gets done.

e. Appointing a permanent secretary to handle communications is often useful.

f. The agenda and all supporting material for the meeting should be distributed before the meeting. When members have a chance to study each item beforehand, they are likely to stick to the point and be ready with informed contributions.

g. Meetings should be started on time, and the time at which they will end should be announced at the outset.

In addition to these procedural steps, managers can follow a number of more people-oriented guidelines to increase the probability of committee success. In this regard, a manager can increase the quality of discussion in committees by:[12]

a. *Rephrasing ideas already expressed.* This rephrasing makes sure that the manager as well as other individuals on the committee have a clear understanding of what has been said.

b. *Bringing a member into active participation.* All committee members represent possible sources of information, and the manager should serve as a catalyst to spark individual participation whenever appropriate.

c. *Stimulating further thought by a member.* The manager should encourage committee members to think ideas through carefully and thoroughly. Only this type of analysis generates high-quality committee output.

Managers should also help the committee avoid a phenomenon called "groupthink."[13] **Groupthink** is the mode of thinking that people engage in when seeking agreement becomes so dominant in a group that it tends to override the realistic appraisal of alternative problem solutions. Groups operate under groupthink when their members are so concerned with being too harsh in their judgments of other group members that objectivity in problem solving is lost. Such groups tend to adopt a softer line of criticism and to seek complete support on every issue, with little conflict generated to endanger the "we-feeling" atmosphere.

Work Teams. **Work teams** are another example of task groups used in organizations. Work teams in the United States have evolved from the problem-solving teams—based on Japanese-style quality circles—that were widely adopted in the 1970s. Problem-solving teams consist of five to twelve volunteer members from different areas of the department who meet weekly to discuss ways to improve quality and efficiency.

Special-purpose teams developed in the early to middle 1980s out of the problem-solving teams. Special-purpose teams typically involve both workers and union representatives who meet together to collaborate on operational decisions at all levels, creating an atmosphere for quality and productivity improvements.

Groupthink is the mode of thinking that people engage in when seeking agreement becomes so dominant in a group that it tends to override the realistic appraisal of alternate problem solutions.

A **work team** is a task group used in organizations to achieve greater organizational flexibility or to cope with rapid growth. Work teams help organizations to be flexible and to cope with rapid growth.

The special-purpose teams laid the foundation for the self-managing work teams of the 1990s that appear to be the wave of the future. These self-managing teams consist of five to fifteen employees who work together to produce an entire product. Members learn all the tasks and rotate from job to job on the project. The teams even take over such managerial duties as scheduling work and vacations and ordering materials. The concept of the work team is a fundamental change in how work is organized, giving the employees control over their jobs.

By employing work teams, the firm draws upon the talent and creativity of all its employees, not just a few maverick inventors or top executives, to make important decisions. As product quality becomes more and more important, managers will need to rely more and more on the team approach in order to stay competitive.[14] Consider a recent situation at Yellow Freight Systems, a shipping company, in which management had a serious concern for enhancing the excellence of service that its customers received.[15] Management established, in essence, a work team to address this concern. The work team was made up of members from many different parts of the company including marketing, sales, operations, and human resources. Over all, the task of the work team was to manage an excellence-in-service campaign that management had initiated.

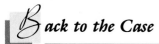

Back to the Case

AT&T management could decide to form a committee to achieve some specific goal. A committee might be formed, for example, on how to enhance the quality of goods and services offered by AT&T. Such a committee could allow various AT&T departments to exchange quality improvement ideas and generate related suggestions to management. Such a committee could improve AT&T decision making in general by encouraging honest feedback from employees about quality issues in the organization, and a committee like this also can be used to get fresh ideas about enhancing product quality and encourage AT&T employees to participate more seriously in improving the quality of goods and services offered by the company. Such a committee can help AT&T management to ensure that all appropriate departments are represented in important quality decisions—when AT&T takes action to improve the quality of a new product, for example, every important angle must be considered, including design, production, marketing, sales, and so on.

In managing such a quality committee at AT&T, management should encourage quality committee members to take certain steps that can help the committee to be successful. After all, although committees *can* be useful, a poorly run committee wastes a lot of time. As an example of steps to be taken, the committee should develop a clear definition of its goals and the limits of its authority. Will the committee merely come up with quality improvement ideas, or should it also take the initial steps toward implementing its ideas?

In addition, the quality committee should not have too few or too many members. Issues must be addressed such as appointing an administrator to handle communications and appointing a chairperson who is good with people-oriented issues. A quality committee needs a chairperson who can rephrase ideas clearly to ensure that everyone understands and who can get members to participate and think about the issues in a way that avoids groupthink. A company like AT&T wants original ideas to come out of committees, not one unanimous opinion that evolved because everyone was avoiding conflict.

Stages of Formal Group Development

Another facet of managing formal groups is understanding the stages of formal group development. In a classic book, Bernard Bass has suggested that group development is a four-stage process influenced primarily by groups learning how to use their resources.[16] Although these stages may not occur sequentially, for the purpose of clarity the discussion that follows assumes that they do. The four stages can be labeled and defined as follows:

1. *The acceptance stage.* It is relatively common for members of a new group initially to mistrust each other somewhat. The acceptance stage occurs only after the initial mistrust within the group has been transformed into mutual trust and the general acceptance of group members by one another.

2. *The communication and decision-making stage.* Once the acceptance stage has been passed, group members are better able to communicate frankly with one another. This frank communication provides the basis for effectively establishing and using some type of group decision-making mechanism.

3. *The group solidarity stage.* Group solidarity comes naturally as the mutual acceptance of group members increases and communication and decision making continue within the group. This stage is characterized by members becoming more involved in group activities and cooperating, rather than competing, with one another. Group members find being a member of the group extremely satisfying and are committed to enhancing the group's overall success.

4. *The group control stage.* A natural result of group solidarity is group control. This stage involves group members attempting to maximize group success by matching individual abilities with group activities and by assisting one another. Flexibility and informality tend to characterize this stage.

In general terms, as a group passes through each of these four stages, it tends to become more mature and more effective—and therefore more productive. The group that reaches maximum maturity and effectiveness is characterized by:[17]

1. *Members functioning as a unit.* The group works as a team. Members do not disturb one another to the point of interfering with their collaboration.

2. *Members participating effectively in group effort.* Members work hard when there is something to do. They usually do not loaf even if they get the opportunity to do so.

3. *Members being oriented toward a single goal.* Group members work for common purposes and thereby do not waste group resources by moving in different directions.

4. *Members having the equipment, tools, and skills necessary to attain the group's goals.* Group members are taught the various parts of their jobs by experts and strive to acquire whatever resources are needed to attain group objectives.

5. *Members asking and receiving suggestions, opinions, and information from one another.* A member who is uncertain about something stops working and asks another member for information. Group members generally talk to one another openly and frequently.

Back to the Case

Managers in companies like AT&T must be patient and understand that it's going to take some time for a new group to develop into a productive working unit. The members in any new work group must start by trusting and accepting one another and then begin communicating and exchanging ideas. Once this acceptance and communication increase, group solidarity and control come naturally. In other words, the group members get involved, cooperate, and try to maximize the group's success.

This is true also with the quality committee that is being used as an example. AT&T management must be patient and let the quality committee mature before management can expect maximum effectiveness and productivity. If given time to grow, the group will function as a unit, members will participate willingly and effectively, and the group will reach valuable decisions about what needs to be done to improve the quality of the goods and services that AT&T offers.

Informal Groups

Informal groups, the second major kind of group that can exist within an organization, are groups that develop naturally as people interact. An **informal group** is defined as a collection of individuals whose common work experiences result in the development of a system of interpersonal relations that extend beyond those established by management.[18] As Figure 16.5 shows, informal group structures can deviate significantly from formal group structures. As in the case of Supervisor A in the figure, an organization member can belong to more than one informal

An **informal group** is a collection of individuals whose common work experiences result in the development of a system of interpersonal relations that extends beyond those established by management.

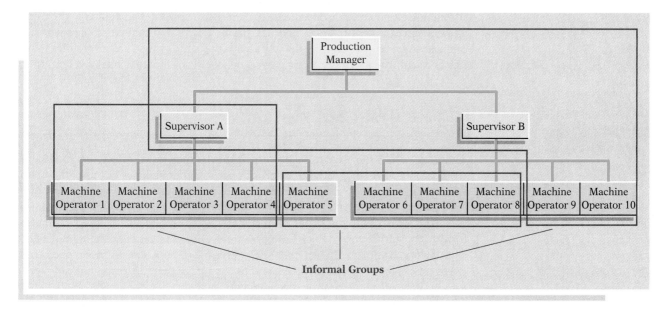

FIGURE 16.5

Three informal groups that deviate significantly from formal groups within the organization

group at the same time. In contrast to formal groups, informal groups typically are not highly structured in terms of procedure and are not formally recognized by management.

The following sections discuss (1) various kinds of informal groups that can exist in organizations, (2) the benefits usually reaped by membership in informal groups, and (3) encouraging the development of informal groups.

Kinds of Informal Groups

An **interest group** is an informal group that gains and maintains membership primarily because of a special concern each member possesses about a specific issue.

A **friendship group** is an informal group that forms in organizations because of the personal affiliation members have with one another.

Informal groups generally are divided into two types: interest groups and friendship groups. **Interest groups** are informal groups that gain and maintain membership primarily because of a special concern each member possesses about a specific issue. An example is a group of workers pressing management for better pay or working conditions. Once the interest or concern that causes an informal group to form has been eliminated, the group tends to disband.

As its name implies, **friendship groups** are informal groups that form in organizations because of the personal affiliation members have with one another. Personal factors such as personal interests, race, gender, and religion serve as foundations for friendship groups. As with interest groups, the membership of friendship groups tends to change over time. Here, however, group membership changes as friendships dissolve or new friendships are made.

Benefits of Informal Group Membership

Informal groups tend to develop in organizations because of various benefits that group members obtain. These benefits include (1) perpetuation of social and cultural values that group members consider important, (2) status and social satisfaction that might not be enjoyed without group membership, (3) increased ease of communication among group members, and (4) increased desirability of the overall work environment.[19] These benefits may be one reason that employees who are on fixed shifts or who continually work with the same groups are sometimes more satisfied with their work than employees whose shifts are continually changing.[20]

Back to the Case

There are also issues regarding informal groups that could affect the success of work groups at AT&T. Employee groups get together at times because of certain issues. For example, the Hispanic employees mentioned in the introductory case have gotten together as a group to increase the opportunities for the professional growth of Hispanics and other minorities at AT&T. And, of course, employees form friendship groups, which ease communication and provide feelings of satisfaction in a company. In general, such informal groups can improve the work environment for everyone involved, and to encourage their development can therefore be very advantageous for management.

Perhaps AT&T management can accelerate the development of a quality committee into a productive unit by placing individuals on this committee who already know and trust one another through membership in one or more informal groups at AT&T. As an example, some members of the newly formed quality committee might know and trust one another immediately as a result of membership in the AT&T Hispanic Employees Association. Under such circumstances, a trust developed among employees through past informal group affiliations could help the formal quality committee to develop into a productive group more quickly.

MANAGING WORK GROUPS

To manage work groups effectively, managers must simultaneously consider the affect of both formal and informal group factors on organizational productivity. This consideration requires three steps: (1) determining group existence, (2) understanding the evolution of informal groups, and (3) maximizing work group effectiveness.

Determining Group Existence

Perhaps the most important step that managers should take in managing work groups is determining what groups exist within the organization and who their members are. **Sociometry** is an analytical tool that managers can use to help determine such information. It can also provide information on the internal workings of an informal group, such as the group leader, the relative status level of various members within the group, and the group's communication networks.[21] This information on informal groups, along with an understanding of the established formal groups as shown on an organization chart, gives managers a complete picture of the group structure.

The procedure involved in performing a sociometric analysis in an organization is quite basic. Various organization members simply are asked, through either an interview or a questionnaire, to name several other organization members with whom they would like to spend some of their free time. A sociogram then is constructed to summarize the informal relationships among group members. **Sociograms** are diagrams that visually link individuals within the group according to the number of times they were chosen and whether the choice was reciprocal.

Figure 16.6 shows two sample sociograms based on a classic study of two groups of boys in a summer camp—the Bulldogs and the Red Devils.[22] An analysis of these sociograms results in several interesting observations. For example, more boys within the Bulldogs than within the Red Devils were chosen as being desirable to spend time with. This probably implies that the Bulldogs are a closer-knit informal group than the Red Devils. Also, communication between L and most other Red Devils members is likely to occur directly, whereas communication between C and other Bulldogs is likely to pass through other group members. Last, the greater the number of times an individual is chosen, the more likely that individual will be the group leader. Thus individuals C and E would tend to be Bulldog leaders, and individuals L and S would tend to be Red Devil leaders.

Sociometric analysis can give managers many useful insights on the informal groups within an organization. Although managers may not want to perform a formal sociometric analysis, they can casually gather information that would indicate what form a sociogram might take in a particular situation. This information can be gathered through inferences made in normal conversations that managers have with other organization members and through observations of how various organization members relate to one another.

Sociometry is an analytical tool that can be used to determine what informal groups exist in an organization and who the members of those groups are.

A **sociogram** is a sociometric diagram that summarizes the personal feelings of organization members about the people in the organization with whom they would like to spend free time.

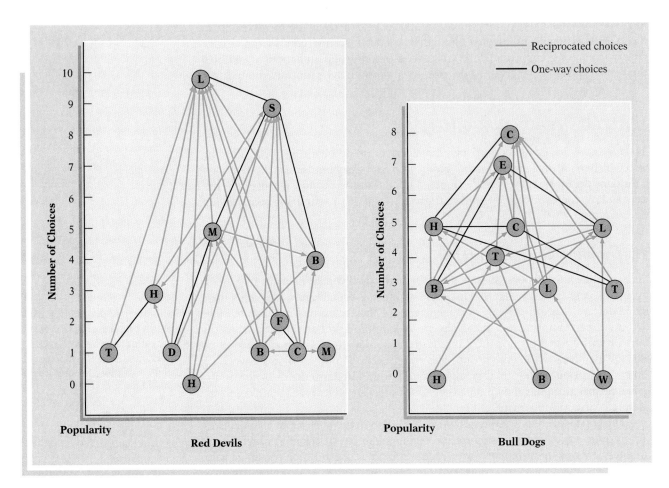

FIGURE 16.6
Sample sociograms

Understanding the Evolution of Informal Groups

Obviously, knowing what groups exist within an organization and what character-izes the membership of those groups is an important prerequisite for managing groups effectively. A second prerequisite is understanding how informal groups evolve, because this gives managers some insights on how to encourage informal groups to develop appropriately within an organization. Naturally, encouraging these groups to develop and maintaining good relationships with work group members can help ensure that organization members support management in the process of attaining organizational objectives.[23]

Perhaps the most widely accepted framework for explaining the evolution of informal groups was developed by George Homans.[24] Figure 16.7 broadly summarizes his theory. According to Homans, the sentiments, interactions, and activities that emerge as part of an informal group result from the sentiments, interactions, and activities that exist within a formal group. In addition, the infor-mal group exists to obtain the consequences of satisfaction and growth for its members. Feedback on whether the consequences are achieved can result in forces that attempt to modify the formal group in order to increase the probability that the informal group will achieve the consequences.

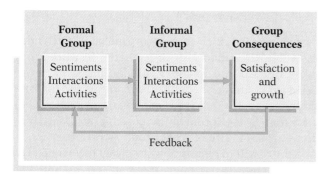

FIGURE 16.7

Homans's ideas on how informal groups develop

An example to illustrate Homans's concept involves twelve factory workers who are members of a formal work group that manufactures toasters. According to Homans, as these workers interact to assemble toasters, they might discover common personal interests that encourage the evolution of informal groups. In turn, these informal groups will tend to maximize the satisfaction and growth of their members. Once established, the informal groups will probably resist changes or established segments of formal groups that threaten the satisfaction and growth of the informal group's members.

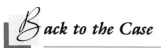 ack to the Case

In order for a company like AT&T to be successful, managers must be able to consider how both formal and informal groups affect organizational productivity. Managers need to determine what informal groups exist, who the group members are, and understand how these groups form. Armed with this information, managers in companies like AT&T can strive to make their work groups more effective.

One way management can get information about the groups at AT&T is to use sociometry. Managers can design a questionnaire asking their employees whom they spend time with and then construct a sociogram to summarize this information. Of course, managers can do a more casual analysis by simply talking to their employees and observing how they interact with one another.

Managers in a company like AT&T should also try to understand how informal groups evolve and realize that an organization's formal structure influences how the informal groups develop within it. For example, let us assume that in one department at AT&T there are thirty people who work on product design. Many of them are interested in sports, have become friends because of this common interest, and work well together as a result. If a manager at AT&T needed to make some changes in this department, he or she should try to accommodate such informal friendship groups to keep group members satisfied. Only with very good reason should a manager of such a department damage the existence of the productive friendship group with actions like transfering one or more informal group members out of the design department.

Maximizing Work Group Effectiveness

Once managers determine which groups exist within an organization and understand how informal groups evolve, they should strive to maximize work group effectiveness. As the following discussion emphasizes, maximizing work group effectiveness requires that managers continue to consider both formal and informal dimensions of the organization.[25]

Figure 16.8 indicates the four factors primarily responsible for collectively influencing work group effectiveness: (1) size of work group, (2) cohesiveness of work group, (3) work group norms, and (4) status of work group members. (The terms *work group* and *formal group* are used synonymously in the sections that follow.)

Size of Work Group

As work group size (the number of members in a work group) increases, forces usually are created within that group that can either increase or decrease its effectiveness.[26] The ideal number of members for a work group depends primarily on the group's purpose.[27] For example, the ideal size for a fact-finding work group usually is set at about fourteen members, and the maximum size for a problem-solving work group is approximately seven members.[28]

Work group size is a significant determinant of group effectiveness because it has considerable impact on three major components of a group: (1) leadership, (2) group members, and (3) group processes. A summary of how these factors can be influenced by group size is presented in Table 16.1.

Managers attempting to maximize group effectiveness by modifying formal group size also should consider informal group factors. For example, a manager may decide that a formal work group should be reduced in size to make it more

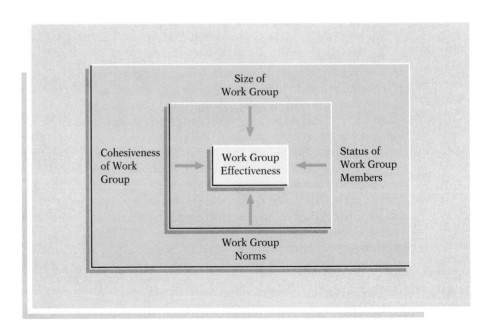

FIGURE 16.8

Primary determinants of work group effectiveness

TABLE 16.1 Possible effects of group size on group leadership, group members, and group processes

Dimensions	Group Size 2–7 Members	8–12 Members	13–16 Members
Leadership			
1. Demand on leader	Low	Moderate	High
2. Differences between leader and members	Low	Low to moderate	Moderate to high
3. Direction of leader	Low	Low to moderate	Moderate to high
Members			
4. Tolerance of direction from leader	Low to high	Moderate to high	High
5. Domination of group interaction by a few members	Low	Moderate to high	High
6. Inhibition in participation by ordinary members	Low	Moderate	High
Group processes			
7. Formalization of rules and procedures	Low	Low to moderate	Moderate to high
8. Time required for reaching decisions	Low to moderate	Moderate	Moderate to high
9. Tendency for subgroup to form	Low	Moderate to high	High

effective. Before making this reduction, however, the manager should consider the existence of informal groups within the formal group. If the manager reduces the size of the formal group by transferring the informal group leader, the effectiveness of the work group could diminish considerably. The slight ineffectiveness of the overly large formal work group might be more advantageous than the greater ineffectiveness that could result from reducing the formal group size and possibly transferring the informal group leader.

Global Highlight: Mazda's Work Group System

At Mazda, management has found that some jobs would require work groups that would be so large and therefore so unproductive that the company has engineered a work group system to handle a job rather than a single work group. According to Sarah Griffin of Mazda Motor Manufacturing (USA), management at the Flat Rock, Michigan, plant has designed and implemented a plan using a series of work groups to better control job injuries within its facility. This work group system involves a department work group for each department at the plant as well as a central work group that monitors, controls, and coordinates the activities of the department work groups. Thus far, this work group system has identified fifty-two jobs that pose significant safety risk to workers because of the excessive bending, reaching, and lifting motions that the jobs require. Joe Galusha, Mazda's safety and health specialist, is encouraged by the initial results of the work groups' system in identifying and eliminating "injury risk" positions within the company. He stresses, however, that the job of the work group system will never really end. Instead, he views the functioning of the work group system as a continuing effort.

Group cohesiveness is the attraction group members feel for one another in terms of the desire to remain a member of a group and to resist leaving it.

Cohesiveness of Work Group

Another factor that can influence work group effectiveness is the degree of cohesiveness of the group. **Group cohesiveness** is the attraction group members feel for one another in terms of the desire to remain a member of the group and to resist leaving it.[29] The greater the desire, the greater the cohesiveness. In general, the cohesiveness of a work group is determined by the cohesiveness of the informal groups that exist within it. Therefore, to manage the degree of cohesiveness that exists within a work group, managers must manage the degree of cohesiveness that exists within the informal groups that constitute the work group.

Group cohesiveness is extremely important to managers because the greater the cohesiveness, the greater the probability the group will accomplish its objectives. In addition, some evidence indicates that groups whose members have positive feelings toward one another tend to be more productive than groups whose members have negative feelings toward one another.[30]

Indicators of high group cohesiveness include the following:[31]

1. The members have a broad, general agreement on the goals and objectives of the informal group.

2. A significant amount of communication and interaction is evident among participating members.

3. There is a satisfactory level of homogeneity in social status and social background among the members.

4. Members are allowed to participate fully and directly in the determination of group standards.

5. The size of the group is sufficient for interaction but is not so large as to stymie personal attention. Normally, the optimum size range of an informal group is from four to seven members.

6. The members have a high regard for their fellow members.

7. The members feel a strong need for the mutual benefits and protection the group appears to offer.

8. The group is experiencing success in the achievement of its goals and in the protection of important values.

Because the cohesiveness of informal groups is such an influential determinant of the cohesiveness of work groups and, as a result, of work group effectiveness, management should assist in the development of informal group cohesiveness whenever possible. (This, of course, assumes that the informal group is attempting to make a constructive contribution to organizational goal attainment.) To this end, managers should attempt to enhance the prestige of existing informal group members, design the overall organization to encourage informal group development, and eliminate organizational barriers to continuing informal group membership over an extended period of time.

If, however, managers determine that an informal group is attempting to attain objectives that are counterproductive to those of the organization, an appropriate strategy would be to attempt to reduce informal group cohesiveness. For example, managers could take action to limit the prestige of existing group members and design the overall organization to discourage further group cohesiveness.

This type of action, however, could result in a major conflict between management and various informal groups that exist within the organization. Over all, managers must keep in mind that the greater the cohesiveness of informal groups with nonproductive objectives, the greater the probability that those nonproductive objectives will be attained.

Work Group Norms

Group norms are a third major determinant of work group effectiveness. In this chapter, **group norms** apply only to informal groups. These norms are appropriate or standard behavior that is required of informal group members. Therefore, they significantly influence the behavior of informal group members in their formal group. According to Hackman, group norms (1) are structured characteristics of groups that simplify the group-influence processes; (2) apply only to behavior, not to private thoughts and feelings of group members; (3) generally develop only in relation to the matters that most group members consider important; (4) usually develop slowly over time; and (5) sometimes apply only to certain group members.[32]

Systematic study of group norms has revealed that there is generally a close relationship between those norms and the profitability of the organization of which the group is a part.[33] Although it would be impossible to state all possible norms that might develop in a group, most group norms relate to one or more of the following: (1) organizational pride, (2) performance, (3) profitability, (4) teamwork, (5) planning, (6) supervision, (7) training, (8) innovation, (9) customer relations, and (10) honesty or security.

Norms usually are divided into two general types: negative and positive. **Negative norms** are required informal group behavior that limits organizational productivity. **Positive norms** are required informal group behavior that contributes to organizational productivity. Examples of negative norms might include stopping work fifteen minutes before quitting time, taking extended coffee breaks, or not rushing to finish work because more will be assigned. Examples of positive norms include doing work correctly the first time and not wasting expensive company materials. The cartoon on page 501 illustrates a negative norm that allows informal group members to agree which nights they will leave work earlier so they can take turns looking good to the boss.

Some managers consider group norms to be of such great importance to the organization that they develop profiles of group norms to assess the norms' organizational impact. Figure 16.9 on page 500 shows a normative profile developed by one company manager. This particular profile is characterized by a number of norm differences. For example, a high level of organizational pride and good customer relations contrast with a lower concern for profitability. What actually happened in this company was that employees placed customer desires at such a high level that they were significantly decreasing organizational profitability to please customers. Once these norms were discovered, management took steps to make the situation more advantageous to the organization.

As the preceding information suggests, a key to managing behavior within a formal work group is managing the norms of the informal groups that exist within the formal group. More specifically, Homans's framework for analyzing group behavior indicates that informal group norms are mainly the result of the characteristics of the formal work group of which the informal group is a part. As a

Group norms are appropriate or standard behavior that is required of informal group members.

Negative norms are informal group standards that limit organizational productivity.

Positive norms are informal group standards that contribute to organizational productivity.

result, changing the existing norms within an informal group means changing the characteristics of the formal work group of which the informal group is a part.

For example, an informal group could have the negative norm: Don't rush the work—they'll just give you more to do. For a manager to change this norm, the factor in the formal work group from which the norm probably arose should be eliminated. The manager might find that this norm is a direct result of the fact that workers are formally recognized within the organization through pay and awards regardless of the amount of work performed. Changing the formal policy so the amount of work accomplished is considered in formal organizational recognition should help dissolve this negative norm. In some situations, norms may be difficult, if not impossible, to change.

Status of Work Group Members

Status is the positioning of importance of a group member in relation to other group members.

Status is the position of a group member in relation to other group members. Over all, an individual's status within a group is determined not only by the person's work or role within the group but by the nonwork qualities the individual brings to the group. Work-related determinants of status include titles, work schedules, and perhaps most commonly, amounts of pay group members receive.[34] Nonwork-related determinants of status include education level, race, age, and sex. Table 16.2 on page 502 entertaining but realistic treatment of how status symbols vary within the formal groups of an organizational hierarchy. These status symbols generally are used within formal work groups to reward individual productivity and to show the different levels of organizational importance.

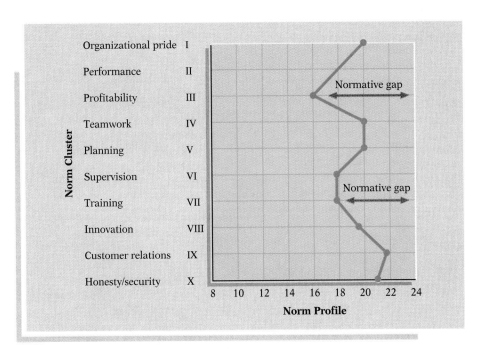

FIGURE 16.9

Sample normative profile

"Come on Scott, be a buddy—look, if you leave the office before me tonight, I'll leave before you any two times you say."

U.S. News & World Report, June 1, 1987. William Hamilton's cartoon is reprinted by permission of Chronicle Features, San Francisco.

To maximize the effectiveness of a work group, managers also should consider the status of members of the informal groups that exist within the formal group. For example, within a formal group, the formal group leaders have higher status than other group members. The informal groups that exist within the formal group also have informal leaders, who generally are different from the formal leader and of higher status than other informal group members. Management usually finds that, to increase productivity within a formal work group, the support of both the formal and the informal leaders must be gained. In fact, some evidence suggests that production is associated more with support from informal group leaders than with support from formal group leaders.[35]

CORPORATE CULTURE

Previous sections of this chapter have focused primarily on managing smaller work groups. This section, on the other hand, discusses corporate culture as an important ingredient in managing all organization members as a total group.

Corporate culture is defined as a set of shared values and beliefs that organization members have regarding the functioning and existence of their organization.[36] The evidence for the type of corporate culture present in any organization can be found by studying its own special combination of status symbols, traditions, history, and physical environment. By understanding the significance of this evidence of corporate culture, management can help to develop a culture that is beneficial to the firm. For example, by looking at the status symbols, the visible, external signs of one's social position that are associated with the various positions in the

Corporate culture is a set of shared values and beliefs that organization members have regarding the functioning and existence of their organization.

TABLE 16.2 How status symbols vary with various levels of the organizational hierarchy

Visible Appurtenances	Top Dogs	VIPs	Brass	No. 2s	Eager Beavers	Hoi Polloi
Briefcases	None—they ask the questions	Use backs of envelopes	Someone goes along to carry theirs	Carry their own—empty	Daily—carry their own—filled with work	Too poor to own one
Desks, office	Custom-made (to order)	Executive style (to order)	Type A, "Director"	Type B, "Manager"	Castoffs from No. 2s	Yellow oak—or castoffs from eager beavers
Tables, office	Coffee tables	End tables or decorative wall tables	Matching tables, type A	Matching tables, type B	Plain work table	None—lucky to have own desk
Carpeting	Nylon—one-inch pile	Nylon—one-inch pile	Wool-twist (with pad)	Wool-twist (without pad)	Used wool pieces—sewed	Asphalt tile
Plant stands	Several—kept filled with strange, exotic plans	Several—kept filled with strange, exotic plants	Two—repotted whenever they take a trip	One medium-sized—repotted annually during vacation	Small—repotted when plant dies	May have one in the department or bring their own from home
Vacuum water bottles	Silver	Silver	Chromium	Plain painted	Coke machine	Water fountains
Library	Private collection	Autographed or complimentary books and reports	Selected references	Impressive titles on covers	Books everywhere	Dictionary
Parking space	Private—in front of office	In plant garage	In company garage—if enough seniority	In company properties—somewhere	On the parking lot	Anywhere they can find a space—if they can afford a car

firm, one can get a feeling for the social hierarchy in the organization. Status symbols such as size and location of one's office, use of executive clubs, and reserved parking are all indicators of the status level of a job.

Traditions and history developed over time in a firm can determine the special way that workers in that particular firm act on a daily basis. Typically, the traditions can help workers know exactly what is expected of them. By developing traditions, managers can therefore help to steer the everyday behaviors that go on.

The firm's physical environment makes a statement about the firm's type of corporate culture. For instance, offices that are closed with few common areas for organization members to meet creates an image of a closed form of culture. A building with open offices and considerable common areas for the employees to interact indicates a more open culture. Whether the doors are consistently closed or open is another clue as to the type of formality that exists in an organization.

The significance of corporate culture for management is that it influences the behavior of everyone within an organization, and if carefully crafted, can have a positive and significant effect on organizational success.[37] If not properly managed, however, corporate culture can help doom an organization to failure. Typically, top management as well as other present or past organizational leaders in an organization are the key agents for influencing corporate culture.

Advice about the way managers should handle corporate culture issues commonly appears in the current management literature.[38] One example of such advice that seems especially practical and helpful suggests that managers can use five primary mechanisms to help develop and reinforce a desired corporate culture. These mechanisms are[39]

1. *What leaders pay attention to, measure, and control.* Leaders can communicate very effectively what their vision of the organization is and what they want done by consistently emphasizing the same issues in meetings, in casual remarks and questions, and in strategy discussions. For example, if product quality is the dominant value to be inculcated in employees, leaders may consistently inquire about the effect of any proposed changes on product quality.

2. *Leaders' reactions to critical incidents and organizational crises.* The manner in which leaders deal with crises can create new beliefs and values and reveal underlying organizational assumptions. For example, when a firm faces a financial crisis but does not lay off any employees, the message may be that the organization sees itself as a "family" that looks out for its members.

3. *Deliberate role modeling, teaching, and coaching.* The behaviors that leaders perform in both formal and informal settings have an important effect on employee beliefs, values, and behaviors. For example, if the CEO regularly works very long hours and on weekends, other managers may respond by spending more of their time at work, too.

4. *Criteria for allocation of rewards and status.* Leaders can quickly communicate their priorities and values by consistently linking rewards and punishments to the behaviors they are concerned with. For example, if a weekly bonus is given for exceeding production or sales quotas, employees may recognize the value placed on these activities and focus their efforts on them.

5. *Criteria for recruitment, selection, promotion, and retirement of employees.* The kinds of people who are hired and who succeed in an organization are those

who accept the organization's values and behave accordingly. For example, if managers who are action oriented and who implement strategies effectively consistently move up the organizational ladder, the organization's priorities should come through loud and clear to other managers.

The corporate culture discussion suggests that managers can influence the type of culture that exists within organizations. In general, a manager must first determine the characteristics of a culture that would be appropriate for an organization and then take calculated and overt steps to encourage the establishment, growth, and maintenance of that culture. Merely allowing corporate culture to develop without planned management influence can result in the appearance of an inappropriate corporate culture that ultimately limits the degree of success that an organization can attain.

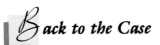

Back to the Case

In managing groups, managers in a company like AT&T should consider the four major factors that influence work group effectiveness. First of all, the size of the work group can be important to its productivity. A twenty-person quality committee would be somewhat large and would probably hamper the group's effectiveness. Managers should consider informal groups before making changes in group size. The quality committee could end up being less productive without one or more of its respected members than it would be if it were slightly too large.

Another important factor that influences work group effectiveness at a company like AT&T is group cohesiveness. Because a more cohesive group will tend to be more effective, AT&T managers should try to increase the cohesiveness of its work groups. Informal groups are very important here, too. AT&T managers can probably increase the cohesiveness of their formal groups by such policies as allowing members to take breaks together or rewarding informal group members for a job well done.

The group norms, or appropriate behaviors required within the informal group, are a third factor that affects the productivity of formal group behavior at a company like AT&T. Because these norms affect company profitability, managers must be aware of them and understand how to influence them within the formal group structure. For example, let us assume that a smaller informal group of workers within a larger department is assembling telephones and cares a great deal about the quality of the phones they produce. Unfortunately, because of its quality norm, informal group members are taking too much time to manufacture high-quality phones. Management could try to improve this norm by giving bonuses to group members who produce phones of better quality in a shorter amount of time. This reward would probably increase the formal group productivity while encouraging a positive norm within the informal group.

Status within the informal groups also affects work group productivity in a company like AT&T. For example, if AT&T managers want to increase production for some group, management should try to encourage the informal group's leaders, as well as the group's formal supervisor. Chances are that targeted group will become more productive only if its informal high-status members support that objective.

Over all, if a company like AT&T wants to maximize work group effectiveness, management must remember both the formal and informal dimensions of its work groups while considering the four main factors that influence work group productivity.

Action Summary

Reread the learning objectives that follow. Each objective is followed by questions. Answering these questions accurately will help you retain the most important concepts discussed in this chapter. After answering each question, check your answer with the answer key at the end of this chapter. (*Hint:* If you have doubt regarding the correct response, consult the page whose number follows the answer.)

Circle:

From studying this chapter, I will attempt to acquire:

1. **A definition of the term *group* as used within the context of management.**
   a. A group is made up of people who interact with one another, perceive themselves to be a group, and are primarily physically aware of one another.   T, F
   b. According to Cartwright and Lippitt, it is not true to say that: (a) groups exist in all kinds of organizations; (b) groups inevitably form in all facets of organizational existence; (c) groups cause undesirable consequences within the organization, so their continued existence should be discouraged; (d) understanding groups can assist managers in increasing the probability that the groups with which they work will cause desirable consequences within the organization; (e) all of the above are true.   a, b, c, d, e

2. **A thorough understanding of the difference between formal and informal groups.**
   a. An informal group is a group that exists within an organization by virtue of management decree.   T, F
   b. A formal group is one that exists within an organization by virtue of interaction among organization members in proximity to one another.   T, F

3. **Knowledge of the types of formal groups that exist in organizations.**
   a. The type of group that generally handles more routine organizational activities is the: (a) informal task group; (b) informal command group; (c) formal task group; (d) formal command group; (e) none of the above.   a, b, c, d, e
   b. Managers should be encouraged to take the following steps to increase the success of a committee: (a) clearly define the goals of the committee; (b) rephrase ideas that have already been expressed; (c) select a chairperson on the basis of ability to run an efficient meeting; (d) a and b; (e) a, b, and c.   a, b, c, d, e

4. **An understanding of how managers can determine which groups exist in an organization.**
   a. The technique of sociometry involves asking people with whom they would like to manage.   T, F

a, b, c, d, e   **b.** A sociogram is defined in the text as: (a) a letter encouraging group partici-
                                pation; (b) a diagram that visually illustrates the number of times that
                                the individuals were chosen within the group and whether the choice was
                                reciprocal; (c) a composite of demographic data useful in determining infor-
                                mal group choices; (d) a computer printout designed to profile psychologi-
                                cal and sociological characteristics of the informal group; (e) none of the
                                above.

                           **5. An appreciation for how managers must evaluate formal and informal
                                groups simultaneously to maximize work group effectiveness.**

a, b, c, d, e   **a.** Which of the following factors has the least influence on the effectiveness
                                of a work group: (a) age of the work group; (b) size of the work group;
                                (c) cohesiveness of the work group; (d) norms of the work group; (e) a
                                and d.

T, F   **b.** Knowing what informal groups exist within an organization and how infor-
                                mal groups evolve are prerequisites for managing groups effectively.

                           **6. Insights about managing corporate culture to enhance organizational
                                success.**

T, F   **a.** The concept of corporate culture usually does not include the set of beliefs
                                that organization members have about their organization and its func-
                                tioning.

a, b, c, d, e   **b.** Mechanisms that managers can use to influence corporate culture include:
                                (a) what leaders pay attention to, (b) criteria that leaders use to make
                                organizational awards, (c) criteria leaders use to select new employees,
                                (d) all of the above, (e) none of the above.

 *Introductory Case Wrap-Up*

"Hispanics Form an Informal Group at AT&T" (p. 480) and its related back-to-the-case sections were written to help you better understand the management concepts contained in this chapter. Answer the following discussion questions about this introductory case to further enrich your understanding of chapter content:

1. Which kind of group would the Hispanic Employees Association at AT&T be classified as? Explain.

2. Should the existence of the Hispanic Association affect the way AT&T managers manage? If so, how? If not, why?

Issues for Review and Discussion

1. How is the term *group* defined in this chapter?
2. Why is the study of groups important to managers?
3. What is a formal group?
4. Explain the significance of linking pins to formal groups in organizations.
5. List and define two types of formal groups that can exist in organizations.
6. Why should managers use committees in organizations?
7. What steps can managers take to ensure that a committee will be successful?

8. Explain how work teams can be valuable to an organization.

9. Describe the stages a group typically goes through as it becomes more mature.

10. What is an informal group?

11. List and define two types of informal groups in organizations.

12. What benefits generally accrue to members of informal groups?

13. What is the relationship between work teams and informal groups?

14. Are formal groups more important to managers than informal groups? Explain.

15. Describe the sociometric procedure used to study informal group membership. What can the results of a sociometric analysis tell managers about members of an informal group?

16. Explain Homans's concept of how informal groups develop.

17. List and define the primary factors that influence work group effectiveness.

18. What is the relationship among formal groups, informal groups, and work group effectiveness?

19. Define corporate culture. Can managers actually build corporate culture? Explain.

Building on What You Know

Directions

Review the Highlight feature as indicated below and answer its corresponding questions. Questions in this section focus on relating a Highlight appearing in this chapter to management concepts that you have learned in a previous chapter.

Review the Ethics Highlight: Calvary Hospital on page 485. In chapter 15 you studied several theories that relate to how managers can provide a motivating work situation for organization members. Considering the situation presented in this Highlight, what human needs might employees be fulfilling by serving on the ethics committee of a hospital? Explain. Would you agree that having an organization member serve on an ethics committee could be a tactic that a manager could use to enrich that person's job? Why? Which of Likert's management systems would probably be most characterized by an ethics committee? Explain.

Action Summary Answer Key

1. a. F, p. 481
   b. c, p. 481
2. a. F, p. 491
   b. F, p. 482
3. a. d, p. 483
   b. e, pp. 486–488
4. a. F, p. 493
   b. b, p. 493
5. a. a, p. 496
   b. T, p. 494
6. a. F, p. 501
   b. d, pp. 501–504

Case Study

The Changing Corporate Culture at Apple Computer

by Leslie Toombs, University of Texas at Tyler, and Leslie Brunetta

Apple Computer, Inc., was one of the great American success stories of the 1980s. Started in a California garage by Steve Jobs and Steve Wozniak, two electronics whiz kids in their early twenties, Apple's mission was to bring computer power to the people. It succeeded. Before Apple, only large companies and well-funded research labs could afford the capital and space to enter the computer age; afterward, personal computers proliferated on millions of desks across the country, in dorm rooms and homes, as well as in offices.

More than just products made Apple revolutionary. At a time when most of corporate America saw Japan's highly disciplined work force undercutting the economic superiority of the United States, Apple achieved global success not in spite of but, it seemed, because of a chaotic corporate culture with its roots in New Age philosophy and Wild West fun. Apple personnel were known for risk taking, informality, outspokenness, team spirit, and a hatred for traditional corporate hierarchies. The corporate headquarters was manic. Phones rang off the hook. Rock music was heard everywhere. Employees at all corporate levels were treated to stress-relief massages. Friday afternoon keg parties featured entertainment such as Huey Lewis or Ella Fitzgerald—live.

Despite appearances, it wasn't all play at Apple—or rather, as Apple employees put it, there was plenty of work, but the work was so exciting, it felt like play. They were known for being zealously committed to Apple's mission, and they tried any method—no matter how unconventional—to advance that mission. Debates about product ideas, about sales figures, about who was meeting for lunch, and about every other aspect of Apple operations raged on a computer mail system open to everybody. Anyone in the company who had an idea could look anywhere in the company for support to get it rolling; there was no need to go up the chain of command—such as it was—for approval.

What made the work so exciting was success. Apple was recognized worldwide as one of the most technologically advanced companies of any kind. Profits soared. By 1984, Apple had gotten too big for Steve Jobs to handle alone (Steve Wozniak had already retired). Moreover, Jobs realized that Apple would soon need a leader with experience managing a mature company in an increasingly competitive market. He recruited John Sculley, a 44-year-old top executive at PepsiCo with a reputation as a marketing genius and a crack manager.

Sculley joined Apple and adopted all aspects of its corporate culture with the vengeance of a new convert. However, by 1984, IBM had already begun to take over the business market for PCs, cutting into Apple's profits and reputation. Apple launched the user-friendly Macintosh in an effort to reclaim the market but failed: Software incompatibilities and a relative lack of power compared to the

IBM PC caused many buyers to reject what was still in many ways a ground-breaking piece of equipment. Added to these problems was the economic recession of 1985, and Apple was suddenly in big trouble. Rifts developed between Jobs and Sculley. Nearly twenty percent of Apple's work force was laid off. In a move that shocked most industry analysts, Sculley ousted Jobs in 1985.

For a few years, Sculley reorganized Apple's structure, hired new top executives, and redirected marketing objectives. Nonetheless, he made a big point of preserving Apple's famous corporate culture. This formula seemed to work; Apple forged what many analysts deemed a remarkable comeback. Yearly sales almost doubled. However, by the late 1980s, Apple faced big problems again, encountering increased competition in all of its markets. Market shares, earnings, and stock prices all slid. Sculley decided it was time to instill a new sense of purpose and discipline in Apple employees.

Many Apple employees felt that Sculley threatened to destroy the very corporate culture that had made the company successful. They complained that the shuffling of top managers and marketing strategies left them with a confused sense of direction. A few top executives with devoted followings were fired, causing further resentment. Unlike the good old days, employees said, there was now a wide chasm between the upper echelons of management and the rank-and-file. While Sculley was laying off lower-level employees, he paid departing top executives multimillion-dollar severance packages.

Both outside analysts and people inside Apple debated whether the Apple culture had truly changed and, if so, how the change would affect the company's fortunes. Some argued that Apple needed to mature and that Sculley was in fact heading in the right direction. Others argued that Apple's past successes had rested as much on its iconoclastic image as on the specific features of its products, and that sales would suffer if the image were tarnished. Only Apple's future sales and profit figures will show who was right.

Discussion Questions

1. Based on the case, how would you describe the set of beliefs that characterize Apple's corporate culture under Jobs and Wozniak?

2. What new beliefs and values do you think Sculley has created with his changes at Apple?

3. Based on the case, how important do you think Apple's corporate culture is to its employees? Why?

4. How do you think the role models offered by Steve Jobs and John Sculley are similar? How are they different?

Kay Unger of the Gillian Group

Kay Unger perceives herself as a group member; as a woman, as a designer, as an entrepreneur, as a family member, her life is in many ways defined by the groups of which she feels herself a part. In 1972, she and partner John Levy founded a fashion design and merchandising concern called "St. Gillian." During the 1980s, Unger changed the corporate name to the Gillian Group. That change reflects a great deal of Unger's view of her work and of her coworkers.

In the first year, St. Gillian's corporate revenues totaled $1.2 million. By 1990, corporate revenues topped $125 million. During a period when recession caused problems throughout the fashion industry, the Gillian Group grew and prospered. During that same time, many small design firms appeared and disappeared, just as hemlines rose and fell. The fashions acceptable to American women, and in particular to American working women, were undergoing tremendous upheaval.

Women had finally made inroads into corporate boardrooms and were unwilling to "dress for success" in pinstripe suits, plain white blouses, and foulard ties any longer. Designs from the haute couture houses of Paris and New York did not suit a working woman's life-style, nor did the extremes they represented, replete with transparent fabrics, layers of frills, or very short skirts. The newest and most chic designs from Milan and Tokyo were equally unsuitable.

Enter Kay Unger. "I know what women who work need. I know the comfort level," she says of her clientele, because "I'm one of *her*. I know who *she* is." That knowledge of her market led Unger to create the sort of clothing working women demanded while other designers were scrambling to adapt to the notion that real clothes could not afford to take their cue from haute couture any longer. Unger's designs have made the Gillian Group one of the forty largest women-owned businesses in the United States. Membership in the club of working women was a key to Gillian's success.

Unger sees another difference, too, in the way working women interact with their coworkers:

> They approach business and get the job done in the same way [as men]; it's their approach to people, I think, that's different. . . . They're really great listeners—I think it's a female thing—and they're extremely organized. Perhaps it's from organizing homes or maybe it's something that's been ingrained in women from times past, but there is a sense of organization that's different. And there are no rules.

Operating outside the bounds of strict policies and rules is also, Unger believes, a common characteristic of entrepreneurs. Unlike businesspeople who work in traditional roles, such as Unger's investment-banker father, she feels that entrepreneurs are more flexible in the routes they chart to success. This helps them to avoid the internal politics and rivalry that many ambitious businesspeople on the rise encounter in established organizational environments. In Unger's opinion, the desire for independence, rather than a specific corporate goal, is key to this group:

"We kind of 'wing it,' do it from the hip, as they say. . . . We each make our own set of rules."

At the Gillian Group, the rules in the design area have been made by Kay Unger. Every two weeks, the designers meet to establish a new "color story"—that is, a block of related or integrated colors that form the core of the new set of clothing designs to be created. After the colors are chosen, the design group breaks into smaller teams centered around designers—Kay Unger herself is the chief designer of the Gillian Group. Those teams are made up of designers, drapers, seamstresses, and models on whom the garments are tried; staff from other areas of the company, such as purchasing and marketing, may also be consulted at this stage. Specific fabrics are chosen that conform to the color story, and the silhouettes—the general shapes of the clothes—are established. Finally, with creative input from the entire group, specific designs are sketched, and prototypes are created.

Kay Unger's employees work in a creative environment, where they are encouraged to express their creativity and explore their talents. On the other hand, when employees don't work out for the Gillian Group, Unger does not hesitate to fire them. John Levy describes her as "sincere, demanding, and tough"; she demands a great deal from herself, and the people working for her learn to follow her example. Her criteria are clear: Do the best work you can, and give extra time and effort. Most important, be flexible in the face of a business that never slows down. To be a success in Kay Unger's world, employees must agree with her when she says, "I love chaos."

Video Case Questions

1. Are design teams at the Gillian Group formal or informal groups? What specific type?
2. Give an example of how groupthink affects sales in the fashion industry. Give an example of how it might negatively affect design at a fashion house such as the Gillian Group.
3. Based on the case, name three mechanisms you believe Kay Unger uses to reinforce the corporate culture at the Gillian Group.
4. Which group would you expect to use more status symbols at Gillian—production, design, or corporate management? Why?

Video Case Activities

1. Using Table 15.2 as a model, prepare a list of examples of positive and negative norms for the following groups of employees at the Gillian Group: clothing models, telephone receptionists, dress designers, and fabric buyers.
2. Consider Homan's concept of how informal groups evolve. Now write a brief description of an informal group that might evolve in the design area at the Gillian Group. Based on your own example, how should management treat this informal group?

PART 4

INTEGRATIVE CASE

*The Navajo Arts and Crafts Enterprise:
Bringing Together Culture and Business*

by Robert E. Kemper, Northern Arizona University

The 1990 U.S. Census lists more than 100,000 Native American Indians living on the 25,000 square mile continuous Navajo reservation that covers parts of Arizona, New Mexico, and Utah, and on the three checkerboard-patterned reservations in northern New Mexico. According to tribal custom, the Navajo people are tied together by *matrilineal clans,* extended family groups linked through the mothers. Women remain the official heads of more than a quarter of Navajo households.

The people feel strong ties to their land; more than eighty percent have always lived on the reservation. However, reservation life is hard: Winters are long and bitter, distances are vast, and water is always in short supply. About fifty percent of reservation homes don't have piped-in water; only twenty-five percent have central heat. At twenty-five years of age or older, two thirds of Navajos are not high school graduates. More than half live below the U.S. poverty line, and unemployment is very high.

Although all U.S. citizens are subject to federal law, Navajos on the reservations are not subject to state laws. The Navajo nation is administered by an elected President and Navajo Tribal Council, with its capital in Window Rock, Arizona. Traditionally, there has been little need for formal government structures; the culture strictly defines appropriate behaviors. Respect for the harmony of living things with each other and their environment are paramount, and respectful, polite behavior is the norm. A Navajo who is ill can be brought back into harmony through traditional healing procedures, although bodily illness is treated by medical methods as well. In government as in medicine, traditions and the new ways have been integrated—not always with success.

The Navajo Arts and Crafts Enterprise (NACE) and the Window Rock Inn are the only corporations to maintain profitable operation under tribal management. The NACE store in Window Rock displays excellent artworks of weaving, silverwork, basketry, woodwork, and paintings that are in demand worldwide. NACE's goal is to further the educational, social, and economic development of the people through development and marketing of traditional tribal arts and crafts. It is administered by a board of directors appointed by the Tribal Council; a general manager is hired by the board. During the late 1970s and early 1980s, the Tribal Council employed consultants from Arthur Andersen to advise NACE and general manager Raymond Smith about personnel and financial practices, to maximize profitability.

Smith had been a member of the famed "Navajo Code Talkers" of World War II and had served on the Tribal Council for twenty years prior to taking the NACE job. He was well liked by employees and well respected among the Navajo people. Following Arthur Andersen's evaluation of NACE, Smith and his staff were trained in the use of appropriate personal computer accounting systems.

Personnel management systems were not so simple, however. Arthur Andersen produced an eighty-page personnel manual, covering every item from hiring and firing to the use of nonexistent corporate credit cards and vehicles. The manual was a generic one, not customized to meet NACE's very specific needs. Nonetheless, Smith adhered to the policies for day-to-day operations, and when he found fault with a particular policy—for example, a sick-leave procedure that did not allow for traditional healing ceremonies—he would ignore it. Generally, his slighting of procedure favored his employees.

However, in the summer of 1986, in accordance with NACE bylaws, Smith refused to purchase some handicrafts from a board member. The board retaliated: Rather than issue Smith's new employment contract scheduled to begin in October, his old contract was extended for a period of ninety days only. During that ninety-day period, Smith was to use his best efforts to achieve the following objectives: (1) to prepare revised employee personnel policies, focusing specifically on leave policies; (2) to prepare written employee evaluations, discuss them with the employees, and submit them to the board; and (3) to develop a written plan for NACE operations, including memoranda setting forth different types of decisions confronting NACE and recommendations for the level at which approval should be made.

Smith met with a local attorney to discuss NACE's difficulties and the board's action. They agreed that the problems concerning personnel procedures and evaluations appeared to stem from the generic Arthur Andersen manual. NACE needed clearly defined policies that could be applied universally, not ignored, but that would be appropriate and fair based on Navajo cultural expectations. The sick-leave policy must incorporate a time allowance for healing ceremonies, for example; appraisal and penalization policies must be modified to work in light of the Navajo's traditional aversion toward confrontation as disrespectful and impolite. In short, the generic personnel policies would only work within the culture for which they were designed. NACE, and all tribal-managed businesses, would need Navajo personnel policies in order to succeed.

Discussion Questions

1. A major goal of tribally administered businesses on the Navajo reservations is employment of Navajos. Given this goal, do you think a store like NACE's run by the tribe should be run differently than an arts and crafts store somewhere else, such as Phoenix?

2. Do you think Raymond Smith acted appropriately in suspending written sick-leave policies to allow those employees who desire it time for traditional healing ceremonies (generally a few days)? Was this the act of a leader or a manager? How might you have handled the situation differently?

3. It is considered rude, a sort of imposition, among the Navajo to touch a stranger. Imagine you are an Arthur Andersen consultant visiting NACE for the first time, and you immediately shake hands with each employee you meet. What impact do you think this might have on your work there?

4. Consider the following motivating strategies: promotion from within, salary bonuses, flextime options, and inclusion in an employee advisory group. Which do you think would work well for NACE employees? Which would not?

The Westinghouse Commercial Nuclear Fuel Division won the Malcolm Baldrige award in 1988 in the manufacturing division. At CNFD, workers and top management directly address quality improvement opportunities and help devise initiatives through their participation in project-oriented teams. About 90% of all workers have undergone quality awareness or quality-related training during the past three years.

Controlling

The purpose of this section is to introduce controlling, the fourth and last major management function. The previous three sections showed that managers must be able to plan, organize, and influence organizational variables. This section will explain that managers must also control these variables in order for their organizations to achieve long-term success. In general, the section will discuss the principles of controlling, the fundamentals of production management and control, and how information relates to the control function.

The discussion of the principles of controlling will open with a definition of *control function*. It will then present the three main steps in controlling and discuss the three main types of control. In addition, it will address the job of a controller and the elements necessary for managers to successfully perform the control function.

Production is an area that requires careful control. Therefore, the discussion of the fundamentals of production management and control will emphasize operations management, productivity, and control tools that relate directly to production control. These tools include management by exception, breakeven analysis, materials requirements planning, and quality control. Quality is discussed from the viewpoints of enhancing productivity and maintaining product excellence.

Lastly, the section will explain how information relates to the control function, what factors influence the value of information, and how managers can use computers for generating and analyzing information. It will also discuss two information-related systems: the management information system (MIS) and the management decision support system (MDSS).

As you study the new material presented in this section, think about how the other functions of management relate to the process of controlling. Once you understand this last major function, you should have a thorough knowledge of how controlling must interact with planning, organizing, and influencing if organizations are to achieve long-term success.

Chapter 17

*S*tudent Learning Objectives

From studying this chapter, I will attempt to acquire:

1. A definition of *control*.

2. A thorough understanding of the controlling subsystem.

3. An appreciation for various kinds of control and for how each kind can be used advantageously by managers.

4. Insights on the relationship between power and control.

5. Knowledge of the various potential barriers that must be overcome for successful control.

6. An understanding of steps that can be taken to increase the quality of a controlling subsystem.

Principles of Controlling

Chapter Outline

CONTROLLING EFFORTS AT BORDEN INC.

Borden Inc., a major food processing company, had to close a portion of its Orlando milk-processing plant several years ago. When operating at full capacity, the plant had employed about 250 workers. The closing of the plant was part of a nationwide effort by Borden to improve its profitability.

"We notified employees that the Orlando processing operation would be consolidated into our Tampa dairy," said Nicholas Iammartino, a spokesman at the company's New York headquarters, in an explanation that the Orlando milk-processing operation would be shut down and the plan that the Tampa dairy operation would make up the lost production.

According to Borden's plan, about 71 of the estimated 250 employees at the Orlando facility would lose their jobs within the next few months as the operation began phasing out. The remaining employees, about 180 people involved in ice cream production, were expected to continue working pending the sale of the facility. Plans called for selling the facility as a going concern.

Borden's plan also called for the selling of fourteen dairy-processing plants in several other states including Ohio, New York, New Mexico, Michigan, Indiana, Kentucky, Georgia, and Wisconsin. In total, such moves enabled Borden to cut its work force from about 46,000 to 39,000 and lower its costs by about $340 million through the mid-1990s.

The milk-processing business is a very tough business to be in.

The milk-processing business is a very tough business to be in. In states like Florida, not enough milk is produced within the state to satisfy milk demand. As a result, some companies have to truck milk into the state, process the milk, and then distribute it to stores.

The extra cost of shipping milk into the state has to be passed on to the consumer, and that puts the price of the milk at a higher price than competitors, who can get all their preprocessed milk within the state. In addition, farmers raise milk prices because of higher grain costs whenever there is dry weather. It is very difficult for milk processors to pass such costs on to the stores because milk retailers often choose to sell milk at a loss in order to attract customers to buy other products.

From Jerry Jackson, "Borden Cuts Back in Orlando," *The Orlando Sentinel* (October 19, 1989), D1.

FUNDAMENTALS OF CONTROLLING

As the scale and complexity of modern work organizations grow, the problem of control in organizations gains in significance.[1] Prospective managers need a working knowledge of the essentials of the controlling function.[2] To this end, the following sections provide a definition of control, a definition of controlling, and a discussion of the various types of control that can be used in organizations.

Defining Control

Stated simply, **control** is making something happen the way it was planned to happen.[3] As implied in this definition, planning and control are virtually inseparable.[4] In fact, the two have been called the Siamese twins of management.[5] According to Robert L. Dewelt:

> The importance of the planning process is quite obvious. Unless we have a soundly charted course of action, we will never quite know what actions are necessary to meet our objectives. We need a map to identify the timing and scope of all intended actions. This map is provided through the planning process.
>
> But simply making a map is not enough. If we don't follow it or if we make a wrong turn along the way, chances are we will never achieve the desired results. A plan is only as good as our ability to make it happen. We must develop methods of measurement and control to signal when deviations from the plan are occurring so that corrective action can be taken.[6]

Over all, managers should continually control, check to make sure that organizational activities and processes are going as planned. Murphy's Law is a lighthearted concept that makes the serious point that managers should continually control. According to **Murphy's Law,** anything that can go wrong will go wrong.[7] This law implies that managers must continually be alert for possible problems within the management system. Even if a management system is operating well one day, the system might erode somewhat over time. Managers must constantly seek feedback that indicates the level at which a system is performing and make corrective changes in the system when they become necessary.

Control is making something happen the way it was planned to happen.

Murphy's Law is a lighthearted observation about organizations indicating that anything that can go wrong will go wrong.

Defining Controlling

Controlling is the process the manager goes through to control.

Controlling is the process managers go through to control. According to Robert Mockler, controlling is

> a systematic effort by business management to compare performance to predetermined standards, plans, or objectives to determine whether performance is in line with these standards and presumably to take any remedial action required to see that human and other corporate resources are being used in the most effective and efficient way possible in achieving corporate objectives.[8]

For example, production workers generally have production goals they must achieve per day and week. At the end of each working day, the number of units produced by each worker is recorded so weekly production levels can be determined. If the weekly totals are significantly below the weekly goals, the supervisor must take action to ensure that actual production levels are equivalent to planned production levels. If production goals are met, the supervisor probably should allow work to continue as it has in the past.

The following sections discuss the controlling subsystem and provide more details about the control process itself.

 ## *B*ack to the *Case*

Borden's activities in this case should be categorized as control. In essence, control is making things happen at Borden the way they were planned to happen. In this case, because profits were not reaching planned levels, management was taking action such as closing milk-processing plants. This action was aimed at ensuring that profits achieved in the future are more in line with planned profit levels. In essence, Borden's control has to be closely related to its planning activities.

Controlling at Borden is the steps or process that management takes in order to control. Ideally, this process at Borden includes a determination of plans, standards, and objectives for milk processing as well as other activities at Borden so that action can be taken to eliminate organizational characteristics that caused deviations from these factors.

The Controlling Subsystem

As with the planning, organizing, and influencing functions described in earlier chapters, controlling can be viewed as a subsystem that is part of the overall management system. The purpose of the controlling subsystem is to help managers enhance the success of the overall management system through effective controlling. Figure 17.1 shows the specific ingredients of the controlling subsystem.

The Controlling Process

As the process (controlling process) segment of Figure 17.2 on page 522 implies, the three main steps of the controlling process are (1) measuring performance, (2) comparing measured performance to standards, and (3) taking corrective action.

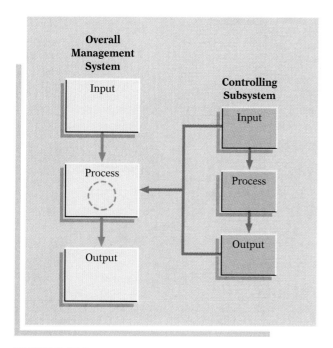

FIGURE 17.1

Relationship between overall management system and controlling subsystem

Measuring Performance. Before managers can determine what must be done to make an organization more effective and efficient, they must measure current organizational performance. And before such a measurement can be taken, some unit of measure that gauges performance must be established and the quantity of this unit generated by the item whose performance is being measured must be observed.

For example, a manager who wants to measure the performance of five janitors first has to establish units of measure that represent janitorial performance, such as the number of floors swept, the number of windows washed, or the number of light bulbs changed. After designating these units of measures for janitorial performance, the manager then has to determine the number of each of these units associated with each janitor. This process of determining the units of measure and the number of units per janitor furnishes the manager with a measure of janitorial performance.

Managers also must keep in mind that a wide range of organizational activities can be measured as part of the control process. For example, the amounts and types of inventory kept on hand are commonly measured to control inventory, and the quality of goods and services being produced is commonly measured to control product quality. Performance measurements also can relate to various effects of production, such as the degree to which a particular manufacturing process pollutes the atmosphere.

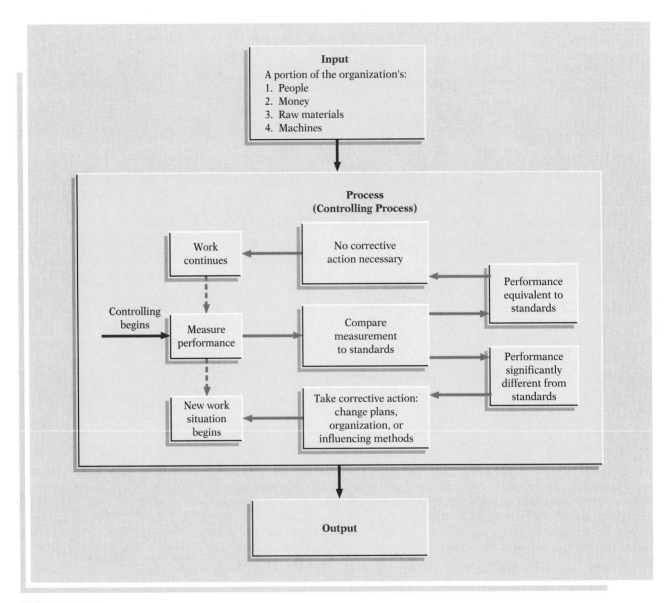

FIGURE 17.2
The controlling subsystem

As one might suspect, the degree of difficulty in measuring various types of organizational performance is determined primarily by the activity being measured. For example, the degree of difficulty in measuring the performance of a highway maintenance worker would differ greatly from the degree of difficulty in measuring the performance of a student enrolled in a college-level management course.[9]

Global Highlight: Controlling Finances at Euro Disneyland

One area in which performance measurements are commonly taken involves the financial affairs of an organization. Certified public accountant Judson Green left the Arthur Young accounting firm to join Walt Disney World in Florida. Today, Green is a senior vice president at Disney and working on the Euro Disneyland project now under construction outside Paris. The French government has extended unprecedented hospitality to Euro Disneyland by offering favorable land deals, tax breaks, and loans with advantageous payback provisions. In addition, decisions that affect the financial affairs of Euro Disney are commonly made by Green in conjunction with people in cities like London and Brussels. In the near future, Disney's focus will shift to developing hotels outside the theme park as well as planning and initiating the building of a second theme park in Europe. A major responsibility of Green's is to monitor or measure the effects of various financial decisions being made for Euro Disney. From such measurements he will encourage company actions that meet or exceed profitability standards while discouraging such actions that do not meet or are below the standards. In essence, Green is responsible for controlling financial activities at Euro Disney.

Comparing Measured Performance to Standards. Once managers have taken a measure of organizational performance, their next step in controlling is to compare this measure against some standard. A **standard** is the level of activity established to serve as a model for evaluating organizational performance. In essence, standards are the yardsticks that determine if organizational performance is adequate or inadequate.[10] Studying operations at General Electric gives insight into the different kinds of standards managers can establish, such as the following:

> A **standard** is the level of activity established to serve as a model for evaluating organizational performance.

1. *Profitability standards.* In general, these standards indicate how much money General Electric would like to make as profit over a given time period—that is, its return on investment. More and more General Electric is using computerized preventative maintenance on its equipment to help maintain profitability standards. Such maintenance programs at General Electric help to reduce labor costs and equipment downtime and thereby help to raise company profits.[11]

2. *Market position standards.* These standards indicate the share of total sales in a particular market that General Electric would like to have relative to its competitors. As an indication of market position standards at General Electric, John F. Welch, Jr., company chairman, announced in 1988 that any product his company offers must have the highest or second highest market share when compared against all products offered by competitors.[12]

3. *Productivity standards.* How much various segments of the organization should produce is the focus of these standards. Management at General Electric has found that one of the most successful methods of convincing organization members to be committed to increasing company productivity is simply to treat them with dignity and make them feel they are part of the General Electric team.[13]

4. *Product leadership standards.* General Electric would like to assume one of the lead positions in its field in product innovation. Product leadership standards indicate what must be done to attain such a position. Reflecting this interest in innovation, General Electric has been a pioneer in developing synthetic diamonds for industrial use. In fact, General Electric is considered by most a leader in this area, having recently found a method for making synthetic diamonds at a purity of 99.9 percent. In all probability, such diamonds will eventually be used as a component of super-high-speed computers.[14]

5. *Personnel development standards.* Standards in this area indicate the type of training programs to which General Electric personnel should be exposed to develop appropriately. General Electric's commitment to sophisticated training technology is an indication of the seriousness with which the company pursues personnel development standards. Company training sessions are commonly supported by sophisticated technology like large-screen projection systems, computer-generated visual aids, combined video and computer presentations, and laser videos.[15]

6. *Employee attitudes standards.* These standards indicate the types of attitudes that General Electric management should strive to develop in its employees. Building attitudes in employees toward enhancing product quality reflects a modern employee attitude standard that General Electric and many other companies are presently striving to achieve.[16]

7. *Social responsibility standards.* General Electric recognizes its responsibility to make a contribution to society. Standards in this area outline the level and types of contributions that should be made. One recent activity at General Electric that reflects social responsibility standards is a renovation of San Diego's Vincent de Paul Joan Kroc center for the homeless. Work teams made up of General Electric employees painted, cleaned, and remodeled a building to create a better facility for a number of San Diego's disadvantaged citizens.[17]

8. *Standards reflecting relative balance between short- and long-range goals.* General Electric recognizes that short-range goals exist to enhance the probability that long-range goals will be attained. These standards express the relative emphasis that should be placed on attaining various short- and long-range goals.[18]

American Airlines has set two very specific standards for appropriate performance of airport ticket offices: (1) at least 95 percent of the flight arrival times posted should be accurate in that actual arrival times do not deviate more than fifteen minutes from posted times, and (2) at least 85 percent of the customers coming to the airport ticket counter do not wait more than five minutes to be serviced. As a general guideline, successful managers pinpoint all important areas of organizational performance and establish corresponding standards in each area.

ℬack to the Case

In theory, Borden's management views controlling activities within the company as a subsystem of the organization's overall management system. For management to achieve organizational control, Borden's controlling subsystem requires a portion of the people, money, raw materials, and machines available within the company.

The process portion of the controlling subsystem at Borden involves management's taking three steps: (1) measuring the performance levels of various productive units, (2) comparing these performance levels to predetermined performance standards for these units, and (3) taking any corrective action necessary to make the planned performance levels consistent with actual performance levels.

Based upon information in the introductory case, areas in which management has developed standards at Borden include a desired profitability level of various milk-processing plants and the availability of preprocessed milk needed to achieve this profit. Because the Orlando plant and other plants throughout the country weren't achieving planned profit levels, or didn't have enough preprocessed milk available within the state in which they operated, management controlled by taking steps to eliminate the plants.

Taking Corrective Action. Once managers have measured actual performance and compared this performance with established performance standards, they should take corrective action if necessary. **Corrective action** is managerial activity aimed at bringing organizational performance up to the level of performance standards. In other words, corrective action focuses on correcting the mistakes in the organization that are hindering organizational performance. Before taking any corrective action, however, managers should make sure that the standards being used were properly established and that the measurements of organizational performance are valid and reliable.

At first glance, it seems fairly simple to state that managers should take corrective action to eliminate **problems**—factors within organizations that are barriers to organizational goal attainment. In practice, however, it may be difficult to pinpoint the problem causing some undesirable organizational effect. For example, a performance measurement may indicate that a certain worker is not adequately passing on critical information to fellow workers. If the manager is satisfied that the communication standards are appropriate and that the performance measurement information is valid and reliable, correction action should be taken to eliminate the problem causing this substandard performance.

However, what exactly is the problem causing substandard communication? Is it that the individual is not communicating because he or she doesn't want to communicate? Or is the person not communicating because the job makes communication difficult? Does the person have the training needed to enable him

Corrective action is managerial activity aimed at bringing organizational performance up to the level of performance standards.

Problems are factors within organizations that are barriers to organizational goal attainment.

A **symptom** is a sign that a problem exists.

or her to communicate in an appropriate manner? The manager must determine whether the individual's lack of communication is a problem in itself or a **symptom**—a sign that a problem exists.[19] For example, the individual's lack of communication could be a symptom of inappropriate job design or a cumbersome organizational structure.

Once an organizational problem has been identified, necessary corrective action can focus on one or more of the three primary management functions of planning, organizing, and influencing. Correspondingly, corrective action can include such activities as modifying past plans to make them more suitable for future organizational endeavors, making an existing organizational structure more suitable for existing plans and objectives, or restructuring an incentive program to make sure that high producers are rewarded more than low producers. In addition, because planning, organizing, and influencing are closely related, there is a good chance that corrective action taken in one area will necessitate some corresponding change in one or both of the other two areas.

A study by Y.K. Shetty surveyed 171 managers from *Fortune's* list of the thirteen hundred largest U.S. industrial and nonindustrial companies.[20] One purpose of the study was to investigate the types of corrective action programs managers use and the frequency with which they are used. Table 17.1 presents the results of this study. The corrective action programs listed in the table are only a sample of such programs, not an exhaustive list.

Quality Highlight: Modern of Marshfield Inc. Capitalizes on CATS

Managers commonly face situations in which they must take corrective actions to improve organizational performance. Although sometimes managers may need to take the corrective action themselves, in some situations, it may be more advantageous or simply necessary to have other organization members take the action, either individually or as a group. For example, William J. Mork, president of Modern of Marshfield Inc. (a custom sofa-sleeper manufacturer in Marshfield, Wisconsin), successfully takes corrective action through groups of organization members. Mork credits 80 to 90 percent of the company's $6 million profits to the impact made by its twelve Corrective Action Teams (CATS). In essence, CATS are small control groups within the company. The groups monitor organizational performance in many different areas and implement corrective action aimed at solving identified organizational problems. A small group of organization members called a Quality Improvement Team oversees and coordinates the efforts of CATS. Mork believes that the success of CATS has had many beneficial effects on the organization, for example: (1) the company has been financially able to pay each employee a bonus, (2) the company has been able to make payments out of profits to debtors and thereby significantly reduce company debt, and (3) company profits have resulted in more cash on hand that the company could use to finance everyday operations. Over all, because Mork believes that having groups take corrective action within his company has contributed significantly to recent organizational success, he will probably continue with his CATS program in the future.

TABLE 17.1 Corrective action programs commonly used by managers
and frequency of use

Corrective Action Program	Frequency of Program Use
Cost reduction	2.3
Employee participation	3.1
Productivity incentives	3.3
Goal setting with productivity focus	3.5
Increased automation	3.8
Quality improvement	3.9
Increased employee training	4.7
Better labor-management relations	4.9
Increased research and development	5.3

Note: The lower the frequency, the higher the relative use of the program.

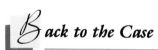

Back to the Case

In determining that corrective action was necessary at Borden, management had to be certain that the action was aimed at organizational problems rather than at symptoms of problems. For example, if too much overhead as a result of having too many milk-processing plants open were the real problem, then the symptom of low profit levels eventually would disappear as a result of the corrective action of closing unneeded milk-processing plants.

Inevitably, corrective action at Borden such as closing milk-processing plants must focus on past planning, organizing, or influencing efforts. How must Borden's plans change now that the Orlando plant has been phased out, or would Borden still need the same number of regional managers in its organization structure even though there are fewer milk-processing plants?

Types of Control

There are three types of management control: (1) precontrol, (2) concurrent control, and (3) feedback control. The type is determined primarily by the time period in which the control is emphasized in relation to the work being performed.

Precontrol

Control that takes place before work is performed is called **precontrol**, or feedforward control.[21] In this regard, management creates policies, procedures, and rules aimed at eliminating behavior that will cause undesirable work results. For example, the manager of a small record shop may find that a major factor in developing return customers is having salespeople discuss various records with

Precontrol is control that takes place before some unit of work is actually performed.

customers. This manager might use precontrol by establishing a rule that salespeople cannot talk to one another while a customer is in the store. This rule is a precontrol because it is aimed at eliminating anticipated problems with salespeople before the salespeople are faced with a customer. Precontrol focuses on eliminating predicted problems.

Concurrent Control

Concurrent control is control that takes place as some unit of work is being performed.

Control that takes place as work is being performed is called **concurrent control.** It relates not only to human performance but also to such areas as equipment performance and department appearance. For example, most supermarkets have rigid rules about the amount of stock that should be placed on the selling floor. In general, these stores want to display generous amounts of all products on the shelves, with no empty spaces. A concurrent control aimed at ensuring that shelves are stocked as planned could be a stock manager's making periodic visual checks throughout a work period to evaluate the status of the sales shelves and, correspondingly, the performance of the stock crew.

Feedback Control

Feedback control is control that takes place after some unit of work has been performed.

Control that concentrates on past organizational performance is called **feedback control.** Managers exercising this type of control are attempting to take corrective action within the organization by looking at organizational history over a specified time period. This history may concentrate on only one factor, such as inventory levels, or on the relationships among many factors, such as net income before taxes, sales volume, and marketing costs.

Figure 17.3 is an example of a report, developed for an oil company, that can serve as the basis for feedback control. This particular report contains graphs that show various trends over a number of years as well as handwritten notes that highlight major trends. Management would use this report to compare actual organizational performance with planned organizational performance and then to take whatever corrective action is necessary to bring together actual and planned performance. Of course, the structure of such reports varies from organization to organization, depending on the various types and forms of information needed to present an overview of specific organizational activities.

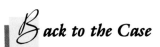

Back to the Case

In controlling Borden, management should use an appropriate combination of precontrol, concurrent control, and feedback control. Precontrol would emphasize the elimination of the factors at Borden that could cause poor annual profitability of milk-processing plants before the year actually begins. Through concurrent control, management would be able to assess the profitability of milk-processing plants at Borden during a particular operation period. Finally, feedback control at

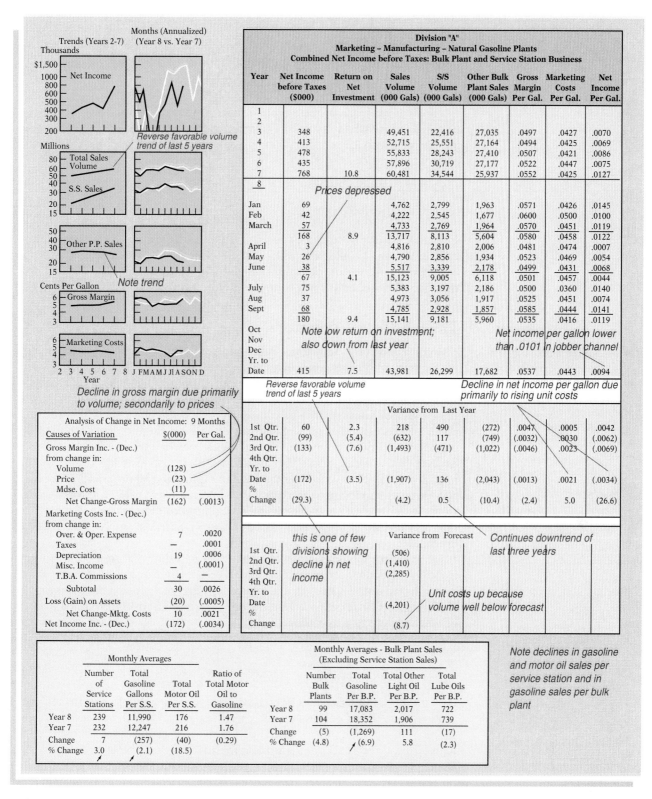

FIGURE 17.3

Example of a report that can serve as the basis for feedback control

Borden would enable management to control at the end of some operating period. In essence, management would improve future performance by analyzing the history of Borden.

Some use of each of these types of control would increase the probability of eliminating profitability problems before those problems become too overwhelming. Borden management must not make the mistake of emphasizing feedback control to the exclusion of concurrent control and precontrol.

THE CONTROLLER AND CONTROL

Organization charts developed for medium- and large-sized companies typically contain a position called controller. The sections that follow explain more about controllers and their relationship to the control function by discussing the job of the controller and how much control is needed within an organization.

The Job of the Controller

The **controller** is the staff individual whose basic responsibility is assisting line managers with the controlling function by gathering appropriate information and generating necessary reports that reflect this information.

The **controller** (also sometimes called the comptroller) is usually a staff person who gathers information that helps managers control. From the preceding discussion, it is clear that managers have the responsibility of comparing planned and actual performance and of taking corrective action when necessary. In smaller organizations, managers may be completely responsible for gathering information about various aspects of the organization and developing necessary reports based on this information. In medium- or large-sized companies, however, the controller handles much of this work. The controller's basic responsibility is assisting line managers with the controlling function by gathering appropriate information and generating reports that reflect this information.[22] The controller usually works with information about the following financial dimensions of the organization: (1) profits, (2) revenues, (3) costs, (4) investments, and (5) discretionary expenses.[23]

The sample job description of a controller in Table 17.2 shows that the controller is responsible for generating information on which a manager can base the exercising of control. Because the controller generally is not directly responsible for taking corrective action within the organization but instead advises a manager of what corrective action should be taken, the controller position is primarily a staff position.

How Much Control Is Needed?

Cost-benefit analysis is the process of comparing the cost of some activity to the benefit or revenue that results from the activity to determine the total worth of the activity to the organization.

As with all organizational endeavors, control activities should be pursued if the expected benefits of performing such activities are greater than the costs of performing them.[24] The process of comparing the cost of any organizational activity with the expected benefit of performing the activity is called **cost-benefit analysis.** In general, managers and controllers should collaborate to determine exactly how much controlling is justified in a given situation.

Figure 17.4 on page 532 shows controlling activity over an extended period of time. According to this figure, controlling costs increase steadily as more and more controlling activities are performed. In addition, because the controlling function requires start-up costs, controlling costs at first usually are greater than

---

TABLE 17.2 Sample job description for a controller in a large company

---

Objectives

The controller (or comptroller) is responsible for all accounting activities within the organization.

Functions

1. *General accounting.* Maintain the company's accounting books, accounting records, and forms. This includes:
   a. Preparing balance sheets, income statements, and other statements and reports.
   b. Giving the president interim reports on operations for the recent quarter and fiscal year to date.
   c. Supervising the preparation and filing of reports to the SEC.
2. *Budgeting.* Prepare a budget outlining the company's future operations and cash requirements.
3. *Cost accounting.* Determine the cost to manufacture a product and prepare internal reports to management of the processing divisions. This includes:
   a. Developing standard costs.
   b. Accumulating actual cost data.
   c. Preparing reports that compare standard costs to actual costs and highlight unfavorable differences.
4. *Performance reporting.* Identify individuals in the organization who control activities and prepare reports to show how well or how poorly they perform.
5. *Data processing.* Assist in the analysis and design of a computer-based information system. Frequently, the data processing department is under the controller, and the controller is involved in management of that department as well as other communications equipment.
6. *Other duties.* Other duties may be assigned to the controller by the president or by corporate bylaws. Some of these include:
   a. Tax planning and reporting.
   b. Service departments such as mailing, telephone, janitors, and filing.
   c. Forecasting.
   d. Corporate social relations and obligations.

Relationships

The controller reports to the vice president for Finance.

---

the income generated from increased controlling. As controlling starts to correct major organizational errors, however, the income from increased controlling eventually equals controlling costs (point X_1 on the graph) and ultimately surpasses them by a large margin.

As more and more controlling activity is added beyond X_1, however, controlling costs and the income from increased controlling eventually become equal again (point X_2 on the graph). As more controlling activity is added beyond X_2, controlling costs again surpass the income from increased controlling. The main reason this last development takes place is that major organizational problems probably have been detected much earlier, and corrective measures taken now are aimed primarily at smaller and more insignificant problems.

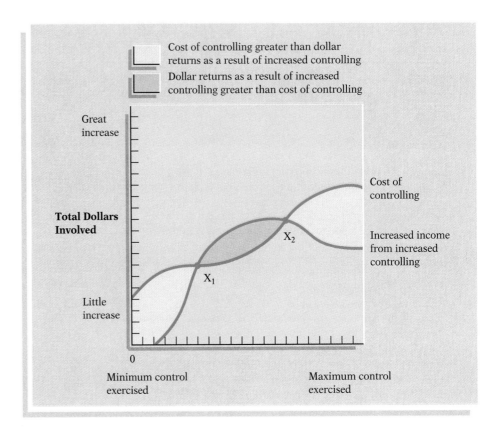

FIGURE 17.4

Value of additional controlling

Ethics Highlight: Environment Defies Control Concept

Managers face situations in which they must decide whether to control by comparing the cost of controlling to the benefits to be gained from controlling. Some decisions about whether to control, on the other hand, should not be based on cost-benefit analysis because their performance is required by law.

In recent times, environmental activists hope to become more proactive in their enforcement tactics and more forcibly to confront companies that are not meeting legislated environmental control standards. They want to exert even more pressure on companies to manufacture, package, and dispose of products in an environmentally safe fashion. Paul R. Thomson, Jr., of the U.S. Environmental Protection Agency says that the EPA will be targeting companies whose environmental violations extend across more than one category—water *and* air, for example. According to Thomson, jail time is now mandatory for federal environmental crimes committed after November 1, 1987. As a result, managers across the nation are giving special attention to controlling organizational activities that could negatively affect the environment and placing much less emphasis on using cost-benefit analysis to determine if such activities should be performed. Managers are now more likely to instruct personnel on what needs to be done to comply with environmental laws and then periodically to audit operations to ensure that the compliance effort is proceeding successfully.

*B*ack to the Case

The job of a controller at Borden would be to gather information for reports that management could use to take corrective action. The controller would not take any corrective action at Borden but would merely advise management as to what corrective action should be taken.

In operating properly, Borden management determines, with the advice of the controller, exactly how much control is necessary at the company; for example, which milk-processing plants seem the most expensive and how this expense is to be reduced. Management should continue to increase controlling at Borden as long as the benefit from the control activities (enhanced profitability) exceeds their cost. Borden management should keep in mind, however, that too much control can cause excessive paperwork in the company and slow decision making to an undesirable level.

POWER AND CONTROL

To control successfully, managers must understand not only the control process itself but also how organization members relate to it. Up to this point, the chapter has emphasized nonhuman variables of controlling. This section focuses on power, perhaps the most important human-related variable in the control process. The following sections discuss power by (1) presenting its definition, (2) elaborating on the total power of managers, and (3) listing the steps managers can take to increase their power over other organization members.

A Definition of Power

Perhaps the two most often confused terms in management are *power* and *authority*. Authority was defined in chapter 10 as the right to command or give orders. The extent to which an individual is able to influence others so that they respond to orders is called **power.** The greater this ability, the more power an individual is said to have.

> **Power** is the extent to which an individual is able to influence others so that they respond to orders.

Obviously, power and control are closely related. To illustrate, after a manager compares actual performance with planned performance and determines that corrective action is necessary, orders usually are given to implement this action. Although the orders are issued through the manager's organizational authority, they may or may not be followed precisely, depending on how much power the manager has over the individuals to whom the orders are addressed.

Total Power of a Manager

The **total power** a manager possesses is made up of two different kinds of power: position power and personal power.[25] **Position power** is power derived from the organizational position a manager holds. In general, moves from lower-level management to upper-level management accrue more position power for a manager. **Personal power** is power derived from a manager's human relationships with others.

> **Total power** is the entire amount of power an individual in an organization possesses, mainly the amount of position power and the amount of personal power possessed by the individual.

Steps for Increasing Total Power

Position power is power derived from the organizational power that one holds.

Personal power is the power derived from the relationship that one person has with another.

Managers can increase their total power by increasing their **position power** or their **personal power.** Position power generally can be increased by a move to a higher organizational position, but managers usually have little personal control over moving upward in an organization. Managers do, however, have substantial control over the amount of personal power they hold over other organization members. John P. Kotter stresses the importance of developing personal power:

> To be able to plan, organize, budget, staff, control, and evaluate, managers need some control over the many people on whom they are dependent. Trying to control others solely by directing them and on the basis of the power associated with one's position simply will not work—first, because managers are always dependent on some people over whom they have no formal authority, and second, because virtually no one in modern organizations will passively accept and completely obey a constant stream of orders from someone just because he or she is the "boss."[26]

To increase personal power, a manager can attempt to develop:[27]

1. *A sense of obligation in other organization members that is directed toward the manager.* If a manager is successful in developing this sense of obligation, other organization members think they should rightly allow the manager to influence them within certain limits. The basic strategy generally suggested to create this sense of obligation is to do personal favors for people.

2. *A belief in other organization members that the manager possesses a high level of expertise within the organization.* In general, a manager's personal power increases as organization members perceive that the manager's level of expertise is increasing. To increase the perceived level of expertise, the manager must quietly make significant achievement visible to others and rely heavily on a successful track record and respected professional reputation.

3. *A sense of identification that other organization members have with the manager.* The manager can strive to develop this identification by behaving in ways that other organization members respect and by espousing goals, values, and ideals commonly held by them. The following description illustrates how a certain sales manager took steps to increase the degree to which his subordinates identified with him:

> One vice-president of sales in a moderate-sized manufacturing company was reputed to be so much in control of his sales force that he could get them to respond to new and different marketing programs in a third of the time taken by the company's best competitors. His power over his employees was based primarily on their strong identification with him and what he stood for. Emigrating to the United States at age seventeen, this person worked his way up "from nothing." When made a sales manager in 1965, he began recruiting other young immigrants and sons of immigrants from his former country. When made vice-president of sales in 1970, he continued to do so. In 1975, 85 percent of his sales force was made up of people whom he hired directly or who were hired by others he brought in.[28]

4. *The perception in other organization members that they are dependent on the manager.* Perhaps the main strategy the manager should adopt in this regard is a clear demonstration of the amount of authority the manager possesses over

organizational resources. Action taken in this regard should emphasize not only influence over resources necessary for organization members to do their jobs but also influence over resources organization members personally receive in such forms as salaries and bonuses. This strategy is aptly reflected in the managerial version of the Golden Rule: "He who has the gold makes the rules."

Back to the Case

For Borden management to be successful in controlling they have to be aware not only of the intricacies of the control process but of how to deal with people as they relate to the control process. With regard to people and control, Borden management has to consider the amount of power held over organization members—that is, their ability to encourage workers to follow orders. Based on the introductory case, many of these orders probably related to taking an additional work at some milk-processing plants and, at other plants, continuing to be productive at non-milk-processing activities while the plants were being sold.

The total amount of power that Borden management possesses comes from the positions they hold and from their personal relationships with other organization members. As an example, Borden's president already has more position power than anyone else in the organization. Therefore, to increase his total power, he would have to develop his personal power. He could attempt to do this by developing (1) a sense of obligation in other organization members toward himself, (2) the belief in other organization members that he has a high level of task-related expertise, (3) a sense of identification that other organization members have with him, and (4) the perception in organization members that they are dependent on him as a manager.

PERFORMING THE CONTROL FUNCTION

Controlling can be a detailed and intricate process, especially as the size of the organization increases. The two sections that follow furnish valuable guidelines for successfully executing this potentially complicated controlling function. These sections discuss potential barriers to successful controlling and making controlling successful.

Potential Barriers to Successful Controlling

Managers should take steps to avoid the following potential barriers to successful controlling:[29]

1. *Control activities can create an undesirable overemphasis on short-term production as opposed to long-term production.* As an example, in striving to meet planned weekly production quotas, a manager might "push" machines in a particular area and not allow these machines to be serviced properly. This kind of management behavior would ensure that planned performance and actual performance are equivalent in the short term but may cause the machines to deteriorate to the point that long-term production quotas are impossible to meet.

2. *Control activities can increase employee frustration with their jobs and thereby reduce morale.* This reaction tends to occur primarily when management exerts too much control. Employees get frustrated because they perceive management as being too rigid in its thinking and not allowing the freedom necessary to do a good job.[30] Another feeling that employees may have from overcontrol is that control activities are merely a tactic to pressure workers to higher production.

3. *Control activities can encourage the falsification of reports.* Employees may perceive management as basing corrective action solely on department records with no regard to extenuating circumstances. (The cartoon below implies that people would sometimes prefer to have management consider extenuating circumstances when controlling.) If this is the case, employees may feel pressured to falsify reports so that corrective action regarding their organizational unit will not be too drastic. For example, actual production may be overstated in order that it will look good to management, or it may be understated to create the impression that planned production is too high, thereby tricking management into thinking that a lighter work load is justified.

A well-publicized example of individuals falsifying control reports involved the Federal Aviation Administration (FAA) and Eastern Airlines.[31] The FAA is a government organization charged with controlling airlines' safety. Part of the controlling process established by the FAA involves airline companies filling out service reports and returning them to the FAA for monitoring and evaluation. Prior to the end of Eastern's existence as a company, Eastern and senior maintenance executives were charged by a federal grand jury with conspiring to falsify aircraft maintenance records and returning improperly maintained

"I guess no man's a hero to his controller—right, Higgins?"

New Yorker, *January 19, 1987, p. 36. Drawing by D. Reilly;*
© *1987 The New Yorker Magazine, Inc.*

aircraft to passenger service. The indictment charged that company managers signed off or coerced aircraft mechanics and mechanics supervisors to sign off on maintenance that had not been completed on fifty-two different occasions. Management may have seen the falsification of maintenance reports as one way of reducing maintenance costs and thereby helping to alleviate Eastern's poor profit performance. In essence, the pressure of poor profits at Eastern Airlines may have caused certain company managers to falsify service reports, making it impossible for the FAA to properly control the airline company.

4. *Control activities can cause the perspective of organization members to be too narrow for the good of the organization.* Although controls can be designed to focus on relatively narrow aspects of an organization, managers must keep in mind that any corrective action should be considered not only in relation to the specific activity being controlled but also in relation to all other organizational units.

   For example, a manager may determine that actual and planned production are not equivalent in a specific organizational unit because of various periods when a low inventory of needed parts causes some production workers to pursue other work activities instead of producing a product. Although the corrective action to be taken in this situation would seem to be simply raising the level of inventory, this probably would be a very narrow perspective of the problem. The manager should seek to answer questions such as the following before any corrective action is taken: Is there enough money on hand to raise current inventory levels? Are there sufficient personnel presently in the purchasing department to effect a necessary increase? Who will do the work the production workers presently are doing when they run out of parts?

5. *Control activities can be perceived as the goals of the control process rather than the means by which corrective action is taken.* Managers must keep in mind that information should be gathered and reports should be designed to facilitate the taking of corrective action within the organization. In fact, these activities can be justified only if they yield some organizational benefit that extends beyond the cost of performing them.

Making Controlling Successful

In addition to avoiding the potential barriers to successful controlling mentioned in the previous section, managers can perform certain activities to make the control process more effective. In this regard, managers should make sure that:

1. *Various facets of the control process are appropriate for the specific organizational activity being focused on.*[32] As an example, standards and measurements concerning a line worker's productivity are much different from standards and measurements concerning a vice president's productivity. Controlling ingredients related to the productivity of these individuals, therefore, must be different if the control process is to be applied successfully.

2. *Control activities are used to achieve many different kinds of goals.* According to Jerome, control can be used for such purposes as standardizing performance, protecting organizational assets from theft and waste, and standardizing product quality.[33] Managers should keep in mind that the control process can be

applied to many different facets of organizational life and that, for the organization to receive maximum benefit from controlling, each of these facets should be emphasized.

3. *Information used as the basis for taking corrective action is timely.*[34] Some time necessarily elapses as managers gather control-related information, develop necessary reports based on this information, decide what corrective action should be taken, and actually take the corrective action. However, information should be gathered and acted on as promptly as possible to ensure that the situation, as depicted by this information, has not changed and that the organizational advantage of corrective action will, in fact, materialize.

4. *The mechanics of the control process are understandable to all individuals who are in any way involved with implementing the process.*[35] Managers should take steps to ensure that people know exactly what information is necessary for a particular control process, how that information is to be gathered and used to compile various reports, what the purposes of various reports actually are, and what corrective actions are appropriate given various possible types of reports. The lesson here is simple: For control to be successful, all individuals involved in controlling must have a working knowledge of how the control process operates.[36]

Back to the Case

In addition to understanding the intricacies of control and how people fit in to the control process, Borden management must be aware of the potential barriers to successful controlling and the action they could take to increase the probability that controlling activities would be successful. That is, to increase the probability that extra work at certain milk-processing plants will be performed efficiently, effectively, and without resistance.

To overcome the potential control-related barriers at Borden, management must balance its emphasis on short-term versus long-term objectives, minimize the negative influence controlling can have on the morale of Borden organization members, eliminate forces that can lead to the falsification of control-related reports, implement a control perspective that has appropriately combined narrow and broad organizational focuses, and stress controlling as a means rather than an end.

With regard to the action that can be taken to increase the probability of effective controlling activities, Borden management must be sure that various facets of its controlling subsystem are appropriate for company activities, that components of the controlling subsystem are flexible and suited to many purposes, that corrective action is based on timely information, and that the controlling subsystem is understood by all organization members involved in its operation.

Action Summary

Reread the learning objectives that follow. Each objective is followed by questions.   *Circle:*
Answering these questions accurately will help you retain the most important
concepts discussed in this chapter. After answering each question, check your
answer with the answer key at the end of this chapter. (*Hint:* If you have doubt
regarding the correct response, consult the page whose number follows the
answer.)

From studying this chapter, I will attempt to acquire:

1. **A definition of *control*.**

   a. Managers must develop methods of measurement to signal when deviations   a, b, c, d, e
   from standards are occurring so that: (a) the plan can be abandoned;
   (b) quality control personnel can be notified; (c) the measurement standards
   can be checked; (d) corrective action can be taken; (e) none of the above.

   b. Control is making something happen the way it was planned to happen.   T, F

2. **A thorough understanding of the controlling subsystem.**

   a. The main steps of the controlling process include all of the following *except:*   a, b, c, d, e
   (a) taking corrective action; (b) establishing planned activities; (c) comparing performance to standards; (d) measuring performance; (e) all of the
   above are steps in controlling.

   b. Standards should be established in all important areas of organizational   T, F
   performance.

3. **An appreciation for various kinds of control and for how each kind can
   be used advantageously by managers.**

   a. Which of the following is not one of the basic types of management control: a, b, c, d, e
   (a) feedback control; (b) precontrol; (c) concurrent control; (d) exception
   control; (e) all are basic types of control.

   b. An example of precontrol established by management would be: (a) rules;   a, b, c, d, e
   (b) procedures; (c) policies; (d) budgets; (e) all of the above are examples.

4. **Insights on the relationship between power and control.**

   a. According to Kotter, controlling others solely on the basis of position   T, F
   power will not work.

   b. The extent to which an individual is able to influence others to respond to   a, b, c, d, e
   orders is: (a) power; (b) sensitivity; (c) authority; (d) communication skills;
   (e) experience.

5. **Knowledge of the various potential barriers that must be overcome for
   successful control.**

   a. Potential barriers to successful controlling can result in: (a) an overemphasis   a, b, c, d, e
   on short-term production as opposed to long-term production; (b) employ-
   ees' frustration with their jobs and thereby reduced morale; (c) the falsification of reports; (d) causing the perception of organization members to be
   too narrow for the good of the organization; (e) all of the above.

   b. Control activities should be seen as the means by which corrective action   T, F
   is taken.

6. An understanding of steps that can be taken to increase the quality of a controlling subsystem.

a, b, c, d, e

a. All of the following are suggestions for making controlling successful *except:* (a) managers should make sure the mechanics of the control process are understood by organization members involved with controlling; (b) managers should use control activities to achieve many different kinds of goals; (c) managers should ensure that control activities are supported by most organization members; (d) managers should make sure that information used as the basis for taking corrective action is timely; (e) all of the above are suggestions.

T, F

b. The standards and measurements concerning a line worker's productivity are much the same as the standards and measurements concerning a vice president's productivity.

$\mathcal{I}$ntroductory Case Wrap-Up

"Controlling Efforts at Borden Inc." (p. 518) and its related back-to-the-case sections were written to help you better understand the management concepts contained in this chapter. Answer the following discussion questions about this introductory case to further enrich your understanding of chapter content:

1. List four areas in which standards should be developed at Borden. Why would standards in these areas be important to company success?

2. Assume that Borden has a controller. From what the case tells about this company, describe five important duties of this controller. Be as specific as you can about how the activities relate to this particular company.

3. Would power be important for managers to possess in ensuring the success of closing some milk-processing plants and shifting work to others? Explain.

Issues for Review and Discussion

1. What is control?
2. Explain the relationship between planning and control.
3. What is controlling?
4. What is the relationship between the controlling subsystem and the overall management system?
5. Draw and explain the controlling subsystem.
6. List and discuss the three main steps of the controlling process.
7. Define the term *standards*.

8. What is the difference between a symptom and a problem? Why is it important to differentiate between a symptom and a problem in controlling?
9. What types of corrective action can managers take?
10. List and define the three basic types of control that can be used in organizations.
11. What is the relationship between controlling and the controller?
12. What basis do managers use to determine how much control is needed in an organization?

13. What is the difference between power and authority? Describe the role of power within the control process.

14. What determines how much power a manager possesses?

15. How can a manager's personal power be increased?

16. Describe several potential barriers to successful controlling.

17. What steps can managers take to ensure that control activities are successful?

Building on What You Know

Directions

Review the Highlight feature as indicated below and answer its corresponding questions. Questions in this section focus on relating a Highlight appearing in this chapter to management concepts that you have learned in a previous chapter.

Review the Quality Highlight: Modern of Marshfield Inc. on p. 526. In chapter 16 you studied about formal groups, informal groups, and maximizing work group effectiveness. Are the CATS groups formal or informal groups? Why? Explain why sociometry could be valuable in choosing organization members to be on a CATS team. As specifically as possible, discuss the steps you would take to apply sociometry in this situation.

Action Summary Answer Key

1. a. d, p. 519   2. a. b, p. 520   3. a. d, p. 527   4. a. T, p. 534   5. a. e, pp. 535–537   6. a. c, pp. 537–538
   b. T, p. 519   b. T, p. 523   b. e, pp. 527–528   b. a, p. 533   b. T, p. 537   b. F, p. 537

Case Study

Measuring Performance at Texaco

by Samuel C. Certo, Rollins College

Texaco's newest gasoline product, System 3, a patented blend of gasoline and seven additive components, is designed to remove the deposits that build up on a car's intake valves; the product is intended to improve the engine's performance. Texaco claims that drivers can improve the performance of their cars by using System 3 gasoline. Texaco's advertising campaign for the product urges drivers to test System 3 by purchasing five tankfuls of the product to see the change in performance for themselves. In order for this campaign to be effective, Texaco realized that the product the customer receives at gasoline pumps throughout the country must be of a consistent quality.

Star Enterprise and Texas Refining and Marketing Inc. (TRMI), two of Texaco's refining and marketing entities, began an extensive testing program to ensure that the gasoline sold at Texaco pumps is the System 3 gasoline that was developed. The testing program also checks to see that the product sold has the proper posted octane and that it is free from any degradation or contamination that might have occurred in the distribution process.

With some 16,000 outlets nationwide, checking the product from every pump nozzle is a staggeringly difficult job, so Star Enterprises and TRMI turned to Southwest Research Institute, an independent, nationally recognized testing company for help. Southwest's hundreds of testers across the country visit randomly selected outlets to collect half-gallon samples of each grade of gasoline in specially prepared and identified galvanized metal containers. The samples are then delivered overnight to Southwest Research's San Antonio, Texas laboratories for chemical analysis and computerized sorting of the data collected. The data are then immediately transferred electronically to Star Enterprise or TRMI field offices. If the test data reveal a problem, testers go back to the problem area, sample the wholesaler's other stations, and investigate to see where the problem originated. If a particular retailer or distributor is at fault, Texaco immediately brings any discrepancy to their attention. If the problem originated at one of Texaco's refineries or somewhere in the distribution system, Texaco's refinery managers are notified, and prompt corrective action is taken.

This product-testing program is only part of Texaco's introduction of a carefully planned quality-improvement program announced in Texaco's 1989 annual report. Texaco's goal is to ensure that things are "done right, on time, every time, in line with customer expectation." Texaco has also set up an oversight committee with representatives from refineries, various marketing groups, transporters, and Texaco's legal department to plan what each department should be doing to control product quality. Potential for problems can occur during the refining and blending process; in any shipment, whether by tanker, barge, pipeline, or truck; as well as at any of the storage facilities. For instance, although the refinery may be turning out the proper product, contamination or comingling may have occurred from another batch of gasoline that preceded the System 3 in the pipeline. The oversight committee meets regularly to find these potential weak links in the chain and to plan ways to ensure the product's integrity.

Texaco's wholesalers and dealers cooperate with and endorse the quality-testing program. Bedford Mitchell, one of Texaco's station dealers makes the following point: "Reputable Texaco wholesalers and dealers don't have any problem with the program. It's good for them. It also assures Texaco customers that they're getting the quality the company advertises." In fact, the wholesale managers encourage even more feedback, good and bad. They want to know whether there are problems and, if so, where they are, so that they can ensure the highest possible product quality.

Discussion Questions

1. Does Texaco use precontrol, concurrent control, or feedback control measures in their total product quality assurance program?

2. How does the testing program help Texaco measure performance, compare the performance to established standards, and then take corrective action?

3. What barriers did Texaco have to overcome in order to implement their testing program?

4. What steps did Texaco take to ensure that its control process was successful?

Frank Olson:
In the Driver's Seat at Hertz

> When I started I was a garage man, I was a rental agent, I was a station manager, I was an office manager, I was a salesman, I was a marketing executive. I worked in finance and I worked in operations. And I think that you can come up in any channel in the organization and grow to become the chief executive. I think you need to sprinkle your career with different responsibilities.

This is the road Frank Olson took to the top at Hertz, the world's largest car rental firm. Like many other American corporate leaders, Olson is convinced that an executive can best chart the company's future by knowing its history and its workings from personal experience. In particular, working his way up the ladder at Hertz enables Olson to identify with the workers whose future he affects—and it allows them to identify with him as well.

Olson started with Hertz at the age of 18 behind the car-rental counter, and he maintains that like each job he has held, the rental counter left its mark on him. He knows what issues will affect the customer and whether the issues are realistic. In the case of advertised prices, for example, Olson argues that generally the prices charged by Hertz end up being as low as those charged by many smaller competitors. However, the competitors advertise low rates and then tack on extra fees once the customer has rented the car. "If you bundled up the aftercharges that occur at these off-airport car loan companies and you compared those to the Hertzes and the Avises, you'd find that the price was no different," he says. "So the perception, in this case, is more important than reality."

Hertz has chosen to build a clientele based on a reputation for reliability and high-quality service, with an underlying assumption that most customers will not be swayed simply by advertised low rates. Large corporate accounts and seasoned business travelers—the vast bulk of rental-car business in the United States—have fallen in line with this strategy, and despite the proliferation of competitors, Hertz remains number one in its industry.

A reputation can be tarnished, however, and goodwill, once lost, is difficult to regain. That is why Frank Olson was devastated by fraud charges brought against his company in 1988. Apparently, customers who returned damaged rental cars had been overcharged on a regular basis for repair work done by or for Hertz. Luckily, Hertz management had located the problem and refunded many of the overcharges before the bad publicity struck, so they were able to mitigate some of the damaging effects. Nonetheless, the company faced $20 million in fines and a difficult time in the press.

Olson learned a lot from that experience:

> What you have to do is constantly reinforce what's right and what's wrong. And you do that by communication directly to the employees from the very top of the organization. You do that by meetings with management to explain to them real

life issues that can occur in business and how it should be handled. You do that by encouraging whistle-blowing, so that if somebody is told to do something wrong, they feel the freedom to raise their hand without fear of reprisal.

Olson identified the problem that cost Hertz so much in money and goodwill as arising from a lack of communication, in terms of both feedback and quality control. Appropriate policies had been in place all along for managing repairs, but management had not involved itself in reviewing actual operations. The policies were not adhered to, and employees were apparently unwilling or afraid to blow the whistle on fellow employees or supervisors.

So, the next issue facing Olson and his now-privately held company is to ensure that operations are appropriately controlled, not simply outlined. He sees Hertz's fall in this case as a mere aberration, and most travel writers agree with him, but there are bigger problems in the industry. Olson is a champion of the move to regulate car-rental advertising to do away with hidden aftercharges and bait-and-switch ploys. He knows that Hertz can stand up to the challenge.

Customer service is the cornerstone of Hertz's success and accounts for double-digit growth figures annually throughout the past thirty years. Frank Olson maintains the respect of his workers by identifying with them, by knowing all aspects of their work, and by being perceived as knowledgeable and honest. He hopes that Hertz will continue to be perceived by its customers as that same sort of leader.

Video Case Questions

1. What sort of standard do you think truth-in-advertising regulations represent?
2. In what way do you think Frank Olson's career development increases his total power at Hertz?
3. Rate the following standards in terms of their relative values at Hertz: employee attitude standards, market-position standards, product-leadership standards, and social-responsibility standards.
4. How can the problem of overcharging for repairs described in the case be avoided in the future?

Video Case Activities

1. Imagine you are a newly appointed manager to the Jackson Hole, Wyoming airport Hertz counter. In summer, you need six full-time employees at the rental desk, but you must determine which three to lay off in winter when business drops off. Prepare a set of standards for measuring your employees' performance to help you justify your decisions.
2. Make a table of precontrol, concurrent control, and feedback control actions for a typical Hertz airport manager. Include at least three actions in each category.

Chapter 18

$\mathscr{S}$ tudent Learning Objectives

From studying this chapter, I will attempt to acquire:

1. Definitions of both *production* and *production control*.

2. An understanding of how productivity and layout patterns relate to the production process.

3. An appreciation for the significance of operations management.

4. Insights on how management by exception and breakeven analysis can be used to control production.

5. An understanding of how quality control and materials requirements planning and control can contribute to production control.

6. Knowledge of how budgets and ratio analysis can be used to achieve overall or broader organizational control.

Production Management
and Control

hapter Outline

PRODUCTION PROBLEMS WITH THE AIRBUS?

It's been one of the more controversial aeronautic introductions since Kitty Hawk. And [recently] the highly automated Airbus A320 jetliner bumped up against still more turbulence. Northwest Airlines, the only U.S. carrier to operate the planes, acknowledged that it has reported suspected malfunctions of the aircraft's flight-control system to the Federal Aviation Administration. The reports come on the heels of two overseas crashes involving the $32 million plane. While both Northwest and the plane's manufacturer say it is safe to fly, the crashes and the reports to the FAA raise questions about its reliability—and the limits of technology. "The controversy is always out there," says Edwin Arbon of the Flight Safety Foundation. "Are we going too far with automation?"

Made by Airbus Industrie, a European consortium, the A320 uses a "fly by wire" computerized system similar to the one in the Air Force's F-16. But just weeks after the fuel-efficient, 150-seat plane was unveiled, its elaborate technology came under scrutiny. During a 1988 air show in France, one of the first models off the production line plunged into a thicket, killing three passengers and injuring about 50. Then, last February, an Indian Airlines A320 crashed near the city of Bangalore, killing 93.

The official cause of both crashes: pilot error. But some pilots and air-safety experts wonder whether the plane's autothrust system, which controls speed, may have contributed to the disasters. They charge that radiation from power lines and other sources could interfere with the system—a serious problem if pilots let their guard down and rely solely on the computer. Says Ken Plunkett of the Aviation Safety Institute, a nonprofit research group: "People may be becoming overconfident with the airbus. They're not [recognizing] its limitations."

> "The controversy is always out there. . . . Are we going too far with automation?"

Cockpit warning: Northwest [spokesperson] Doug Miller says passengers have always been safe on the airline's eight-plane A320 fleet. Still, after the Indian Airlines disaster, Northwest issued a bulletin that alerted pilots to possible glitches in the plane's cockpit computer. In addition, the Minneapolis *Star Tribune* reported, Northwest filed 39 FAA "service difficulty" reports concerning its fleet. Many reports involve such minor problems as malfunctioning cabin lights; others are more substantive. In one case, a pilot disconnected the autopilot because he mistakenly believed he was descending too rapidly.

Both Northwest and the FAA insist the glitches are typical of new planes. Northwest's Miller calls the troubles "teething" problems while the FAA's Mort Edelstein refers to them as "bugs." Airline officials say those bugs are well on their way to being eliminated. In fact, they are betting more than $500 million on the prospect. The airline plans to add 17 other A320s to its fleet—and has options to buy 75 more.

This case is excerpted from Annetta Miller and Karen Springen, "A Bumpy Ride for the Airbus A20," *Newsweek,* May 21, 1990, 69.

The introductory case describes the reporting of many relatively minor, as well as more serious, defects associated with the Airbus A320. Assuming that the reports are valid, the European group that produces this airplane, Airbus Industrie, may be experiencing production-related problems concerning autothrust systems, cockpit computers, and serviceability. This chapter is designed to help managers in companies like Airbus Industrie, who are confronted with the need to eliminate defects in products, or with other production-related problems.

This chapter emphasizes the fundamentals of **production control**—ensuring that an organization produces goods and services as planned. The three primary discussion areas in the chapter are (1) production, (2) operations management, and (3) production and control.

Production control ensures that an organization produces goods and services as planned.

PRODUCTION

To reach organizational goals, all managers must plan, organize, influence, and control to produce some type of goods or services. Naturally, these goods and services may vary significantly from organization to organization. This section of the chapter defines *production* and discusses productivity and the production facility.

Defining Production

Production is the transformation of organizational resources into products.[1] In this definition, *organizational resources* are all assets available to a manager to generate products, *transformation* is the set of steps necessary to change these resources into products, and *products* are various goods or services aimed at meeting human needs. Figure 18.1 on page 550 contains examples of organizational resources (inputs), transformation processes, and goods and services produced (outputs) for each of three different types or organizations.

Production is the transformation of organizational resources into products.

Productivity

Productivity is an important consideration in designing, evaluating, and improving modern production systems. The two sections that follow define *productivity* and discuss robotics, a means of increasing productivity.

Defining Productivity

Productivity is the relationship between the total amount of goods or services being produced (output) and the organizational resources needed (input) to produce them. This relationship is usually expressed by the following equation:[2]

$$\text{Productivity} = \frac{\text{Outputs}}{\text{Inputs}}$$

Productivity is the relationship between the amount of goods or services produced and the organizational resources needed to produce them.

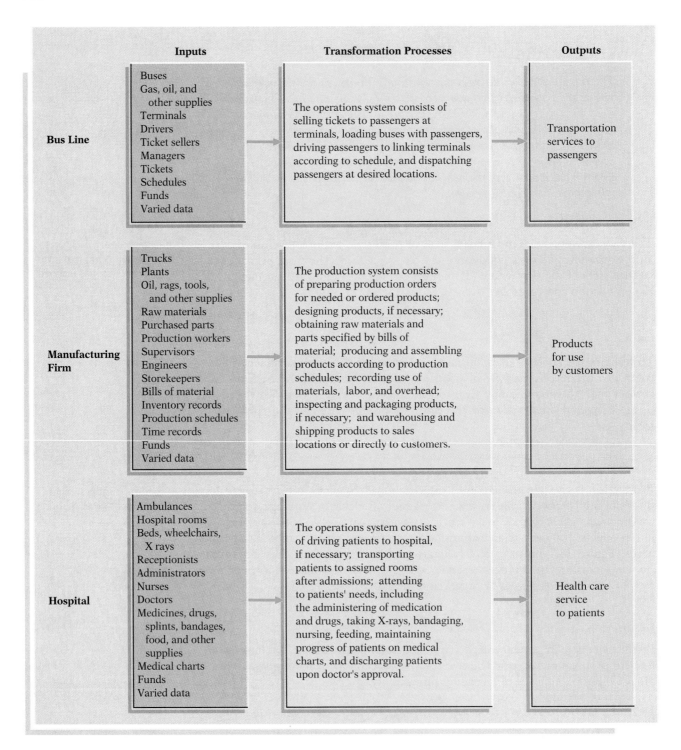

FIGURE 18.1

Inputs, transformation processes, and outputs for three different types of organizations

The higher the value of the ratio of outputs to inputs, the higher the productivity of the operation.

Although managers should continually strive to make their production processes as productive as possible, it is no secret that over the last twenty years the rate of productivity growth related to production management and innovation in manufacturing within the United States has lagged significantly behind that of countries such as Japan, West Germany, and France.[3] Some of the more traditional strategies for increasing productivity include (1) improving the effectiveness of the organizational work force through training, (2) improving the production process through automation, (3) improving product design to make products easier to assemble, (4) improving the production facility by purchasing more modern equipment, and (5) improving the quality of workers hired to fill open positions.

Quality and Productivity

Quality can be defined as how well a product does what it is intended to do—how closely it satisfies the specifications to which it is built. In a broad sense, quality is a degree of excellence on which products or services can be ranked on the basis of selected features or characteristics.

During the last several years, managerial thinking about the relationship between quality and productivity has changed drastically. Managers once saw little relationship between improving quality and increasing productivity. Improving quality was viewed largely as a controlling activity that took place somewhere near the end of the production process. Because this emphasis on improving quality typically resulted in merely rejecting a number of finished products that could otherwise be offered to customers, efforts to improve product quality were generally believed to lower productivity. Many earlier managers chose to achieve higher levels of productivity simply by producing a greater number of products given some fixed level of available resources.

Management theorists have more recently found that improving product quality during all phases of a production process actually improves the productivity of the system that manufactures the product.[4] As early as 1948 Japanese companies observed that such improvements in product quality normally resulted in improved productivity. How does this happen? According to Dr. W. Edwards Deming, a world-renowned quality expert, a serious and consistent quality focus normally reduces nonproductive variables like the reworking of products, production mistakes, delays and production snags, and poor use of time and materials.

According to Deming, the advantages to improving product quality do not end merely with improved productivity. Productivity improvements typically result in an organization that can capture a significant share of a market because the company suddenly possesses a better product at a lower price. In essence, Deming believes that a manager who seriously focuses on improving product quality throughout all phases of a production process initiates a set of chain reactions that benefits not only the organization but the society in which the organization exists. The complete set of Deming's chain reactions appears in Figure 18.2.

Robotics: A Means of Increasing Productivity

Basically, the preceding sections introduced the topic of productivity within organizations. Robotics shows promising signs of increasing organizational productivity in a revolutionary way.

Quality is the extent to which a product reliably does what it is intended to do.

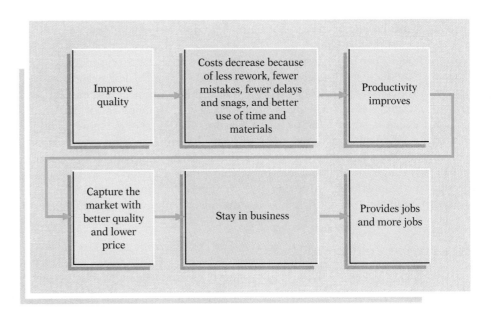

FIGURE 18.2
Deming's chain reactions to improving product quality.

Robotics is the study of the development and use of robots.

A robot is a flexible machine with the ability to hold, move, or grab items that functions through electronic impulses that activate motors or switches.

Robotics is the area of study dealing with the development and use of robots. A **robot** is a flexible machine with the ability to hold, move, or grab items that functions through electronic impulses that activate motors or switches. Three of today's most commonly used applications of robots during production are presented in Table 18.1. The role of the robot of the future, however, will become far more complex in industrial applications, as robot manufacturers master higher

TABLE 18.1 Three common applications of robots during production

Robot Operations	*Description of Operations*
Assembly operations	Activities involved in constructing products. Various types of welding, parts insertion, wiring, and soldering are stressed. The automobile industry and the electronics industry commonly use robots for assembly operations.
Materials handling operations	Activities that involve moving materials from one point to another during the manufacturing process—including point-to-point transfers, machine loading, and loading and unloading palletized goods. Materials handling is one area where growth in robotics is anticipated for smaller manufacturing firms.
Spraying operations	Activities that involve applying necessary liquids during various stages of the production process. The application of paint, stain, lacquer, sealants, and rustproofing is common. Automobile and major appliance manufacturers are among the largest users of robots for spraying operations.

levels of robot design. The use of robots as standalone pieces of manufacturing equipment will diminish in importance. Linking robots to many forms of production in order to achieve full factory automation will be stressed.[5]

Naturally, there are potential advantages and disadvantages to using robots to perform work functions. One advantage, of course, is that robots can take over boring factory jobs and allow people to perform more interesting and more motivating jobs. One disadvantage is that because workers are generally threatened by job loss, the use of robots can strain relations between management and labor.[6]

Global Highlight: GMFancu Focuses on Robotics

Managers face situations that may allow them to increase productivity through the use of robotics. In addition to enhancing productivity, the application of robots to work situations may be a critical factor in enabling organizations to compete with Japanese firms in the future.

Although robots were invented in the United States and although the country still leads in advanced robotics research, Japan leads in the practical use of robots. Japanese companies of all sizes use robots because they make it easier to quickly alter a production line in order to make several different models of a product. One of the few profitable U.S. robot companies in GMFancu, a joint venture between General Motors (GM) and Fancu, a Japanese robot manufacturer. According to GMFancu officials, robots are more than a substitute for human labor because robots can perform some jobs better than people can. As electronics components become smaller and smaller, robots are becoming an essential ingredient for the production of such items as watches and videocassette recorders. Overblown expectations for the use of robots in manufacturing situations as well as higher return requirements for dollars invested in robots are two primary reasons why robotics has not been as popular in the United States as in Japan. The key to competing with Japanese manufacturers in the future may be to find better uses of robots in various manufacturing situations.

The Production Facility: Layout Patterns

In addition to understanding the production process and how productivity relates to it, managers also should be aware of various layout patterns that can be used within a production facility. A **layout pattern** is the overall arrangement of machines, equipment, materials handling areas, aisles, service areas, storage areas, and work stations within a production facility. The primary objective of a layout is to optimize the arrangement of these variables so their total contribution to the production process is maximized.[7] There are three basic layout patterns:

1. **Process layout** is a layout pattern based primarily on the grouping of similar types of equipment. Hospitals, automobile repair shops, and department stores use process layout.

A **layout pattern** is the overall arrangement of machines, equipment, materials handling, aisles, service areas, storage areas, and work stations within a production facility. A layout pattern is an arrangement of a number of variables to maximize productivity.

A **process layout** is a layout pattern based primarily on grouping together similar types of equipment.

A **product layout** is a layout pattern based mostly on the progressive steps by which the product is made.

A **fixed position layout** is a layout pattern that has workers, tools, and materials rotating around a stationary product.

2. **Product layout** is a layout pattern based on the progressive steps by which a product is made. The automobile assembly line and furniture manufacturing are areas where product layout is used.

3. **Fixed position layout** is a layout pattern that, because of the weight or bulk of the product being manufactured, has workers, tools, and materials rotating around a stationary product. Ships and airplanes usually are manufactured with the fixed position layout.

Figure 18.3 illustrates each of the three basic layout patterns.

In practice, what constitutes the best, or most appropriate, layout pattern differs from organization to organization. There are, however, several criteria for judging the effectiveness and efficiency of a layout pattern, regardless of the organization in which it exists. Several of these criteria are listed in Table 18.2.[8]

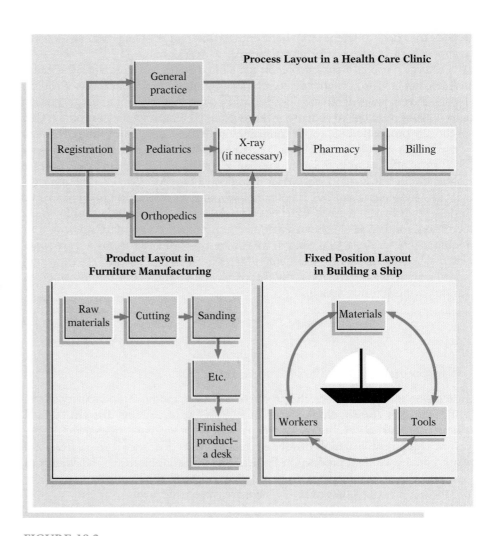

FIGURE 18.3
Three basic layout patterns

TABLE 18.2 Criteria for effective and efficient plant layout

Effective and efficient plant layout has:

1. Straight aisles to minimize worker and materials movement
2. Minimum handling of materials between manufacturing or assembly operations
3. Short distances over which materials must be moved
4. Beginning production steps occurring as close as possible to the place where resources are received from suppliers
5. Ending production steps occurring as close as possible to the place where finished goods are shipped to customers
6. Adequate storage for tools and equipment
7. The ability to be changed easily as circumstances change
8. Maximum use of all production facilities
9. Desirable levels of control for production nuisances, such as noise, dust, and heat
10. An effective and efficient system for scrap removal

OPERATIONS MANAGEMENT

Operations management deals with managing production in organizations. The sections that follow define *operations management* and discuss the steps involved in its use.

Defining Operations Management

According to Chase and Aquilano, **operations management** is the performance of the managerial activities entailed in selecting, designing, operating, controlling, and updating production systems.[9] Figure 18.4, page 556, describes these activities and categorizes them as being either periodic or continual. The distinction between periodic and continual activities is based on the relative frequency of their performance: Periodic activities are performed from time to time, and continual activities are performed essentially without interruption.

Operations management is the process of managing production in organizations.

Steps in Operations Management

There are four major steps to managing production successfully. Normally, these steps should be performed in the following order:

Step 1: Production planning. **Production planning** is determining the type and amount of resources needed to produce specified goods or services. It is the foundation step in operations management in that it determines to a large degree the effectiveness of the operations management steps that follow. Other issues involved in production planning are (1) how much to produce, (2) what level inventory should be kept at, and (3) what materials should be ordered and from which suppliers.

Production planning is determining the type and amount of resources needed to produce specified goods or services.

Step 2: Routing. **Routing** is determining the sequence in which work must be completed to produce specified goods or services. In essence, routing determines the path through a plant that materials acquired during production planning

Routing is determining the sequence in which work must be completed to produce specified goods or services.

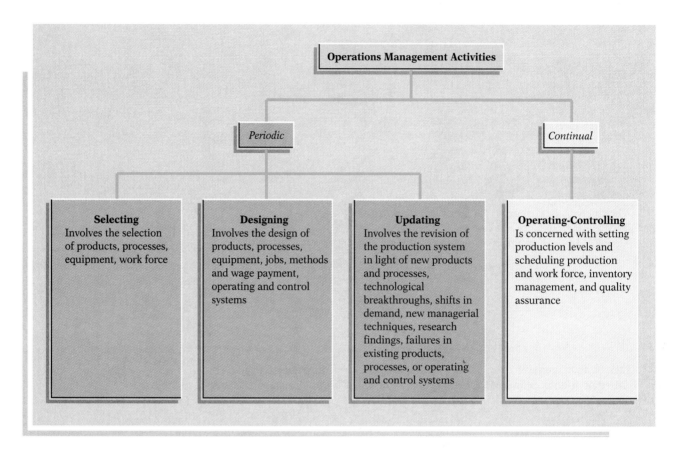

FIGURE 18.4
Major activities performed to manage production

must take to become finished products. For example, wood acquired to produce furniture must be cut, sanded, glued, painted, and so on.

Step 3: Scheduling. **Scheduling** is the process of (1) formulating detailed listings of activities that must be performed to accomplish a task, (2) allocating resources necessary to complete the task, and (3) setting up and following timetables for completing the task. Gantt charts and PERT networks are two useful scheduling tools.[10]

Step 4: Dispatching. **Dispatching** is issuing orders to the individuals involved in producing goods or services. It takes the results of production planning, routing, and scheduling and puts them into operation within the organization.

Back to the Case

The presence of defects in the Airbus A320, as presented in the introductory case, may be a result of the way in which resources such as people, equipment, and materials at Airbus Industrie are transformed into products.

Although the level of productivity at Airbus Industrie is not specifically mentioned in the case, company managers must strive to increase it to obtain the

Scheduling is the process of formulating detailed listings of activities needed to accomplish a task, allocating resources to complete the task, and determining timetables for completing the task.

Dispatching is issuing orders to the individuals involved in producing goods or services.

maximum number of products manufactured for the level of resources invested in the production process. In striving to increase productivity at Airbus Industrie, managers can take such actions as implementing more effective training programs for employees and being more selective in hiring people. In addition, Airbus Industrie managers should evaluate the possibility of using robots to produce products. Besides increasing productivity, robots probably would make fewer production errors than humans.

Fixed position layout is probably the layout pattern used at Airbus Industrie to manufacture the Airbus A320. In general, airplane manufacturers have found that it is impossible to assemble airplanes using progressive steps, a type of assembly-line situation. The process layout, grouping production around similar types of equipment, would also generally be inadvisable for manufacturing the Airbus A320. Instead, the most effective and efficient production process for airplanes has traditionally been the fixed position layout, rotating workers, materials, and tools around a single Airbus A320.

As the introductory case implies, managers at Airbus Industrie must spend much time managing production, or performing operations management activities. In essence, these managers are involved in selecting, designing, operating, controlling, and updating the Airbus A320 production process. To carry out their operations management responsibilities, Airbus Industrie managers perform the sequential steps of production planning, routing, scheduling, and dispatching.

PRODUCTION AND CONTROL

A **control tool** is a specific procedure or technique that presents pertinent organizational information in a way that helps managers develop and implement appropriate control strategy. That is, it helps managers pinpoint the organizational strengths and weaknesses on which a useful control strategy must focus. This section discusses specific control tools for production as well as tools for broader organizational control.

A **control tool** is a specific procedure or technique that presents pertinent organizational information in such a way that a manager is aided in developing and implementing appropriate control strategy.

Control Tools for Production

Some of the best-known and most commonly used control tools are (1) management by exception, (2) management by objectives, (3) breakeven analysis, (4) materials requirements planning and control, and (5) quality control. The specific purpose of these tools is to control the production of organizational goods and services.

Management by Exception

Management by exception is a control technique that allows only significant deviations between planned and actual performance to be brought to a manager's attention.[11] Actually, management by exception is based on the exception principle, a management principle that appears in early management literature.[12] The exception principle recommends that subordinates handle all routine organizational matters, leaving managers to handle only nonroutine, or exceptional, organizational issues.

Management by exception is a control tool that allows only significant deviations between planned and actual performance to be brought to the manager's attention.

Although exceptional issues might be uncovered when managers themselves detect significant deviation between standards and performance, some managers establish rules to ensure that exceptional issues surface as a matter of normal operating procedure. It is important to establish the rules carefully, so that a true deviation is always brought to the manager's attention. Two examples of such rules are the following:[13]

1. A department manager must immediately inform the plant manager if actual weekly labor costs exceed estimated weekly labor costs by more than 15 percent.

2. A department manager must immediately inform the plant manager if actual dollars spent plus estimated dollars to be spent on a special project exceed the funds approved for the project by more than 10 percent.

These two rules focus on production-related expenditures. However, such rules can be established in virtually any organizational area.

If appropriately administered, management by exception yields the added advantage of ensuring the best use of a manager's time. Because it brings only significant issues to the manager's attention, the possibility that the manager will spend valuable time working on relatively insignificant issues is automatically eliminated.

Of course, the significant issues brought to the manager's attention could be organizational strengths as well as organizational weaknesses. The manager should try to eliminate the weaknesses and reinforce the strengths.

Management by Objectives

Management by objectives, as discussed in Chapter 4, is a control tool in which the manager assigns a specialized set of objectives and action plans to the workers and then rewards the individuals on the basis of how close they come to reaching their goals. It is a control technique that has been implemented successfully in some corporations in order to use an employee-participative means to improve productivity.

Breakeven Analysis

Breakeven analysis is a control tool that summarizes the various levels of profit or loss associated with various levels of production.

Another production related control tool commonly used by managers is breakeven analysis. **Breakeven analysis** is the process of generating information that summarizes various levels of profit or loss associated with various levels of production. The following sections discuss (1) the basic ingredients of breakeven analysis, (2) the types of breakeven analysis available to managers, and (3) the relationship between breakeven analysis and controlling.

Basic Ingredients of Breakeven Analysis. Breakeven analysis typically includes reflection, discussion, reasoning, and decision making relative to the following seven major ingredients:

Fixed costs are expenses incurred regardless of the number of products produced.

1. *Fixed costs.* **Fixed costs** are expenses incurred by the organization regardless of the number of products produced. Some examples are real estate taxes, upkeep to the exterior of a business building, and interest expenses on money borrowed to finance the purchase of equipment.

2. *Variable costs.* Expenses that fluctuate with the number of products produced are called **variable costs.** Some examples are costs of packaging a product, costs of materials needed to make the product, and costs associated with packing products to prepare them for shipping.

3. *Total costs.* **Total costs** are simply the sum of fixed costs and variable costs associated with production.

4. *Total revenue.* **Total revenue** is all sales dollars accumulated from selling manufactured products or services. Naturally, total revenue increases as more products are sold.

5. *Profits.* **Profits** are defined as the amount of total revenue that exceeds the total costs of producing the products sold. The following cartoon lightheartedly makes the point that although profit is easily defined, it is much more difficult to earn.

6. *Loss.* **Loss** is the amount of the total costs of producing a product that exceeds the total revenue gained from selling the product.

7. *Breakeven point.* The **breakeven point** is the situation wherein the total revenue of an organization equals its total costs—that is, the point at which the organization is generating only enough revenue to cover its costs. The company is neither gaining a profit nor incurring a loss.

Types of Breakeven Analysis.   There are two somewhat different procedures for determining the same breakeven point for an organization: algebraic breakeven analysis and graphic breakeven analysis.[14]

Variable costs are expenses that fluctuate with the number of products produced.

Total costs are the sum of fixed costs and variable costs.

Total revenue is all sales dollars accumulated from selling goods or services that are produced.

Profits are the amount of total revenue that exceeds total costs.

Loss is the amount of the total costs of producing a product that exceeds the total revenue.

The **breakeven point** is the situation wherein the total revenue of an organization equals its total costs.

"We've got a situation here that has never come up — we're making more money than we're spending."

Algebraic Breakeven Analysis. The following simple formula is commonly used to determine the level of production at which an organization breaks even:

$$BE = \frac{FC}{P - VC}$$

where—

BE = the level of production at which the firm breaks even
FC = total fixed costs of production
 P = price at which each individual unit is sold to customers
VC = variable costs associated with each product manufactured and sold

Two sequential steps must be followed in using this formula to calculate a breakeven point. First, the variable costs associated with producing each unit must be subtracted from the price at which each unit will sell. The purpose of this calculation is to determine how much of the selling price of each unit sold can go toward covering total fixed costs incurred from producing all products. The second step is to divide the remainder calculated in the first step into total fixed costs. The purpose of this calculation is to determine how many units must be produced and sold to cover fixed costs. This number of units is the breakeven point for the organization.

For example, a book publisher could face the fixed costs and variable costs per paperback book presented in Table 18.3. If the publisher wants to sell each book for $12, the breakeven point could be calculated as follows:

$$BE = \frac{\$88,800}{\$12 - \$6}$$

$$BE = \frac{\$88,800}{\$6}$$

$$BE = 14,800 \text{ copies}$$

This calculation indicates that if expenses and selling price remain stable, the book publisher will incur a loss if book sales are fewer than 14,800 copies, will break even if book sales equal 14,800 copies, and will make a profit if book sales exceed 14,800 copies.

Graphic Breakeven Analysis. Graphic breakeven analysis entails the construction of a graph that shows all the critical elements in a breakeven analysis. Figure 18.5 is a breakeven graph for the book publisher. Note that in a breakeven graph, the total revenue line starts at zero.

TABLE 18.3 Fixed costs and variable costs for a book publisher

Fixed Costs (Yearly Basis)		*Variable Costs per Book Sold*	
1. Real estate taxes on property	$ 1,000	1. Printing	$2.00
2. Interest on loan to purchase equipment	5,000	2. Artwork	1.00
3. Building maintenance	2,000	3. Sales commission	.50
4. Insurance	800	4. Author royalties	1.50
5. Salaried labor	80,000	5. Binding	1.00
Total fixed costs	$88,800	Total variable costs per book	$6.00

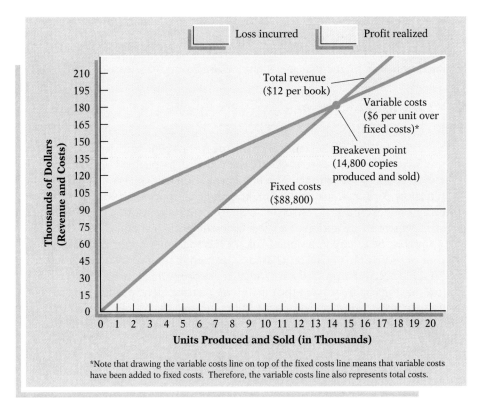

FIGURE 18.5

Breakeven analysis for a book publisher

Using the Algebraic and Graphic Breakeven Methods. Both the algebraic and the graphic methods of breakeven analysis for the book publisher result in the same breakeven point—14,800 books produced and sold. However, the processes used to arrive at the point are quite different.

The situation managers face usually determines which breakeven method they should use. For example, if managers simply desire a quick yet accurate determination of a breakeven point, the algebraic method generally suffices. If they prefer a more complete picture of the cumulative relationships between the breakeven point, fixed costs, and escalating variable costs, the graphic breakeven method probably is more useful. The book publisher could quickly and easily see from Figure 18.5 the cumulative relationships of fixed costs, escalating variable costs, and potential profit and loss associated with various levels of production.

Control and Breakeven Analysis. Breakeven analysis is a useful control tool because it helps managers understand the relationships between fixed costs, variable costs, total costs, and profit and loss within an organization. Once these relationships are understood, managers can take steps to modify one or more of the variables to reduce significant deviation between planned and actual profit levels.[15] Increasing costs or decreasing selling prices have the overall effect of increasing the number of units an organization must produce and sell to break even. Conversely, the managerial strategy for decreasing the number of products an organization must produce and sell to break even entails lowering or stabilizing fixed and variable costs or increasing the selling price of each unit. The exact breakeven control strategy a particular manager should develop and implement is dictated primarily by the manager's unique organizational situation.

Back to the Case

There are useful production control tools that Airbus Industrie management could use to ensure that the Airbus A320 is produced as planned. Management by exception is one of these tools. The implementation of management by exception would allow Airbus Industrie workers to handle all routine production issues and to bring only exceptional matters to management's attention. The successful use of management by exception at Airbus Industrie probably would be characterized by a number of carefully designed rules. One such rule might be that when 10 percent or more of materials purchased to be used in the production of the Airbus A320 are defective, a production worker must bring this fact to the attention of the production supervisor and the purchasing manager. The production supervisor could then inspect products more carefully to ensure that a significant number are not manufactured with defective parts, and the purchasing manager could contact the supplier for an upgrading of future delivered materials and an allowance for defective materials already delivered.

In addition to management by exception, Airbus Industrie management could use breakeven analysis as a control tool. Breakeven analysis would furnish management with information about various levels of profit or loss associated with various levels of production. To use breakeven analysis, Airbus Industrie management would have to determine the total fixed costs necessary to operate a production facility, the price at which each plane is to be offered, and the variable costs associated with producing each of the planes.

For example, if Airbus Industrie management wanted to determine how many Airbus A320s had to be sold before the company would break even on that product alone, management could arrive at the breakeven point algebraically by following three steps. First, management would have to total all fixed costs attributable to the Airbus A320—for example, lighting expenses and real estate taxes. Second, Airbus Industrie management would have to total all variable costs associated with manufacturing and selling each Airbus A320 and subtract this total from the price at which each unit is to be sold. Variable costs would include such expenses as the costs of materials and labor needed to produce the plane. Finally, management would have to divide the answer calculated in step 2 into the answer derived in step 1. This figure would tell management how many A320s had to be sold to break even.

Airbus Industrie management also could arrive at this breakeven point by constructing a graph that showed fixed costs, variable costs, and selling price. The graph probably would provide management with a more useful picture for formulating profit-oriented production plans.

Materials Requirements Planning and Control

Materials requirements planning is another control tool that can increase the effectiveness and efficiency of the production process. **Materials requirements plan-**

ning is the process of creating schedules that identify specific parts and materials required to produce an item, the exact quantities of each needed to enhance the organizational production process, and the dates when orders for these quantities should be released to suppliers and be received for best timing within the production cycle.[16]

Figure 18.6 shows the main elements of a materials requirements planning system. As can be seen from this figure, the computer can be an important part of the materials requirements planning process. Input data for the computer come from three main sources: (1) a master production schedule based on orders from consumers, sales forecasts or product demand, and plant capacity; (2) a bill of material file that considers product design changes in determining the types and quantities of materials needed within the production process; and (3) an inventory file that shows the types and quantities of materials presently on hand. The computer then generates output reports that indicate what materials should be ordered or canceled as well as what materials should be expedited or de-expedited.

Naturally, materials requirements planning is closely related to materials requirements control. **Materials requirements control** is simply the process of making things happen the way they were planned to happen in materials requirements planning.

Materials requirements planning (MRP) is the process that identifies the specific parts and materials required to produce an item, the exact quantities of each needed, and schedules for obtaining these items for greatest production efficiency.

Materials requirements control is the process of making things happen the way they were planned to happen in materials requirements planning.

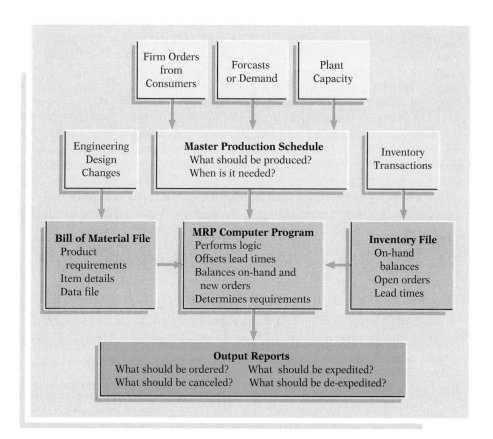

FIGURE 18.6

Basic elements of a materials requirements planning system

Just-in-Time Inventory Control

Just-in-time (JIT) inventory control is a control technique that reduces inventories to a minimum by arranging for them to be delivered to the production facility "just in time" to be used. The concept, developed primarily by the Toyota Motor Company of Japan,[17] is also called "zero inventory" and "kanban"—the latter a Japanese term referring to purchasing raw materials by using a special card ordering form.

JIT is based on the management philosophy that products should be manufactured when customers need them and in the quantities customers need them in order to minimize levels of raw materials and finished goods inventories kept on hand.[18] Over all, JIT emphasizes maintaining operations within a company by using only the resources that are absolutely necessary to meet customer demand.

JIT works best in companies that manufacture relatively standardized products and that have consistent product demand. Such companies can comfortably order materials from suppliers and assemble products in several small, continuous batches. The result is a smooth, consistent flow of purchased materials and assembled products and little inventory buildup. Companies that manufacture nonstandardized products that have sporadic or seasonal demand generally must face more irregular purchases of raw materials from suppliers, more uneven production cycles, and greater accumulations of inventory.

If implemented successfully, JIT can enhance organizational performance in several important ways. First, it can reduce unnecessary labor expenses generated by products manufactured but not sold. Second, it can minimize the tying up of monetary resources needed to purchase production related materials that do not result in sales on a timely basis.[19] Third, it can help management minimize expenses normally associated with maintaining an inventory—for example, storage and handling costs. Better inventory management and improved control of labor costs are two of the most commonly cited benefits of JIT.[20]

Many U.S. businesses are adopting JIT as a means of improving organizational performance.[21] General Motors has used JIT since 1980 and has slashed its annual inventory related costs from $8 billion to $2 billion. One American Motors plant has cut its inventories to less than one day's supply, compared to the more usual six-day reserve. Recent reports indicate that the use of JIT is spreading from the automotive industry to other industries—for example, the small appliances industry. General Electric and RCA are two small appliance firms seriously experimenting with JIT.[22]

Experience indicates that successful JIT programs tend to have certain common characteristics:[23]

1. *Closeness of suppliers.* Manufacturers using JIT find it beneficial to have suppliers of raw materials within short distances of them. As companies begin to order smaller quantities of raw materials, suppliers sometimes must be asked to make one or more deliveries per day. Short distances make multiple deliveries per day feasible.

2. *High quality of materials purchased from suppliers.* Manufacturers using JIT find it difficult to overcome problems caused by defective materials purchased from suppliers. Since the materials inventory is kept small, defective materials may mean that the manufacturer must wait until the next delivery from the supplier

before the production process can continue. Such production slowdowns can be disadvantageous, causing late delivery to customers or lost sales because finished products are unavailable.

3. *Well-organized receiving and handling of materials purchased from suppliers.* Companies using JIT must be able to receive and handle raw materials effectively and efficiently. Such materials must be available for the production process where and when they are needed. Naturally, if the materials are not available, extra costs are built into the production process.

4. *Strong management commitment.* Management must be strongly committed to the concept of JIT. The system takes time and effort to plan, install, and improve—and is therefore expensive to implement. Management must be willing to commit funds to initiate the JIT system and to support it once it is functioning.

Quality Control

Quality control is the process of making the quality of finished goods and services what it was planned to be. Managers compare the quality of goods or services produced to organizational quality standards and take steps to maintain the level of product quality dictated by the situation.[24] Two management tools for controlling product quality are quality circles and inspection.

Quality control is the process of ensuring the quality of finished goods and services.

Quality Highlight: Tupperware Quality Not Enough

In addition to maintaining the quality of goods and services offered to customers, managers must attend to other aspects of the organization if it is to be successful. For example, at Tupperware, a worldwide manufacturer of high-quality plastic kitchenware products, management recently found that quality efforts must be supplemented by efforts in other areas.

Irene McLaughlin, an independent Tupperware dealer for the past fifteen years, swears that she can detect, even with her eyes closed, the quality difference between her Tupperware® brand products and those of her largest competitor, Rubbermaid. According to McLaughlin, her products are of obviously superior quality to those of Rubbermaid. Despite this quality difference, Tupperware has not impressed as many buyers as it would like at the national level. Critics say that a cumbersome distribution system, lack of new products, and a high price structure have stunted growth at Tupperware during the past decade. Sagging sales have forced the company to terminate about 15 percent of the employees in U.S. operations. Few would argue with the fact that Tupperware® products are of very high quality. Instead, most would argue that if an organization like Tupperware is to be successful, it must complement its outstanding quality control program with efforts in other areas such as new product development and effective and efficient product distribution.

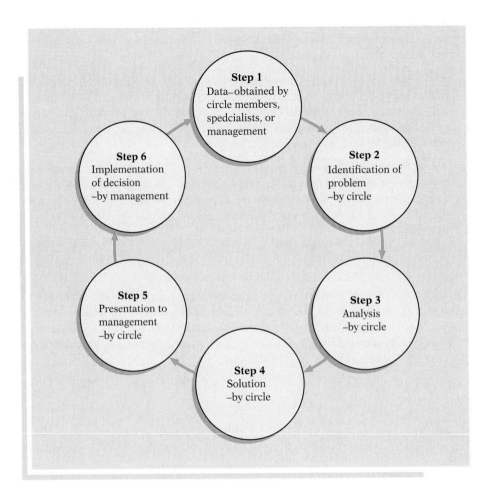

FIGURE 18.7

The roles of management and circle members in the quality circle problem-solving process

Quality circles are small groups of workers that meet regularly with management to discuss quality related problems.

Quality Circles

Recently, managers have involved all of a company's employees in quality control. In general, management solicits the ideas of employees in judging and maintaining product quality. This trend toward more involvement of employees in quality control developed from a control system originating in Japan called quality circles. Although many corporations are now moving beyond the concept of the quality circle to the concept of the work team, as discussed in Chapter 16, many of the ideas generated from quality circles continue to be valid. **Quality circles** are simply small groups of workers who meet regularly to discuss and help solve quality-related problems. Solutions to the problems are communicated directly to management at a formal presentation session. Figure 18.7 shows the roles of management and circle members in the quality circle problem-solving process.

Most quality circles are similar in the way they operate. Each circle is usually under twenty members in size, and leaders of the circles are not necessarily the members' supervisors. Members are generally from a common work site or task area, and their focus is operational problems rather than interpersonal ones. Although the problems are sometimes assigned by management, they can also be uncovered by the group itself.[25]

Inspection

Inspection is a more traditional method managers use to control product quality. Inspection is simply examining and grading finished products, components, or products at any stage of production.[26] The result of inspection is to discard products or components that do not meet preestablished quality standards. By discarding substandard parts or finished products, the organization maintains the planned quality of products that are finally sold.

Managers must determine not only what products or product components to inspect but also how many units or components to inspect. One method of addressing this question is called statistical quality control.[27] **Statistical quality control** is a process used to determine how many units of a product should be inspected to calculate a probability that the total number of units meets organizational quality standards. Although managers limit inspection expenses by not examining all units, they must be careful to ensure that the number of units inspected gives an accurate measurement of the quality of the products being produced.

Statistical quality control is the process used to determine the percentage of products produced that must be inspected to calculate a probability that all products meet quality standards.

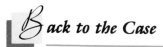

ack to the Case

Two additional production control tools that probably would be useful to Airbus Industrie management are materials requirements planning and control and quality control. Materials requirements planning for the Airbus A320 would involve creating work schedules that identify the specific parts and materials necessary to produce the airplane, determining the quantities of each needed to get maximum use of the Airbus A320 production system, and pinpointing dates when orders for these items should be released and materials actually received from suppliers. Airbus Industrie management undoubtedly would find that the materials requirements planning process for the A320 would be so complex that the use of a computer to organize and manage it would be invaluable.

Materials requirements control at Airbus Industrie would require that management follow up to make sure that events occur as planned during the process of materials requirements planning. If shipments of materials are not arriving as planned, for example, Airbus Industrie management must contact suppliers to expedite deliveries.

Because the most serious issue at Airbus Industrie as depicted in the introductory case is that of poor-quality products, quality control should be an important concern. Company management must plan for some desirable level of quality—neither too high nor too low—and then take steps to ensure that planned levels of quality are indeed present in the finished airplanes. An important part of this quality control process would involve inspection. Airbus Industrie management first must determine what should be inspected—materials purchased for inventory, materials available from various suppliers, units at different stages of Airbus A320 production, or finished Airbus A320s. Then management must decide how many should be inspected—every A320 plane in production, all materials purchased from all suppliers, or only some proportion of each. Statistical quality control is a tool Airbus Industrie management can use to minimize inspection expenses without sacrificing the measurement accuracy for product quality.

Tools for Broader Organizational Control

The control tools already discussed are commonly applied directly to the production process. The following sections discuss control tools that do not relate as directly to the production process: budgets and ratio analysis. Because the production process has an effect on virtually all phases of organizational existence, however, a thorough understanding of the production process is a prerequisite for the successful use of even these control tools.

Budgets

A **budget** is a control tool that outlines how funds will be obtained and spent in a given period.

As described in chapter 8, a budget is a single-use financial plan that covers a specified length of time. The **budget** of an organization is the financial plan outlining how funds in a given period will be obtained and spent.

In addition to being a financial plan, however, a budget is also a control tool.[28] As managers gather information on actual receipts and expenditures within an operating period, significant deviations from budgeted amounts may be uncovered. In such a case, managers can develop and implement a control strategy aimed at making actual performance more consistent with planned performance. This, of course, assumes that the plan contained in the budget is appropriate for the organization.

An illustration of how a budget can be used as an organizational plan as well as an organizational control tool is the following fictitious situation concerning a Father Walter James, rector and manager of St. Matthew's Church. In response to organizational objectives, Father James developed a simple budget for St. Matthew's (see Table 18.4). The budget is actually Father James's financial plan of how money will be spent to achieve organizational objectives.

In addition, however, Father James can use this budget as a control tool. For example, as actual office supplies and expenses approach their maximum budgeted allowance of $2,250 during an operating period, Father James conceivably can take steps to minimize further expenditures in this area. Or, after analyzing the entire situation carefully, Father James may decide to increase the budgeted amount for office supplies and expenses. Because the total amount of resources for this church or any other organization probably is fixed, an increase in the budgeted amount for one expense typically requires an equal decrease in the budgeted amount for another expense. For example, increasing the budgeted allowance for office supplies and expenses from $2,250 to $3,250 would require a $1,000 reduction in the budgeted amounts for other organizational expenses.

The following sections discuss potential pitfalls of budgets and people considerations in using budgets.

Potential Pitfalls of Budgets. To maximize the benefits of using budgets, managers must be able to avoid several potential pitfalls. These pitfalls include:

1. *Placing too much emphasis on relatively insignificant organizational expenses.* In preparing and implementing a budget, managers should allocate more time for dealing with significant organizational expenses and less time for relatively insignificant organizational expenses. For example, the amount of time managers spend on developing and implementing a budget for labor costs typically should be much more than the amount of time managers spend on developing and implementing a budget for office supplies.

TABLE 18.4 Operating budget for St. Matthew's Church

St. Matthew's Operating Budget
Year 1992

Disbursements		Receipts		
Diocesan assessment	$ 17,220.00	For general purposes:		
Clergy salary	26,368.00	Plate offerings	$ 501.47	
Secretary salary	7,200.00	Pledge payments	74,761.11	
Sexton	6,463.00	Parish organizations:		
Organist/St. Matthew's		Treasure House	1,320.00	
choirmaster salary	4,576.00	St. Thomas's Guild	2,019.32	
Social security	2,000.00	From diocese	325.00	
Housing allowance	3,000.00	Other miscellaneous sources	828.59	
Auto lease	3,072.00	Investment income	16,645.00	$ 96,400.49
Auto gas allowance	1,100.00			
Pastoral care	350.00	For special parish use:		
Pension premium	3,500.00	Communion alms	1,240.19	
Utilities	7,920.00	Building fund (steeple repair)	1,050.00	
Housekeeping	2,400.00	Designated gifts and memorials	1,239.25	
Repairs to property		Miscellaneous sources	485.00	$ 4,014.44
(bldg. fund)	5,000.00			
Telephone	1,760.00	For work outside parish	$ 152.55	
Office supplies & expenses	2,250.00	Nonincome receipts:		
Postage	700.00	From endowment trust		
Bulletins & printing	1,500.00	transfers		$ 13,552.75
Kitchen supplies & expense	3,000.00	Day school		16,918.28
Organ maintenance	200.00	Total receipts		$131,038.51
T.H. Greater Fed. of Churches	2,600.00			
Church school				
Worship commission				
Planning commission				
Social concerns commission				
Youth commission				
Rector's funds (music, adult				
education, special programs)	4,500.00			
Other expenses	3,200.00			
Convention delegate expense	800.00			
Insurance	5,500.00			
Sexton's insurance	500.00			
Clergy assistance	1,000.00			
Altar supplies	2,000.00			
Garden maintenance	500.00			
Total Disbursements	$120,179.00			

2. *Increasing budgeted expenses year after year without adequate information.* It does not necessarily follow that items contained in last year's budget should be increased this year. Perhaps the best-known method developed to overcome this potential pitfall is zero-base budgeting.[29] Zero-base budgeting is the planning and budgeting process that requires managers to justify their entire budget requests in detail rather than simply to refer to budget amounts established in previous years.[30]

Zero-base budgeting requires managers to justify their entire budget request in detail rather than simply referring to budget amounts established in previous years.

Some management theorists believe **zero-base budgeting** is a more complete management tool than more traditional budgeting, which simply starts with the budget amount established in the prior year,[31] because more focused identification and control of each budget item is emphasized. This tool, however, will be implemented successfully only if management is able to explain adequately what zero-base budgeting is and how it will be used within a particular organization.[32] One of the earliest and most commonly cited successes in implementing a zero-base budgeting program was in the Department of Agriculture's Office of Budget and Finance. The instructions used to implement this program, still a good model for implementing a zero-base budgeting process today, were as follows:

> A new concept has been adopted for [this year's] agency estimates; namely, that of zero-base budgeting. This means that all programs will be reviewed from the ground up and not merely in terms of changes proposed for the budget year. . . . The total work program of each agency must be subjected to an intensive review and evaluation. . . . Consideration must be given to the basic need for the work contemplated, the level at which the work should be carried out, the benefits to be received, and the costs to be incurred.
>
> The fact that certain activities have been carried out for a number of years will not, per se, adequately justify their continuation. Nor will the fact that programs are prescribed by statutory law necessarily be a controlling consideration. Program goals based on statutes enacted to meet problems or needs that are today of lesser priority must be reevaluated in terms of present conditions.
>
> It is implied in the zero-base budget approach that the need for programs and their recommended magnitude in [this] fiscal year . . . be clearly and specifically demonstrated. . . . The justification should be prepared on the assumption that all information needed for making budget decisions should be included.[33]

3. *Ignoring the fact that budgets must be changed periodically.* Managers should recognize that such factors as costs of materials, newly developed technology, and product demand constantly are changing and that budgets should be reviewed and modified periodically in response to these changes. A special type of budget called a variable budget is sometimes used to determine automatically such needed changes in budgets. **Variable budgets** outline various levels of resources to be allocated for each organizational activity, depending on the level of production within the organization. It follows, then, that a variable budget automatically indicates increases or decreases in the amount of resources allocated for various organizational activities, depending on whether production levels increase or decrease. Variable budgets also have been called flexible budgets.

Variable budgets are budgets that outline various levels of resources to be allocated for each organizational activity, depending on the level of production within the organization. Also called flexible budgeting.

People Considerations in Using Budgets. Many managers believe that although budgets are valuable planning and control tools, they can result in major human relations problems in an organization. For example, in a classic article by Chris Argyris, budgets are shown to build pressures that unite workers against management, cause harmful conflict between management and factory workers, and create tensions that result in worker inefficiency and worker aggression against management.[34] Depending on the severity of such problems, budgets may result in more harm to the organization than good.

Several strategies have been suggested to minimize the human relations problems caused by budgets. The most often recommended strategy is to design and implement appropriate human relations training programs for finance personnel, accounting personnel, production supervisors, and all other key people involved in the formulation and use of budgets. These training programs should be designed to emphasize both the advantages and disadvantages of applying pressure on people through budgets and the possible results of using budgets to imply organization member success or failure.[35]

Ethics Highlight: Arco Budgets for Social Responsibility

Managers face situations in which they must budget or plan how funds will be both obtained and spent in a given period. Although managers have traditionally planned for how they will spend money in areas like marketing and production, one nontraditional area in which more and more modern managers are planning for how to spend money is social responsibility.

One company that has notable experience in budgeting in the social responsibility area is Arco. The Arco Foundation has played a very important role in corporate philanthropy and social responsibility in recent years. As did most other major oil companies, Arco experienced a period of sagging profits in the mid-1980s. Now, the company focuses on business in oil, gas, and coal while serving a new, smaller market in five midwestern states. Recent reports show that over a five-year period Arco's annual social responsibility grants program is up from $7.5 million to nearly $35 million. In addition, company management is aiming in the future to reach and maintain a contribution budget of 2 percent of pretax net income. Areas that have benefited from Arco's social responsibility contributions include higher education, the arts, neighborhood and economic development, and the environment. For example, an Arco Foundation Grant provides funding for the MESA program, which offers educational enrichment opportunities to stimulate student interest in math and science. The company's chairman, Lodrick Cook, has indicated that Arco will continue to budget for expenditures in the area of social responsibility.

Back to the Case

Budgets are control tools available to Airbus Industrie management for broader organizational control. The prerequisite for gaining maximum benefit from the use of these tools is a thorough understanding of the company's production process.

A budget would be Airbus Industrie's financial plan indicating how much money should be spent on such items as salaries, materials, and equipment. The budget, once prepared, would be a source of information to Airbus management regarding what steps for control, if any, should be taken. For example, if 60 percent of the annual allowance for production workers is already used up and 70 percent of the year still remains, Airbus Industrie management must assess the situation carefully to determine what, if anything, must be done. Management could decide to cut wages, lay off certain workers, or increase the salary allowance in the budget and decrease the monetary commitment to some other budget item, such as advertising.

To use budgets successfully, Airbus Industrie management must focus on significant expenses rather than minor ones, attempt to rejustify budgeted expenses at the company each time a budget is revised, and change the amounts allocated to various budgeted expenses as conditions change. Airbus Industrie management also must keep in mind that budgets can cause human relations problems and that training focusing on how to minimize such problems should be provided for all people involved in formulating and using Airbus Industrie budgets.

Ratio Analysis

The second tool for broader organizational control is ratio analysis.[36] A *ratio* is a relationship between two numbers that is calculated by dividing one number into the other. **Ratio analysis** is the process of generating information that summarizes the financial position of an organization through the calculation of ratios based on various financial measures that appear on the organization's balance sheet and income statements.[37] The ratios available to managers for controlling organizations typically are divided into four categories: (1) liquidity ratios, (2) leverage ratios, (3) activity ratios, (4) profitability ratios.

Liquidity Ratios. Ratios that indicate an organization's ability to meet upcoming financial obligations are called **liquidity ratios.** The better an organization is at meeting these obligations, the more liquid it is said to be. As a general rule, organizations should be liquid enough to meet their obligations, yet not so liquid that too many financial resources are sitting idle in anticipation of meeting upcoming debts. The two main types of liquidity ratios are the current ratio and the quick ratio.

The **current ratio** is calculated by dividing the dollar value of the organization's current assets by the dollar value of its current liabilities:

$$\text{Current ratio} = \frac{\text{Current assets}}{\text{Current liabilities}}$$

Current assets typically include cash, accounts receivable, and inventory. Current liabilities generally include accounts payable, short-term notes payable, and any other accrued expenses. The current ratio indicates to managers the organization's ability to meet its financial obligations in the short term.

The **quick ratio,** sometimes called the acid-test ratio, is computed by subtracting inventory from current assets and then dividing the difference by current liabilities:

$$\text{Quick ratio} = \frac{\text{Current assets} - \text{Inventory}}{\text{Current liabilities}}$$

The quick ratio is the same as the current ratio except that it does not include inventory in current assets. Because inventory can be difficult to convert into money or securities, the quick ratio gives managers information on the organization's ability to meet its financial obligations with no reliance on inventory.

Leverage Ratios. **Leverage ratios** indicate the relationships between organizational funds supplied by the owners of an organization and organizational funds supplied by various creditors. The more organizational funds furnished by creditors, the more leverage an organization is said to be employing. As a general

Ratio analysis is a control tool that summarizes the financial position of an organization by calculating ratios based on various financial measures.

Liquidity ratios are the ratios that indicate an organization's ability to meet upcoming financial obligations.

The **current ratio** is the liquidity ratio that indicates the organization's ability to meet its financial obligations in the short run.

The **quick ratio** is the liquidity ratio that indicates an organization's ability to meet its financial obligations with no reliance on inventory.

Leverage ratios are the ratios that indicate the relationship between organizational funds supplied by the owners of an organization and organizational funds supplied by creditors.

guideline, an organization should use leverage to the extent that borrowed funds can be used to generate additional profit without a significant amount of organizational ownership being established by creditors. Perhaps the two most commonly used leverage ratios are the debt ratio and the times interest earned ratio.

The **debt ratio** is calculated by dividing total organizational debt by total organizational assets:

$$\text{Debt ratio} = \frac{\text{Total debts}}{\text{Total assets}}$$

In essence, this ratio gives the percentage of all organizational assets provided by organizational creditors.

The kind of business an organization is in may help to determine whether a particular debt ratio is too high. As an example, the debt ratio at Unisys Corporation, a company that designs and manufactures computer-related equipment, recently reached 41.7 percent.[38] Some think that this level of financing is somewhat high for Unisys because no one knows for sure what kind of computers will be popular in ten years, and the ability of Unisys to repay this level of debt therefore becomes questionable. In contrast, this level of debt would probably be considered more acceptable for a basic food processing company like Heinz. Because many products Heinz now offers, such as ketchup, will probably still be in demand in ten years, the company's ability to repay its debt is less suspect.

The **times interest earned ratio** is calculated by dividing gross income, or earnings before interest and taxes, by the total amount of organizational interest charges incurred from borrowing needed resources:

$$\text{Times interest earned ratio} = \frac{\text{Gross income}}{\text{Interest charges}}$$

This ratio indicates the organization's ability to pay interest expenses directly from gross income.

Activity Ratios. **Activity ratios** indicate how well an organization is selling its products in relation to its available resources. Obviously, management's goal is to maximize the amount of sales per dollar invested in organizational resources. Three main activity ratios are (1) inventory turnover, (2) fixed assets turnover, and (3) total assets turnover.

Inventory turnover is calculated by dividing organizational sales by inventory:

$$\text{Inventory turnover} = \frac{\text{Sales}}{\text{Inventory}}$$

This ratio indicates whether an organization is maintaining an appropriate level of inventory in relation to its sales volume. In general, as sales volume increases or decreases, an organization's inventory level should fluctuate correspondingly.

Fixed assets turnover is calculated by dividing fixed assets, or plant and equipment, into total sales:

$$\text{Fixed assets turnover} = \frac{\text{Sales}}{\text{Fixed assets}}$$

This ratio indicates the appropriateness of the amount of funds invested in plant and equipment relative to the level of sales.

The **debt ratio** is the leverage ratio that indicates the percentage of all organizational assets provided by organizational creditors.

Times interest earned ratio is the leverage ratio that indicates an organization's ability to pay interest expenses directly from gross income.

Activity ratios are ratios that indicate how well an organization is selling its products in relation to its available resources.

Inventory turnover is the activity ratio that indicates whether an organization is maintaining an appropriate level of inventory in relation to its sales volume.

Fixed assets turnover is the activity ratio that indicates the appropriateness of the amount of funds invested in plant and equipment relative to the level of sales.

Total assets turnover is the activity ratio that indicates the level of funds an organization has tied up in all assets relative to its rate of sales.

Profitability ratios are the ratios that indicate the ability of an organization to generate profits.

Profit to sales ratio is the profitability ratio that indicates whether the organization is making an adequate net profit in relation to the total dollars coming into the organization.

Profit to total assets ratio is the profitability ratio that indicates whether the organization is realizing enough net profit in relation to the total dollars invested in assets.

Total assets turnover is calculated by dividing sales by total assets:

$$\text{Total assets turnover} = \frac{\text{Sales}}{\text{Total assets}}$$

The focus of this ratio is on the appropriateness of the level of funds the organization has tied up in all assets relative to its rate of sales.

Profitability Ratios. **Profitability ratios** focus on assessing overall organizational profitability and improving it wherever possible. Major profitability ratios include the profit to sales ratio and the profit to total assets ratio.

The **profit to sales ratio** is calculated by dividing the net profit of an organization by its total sales:

$$\text{Profit to sales ratio} = \frac{\text{Net profit}}{\text{Sales}}$$

This ratio indicates whether the organization is making an adequate net profit in relation to the total dollars coming into the organization.

The **profit to total assets ratio** is calculated by dividing the net profit of an organization by its total assets:

$$\text{Profit to total assets ratio} = \frac{\text{Net profit}}{\text{Total assets}}$$

This ratio indicates whether the organization is realizing enough net profit in relation to the total dollars invested in assets.

Using Ratios to Control Organizations. Managers can use ratio analysis in three ways to control an organization.[39] First, managers should evaluate all ratios simultaneously. This strategy ensures that managers will develop and implement a control strategy appropriate for the organization as a whole rather than one that suits only one phase or segment of the organization.

Second, managers should compare computed values for ratios in a specific organization with the values of industry averages for those ratios. (The values of industry averages for the ratios can be obtained from Dun & Bradstreet; Robert Morris Associates, a national association of bank loan officers; the Federal Trade Commission; and the Securities and Exchange Commission.) Managers can increase the probability of formulating and implementing appropriate control strategies by comparing their financial situation to that of competitors.

Third, managers' use of ratios to control an organization also should involve trend analysis. Managers must remember that any set of ratio values is actually only a determination of relationships that exist in a specified time period, perhaps a year. To use ratio analysis to its maximum advantage, values for ratios should be accumulated for a number of successive time periods to uncover specific organizational trends. Once these trends are uncovered, managers can formulate and implement appropriate strategies for dealing with them.

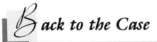

Back to the Case

Ratio analysis is another tool available to Airbus Industrie managers for broader organizational control. Ratio analysis would indicate the financial position of Airbus Industrie by determining relationships between various financial factors on the company's income statement and balance sheet. More specifically, Airbus Industrie management could use liquidity ratios to determine the company's ability to pay its debts, leverage ratios to indicate the appropriateness of the amount of debt used to run the company, activity ratios to indicate the level of activity at the company relative to its resources, and profitability ratios to indicate the appropriateness of Airbus Industrie's profit level.

As with all control tools, Airbus Industrie's management must use these ratios as a basis for a more subjective development and implementation of appropriate control strategies. Company management should evaluate all ratio information simultaneously, compare Airbus Industrie ratio values to the values of industry averages for the same ratios, and analyze ratio values for several successive time periods to identify and control any financial trends that might exist at Airbus Industrie.

Action Summary

Reread the learning objectives that follow. Each objective is followed by questions. Answering these questions accurately will help you retain the most important concepts discussed in this chapter. After answering each question, check your answer with the answer key at the end of this chapter. (*Hint:* If you have doubt regarding the correct response, consult the page whose number follows the answer.)

Circle:

From studying this chapter, I will attempt to acquire:

1. **Definitions of both *production* and *production control*.**
   a. *Production* is defined simply as the transformation of organizational resources into: (a) profits; (b) plans; (c) forecasts; (d) processes; (e) products.   a, b, c, d, e
   b. *Production control* is ensuring that an organization produces goods and services as planned.   T, F

2. **An understanding of how productivity and layout patterns relate to the production process.**
   a. The ratio that defines productivity is: (a) inputs/outputs; (b) outputs/profit; (c) outputs/inputs; (d) profits/inputs; (e) none of the above.   a, b, c, d, e
   b. Improving product quality does not normally lead to improvement in productivity.   T, F
   c. Which of the following layout patterns is usually used to manufacture airplanes: (a) process layout; (b) product layout; (c) fixed position layout; (d) customer layout; (e) assembly-line layout.   a, b, c, d, e

3. **An appreciation for the significance of operations management.**
   a. Which of the following is *not* one of the operations management activities: (a) selecting; (b) designing; (c) updating; (d) operating-controlling; (e) all of the above are operations management activities.   a, b, c, d, e
   b. Scheduling is the first step to be taken in operations management.   T, F

4. **Insights concerning how management by exception and breakeven analysis can be used to control production.**

T, F

   a. Management by exception is a control technique that allows only significant deviations between planned and actual performance to be brought to the manager's attention.

a, b, c, d, e

   b. The overall effect on the breakeven point of increasing costs or decreasing selling prices is that: (a) the number of products an organization must sell to break even increases; (b) the amount of profit a firm will receive at a fixed number of units sold increases; (d) the number of products an organization must sell to break even decreases; (d) a and b; (e) there is no effect on the breakeven point.

5. **An understanding of how quality control and materials requirements planning and control can contribute to production control.**

a, b, c, d, e

   a. A process used to determine how many units of a product from a larger number should be inspected to calculate a probability that the total number of units meets organizational quality standards is: (a) quality control; (b) materials requirements planning; (c) materials requirements control; (d) statistical quality control; (e) all of the above.

T, F

   b. Quality circles generally have circle members identifying problems and management then finding solutions to those problems.

a, b, c, d, e

   c. Input data for the computer in a materials requirements planning system come from all of the following sources except: (a) an accounts receivable file; (b) a master production schedule; (c) a bill of material file; (d) an inventory file; (e) all of the above are sources.

6. **Knowledge of how budgets and ratio analysis can be used to achieve overall or broader organizational control.**

a, b, c, d, e

   a. Potential pitfalls of using budgets as control tools include: (a) too much emphasis placed on relatively insignificant organizational expenses; (b) changing budgets periodically; (c) increasing budgeted expenses year after year without adequate information; (d) a and c; (e) a and b.

a, b, c, d, e

   b. Which of the following is an activity ratio: (a) inventory turnover ratio; (b) current ratio; (c) debt ratio; (d) quick ratio; (e) times interest earned ratio.

 ntroductory Case Wrap-Up

"Production Problems with the Airbus?" (p. 548) and its related back-to-the-case sections were written to help you better understand the management concepts contained in this chapter. Answer the following discussion questions about this introductory case to further enrich your understanding of chapter content:

1. What problems could be causing plane defects at

Airbus Industrie? List as many problems as possible.

2. What would you do to solve the problems identified in question 1?

3. Does the recurrence of defects in the Airbus A320 represent a serious situation for Airbus Industrie? Explain fully.

Issues for Review and Discussion

1. Define both *production* and *production control.*

2. Thoroughly explain the equation used to define productivity.

3. Discuss several traditional strategies that managers can use to increase organizational productivity.

4. Discuss the relationship between quality and productivity.

5. Discuss the importance of robots in building productive organizations in the future.

6. What is a layout pattern, and what is its relationship to productivity?

7. Name the three basic types of layout patterns and give an example of each.

8. List five criteria for efficient and effective plant layout and explain how each can contribute to increasing productivity.

9. Explain the term *operations management* as well as the major managerial activities involved in operations management.

10. What steps usually are recommended to manage production successfully? Be sure to discuss each step as well as the relationships among the steps.

11. What is a control tool?

12. Define *management by exception* and describe how it can help managers control production.

13. List and define seven major ingredients of breakeven analysis.

14. How can managers use breakeven analysis as an aid in controlling production?

15. What is materials requirements planning, and how can it aid in production control?

16. Discuss how quality circles normally operate. What purpose do they serve?

17. Define *statistical quality control* and describe its role in production control.

18. Define *budget*. How can managers use a budget to control an organization?

19. List three potential pitfalls of budgets.

20. What is ratio analysis?

21. List and define the four basic types of ratios.

22. What can the profit to sales ratio and the profit to total assets ratio tell managers about organizational profitability?

23. What guidelines would you recommend to managers using ratio analysis to control an organization?

Building on What You Know

Directions

Review the Highlight feature as indicated below and answer its corresponding questions. Questions in this section focus on relating a Highlight appearing in this chapter to management concepts that you have learned in a previous chapter.

Review the Global Highlight: GMFancu on page 553. In chapter 17 you studied about various types of controlling and how power is related to control. If you were introducing the use of robots in an organization, which type of control (precontrol, concurrent control, or postcontrol) would you emphasize most in attempting to preserve product quality? Explain. Give an example of one action that you might take in order to precontrol, concurrent control, and postcontrol in this situation. Would the amount of power that you possess be important to you in introducing the robots in your company? Explain.

Action Summary Answer Key

1. a. e, p. 549
   b. T, p. 549

2. a. c, p. 549
   b. F, p. 551
   c. c, p. 554

3. a. e, p. 555
   b. F, pp. 555–556

4. a. T, p. 557
   b. a, p. 561

5. a. d, p. 567
   b. F, p. 566
   c. a, p. 563

6. a. d, pp. 568–570
   b. a, p. 573

Case Study

Caterpillar's Factory, A Star

by Mary S. Thibodeaux, University of North Texas

According to a recent *Fortune* article, many U.S. companies have relegated their factories to the status of "just another cost center," but for Caterpillar ("Cat"), the world's largest producer of earth-moving construction equipment, the factory is a star. In an effort to recover from financial problems experienced in the 1980s, Cat is hard at work training employees to work with new robots, computerized assembly machinery, and new ways of thinking and behaving. Materials handling equipment is now broken into thirteen profit centers (down from twenty-two plants) and has brought together on the factory floor the design engineers and marketing and pricing personnel to work alongside production workers. Cat is now able to focus its "three key aspects of manufacturing"—people, process, and design—all together. The new factory design is called "PWAF (pee-waf)," for plant with a future.

Business Week reports that Cat's goal is "a 20 percent cut in total manufacturing costs—about $1.5 billion a year—when its plant update is finished in late 1992 or 1993." Plants, suppliers, and dealerships will be linked by a global electronic information network. The idea is to make Cat one of the most efficient producers of earth-moving equipment.

What is so different about PWAF? Consider the old plants: Bins of parts sat in work-in-process inventory for weeks at a time. Parts were shuttled back and forth between buildings, losing time and money. The process seemed haphazard at best. PWAF plans are based on cell production.

In a nonrefurbished section of one transmission factory stands an assembly line of 35 machine tools, each with at least one operator. Only one kind of case can be worked on at a time, with a two- to forty-eight-hour setup time for each new casing. On the other side of the plant, the cellular system is in use. Each cell does its own milling, drilling, sorting, etc. However, because the cells are designed to handle several different cases, the setup time per case is reduced to a few seconds. Pierre Guerindon, creator of PWAF, says the work time to produce each transmission has been cut from 90 days down to 15!

To assist with installing the changes, Caterpillar has established corporate manufacturability teams, including representatives from purchasing, manufacturing, and engineering; the teams meet monthly. Simplification is emphasized in product designs, manufacturing processes, and operating procedures. It costs less. Competition from companies such as Komatsu, Ltd., puts pressure on Caterpillar to get things right the first time and to get the most out of scarce resources. Cat is now simplifying virtually all areas of its operations.

In an industry where most companies are organized by function, Cat's new system requires multifunctionalized interaction. At Cat, team building across function lines closely resembles a matrix organizational philosophy.

Suppliers are also involved in the process from an early stage of product design. This is because new inventory controls are based on just-in-time (JIT) methods; trust and commitment are necessary between Cat and suppliers. The relationship is solidified by the Caterpillar Supplier Certification program begun in the late 1970s. Certification can take as long as two years, and is under continuous review.

Caterpillar is not known traditionally as an industry pacesetter, as it allows its competitors to lead in both product design and customer complaints. Once technology has been developed and problems ironed out by trial-and-error elsewhere, Caterpillar introduces trouble-free products that enhance the company's reputation for high quality. Products must not only be high in quality, but also capital intensive and capable of benefiting from high technology, and they must fit into Cat's distribution system.

The dealer network and distribution system has been a key contributor to Cat's success. Caterpillar parts are distributed through a network of twenty-two facilities in ten countries. Products are sold and serviced through a global network of approximately 225 independent dealers and one company-owned dealership. Dealers, for the most part, strongly support Cat's policies and are very loyal.

Like many other multinational enterprises, Caterpillar has a need to communicate with some dealer service personnel who speak little or no English. This communication problem is magnified by a degree of technical product sophistication that makes it hard even for an experienced service technician to rely solely on retained skills and knowledge. So, in addition to translating its more than 20,000 technical publications into French, German, Spanish, and Portuguese, Cat has developed "Caterpillar Fundamental English." This language consists of about 850 words of correct, simple English, used to create a standard single version of any service publication for immediate use worldwide.

Company officials assert that Caterpillar has committed itself to a long-term point of view and will continue with its plant modernization program. They expect to realize major benefits from a new emphasis on product design and annual quality-improvement programs—and from simplification.

Discussion Questions

1. In moving from a traditional American system of manufacturing to a flexible, JIT/Japanese style, do you think Caterpillar is trying to do too much too quickly based on the information presented? Why or why not?

2. Which layout pattern did the old Caterpillar system of manufacture most closely resemble? What about the PWAF system?

3. Describe the JIT system, and explain how it benefits Caterpillar's PWAFs.

4. Consider the algebraic equation for breakeven analysis:

    BE = Fixed costs/(Price minus Variable Costs).

How do you think Caterpillar's PWAF system will lower the breakeven point of manufacture most directly in the long run?

Profits and People: Robert Rich of Rich Products

Robert Rich, although still in his forties, is the president of Rich Food Products, Inc., one of the largest industries in Buffalo, New York. He is a second-generation leader; the company was founded in 1945 by his father, Robert Rich, Sr., who continues to serve as its chair.

Like many children in family businesses, Rich was set to work learning the business from the ground up. He recalls,

> I've worked in every phase of the business. I used to work loading trucks in the summertime and I've worked in the plant several summers as well. I think it's literally impossible for anyone to make decisions about any part of a business if they haven't worked in that part of the business.

However, the part of the business he enjoys most is the sound of the shop floor: "It's very loud out here, but this sounds to me like jobs for the people in the community." With calculated and well-managed expansion through both growth strategies and new acquisitions, Rich Food Products has grown and created many new jobs in Buffalo and around the country. Rich Products now operates 38 production facilities, all dedicated to processing and packaging frozen and preserved food products that range from Coffee Rich, the company's first and flagship product, to barbecued beef and bakery products.

The Riches made a commitment to automation early in the corporation's development and have continued to invest in the latest technology available for food processing, packaging, and shipping. Measuring, mixing, wrapping, and labeling are all tasks that can be handled more quickly by machines than by people. In Rich's factories, machines do the cooking, and people run the machines.

Materials-requirement planning is especially important to a company involved with food products because spoilage is a crucial consideration when inventories of perishable raw materials are involved. Frozen and dried substitutes for fresh ingredients are not universally acceptable, so many fresh materials are required every day.

Therefore, planning ahead to identify necessary quantities and factory shelf life of raw materials or ingredients is a high priority for all thirty-eight Rich Food Products facilities. Scheduling the purchases, shipping, delivery, and timely off-loading is also crucial. Just-in-time (JIT) inventory control methods could have been invented for the business of processing food products.

Another important aspect of JIT methods is the factory shelf life of the finished product. Even deep-frozen food has a limited life span before it begins deterioration, and Robert Rich does not want his name associated with freezer-burned or tasteless food. JIT inventory control systems can continue to be useful after production, too, because they can be designed to make production schedules as well as raw-material orders conform to advance sales projections. For example, if a major supermarket chain plans to increase promotions for frozen diet entrées and decrease their inventory of frozen pizzas in April, as a part of "National Weight Loss Month," their advance orders provide input to the JIT projections, which in turn enable the factory to reduce orders for pizza materials and increase orders for skim milk and reduced-calorie cheese.

Tight controls over all aspects of production, from JIT shipping of raw materials to carefully selected servicing downtime for shop floor machinery, are integral to the success of Rich Food Products. Like many successful businesspeople, Robert Rich is impatient with people and with systems that do not recognize the need for these controls:

> I think that most people in business are used to having a timetable, moving along, maybe even being arbitrary at times to get things done. . . . I think the best thing that our company, for example, can do politically is do what we do best and provide jobs for our area, and that's the life blood of business. I think that's the goal of business.

Rich is a leader who prides himself on developing not only new opportunities and jobs, but also the capabilities of his employees. His pride in his community and in his company is evident to them, and that in turn motivates them to be proud of what they do. Pride in a high-quality product is a great spur to productivity—one Rich knows from personal experience. Pride in personal achievement is another spur he wants his people to feel, too. "One of my major objectives is to . . . be there when people need me, but make sure that they're being given the decision-making power, that they're being paid to perform."

Video Case Questions

1. A primary goal for Rich Food Products is to provide new jobs through organizational growth. Deming's chain reaction shows providing new jobs as a final outcome of improving quality. Give two examples of ways in which a Rich factory might improve quality to achieve this goal.

2. List three possible uses for robotics in one of the Rich Products facilities.

3. Assume that Rich Food Products has just acquired a major producer of bakery products. In the weeks immediately following this acquisition, how do you think the current ratio, the quick ratio, and the debt ratio will be affected?

4. When Rich Products upgrades the automation in a production facility, the fixed costs for that facility increase. In order to maintain the same breakeven point, what changes can be made in other aspects of the facility's business? What would you recommend?

Video Case Activities

1. Consult Figure 18.1, which shows inputs, transformation processes, and outputs for three very different sorts of industries. Robert Rich is very interested in baseball; he owns the Buffalo Bisons, the AAA farm team for the Pittsburgh Pirates. Prepare a figure like Figure 18.1 in the text, showing the input-to-output process for the Bisons.

2. Design a sample layout for a Rich factory producing frozen potato products, specifically both french-fried potatoes and hash-brown patties. Include ingredient storage areas, food-preparation areas (handling and cooking), packaging areas, storage for finished products, and a shipping area.

Chapter 19

Student Learning Objectives

From studying this chapter, I will attempt to acquire:

1. An understanding of the relationship between data and information.

2. Insights on the main factors that influence the value of information.

3. Knowledge of some potential steps for evaluating information.

4. An appreciation for the role of computers in handling information.

5. An understanding of the importance of a management information system (MIS) to an organization.

6. A feasible strategy for establishing an MIS.

7. Information about what a management decision support system is and how it operates.

Information

 hapter Outline

CONSOLIDATED INSURANCE GROUP CHANGES TO PCs TO MANAGE INFORMATION

Consolidated Insurance Group recently pulled the plug on the IBM 3090 mainframe at its Wilmington, Del., headquarters. Technicians drained the cooling fluid and wheeled the minivan-length computer out on a dolly. Wayne Read, data processing chief, shut off the air conditioners that kept the glass-walled computer room at a constant 67° [F]. Now he's planning a party to celebrate the company's conversion from the $3 million mainframe to a $300,000 network of personal computers.

Sitting in a cramped room is the heart of the new system: seven powerful PCs—the "servers" that control the central data bases—and the disk drives that store much of its data. But most of its muscle is in 150 desktop PCs. And the PC users love it. Instead of queuing up and eventually getting a lengthy report from the mainframe, they use their own software to tap the corporate data base. They get the information electronically, pick the parts they want, and print them out on a desk-side printer.

In switching to PCs, Consolidated Insurance appears to be in the vanguard of a revolution.

Many users "are very excited" about getting information so quickly, Mr. Read says. "With mainframes, you wait a day or two. Then, you may not like it and have another two-day turnaround."

In switching to PCs, Consolidated Insurance appears to be in the vanguard of a revolution. Personal computers have been the fastest-growing sector of the computer industry for a decade, of course, but most of them have taken on new tasks or replaced typewriters and cash registers rather than doing the heavy lifting performed by mainframes. Sending out bills, tracking corporate accounts, and managing payables and receivables has been considered too important to entrust to small computers. PC buffs talked about getting rid of mainframes, but few companies did so.

Even five years ago, any notion of replacing a mainframe with PCs was heresy. And impossible: PCs weren't powerful enough. But as PCs get ever faster and remain astonishingly cheap, more and more companies are concluding that their mainframes are dinosaurs. They cost too much; some run as high as $20 million. And PCs, besides being far cheaper, can do some jobs *better* than mainframes can. So, at long last, PCs are beginning to move into the core mainframe markets, the corporate data processing centers.

Dropping mainframes isn't painless. At Consolidated Insurance, which expects to cut annual operating costs by $1 million, 30 people used to do mainframe work and write new software when users asked for different information. Now, just 10 staffers are left; the rest started job-hunting as soon as they learned of the move to PCs. "You have people who have been in mainframe data processing for 15 or 20 years. They elected to leave because that's where they want to continue to make their living."

WHAT'S AHEAD

The introductory case discusses a decision at Consolidated Insurance Group to improve the management of information within the company by changing from an IBM mainframe computer to a network of personal computers. Management has concluded that higher-quality information can be generated at a more reasonable cost using the PCs as opposed to the mainframe. This chapter's discussion emphasizes the process involved in making such a decision in organizations.

Controlling is the process of making things happen as planned. Of course, managers cannot make things happen as planned if they lack information on the manner in which various events in the organization occur. This chapter discusses the fundamental principles of handling information in an organization by first presenting the essentials of information and then examining both the management information system (MIS) and the management decision support system (MDSS).

ESSENTIALS OF INFORMATION

The process of developing information begins with the gathering of some type of facts or statistics, called **data.** Once gathered, data typically are analyzed in some manner. In general terms, **information** is the conclusions derived from data analysis. In management terms, information is the conclusions derived from the analysis of data that relate to the operation of an organization. As examples to illustrate the relationship between data and information, managers gather data regarding pay rates that individuals are receiving within industries to develop information about how to develop competitive pay rates,[1] data regarding hazardous-materials accidents in order to gain information about how to improve worker safety,[2] and data regarding customer demographics in order to gain information about product demand in the future.[3]

Data are facts or statistics.
Information is the set of conclusions derived from data analysis.

The information that managers receive heavily influences managerial decision making, which in turn determines the activities that will be performed within the organization, which in turn dictate the eventual success or failure of the organization.[4] Some management writers consider information to be of such fundamental importance to the management process that they define *management* as the process of converting information into action through decision making.[5] The following sections discuss (1) factors that influence the value of information, (2) how to evaluate information, and (3) computer assistance in using information.

Factors Influencing the Value of Information

Some information is more valuable than other information.[6] The value of information is defined in terms of the benefit that can accrue to the organization through the use of the information. The greater this benefit, the more valuable the information.

Four primary factors determine the value of information: (1) information appropriateness, (2) information quality, (3) information timeliness, and (4) information quantity. In general, management should encourage the generation, distribution, and use of organizational information that is appropriate, of high quality, timely, and of sufficient quantity. Following this guideline will not necessarily guarantee sound decisions, but it will ensure that important resources necessary to make such decisions are available.[7] Each of the factors that determine information value is discussed in more detail in the paragraphs that follow.

Information Appropriateness

Information appropriateness is defined in terms of how relevant the information is to the decision-making situation faced by the manager. If the information is quite relevant, then it is said to be appropriate. Generally, as the appropriateness of information increases, the value of that information increases.

Figure 19.1 shows the characteristics of information appropriate for the following common decision-making situations: (1) operational control, (2) management control, and (3) strategic planning.[8]

Operational control decisions relate to assuring that specific organizational tasks are carried out effectively and efficiently. Management control decisions relate to obtaining and effectively and efficiently using the organizational resources necessary to reach organizational objectives. Strategic planning decisions relate to determining organizational objectives and designating the corresponding action necessary to reach them.

As Figure 19.1 shows, characteristics of appropriate information change as managers shift from making operational control decisions to making management

Information appropriateness is the degree to which information is relevant to the decision-making situation that faces the manager.

Characteristics of Information	Operational Control	Management Control	Strategic Planning
Source	Largely internal	→	External
Scope	Well defined, narrow	→	Very wide
Level of aggregation	Detailed	→	Aggregate
Time horizon	Historical	→	Future
Currency	Highly current	→	Quite old
Required accuracy	High	→	Low
Frequency of use	Very frequent	→	Infrequent

FIGURE 19.1

Characteristics of information appropriate for decisions related to operational control, management control, and strategic planning

control decisions to making strategic planning decisions. Strategic planning decision makers need information that focuses on the relationship of the organization to its external environment, emphasizes the future, is wide in scope, and presents a broad view. Appropriate information for this type of decision is usually old and not completely accurate.

Information appropriate for making operational control decisions has dramatically different characteristics than information appropriate for making strategic planning decisions. Operational control decision makers need information that focuses for the most part on the internal organizational environment, emphasizes the performance history of the organization, and is well defined, narrow in scope, and detailed. In addition, appropriate information for this type of decision is both highly current and highly accurate.

Information appropriate for making management control decisions generally has characteristics that fall somewhere between the extreme characteristics of appropriate operational control information and appropriate strategic planning information.

Information Quality

The second primary factor that determines the value of information is **information quality**—the degree to which information represents reality. The more closely information represents reality, the higher the quality and the greater the value of the information. In general, the higher the quality of information available to managers, the better equipped the managers are to make appropriate decisions and the greater the probability that the organization will be successful over the long term. Perhaps the most significant factor in producing poor-quality information is data contamination. An issue like inaccurate data gathering can result in information that is of very low quality—a poor representation of reality.[9]

Information quality is the degree to which information represents reality.

Information Timeliness

Information timeliness, the third primary factor that determines the value of information, is the extent to which the receipt of information allows decisions to be made and action to be taken so the organization can gain some benefit from possessing the information. Information received by managers at a point when it can be used to the advantage of the organization is said to be timely.

For example, a product may be selling poorly because its established market price is significantly higher than that of competitive products. If this information is received by management after the product has been discontinued, the information will be untimely. If, however, it is received soon enough to adjust the selling price of the product and thereby significantly increase sales, it will be timely.

Information timeliness is the extent to which the receipt of information allows decisions to be made and action to be taken so the organization can gain some benefit from possessing the information.

Information Quantity

The fourth and final determinant of the value of information is **information quantity**—the amount of decision-related information managers possess. Before making a decision, managers should assess the quantity of information they possess that relates to the decision being made. If this quantity is judged to be insufficient, more information should be gathered before the decision is made. If the amount of information is judged to be as complete as necessary, managers can feel justified in making the decision.

Information quantity is the amount of decision-related information a manager possesses.

Evaluating Information

Evaluating information is the process of determining whether the acquisition of specified information is justified. As with all evaluations of this kind, the primary concern of management is to weigh the dollar value of benefit gained from using some quantity of information against the cost of generating that information.

According to the flowchart in Figure 19.2, the first major step in evaluating

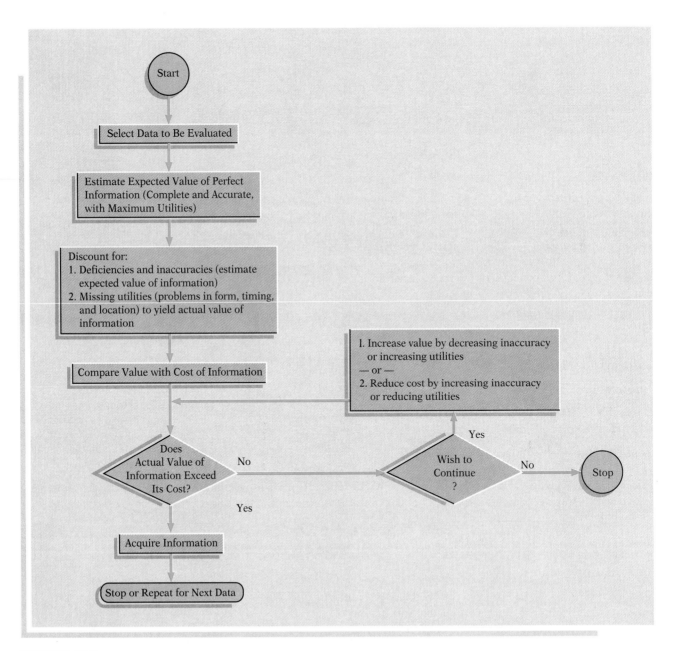

FIGURE 19.2
Flowchart of main activities in evaluating information

TABLE 19.1 Characteristics that tend to limit the usefulness of information and how to eliminate them

Characteristics That Tend to Limit the Usefulness of Information	Possible Actions to Eliminate These Characteristics*
Language or format not understood	Translate, revise, or change format
Volume excessive: Time required to examine information exceeds the intuitive estimate of the value of the contents	Condense
Received before need perceived	Store for possible future need
Received after needed	Ensure against future occurrence
Inaccessible	Create access
Time or cost of access excessive	Relocate data, change access
No right of use, or closed communication channels because of conflicting subunit goals, authority relationships, and so forth	Relocate information; alter or open transmission channels; change relationships

*The organization will incur some additional cost by taking one or more of these actions.

organizational information is to determine the value of that information by pinpointing the data to be analyzed and then determine the expected value or return to be received from obtaining perfect information based on these data. Next, this expected value should be reduced by the amount of benefit that will not be realized because of deficiencies and inaccuracies expected to appear in the information.

Then the expected value of organizational information should be compared with the expected cost of obtaining that information. If the expected cost does not exceed the expected value, the information should be gathered. If it does exceed the expected value, managers either must increase the information's expected value or decrease its expected cost before the information gathering can be justified. If neither of these objectives is possible, management cannot justify gathering the information.

One generally accepted strategy for increasing the expected value of information is to eliminate the characteristics of the information that tend to limit its usefulness. Table 19.1 lists some of these characteristics and the possible actions management can take to eliminate them.

 ack to the Case

Information at Consolidated Insurance Group can be defined as the conclusions derived from the analysis of data relating to the way in which the company operates. The case implies that managers at Consolidated Insurance Group will be better able to make sound decisions, including better control decisions, because of the improved data handling achieved by its new network of PCs.

One important factor in evaluating the general advisability of changing from a mainframe to a PC network would be the overall impact of the change on the value of information that company managers would receive. Evidently, management at Consolidated Insurance Group determined that changing from a mainframe to a PC network would enhance the value of information that organization members would receive, and at a reasonable cost. That is, for a reasonable cost, the change would enhance the appropriateness, quality, timeliness, and quantity of information that organization members would be able to use. Overall, management believed that the benefits of making the change to the PCs would outweigh the costs of making the change and therefore implemented the change.

Computer Assistance in Using Information

Managers have an overwhelming amount of data to gather, analyze, and transform into information before making numerous decisions. In fact, many managers in the United States as well as in the United Kingdom and other foreign countries are currently complaining that they are overloaded with information.[10] A computer is a tool managers can use to assist in the complicated and time-consuming task of generating this information. A **computer** is an electronic tool capable of accepting data, interpreting data, performing ordered operations on data, and reporting on the outcome of these operations. Computers give managers the ability to store vast amounts of financial, inventory, and other data so that the data will be readily accessible for making day-to-day decisions. Table 19.2 lists several specific computer operations for handling information.

The sections that follow discuss the main functions of computers and possible pitfalls in using computers.

A **computer** is an electronic tool capable of accepting data, interpreting data, performing ordered operations on data, and reporting on the outcome of these operations. Computers are extremely helpful in generating information from raw data.

Main Functions of Computers

A computer function is a computer activity that must be performed to generate organizational information. Computers perform five main functions: (1) input, (2) storage, (3) control, (4) processing, and (5) output. The relationships among these functions are shown in Figure 19.3 on page 592.

The **input function** consists of computer activities through which the computer enters the data to be analyzed and the instructions to be followed to analyze the data appropriately. As Figure 19.3 shows, the purpose of the input function is to provide data and instructions to be used in the performance of the storage, processing, control, and output functions.

The **storage function** consists of computer activities involved with retaining the material entered into the computer during the performance of the input function. The storage unit, or memory, of a computer is similar to the human memory in that various facts can be stored until they are needed for processing. In addition, facts can be stored, used in processing, and then restored as many times as necessary. As Figure 19.3 demonstrates, the storage, processing, and control activities are dependent on one another and ultimately yield computer output.

The five main functions of computers are:
1. The **input function**—computer activities through which the computer enters the data to be analyzed and the instructions to be followed to analyze the data appropriately.

2. The **storage function**—computer activities involved with retaining the material entered into the computer during the performance of the input function.

TABLE 19.2 Computer operations that assist management in handling information

Operation	How a Computer Can Aid Managers
Billing	Control of buying, inventory, selling; rapid paying cycle; improved cash position; data about customers, products, items, costs, prices, sales representatives, sales statistics
Accounts receivable	Shorten average collections of accounts receivables; highlight past-due statements, improve cash flow, invoice summary
Sales analysis	Review sales volume on the basis of profit contributions as well as gross profit contribution; compute sales representatives' commission plans; pinpoint sales improvement for customers and sales representatives
Inventory	Provide control of inventory, generation of distribution-by-value report—that is, quantity sold annual sales are accumulated and printed as percentage of total number of items and total annual sales; pinpoint marginal items; segment inventory; establish order quantities and order points; cycle reviewing of vendor lines
Payroll	Construct payroll accounting system; produce reports to management, employees, government agencies; reduce peak workloads, strengthen managerial control over human resources
Materials planning	Determine components requirements; plan inventory per item by time period; determine how change in order quantity or delivery will affect production schedule; consolidate requirements of multiple-use items; reduce materials planning costs
Purchasing	Provide performance figures by item, supplier, and buyer in terms of cost, quality, and delivery; achieve tangible savings by meeting discount dates through faster processing of invoices; simplify analysis of historical data, expedite purchase orders based on production shortages and late deliveries
Dispatching and shop floor control	Reduce expediting costs because job status records are current; give early notification of exceptions requiring corrective action plus daily revisions of order priority by machine group
Capacity planning and operation scheduling	Make available labor requirements by time period in time to take corrective action; provide immediate information about effect of changes on work orders, simplified planning on availability of tools, realistic order release dates

Ethics Highlight: Burroughs Computerizes Benefits Information

Managers commonly face the situation of storing data in computers. One issue that must be faced in this situation is the ethical consideration of how management will keep private and personal data about organization members from being accessed by inappropriate individuals. Burroughs Wellcome, a large pharmaceutical company in North Carolina, has successfully dealt with this issue of maintaining employee privacy in its system of computer data storage.

At Burroughs Wellcome, rather than dedicating a large portion of the human resource department staff to answering routine questions about company benefits on a regular basis, management uses a computer-based system to answer such employee queries. Questions are answered consistently and accurately, twenty-four hours a day, seven days a week. More personal questions from employees can focus on specific questions regarding wages and wage rates as well as medical benefits. More general questions can also be asked regarding issues like job openings that exist within the company, weather-related plant closings, and holiday schedules. This system used at Burroughs even has a voice-response capability so that employee questions can get an oral response. The voice-response system is sophisticated enough to select, retrieve, and report responses from a large pool of data, yet simple enough to be accessed by a touch-tone telephone. Concern about the ethical issue of employee privacy is adequately addressed in the Burroughs system. Employees are issued personal identification numbers. No one can ask or access information about a specific employee without using the identification number issued to that employee.

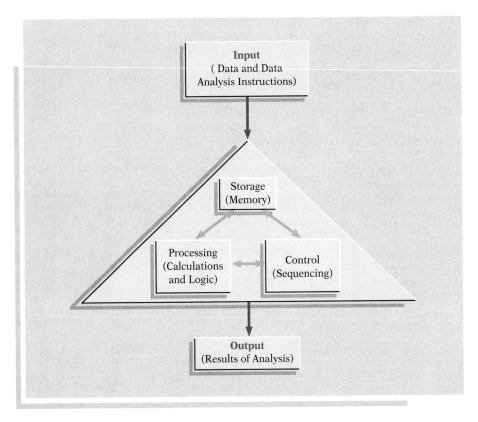

FIGURE 19.3

Relationships among the five main functions of a computer

The **processing function** consists of the computer activities involved with performing both logic and calculation steps necessary to analyze data appropriately. Calculation activities include virtually any numeric analysis. Logic activities include such analysis as comparing one number to another to determine which is larger. Data, as well as directions for processing the data, are furnished by input and storage activities.

Computer activities that dictate the order in which other computer functions are performed compose the **control function.** Control activities indicate (1) when data should be retrieved after storage, (2) when and how the data should be analyzed, (3) if and when the data should be restored after analysis, (4) if and when additional data should be retrieved, and (5) when output activities (described in the next paragraph) should begin and end.

The **output function** comprises the activities that take the results of the input, storage, processing, and control functions and transmit them outside the computer. These results can appear in such diverse forms as data on magnetic tape or characters typed on paper. Obviously, the form in which output appears is determined primarily by how the output is to be used. Output that appears on magnetic tape, for example, can be used as input for another computer analysis but is of little value for analysis by human beings.

3. The **processing function**—computer activities involved with performing the logic and calculation steps necessary to analyze data appropriately.

4. The **control function**—computer activities that dictate the order in which other computer functions are performed.

5. The **output function**—computer activities that take the results of input, storage, processing, and control functions and transmit them outside the computer.

Possible Pitfalls in Using Computers

The computer is a sophisticated management tool with the potential of making a significant contribution to organizational success. For this potential to materialize, however, the following possible pitfalls should be avoided:

1. *Thinking that a computer is capable of independently performing creative activities.* A computer does not lessen the organization's need for a manager's personal creative ability and professional judgment.[11] A computer is capable only of following precise and detailed instructions provided by the computer user. The individual using the computer must tell the computer exactly what to do, how to do it, and when to do it. Computers are simply pieces of equipment that must be directed very precisely by computer users to perform some function.

2. *Spending too much money on computer assistance.*[12] In general, computers can be of great assistance to managers. The initial cost of purchasing a computer as well as updating it when necessary, however, can be very high.[13] Managers need to keep comparing the benefit obtained from computer assistance with the cost of obtaining this assistance. In essence, an investment in a computer should be expected to help the organization generate enough added revenue to not only finance the computer, but also contribute an acceptable level of net profit.[14]

3. *Overestimating the value of computer output.* Some managers fall into the trap of assuming that they have "the answer" once they have received information generated by computer analysis. The cartoon on the next page illustrates problems that can arise when organization members think that computers generate "the answer." Managers must recognize that computer output is only as good as the quality of data and directions for analyzing the data that human beings have put into the computer. Inaccurate data or inappropriate computer instructions yield useless computer output. A commonly used phrase to describe such an occurrence is "garbage in, garbage out."

'Sorry, but according to our brand-new $40,000 computer, we don't have any paintbrushes — and if we did, it wouldn't know how much to charge for one.'

Orlando Sentinel (May 1, 1989).

 ack to the Case

The central issue in comparing a mainframe and a PC network in an organization focuses on how the two alternatives vary on the basis of accepting data, interpreting data, performing operations on the data, and reporting on the outcome of these operations. A number of facts in the case illustrate differences along these lines. In terms of the mainframe, it required a cooling fluid to make sure that it didn't overheat, a special temperature-controlled room, about a day, on average, to get generated reports to managers who ordered them, and then required another day or two if the report had to be somewhat redesigned. In terms of the PC network, it has the advantages of requiring less temperature control and less specially tailored physical space, it enables managers to get into the company database directly by using their own software, and it allows managers to receive reports almost instantaneously at printers positioned next to their personal computers.

The PC network at Consolidated Insurance Group is capable of not only storing and processing data related to performing functions such as control at the company, but of handling additional operations related to such areas as payroll, sales analysis, billing, and purchasing. Essentially, the PC network seems to be able to do what the mainframe does, and in a lot of cases to do it better, at a cost of $300,000, as opposed to the $3 million mainframe. As was true with using a mainframe, however, Consolidated Insurance Group members should keep in mind that the PC network is incapable of performing creatively and therefore its output should be scrutinized carefully and never used as "the answer."

THE MANAGEMENT INFORMATION SYSTEM (MIS)

In simple terms, a **management information system (MIS)** is a network established within an organization to provide managers with information that will assist them in decision making. The following, more complete definition of an MIS was developed by the Management Information System Committee of the Financial Executives Institute:

> An MIS is a system designed to provide selected decision-oriented information needed by management to plan, control, and evaluate the activities of the corporation. It is designed within a framework that emphasizes profit planning, performance planning, and control at all levels. It contemplates the ultimate integration of required business information subsystems, both financial and nonfinancial, within the company.[15]

The title of the specific organization member responsible for developing and maintaining an MIS varies from organization to organization. In smaller organizations, a president or vice president may possess this responsibility. In larger organizations, an individual with a title such as "director of information systems" may be solely responsible for appropriately managing an entire MIS department. The term *MIS manager* is used in the sections that follow to indicate the person within the organization who has the primary responsibility for managing the MIS. The term *MIS personnel* is used to designate the nonmanagement individuals within the organization who possess the primary responsibility of actually operating the MIS. Examples of nonmanagement individuals are computer operators and computer programmers. The sections that follow describe an MIS more fully and outline the steps managers take to establish an MIS.

A **management information system (MIS)** is a network established in an organization to provide managers with information that will assist them in decision making. An MIS gets information to where it is needed.

Global Highlight: Pohang Iron & Steel Company Needs a Complex MIS

Managers face situations involving the use of a management information system in managing activities at virtually all levels of an organization. This description implies that although an MIS may be relatively simple, some managers also have to face a situation of developing and using a very complex MIS, especially if their organizations are of significant size.

Management at the Pohang Iron & Steel Company in Korea faced the challenge of developing a complex MIS in order to manage its organizational activities efficiently and effectively. A complex MIS was needed primarily as a result of the large size of the company and the complexity of the activities involved in manufacturing steel. The company's MIS system permits managers to monitor any phase of the steel production process. In addition, the system continually monitors about 60,000 items that are critical in controlling production costs and, at specified intervals, automatically updates the status of these items. To best interpret and react to information that flows on its MIS, management uses regularly scheduled video conferences with organization members in different locations. Pohang is the only Korean company to use regularly scheduled video conferences in this fashion. Pohang was founded in 1973 by the government of the Republic of Korea and is now the second largest and most competitive steelmaker in the world. The company's success is largely credited to its development and use of its sophisticated MIS.

Describing the MIS

The MIS is perhaps best described by a summary of the steps necessary to properly operate an MIS and by a discussion of the different kinds of information various managers need to make job-related decisions.

Operating the MIS

MIS personnel generally perform six sequential steps to properly operate an MIS.[16] (Figure 19.4 summarizes the steps and indicates the order in which they are performed.) The first step is to determine what information is needed within the organization, when it will be needed, and in what form it will be needed. Because the basic purpose of the MIS is to assist management in making decisions, one way to begin determining management information needs is to analyze (1) decision areas in which management makes decisions, (2) specific decisions within these decision areas that management actually must make, and (3) alternatives that must be evaluated to make these specific decisions. Table 19.3 presents such an analysis for a manager making decisions related to production and operations management.

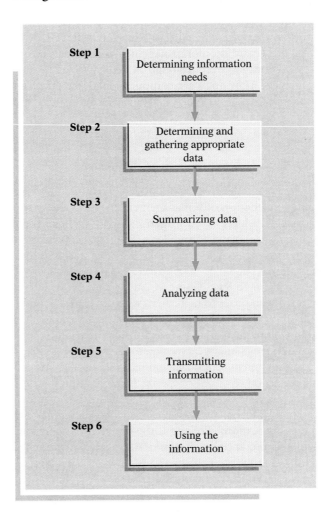

FIGURE 19.4

The six steps necessary to operate an MIS properly in order of their performance

TABLE 19.3 Decision areas, decisions, and alternatives related to production and operations management

Decision Areas	Decisions	Alternatives
Plant and equipment	Span of process	Make or buy
	Plant size	One big plant or several smaller ones
	Plant location	Locate near markets or locate near materials
	Investment decisions	Invest mainly in buildings, or equipment, or inventories, or research
	Choice of equipment	General-purpose or special-purpose equipment
	Kind of tooling	Temporary, minimum tooling or "production tooling"
Production planning and control	Frequency of inventory taking	Few or many breaks in production for buffer stocks
	Inventory size	High inventory or a lower inventory
	Degree of inventory control	Control in great detail or in lesser detail
	What to control	Controls designed to minimize machine downtime, or labor cost, or time in process, or to maximize output of particular products or material usage
	Quality control	High reliability and quality or low costs
	Use of standards	Formal, or informal, or none at all
Labor and staffing	Job specialization	Highly specialized or not highly specialized
	Supervision	Technically trained first-line supervisors or nontechnically trained supervisors
	Wage system	Many job grades or few job grades; incentive wages or hourly wages
	Supervision	Close supervision or loose supervision
	Industrial engineers	Many or few industrial engineers
Product design/ engineering	Size of product line	Many customer specials, or few specials, or none at all
	Design stability	Frozen design or many engineering change orders
	Technological risk	Use of new processes unproved by competitors or follow-the-leader policy
	Engineering	Complete packaged design or design-as-you-go approach
	Use of manufacturing engineering	Few or many manufacturing engineers
Organization and management	Kind of organization	Functional, or product focus, or geographical, or other
	Executive use of time	High involvement in investment, or production planning, or cost control, or quality control, or other activities
	Degree of risk assumed	Decisions based on much or little information
	Use of staff	Large or small staff group
	Executive style	Much or little involvement in detail; authoritarian or nondirective style; much or little contact with organization

The second major step in operating the MIS is pinpointing and collecting the data that will yield needed organizational information. This step is just as important as determining the information needs of the organization. If collected data do not relate properly to information needs, it will be impossible to generate needed information.

After the information needs of the organization have been determined and appropriate data have been pinpointed and gathered, summarizing the data and analyzing the data are, respectively, the third and fourth steps MIS personnel generally should take to properly operate an MIS. It is in the performance of these steps that MIS personnel find computer assistance of great benefit.

The fifth and sixth steps are transmitting the information generated by data analysis to appropriate managers and having the managers actually use the information. The performance of these last two steps results in managerial decision making. Although each of the six steps is necessary if an MIS is to run properly, the time spent on performing each step naturally will vary from organization to organization.

Different Managers Need Different Kinds of Information

For maximum benefit, an MIS must collect relevant data, transform that data into appropriate information, and transmit that information to the appropriate managers. Appropriate information for one manager within an organization, however, may not be appropriate information for another. Robert G. Murdick suggests that the degree of appropriateness of MIS information for a manager depends on the activities for which the manager will use the information, the organizational objectives assigned to the manager, and the level of management at which the manager functions.[17] All of these factors, of course, are closely related.

Murdick's thoughts on this matter are best summarized in Figure 19.5. As can be seen from this figure, because the overall job situations of top managers, middle managers, and first-line managers are significantly different, the kinds of information these managers need to satisfactorily perform their jobs also are significantly different.

Back to the Case

The comparison of the mainframe and the PC network at Consolidated Insurance Group should include an analysis of each as the main ingredient of the company's MIS. The MIS at Consolidated is the organizational network established to provide managers with information that helps them make job-related decisions. In using a mainframe, the Consolidated MIS would necessitate the use of several MIS personnel who would help determine information needs at the company, help determine and collect appropriate Consolidated data, summarize and analyze these data, transmit analyzed data to appropriate Consolidated managers, and generally help managers in interpreting received MIS information. By changing to the PC network, Consolidated Insurance Group could cut about thirty MIS personnel needed to operate the mainframe-based MIS. Only about ten MIS workers would continue to be needed with the new PC-based MIS. Over all, in terms of MIS personnel needed to maintain and operate an MIS, the cost of operating the new PC-based MIS is significantly lower than the cost of operating the mainframe-based MIS.

Establishing an MIS

The process of establishing an MIS involves four stages: (1) planning for the MIS, (2) designing the MIS, (3) implementing the MIS, and (4) improving the MIS.

Organizational Level	Type of Management	Manager's Organizational Objectives	Appropriate Information from MIS	How MIS Information Is Used
1. Top management	CEO, president, vice president	Survival of the firm, profit growth, accumulation and efficient use of resources	Environmental data and trends, summary reports of operations, "exception reports" of problems, forecasts	Corporate objectives, policies, constraints, decisions on strategic plans, decisions on control of the total company
2. Middle management	Middle managers such as marketing, production, and financial	Allocation of resources to assigned tasks, establishment of plans to meet operating objectives, control of operations	Summaries and exception reports of operating results, corporate objectives, policies, contraints, decisions on strategic plans, relevant actions and decisions of other middle managers	Operating plans and policies, exception reports, operating summaries, control procedures, decisions on resource allocations, actions and decisions related to other middle managers
3. First-line management	First-line managers whose work is closely related	Production of goods to meet marketing needs, supplying budgets, estimates of resource requirements, movement and storage of materials	Summary reports of transactions, detailed reports of problems, operating plans and policies, control procedures, actions and decisions of related first-line managers	Exception reports, progress reports, resource requests, dispatch orders, cross-functional reports

FIGURE 19.5

Appropriate MIS information under various sets of organizational circumstances

Planning for the MIS

The planning stage is perhaps the most important stage of establishing an MIS. Commonly cited factors that make planning for the establishment of an MIS an absolute necessity are the typically long periods of time needed to acquire MIS-related data-processing equipment and to integrate it within the operation of the organization, the difficulty of hiring competent operators of the equipment, and the major amounts of financial and managerial resources typically needed to operate an MIS.[18]

The specific types of plans for an MIS vary from organization to organization. However, a sample plan for the establishment of an MIS at General Electric is shown in Figure 19.6. This particular plan, of course, is abbreviated. Much more detailed outlines of each of the areas in this plan would be needed before it could be implemented. It is interesting to note that this plan includes a point (about a third of the way down the figure) at which management must decide if there is enough potential benefit to be gained from the existence of the MIS to continue the process of establishing it. This particular plan specifies that if management decides there is not sufficient potential benefit to be gained by establishing the MIS, given its total costs, the project should be terminated.

Designing the MIS

Although data processing equipment is normally an important ingredient of management information systems, the designing of an MIS should not begin with a comparative analysis of the types of such equipment available. Many MIS managers mistakenly think that data processing equipment and an MIS are synonymous.

Stoller and Van Horn indicate that, because the purpose of an MIS is to provide information that will assist managers in making better decisions, the designing of an MIS should begin with analysis of the kinds of decisions the managers actually make in a particular organization.[19] These authors suggest that designing an MIS should consist of four steps: (1) defining various decisions that must be made to run an organization, (2) determining the types of existing management policies that may influence the ways in which these decisions should be made, (3) pinpointing the types of data needed to make these decisions, and (4) establishing a mechanism for gathering and appropriately processing the data to obtain needed information.

Implementing the MIS

The third stage in the process of establishing an MIS within an organization is implementation—that is, putting the planned for and designed MIS into operation. In this stage, the equipment is acquired and integrated into the organization. Designated data are gathered, analyzed as planned, and distributed to appropriate managers within the organization. Line managers make decisions based on the information they receive from the MIS.

Management of the implementation process of the MIS can determine the ultimate success or failure of the system.[20] To help ensure that this process will be successful, management can attempt to find an executive sponsor—a high-level manager who understands and supports the MIS implementation process. The support of such a sponsor will be a sign to all organization members that the MIS implementation is important to the organization and that all organization members should cooperate in making the implementation process successful. In addition, making sure that the MIS is as simple as possible and serves information needs of management is critical in making successful implementation of an MIS. If the MIS is overly complicated or does not meet information needs of management, the implementation will meet with much resistance and will probably have only limited success.

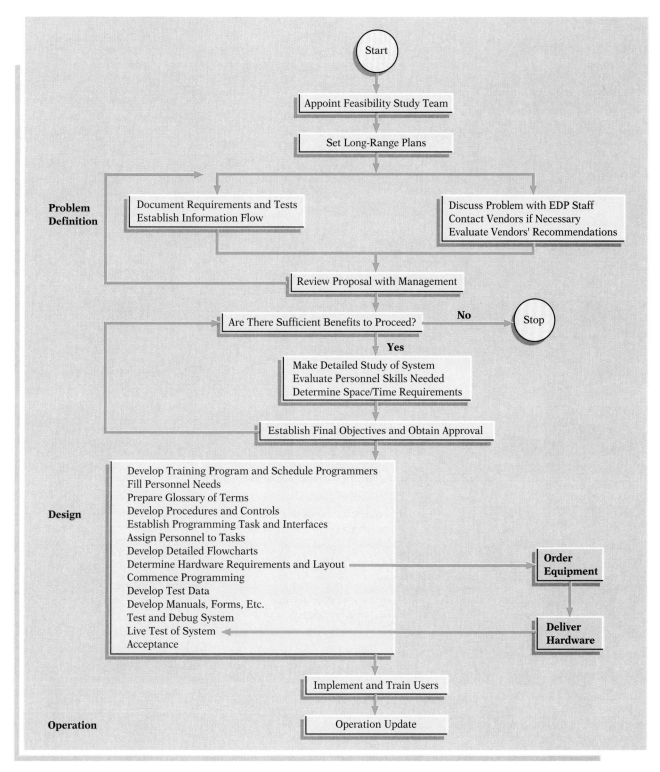

FIGURE 19.6
Plan for establishing an MIS at General Electric

Improving the MIS

Once the MIS is operating, MIS managers should continually strive to maximize its value. The two sections that follow provide insights on how MIS improvements might be made.

Symptoms of Inadequate MIS. To improve an MIS, MIS managers must first find symptoms or signs that the existing MIS is inadequate. A list of such symptoms, developed by Bertram A. Colbert, a principal of Price Waterhouse & Company, is presented in Table 19.4.[21]

Colbert divides the symptoms into three types: (1) operational, (2) psychological, and (3) report content. Operational symptoms and psychological symptoms relate, respectively, to the operation of the organization and the functioning of organization members. Report content symptoms relate to the actual makeup of the information generated by the MIS.

Although the symptoms in the table are clues that an MIS is inadequate, the symptoms themselves may not actually pinpoint MIS weaknesses. Therefore, after such symptoms are detected, MIS managers usually must gather additional information to determine what MIS weaknesses exist. Answering questions such as

TABLE 19.4 Symptoms of an inadequate MIS

Operational	*Psychological*	*Report Content*
Large physical inventory adjustments	Surprise at financial results	Excessive use of tabulations of figures
Capital expenditure overruns	Poor attitude of executives about usefulness of information	Multiple preparation and distribution of identical data
Inability of executives to explain changes from year to year in operating results	Lack of understanding of financial information on part of nonfinancial executives	Disagreeing information from different sources
Uncertain direction of company growth	Lack of concern for environmental changes	Lack of periodic comparative information and trends
Cost variances unexplainable	Executive homework reviewing reports considered excessive	Lateness of information
No order backlog awareness		Too little or excess detail
No internal discussion of reported data		Inaccurate information
Insufficient knowledge about competition		Lack of standards for comparison
Purchasing parts from outside vendors when internal capability and capacity to make is available		Failure to identify variances by cause and responsibility
Record of some "sour" investments in facilities, or in programs such as R&D and advertising		Inadequate externally generated information

the following would be of some help to MIS managers in determining these weaknesses:[22]

1. Where and how do managers get information?

2. Can managers make better use of their contacts to get information?

3. In what areas is managers' knowledge weakest, and how can managers be given information to minimize these weaknesses?

4. Do managers tend to act before receiving information?

5. Do managers wait so long for information that opportunities pass them by and the organization becomes bottlenecked?

Typical Improvements to an MIS. MIS inadequacies vary from situation to situation, depending on such factors as the quality of an MIS plan, the appropriateness of an MIS design, and the kinds of individuals operating an MIS. However, several activities have the potential of improving the MIS of most organizations:

1. *Building cooperation among MIS personnel and line managers.*[23] Cooperation of this sort encourages line managers to give MIS personnel honest opinions of the quality of information being received. Through this type of interaction, MIS designers and operators should be able to improve the effectiveness of an MIS.

2. *Constantly stressing that MIS personnel should strive to accomplish the purpose of the MIS—providing managers with decision-related information.* In this regard, it probably would be of great benefit to hold line managers responsible for continually educating MIS personnel on the types of decisions organization managers make and the corresponding steps taken to make these decisions. The better MIS personnel understand the decision situations that face operating managers, the higher the probability that MIS information will be appropriate for decisions these managers must make.

3. *Holding, wherever possible, both line managers and MIS personnel accountable for MIS activities on a cost-benefit basis.*[24] This accountability reminds line managers and MIS personnel that the benefits the organization receives from MIS functions must exceed the costs. In effect, this accountability emphasis helps increase the cost consciousness of both line managers and MIS personnel.

4. *Operating an MIS in a "people conscious" manner.* An MIS, like the formal pyramidal organization, is based on the assumption that organizational affairs can and should be handled in a completely logical manner. Logic, of course, is important to the design and implementation of an MIS. In addition, however, MIS activities also should include people considerations.[25] After all, even if MIS activities are well thought out and completely logical, an MIS can be ineffective simply because people do not use it as intended.

According to Dickson and Simmons, several factors can cause people to resist using an MIS.[26] A summary of these factors according to working groups is presented in Table 19.5 on page 604. This table implies that for managers to improve MIS effectiveness, they may have to take steps to reduce such factors as threats to power and status that might be discouraging MIS use.

TABLE 19.5 Causes for four different working groups' resistance to an MIS

	Operating (Nonclerical)	Operating (Clerical)	Operating Management	Top Management
Threats to economic security		X	X	
Threats to status or power		X	X*	
Increased job complexity	X		X	X
Uncertainty or unfamiliarity	X	X	X	X
Changed interpersonal relations or work patterns		X*	X	
Changed superior-subordinate relationships		X*	X	
Increased rigidity or time pressure	X	X	X	
Role ambiguity		X	X*	X
Feelings of insecurity		X	X*	X*

X = The reason is possibly the cause of resistance to MIS development.
X* = The reason has a strong possibility of being the cause of resistance.

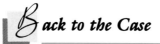

Back to the Case

Consolidated Insurance Group is shifting from a mainframe-based MIS to a PC-based MIS. In making such a change, the company can probably gain significantly by carefully planning the way in which the new MIS would be established. For example, the following questions about the planning stage of Consolidated's new MIS would be useful: Is an appropriate PC-based system being acquired and integrated? Does the company need new MIS personnel, or will present MIS personnel require further training in order to operate the new MIS? Will managers need additional training in order to operate the new PC-based MIS?

About the design and implementation stages of Consolidated's new MIS, management should seek answers to such questions as: How do we design the new MIS based on managerial decision making? How can we ensure that the new MIS as designed and implemented will be functional?

Concerning the new PC-based MIS at Consolidated Insurance Group, managers as well as MIS personnel should continually try to improve it. All users of the new MIS should be aware of the symptoms of an inadequate MIS and should constantly attempt to pinpoint and eliminate corresponding MIS weaknesses. Suggestions for improving the new MIS could include: (1) building additional cooperation between MIS managers, MIS personnel, and line managers; (2) stressing that the purpose of the MIS is to provide managers with decision-related information; (3) using cost-benefit analysis to evaluate MIS activities; and (4) ensuring that the MIS operates in a people-conscious manner.

THE MANAGEMENT DECISION SUPPORT SYSTEM (MDSS)

Traditionally, the MIS that uses electronic assistance in gathering data and providing related information to managers has been invaluable. This MIS assistance has been especially useful in areas where programmed decisions (see chapter 6) are necessary, because the computer continually generates the information that helps managers make these decisions. An example is using the computer to track cumulative labor costs by department. The computer can be used to automatically gather and update the cumulative labor costs per department, compare the costs to corresponding annual budgets, and calculate the percentage of the budget that each department has reached to date. Such information would normally be useful in controlling departmental labor costs.

Closely related to the MIS is the **management decision support system (MDSS)**—an interdependent set of decision aids that help managers make non-programmed decisions (see chapter 6).[27] Figure 19.7 illustrates possible components of the MDSS and describes what they do. The MDSS is typically characterized by the following:[28]

1. *One or more corporate databases.* A **database** is a reservoir of corporate facts consistently organized to fit the information needs of a variety of organization members. These databases (also termed corporate databases) tend to contain facts about all of the important facets of company operations, including financial as well as nonfinancial information. These facts are used to explore issues important to the corporation. For example, a manager might find it helpful to use facts from the corporate database to forecast profits for each of the next three years.

A **management decision support system (MDSS)** is an interdependent set of computer-oriented decision aids that help managers make non-programmed decisions.

1. Corporate databases. A **database** is a reservoir of corporate facts consistently organized to fit the information needs of a variety of organization members.

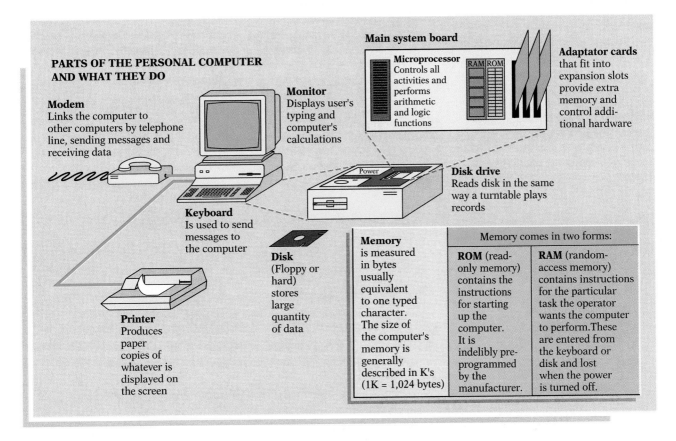

FIGURE 19.7

Possible components of a management decision support system (MDSS) and what they do

2. User databases. A user database is a database developed by an individual manager or other user.

2. *One or more user database.* In addition to the corporate database, an MDSS tends to contain several additional user databases. A **user database** is a database developed by an individual manager or other user. These databases may be derived from but are not necessarily limited to the corporate database. They tend to address specific issues peculiar to the individual users. For example, a production manager might be interested in exploring the specific issue of lowering production costs. To do so, the manager might build a simple user database that includes departmental facts about reject rates of materials purchased from various suppliers. The manager might be able to lower production costs by eliminating the materials from the suppliers with the highest reject rates.

3. Model databases. A **model base** is a collection of quantitative computer programs that can assist management decision support system (MDSS) users in analyzing data within databases.

3. *A set of quantitative tools stored in a model base.* A **model base** is a collection of quantitative computer programs that can assist MDSS users in analyzing data in databases. For example, the production manager discussed in item 2 might use a correlation analysis program stored in a model base to accurately determine any relationships that might exist between reject rates and the materials from various suppliers.

"What if" analysis is the simulation of a business situation over and over again using somewhat different data for selected decision areas.

One desirable feature of a model base is its ability to allow the user to perform **"what if" analysis**—the simulation of a business situation over and over again using somewhat different data for selected decision areas. For example, a manager might first determine the profitability of a company under present conditions. The manager might then ask *what* would happen *if* materials costs increased by 5 percent. Or *if* products were sold at a different price. Popular programs such as Lotus 1–2–3 and the Interactive Financial Planning System (IFPS)[29] allow managers to ask as many "what if's" as they want to and to save their answers without changing their original data.

4. Dialogue capability. A **dialogue capability** is the ability of a management decision support system (MDSS) user to interact with a management decision support system.

4. *A dialogue capability.* The ability of an MDSS user to interact with an MDSS is **dialogue capability.** Such interaction typically involves extracting data from a database, calling various models stored in the model base, and storing analysis results in a file. How this dialogue capability interacts with other MDSS ingredients is depicted in Figure 19.8.

Quality Highlight: Mrs. Fields, Inc.'s Sophisticated Database Allows Quick Responses

A company must do more than produce high-quality products if it is to meet the needs of its customers. If a company cannot respond promptly and efficiently to customer needs—and wants—it cannot provide the level of quality that customers seek. For example, an office equipment manufacturer that specializes in providing mechanical typewriters and calculators of the finest quality meets the needs of very few contemporary business customers. Though few companies are as insensitive to their consumers as this hypothetical office equipment manufacturer, few are as responsive to consumers as is Mrs. Fields, Inc.

Mrs. Fields, Inc., with home offices in Park City, Utah, has grown from one woman's idea to a corporation that operates more than 500 Mrs. Fields Cookie Stores and over 100 La Petite Boulangerie bakery and sandwich stores. Mrs. Fields's corporate database can be readily accessed at any time by any of the

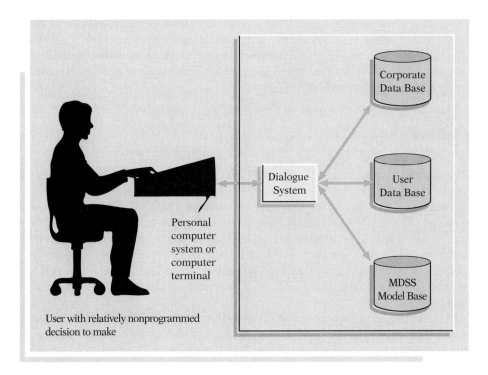

FIGURE 19.8

How dialogue capability interacts with other MDSS ingredients

appropriate organization members at any of the Mrs. Fields locations. The database, acknowledged as one of the most sophisticated information systems in retailing, contains modules supporting a variety of managerial tasks. Just a few of the ways in which managers use the database are

- To prepare for interviews with prospective employees
- To train existing employees
- To plan work schedules, both in stores and in production
- To compile financial reports, submit data for inclusion in such reports, and obtain information from these reports
- To transmit a variety of information within the corporation, whether among retail outlets, among production units, or between retail and production personnel

Data from each location is transmitted to the company headquarters each day, allowing frequent compilation of reports. The information from these reports is then added to the database and made available to persons at every level of management throughout the company. The quality of the Mrs. Fields database has helped the company to cultivate and nurture a reputation for high-quality products and excellent responsiveness to consumers, which has allowed it to become a leader in the industry.

The continued technological developments related to microcomputers have made the use of the MDSS concept feasible and its application available to virtually all managers. In addition, the continued development of extensive software to support information analysis related to more subjective decision making is contributing to the popularity of MDSS.

Back to the Case

The introductory case indicates that with the new PC-based MIS at Consolidated Insurance Group, managers are now able to use their own software to tap into the corporate data base. The preceding information about MDSS emphasizes this concept. In order for Consolidated to gain maximum advantage from its new MIS, its managers should be able to use an MDSS efficiently and effectively. Because some managers may not be familiar with the MDSS concept, they may have to undergo training aimed at understanding and using the MDSS. Company managers should know how to use the MDSS to help them make both programmed and nonprogrammed decisions.

In building and using the most advantageous PC-based MIS possible, Consolidated management should ensure that MIS users within the company have adequate equipment to operate and use an MDSS and adequate access to a corporate database, and are properly employing user databases, have appropriate model bases available, and have adequate dialogue capability within the company's MDSS. If Consolidated Insurance Group's management is successful in ensuring that these issues reflect MDSS use within the company, then the probability is high that the company MDSS is being properly used. If, on the other hand, management is not successful in ensuring that these issues reflect MDSS use within the company, management could improve operations within Consolidated by encouraging organization members to appropriately use an MDSS.

Action Summary

Circle:

Reread the learning objectives that follow. Each objective is followed by questions. Answering these questions accurately will help you retain the most important concepts discussed in this chapter. After answering each question, check your answer with the answer key at the end of this chapter. (*Hint:* If you have doubt regarding the correct response, consult the page whose number follows the answer.)

From studying this chapter, I will attempt to acquire:

1. **An understanding of the relationship between data and information.**

a, b, c, d, e   **a.** Data can be: (a) information; (b) opinion; (c) premises; (d) facts; (e) gossip.

a, b, c, d, e   **b.** Information can be defined as conclusions derived from: (a) data analysis; (b) opinion; (c) premises; (d) gossip; (e) none of the above.

2. **Insights on the main factors that influence the value of information.**

   a. All of the following are primary factors determining the value of infor-   a, b, c, d, e
   mation except: (a) appropriateness; (b) expense; (c) quality; (d) timeliness;
   (e) quantity.

   b. The appropriateness of the information increases as the volume of the infor-   T, F
   mation increases.

3. **Knowledge of some potential steps for evaluating information.**

   a. All of the following are main activities in evaluating information except: a, b, c, d, e
   (a) acquiring information; (b) comparing value with cost of information;
   (c) selecting data to be evaluated; (d) using information in decision making;
   (e) discounting expected value for deficiencies and inaccuracies.

   b. The primary concern of management in evaluating information is the dol-   T, F
   lar value of the benefits gained compared to the cost of generating the
   information.

4. **An appreciation for the role of computers in handling information.**

   a. All of the following are main computer functions except: (a) input;   a, b, c, d, e
   (b) storage; (c) control; (d) heuristic; (e) output.

   b. All of the following are possible pitfalls in using the computer except: a, b, c, d, e
   (a) thinking that a computer is independently capable of creative activities;
   (b) failing to realize that a computer is capable only of following precise
   and detailed instructions; (c) training and retraining all computer operating
   personnel; (d) spending too much money on computer assistance; (e) overestimating the value of computer output.

5. **An understanding of the importance of a management information system
   (MIS) to an organization.**

   a. A management information system is a network established within an orga-   T, F
   nization to provide managers with information that will assist them in decision making.

   b. "Determining information needs" is which of the steps necessary to operate   a, b, c, d, e
   an MIS: (a) first; (b) second; (c) third; (d) fourth; (e) none of the above.

6. **A feasible strategy for establishing an MIS.**

   a. All of the following are stages in the process of establishing an MIS except: a, b, c, d, e
   (a) planning; (b) designing; (c) improving; (d) implementing; (e) all of the
   above are stages.

   b. Which of the following activities has the potential of improving an MIS: a, b, c, d, e
   (a) stressing that MIS personnel should strive to accomplish the purpose of
   an MIS; (b) operating an MIS in a "people conscious" manner; (c) encouraging line managers to continually request additional information through
   the MIS; (d) a and b; (e) all of the above.

7. **Information about what a management decision support system is and
   how it operates.**

   a. A management decision support system is a set of decision aids aimed at   T, F
   helping managers make nonprogrammed decisions.

   b. There is basically no difference between a corporate database and a user   T, F
   database.

   c. Dialogue capability allows the MDSS user to interact with an MIS.   T, F

Introductory Case Wrap-Up

"Consolidated Insurance Group Changes to PCs to Manage Information" (p. 584) and its related back-to-the-case sections were written to help you better understand the management concepts contained in this chapter. Answer the following discussion questions about this introductory case to further enrich your understanding of chapter content:

1. If you were a manager at Consolidated, would you rather work with the mainframe-based or the PC-based MIS? Why?

2. Name three issues on which management's plan for implementing the new PC-based MIS should focus. Discuss the importance of each issue.

3. The main steps of the controlling process are measuring performance, comparing performance to standards, and taking corrective action. Discuss a possible role of the new MIS at Consolidated in each of these steps.

Issues for Review and Discussion

1. What is the difference between data and information?

2. List and define four major factors that influence the value of information.

3. What are operational control decisions and strategic planning decisions? What characterizes information appropriate for making each of these decisions?

4. Discuss the major activities involved in evaluating information.

5. What factors tend to limit the usefulness of information, and how can these factors be overcome?

6. Is a computer a flexible management tool? Explain.

7. How do the main functions of a computer relate to one another?

8. Summarize the major pitfalls managers must avoid when using a computer.

9. Define *MIS* and discuss its importance to management.

10. What steps must be performed to operate an MIS properly?

11. What major steps are involved in establishing an MIS?

12. Why is planning for an MIS such an important part of establishing an MIS?

13. Why does the designing of an MIS begin with analyzing managerial decision making?

14. How should managers use the symptoms of an inadequate MIS as listed in Table 19.4?

15. How could building cooperation between MIS personnel and line managers improve an MIS?

16. How can management use cost-benefit analysis to improve an MIS?

17. Describe five possible causes of resistance to using an MIS. What can managers do to ensure that these causes do not affect their organization's MIS?

18. How does an MDSS differ from an MIS? Define *"what if" analysis* and give an illustration of how a manager might use it.

Building on What You Know

Directions

Review the Highlight feature as indicated below and answer its corresponding questions. Questions in this section focus on relating a Highlight appearing in this chapter to management concepts that you have learned in a previous chapter.

Review the Quality Highlight: Mrs. Fields, Inc. on page 606. In chapter 18 you studied about quality and quality control. Do you think that the accessibility feature of the Mrs. Fields database would influence company efforts to control product quality? Explain. Assuming that Mrs. Fields uses quality circles, how could such a database enhance the operation of the circles?

Action Summary Answer Key

1. a. d, p. 585
   b. a, p. 585

2. a. b, p. 586
   b. F, pp. 586–587

3. a. d, pp. 588–589
   b. T, p. 588

4. a. d, p. 590
   b. c, p. 593

5. a. T, p. 595
   b. a, p. 596

6. a. e, p. 598
   b. d, p. 603

7. a. T, p. 605
   b. F, pp. 605–606
   c. F, p. 606

Case Study

Managing Information:
General Colin Powell

by Robert E. Kemper, Northern Arizona University

On August 2, 1990, the army of Iraq invaded the emirate of Kuwait, a tiny, oil-rich country to the south. The invasion followed weeks of military buildup along the Iraqi–Kuwaiti border, a buildup that had been carefully tracked by satellites and by earthbound intelligence gathering. In response to Iraq's threat of extended aggression against the kingdom of Saudi Arabia, west of Kuwait, forces from a coalition of allies led by the United States and including many NATO and Middle Eastern nations were gathered in and around the Persian Gulf. This constituted Operation Desert Shield, a position taken to convince Iraq that further aggression would be dangerous, and that Kuwait's government must be restored. Meanwhile diplomatic efforts and economic sanctions were underway toward the same end.

When Iraq did not withdraw from Kuwait by the deadline established by the coalition, the allied forces attacked. Operation Desert Storm began on January 16, 1991. Allied commanders in the Persian Gulf theater reported to U.S. General Norman Schwarzkopf; a subchain of command for Arab forces was established under Saudi Lieutenant General Prince Khalid bin Sultan.

The architect of allied actions, however, was in Washington, DC: U.S. Chairman of the Joint Chiefs of Staff General Colin Powell. The Chairman serves as senior military advisor to the Bush administration and creates a bridge between political decisions made in the White House and military strategy in the field.

From August onward, Chairman Powell, Secretary of State James Baker, and Secretary of Defense Dick Cheney had crisscrossed Europe and the Middle East. Baker and Cheney pursued diplomatic ends while Powell coordinated military preparation with his counterparts. In Washington, National Security Advisor Brent Scowcroft coordinated incoming intelligence reports. Powell had served as President Ronald Reagan's National Security Advisor and knew the business of intelligence handling well, too.

On January 16, the deadline past, Chairman Powell was in charge. His military doctrine was simply stated: "Strike suddenly, decisively, and in sufficient force to resolve the matter. Do it quickly, and do it with minimum loss of [coalition] life." He and his coworkers had spent five months in meticulous preparation for a war they had hoped never to fight, and they were ready to strike.

Powell had a second battle to fight in January, 1991, however. U.S. and allied press representatives were furious to find that allied commanders would not allow the press free access to war zones and troops in the field. Instead, small pools of press members were attached to each major military unit. A few renegades evaded the controls, but for the first time, the majority of press access to a war would be controlled by the military.

Powell said that his reasons were straightforward and did not involve political censorship, as some press leaders accused. According to Powell, the world had changed since the Vietnam War era. Live reporting of battles and troop movements were not only possible, they would now be expected. The allies might as well telephone Baghdad direct with plans for advances and targets. To limit information flow to Iraqi commanders, it was necessary to limit reporting—in effect, to keep the world from having access to military data. Allowing free press access would undoubtedly prolong the war and raise the fatalities, Powell argued; the Bush administration supported him.

In the early weeks of Desert Storm, allied air attacks aimed at three main targets: Iraqi aircraft and airfields, highways that could be used to move troops and support supplies to the fronts, and Iraq's internal communication systems. The goal was to knock out any Iraqi central command or control, while obliterating its air power. Powell reasoned that without a flow of information, Baghdad would be unable to raise effective defenses against allied movements, and certainly Iraq could not mount an offense of its own. He was right.

Nonetheless, data and information flowing to Washington and other allied capitals were immediate, continuous, and plentiful. Computer-based information systems formed the backbone of Washington's military management. The central source for military information reaching the Pentagon was the Worldwide Military Command and Control System, a global network. Battle information was gathered electronically and routed through the Airborne Battlefield Command Control Center, which provides primary support to coordination of air, land, and sea actions.

In direct support of troops are four subsidiary systems. The Joint Deployment System manages the movement of materiel for all U.S. armed services; the Stock Control and Distribution Program sends Air Force supplies in particular where they are needed. The Military Aircraft Command Information Processing System tracks transport and cargo planes supporting military operations. The Tactical Army Combat Service Support Computer Systems maintain up-to-date records of personnel deployments and medical supplies.

Based on information from these and other sources, General Schwarzkopf and his allied commanders determined battle tactics and strategy. A computer-driven system was helpful here, also: The Modern Age Planning Program was used to simulate battle scenarios. However, war games are only as good as the information that is fed to them, and even General Schwarzkopf's command was surprised by some Iraqi weaknesses and by the devastating results achieved by knocking out Iraqi communications. There is no question that the war was won by pilots, artillery personnel, tank crews, and soldiers. However, it could not have been won at so little human cost to the United States and its allies without information control systems supporting supply, personnel, medical, and intelligence activities.

Discussion Questions

1. In the context of this case, give two examples showing the difference between data and information.

2. In briefings during the early days of the Gulf War, General Powell cautioned against adding up allied pilots' reports of destroyed Iraqi aircraft to reach an assumption of air superiority. Why do you think he felt this was an inappropriate use of the data supplied by those reports?

3. Why do you think it was necessary for Chairman Powell, Secretary Baker, and Secretary Cheney all to meet with leaders of European and Middle Eastern allies during the months from August, 1990, until January, 1991?

4. Consider the Military Aircraft Command Information Processing System as a management information system (MIS). What are its goals? What do you think the major challenges might be for such a system?

The Shape of the World: Hammond Atlases

Caleb Dean Hammond III is the president of Hammond, Inc., a company that has produced maps and atlases since 1900. His father serves the company as chair of the board; his wife Kathy is vice president and chief operating officer. Nonetheless, the almost century-long family orientation of this company does not mean that it is slow to adapt. Indeed, in the map business, quick changes and flexibility are part of everyday life.

In 1990, following the Iraqi invasion of Kuwait, the world's interest centered on the Middle East. U.S. service personnel from all over the globe were being sent to an area of which they and their families had only passing knowledge. The Hammonds responded immediately, preparing a *Middle East Crisis Atlas* to help introduce and guide them, to give "a true graphic sense of where they are and, hopefully, what they are doing there," as Dean Hammond relates.

To publish pictures of a rapidly changing world as quickly as possible is a challenge that all map- and atlas-makers face. In recent years, this aspect of their business has been changed by computer aids. Although artists and graphic designers are still integral to the business of cartography, mathematicians, physicists, and engineers have now joined the team as well. Political and factual changes are now easily made by inputing updated data into computer databases. Hammond has invested in a highly sophisticated database and map-drawing system that contains the equivalent of 150 person-years of information. Raw data is entered in terms of latitudes and longitudes, and the computer prepares a map based on that data; information can be provided about such disparate values as population statistics, volumes of rainfall or river flow, and political shifts.

The ease of updating provided by the computer system is particularly important to the preparation of atlases, which generally reflect a great deal of population-oriented information. An atlas may include as many as 8,000 changes from one edition to the next; regular updating of the computer database makes most of these changes fairly painless to accomplish. Dean Hammond says,

> The fact for me that is the most exciting, I believe, is the transfer of information to the electronic side of things because we are now able to deliver far better data in all languages in digital as well as print media, and there's an enormous market out there.

In addition, computer assistance is important to more than just the speedy updating of geographical information. Hammond, Inc., also relies on information systems to run other corporate divisions. Hammond's salespeople, for example, use the systems to track prospect lists and client information, including contacts, dates of sales calls and follow-up timings, past order history, and so on.

Others use computer databases to track inventories, compare inventories to sales orders, order new printings when necessary, and schedule deliveries. Tight inventory control is especially important to a company such as Hammond because the world is always changing. Maps and atlases must be timely in order to be salesworthy; a large inventory of outdated publications represents a waste of money.

"People are watching world events," says Dean Hammond, "and we have to respond and, in some cases, to lead the understanding of what those events mean." As a thoroughly modernized company in the old-world science of cartography, Hammond, Inc., stands ready and willing to meet that challenge.

Video Case Questions

1. Give two examples of how Hammond managers might use the what-if capabilities of MDSS software?

2. How do you think Hammond, Inc., justified the expense of a computerized map-making system such as the one they purchased to their shareholders?

3. Of the following four factors—appropriateness, quality, timeliness, and quantity—affecting the value of information, which do you think is (are) most important to Hammond, Inc.? Why?

Video Case Activities

1. Assume you are preparing an atlas entry on a brand-new nation, which has just emerged in the Caribbean as a result of immigration to a previously uninhabited island. Prepare a list of 20 pieces of basic data about the nation, and then prepare a brief paragraph relating information about the nation from those data.

2. You have just been put in charge of a new subsidiary of Hammond, Inc. Your subsidiary will design and, eventually, implement a new computer-accessed atlas, which is published to and accessible through a satellite-connected computer network rather than published in print as a book. How will you use an MIS to set up your subsidiary? Prepare a brief explanation to present to the board of directors.

PART 5

INTEGRATIVE CASE

Buy Me a Light—A Mag Light

by Robert E. Kemper, Northern Arizona University

Tony Maglica decided to build the perfect flashlight. With his name (or part of it) on every one, his ego would accept no less. There was an unanswered need for a flashlight that people could rely on to work whenever they turned it on, and Tony Maglica responded. He created a market niche—high-quality flashlights with a sleek appearance that speaks of good design.

The Maglight is, by any measure, the best flashlight there is, a state-of-the-art flashlight. "The light had to be distinguished, beautiful, a showpiece," Maglica says. "I wanted people to be proud to give it as a gift. Besides, if you are designing something to last a long time, you have to build it so that people are willing to look at it for a long time." Not surprisingly, Maglight prices are state-of-the-art as well.

Each year, thanks to word of mouth and consistent quality, the number of people who recognize the Mag name increases. Magazines like *Fortune* include Mag on its list of the best U.S.-made products, and the Maglight has appeared in books that celebrate the best of U.S. design. It has become a status symbol.

Maglights are sold through independent representatives. The company's best-seller, the Mini-Mag, retails for about $16.95, double the price of a typical flashlight. Their top-of-the-line model, complete with AC converter, battery pack, and wall mounting bracket, can run as high as $150. Of necessity, Maglica deals exclusively with high-end salespeople who specialize in explaining why this product should cost more than the alternatives.

In designing the initial flashlight, Maglica required an extremely close tolerance to ensure the parts would fit together well. He also specified safeguards to eliminate some traditional reasons for flashlight failure. For example, batteries leak over time and the corrosive battery acid eventually dissolves most on–off switches, rendering the flashlight useless. In his prototype, Maglica created a switch that rubs off the battery-acid buildup every time the light is flicked on or off.

The design was clever, but there was no manufacturing equipment on the market to meet Mag's specifications. To meet his quality requirements, Maglica had to build his own equipment, which meant an investment of time and money. Nonetheless, everywhere you look at Mag Instruments, Inc., you find a commitment to quality production, to strict quality control—and Mag did $70 million worth of business in 1989.

Just inside the Mag Instruments factory door are open boxes marked "Scrap"; they are first to catch your eye. They are full of flashlights that Mag's quality inspectors have rejected—some days, up to $80,000 worth. Perhaps the flashlights work, but their housings are loose—scrap the entire batch. Surely this commitment to quality must pay off.

The keys to Mag's success are its unique design and its manufacturing process. Both are patent protected, and Maglica has employed an army of attorneys to keep them from being duplicated. Since 1983, Maglica has spent $16 million in lawyers' fees on suits against not only copycat companies but also retailers who sold the copies. Mag constantly searches the marketplace for imitators.

In fact, with its commitment to upscale design and high-quality production, Mag has to some extent painted itself into a corner. To allow competition, to change its marketing strategy, or to downgrade its market position would risk everything Maglica has created since entering business in 1978. So Maglica and his wife Claire live and breathe their business. Married for ten years, they take separate vacations so there will always be a Maglica minding the store. No one can be hired without being approved first by Tony Maglica— These people will determine his company's reputation, and he wants to meet them.

Mag Instruments pays an average $1 more per hour than their employees could make at similar jobs. Yet even so, it is hard to attract workers. "Working with screw machines is becoming a dying trade," says Maglica. So now the company has set up a training school for unskilled but willing workers. Maglica has no idea what the program will cost, however: "That would be the wrong way of looking at it. The question I ask myself is, what will this cost me if I do not do it?"

Of course, the Maglicas did not know the cost of their quality vigilance when Tony Maglica designed his first flashlight. They only knew they wanted to build the best flashlight the world had ever seen. That plan might have been fatal—what if they had built the perfect light, and no one cared? "We all take pride in what we are doing," says Claire Maglica. "Maybe it's our

naïvete, but we define success as putting out the best products we can." For now, their commitment is paying off; people are willing to pay for the best.

Discussion Questions

1. Give examples of each type of control (precontrol, concurrent control, and feedback control) used at Mag Instrument, Inc., to ensure the market position of Maglights.

2. If you were to perform cost–benefit analysis at Mag Instruments, where on the curve of payback do you think controlling might fall, according to the case? Why?

3. Consider the principle of Deming's chain reaction discussed in Chapter 18. How do you think this applies to the Maglica's new training program?

4. The Maglicas evidently rely on inspection as a major form of quality control. How might they use quality circles in their factory? Do you think this would be helpful?

5. The acquisition of information can be very costly. Scouring the marketplace for possible patent infringement, for example, must cost Mag Instruments a fair amount of money annually. Is the cost of acquiring this information justified? Why or why not?

The Business Products and Systems Division of **The Xerox Corporation** won the Malcolm Baldrige award in 1989. Xerox was recognized for its success in implementing a process that they call *Leadership Through Quality*, in which quality is defined as "meeting customer requirements."

Topics for Special Emphasis

The first five sections of this text introduced the subject of management and presented detailed discussions of the four major management functions. The purpose of this section is to emphasize carefully selected topics that present special challenges for modern managers. This last portion of the text covers international management, and quality as a means of building competitive organizations.

The discussion of international management defines *international management* and *multinational corporations,* explains the complexities and risks involved in managing internationally, and examines, through a study of Japanese management techniques, how the four management functions and the process of comparative management relate to the field of international management. The increasing importance of international management is emphasized.

Quality is discussed from the viewpoint of maintaining organizational competitiveness through company-wide quality (CWQ), building excellence into all functions performed by an organization. This section discusses the importance of a quality focus within an organization and presents advice on how to achieve CWQ from internationally recognized experts like Philip B. Crosby, W. Edwards Deming, and Joseph M. Juran. The relationship between strategic planning and quality is discussed as well as management skills necessary for achieving CWQ.

Once you have studied the final section of this text, you should understand the most important principles of modern management. The purpose of this text was to introduce you to these principles and to prepare you for becoming a manager in the future. Keep this text in your professional library as a reference book that can help you meet the many challenges you will face throughout your management career.

Chapter 20

ꞇtudent Learning Objectives

From studying this chapter, I will attempt to acquire:

1. An understanding of international management and its importance to modern managers.

2. An understanding of what constitutes a multinational corporation.

3. Insights concerning the risk involved in investing in international operations.

4. Knowledge about planning and organizing in multinational corporations.

5. Knowledge about influencing and controlling in multinational corporations.

6. Insights about what comparative management is and how it might help managers do their jobs better.

7. Ideas on how to be a better manager through the study of Japanese management techniques.

International Management

Chapter Outline

Introductory Case

TOYS "Я" US FOCUSES ON JAPAN

For the past few years, Toys "Я" Us, a toys retailer, has been focusing on expansion through international sales. Company growth in international sales has increased steadily from 1987 to 1989 and is expected to continue to climb in the early 1990s. In 1989, Toys "Я" Us opened stores in such locations as Puerto Rico, Canada, France, the United Kingdom, and Germany.

Recently, the company chose a new foreign target for expansion. Toys "Я" Us Inc. opened a number of its huge discount toy stores in Japan. The expansion marks the first attempt by a large American retailer to open its own store in Japan—and local vendors became angry and ready to fight. By using a law that is at the center of U.S.-Japan trade tensions, they hoped to protect their small-scale business by keeping Toys "Я" Us out.

Local opposition can be deadly in Japan.

Toy wholesalers and industry associations throughout Japan were concerned that the U.S. company's aggressive plans to eventually open 100 stores nationwide would disrupt their market. Japan's 800 billion yen ($5.52 billion) toy market is crowded by thousands of mom-and-pop operations that eke out a living from shops with floor space of no more than about 3,200 square feet. In contrast, Toys "Я" Us, which built a 54,000-square-foot store for Niigata City, has about 480 toy supermarkets throughout the world and annual sales of around $4.75 billion.

"This is not just a local problem: Toys "Я" Us will have a big impact on the entire toy industry," said a Niigata toy wholesaler. "We are opposed to their plan." The wholesaler, who declined to be identified, plans to meet with others in the industry to plot a strategy against the U.S. intruder.

Such local opposition can be deadly in Japan, and not just for a toy retailer. Under what's called "the large-scale retail law," retailers who want to open stores with more than 500 square meters, or 5,400 square feet, of floor space must obtain approval from other retailers in the area. In the past, many of the fights became nasty—with local shops stalling, sometimes for as long as 10 years. While some would-be entrants negotiate to win approval for smaller stores, many just plain give up. (The law doesn't stipulate how long a period can be set aside to hear complaints, but they

drag on even for large Japanese retailers. Knowing that, foreign companies haven't been lining up to try to crack the Japan market.)

Despite the local opposition in Japan, Toys "Я" Us says it is still "moving along" with plans to open even five or six stores in Japan in 1991, says Michael Goldstein, vice chairman. He does concede, though, that "a lot will depend on whether the Japanese government will relax their rules." He adds: "We think we're going to expand the market there for toys. It'll be good for us, good for our suppliers, and will be good for Japan in that we're going to bring a diversity of products for Japanese consumers.

There are rare cases of Japanese businesses that welcome the foreign pressure. "We are in favor of allowing big discount chains to move into a local area," says an official at one of the country's leading retail chains. "It's good for the customers. And it will stimulate the industry."

This case is from Kathryn Graven, "For Toys "Я" Us, Japan Isn't Child's Play," *Wall Street Journal* (February 7, 1990), B1, B6.

WHAT'S AHEAD

The introductory case illustrates the recent history of Toys "Я" Us, an American-based toy retailer, in the international management arena and Japanese-based resistance that the company is facing in attempting to expand into Japan. Any organization could face such resistance from foreign nationals when attempting to expand into a foreign country. The material in this chapter provides insights about the international management process and highlights how such resistance fits into that process. Major topics covered are fundamentals of international management, the multinational corporation, management functions and multinational corporations, and comparative management.

FUNDAMENTALS OF INTERNATIONAL MANAGEMENT

International management is simply the performance of management activities across national borders. International management entails reaching organizational objectives by extending management activities to include an emphasis on organizations in foreign countries.

In practice, this emphasis may take any of several different forms and can vary from simply analyzing and fighting competition in foreign markets to establishing a formal partnership with a foreign company. AMP, Inc., for an example, is a company fighting competition in a foreign market. AMP, Inc., a manufacturer of electrical parts, is headquartered in Harrisburg, Pennsylvania. Over all, the company is profitable and efficient, and has achieved outstanding success by gaining control of 15 to 20 percent of its multinational market. The company has factories in seventeen countries because experience showed that competitors could best be beaten in foreign markets by a company's actually producing products within market areas. For AMP, Inc., each overseas subsidiary is staffed entirely by local citizens.[1] An example of a formal partnership is National Steel, a U.S. company that has formed an equal partnership with Nippon Kokan, a Japanese steel company, in an effort to gain a competitive advantage over other world steel producers.[2]

Outstanding progress in areas such as transportation, communication, and technology makes access to foreign countries more feasible and attractive as time passes. As a result, many modern managers face numerous international issues that can have a direct and significant effect on organizational success. For example, the following situation was facing managers at Xerox about ten years ago.

> Xerox corporation is racing to meet deadlines at once. It must slim its copier business fast enough to beat the Japanese. Japanese competition in small copiers, a nagging worry since the mid-1970s, has shrunk Xerox's market share in America to roughly half of total copier revenue. In Europe, its other big market, Xerox has only a quarter of the revenues. Xerox has had to accept slimmer profit margins to stop the rot.[3]

International management is performing management activities across national borders.

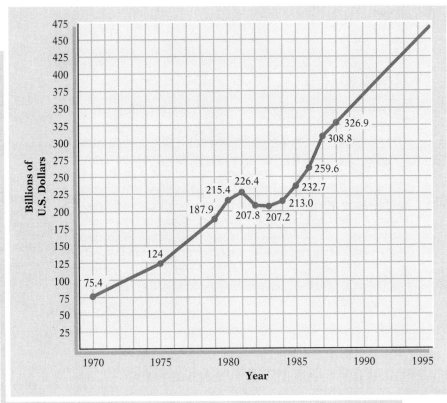

FIGURE 20.1
Growth in U.S. investment
(Author's forecast based on past data.)

The notable trend that already exists in the United States and other countries toward developing business relationships in and with foreign countries is expected to accelerate even more in the future.[4] As Figures 20.1 and 20.2 indicate, U.S. investment in foreign countries and investment by foreign countries in the United States has been growing since 1970 and is expected to continue growing. Information of this nature has caused many management educators as well as practicing managers to voice the opinion that an understanding of international management is necessary for a thorough and contemporary understanding of the fundamentals of management.[5]

NOT TO BE OUTDONE BY FRANCE AND ENGLAND, THE UNITED STATES AND SPAIN BUILD A BRIDGE.

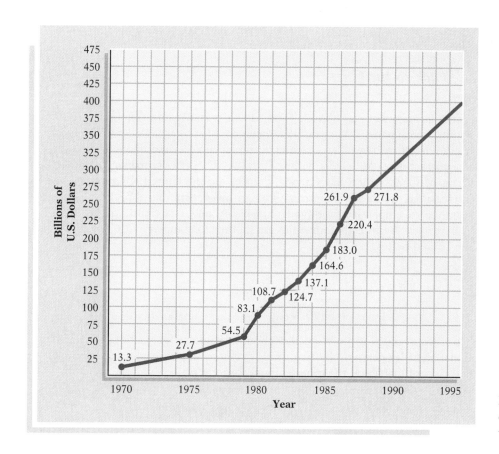

FIGURE 20.2

Growth in foreign investment in
the United States
(Author's forecast based on past data.)

*E*thics Highlight: U.S. Companies Send Hazardous Waste to Mexico

The export of hazardous wastes by companies in more developed countries to companies in less-developed countries is becoming commonplace. For example, U.S. companies commonly send large quantities of such waste to Mexico for disposal by Mexican companies. Although accidents related to this business could cause extensive environmental damage and even result in a loss of human life in one or more countries, useful international legislation governing this type of business is virtually nonexistent.

Perhaps partly in response to the absence of such legislation, public controversy surrounding international trade in the disposal of hazardous wastes emphasizes ethical issues. Individuals demonstrating against the disposal of hazardous wastes in their areas insist that they have a right to a livable environment that is free of hazardous waste disposal sites. Citizens of underdeveloped countries charge that the dumping of hazardous wastes in their countries by developed countries is simply another means of racism and should be halted immediately.

In facing this international hazardous waste disposal situation, managers should ensure that interests of domestic and foreign societies are protected along with interests of their organizations. Although much of this protection may be voluntary at this time, the evolution of legislation in this area will undoubtedly require such protection in the future.

*B*ack to the Case

As the introductory case shows, Toys "Я" Us is an organization involved in international management. The company experienced substantial sales in foreign countries even before Toys "Я" Us entered the Japanese market from a site located in that marketplace. Managers within Toys "Я" Us perform management activities across national borders like Canada, France, and the United Kingdom. Given the international trend toward greater foreign investment, Toys "Я" Us is likely to continue to emphasize worldwide expansion, and this trend will no doubt be characterized by foreign companies attempting to compete with Toys "Я" Us in the United States.

THE MULTINATIONAL CORPORATION

This section presents more specifics about managing organizations in the international arena by defining *multinational corporation* and discussing the complexities and risks of managing the multinational corporation.

Defining the Multinational Corporation

The term *multinational corporation* first appeared in the dictionary about 1970 and has been defined in several ways in conversation and textbooks alike. For the purposes of this text, a **multinational corporation** is a company that has significant operations in more than one country. In essence, a multinational corporation is an organization that is involved in doing business at the international level. It carries out its activities on an international scale that disregards national boundaries and on the basis of a common strategy from a corporation center.[6]

A list of multinational corporations in this country would include such companies as Ford, General Motors, Mobil Oil, Firestone Tire, and Massey-Ferguson. A Massey-Ferguson executive has described his company's international involvement as combining French-made transmissions, British-made engines, Mexican-made axles, and U.S.-made sheet metal parts to produce in Detroit a tractor for sale in Canada.[7] Examples of foreign multinational corporations that have various levels of ownership in certain companies located in the United States are presented in Table 20.1. As the table implies, foreign revenue, related profit, and foreign assets owned can be significant for multinational corporations.

Neil H. Jacoby explains that companies go through six stages to reach the highest degree of multinationalization (see Table 20.2).[8] As the table indicates, companies can range from slightly multinationalized organizations that simply export products to a foreign country to highly multinationalized organizations that have some of their owners in other countries.

In general, the larger the organization, the greater the likelihood that it participates in international operations of some sort. Companies such as General Electric, Lockheed, and du Pont, which have annually accumulated over $1 billion from export sales, support this generalization. Exceptions, however, also exist. BRK Electronics, for example, a small firm in Aurora, Illinois, has won a substantial share of world sales of smoke detectors. By setting up local distributors in Italy,

A **multinational corporation (MNC)** is a company that has significant operations in more than one country.

TABLE 20.1 The effect of foreign operations on several multinational organizations

Company	Foreign Revenue as Percent of Total	Foreign Profit as Percent of Total Profits	Foreign Assets as Percent of Total Profits
Citicorp	49.8	51.2	53.7
Coca-Cola	38.0	55.6	25.3
Colgate Palmolive	52.3	48.1	38.4
Dow Chemical	53.6	55.3	45.9
Exxon	69.4	55.4	43.0
Gillette	51.8	54.0	45.5
IBM	40.4	39.4	36.1
Texaco	50.1	46.1	30.1

France, and England, BRK caused its export sales to climb from $124,000 in one year to $4 million five years later.[9] An increasing number of smaller organizations are becoming involved in international operations.

Complexities of Managing the Multinational Corporation

The definition of *international management* and the discussion of what constitutes a multinational corporation clearly demonstrate that international management and domestic management are quite different. International management differs from domestic management because it involves operating:[10]

1. Within different national sovereignties.

2. Under widely disparate economic conditions.

3. Among people living within different value systems and institutions.

4. In places experiencing the industrial revolution at different times.

5. Often over greater geographical distance.

6. In national markets varying greatly in population and area.

TABLE 20.2 Six stages of multinationalization

Stage 1	Stage 2	Stage 3	Stage 4	Stage 5	Stage 6
Exports its products to foreign countries	Establishes sales organizations abroad	Licenses use of its patents and know-how to foreign firms that make and sell its products	Establishes foreign manufacturing facilities	Multinationalizes management from top to bottom	Multinationalizes ownership of corporate stock

Figure 20.3 shows some of the more important management implications of the six variables and some of the relationships among them. For example, according to the "different national sovereignties" variable, different national sovereignties generate different legal, monetary, and political systems. In turn, each legal system implies a unique set of rights and obligations involving property, taxation, antitrust (control of monopoly) law, corporate law, and contract law. These, in turn, require the firm to acquire new skills to assess the international legal considerations. The skills are new in the sense of being different from those required in a purely domestic setting.

Global Highlight: U.S. Companies in China

China is an example of a country in which U.S. managers typically find special challenge in developing interpersonal working relationships and in simply living in the general environment. U.S. managers indicate that there are barriers to the development of personal relationships with Chinese employees. The most significant of these barriers seems to be fear and suspicion of U.S. managers by the Chinese. Because delegation of authority to Chinese workers has not been commonplace in the Chinese society, actions by U.S. managers to delegate seem to make these barriers more formidable. To compound the challenges and frustrations in the workplace, U.S. managers report that simply living in China is difficult. There is a general lack of privacy, a lack of entertainment in after-work hours, and difficulty in arranging for personal travel.

Over all, the challenges and difficulties of managing in a foreign organization seem to be compounded by the challenges and difficulties of living in a foreign society. Special training programs are being designed and implemented to help U.S. managers more successfully handle these difficulties and challenges in China as well as in other countries. Many organizations require that U.S. managers undergo such training before they can qualify for a foreign assignment.

Risk and the Multinational Corporation

Naturally, developing a multinational corporation requires a substantial investment in foreign operations. Normally, managers who make foreign investments believe that such investments (1) reduce or eliminate high transportation costs; (2) allow participation in the rapid expansion of a market abroad; (3) provide foreign technical, design, and marketing skills; and (4) earn higher profits.[11]

Many managers decide to internationalize their companies, however, without having an accurate understanding of the risks involved in making such a decision.[12] For example, political complications involving the **parent company** (the company investing in the international operations) and various factions within the **host country** (the country in which the investment is made) could keep the desirable

The **parent company** is the company investing in international operations.

The **host country** is the country in which an investment is made by a foreign company.

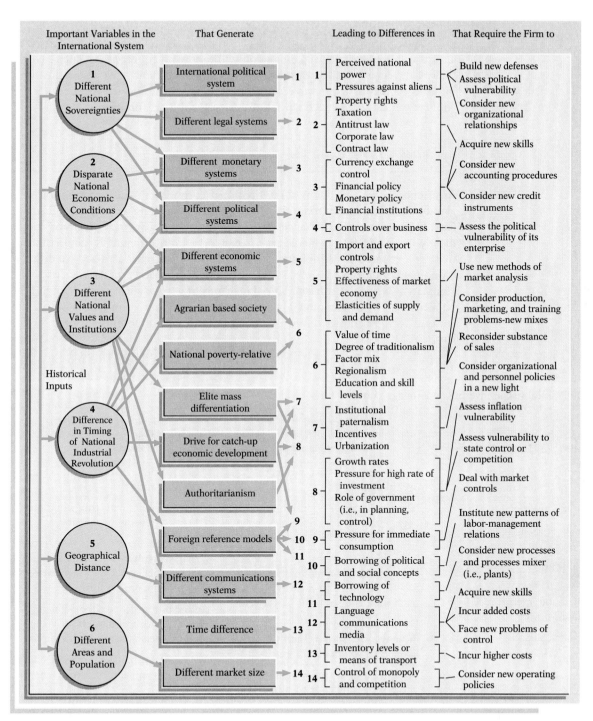

FIGURE 20.3

Management implications based on six variables in international systems
and relationships among them

outcomes in the preceding paragraph from materializing. Table 20.3 lists various possible sources of political risk, several groups within the host country that might generate the risk, and possible effects of the risk on the investing organization.

The likelihood of desirable outcomes related to foreign investments probably always will be somewhat uncertain and will vary from country to country. Nevertheless, managers faced with making a foreign investment must assess this likelihood as accurately as possible. Obviously, a poor decision to invest in another country can cause serious financial problems for the organization.

*B*ack to the Case

In essence, Toys "Я" Us is a multinational corporation—an organization with significant operations in more than one country. Managing at Toys "Я" Us under such international circumstances is a complex matter. This complexity is caused mostly by Toys "Я" Us managers' managing within different foreign countries that are separated by significant distances and that are characterized by different economic conditions, people, levels of technology, market sizes, and laws. The company's expansion attempt into Japan meeting laws such as the "large scale retailer law," which requires approval from its Japanese competitors before any company can be admitted into the country, illustrates how unusual some foreign laws can be.

TABLE 20.3 Political risk in investing in a foreign country

Sources of Political Risk	Groups through Which Political Risk Can Be Generated	Political Risk Effects: Types of Influence on Business Operations
Competing political philosophies (nationalism, socialism, communism)	Government in power and its operating agencies	Confiscation: Loss of assets without compensation
Social unrest and disorder	Nonparliamentary opposition groups (e.g., anarchist or guerilla movement working from within or outside of country)	Expropriation with compensation: Loss of freedom to operate
Vested interests of local business groups		Operational restrictions: Market shares, product characteristics, employment policies, locally shared ownership, and so forth
Recent and impending political independence	Nonorganized common interest groups: students, workers, peasants, minorities, and so forth	
Armed conflicts and internal rebellions for political power		Loss of transfer freedom: Financial (e.g., dividends, interest payments), goods, personnel, or ownership rights
New international alliances	Foreign governments or intergovernment agencies such as the European Economic Community	Breaches or unilateral revisions in contracts and agreements
	Foreign governments willing to enter into armed conflict or to support internal rebellion	Discrimination, such as taxes, compulsory subcontracting
		Damage to property or personnel from riots, insurrections, revolutions, and wars

Naturally, management at Toys "Я" Us is attempting to minimize risk in its past decisions to make foreign investments in countries like Canada and France as well as its present decision to expand into Japan. In the past several years, these countries are generally considered to be relatively stable from an economic viewpoint and potentially profitable markets for foreign investors. In addition, the political situation between the United States and these countries seems mostly friendly and relatively stable. Of course, political situations can change quickly and the political relationship between the United States and these countries should be constantly monitored by Toys "Я" Us. On such additional risk-oriented dimensions as economy and social factors, Toys "Я" Us management obviously has decided that foreign investments represent a tolerable amount of risk when weighed against the prospect of increased return from foreign operations. This decision is probably best illustrated through Toys "Я" Us moving ahead to try to open new stores in Japan despite local opposition.

MANAGEMENT FUNCTIONS AND MULTINATIONAL CORPORATIONS

The sections that follow discuss the four major management functions—planning, organizing, influencing, and controlling—as they occur at multinational corporations.

Planning for Multinational Corporations

Planning was defined in chapter 5 as determining how the management system will achieve its objectives. This definition is applicable to the management of both domestic and multinational organizations. In general, such management tools as policies, procedures, rules, budgets, forecasting, Gantt charts, and the program evaluation and review technique (PERT) are equally valuable in planning for either domestic or multinational organizations.

Perhaps the primary difference between planning in multinational versus domestic organizations involves strategic planning. Organizational strategy for the multinational organization must include provisions that focus on the international arena, whereas such strategy for a purely domestic organization does not. Increased environmental uncertainties along with a growing sense of international competition are causing more and more managers to carefully evaluate internationalization as an organizational strategy. The most significant challenge facing modern managers may be how to plan strategically in order to survive in a multinational business world.[13]

To develop appropriate international strategies, managers explore issues such as (1) establishing a new sales force in a foreign country, (2) developing new manufacturing plants in other countries through purchase or construction, (3) financing international expansion, and (4) determining which countries represent the most suitable candidates for international expansion. Although international strategies vary, most include some emphasis on one or more of the following areas: imports/exports, license agreements, direct investing, and joint ventures.

Imports/Exports

Importing is buying goods or services from another country.

Exporting is selling goods or services to another country.

Strategy in imports/exports emphasizes reaching organizational objectives by **importing** (buying goods or services from another country) or **exporting** (selling goods or services to another country).

Organizations of all sizes are importing and exporting. On the one hand, there are very small organizations, such as People's Car Company, which is made up basically of two people who import cars from Mexico to be sold to American dealers for resale.[14] On the other hand, there are extremely large and complex organizations, such as Eastman Kodak, which exports photographic products to a number of foreign countries.[15]

License Agreements

A **license agreement** is a right granted by one company to another to use its brand name, technology, product specifications, and so on, in the manufacture or sale of goods and services.

A **license agreement** is a right granted by one company to another to use its brand name, technology, product specifications, and so on in the manufacture or sale of goods and services. Naturally, the company to which the license is extended pays some fee for the privilege. International strategy in this area involves reaching organizational objectives through either the purchase or sale of licenses at the international level.

For example, Ohio Mattress Company, a relatively small mattress manufacturer, has generated outstanding profits by making and selling Sealy bedding in Ohio, Texas, and Puerto Rico. A license purchased by Ohio Mattress from Sealy gives Ohio Mattress the right to manufacture and sell Sealy's well-known products.[16]

Direct Investing

Direct investing is using the assets of one company to purchase the operating assets of another company.

Direct investing is using the assets of one company to purchase the operating assets (for example, factories) of another company. International strategy in this area emphasizes reaching organizational objectives through the purchase of operating assets of a company in another country.

For example, Robinson Nugent, Inc., of New Albany, Indiana, manufactures sophisticated electronic parts that are used in other products assembled by high-tech manufacturers throughout the world. The company opened a manufacturing facility in Delemont, Switzerland, in an effort to maintain its share of the European market. Over all, the company believes that this Swiss plant has had a good effect on European sales and has even increased demand for exports from the United States to Europe by 40 percent.[17]

Joint Ventures

An **international joint venture** is a partnership formed by a company in one country with a company in another country for the purpose of pursuing some mutually desirable business undertaking.

An **international joint venture** is a partnership formed by a company in one country with a company in another country for the purpose of pursuing some mutually desirable business undertaking. International strategy that includes joint ventures emphasizes the attainment of organizational objectives through partnerships with foreign companies.

Joint ventures between car manufacturers in Europe are becoming more and more common as companies strive for greater economies of scale and higher standards in product quality and delivery. Renault, for example, formulated a network of deals for diesel engines from Fiat, gasoline engines from Volvo, forgings and castings from Peugeot, and gearboxes from Volkswagen.[18]

Organizing Multinational Corporations

Organizing was defined in chapter 9 as the process of establishing orderly uses for all resources within the organization. This definition applies equally to the management of either domestic or multinational organizations. Two organizing topics regarding multinational corporations, however, bear further discussion. These topics are organization structure and the selection of managers.

Organization Structure

Organization structure was defined in chapter 8 as established relationships among resources within the management system, and the *organization chart* is the graphic illustration of organization structure. Chapter 9 also noted that departments shown on organization charts are most commonly established according to function, product, territory, customers, or manufacturing process. Internationally oriented organizations also normally establish structure based on these five areas (see Figure 20.4 on p. 634).

As with domestic organizations, there is no best way to organize all multinational corporations. Instead, managers of these organizations must analyze the multinational circumstances that confront them and develop an organization structure that best suits the circumstances.

Selection of Managers

For multinational organizations to thrive, they must of course have competent managers. One important characteristic that is believed to be a primary determinant of how competently managers can guide multinational organizations is their attitude toward how such organizations should operate.

Over the years, management theorists have identified three basic managerial attitudes toward the operations of multinational corporations: ethnocentric, polycentric, and geocentric.[19] The **ethnocentric attitude** reflects a belief that multinational corporations should regard home country management practices as superior to foreign country management practices. Managers with an ethnocentric attitude seem prone to making the mistake of stereotyping home country management practices as sound and reasonable and foreign management practices as faulty and unreasonable.[20] The **polycentric attitude** reflects a belief that because foreign managers are closer to foreign organizational units, they probably understand them better, and therefore foreign management practices should generally be viewed as more insightful than home country management practices. Managers with a **geocentric attitude** believe that the overall quality of management recommendations, rather than the location of managers, should determine the acceptability of management practices used to guide multinational corporations.

Understanding the potential worth of these three attitudes within multinational corporations is extremely important. The ethnocentric attitude, although perhaps having the advantage of keeping the organization simple, generally causes

The **ethnocentric attitude** is the attitude that reflects a belief that multinational corporations should regard home country management practices as superior to foreign country management practices.

The **polycentric attitude** is the attitude that reflects a belief that because foreign managers are closer to foreign organizational units, they probably understand them better—and therefore foreign management practices generally should be viewed as more insightful than home country management practices.

The **geocentric attitude** is the attitude that reflects a belief that the overall quality of management recommendations, rather than the location of managers, should determine the acceptability of management practices used to guide multinational corporations. The geocentric attitude generally is considered most appropriate for long-term organizational success.

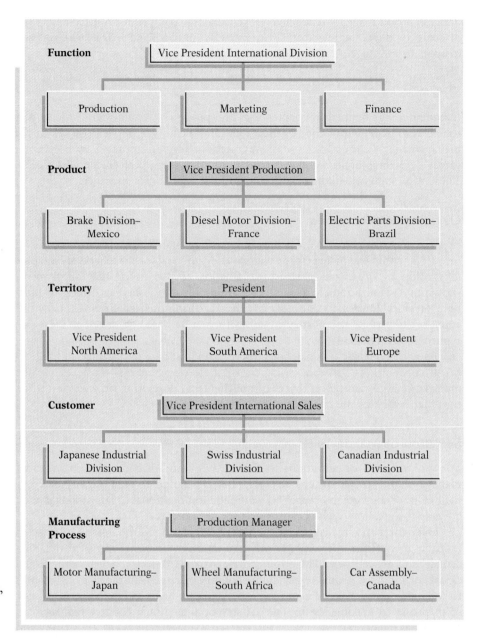

FIGURE 20.4

Partial multinational organization charts based on function, product, territory, customers, and manufacturing process

organizational problems, because feedback from foreign operations is eliminated. In some cases, the ethnocentric attitude even causes resentment toward the home country within the foreign society. The polycentric attitude can create the advantage of tailoring the foreign organizational segment to its culture, but it can lead to the sizable disadvantage of creating numerous individually run, relatively unique, and therefore difficult to control foreign organizational segments.

The geocentric attitude is generally thought to be the most appropriate for managers in multinational corporations. This attitude promotes collaboration between foreign and home country management and encourages the development of managerial skill regardless of the organizational segment or country in which managers operate. An organization characterized by the geocentric attitude generally incurs high travel and training expenses, and many decisions are made by consensus. Although risks such as the wide distribution of power in such an organization are real, payoffs such as better-quality products, worldwide utilization of the best human resources, increased managerial commitment to worldwide organizational objectives, and increased profit generally outweigh potential harm. Over all, managers with a geocentric attitude create organizations that contribute more to the long-term success of the multinational corporation. Table 20.4 compares in more detail the types of organizations generally created by managers who possess ethnocentric, polycentric, and geocentric attitudes.

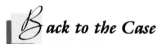

Back to the Case

Planning tools such as policies and procedure are equally valuable at Toys "Я" Us in managing either domestic or foreign operations. Being a multinational corporation, Toys "Я" Us has strategies that focus on the international sector, whereas a totally domestic organization would not. Such strategies could include having Toys "Я" Us buy toys (import) from foreign toy manufacturers for sale in the

TABLE 20.4 Different organizational characteristics typical of ethnocentric, polycentric, and geocentric

Organizational Characteristics	Managerial Attitudes		
	Ethnocentric	Polycentric	Geocentric
Complexity of organization	Complex in home country, simple in subsidiaries	Varied and independent	Increasingly complex and interdependent
Authority, decision making	High in headquarters	Relatively low in headquarters	Aim for a collaborative approach between headquarters and subsidiaries
Evaluation and control	Home standards applied for persons and performance	Determined locally	Find standards that are universal and local
Rewards and punishments, incentives	High in headquarters, low in subsidiaries	Wide variation; can be high or low for subsidiary performance	International and local executives rewarded for reaching local and worldwide objectives
Communicating, information flow	High volume to subsidiaries: orders, commands, advice	Little to and from headquarters, little between subsidiaries	Both ways and between subsidiaries: heads of subsidiaries part of management team
Identification	Nationality of owner	Nationality of host country	Truly international company but identifying with national interests
Perpetuation (recruiting, staffing, development)	Recruit and develop people of home country for key positions everywhere in the world	Develop people of local nationality for key positions in their own country	Develop best people everywhere in the world for key positions everywhere in the world

United States, sell the rights (license agreements) to a foreign company to use the name Toys "Я" Us in selling toys, purchase operating toy stores in other countries and convert them to Toys "Я" Us stores (direct investing), or enter a partnership (joint venture) with a foreign company to pursue some mutually desirable toy-selling opportunity.

Regarding organizing a multinational corporation such as Toys "Я" Us, organization structure generally should be based on one or more of the important variables of function, product, territory, customers, or manufacturing process. Toys "Я" Us managers must consider all of the variables within the situations that confront them and then design the organization structure that is most appropriate for those situations.

Over the long term, management at Toys "Я" Us should try to select for multinational positions the managers who possess geocentric attitudes, as opposed to polycentric or ethnocentric attitudes. Such managers would tend to build operating units in, say, Japan and the United Kingdom that would use the best human resources available and be highly committed to the attainment of organizational objectives.

Influencing People in Multinational Corporations

Influencing was defined in chapter 13 as guiding the activities of organization members in appropriate directions through such activities as communicating, leading, motivating, and managing groups. Influencing people in a multinational corporation, however, is more complex and challenging than in a domestic organization.

The factor that probably contributes most to this increased complexity and challenge is culture. **Culture** is the total characteristics of a given group of people and their environment. Factors generally designated as important components of a culture include customs, beliefs, attitudes, habits, skills, state of technology, level of education, and religion. As a manager moves from a domestic corporation involving basically one culture to a multinational corporation involving several, the task of influencing usually becomes progressively more difficult.

To successfully influence people, managers in multinational corporations should:

1. *Acquire a working knowledge of the languages used in countries that house foreign operations.* Multinational managers attempting to operate without such knowledge are prone to making costly mistakes. For example, one American company was shaken when it discovered that the Spanish brand name of the well-known cooking oil it had just introduced in Latin America translated as "jackass oil."[21] Naturally, such a mistake could have been avoided if the management of this organization had had a working knowledge of the Spanish language.

2. *Understand the attitudes of people in countries that house foreign operations.* An understanding of these attitudes can help managers design business practices that are suitable for unique foreign situations. For example, Americans generally accept competition as a tool to encourage people to work harder. As a result, U.S. business practices that include some competitive aspects seldom create significant disruption within organizations. Such practices, however, could cause disruption if introduced in either Japan or the typical European country. Table 20.5 compares the American, European, and Japanese attitudes toward competition in more detail.

Culture is the total characteristics of a given group of people and their environment.

TABLE 20.5 Comparison of American, European, and Japanese viewpoints on competition

Competition	Typical American Viewpoints	Typical European Viewpoints	Typical Japanese Viewpoints
Nature of competition	Competition is a strong moral force; it contributes to character building.	Competition is neither good nor bad.	There is conflict inherent in nature. To overcome conflicts, individuals must compete; but our final goal is harmony with nature and other human beings.
Business competition compared	Business competition is like a big sport game.	Business competition affects the livelihood of people and quickly develops into warfare.	The company is like a family. Competition has no place in a family. Aggressive action against competitors in the marketplace is for the survival and growth of the company.
Motivation	One cannot rely on an employee's motivation unless extra monetary inducements for hard work are offered in addition to a base salary or wage.	A key employee is motivated by the fact that he or she has been hired by the company.	Same as the European viewpoint.
Reward system	Money talks. A person is evaluated on the basis of his or her image (contribution) to the company. High tipping in best hotels, restaurants, and so on, is expected.	An adequate salary, fringe benefits, opportunities for promotion, but no extra incentives—except in sales. Very little tipping (normally, a service charge is included in added-value tax).	Same as the European viewpoint.
Excessive competition	Competition must be tough for the sale of the general welfare of society. No upper limit on the intensity and amount of competition is desirable.	Too much competition is destructive and is in conflict with brotherly love and the Christian ethic.	Excessive competition is destructive and can create hatred. Only restrained competition leads to harmony and benefits society.
Hiring policy	Aggressive individuals who enjoy competition are ideal employees. Individuals who avoid competition are unfit for life and company work.	Diversity of opinion. How competitiveness or aggressive behavior of an individual is viewed varies with national idealogy and the type of work. In England, it is not a recommendation to describe a job applicant as being aggressive.	Individuals are hired usually not for specific jobs but on the basis of their personality traits and their ability to become honorable company members. Team play and group consensus are stressed.

3. *Understand the needs that motivate people in countries housing foreign operations.* For managers in multinational corporations to be successful in motivating people in different countries, they must present these individuals with the opportunity to satisfy personal needs while being productive within the

organization. In designing motivation strategies, multinational managers must understand that people in different countries often have different personal needs. For example, people in Switzerland, Austria, Japan, and Argentina tend to have high security needs, whereas people in Denmark, Sweden, and Norway tend to have high social needs. People in Great Britain, the United States, Canada, New Zealand, and Australia tend to have high self-actualization needs.[22] Thus, to be successful at influencing, multinational managers must understand their employees' needs and mold such organizational components as incentive systems, job design, and leadership style to correspond to these needs.

Controlling Multinational Corporations

Controlling was defined in chapter 17 as making something happen the way it was planned to happen. As with domestic corporations, control in multinational corporations requires that standards be set, performance be measured and compared to standards, and corrective action be taken if necessary. In addition, control in such areas as labor costs, product quality, and inventory is important to organizational success regardless of whether the organization is domestic or international.

Control of a multinational corporation has additional complexities. First, there is the problem of different currencies. Management must decide how to compare profit generated by organizational units located in different countries and therefore expressed in terms of different currencies.

Another complication is that organizational units in multinational corporations are generally more geographically separated. This increased distance normally makes it difficult for multinational managers to keep a close watch on operations in foreign countries. For example, physical distance certainly contributed to the adverse publicity PepsiCo received when an employee in Pepsi's overseas bottling branch blew the whistle on an elaborate scam that had puffed up unit profits for several previous years. Using stacks of false documents, finance staffers in the Philippines and Mexico had overstated assets and profits and deferred expenses. As a result, PepsiCo's financial position was overstated by $224 million.[23]

One action managers are taking to help overcome the difficulty of monitoring geographically separated foreign units is to carefully design the communication network or management information system that links them. A significant part of this design is to require all company units to acquire and install similar MIS equipment in all offices, both foreign and domestic, in an effort to ensure the likelihood of network hookups when communication becomes necessary. In addition, such standardization of MIS equipment seems to provide the advantages of facilitating communication among all foreign locations as well as making MIS equipment repair and maintenance problems more understandable, more easily solved, and therefore less expensive.[24]

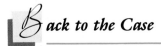

Back to the Case

Influencing people at Toys "Я" Us must be a complicated process. The culture of people in Canada, Puerto Rico, France, the United Kingdom, and Japan, as well as the United States, must be thoroughly understood. Toys "Я" Us managers of foreign operations must have a working knowledge of the languages spoken in the country and an understanding of the attitudes and personal needs that motivate individuals within the foreign work force. If motivation strategy is to be successful for Toys "Я" Us as a whole, rewards used to motivate French workers may need to be much different from rewards used to motivate Canadian workers.

The control process at Toys "Я" Us should involve standards, measurements, and needed corrective action just as it should within a domestic company. The different currencies used in countries like France, the United States, the United Kingdom, and Canada, however, tend to make control more complicated for Toys "Я" Us than for a domestic organization. The significant distance of all of the other countries from the United States also tends to complicate control at Toys "Я" Us.

COMPARATIVE MANAGEMENT: AN EMPHASIS ON JAPANESE MANAGEMENT

Perhaps the most popular international management topic today is comparative management. The sections that follow define *comparative management* and provide insights on Japanese management practices that can be of value to U.S. managers.

Defining Comparative Management

Comparative management is the study of the management process in different countries to examine the potential of management action under different environmental conditions. Whereas international management focuses on management activities across national borders,[25] comparative management analyzes management practices in one country for their possible application in another country.[26]

The sections that follow discuss motivation and management practice insights that were formulated by analysis of Japanese management methods. These insights currently are being applied by many U.S. managers.

Comparative management is the study of the management process in different countries to examine the potential of management action under different environmental conditions.

Quality Highlight: The Deming Prize—No Longer a Stranger at Home

Japan's most prestigious quality assurance award, the Deming Prize, honors the American, W. Edwards Deming. Deming is a statistician and quality control expert. Deming's work in statistical quality measures created a devotion to quality control that has become ingrained in Japanese industrial culture. Until recently, however, Deming's native country ignored his work. His namesake prize had eluded U.S. companies until Florida Power and Light (FPL) made history by winning the Deming Prize last month.

Established in 1951 by the Japanese Union of Scientists and Engineers, the Deming Prize goes to organizations that demonstrate a successful, companywide quality control program. The award has helped establish total quality techniques in nearly every aspect of Japanese industry. Many Japanese organizations enter the grueling application procedure to streamline and upgrade internal quality procedures to a level worthy of securing the award. This nationwide acceptance has resulted in the massive improvements in manufacturing quality that have helped Japanese industry take giant strides in the global market.

The Deming has three categories: Japanese individuals, Japanese organizations, and overseas companies. The third category was a response, in 1986, to the growing non-Japanese interest in quality.

FPL learned from Japan's Kansai Electric Power Company, the first service firm to win a Deming in 1984. FPL launched an all-out effort to win the prize after CEO John J. Hudiburg and a team of FPL managers visited Kansai and other Japanese firms several years ago.

According to Donald F. Borgschulte, FPL's director of systems and programming, completing the grueling challenge process was satisfaction enough.

"Just being in the competition vastly improved the company's quality improvement process," Borgschulte said.

"The challenge for the Deming Prize has accelerated a new management process from two years to 6–10 months. The outcome was almost irrelevant."

Insights from Japanese Motivation Strategies

The one country that is being studied the most from a comparative management viewpoint is Japan, and knowledge of the overall success of today's Japanese managers is widespread.[27] Perhaps the most analyzed area of this success deals with how Japanese managers effectively motivate organization members. So successful are the Japanese in this area that Americans are traveling to Japan to try to gain insights on Japanese motivation strategies.[28]

Japanese managers seem to be able to motivate their organization members by:

1. *Hiring employees for life rather than for some shorter period of time.* A close relationship between workers and the organization is built through this lifetime employment. Because workers know that they have a guaranteed job and that their future is therefore heavily influenced by the future of the organization, they are willing to be flexible and cooperative.[29]

2. *Elevating employees to a level of organizational status equal to that of management.* In Japanese factories, employees at all levels wear the same work clothes, eat in the same cafeteria, and use the same restrooms.[30]

3. *Making employees feel that they are highly valued by management and that the organization will provide for their material needs.*[31] New workers and their relatives attend a ceremony at which the company president welcomes them to the firm. The newcomers often live in company-built housing for several years until they can afford to buy their own housing. Also, much employee life outside work is spent in company social clubs, with weddings and receptions often being held in company facilities. Some Japanese companies even help pay for wedding expenses.

Japanese managers obviously go to great lengths to build positive working relationships with their employees. In addition, there is some evidence that similar actions have been applied successfully by Japanese managers in motivating American employees at the Sony plant in San Diego.[32] Because the general Japanese culture has been shown to be a significant factor influencing the success of Japanese management,[33] however, managers of other countries should imitate Japanese actions with extreme caution.[34] After all, what Japanese workers find desirable or need-satisfying may not be the same as what workers from other countries find desirable or need-satisfying.[35]

Insights from Japanese Management Practices: Theory Z

Given the success of organizations such as Nissan and Sanyo, many U.S. management writers have been carefully analyzing Japanese organizations and comparing them to American organizations. The purpose is to make recommendations about how Japanese management practices can be used to improve the operation of American organizations.

One such recommendation, called Theory Z, was introduced by William Ouchi in 1981.[36] **Theory Z** suggests that significant management practices in the United States and Japan be combined into one middle-ground, improved framework. Ouchi studied the following management practices in U.S. and Japanese organizations: (1) the length of time workers were employed, (2) the way decisions were made, (3) where responsibility existed, (4) the rate at which employees were evaluated and promoted, (5) the type of control tools used, (6) the degree to which employees had specialized career paths, and (7) the type of concern shown for employees. Figure 20.5 summarizes Ouchi's findings about how management practices differ in U.S. and Japanese organizations.

Theory Z is the effectiveness dimension that implies that managers who use either Theory X or Theory Y assumptions when dealing with people can be successful, depending on their situation.

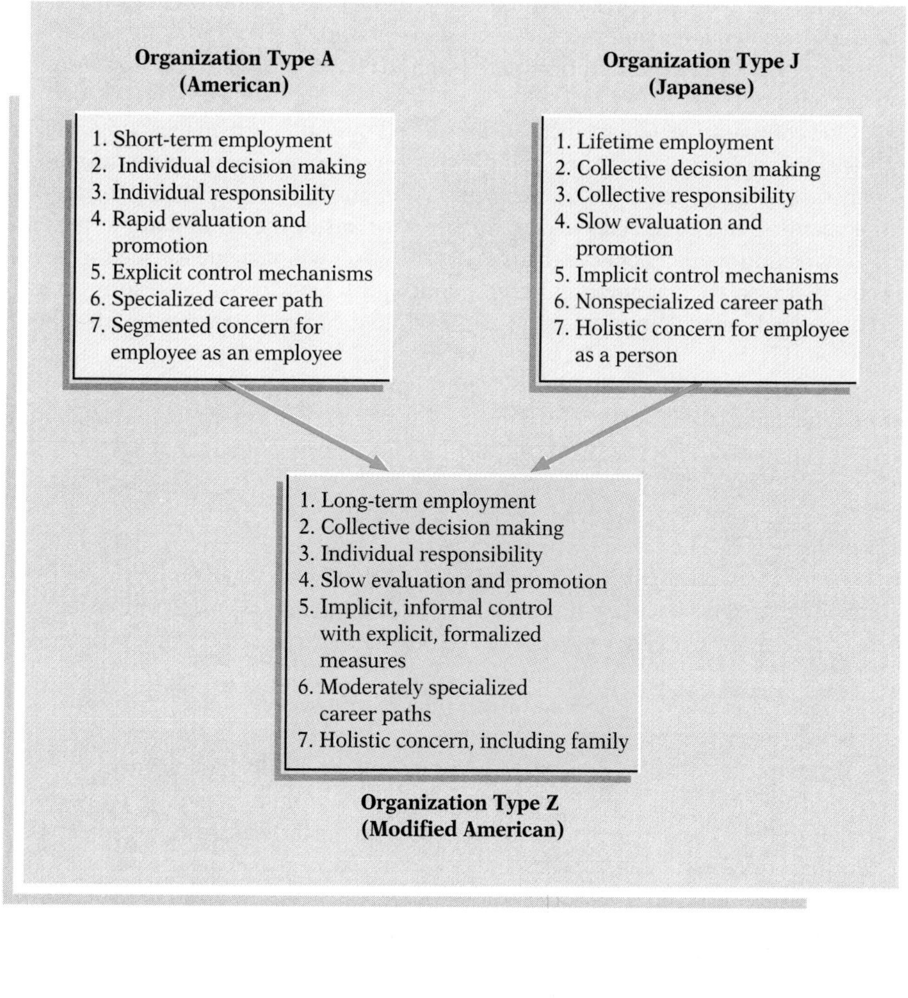

Organization Type A (American)
1. Short-term employment
2. Individual decision making
3. Individual responsibility
4. Rapid evaluation and promotion
5. Explicit control mechanisms
6. Specialized career path
7. Segmented concern for employee as an employee

Organization Type J (Japanese)
1. Lifetime employment
2. Collective decision making
3. Collective responsibility
4. Slow evaluation and promotion
5. Implicit control mechanisms
6. Nonspecialized career path
7. Holistic concern for employee as a person

Organization Type Z (Modified American)
1. Long-term employment
2. Collective decision making
3. Individual responsibility
4. Slow evaluation and promotion
5. Implicit, informal control with explicit, formalized measures
6. Moderately specialized career paths
7. Holistic concern, including family

FIGURE 20.5

Combining significant American and Japanese management practices to form the Type Z organization

In addition, the figure contains Ouchi's suggestions for how to integrate American and Japanese management practices to develop a new, more successful American organization, called a Type Z organization. According to Ouchi, the Type Z organization is characterized by the "individual responsibility" of American organizations as well as the "collective decision making, slow evaluation and promotion, and holistic concern for employees" of Japanese organizations. The length of employment, control, and career path characteristics of the Type Z organization are essentially compromises between American and Japanese organizations.

In a very short time, Ouchi's Theory Z concept gained popularity not only among management theoreticians but also among practicing managers. Anecdotes abound about how the application of Theory Z principles has aided managers in such organizations as Chrysler and Mead Merchants.[37] However, some question has arisen regarding the quality of Ouchi's research methods,[38] and the validity of his Theory Z conclusions has been questioned. Much more investigation is needed before Ouchi's Theory Z can be conclusively evaluated.

Back to the Case

Managers at Toys "Я" Us undoubtedly are involved with comparative management. In this regard, they study the management practices in foreign operations for the purpose of applying them to improve operations at Toys "Я" Us. Company managers usually take a number of trips annually to see firsthand how foreign operations are run.

One comparative management insight that Toys "Я" Us managers might want to consider applying within their company involves Japanese motivation strategies. Japanese managers seem to be very successful in motivating their workers by implementing such strategies as elevating the workers to the same status as managers and making workers believe that the organization will provide for their material needs. Because the Japanese culture is much different from the culture of the French, the United Kingdom, and of the United States and others with whom Toys "Я" Us deals, Toys "Я" Us managers should be careful in applying Japanese methods to workers in other countries. If Toys "Я" Us is successful in opening stores in Japan, applying motivation insights acquired from watching successful Japanese managers operate would probably be very valuable to the Toys "Я" Us Japanese stores.

Another comparative management insight that could be valuable to Toys "Я" Us managers is Theory Z, which suggests a blend of American and Japanese management practices. With Theory Z, Toys "Я" Us managers could make their company more successful by implementing such strategies as hiring employees for the long term and having only moderately specialized career paths for workers. If Theory Z is to be implemented in a non-Japanese company, however, the worth and impact of the concept should be carefully monitored. More research is needed to test Theory Z's true worth.

JIT, another Japanese concept, could prove to be a valuable inventory-control method for Toys "Я" Us. Keeping inventory to a minimum by ordering toys from suppliers only as they are needed for sale could significantly enhance organizational performance. Minimizing storage and handling costs related to inventories and engaging only the organizational resources needed to meet customer needs are advantages that Toys "Я" Us could gain by using JIT.

Action Summary

Reread the learning objectives that follow. Each objective is followed by questions. Answering these questions accurately will help you retain the most important concepts discussed in this chapter. After answering each question, check your answer with the answer key at the end of this chapter. (*Hint:* If you have doubt regarding the correct response, consult the page whose number follows the answer.)

Circle:

From studying this chapter, I will attempt to acquire:

1. **An understanding of international management and its importance to modern managers.**

   a. To reach organizational objectives, management may extend its activities to include an emphasis on organizations in foreign countries. T, F

   b. It has been estimated that by 1995 the investments in foreign countries made by U.S. companies will be: (a) $275 billion; (b) $213 billion; (c) $124 billion; (d) $75 billion; (e) none of the above. a, b, c, d, e

2. **An understanding of what constitutes a multinational corporation.**

   a. According to Jacoby, the first stage in a corporation's multinationalization is when the corporation: (a) multinationalizes ownership of corporate stock; (b) multinationalizes management from top to bottom; (c) establishes foreign manufacturing facilities; (d) establishes sales organizations abroad; (e) exports its products. a, b, c, d, e

   b. In general, the smaller the organization, the greater the likelihood that it participates in international operations of some sort. T, F

3. **Insights concerning the risk involved in investing in international operations.**

   a. Managers who make foreign investments believe that such investments: (a) reduce or eliminate high transportation costs; (b) allow participation in the rapid expansion of a market abroad; (c) provide foreign technical, design, and marketing skills; (d) earn higher profits; (e) a, b, c, and d. a, b, c, d, e

   b. A manager's failing to understand the different national sovereignties, disparate national conditions, and different national values and institutions can lead to poor investment decisions. T, F

4. **Knowledge about planning and organizing in multinational corporations.**

   a. The primary difference between planning in multinational versus domestic organizations probably involves operational planning. T, F

   b. The feeling that multinational corporations should regard home country management practices as superior to foreign country practices is known as which of the following attitudes: (a) egocentric attitude; (b) ethnocentric attitude; (c) polycentric attitude; (d) geocentric attitude; (e) isocentric attitude. a, b, c, d, e

5. **Knowledge about influencing and controlling in multinational corporations.**

   a. The factor that probably contributes most to the increased complexity and challenge of influencing in multinational organizations is: (a) language; (b) attitudes; (c) personal needs; (d) culture; (e) none of the above. a, b, c, d, e

   b. Different currencies and distance are the two major contributors to the difficulty of controlling in multinational corporations. T, F

6. **Insights about what comparative management is and how it might help managers do their jobs better.**

T, F
a. Comparative management emphasizes analyzing management practices in one country to determine how to best counteract the effectiveness of a foreign competitor.

a, b, c, d, e
b. A group of American autoworkers visiting a Toyota plant in Japan to gather ideas that can be applied in their plant back home is an example of: (a) industrial sabotage; (b) comparative management; (c) kibutshi; (d) foreign intervention; (e) none of the above.

7. **Ideas on how to be a better manager through the study of Japanese management techniques.**

T, F
a. Since the Japanese have been so successful and there is little relationship between their culture and their success, American management would be wise to immediately implement the Japanese techniques.

a, b, c, d, e
b. Which of the following is *not* one of the significant management practices that Ouchi studied in American and Japanese organizations: (a) the length of time workers were employed; (b) the way in which decisions were made; (c) the type of incentive plan used; (d) where responsibility existed within the organization; (e) the rate at which employees were evaluated and promoted.

T, F
c. JIT emphasizes the improvement of organizational performance primarily through more accurate sales forecasts.

Introductory Case Wrap-Up

"Toys "Я" Us Focuses on Japan" (p. 622) and its related back-to-the-case sections were written to help you better understand the management concepts contained in this chapter. Answer the following discussion questions about this introductory case to further enrich your understanding of chapter content:

1. Do you think that at some point in your career you will become involved in international management? Explain.

2. Assuming that you will be involved in managing a Toys "Я" Us store in Japan, what challenges do you think will be the most difficult for you to meet? Why?

3. Evaluate the following statement: Toys "Я" Us can learn to manage its organizations better by studying how successful toy stores are managed in other countries.

Issues for Review and Discussion

1. Define *international management*.
2. How significant is the topic of international management to the modern manager? Explain fully.
3. What is meant by the term *multinational corporation*?
4. List and explain four factors that contribute to the complexity of managing multinational corporations.
5. Should managers be careful in making investments in foreign operations? Explain.

6. List and define four areas in which managers can develop internationally oriented strategies.

7. What is the difference between direct investing and joint ventures at the international level?

8. Draw segments of organization charts that organize a multinational corporation on the basis of product, function, and customers.

9. Is there one best way to organize all multinational corporations? Explain fully.

10. What are the differences between ethnocentric, polycentric, and geocentric attitudes? Describe advantages and disadvantages of each.

11. How does culture affect the international management process?

12. Discuss three suggestions that would be helpful to a manager attempting to influence organization members in different countries.

13. How does geographic distance relate to controlling multinational corporations?

14. How can comparative management help managers of today?

15. What insights can be learned from Japanese managers about ways to motivate people? Should caution be exercised by a Canadian manager in applying these insights? Explain.

16. Discuss what is meant by Theory Z. How much value should a manager place on the Theory Z concept? Explain.

Building on What You Know

Directions

Review the Highlight feature as indicated below and answer its corresponding questions. Questions in this section focus on relating a Highlight appearing in this chapter to management concepts that you have learned in a previous chapter.

Review the Quality Highlight: The Deming Prize—No Longer a Stranger at Home on page 639. In chapter 19 you studied about management information systems. Would a management information system be an important part of a Japanese company's winning the Deming Prize? Explain. How critical would a Management Decision Support System be in winning the prize? Explain.

Action Summary Answer Key

1. a. T, p. 623
   b. a, p. 624

2. a. e, p. 627
   b. F, p. 626

3. a. e, p. 628
   b. T, pp. 628–629

4. a. F, p. 631
   b. b, p. 633

5. a. d, p. 636
   b. T, p. 638

6. a. F, p. 639
   b. b, p. 639

7. a. F, pp. 640–641
   b. c, p. 641
   c. F, p. 642

Case Study

Maquiladoras:
An International Case Study

by Mary S. Thibodeaux, University of North Texas

Edward Shepherd, an unemployed worker in Detroit, is very disturbed about the thousands of *maquiladoras* (U.S.-owned factories operating in Mexico) springing up in Mexico. Because of them, the managers of his company closed his plant, laid off the workers making $9 and $12 per hour, and moved the manufacturing facility to Juarez, Mexico, where they pay workers approximately $1 per hour.

The Mexican word *maquiladora* (also referred to as a "twin plant") is derived from a Spanish word used in Colonial Mexico. Today, *maquiladora* is used to mean a production facility that operates in Mexico and manufactures, assembles, or produces raw materials that have been temporarily imported into Mexico, in-bond and duty-free. Because the parts are generally used to manufacture goods for export, the imported parts are placed "in-bond" to avoid taxes. When these finished products are exported from Mexico, no export fee or value-added tax is charged by the Mexican government.

Thousands of American producers are pouring into Mexico to participate in this program. The list includes General Motors, Ford, Eastman Kodak, Chrysler, International Telephone and Telegraph, General Electric, and many others. Actually, only about sixty-eight percent of the *maquila* plants are owned by U.S. firms; many other countries are participating in the program as well. Firms from Britain, Finland, Spain, France, and Holland have established operations in Mexico, and the percentage of Japanese firms in Mexico (presently two percent of the total) are increasing.

The *maquiladora* program started around 1960 and was formulated into law in 1971 as the Border Industrialization Program (BIP). Although approximately ninety percent of *maquila* plants are adjacent to the U.S.–Mexican border from San Diego to Brownsville, Texas, the products can be produced in the interior of Mexico with no restrictions. Up to twenty percent of the products can be sold in Mexico, and the plants are exempt from the requirement of fifty-one percent Mexican ownership. These plants, estimated now at approximately 2,000, employ half a million Mexicans, paying them an average of $5 to $8 a day.

Firms that manufacture in Mexico under the *maquiladora* program and distribute in this country can achieve several strategic and competitive advantages. Among these advantages are (1) labor cost, (2) logistics, (3) transportation, and (4) skilled personnel.

The cost of labor is among the lowest in the world. In 1989, the average wage was $1.57 per hour, compared to $1.79 in Korea. It is customary to pay *maquila* workers at the legal minimum wage for Mexican workers.

Because an important component of manufacturing some labor-intensive goods is people, companies benefit from the ability to ship raw materials to any part of Mexico for assembly. This allows for excellent cost control, product flow, and flexibility. In addition, a U.S. company can easily link its existing operations to the *maquila* via highway, rail, air, etc. Finally, there is an excellent supply of qualified and trained managers, engineers, and technicians available to work in the *maquila*. Although the wages and salaries are less than their American counterparts, benefits are generous. For instance, these professionals may live on either side of the border, allowing families to take advantage of educational, cultural, and economic benefits of both countries.

Maquiladoras are not without problems. In February, 1991, a coalition of religious, environmental, and labor groups launched a new corporate offensive aimed at pushing U.S. manufacturers to improve the health, safety, and working conditions at their border plants. The Coalition for Justice in the Maquiladoras, naming such companies as GM, ITT, and GE, charged that these companies save money by operating below the minimum standards imposed in the United States. In responding to such charges, a General Motors spokesperson stated, "We comply with [each country's] cultural norms."

The new government officials in Mexico, though, want more for their workers. The Mexican president has stated on several occasions that with its high rate of literacy (eighty-seven percent), Mexico can now be more than a giant assembly line. The officials are seriously considering free trade between Mexico and the U.S., with the accompanying benefits and costs to companies and populations in both countries. It is very clear to informed observers that a free-trade pact with Mexico would stimulate a rapid and increasingly complex movement of investment throughout Mexico.

Discussion Questions

1. Does a company have a legal and/or ethical obligation to meet the requirements of a host country? Should a company go beyond the requirements that have been established in a developing country?

2. What are some possible benefits and costs to American countries of engaging in free trade with Mexico?

3. Even though values differ from country to country, should a U.S. company follow its own management practices or those of the host country?

4. What are the risks and benefits for multinational companies running *maquiladoras* in Mexico?

From Soda Pop to Power: Donald Kendall, Former Chair of PepsiCo

Most Americans would be surprised to learn that PepsiCo is more than the second largest producer of cola drinks worldwide—much, much more. PepsiCo is a multinational power of some note. Its divisions include Pepsi, Pizza Hut, Kentucky Fried Chicken, and Taco Bell as well as innumerable smaller concerns. Its annual operating budgets exceed those of many nations where its products are sold. Projections of 1990 sales topped $18 billion.

When Donald Kendall joined Pepsi as a syrup salesperson in 1947, however, Pepsi was simply a soft-drink company. Within a decade, Kendall had become president of Pepsi International, a young offshoot of the parent company, making inroads in the soft-drink markets of 60 countries around the world. Under Kendall, Pepsi International invaded more than 60 additional international markets, and sales tripled.

In 1958, shortly after Kendall took over Pepsi International, he grabbed the opportunity to make history. The United States was invited to participate in a business–culture exhibit in Moscow, and Coca-Cola was invited to attend. United States's attitudes toward the Union of Soviet Socialist Republics (U.S.S.R.) at the time were frigid—the Cold War was in full swing. Coca-Cola, although in business in the U.S.S.R., declined the invitation. Pepsi took the challenge. In the most famous taste test of the 1950s, Kendall offered U.S.S.R. premier Nikita Khrushchev the chance to compare Pepsi bottled in New York to Pepsi bottled in the U.S.S.R. Press reporters and photographers lapped it up as Khrushchev and then Vice President Richard Nixon downed Pepsi after Pepsi. Pepsi had conquered the U.S.S.R. cola market and the international headlines in one afternoon.

Pepsi went on to become the first American product to be completely manufactured in the U.S.S.R., with an innovative trade agreement that allows Pepsi to export the U.S.S.R.'s Stolichnaya vodka rather than rubles in payment for Pepsi's imported cola and cola ingredients. Similar approaches have been used successfully by other Pepsi divisions and are now being copied by competitors. Pepsi now runs 26 fully operational plants in the U.S.S.R., and in 1990, Pepsi signed contracts to build 28 more—an additional $3 billion investment.

Pepsi also deals directly with the distilleries creating Stolichnaya, rather than purchasing through middlepersons, as other vodka importers must. As a result, they are able to reduce communication difficulties and time lags. Recently, Pepsi introduced a new, upscale Stolichnaya vodka to the American market. Working directly with factories in Russia, they were able to develop new label and bottle designs and the equipment to create them in only six months—a process that in the past in the U.S.S.R. would have taken years.

Although he moved on from Pepsi International to a larger arena in 1965, Kendall keeps an eye on Pepsi's international activities. He sees innovative marketing and trade strategies as keys to Pepsi's phenomenal growth. Pepsi, and later PepsiCo, learned early to think globally and not in terms of simply exporting homegrown goods. Kendall sees Pepsi's biggest opportunities as existing in overseas markets still dominated by Coca-Cola. Domestic (U.S.) sales of Pepsi and Coca-Cola are almost even.

Kendall and Herman Lay, founder of Frito-Lay, were responsible for creating PepsiCo in 1965 when their two companies merged. Kendall served as the new company's chief executive officer and chair until 1986; he keeps his hand in now as chair of the executive committee of PepsiCo's board of directors. During those two decades, Kendall charted the course that has led PepsiCo to giant stature.

"We try to build divisional pride in the divisions," he explains. "They all have their own individual headquarters and they have pride of the division, and I think that's one of the reasons they've all been successful. We haven't tried to make them all fit the same pattern." Instead, PepsiCo allows its divisions to operate as if they were smaller multinationals. This retains a sense of independence and gives each division the opportunity to grow and move flexibly as its own best interests dictate.

During Donald Kendall's chairship, PepsiCo set a new course at home, as well, by becoming the first U.S. corporation to appoint an African-American vice president. This created problems in some markets in the South, but Kendall knew it was the right thing to do. His attitude toward PepsiCo's people—all 220,000 of them worldwide—parallels his attitude toward PepsiCo's divisions: "We should give everybody an opportunity."

Video Case Questions

1. Does PepsiCo meet the definition of a multinational corporation? Did Pepsi International meet this definition at the time Kendall was its president? Why or why not?
2. Do you think PepsiCo's management attitudes are primarily ethnocentric, polycentric, or geocentric? Why?
3. How has Pepsi avoided the economic peculiarity of trading for rubles, relatively worthless overseas, in its U.S.S.R. operations?
4. How might comparative management techniques be used to benefit PepsiCo divisions internationally?

Video Case Activities

1. Prepare a partial organizational chart for three PepsiCo divisions based on function and another chart based on territory. Which is more likely to rely on a geocentric management attitude?
2. Review Table 20.4. For each organizational characteristic shown, which attitude is most likely to be present in Pepsi's Soviet operations?

Chapter 21

Student Learning Objectives

From studying this chapter, I will attempt to acquire:

1. An understanding of the relationship between quality and companywide quality.

2. An appreciation of the importance of quality.

3. Insight about how to achieve quality.

4. An understanding of how strategic planning can be used to promote quality.

5. Knowledge about management skills that relate to achieving quality.

6. Insights about special situations that could affect the achievement of quality.

Quality: Building Competitive Organizations

 *hapter Outline*

DISNEY WORLD: ATTENTION TO QUALITY

Disney World, a theme park near Orlando, Florida, is a commonly used example of a company facility that is managed with constant attention to establishing and maintaining high quality in all of its operations. Undoubtedly, Disney's constant focus on quality has helped to build its market appeal throughout the world. Recent polls indicate that Disney World is now the number 1 honeymoon destination in the world.

Disney has taken a lush tropical wilderness and turned it into the most technologically innovative theme park in the world. State-of-the-art attractions like Space Mountain and Journey into Imagination continually amaze park guests.

Although attention to high-quality attractions is critically important in the Disney formula for success, attention to excellence in other areas is perhaps an even

> Disney's constant focus on quality has helped to build its market appeal throughout the world.

more important ingredient of the Disney experience. Customer surveys rank park attractions number 3 in the hearts of customers. What customers like even more than the attractions are the friendliness of Disney employees and the cleanliness that makes Disney World seem to shine. Customers apparently believe that Disney World is an almost perfect example of order and efficiency and enjoy being able to experience it.

Disney is such an accepted authority on how to maintain high quality in even the most seemingly insignificant aspects of organizational operations that the company has been successful in offering "Disney Quality Service Seminars." Executives from other companies pay to attend the seminars to find out exactly how Disney maintains its focus on quality. The executives adapt concepts learned in the seminars to their own businesses.

One point made in the seminars is that Disney emphasizes its orientation process for new hires as an opportunity to begin building high-quality customer

relations. As an example, Disney's orientation emphasizes the importance of courtesy in interacting with customers and of thinking of park visitors as personal guests rather than customers. Chico Lager, the chief executive officer of Ben & Jerry Homemade Inc., recently attended the Disney seminar and came away with the commitment to revamp entirely his company orientation program to make it more consistent with company philosophy and values.

Disney's experience tells us that attention to less-significant aspects of organizational operations can be instrumental in maintaining customer perception of the quality of all company goods or services. This is the lesson that Disney is teaching to executives from other companies.

This case is based on Jeanne C. Meister, "Companies Weave the Disney 'Magic' into Their Own Businesses," *Marketing News* 24 (February 5, 1990), 12–13; and Charles Leerhsen, "How Disney Does It," *Newsweek*, April 3, 1989.

FUNDAMENTALS OF QUALITY

Quality was defined earlier in this text as how well a product does what it is supposed to do—how closely and reliably it satisfies the specifications to which it is built. In general, quality was presented as the degree of excellence on which products or services can be ranked. This chapter expands the subject of product quality.

Quality is how well a product does what it is supposed to do—how closely and reliably it satisfies the specifications to which it is built.

Defining Company-wide Quality

Company-wide quality (CWQ) is the continuous process of involving all organization members in ensuring that every activity related to the production of goods or services has an appropriate role in establishing product quality.[1] In essence, all organization members emphasize the appropriate performance of activities throughout the company in order to maintain the quality of products offered by the company. Under the CWQ concept, all organization members work both individually and collectively to maintain the quality of products offered to the marketplace.

Although the CWQ movement actually began in the United States, the establishment, growth, and development of the movement throughout the world is largely credited to the Japanese. The Japanese believe that a CWQ program must include the cooperation of all people within a company. Top managers, middle managers, supervisors, and workers throughout a company must strive together to ensure that all phases of company operations appropriately affect product quality. Such operations include areas like market research, research and development, product planning, design, production, purchasing, vendor management, manufacturing, inspection, sales, after-sales customer care, financial control, personnel administration, and company training and education.

Company-wide quality (CWQ) is the continuous process of involving all organization members in ensuring that every activity related to the production of goods and services has an appropriate role in establishing product quality.

Quality Highlight: Cadillac Implements Simultaneous Engineering

In 1985, the Cadillac Motor Car Division of General Motors Corporation began a sweeping program, called Simultaneous Engineering, to improve quality, cut costs, and sell more cars. The program improves quality by involving everyone from the factory worker to the dealer to the customer in the manufacture and production of Cadillac cars. In 1990, Cadillac won the Malcolm Baldrige National Quality Award. The program involves more than 700 employees and supplier representatives, grouped into teams that monitor quality and production. The teams participate in the preparation of Cadillac's annual business plan, are given continuous education, attend weekly team meetings, and are given financial incentives as well, amounting to about $9.3 million in 1989.

To put employees in the customers' shoes, Cadillac began sending hourly and salaried workers to auto shows to talk with customers and potential customers and began working directly with selected dealers to resolve customer problems. External suppliers were also brought into the program to serve on Product Improvement and Development Teams.

Improved product quality has meant that Cadillac offers customers a much stronger warranty. At the same time, warranty-related costs for the company, during the first year of ownership, have dropped sharply.

In 1985, 70 percent of customers gave Cadillac favorable ratings on satisfaction, service, and total owner experience. In 1989, 86 percent gave favorable ratings.

But the biggest benefit, says Cadillac General Manager, John Grettenberger, has been the improvement in attitude among employees. "When you go into plants and offices," he says, "you see people smiling again."

The CWQ concept has been adopted by a majority of firms throughout Japan. In fact, CWQ is generally credited with being a major factor in Japan's undeniable success in establishing that country as a major competitor in the world marketplace. Although U.S. firms seem to be moving somewhat toward accepting and implementing the CWQ concept, there are some basic differences between the U.S. and Japanese positions on establishing and maintaining companywide quality. Table 21.1 demonstrates some of these basic differences.

In essence, CWQ is a means to the end of product quality. The excellence or quality of all management activities (planning, organizing, influencing, and controlling) inevitably influences the quality of final goods or services offered by organizations to the marketplace. In general, the more effective a CWQ program within an organization, the higher the quality of goods and services that an organization can offer to the marketplace. The Quality Highlight feature has been used throughout this text to illustrate that quality is related to planning, organizing, influence, and controlling issues. Highlight capsules covered in this book that focus on quality-related activities are enumerated in Table 21.2 on page 656.

TABLE 21.1 U.S. and Japanese positions on CWQ

United States Position	Japanese Position
Quality is a function of how well the product or service meets the specifications.	Same as the U.S. position.
Quality depends on all departments—from purchasing to engineering design to production to shipping to service.	Same as the U.S. position.
The quality goal is to reach a present percentage of defectives.	Accept no defects—insist on perfection.
Quality goals are set one fiscal year at a time.	Strive to improve quality consistently, not once a year, but all the time.
There is an optimal level of quality. Customers will not pay for a higher level.	Increasing quality all the time will increase market share and spur new market demand.
Control quality is done through inspections during production and through final inspection of completed lots.	Every production worker is responsible for inspection, even if this means stopping the assembly line to correct an observed defect.
Use statistical sampling methods to inspect large lots of completed products.	Inspect each piece as it is produced to catch defects before a whole lot is poorly made. Keep inventory low, using the just-in-time concept.
Set acceptable quality levels (AQL) based on sampling tables. These levels are stated in number of defects per 100 units produced.	Reject sampling tables, because no level of defects is acceptable. Express defects in number of defects per 1,000,000 units produced.
Use a random sample, typically of size $n = 5$, to check for process stability.	Use a sample of $n = 2$, consisting of the first piece and last piece produced in each lot to assure stability.
The quality control (QC) department is responsible for testing and inspection.	The QC department monitors quality, but also teaches and spreads QC information. Actual inspection by workers.
Rework of defective units is done on a separate rework line with its own staff.	Workers or groups correct their own errors, even if they have to stay late. (In reality, very few reworks are needed because of total quality control.)
Janitors keep workplaces clean.	Workers themselves are responsible for housekeeping of their work areas.

TABLE 21.2 Management Highlights in this book that illustrate the concern for quality throughout all phases of management

Baldrige Award Exemplifies Quality (p. 47)

Xerox Corporation (p. 64)

A High-Quality MBO Program at Boehringer Mannheim Company (p. 123)

LL Bean Uses Management Sciences Techniques to Improve the Quality of Employee Scheduling (p. 136)

PepsiCo High-Quality Training Focuses on Making Risky Decisions (p. 174)

Harley Davidson Strives For High Quality (p. 202)

Georgetown, Kentucky, Is Chosen as a High-Quality Plant Site (p. 231)

Improving the Quality of Coordination at Nike Affects Company Success (p. 269)

High-Quality Job Design Is a Key to Productivity at Motorola (p. 287)

Aetna Life & Casualty Company Increases the Quality of Training Lectures (p. 331)

Union Carbide Disaster Brings Structural Change (p. 355)

Milliken & Co. Motivates Employees to Excel (p. 388)

Nucor Corp's Chief Motivates Employees Through Leadership (p. 431)

Recognition, Growth, and Advancement Yield High-Quality Enrichment Programs at Apple (p. 465)

Quality Training at Eastman Kodak Focuses on Managing Groups (p. 482)

William J. Mork Uses Corrective Action Teams to Improve Quality (p. 526)

Quality Effort Must Be Supplemented at Tupperware (p. 565)

Accessibility Yields High Quality Database at Mrs. Fields, Inc. (p. 606)

The Deming Prize—No Longer a Stranger at Home (p. 639)

Cadillac Implements Simultaneous Engineering (p. 654)

The Importance of Quality

Many managers and management theorists believe that organizations without high-quality products will be unable to compete in the world marketplace of today. A writer in *Business Week* supports this belief:[2]

> Quality. Remember it? American manufacturing has slumped a long way from the glory days of the 1950s and '60s when "Made in the U.S.A." proudly stood for the best that industry could turn out. . . . While the Japanese were developing remarkably higher standards for a whole host of products, from consumer electronics to cars and machine tools, many U.S. managers were smugly dozing at the switch. Now, aside from aerospace and agriculture, there are few markets left where the U.S. carries its own weight in international trade. For American industry, the message is simple: Get Better or Get Beat.

Producing high-quality products is not an end in itself. Successfully offering high-quality goods and services to the marketplace typically results in three important benefits for the organization: a positive company image, lower costs and higher market share, and decreased product liability costs.

Positive Company Image

To a significant extent, an organization's reputation for high quality results in a positive image for the organization, a point the cartoon successfully makes.

Over all, organizations gain many advantages from having a positive company image. A positive image, for example, can be instrumental in recruiting valuable new employees, accelerating sales of a product newly offered to the marketplace, and obtaining needed loans from financial institutions. To summarize, high-quality products generally result in a positive company image, which in turn results in numerous organizational benefits.

Lower Costs and Higher Market Share

Activities that support product quality benefit the organization by yielding lower costs and greater market share. Figure 21.1 on page 658 illustrates this point. According to the top half of this figure, greater market share or gain in product sales is a direct result of customer perception of improved product quality. According to the bottom half of the figure, activities within an organization that contribute to product quality result in such benefits as increased productivity, lower rework and scrap costs, and lower warranty costs, which in turn result in lower manufacturing costs and lower costs of servicing products after they are sold. The figure also makes the important point that both greater market share and lower costs attributed to high quality normally result in greater organizational profits.

Decreased Product Liability Costs

Product manufacturers are increasingly facing legal suits over damages caused by faulty products. Organizations that design and produce faulty products are being held liable in the courts for damages resulting from the use of such products. As

Well, as a last ditch measure, we could improve corporate image by improving the product."

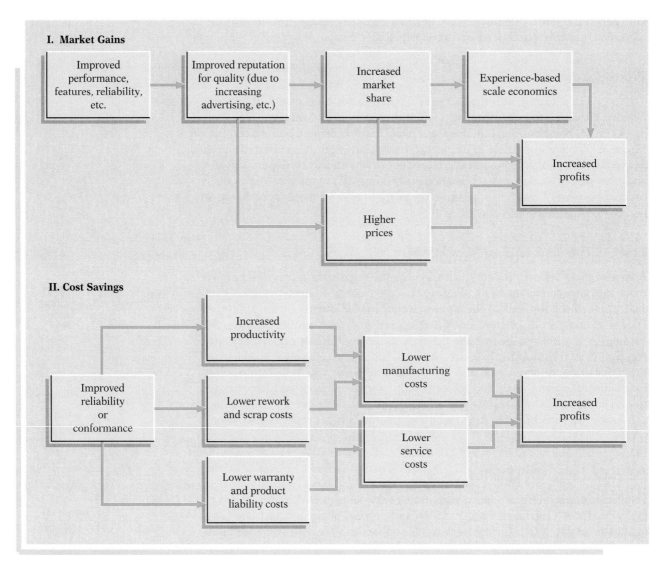

FIGURE 21.1

CWQ typically results in lower costs and greater market share

a dramatic example, Pfizer, a company that develops mechanical heart valves, has recently settled an estimated 180 lawsuits by heart-implant patients claiming that valves used in their implants were faulty.[3] Successful CWQ efforts typically result in improved products and product performance. Naturally, the normal result of improved products and product performance is lower product liability costs.

Recognizing the importance of all of these benefits of quality, in recent years there has been an increased emphasis throughout our society on achieving high-quality products. Evidencing this trend, in 1988 the United States presented its first national awards for quality achievement within organizations. Known as the **Malcolm Baldrige National Quality Awards,** Motorola, Globe Metallurgical, and Westinghouse Electric's Commercial Nuclear Fuel Division won the award in 1988; in 1989, Milliken and Xerox won the award; and the 1990 winners were the

Malcolm Baldrige National Quality Awards are the national awards given in the U.S. to companies doing exemplary work in the area of quality.

Cadillac Motor Car Division of General Motors Corporation, IBM of Rochester, Federal Express Corporation, and the Wallace Company, a small chemical company.

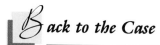

Back to the Case

Based upon the information that we have, product quality at Disney World can be defined in terms of the extent to which customer needs are satisfied through the entertainment experience provided at the theme park. Companywide quality at Disney is a result of the process of involving all workers from all organizational levels in providing a high-quality experience to customers.

Clearly, many different kinds of workers at Disney World have a significant role in determining the quality of the entertainment that park visitors receive. Although the technological marvel of ride attractions within the park is an obvious dimension of the quality of experience provided customers, company research shows that employee friendliness to customers as well as park cleanliness are more important determinants of quality in the customers' minds. This information indicates that engineers who design and install rides, ticket booth workers who sell admissions tickets, and attendants who dispose of trash all play a critical role in establishing the level of product quality that Disney World offers its customers.

In the international marketplace of today, it is extremely important even for a company as successful as Disney to maintain a reputation of high product quality. Such a reputation typically results in a positive image for the company as a whole and can make it easier for management to recruit competent employees, to lower costs and gain the higher market share that can enhance company profits, and to decrease product liability costs.

Achieving Quality

Ensuring that all company operations play a productive role in maintaining product quality seems like an overwhelming task. Although the task is indeed formidable, several useful and valuable guidelines have been formulated to make the task more achievable. Advice from three internationally acclaimed experts—Philip B. Crosby, W. Edwards Deming, and Joseph M. Juran—on how to achieve product quality is summarized in the sections that follow.[4]

Crosby's Advice on Achieving Quality

Philip B. Crosby is generally known throughout the world as an expert in the area of quality and is accepted as a pioneer of the quality movement in the United States.[5] Crosby's work provides managers with valuable insights regarding how to achieve product quality: According to Crosby an organization must be "injected" with certain ingredients relating to integrity, systems, communications, operations, and policies. By adding these ingredients to an organization, the organization should be able to achieve significant progress in achieving product quality. Crosby calls these ingredients the "vaccination serum" that prevents the disease of low companywide quality. The ingredients of the Crosby Vaccination Serum are presented in Table 21.3 on page 660.

Integrity

A. The chief executive officer is dedicated to having the customer receive what was promised, believes that the company will prosper only when all employees feel the same way, and is determined that neither customers nor employees will be hassled.

B. The chief operating officer believes that management performance is a complete function requiring that quality be "first among equals"—schedule and cost.

C. The senior executives, who report to those in A and B, take requirements so seriously that they can't stand deviations.

D. The managers, who work for the senior executives, know that the future rests with their ability to get things done through people—right the first time.

E. The professional employees know that the accuracy and completeness of their work determines the effectiveness of the entire work force.

F. The employees as a whole recognize that their individual commitment to the integrity of requirements is what makes the company sound.

Systems

A. The quality management function is dedicated to measuring conformance to requirements and reporting any differences accurately.

B. The quality education system (QES) ensures that all employees of the company have a common language of quality and understand their personal roles in causing quality to be routine.

C. The financial method of measuring nonconformance and conformance costs is used to evaluate processes.

D. The use of the company's services or products by customers is measured and reported in a manner that causes corrective action to occur.

E. The companywide emphasis on defect prevention serves as a base for continual review and planning that utilizes current and past experience to keep the past from repeating itself.

Communications

A. Information about the progress of quality improvement and achievement actions is continually supplied to all employees.

B. Recognition programs applicable to all levels of responsibility are a part of normal operations.

C. Each person in the company can, with very little effort, identify error, waste, opportunity, or any concern to top management quickly—and receive an immediate answer.

D. Each management status meeting begins with a factual and financial review of quality.

Operations

A. Suppliers are educated and supported in order to ensure that they will deliver services and products that are dependable and on time.

B. Procedures, products, and systems are qualified and proven prior to implementation and then continually examined and officially modified when the opportunity for improvement is seen.

C. Training is a routine activity for all tasks and is particularly integrated into new processes and procedures.

Policies

A. The policies on quality are clear and unambiguous.

B. The quality function reports on the same level as those functions that are being measured and has complete freedom of activity.

C. Advertising and all external communications must be completely in compliance with the requirements that the products and services must meet.

Deming's Advice on Achieving Quality

W. Edwards Deming was originally trained as a statistician and began teaching statistical quality control in Japan shortly after World War II. He is recognized internationally as a primary contributor to Japanese quality-improvement programs. Deming advocates that the way to achieve product quality is to continuously improve the design of a product and the process used to manufacture it. According to Deming, top management has the primary responsibility for achieving product quality. Deming advises that management follow fourteen points to achieve a high level of success in improving and maintaining product quality:[6]

Dr. Deming's 14 Points

1. Create and publish to all employees a statement of the aims and purposes of the company or other organization. The management must demonstrate constantly their commitment to this statement.

2. Learn the new philosophy, top management and everybody.

3. Understand the purpose of inspection, for improvement of processes and reduction of cost.

4. End the practice of awarding business on the basis of price tag alone.

5. Improve constantly and forever the system of production and service.

6. Institute training.

7. Teach and institute leadership.

8. Drive out fear. Create trust. Create a climate for innovation.

9. Optimize toward the aims and purposes of the company the efforts of teams, groups, staff areas.

10. Eliminate exhortations for the work force.

11. a. Eliminate numerical quotas for production. Instead, learn and institute methods for improvement.

    b. Eliminate MBO. Instead, learn the capabilities of processes, and how to improve them.

12. Remove barriers that rob people of pride of workmanship.

13. Encourage education and self-improvement for everyone.

14. Take action to accomplish the transformation.

Ethics Highlight: American Marketing Association Promotes "Zero Defects" Ethics

Deming advises that management should strive for zero defects within its production process. That is, as they produce their products companies should emphasize that no mistakes can be tolerated. Although the concept of zero defects is normally thought of as applying to manufacturing situations, the American Marketing Association (AMA) is an example of an organization that encourages the application of this concept to the area of ethics.

The AMA is a professional organization established and maintained to meet the needs of professional marketing managers. The AMA recently adopted a new code of ethics that describes the responsibilities of such managers and the rights and duties of individuals involved in the marketing process. As with any code of ethics, the AMA Code will have impact only if managers understand it, become committed to it, and comply with it. If the AMA had its way, a company or person is reputable only if it has high standards for quality products and services and has demonstrated constant emphasis on maintaining high ethical practices.

The AMA's philosophy about ethics indicates that an emphasis on high-quality ethics should be a component of every quality program. Naturally, maintaining high ethical practices within an organization is not an easy task to accomplish. One philosophy that can help managers to accomplish this task, however, is to adopt a zero-defects philosophy about ethical practices. That is, managers will strive to eliminate every ethical practices mistake in their organizations.

Juran's Advice on Achieving Quality

Joseph M. Juran taught quality concepts to the Japanese and has been a significant force in the quality focus throughout the world. Juran's philosophy emphasizes that management should pursue the mission of quality improvement and maintenance on two levels: (1) the mission of the firm as a whole to achieve and maintain high quality; and (2) the mission of individual departments within the firm to achieve and maintain high quality.

According to Juran, quality improvement and maintenance is a clear process. Managers must be involved with studying symptoms of quality problems, pinpointing the quality problems implied by the symptoms, and applying solutions to these problems. For maximum effect of a quality effort, strategic planning for quality should be similar to an organization's strategic planning for any other organizational issue like finance, marketing, or human resources; that is, strategic planning for quality should include setting short-term and long-term quality goals, comparing quality results with quality plans, and integrating quality plans with other corporate strategic areas. More discussion on the relationship between quality and strategic planning follows.

 ack to the Case

Information in the chapter gives insights on how an organization like Disney World can achieve high product quality. Based upon the ideas of Philip Crosby, Disney management can achieve its high product quality through a focus such as complete dedication to quality, having quality-oriented systems, constantly discussing and monitoring quality in its communications, making sound quality-oriented operations decisions regarding issues such as which suppliers to use, and setting clear policies emphasizing guidelines for achieving a high-quality product.

Based upon the ideas of Deming, Disney World can achieve its quality product by constantly improving the design of the entertainment experience and the process used to actually provide the experience to its customers. Taking such actions as constantly focusing on the purpose of improving product quality, promoting cooperation to facilitate the development of product quality, and emphasizing teamwork as a means to product quality are all management activities that must be instrumental in achieving high product quality in the theme park.

Based on the ideas of Juran, Disney World can achieve its high-quality product by emphasizing that maintaining product quality is the challenge of the entire organization as well as of individual departments. In addition, Disney World can maintain product quality because all organization members constantly search for symptoms that are signals of quality problems and then take action to solve whatever quality problems those symptoms suggest.

It would be difficult to conclude that the thoughts of any one of these three theorists completely outlines how an organization like Disney World can achieve product quality. Instead, managers should collectively use all of their ideas in formulating a best way to establish product quality within a particular organization.

QUALITY THROUGH STRATEGIC PLANNING

Managers in most organizations spend significant amounts of time and effort on strategic planning. If designed properly, strategic planning can play an important role in establishing and maintaining product quality.[7] As you recall, strategic planning has been defined as long-range planning that focuses on the organization as a whole. The following sections focus on the steps of the strategic management process and discuss how each step can be used to encourage product quality.

Environmental Analysis and Quality

The initial step of the strategic management process is environmental analysis. *Environmental analysis* is defined in chapter 7 as the study of organizational environment to pinpoint factors that can significantly influence organizational operations. In establishing the role of environmental analysis to enhance product quality, special attention can be given to studying quality-related environmental factors. Consumer expectations about product quality, the quality of products offered by competitors, and special technology being developed to enhance the quality of organizational activities are all examples of such factors.

Suppliers are often given special attention during environmental analysis by managers who stress quality. Suppliers are those companies that sell materials to be used in the final assembly of a product by another company. As an example, General Motors has many suppliers who furnish the company with parts that are then used in the final assembly of GM automobiles. Basically, the satisfactory performance of a final product will be only as good as the quality of parts obtained from company suppliers. Defective parts from suppliers can result in delayed delivery schedules, reduced sales, and reduced productivity. Special study of suppliers during environmental analysis can alert management to suppliers who can help to improve product quality through the quality of the parts that they furnish.

Establishing Organizational Direction and Quality

In this step of the strategic management process the results of environmental analysis are used as the basis for determining the path that the organization will take in the future. This path is then documented and distributed throughout the organization in the form of a mission statement and related objectives. Assuming that environmental analysis results indicate that product quality is important for an organization, a manager can use an organizational mission statement and its related objectives to give general direction to organization members regarding the organization's focus on product quality. The following is an example of a mission statement used to encourage companywide quality by Charles Steinmetz, president of All America Inc., the largest privately owned pest control company in the United States:[8]

> All America Termite & Pest Control, Inc., operating as Sears Authorized Termite & Pest Control, was founded to provide the residential market a once-a-year pest control service as well as premium termite protection.
>
> The purpose of our company is to provide our customers the highest quality of customer service available in our industry while providing unlimited personal and financial potential to our employees.
>
> We will commit the time, energy, expertise, and resources needed to provide premier customer service. Furthermore, we realize there are no other choices, options, or alternatives in our pursuit of quality.
>
> This requires us to give each customer full value for his or her money and to provide that value the first time and every time we have an opportunity to be of service.
>
> We will resolve any customer problems quickly, whether real and apparent or hidden or imaginary. If for any reason we cannot satisfy any customer, we will stand behind our satisfaction or money-back guarantee.
>
> Our commitment to our employees is no less important. We will provide all employees with the training necessary for them to become proficient at their job as well as proper equipment, safe materials, and a safe working environment.
>
> We will provide ample personal and family benefits to provide reasonable security and offer unlimited compensation, significant opportunity for advancement, and an environment that limits success only by the limits of each employee's hard work, dedication, and capabilities.

In studying how different companies establish the direction of a product quality focus, it becomes apparent that different companies define product quality in different ways. For example, at some companies product quality is defined as a stronger product that will last longer, or as a heavier, more durable product. At other companies, product quality can be the degree to which a product conforms to design specifications, or product excellence at an acceptable price and at an acceptable cost. In still other companies, quality is defined as the degree to which a product meets consumer tastes. Whatever management decides that its definition of product quality might be, this definition must be communicated to all organization members in order that they might work together in a focused and efficient way to achieve predetermined product quality.

Strategy Formulation and Quality

After determining organizational direction, the next step of the strategic management process is strategy formulation, deciding what steps should be taken to best deal with competitors. Incorporating the issue of product quality as part of the focus of a SWOT analysis (Strengths, Weaknesses, Opportunities, Threats) can help managers develop quality-based strategies. As an example, it may be pointed out as a result of a SWOT analysis that organization members are not adequately trained to deal with certain product quality issues. Naturally, a strategy based on this organizational weakness would be to improve quality-oriented training.[9] Answering questions like the following can help managers to determine the specifics of a quality-related SWOT analysis:

Is the quality responsibility throughout the company relegated to a quality control department, or do all functions in the company have responsibility for maintaining CWQ?

How much emphasis is placed on satisfying the customers?

Is CWQ an important element in a company's strategic plan?

Does the company recognize that productivity can be improved by improving CWQ?

Is the quality of suppliers considered to be a factor in improving CWQ?

Strategy Implementation and Quality

When the results of environmental analysis indicate that product quality is important for an organization, that product quality direction has been established through its mission statement and related objectives, and that strategy has been developed for achieving or maintaining product quality, management is ready to implement its product quality strategy. Implementation merely requires putting product quality strategy into action.

Although implementing product quality strategy seems like a straightforward step, in reality it is quite complex. In order for managers to be successful at implementing product quality strategy, they must meet challenges like being sensitive to the fears and frustrations of employees in implementing new strategy, providing organizational resources needed to implement the strategy, monitoring implementation progress, and creating and using a network of individuals throughout the organization who can be helpful in overcoming implementation barriers.

Two tools managers commonly use to implement product quality strategy are policies and organizational structure. Each of these tools is discussed further in the following sections.

Policies for Quality.   A policy is defined in chapter 8 as a standing plan that furnishes broad, general guidelines for channeling management thinking toward taking action consistent with reaching *organizational* objectives. A quality-oriented policy is a special type of policy. A **quality-oriented policy** is a standing plan that furnishes broad, general guidelines for channeling management thinking toward taking action consistent with reaching *quality* objectives. Quality-oriented policies can be made in virtually any organizational area and can focus on issues like the quality of new employees recruited, the quality of plans developed within the organization, the quality of decision-related information gathered and distributed

A **quality-oriented policy** is a standing plan that furnishes broad, general guidelines for channeling management thinking toward taking action consistent with reaching quality objectives.

Quality-oriented structures are the designated relationships among organizational resources that emphasize the achievement of quality objectives.

within the organization, the quality of parts from suppliers to be used in the final assembly of products, and the quality of training used to prepare employees to work in foreign subsidiaries.

Structure for Quality. Structure is defined in chapter 9 as designated relationships among resources of the management system. A **quality-oriented structure** is designated relationships among organizational resources that emphasize the achievement of quality objectives.

One means of illustrating relationships among organizational resources as they are intended to help management accomplish product-quality objectives is an organization chart, a graphic illustration of structure. Figure 21.2 illustrates how an organization chart can be designed to involve a focus on product quality throughout an organization. This particular chart indicates a CWQ Committee above the president that reports to the company board of directors. In addition, a Presidential Quality Committee reports to the president, and a CWQ vice president maintains a constant quality focus throughout lower levels of the organization. The chart clearly makes the point that an emphasis on maintaining product quality requires resources and focus throughout all levels of the organization.

Strategic Control and Quality

Strategic control emphasizes monitoring the strategic management process to make sure that it is operating properly. In terms of product quality, strategic control would focus on monitoring company activities to ensure that product quality strategies are operating as planned. In achieving strategic control in the

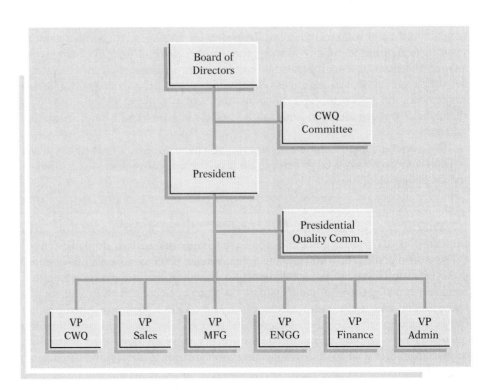

FIGURE 21.2

A partial organization chart emphasizing companywide quality area of product quality, management must measure how successful it has become in achieving product quality.

Insights offered by Philip Crosby state that in order to control efforts in achieving product quality, several organizational areas should be monitored. These areas include management's understanding and attitude toward quality, how quality appears within an organization, how organizational problems are handled, the cost of quality as a percentage of sales, quality improvement actions taken by management, and how management summarizes the organization's quality position.

According to Crosby, organizations go through five successive stages of quality maturity as they approach the maximum level of quality in all phases of organizational activity. Each of the stages represents variations of the above monitoring areas. Figure 21.3 on page 668 depicts Crosby's five stages of quality and the different variations of monitoring areas represented with each stage. Figure 21.3 is actually a rating instrument called the Quality Management Maturity Grid. Strategic control concerning quality would focus on ensuring that an organization evolves to Stage V of the Quality Management Maturity Grid.

Global Highlight: Ford of Canada Reaps Rewards of Quality

Ford of Canada is an example of a company that has emphasized quality within its strategic management process. In analyzing factors in the organizational environment like competitive products and competitors, Ford management determined that the company should adopt a strategy of increasing its level of product quality. The company's newly developed emphasis on quality was described and circulated throughout the company in a formal document called "Mission, Values, and Guiding Principles." In essence, this document was a mission statement that aimed and encouraged the efforts of all managers in the direction of improving product quality. In implementing its strategy to increase product quality, Ford initiated a broad range of programs worldwide that were designed to build a higher quality of trucks and automobiles. The slogan "Quality is Job #1 at Ford" captures in a nutshell the campaign that began the company-wide quality program at Ford. The company has tightened quality control in its plants and spent much money training employees to spot and react to quality problems during the manufacturing process. Perhaps the most important element of Ford's global quality effort is that it involves employees in designing and implementing the quality program. Largely as a result of its efforts, in 1988 Ford recorded its third consecutive year of worldwide profits. Also largely as a result of its quality efforts, since 1980, Ford's breakeven point has been reduced by 40 percent in North America and 25 percent worldwide.

Back to the Case

According to the preceding information, strategic planning is a tool that managers in an organization like Disney World can use to achieve product quality. Strategic planning employs strategies and tactics to help management focus on what must be done to maintain product quality in both the long run and the short run.

QUALITY MANAGEMENT MATURITY GRID

Rater _____ Unit _____

Measurement Categories	Stage I: Uncertainty	Stage II: Awakening	Stage III: Enlightenment	Stage IV: Wisdom	Stage V: Certainty
Management understanding and attitude	No comprehension of quality as a management tool. Tend to blame quality department for "quality problems."	Recognizing that quality management may be of value but not willing to provide money or time to make it all happen.	While going through quality improvement program learn more about quality management; becoming supportive and helpful.	Participating. Understand absolutes of quality management. Recognize their personal role in continuing emphasis.	Consider quality management an essential part of company system.
Quality organization status	Quality is hidden in manufacturing or engineering departments. Inspection probably not part of organization. Emphasis on appraisal and sorting.	A stronger quality leader is appointed but main emphasis is still on appraisal and moving the product. Still part of manufacturing or other.	Quality department reports to top management, all appraisal is incorporated, and manager has role in management of company.	Quality manager is an officer of company; effective status reporting and preventive action. Involved with consumer affairs and special assignments.	Quality manager on board of directors. Prevention is main concern. Quality is a thought leader.
Problem handling	Problems are fought as they occur; no resolution; inadequate definition; lots of yelling and accusations.	Teams are set up to attack major problems. Long-range solutions are not solicited.	Corrective action communication established. Problems are faced openly and resolved in an orderly way.	Problems are identified early in their development. All functions are open to suggestion and improvement.	Except in the most unusual cases, problems are prevented.
Cost of quality as % of sales	Reported: unknown Actual: 20%	Reported: 3% Actual: 18%	Reported: 8% Actual: 12%	Reported: 6.5% Actual: 8%	Reported: 2.5% Actual: 2.5%
Quality improvement actions	No organized activities. No understanding of such activities.	Trying obvious "motivational" short-range efforts.	Implementation of the 14-step program with thorough understanding and establishment of each step.	Continuing the 14-step program and starting Make Certain.	Quality improvement is a normal and continued activity.
Summation of company quality posture	"We don't know why we have problems with quality."	"Is it absolutely necessary to always have problems with quality?"	"Through management commitment and quality improvement we are identifying and resolving our problems."	"Defect prevention is a routine part of our operation."	"We know why we do not have problems with quality."

FIGURE 21.3 The Quality Management Maturity Grid

Management of an organization like Disney World can use strategic planning to further product quality by emphasizing quality throughout the strategic management process. During environmental analysis, for example, management can strive to discover information like the level of quality park visitors expect and technological improvements that might be employed to make the quality of ride experiences even greater. Given such information, management of an organization like Disney World can decide the direction that product quality should pursue and then use a mission statement and related goals to communicate this direction to all other organization members. Normally, related product quality strategy should then be developed, implemented, and controlled to make sure that it is working.

MANAGEMENT SKILLS FOR ACHIEVING QUALITY

To manage successfully, managers should apply both knowledge of systems theory and the four basic management functions to management situations that they face. Three management skills related to the application of this knowledge are systems skill, functional skill, and situational analysis skill. The following sections discuss each of these skills with special focus on their relationships to achieving product quality.

Systems Skill and Quality

Systems skill is the ability to view and manage a business or some other concern as a number of components that work together and function as a whole to achieve some objective. In essence, the systems approach to management is a way of analyzing and solving managerial problems.[10] Managers analyze problems and implement solutions only after examining the system parts related to the problems and evaluating the effect of each solution on the functioning of all the parts.[11]

Systems skill is extremely important in achieving product quality. Only after managers understand the "big picture" or how all parts of the organization work together to produce goods or services can managers adequately focus on improving product quality. In essence, managers must understand completely the effect that making a change to the production process will have on other company issues like jobs, new suppliers that may be needed as a result of a production change, or scheduling changes that may necessarily follow as a result of a production change. Without such understanding, it is quite possible that a change in the production process intended to increase product quality actually would cause significant quality problems in other areas and thereby actually reduce product quality.

> **Systems skill** is the ability to view and manage a business or some other concern as a number of components that work together and function as a whole to achieve some objective.

Functional Skill and Quality

Functional skill is the ability to apply appropriately the concepts of planning, organizing, influencing, and controlling to the operation of a management system. The application of these four basic functions is of such vital concern to management that this study presents them as subsystems of the overall management system (Figure 21.4, p. 670).

Generally, product quality can be improved through improvements in organizational planning, organizing, influencing, and controlling. Relevant improvements in these functional areas might include better scheduling of workers to allow workers to perform jobs they do best, better designing of organization structure

> **Functional skill** is the ability to apply appropriately the concepts of planning, organizing, influencing, and controlling to the operation of a management system.

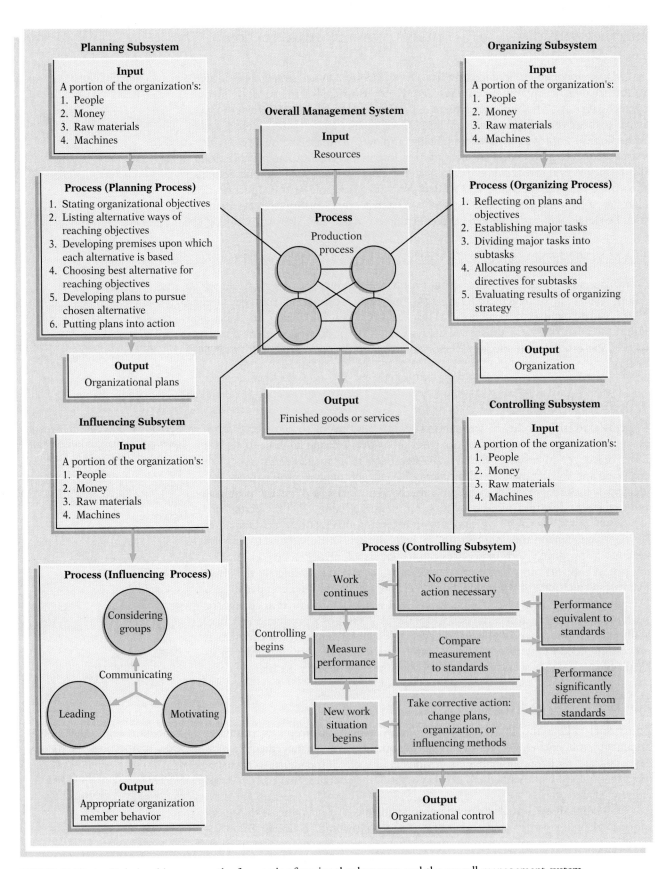

FIGURE 21.4 Relationships among the four major functional subsystems and the overall management system

to focus resources on quality issues, better designing of incentive programs to reward organization members for improving product quality, and improved information systems to furnish managers better data relevant to controlling product quality.

Special Quality Situations

Situational analysis skill is the ability to apply both systems theory and functional theory to the particular situations managers face. This skill emphasizes that managers must thoroughly understand their own unique management situations before they can use systems and functional skills to their best advantage. Obviously, the importance of situational analysis skill is supported by the thoughts and ideas of the contingency approach to management.

Situational analysis skill regarding product quality is the ability to apply both systems theory and functional theory to product quality situations that managers face. In the case of product quality, managers must thoroughly understand their own unique quality situation before they can use systems and functional skills to their best advantage. A few important situational variables that many managers now face or may face in the future in striving for product quality are (1) an aging work force, (2) a shrinking work force, (3) the quality of work life, (4) women in management, and (5) work force diversity. The relationship of product quality to each of these variables is discussed in the following sections.

Situational analysis skill is the ability to apply both systems theory and functional theory to the particular situations managers face.

An Aging Work Force.   Over all, the work force of today is getting older. As shown in Figure 21.5 on page 672, the increase in the average age of the work force is projected to occur mainly as a result of a significant increase in the number of workers twenty-five to fifty-four years old.

An aging work force has many implications for maintaining product quality. Such issues as organizations having to become more competitive in hiring talented older employees, because the supply of younger employees is shrinking, and managers having to become more sensitive to the needs and concerns of older workers are certainly important in maintaining product quality. Trying to maintain product quality with an aging work force will probably increase the importance of wellness programs.[12] **Wellness programs** are special activities within an organization designed to keep organization members in good health. It is a fact that as workers become older they become absent from jobs more often due to sickness and chronic illnesses. Wellness programs can include health assessment of employees, strategies to stop smoking, exercise programs, suggestions on handling stress, and general health education. Wellness programs can help management minimize absenteeism due to illness of an older work force and thereby help to maintain continuity of product quality efforts.

Wellness programs are special activities within an organization designed to keep organization members in good health.

A Shrinking Work Force.   The work force of tomorrow will undoubtedly be smaller than the work force of today. As Figure 21.6 on page 673 demonstrates, labor force growth has been slowing down for several years. A decreasing national population rate is generally cited as the basis for the predicted smaller work force of the future. In fact, the population and the work force are growing more slowly than at any time since the 1930s.[13]

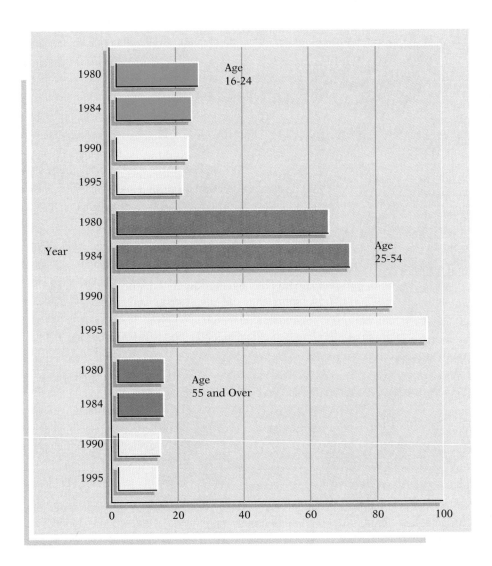

FIGURE 21.5

Comparison of the number of workers in three age groups from 1980 projected through the mid-1990s

A shrinking work force certainly has implications for maintaining product quality. Management needs appropriate workers to maintain product quality, and a shrinking work force makes it more difficult for management to get those workers. To increase the probability that needed workers are obtained, management should expend more effort on human resource planning. Such effort would help management to compete better with other firms in recruiting needed employees. Increased effort in determining the kinds of organization members that will be needed, when they will be needed, and where they will come from will all help to ensure product quality in periods of short labor supply.

Quality of work life is the degree of opportunity of workers to make decisions that influence their work situation.

Quality of Work Life. The modern work force shows more interest in quality of work life than any other work force in our history. **Quality of work life** is the degree of opportunity of workers to make decisions that influence their work

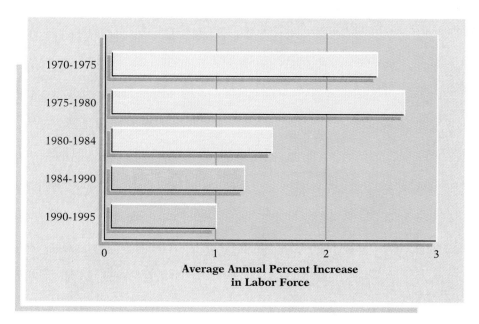

FIGURE 21.6

Labor force growth rate projected through the mid-1990s

situation. The greater the opportunity of workers to make such decisions, the higher the quality of work life is said to be. Workers would like to make decisions that tend to create the following:[14]

1. Jobs that are interesting, challenging, and responsible.

2. Worker rewards through fair wages and recognition for worker contributions.

3. Workplaces that are clean, safe, quiet, and bright.

4. Minimal but available supervision.

5. Secure jobs that promote the development of friendly relationships with other system members.

6. Organizations that provide for personal welfare and medical attention.

A high quality of work life is normally a prerequisite for achieving and maintaining high product quality. Without a high-quality work life, management is simply making it more difficult to get workers excited about product quality. When management fails to focus on developing a high-quality work life, workers are likely to view management's product quality focus as mostly aimed at squeezing more out of workers without really caring about them.

Women in Management. As Figure 21.7 on page 674 shows, women are expected to account for over three-fifths of the labor force growth from 1990 to 1995. Moreover, women's participation in maintaining quality within organiza-

674   PART SIX   TOPICS FOR SPECIAL EMPHASIS

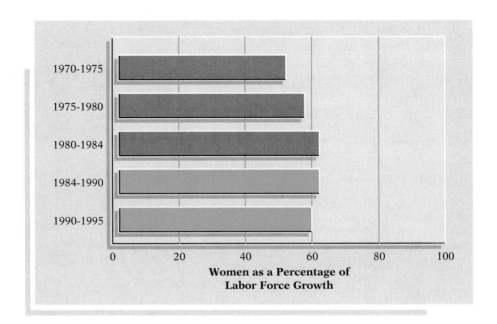

FIGURE 21.7

Women as a major factor in
labor force growth through
the mid-1990s

tions will continue to grow. By the year 2000, 47 percent of the work force will
be women, and 61 percent of women within our society will be employed.[15]

It is noteworthy that the effect of the rising numbers of women in the labor
force has been felt in management ranks. Over the past two decades, the "face" of
management has changed dramatically. Now that "face" is female more than one-
third of the time.[16] Although many women would agree that women have made
noticeable progress in accelerating their management careers in the past few years,
most also believe that a long way remains to go before their status will equal that
of their male counterparts. Some of their most serious concerns are equal pay for
equal work, maternity leave, and job discrimination.[17]

Work-Force Diversity. The labor force of the future in the United States
will change drastically over the next several years. As an indicator of this changing
work force, the percentage of whites in the total U.S. population is expected to
fall below 50 percent.[18]

Perhaps the most significant characteristic of this changing labor force will be
its diversity. The share of white males of the total labor force will shrink from 51
percent in 1980 to 45 percent in the year 2000. As Figure 21.8 indicates, by the
year 2000, women as well as other minorities will become a greater percentage of
the work force. These other minorities include groups like African-Americans,
Hispanic-Americans, Native Americans, and Asian-Americans. Perhaps the diversity of this labor force is typified in the following excerpt, which claims to reflect
the work force of the future:[19]

> Harold Epps, who runs the Digital Equipment Corporation plant that makes
> computer keyboards, manages the work force of the future. The Boston factory's
> 350 employees come from 44 countries and speak 19 languages. When the plant
> issues written announcements, they are printed in English, Chinese, French, Span-
> ish, Portuguese, Vietnamese, and Haitian Creole.

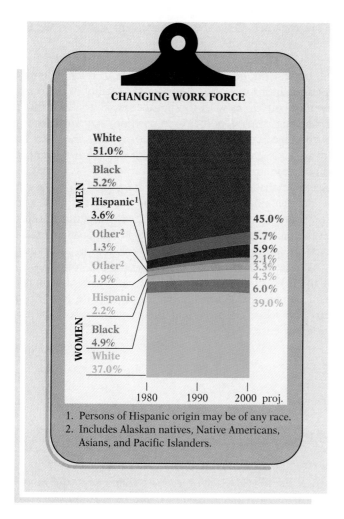

CHANGING WORK FORCE

MEN		WOMEN	
White 51.0%	→ 45.0%		
Black 5.2%	→ 5.7%		
Hispanic[1] 3.6%	→ 5.9%		
Other[2] 1.3%	→ 2.1%		
Other[2] 1.9%	→ 3.3%		
Hispanic 2.2%	→ 4.3%		
Black 4.9%	→ 6.0%		
White 37.0%	→ 39.0%		

1980   1990   2000 proj.

1. Persons of Hispanic origin may be of any race.
2. Includes Alaskan natives, Native Americans, Asians, and Pacific Islanders.

FIGURE 21.8

Women and other minorities will continue to grow as a percentage of the total work force through the year 2000

Diversity in the workplace has important implications for maintaining high product quality. One of the most challenging management tasks regarding worker diversity is to build people from many different cultures into a productive work team that focuses on product quality.[20] To build such a work team, managers must stimulate within each organization member an awareness of and appreciation for the culture and heritage of every other organization member. Cross-cultural training programs can be specially designed and implemented to build this awareness and appreciation within organizations.[21]

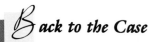 *ack to the Case*

The kinds of skills that management of an organization like Disney World must have in order to achieve product quality include systems skill—the ability to see how different components of the theme park like the Magic Kingdom, EPCOT, and the MGM Studios work together. Only after management is able to see the big picture can it adequately address product-quality issues.

Management such as that of Disney World must also have functional skill—the ability to use planning, organizing, influencing, and control to reach a desired level of product quality. Setting appropriate standards for the quality of customer relations (planning), providing employees with training necessary to reach those standards (organizing), rewarding employees for reaching those standards (influencing), and monitoring employee customer relations to see how they can be improved (controlling) are all ways that Disney management can use management functional skill to focus on attaining product quality.

To achieve product quality, management of an organization like Disney World must also have situational analysis skill—the ability to apply both systems skill and functional skill to specific quality issues. Such quality-related issues that Disney World management might face include how to best manage professional engineers to ensure that they are given an appropriate amount of job freedom in addressing product quality, the use of a wellness program in furthering the contribution of older park employees to product quality, and the development of women, African-Americans, Hispanic-Americans, Asian-Americans, and other minorities into cohesive work groups that focus on providing theme park visitors with a high-quality entertainment experience.

Action Summary

Circle:

Reread the learning objectives that follow. Each objective is followed by questions. Answering these questions accurately will help you to retain most important concepts discussed in this chapter. After answering each question, check your answer with the answer key at the end of the chapter. (*Hint:* If you have doubt regarding the correct response, consult the page whose number follows the answer.)

From studying this chapter, I will attempt to acquire:

1. **An understanding of the relationship between quality and companywide quality (CWQ).**

T, F
    a. Over all, product quality and companywide quality are the same.

a, b, c, d, e
    b. A CWQ program is *not* characterized by: (a) a continual process, (b) efforts by all organization members, (c) a focus on only a few critical work activities; (d) a focus on the production process, (e) efforts to involve organization members.

2. **An appreciation of the importance of quality.**

T, F
    a. High product quality can result in reduced costs but generally not increased market share.

T, F
    b. Increasing product quality can reduce product liability costs for an organization.

3. **Insight about how to achieve quality.**

   a. According to Crosby, in order to achieve quality, an organization must contain critical ingredients relating to: (a) integrity, (b) systems, (c) communications, (d) operations, (e) all of the above.   a, b, c, d, e

   b. According to Deming, a company can improve its product quality by choosing suppliers based on quality and not on price alone.   T, F

   c. According to Juran, a company can improve its product quality by focusing on the quality of the organization as a whole as well as the quality of individual departments.   T, F

4. **An understanding of how strategic planning can be used to promote quality.**

   a. Establishing an appropriate mission statement is important in achieving quality.   T, F

   b. Establishing and using appropriate policies and organization structure are important steps in quality-oriented strategy formulation.   T, F

5. **Knowledge about management skills that relate to achieving quality.**

   a. In general, systems skill is slightly more important in achieving product quality than is functional skill.   T, F

   b. Situational analysis skill is the ability to apply both systems theory and functional theory to particular situations managers face.   T, F

6. **Insights about special situations that could affect the achievement of quality.**

   a. In the future, planning for product quality should probably consider issues such as more women rising to the status of management and the increasing diversity of the work force.   T, F

   b. Wellness programs as a factor in improving product quality are most closely related to: (a) changing professional workers, (b) an aging work force, (c) a shrinking work force, (d) women in management, (e) the diversity of the work force.   a, b, c, d, e

Introductory Case Wrap-Up

"Disney World: Attention to Quality" (p. 652) and its related back-to-the-case sections were written to help you better understand the management concepts contained in this chapter. Answer the following discussion questions about the introductory case to further enrich your understanding of chapter content:

1. Can a successful CWQ program at Disney decrease the company's product liability costs? If not, why not? If so, how?

2. How does Crosby's advice relate to ensuring high-quality company activities at Disney in the future?

3. What steps can Disney take to ensure that work-force diversity will not significantly lower the quality of company operations?

Issues for Review and Discussion

1. What is the difference between product quality and companywide quality (CWQ)?

2. Is a successful CWQ program important to an organization? Explain.

3. Discuss three benefits that are the result of achieving high product quality.

4. What advice does Crosby give on achieving quality?

5. What advice does Deming give on achieving quality?

6. What advice does Juran give on achieving quality?

7. Discuss how establishment of organizational direction as a step of the strategic management process can be used to improve the success of an effort to raise product quality.

8. Can quality be a significant component of a company's strategy? Explain.

9. Discuss the significance of policies and organization structure as components of an effort to maintain product quality.

10. Based on Crosby's "five successive stages of quality maturity," how would you control CWQ efforts in an organization?

11. Discuss the importance of systems skill in achieving product quality.

12. Discuss the importance of functional skill in achieving product quality.

13. How might an aging work force influence management's efforts to raise product quality?

14. Discuss the importance in the year 2000 of wellness programs in maintaining product quality.

15. How does quality of work life relate to maintaining product quality?

16. As part of your efforts to increase product quality, would you try to minimize possible problems that can result from men and women working together? Why?

17. Would you be concerned with work-force diversity in a program aimed at enhancing product quality? Why or why not? If you would be concerned, what action would you take?

Building on What You Know

Directions

Review the Quality Highlight as indicated below and answer its corresponding questions. Questions in this section focus on relating a Highlight appearing in this chapter to management concepts that you have learned in a previous chapter.

Review the Quality Highlight: Cadillac Implements Simultaneous Engineering on p. 654. In chapter 20, International Management, you studied about managing when different countries are involved. In what way(s) do Cadillac's tactics to improve product quality seem consistent with Japanese motivation strategies? In what way(s) do they seem inconsistent? In what way(s) do they seem consistent and inconsistent with Theory Z? Do you believe that Cadillac's tactics to improve quality would be successful if used by Toyota managers in Japan? Why?

Action Summary Answer Key

1. a. F, p. 653
    b. c, p. 653

2. a. F, pp. 656–657
    b. T, pp. 657–658

3. a. e, pp. 659–660
    b. T, p. 661
    c. T, p. 662

4. a. T, pp. 663–664
    b. F, pp. 665–666

5. a. F, p. 669
    b. T, p. 671

6. a. T, p. 671
    b. b, p. 671

Case Study

If It Isn't Broken at Florida Power and Light, They Fix It Anyway

by Robert E. Kemper, Northern Arizona University

Since 1983, Florida Power and Light (FPL)—which in 1989 had $4.9 billion in operating revenue—has spent millions to improve services to customers. FPL is the fourth largest investor-owned utility in the United States, servicing more than three million customers in a territory that includes four of the ten fastest-growing metropolitan areas in the country.

FPL generates, transmits, distributes, and sells electric energy, and its quest for quality improvement never ends. FPL has made impressive strides toward improving customer service. The Florida Public Service Commission received 2,100 service and billing complaints concerning FPL in 1984, 900 in 1988, 750 in 1989, and less than 500 in 1990. FPL cuts complaints at a rate of fifteen to twenty percent a year, with a target of getting complaints below one percent on an annual basis.

FPL's quality service is not just hype dreamed up by the marketing department and followed by a few workers. At the nation's fastest-growing utility—located in a state whose population has grown an explosive thirty-one percent since 1980—quality involves every one of FPL's 15,000 workers.

Marshall McDonald, FPL's former chief executive officer, became interested in quality improvement in the early 1980s, following a three-week visit to Kansai Electric Power Company, one of Japan's largest utilities. McDonald liked what he saw there, and he persuaded FPL's employees to march to the quality beat. FPL started by encouraging the formation of quality teams—worker-led groups assembled to identify and solve specific problems. Top management also continued to visit Kansai, setting up a cross-training program and garnering advice from Kansai consultants. The Japan trips and return visits made a vast overall impression that quality assurance completely pervades the Japanese way of life.

Training was one of the most crucial factors in improving service to customers. Structured quality methodology replaced the freewheeling brainstorming American style of innovation. Moving to quality service as a way of life was a complete change of philosophy, especially for FPL's middle managers. Once FPL emphasized training and showed how to use the new tools, it became very simple to do things that improved customer satisfaction.

The backbone of FPL's quality program is information and the technology used to collect and deliver it. For a company that produces electric power, quality might appear to be an intangible, but FPL works with users to select and track critical quality indicators of light and power services. FPL uses technology to measure critical success factors; employees decide what they want to achieve, establish measurable service targets, and then track how they are doing.

For example, FPL decided to improve its 30-minute delay between the time a customer calls FPL to report a problem and the issuance of a repair order. Today, the time has dropped to less than six minutes. The time an FPL customer is without electric service has dropped from an average of 100 minutes per year in the early 1980s to forty-eight minutes per year today. The number of unplanned days off-line for FPL's nuclear units dropped by fifty-seven percent in 1988 compared with 1987.

FPL service managers study important data and, based on their analyses of past problems, they can prevent future problems. For example, data indicated that lightning was the main cause of service interruptions. Investigators then discovered that transformers were inadequately grounded; this led to better grounding and fewer power interruptions.

In 1989, Florida Power and Light became the first American company to win Japan's Deming Prize for foreign companies. The prize, which has been offered to Japanese corporations since 1951, was named for U.S. statistician W. Edwards Deming. FPL treats Deming's teachings as gospel, and employees have responded to the new direction of the company. Indexes of quality, such as customer complaints, employee safety, and duration of outages, have shown that FPL has indeed become a quality-oriented company.

Discussion Questions

1. What were the key activities that FPL used to pursue quality as an organizational mission?
2. What role did the teachings of W. Edwards Deming play in FPL's improved electric service?
3. List and describe the most important companywide quality efforts by employees at FPL.
4. In your opinion, how did winning the prestigious Deming Prize affect FPL?

David Kearns of Xerox: Taking a Long, Hard Look at the Competition

The Xerox Corporation hit the ground running in 1959, with the introduction of a brand-new idea in office machinery, the copier. Xerox had invented a totally revolutionary machine, one that would change the face of business completely, and the company was flying high. Xerox updated the product as needed but made few innovations.

By the mid-1970s, though, both Japanese and American competitors had begun to cut deeply into Xerox's market. Profits dropped substantially. When David Kearns became chair of Xerox in 1982, he confronted the huge challenge of trying to regain dominance in a market now loaded with cheap competitive products.

Like many other American businesspeople, Kearns believed that the Japanese copiers were exactly that—cheap. He was surprised when his engineers took one apart to find that the quality of the Japanese-made machines was quite high. They found that the individual parts were better made, and the copier was more reliable. For every single production supplier the Japanese company used, Xerox used nine, and the Xerox machine had seven times as many manufacturing defects. Even more frightening, the copier was being sold in Japan for the same price it cost Xerox to build a copier in America!

Kearns realized that Xerox must change its operations radically just to compete with its new competitors, much less to regain market share. The key, he decided, was "changing expectations . . . you have to set a new expectation level that's so much above where you currently are, that is the hardest thing." Changing expectations at Xerox meant simplifying management by removing middle layers to build a trimmer, flatter organizational structure. This brought with it more direct and open communications companywide. More importantly, it also brought a new sense among surviving Xerox employees that excess bureaucracy was a thing of the past, and the new Xerox would be an active, positive, forward-moving place to work.

The shock of not measuring up to the competition also provided the impetus for Xerox's radical benchmarking approach to management. *Benchmarking* means comparing your product and production techniques to those of other companies that do the same things you do. To improve your warehousing techniques through benchmarking, for example, you study the techniques of another company that runs their warehousing operation very successfully. Then you imitate them.

Warehousing was among other problem areas costing Xerox profits. Kearns assigned a staff member to locate a company with a successful warehouse–distribution system; the name L. L. Bean kept cropping up. So a team of three Xerox consultants studied L. L. Bean's methods and applied them at Xerox: The net result was a three- to five-percent gain in profit.

Billing and collection also presented difficulties for Xerox. Kearns sent a team to study those operations at American Express, where collections are handled very efficiently. Xerox now applies the American Express techniques to their own operations.

Xerox has gone on to apply benchmarking to most departments, in an effort to streamline internal operations, cut costs, and raise profits. Kearns has also instituted an active program of management by objectives (MBO). It is important to him that Xerox's people have a clear understanding of corporate objectives and a real commitment to both corporate and personal objectives that will help achieve the corporate goals. MBO is a program that David Kearns sees as integral to high-quality operations because a work force that is proud of its products, proud of its operation, and committed to its leadership will not produce an inferior product.

Kearns wants Xerox to stand for three things—innovation, integrity, and quality—and of these three, quality is most important to him. When he ran the company's overseas operations during the 1970s, he came into contact with the Japanese methods of quality control. He feels he has learned a lot from their way of doing business, and in particular from their commitment to "total quality." To produce an acceptable percentage of high-quality products is no longer enough for Xerox; each machine should perform up to standard. "Because if you have to do things over," Kearns says, "the cost is extraordinarily high."

Video Case Questions

1. How does Deming's advice about achieving high quality apply to Kearns's taking apart a Japanese copier?

2. At what stage in Crosby's five stages of quality maturity do you think Xerox falls? Why?

3. What specific technique does Xerox use to follow Juran's advice at a departmental, rather than a companywide, level?

4. Why do you think it was important that Xerox noted, on dissecting its Japanese competition, that the competitors used only one supplier for every nine used by Xerox?

Video Case Activities

1. Consider the fourteen points for quality improvement suggested by Deming. Give an example for any five of these points, showing how Kearns might improve Xerox's product quality.

2. Assume you are preparing a SWOT analysis for Xerox, and concentrate on quality issues. List at least one quality-related item for each category, based on this case.

PART 6

INTEGRATIVE CASE

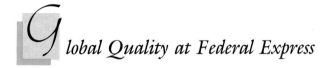

Global Quality at Federal Express

by Robert E. Kemper, Northern Arizona University

Federal Express has a global vision. It no longer recognizes outdated geographic, political, and trade barriers the world over. It intends to provide the products and services to match these new economic realities.

Federal Express is convinced that its strategy to expand globally to meet the need for time-definite international service is sound. Three significant actions during 1989–1990 moved it closer to its mission:

1. It integrated Tiger International into its network, and it introduced its first around-the-world Boeing 747 flight. The addition of this route provides scheduled service between Asia, the Middle East, and Europe and adds to the available capacity in the Asia-to-Europe and the U.S. markets.

2. It introduced three new services in the marketplace:
   a. The International Distribution Service offering the fastest, time-definite international service for freight shipments between Asia, Europe, and the U.S. and between South America and the U.S.
   b. A domestic U.S. Heavyweight Service, designed to deliver items above its traditional piece limit of 150 pounds by the second business day.
   c. The new Collect on Delivery Service that provides the fastest payment return in the industry.

3. It continued its devotion of substantial resources to refining its quality-improvement process. It now depends even more heavily on employee-based quality action teams to determine causes of problems and to offer solutions.

Since 1987, overall customer satisfaction with Federal Express's domestic service has averaged better than ninety-five percent, and its international service has rated a satisfaction score of about ninety-four percent. In an independently conducted survey of air-express industry customers, fifty-three percent gave Federal

Express a perfect score, as compared with thirty-nine percent for the next-best competitor.

Today, approximately 90,000 Federal Express employees, at more than 1,650 sites process 1.5 million shipments daily, all of which must be tracked in a central information system, sorted in a short time at facilities in Memphis, Indianapolis, Newark, Oakland, Los Angeles, Anchorage, and Brussels, and delivered by a highly decentralized distribution network. The firm's air cargo fleet is the world's largest.

Through a quality-improvement process focusing on twelve service quality indicators (SQIs), all tied to customer expectations and articulated at all levels of its international business, the Memphis-based firm continues to set higher standards for service and customer satisfaction. Measuring themselves against a 100-percent service standard, managers and employees strive to improve all aspects of the way Federal Express does business.

To spur progress toward its ultimate target of 100-percent customer satisfaction, Federal Express has set up cross-functional teams for each service component. A senior executive leads each team and assures the involvement of frontline employees, support personnel, and managers from all parts of the corporation when needed. Two of these corporatewide teams have a network of over 1,000 employees working on improvements.

The company's advanced computer, including the Super Tracker (a hand-held computer used for scanning a shipment's bar code), and tracking systems gather performance data every time a package changes hands between pick-up and delivery. Rapid analysis of data from the firm's far-flung operations yields daily SQI reports transmitted to workers at all Federal Express sites. Management meets daily to discuss the previous day's performance and tracks weekly, monthly, and annual trends. Analysis of data contained in the company's more than thirty major databases assists quality action teams (QATs) in locating the root causes of problems that surface in SQI reviews. Extensive customer and internal data are used by cross-functional teams involved in the company's new product-introduction process.

Federal Express's "People–Service–Profit" philosophy guides management policies and actions. The company has a well-developed and thoroughly deployed management evaluation system called "SFA" (survey/feedback/action), which involves a *survey* of employees, *analysis* of each work group's results by the work group's manager, and a discussion between the manager and the work group to develop written *action* plans for the manager to improve and become more effective. Data from the SFA process are aggregated at all levels of the organization for use in policy making.

Federal Express's adherence to a management philosophy emphasizes people, service, and profit, in that order, and results in high levels of customer satisfaction. Sales growth was rapid, too, with annual revenues topping $1 billion within ten years of the company's founding.

Employees are encouraged to be innovative and to make decisions that advance quality goals. Federal Express provides employees with the information and technology they need to continuously improve their performance. An example is the digitally assisted dispatch system (DADS), which communicates to some 30,000 couriers through screens in their vans. The system enables quick response to pick-up and delivery dispatches and allows couriers to manage their time and routes with high efficiency.

Training of frontline personnel is a responsibility of managers, and "recurrency training" is a widely used instrument for improvement. Teams regularly assess training needs, and a worldwide staff of training professionals devise programs to address those needs. To aid this effort, Federal Express has developed an interactive video system for employee instruction. An internal television network, accessible throughout the company, also serves as an important avenue for employee education.

More than any other year in its seventeen-year history, fiscal 1990 demonstrated Federal Express's absolute commitment to creating the most capable, extensive, and reliable express transportation company in the world.

Discussion Questions

1. Why should a successful domestic corporation such as Federal Express consider entering the global market?

2. What are the various alternatives for expanding from a domestic-oriented corporation to a global-oriented corporation? Did Federal Express make the correct decision when it implemented its global strategy?

3. As a Malcolm Baldrige National Quality Award Winner, what advantage does Federal Express have over its competition? Explain.

4. If Federal Express were faced with a decision that required it to choose between quality and global expansion, which would you recommend? Explain.

Glossary

This glossary contains important management terms and their definitions as used in this text. Since it is sometimes difficult to understand a term fully simply by reading its definition, page numbers after each definition indicate where a more complete discussion of the term can be found.

Accountability Management philosophy that individuals are held liable, or accountable, for how well they use their authority and live up to their responsibility of performing predetermined activities. (page 296)

Activities In the PERT network, specified sets of behavior within a project. (page 240)

Activity ratios In ratio analysis, ratios that indicate how well an organization is selling its products in relation to its available resources. (page 573)

Affirmative action programs In the area of equal employment opportunity, programs whose basic purpose is to eliminate barriers against and increase opportunities for underutilized or disadvantaged individuals. (page 323)

Alderfer's ERG Theory An explanation of human needs that divides them into three basic types: existence needs, relatedness needs, and growth needs. (page 456)

Appropriate human resources The individuals in the organization who make a valuable contribution to management system goal attainment. (page 315)

Argyris's maturity-immaturity continuum A concept that furnishes insights on human needs by focusing on an individual's natural growth process from immaturity to maturity. (page 456)

Assessment centers Programs in which participants engage in and are evaluated on a number of individual and group exercises constructed to simulate important activities at the organizational levels to which these participants aspire. (page 327)

Authority The right to perform or command. (page 290)

Behavioral approach to management Management approach that emphasizes increasing organizational success by focusing on human variables within the organization. (page 43)

Behavior modification Program that focuses on managing human activity by controlling the consequences of performing that activity. (page 466)

Breakeven analysis Control tool based on the process of generating information that summarizes various levels of profit or loss associated with various levels of production. (page 558)

Breakeven point The situation wherein the total revenue of an organization equals its total costs. (page 559)

Budget Control tool that outlines how funds in a given period will be spent, as well as how they will be obtained. (pages 228, 568)

Bureaucracy Management system with detailed procedures and rules, a clearly outlined organizational hierarchy, and, mainly, impersonal relationships among organization members. (page 261)

Business ethics Involve the capacity to reflect on values in the corporate decision-making process, to determine how these values and decisions affect the various stakeholder groups, and to establish how managers can use these observations in day-to-day company management.

Business portfolio analysis The development of business related strategy that is based primarily on the market share of businesses and the growth of markets in which businesses exist. (page 202)

Career An individual's perceived sequence of attitudes and behaviors associated with the performance of work related experiences and activities over the span of the person's working life. (page 16)

Career plateauing A period of little or no apparent progress in the growth of a career. (page 17)

Centralization The situation in which a minimal number of job activities and a minimal amount of authority are delegated to subordinates. (page 300)

Change agent Anyone inside or outside the organization who tries to modify an existing organizational situation. (page 351)

Changing The second of Kurt Lewin's three related conditions, or states, that result in behavioral change—the state in which individuals begin to experiment with performing new behaviors. (page 363)

Changing an organization The process of modifying an existing organization to increase organizational effectiveness. (page 349)

Classical approach to management Management approach that emphasizes organizational efficiency to increase organizational success. (page 35)

Classical organizing theory The cumulative insights of early management writers on how organizational resources can best be used to enhance goal attainment. (page 261)

Closed system System that is not influenced by and does not interact with its environment (page 49)

Code of Ethics A formal statement that acts as a guide for making decisions and acting within an organization.

Command groups Formal groups that are outlined in the chain of command on an organization chart. (page 483)

Commitment principle Management guideline that advises managers to commit funds for planning only if they can anticipate, in the foreseeable future, a return on planning expenses as a result of the long-range planning analysis. (page 189)

Committee Task group that is charged with performing some type of specific activity. (page 484)

Communication The process of sharing information with other individuals. (page 389)

Communication effectiveness index Intended message reactions divided by the total number of transmitted messages. (page 395)

Communication macrobarriers The factors that hinder successful communication and that relate primarily to the communication environment and the larger world in which communication takes place. (page 391)

Communication microbarriers The factors that hinder successful communication and that relate primarily to such variables as the communication message, the source, and the destination. (page 393)

Company-wide quality (CWQ) The continuous process of involving all organization members in ensuring that every activity related to the production of goods and services has an appropriate role in establishing product quality. (page 653)

Comparative management The study of the management process in different countries to examine the potential of management action under different environmental conditions. (page 639)

Complete certainty condition The decision-making situation in which the decision maker knows exactly what the results of an implemented alternative will be. (page 173)

Complete uncertainty condition The decision-making situation in which the decision maker has absolutely no idea what the results of an implemented alternative will be. (page 173)

Comprehensive analysis of management Studying the management function as a whole.

Computer Electronic tool capable of accepting data, interpreting data, performing ordered operations on data, and reporting on the outcome of these operations. (page 590)

Conceptual skills Skills that involve the ability to see the organization as a whole. (page 14)

Concurrent control Control that takes place as some unit of work is being performed. (page 528)

Consensus Agreement on a decision by all individuals involved in making the decision. (page 165)

Consideration behavior Leadership behavior that reflects friendship, mutual trust, respect, and warmth in the relationship between the leader and the followers. (page 426)

Content theories of motivation Explanations of motivation that emphasize internal characteristics of people. (page 449)

Contingency approach to management Management approach that emphasizes that what managers do in practice depends on a given set of circumstances—a situation. (page 48)

Contingency theory of leadership Leadership concept that hypothesizes that, in any given leadership situation, success is determined primarily by (1) the degree to which the task being performed by the followers is structured, (2) the degree of position power possessed by the leader, and (3) the type of relationship that exists between the leader and the followers. (page 432)

Control Making something happen the way it was planned to happen. (page 519)

Control function Computer activities that dictate the order in which other computer functions are performed. (page 593)

Controller Staff individual whose basic responsibility is assisting line managers with the controlling function by gathering appropriate information and generating necessary reports that reflect this information. (page 530)

Controlling The process the manager goes through to control. (page 520)

Control tool Specific procedure or technique that presents pertinent organizational information in such a way that a manager is aided in developing and implementing appropriate control strategy. (page 557)

Coordination The orderly arrangement of group effort to provide unity of action in the pursuit of a common purpose. (page 268)

Corporate culture A set of shared values and beliefs that organization members have regarding the functioning and existence of their organization. (page 501)

Corporate database *See* Database.

Corporate social responsibility The managerial obligation to take action that protects and improves the welfare of society as a whole and organizational interests as well. (page 63)

Corrective action Managerial activity aimed at bringing organizational performance up to the level of performance standards. (page 525)

Cost-benefit analysis The process of comparing the cost of some activity to the benefit or revenue that results from the activity to determine the total worth of the activity to the organization. (page 530)

Cost leadership A strategy that focuses on making an organization more competitive by producing its products more cheaply than competitors can. (page 206)

Critical path The sequence of events and activities within a program evaluation and review technique (PERT) network that requires the longest period of time to complete. (page 241)

Critical question analysis Strategy development tool composed mainly of four questions: What are the purposes and objectives of the organization? Where is the organization presently going? In what kind of environment does the organization presently exist? What can be done to better achieve organizational objectives in the future? (pages 200–201)

Culture The total characteristics of a given group of people and their environment. (page 636)

Current ratio The liquidity ratio that indicates the organization's ability to meet its financial obligations in the short run. (page 572)

$$\text{Current ratio} = \frac{\text{Current assets}}{\text{Current liabilities}}$$

Data Facts or statistics. (page 585)

Database A reservoir of corporate facts consistently organized to fit the information needs of a variety of organization members. Also termed corporate database. (page 605)

Debt ratio The leverage ratio that indicates the percentage of all organizational assets provided by organizational creditors. (page 573)

$$\text{Debt ratio} = \frac{\text{Total debts}}{\text{Total assets}}$$

Decentralization The situation in which a significant number of job activities and a maximum amount of authority are delegated to subordinates. (page 300)

Decision Choice made between two or more available alternatives. (page 161)

Decision-making process The steps a decision maker takes to make a decision. (page 168)

Decision tree Graphic decision-making tool typically used to evaluate decisions containing a series of steps. (page 176)

Decline stage The fourth and last stage in career evolution, which occurs near retirement and during which individuals about sixty-five years of age or older show declining productivity. (page 18)

Decoder/destination The person or people in the interpersonal communication situation with whom the source/encoder attempts to share information. (page 390)

Delegation The process of assigning job activities and related authority to specific individuals in the organization. (page 297)

Demographics The statistical characteristics of a population. (page 193)

Department Unique group of resources established by management to perform some organizational task. (page 263)

Departmentalization The process of establishing departments in the management system. (page 263)

Dialogue capability The ability of a management decision support system (MDSS) user to interact with a management decision support system. (page 606)

Differentiation A strategy that focuses on making an organization more competitive by developing a product(s) that customers perceive as being different from products offered by competitors. (page 205)

Direct investing Using the assets of one company to purchase the operating assets of another company. (page 632)

Dispatching Issuing orders to the individuals involved in producing goods or services. (page 556)

Divestiture Strategy generally adopted to eliminate a strategic business unit that is not generating a satisfactory amount of business and has little hope of doing so in the future. (page 207)

Division of labor The assignment of various portions of a particular task among a number of organization members. (page 267)

Downward organizational communication Communication that flows from any point on an organization chart downward to another point on the organization chart. (page 399)

Economics Science that focuses on understanding how people of a particular community or nation produce, distribute, and use various goods and services. (page 192)

Employee-centered behavior Leader behavior through which the leader focuses primary attention on subordinates as people. (page 428)

Environmental analysis Study of the organizational environment to pinpoint environmental factors that can significantly influence organizational operations. (page 191)

Equal Employment Opportunity Commission (EEOC) Agency established to enforce the laws that regulate recruiting and other managerial practices. (page 323)

Equity theory of motivation An explanation of motivation that emphasizes an individual's perceived fairness of an employment situation and how perceived inequities can cause certain behaviors. (page 451)

Establishment stage The second stage in career evolution, during which individuals of about twenty-five to forty-five years of age typically start to become more productive or higher performers. (page 17)

Esteem needs Maslow's fourth set of human needs—including the desires for self-respect and respect from others. (page 455)

Ethics Our concern for good behavior; our obligation to consider not only our own personal well-being but also that of other human beings. (page 86)

Ethnocentric attitude Attitude that reflects a belief that multinational corporations should regard home country management practices as superior to foreign country management practices. (page 633)

Events In the PERT network, the completions of major product tasks. (page 240)

Expected value Measurement of the anticipated value of some event; determined by multiplying the income an event would produce by its probability of making that income. (page 121)

Exploration stage The first stage in career evolution, which occurs at the beginning of a career and is characterized by self-analysis and the exploration of different types of available jobs by individuals of about fifteen to twenty-five years of age. (page 16)

Exporting Selling goods or services to another country. (page 632)

Extrinsic rewards Rewards that are extraneous to the task accomplished. (page 453)

Feedback In the interpersonal communication situation, the decoder/destination's reaction to a message. (page 395)

Feedback control Control that takes place after some unit of work has been performed. (page 528)

Financial objectives Organizational targets relating to monetary issues. (page 115)

Fixed assets turnover The activity ratio that indicates the appropriateness of the amount of funds invested in plant and equipment relative to the level of sales. (page 573)

$$\text{Fixed asset turnover} = \frac{\text{Sales}}{\text{Fixed assets}}$$

Fixed costs Expenses incurred by an organization regardless of the number of products produced. (page 558)

Fixed position layout Layout pattern that, because of the weight or bulk of the product being manufactured, has workers, tools, and materials rotating around a stationary product. (page 554)

Flat organization chart Organization chart that is characterized by few levels and relatively large spans of management. (page 272)

Flextime Program that allows workers to complete their jobs within a workweek of a normal number of hours that they schedule themselves. (page 465)

Focus A strategy that emphasizes making an organization more competitive by targeting a particular customer. (page 206)

Forecasting Planning tool used to predict future environmental happenings that will influence the operation of the organization. (page 233)

Formal group Group that exists in an organization by virtue of management decree to perform tasks that enhance the attainment of organizational objectives. (page 482)

Formal organizational communication Organizational communication that follows the lines of the organization chart. (page 399)

Formal structure Relationships among organizational resources as outlined by management. (page 262)

Friendship groups Informal groups that form in organizations because of the personal affiliation members have with one another. (page 492)

Functional authority The right to give orders within a segment of the management system in which the right is normally nonexistent. (page 295)

Functional objectives Targets relating to key organizational functions. (page 116)

Functional similarity method Method for dividing job activities in the organization. (page 286)

Functional skill Skill involving the ability to apply appropriately the concepts of planning, organizing, influencing, and controlling to the operation of a management system. (page 669)

Gangplank   Communication channel extending from the organizational division to another but not shown in the lines of communication outlined on an organization chart. (page 274)

Gantt chart   Scheduling tool composed essentially of a bar chart with time on the horizontal axis and the resource to be scheduled on the vertical axis. (page 239)

General environment   The level of an organization's external environment that contains components normally having broad long-term implications for managing the organization. (page 192)

Geocentric attitude   Attitude that reflects a belief that the overall quality of management recommendations, rather than the location of managers, should determine the acceptability of management practices used to guide multinational corporations. (page 633)

Geographic contiguity   The degree to which subordinates are physically separated. (page 210)

Goal integration   Compatibility between individual and organizational objectives. (page 111)

Graicunas's formula   Formula that makes the span of management point that as the number of a manager's subordinates increases arithmetically, the number of possible relationships between the manager and the subordinates increases geometrically. (page 271)

Grapevine   Network for informal organizational communication. (page 402)

Grid organization development (grid OD)   Commonly used organization development technique based on a theoretical model called the managerial grid. (page 358)

Group   Any number of people who (1) interact with one another, (2) are psychologically aware of one another, and (3) perceive themselves to be a group. (page 481)

Group cohesiveness   The attraction group members feel for one another in terms of the desire to remain a member of the group and to resist leaving it. (page 498)

Group norms   Appropriate or standard behavior that is required of informal group members. (page 499)

Groupthink   The mode of thinking that people engage in when seeking agreement becomes so dominant in a group that it tends to override the realistic appraisal of alternate problem solutions. (page 488)

Growth   Strategy adopted by management to increase the amount of business that a strategic business unit is currently generating. (page 207)

Hierarchy of objectives   The overall organizational objective(s) and the subobjectives assigned to the various people or units of the organization. (page 117)

Host country   The country in which an investment is made by a foreign company. (page 628)

Human resource inventory   Accumulation of information concerning the characteristics of organization members; this information focuses on the past performance of organization members as well as on how they might be trained and best used in the future. (page 319)

Human resource planning   Input planning that involves obtaining the human resources necessary for the organization to achieve its objectives. (page 232)

Human resources   *See* Appropriate human resources.

Human skills   Skills involving the ability to build cooperation within the team being led. (page 14)

Hygiene, or maintenance, factors   Items that influence the degree of job dissatisfaction. (page 463)

Importing   Buying goods or services from another country. (page 632)

Individual objectives   Personal goals that each organization member would like to reach as a result of personal activity in the organization. (page 111)

Influencing   The process of guiding the activities of organization members in appropriate directions, involving the performance of four primary management activities: (1) leading, (2) motivating, (3) considering groups, and (4) communicating. (page 385)

Informal group   A collection of individuals whose common work experiences result in the development of a system of interpersonal relations that extends beyond those established by management. (page 491)

Informal organizational communication   Organizational communication that does not follow the lines of the organization chart. (page 402)

Informal structure   Patterns of relationships that develop because of the informal activities of organization members. (page 263)

Information   Conclusions derived from data analysis. (page 585)

Information appropriateness   The degree to which information is relevant to the decision-making situation that faces the manager. (page 586)

Information quality   The degree to which information represents reality. (page 587)

Information quantity   The amount of decision related information a manager possesses. (page 587)

Information timeliness   The extent to which the receipt of information allows decisions to be made and action to be taken so the organization can gain some benefit from possessing the information. (page 587)

Input function   Computer activities through which the computer enters the data to be analyzed and the instructions to be followed to analyze the data appropriately. (page 590)

Input planning   Development of proposed action that will furnish sufficient and appropriate organizational resources for reaching established organizational objectives. (page 229)

Interest groups   Informal groups that gain and maintain membership primarily because of special concern each member possesses about a specific issue. (page 492)

Intermediate-term objectives   Targets to be achieved within one to five years. (page 114)

Internal environment   The level of an organization's environment that exists inside the organization and normally has immediate and specific implications for managing the organization. (page 197)

International joint venture   A partnership formed by a company in one country with a company in another country for the purpose of pursuing some mutually desirable business undertaking. (page 632)

International management   Performing management activities across national borders. (page 623)

Intrinsic rewards   Rewards that come directly from performing a task. (page 453)

Inventory turnover   The activity ratio that indicates whether an organization is maintaining an appropriate level of inventory in relation to its sales volume. (page 573)

$$\text{Inventory turnover} = \frac{\text{Sales}}{\text{Inventory}}$$

Job analysis Technique commonly used to gain an understanding of what a task entails and the type of individual who should be hired to perform the task. (page 316)

Job description Specific activities that must be performed to accomplish some task or job. (pages 285, 316)

Job enlargement The process of increasing the number of operations an individual performs in a job. (page 462)

Job enrichment The process of incorporating motivators into a job situation. (page 463)

Job rotation The process of moving individuals from one job to another and not requiring individuals to perform only one job over the long term. (page 462)

Job specification Characteristics of the individual who should be hired to perform a specific task or job. (page 316)

Job-centered behavior Leader behavior through which the leader focuses primary attention on the work a subordinate is doing. (page 427)

Jury of executive opinion method Method of predicting future sales levels primarily by asking appropriate managers to give their opinions on what will happen to sales in the future. (page 235)

Just-in-time (JIT) inventory control An inventory control technique that reduces inventories to a minimum by arranging for them to be delivered to the production facility just in time to be used. (page 564)

Lateral organizational communication Communication that flows from any point on an organization chart horizontally to another point on the organization chart. (page 400)

Layout patterns The overall arrangement of machines, equipment, materials handling, aisles, service areas, storage areas, and work stations within a production facility. (page 553)

Leader flexibility The ability of leaders to change their leadership styles. (page 432)

Leadership The process of directing the behavior of others toward the accomplishment of objectives. (page 415)

Leadership style Behavioral pattern a leader establishes while guiding organization members in appropriate directions. (page 427)

Lecture Primarily one-way communication situation in which an instructor trains by orally presenting information to an individual or group. (page 330)

Level dimension (of plans) The level of the organization at which plans are aimed. (page 224)

Leverage ratios In ratio analysis, the ratios that indicate the relationship between organizational funds supplied by the owners of an organization and organizational funds supplied by creditors. (page 572)

License agreement Right granted by one company to another to use its brand name, technology, product specifications, and so on in the manufacture or sale of goods and services. (page 632)

Life cycle theory of leadership Leadership concept that hypothesizes that leadership styles should reflect primarily the maturity level of the followers. (page 428)

Line authority The right to make decisions and to give orders concerning the production-, sales-, or finance-related behavior of subordinates. (page 291)

Liquidity ratios In ratio analysis, the ratios that indicate an organization's ability to meet upcoming financial obligations. (page 572)

Long-term objectives Targets to be achieved within five to seven years. (page 114)

Loss The amount of the total costs of producing a product that exceeds the total revenue gained from selling the product. (page 559)

Maintenance stage The third stage in career evolution, during which individuals of about forty-five to sixty-five years of age become more productive, stabilize, or become less productive. (page 17)

Malcolm Baldrige National Quality Awards National awards given in the U.S. to companies doing exemplary work in the area of quality. (page 658)

Management The process of reaching organizational goals by working with and through people and other organizational resources. (page 8)

Management by exception Control tool that allows only significant deviations between planned and actual performance to be brought to the manager's attention. (page 557)

Management by objectives (MBO) Management approach that uses organizational objectives as the primary means by which to manage organizations. (page 121)

Management decision support system (MDSS) An interdependent set of computer-oriented decision aids that help managers make nonprogrammed decisions. (page 605)

Management functions Activities that make up the management process, including planning, organizing, influencing, and controlling. (page 9)

Management information system (MIS) Network established in an organization to provide managers with information that will assist them in decision making. (page 595)

Management inventory card Form used in compiling a human resource inventory—containing an organizational history of an individual and an explanation of how the individual might be used in the future. (page 319)

Management manpower replacement chart Form used in compiling a human resource inventory—people-oriented and presenting a total composite view of the individuals whom management considers significant to human resource planning. (page 319)

Management responsibility guide Tool that can be used to clarify the responsibilities of various managers in the organization. (page 288)

Management science approach Management approach that emphasizes the use of the scientific method and quantitative techniques to increase organizational success. (page 45)

Management system Open system whose major parts are organizational input, organizational process, and organizational output. (page 50)

Managerial effectiveness   The degree to which management attains organizational objectives. (page 12)

Managerial efficiency   The degree to which organizational resources contribute to productivity. (page 12)

Managerial grid   Theoretical model based on the premise that concern for people and concern for production are the two primary attitudes that influence management style. (page 358)

Materials requirements control   The process of making things happen the way they were planned to happen in materials requirements planning. (page 563)

Materials requirements planning (MRP)   Creating schedules that identify the specific parts and materials required to produce an item, the exact quantities of each needed to enhance the production process, and the dates when orders for these quantities should be released to suppliers and be received for best timing in the production cycle. (page 563)

Matrix organization   Traditional organizational structure that is modified primarily for the purpose of completing some type of special project. (page 355)

Maturity   As used in the life cycle theory of leadership, an individual's ability to independently perform the job, to assume additional responsibility, and to desire success. (page 428)

McClelland's Acquired-Needs Theory   An explanation of human needs that focuses on desires for achievement, power, and affiliation as needs that people develop as a result of their life experiences. (page 457)

Means-ends analysis   The process of outlining the means by which various objectives, or ends, in the organization can be achieved. (page 120)

Message   Encoded information that the source/encoder intends to share with others. (page 390)

Message interference   Stimuli that compete with the communication message for the attention of the decoder/destination. (page 393)

Mission statement   A written document developed by management, normally based upon input by managers as well as nonmanagers, that describes and explains what the mission of an organization actually is. (page 199)

Model base   A collection of quantitative computer programs that can assist management decision support system (MDSS) users in analyzing data within databases. (page 606)

Motion study   Finding the one best way to accomplish a task by analyzing the movements necessary to perform the task. (page 38)

Motivating factors   Items that influence the degree of job satisfaction. (page 463)

Motivation   The inner state that causes an individual to behave in a way that ensures the accomplishment of some goal. (page 449)

Motivation strength   Individual's degree of desire to perform a behavior. (page 451)

Multinational corporation (MNC)   Company that has significant operations in more than one country. (page 626)

Murphy's Law   A lighthearted observation about organizations indicating that anything that can go wrong will go wrong. (page 519)

Needs-goal model   Motivation model that hypothesizes that felt needs cause human behavior. (page 450)

Negative norms   Informal group standards that limit organizational productivity. (page 499)

Negative reinforcement   Reward that is the elimination of an undesirable consequence of behavior. (page 467)

Nonprogrammed decisions   Decisions that typically are one-shot occurrences and usually are less structured than programmed decisions. (page 162)

Nonverbal communication   The sharing of ideas without the use of words. (page 397)

On-the-job training   Training technique that blends job related knowledge with experience in using that knowledge in the job. (page 333)

Open system   System that is influenced by and is constantly interacting with its environment. (page 49)

Operating environment   Level of the organization's external environment that contains components normally having relatively specific and immediate implications for managing the organization. (page 195)

Operational objectives   Objectives that are stated in observable or measurable terms. (page 119)

Operations management   The process of managing production in organizations. (page 555)

Organizational communication   Interpersonal communication in organizations. (page 399)

Organizational mission   The purpose for which or the reason why an organization exists. (page 198)

Organizational objectives   Targets toward which the open management system is directed. (page 107)

Organizational purpose   What the organization exists to do, given a particular group of customers and customer needs. (page 107)

Organizational resources   Assets available for activation during normal operations, among which are human resources, monetary resources, raw materials resources, and capital resources. (page 10)

Organization chart   Graphic representation of organizational structure. (page 261)

Organization development   Process that emphasizes changing an organization by changing organization members and that bases these changes on an overview of structure, technology, and all other organizational ingredients. (page 358)

Organizing   The process of establishing orderly uses for all resources in the organization. (page 257)

Output function   Computer activities that take the results of input, storage, processing, and control functions and transmit them outside the computer. (page 593)

Overlapping responsibility   Situation in which more than one individual is responsible for the same activity. (page 286)

Parent company   The company investing in international operations. (page 628)

Path-goal theory of leadership   A theory of leadership that suggests the primary activity of a leader should be to make desirable and achievable rewards available to organization members as a result of attaining organizational goals and to clarify the kinds of behavior that must be performed to earn those rewards. (page 434)

People change   Changing certain aspects of organization members to increase organizational effectiveness. (page 358)

People factors   Attitudes, leadership skills, communication skills, and all other characteristics of the organization's employees. (page 353)

Perception Interpretation of a message as observed by an individual. (page 394)

Performance appraisal The process of reviewing past productive activity to evaluate the contribution individuals have made toward attaining management system objectives. (page 334)

Personal power Power derived from the relationship that one person has with another. (page 534)

PERT *See* Program evaluation and review technique (PERT). (page 240)

Physiological needs Maslow's first set of human needs—for the normal functioning of the body—including the desire for water, food, rest, sex, and air. (page 454)

Plan Specific action proposed to help the organization achieve its objectives. (page 223)

Plan for planning Listing of all steps that must be taken to plan for an organization. (page 143)

Planning The process of determining how the management system will achieve its objectives. (page 135)

Planning tools Techniques managers can use to help develop plans. (page 233)

Plant facilities planning Input planning that involves developing the type of work facility an organization will need to reach its objectives. (page 229)

Policy Standing plan that furnishes broad guidelines for channeling management thinking in specified directions. (page 225)

Polycentric attitude Attitude that reflects a belief that since foreign managers are closer to foreign organizational units, they probably understand them better—and therefore that foreign management practices generally should be viewed as more insightful than home country management practices. (page 633)

Porter-Lawler model Motivation model that hypothesizes that felt needs cause human behavior and that motivation strength is determined primarily by the perceived value of the result of performing the behavior and the perceived probability that the behavior performed will cause the result to materialize. (page 452)

Position power Power derived from the organizational position that one holds. (page 534)

Position replacement form Form used in compiling a human resource inventory—summarizing information about organization members who could fill a position should it open. (page 319)

Positive norms Informal group standards that contribute to organizational productivity. (page 499)

Positive reinforcement Reward that is a desirable consequence of behavior. (page 467)

Power The extent to which an individual is able to influence others so they respond to orders. (page 533)

Precontrol Control that takes place before some unit of work is actually performed. (page 527)

Premises Assumptions on which alternative ways of accomplishing objectives are based. (page 138)

Principle of supportive relationships Management guideline that indicates that all human interaction with an organization should build and maintain the sense of personal worth and the importance of those involved in the interaction. (page 470)

Principle of the objective Management guildeline that recommends that before managers initiate any action, organizational objectives should be clearly determined, understood, and stated. (page 114)

Probability theory Decision-making tool used in risk situations—situations in which the decision maker is not completely sure of the outcome of an implemented alternative. (page 175)

Problems Factors within organizations that are barriers to organizational goal attainment. (page 525)

Procedure Standing plan that outlines a series of related actions that must be taken to accomplish a particular task. (page 226)

Processing function Computer actvities involved with performing the logic and calculation steps necessary to analyze data appropriately. (page 593)

Process layout Layout pattern based primarily on grouping together similar types of equipment. (page 553)

Process theories of motivation Explanations of motivation that emphasize how individuals are motivated. (page 449)

Production The transformation of organizational resources into products. (page 549)

Production control Ensuring that an organization produces goods and services as planned. (page 549)

Production planning Determining the type and amount of resources needed to produce specified goods or services. (page 555)

Productivity The relationship between the total amount of goods or services being produced (output) and the organizational resources needed (input) to produce the goods or services. (page 549)

Product layout Layout pattern based mostly on the progressive steps by which the product is made. (page 554)

Product life cycle Five stages through which most new products and services pass—introduction, growth, maturity, saturation, and decline. (page 236)

Product-market mix objectives Objectives that outline which products and the relative number or mix of these products the organization will attempt to sell. (page 115)

Profitability ratios In ratio analysis, the ratios that indicate the ability of an organization to generate profits. (page 574)

Profits The amount of total revenue that exceeds total costs. (page 559)

Profit to sales ratio The profitability ratio that indicates whether the organization is making an adequate net profit in relation to the total dollars coming into the organization. (page 574)

$$\text{Profit to sales ratio} = \frac{\text{Net profit}}{\text{Sales}}$$

Profit to total assets ratio The profitability ratio that indicates whether the organization is realizing enough net profit in relation to the total dollars invested in assets. (page 574)

$$\frac{\text{Profit to}}{\text{total assets ratio}} = \frac{\text{Total assets}}{\text{Net profits}}$$

Program Single-use plan designed to carry out a special project in an organization. (page 226)

Program evaluation and review technique (PERT) Scheduling tool that is essentially a network of project activities showing estimates of time necessary to complete each activity and the sequential relationship of activities that must be followed to complete the project. (page 240)

Programmed decisions Decisions that are routine and repetitive and that typically require specific handling methods. (page 161)

Programmed learning Technique for instructing without the presence of a human instructor—small pieces of information requiring responses are presented to individual trainees. (page 331)

Punishment The presentation of an undesirable behavioral consequence or the removal of a desirable one that decreases the likelihood of the behavior continuing. (page 467)

Quality How well a product does what it is supposed to do—how closely and reliably it satisfies the specifications to which it is built. (page 653)

Quality circles Small groups of workers that meet regularly with management to discuss quality related problems. (page 566)

Quality control The process of making the quality of finished goods and services what it was planned to be. (page 565)

Quality of work life Opportunity of workers to make decisions that influence their work situation. (page 672)

Quality-oriented policy A standing plan that furnishes broad, general guidelines for channeling management thinking toward taking action consistent with reaching quality objectives. (page 665)

Quality-oriented structure Designated relationships among organizational resources that emphasize the achievement of quality objectives. (page 666)

Quick ratio The liquidity ratio that indicates an organization's ability to meet its financial obligations with no reliance on inventory. (page 572)

$$\frac{\text{Quick}}{\text{ratio}} = \frac{\text{Current assets} - \text{Inventory}}{\text{Current liabilities}}$$

Ratio analysis Control tool based on the process of generating information that summarizes the financial position of an organization by calculating ratio based on various financial measures appearing on balance sheets and income statements. (page 572)

Recruitment The initial screening of the total supply of prospective human resources available to fill a position. (page 316)

Refreezing The third of Kurt Lewin's three related conditions, or states, that result in behavioral change—the state in which an individual's experimentally performed behaviors become part of the person. (page 363)

Relevant alternatives Alternatives that are considered feasible for implementation and for solving an existing problem. (page 167)

Repetitiveness dimension (of plans) The extent to which plans are used again and again. (page 223)

Responsibility The obligation to perform assigned activities. (page 285)

Responsibility gap Situation in which certain organizational tasks are not included in the responsibility area of any individual organization member. (page 286)

Retrenchment Strategy adopted by management to strenghten or protect the amount of business a strategic business unit is currently generating. (page 207)

Risk condition The decision-making situation in which the decision maker has only enough information to estimate how probable the outcome of implemented alternatives will be. (page 173)

Robot A flexible machine with the ability to hold, move, or grab items that functions through electronic impulses that activate motors or switches. (page 552)

Robotics The area of study dealing with the development and use of robots. (page 552)

Routing Determining the sequence in which work must be completed to produce specified goods or services. (page 555)

Rule Standing plan that designates specific required action. (page 226)

Sales force estimation method Method of predicting future sales levels primarily by asking appropriate salespeople for their opinions of what will happen to sales in the future. (page 235)

Scalar relationships The chain of command positioning of individuals on an organization chart. (page 273)

Scheduling The process of formulating detailed listings of activities that must be performed to accomplish a task, allocating resources necessary to complete the task, and setting up and following timetables for completing the task. (pages 239, 556)

Scientific management Management approach that emphasizes the one best way to perform a task. (page 36)

Scientific method Problem-solving method that entails the following sequential steps: (1) observing a system, (2) constructing a framework that is consistent with the observations and from which the consequences of changing the systems can be predicted, (3) predicting how various changes would influence the system, and (4) testing to see if these changes influence the system as intended. (page 46)

Scope dimension (of plans) The portion of the total management system at which the plans are aimed. (page 223)

Scope of the decision The proportion of the total management system that a particular decision will affect. (page 163)

Security, or safety, needs Maslow's second set of human needs—reflecting the human desire to keep free from physical harm. (page 454)

Selection Choosing an individual to hire from all of those who have been recruited. (page 324)

Self-actualization needs Maslow's fifth set of human needs—reflecting the human desire to maximize potential. (page 455)

Serial transmission The passing of information from one individual through a series of individuals. (page 400)

Short-term objectives Targets to be achieved in one year or less. (page 114)

Signal A message that has been transmitted from one person to another. (page 390)

Single-use plans Plans that are used only once or several times because they focus on organizational situations that do not occur repeatedly. (page 225)

Site selection Determining where a plant facility should be located. (pages 229, 230)

Situational analysis skill Skill involving the ability to apply both systems theory and functional theory to the unique conditions of a particular organizational situation. (page 671)

Situational approach to leadership Relatively modern view of leadership that suggests that successful leadership requires a unique combination of leaders, followers, and leadership situations. (page 418)

Social audit The process of measuring the social responsibility activities of an organization. (page 83)

Social needs Maslow's third set of human needs—reflecting the human desire to belong, including the desire for friendship, companionship, and love. (page 455)

Social obligation approach Approach to meeting social obligations that reflects an attitude that considers business to have primarily economic purposes and confines social responsibility activity mainly to conformance to existing legislation. (page 76–77)

Social responsibility approach Approach to meeting social obligations that is characterized by an attitude that considers business as having both societal and economic goals. (page 76–77)

Social responsiveness The degree of effectiveness and efficiency an organization displays in pursuing its social responsibilities. (page 73)

Social responsiveness approach Approach to meeting social obligations that reflects an attitude that considers business to have societal and economic goals as well as the obligation to anticipate upcoming social problems and to work actively toward preventing their appearance. (page 76–77)

Social values The relative degrees of worth society places on the manner in which it exists and functions. (page 193)

Sociogram Sociometric diagram that summarizes the personal feelings of organization members about the people in the organization with whom they would like to spend free time. (page 493)

Sociometry Analytical tool that can be used to determine what informal groups exist in an organization and who the members of those groups are. (page 493)

Source/encoder The person in the interpersonal communication situation who originates and encodes information that the person wants to share with others. (page 390)

Span of management The number of individuals a manager supervises. (page 270)

Stability Strategy adopted by management to maintain or slightly improve the amount of business a strategic business unit is generating. (page 207)

Staff authority The right to advise or assist those who possess line authority. (page 292)

Standard The level of activity established to serve as a model for evaluating organizational performance. (page 523)

Standing plans Plans that are used over and over because they focus on organizational situations that occur repeatedly. (page 225)

Statistical quality control Process used to determine how many products from a larger number should be inspected to calculate a probability that the total number of products meets organizational quality standards. (page 567)

Status The positioning of importance of a group member in relation to other group members. (page 500)

Storage function Computer activities involved with retaining the material entered into the computer during the performance of the input function. (page 590)

Strategic business unit (SBU) In business portfolio analysis, a significant organizational segment that is analyzed to develop organizational strategy aimed at generating future business or revenue. (page 203)

Strategic control The last step of the strategy management process, monitoring and evaluating the strategy management process as a whole in order to make sure that it is operating properly. (page 208)

Strategy implementation The fourth step of the strategy management process, putting formulated strategy into action. (page 207)

Strategic planning Long-term planning that focuses on the organization as a whole. (page 189)

Strategy Broad and general plan developed to reach long-term organizational objectives. (page 189)

Strategy formulation The process of determining appropriate courses of action for achieving organizational objectives and thereby accomplishing organizational purpose. (page 200)

Strategy management The process of ensuring that an organization possesses and benefits from the use of an appropriate organization strategy. (page 190)

Stress The bodily strain that an individual experiences as a result of coping with some environmental factor. (page 365)

Stressor Environmental demand that causes people to feel stress. (page 368)

Structural change Type of organizational change that emphasizes modifying an existing organizational structure. (page 354)

Structural factors Organizational controls, such as policies and procedures. (page 353)

Structure Designated relationships among resources of the management system. (page 261)

Structure behavior Leadership activity that (1) delineates the relationship between the leader and the leader's followers or (2) establishes well-defined procedures that the followers should adhere to in performing their jobs. (page 426)

Suboptimization Condition wherein organizational subobjectives are conflicting or not directly aimed at accomplishing overall organizational objectives. (page 118)

Subsystem System created as part of the process of the overall management system. (page 140)

Successful communication Interpersonal communication situation in which the information the source/encoder intends to share with the decoder/destination and the meaning the decoder destination derives from the transmitted message are the same. (page 391)

Suppliers Individuals or agencies that provide organizations with resources needed to produce organizational goods or services. (page 196)

SWOT analysis Strategy development tool that matches internal organizational strengths and weaknesses with external opportunities and threats. (page 201)

Symptom Sign that a problem exists. (page 526)

System Number of interdependent parts functioning as a whole for some purpose. (page 49)

System approach to management Management approach based on general system theory—the theory that to understand fully the operation of an entity, the entity must be viewed as a system. (page 49)

Systems skill The ability to view and manage a business or some other concern as a number of components that work together and function as a whole to achieve some objective. (page 669)

Tactical planning Short-range planning that emphasizes current operations of various parts of the organization. (page 209)

Tall organization chart Organization chart that is characterized by many levels and relatively small spans of management. (page 272)

Task groups Formal groups of organization members who interact with one another to accomplish mostly nonroutine organizational tasks (members of any one task group can and often do come from various levels and segments of an organization). (page 484)

Technical skills The ability to apply specialized knowledge and expertise to work related techniques and procedures. (page 14)

Technological change Type of organizational change that emphasizes modifying the level of technology in the management system. (page 354)

Technological factors Any types of equipment or processes that assist organization members in the performance of their jobs. (page 353)

Theory X Set of essentially negative assumptions about the nature of people. (page 460)

Theory Y Set of essentially positive assumptions about the nature of people. (page 460)

Theory Z Effectiveness dimension that implies that managers who use either Theory X or Theory Y assumptions when dealing with people can be successful, depending on their situation. (pages 460, 641)

Time dimension (of plans) The length of time plans cover. (page 223)

Time series analysis method Method of predicting future sales levels by analyzing the historical relationship in an organization between sales and time. (page 236)

Times interest earned ratio The leverage ratio that indicates an organization's ability to pay interest expenses from gross income. (page 573)

$$\frac{\text{Times interest}}{\text{earned ratio}} = \frac{\text{Gross income}}{\text{Interest charges}}$$

Total assets turnover The activity ratio that indicates the appropriateness of the level of funds an organization has tied up in all assets relative to its rate of sales. (page 574)

$$\frac{\text{Total assets}}{\text{turnover}} = \frac{\text{Sales}}{\text{Total assets}}$$

Total costs The sum of fixed costs and variable costs associated with production. (page 559)

Total power The entire amount of power an individual in an organization possesses, mainly the amount of position power and the amount of personal power possessed by the individual. (page 533)

Total revenue All sales dollars accumulated from selling goods or services that are produced. (page 559)

Training The process of developing qualities in human resources that ultimately will enable them to be more productive and thus to contribute more to organizational goal attainment. (page 328)

Training need Information or skill area of an individual or group that requires further development to increase the organizational productivity of the individual or group. (page 328)

Trait approach to leadership Outdated view of leadership that sees the personal characteristics of an individual as the main determinants of how successful the individual could be as a leader. (page 416)

Transformational leadership Leadership that inspires organizational success by profoundly affecting followers' beliefs in what an organization should be, as well as followers' values like justice and integrity. (page 435)

Triangular management Management approach that emphasizes using information from the classical, behavioral, and management science schools of thought to manage the open management system. (page 51)

Trust Followers' belief in and reliance on the ability and the integrity of the leader. (page 436)

Unfreezing The first of Kurt Lewin's three related conditions, or states, that result in behavioral change—the state in which individuals experience a need to learn new behaviors. (page 363)

Unity of command Management principle that recommends that an individual have only one boss. (page 274)

Universality of management skills The idea that the principles of management are universal, or applicable to all types of organizations and organizational levels. (page 15)

Unsuccessful communication Interpersonal communication situation in which the information the source/encoder intends to share with the decoder/destination and the meaning the decoder/destination derives from the transmitted message are different. (page 391)

Upward organizational communication Communication that flows from any point on an organization chart upward to another point on the organization chart. (page 400)

User database Database developed by an individual manager or other user. (page 606)

Variable budgets Budgets that outline various levels of resources to be allocated for each organizational activity, depending on the level of production within the organization. Also called flexible budgets. (page 570)

Variable costs Organizational expenses that fluctuate with the number of products produced. (page 559)

Verbal communication The sharing of ideas through words. (page 397)

Vroom expectancy model Motivation model that hypothesizes that felt needs cause human behavior and that motivation strength depends on an individual's degree of desire to perform a behavior. (page 450)

Wellness programs Special activities within an organization designed to keep organization members in good health. (page 671)

"What if" analysis The simulation of a business situation over and over again using somewhat different data for selected decision areas. (page 606)

Work team Task group used in organizations to achieve greater organizational flexibility or to cope with rapid growth. (page 488)

Zero-base budgeting The planning and budgeting process that requires managers to justify their entire budget request in detail rather than simply to refer to budget amounts established in previous years. (page 570)

Endnotes

CHAPTER 1

1. Peter F. Drucker, "Management's New Role," *Harvard Business Review* (November/December 1969), 54.
2. U.S. Bureau of the Census, *Statistical Abstract of the United States,* 108th ed. (Washington, D.C.: Government Printing Office, 1987), 230.
3. Dana Wechsler, "Just Deserts," *Forbes.* May 28, 1990, 208.
4. Robert Albanese, *Management* (Cincinnati: Southwestern, 1988), 8.
5. For a more detailed description of each of these definitions of management, see Dalton E. McFarland, *Management: Principles and Practice,* 4th ed. (New York: Macmillan, 1974), 6–10.
6. Robert L. Katz, "Skills of an Effective Administrator," *Harvard Business Review* (January/February 1955), 33–41.
7. Ruth Davidhizar, "The Two-Minute Manager," *Health Supervisor* 7 (April 1989), 25–29.
8. For an article that demonstrates how important human skills are for middle managers, see also Philip A. Rudolph and Brian H. Kleiner, "The Art of Motivating Employees," *Journal of Managerial Psychology* 4 (1989), i–iv.
9. Henri Fayol, *General and Industrial Management* (London: Sir Isaac Pitman & Sons, 1949).
10. B.C. Forbes, *Forbes.* March 15, 1976, 128.
11. Douglas T. Hall, *Careers in Organizations* (Santa Monica, Calif.: Goodyear Publishing, 1976), 4.
12. John Ivancevich and Michael T. Matteson, *Organizational Behavior and Management* (Homewood, Ill.: BPI/Irwin, 1990), 593–95.
13. John W. Slocum, Jr., William L. Cron, and Linda C. Yows, "Whose Career Is Likely to Plateau?" *Business Horizons* (March/April 1987), 31–38.
14. Lynn Slavenski, "Career Development: A Systems Approach," *Training and Development Journal* (February 1987), 56–59.
15. Joseph E. McKendrick, Jr., "What Are You Doing the Rest of Your Life?" *Management World* (September/October 1987), 2.
16. Carl Anderson, *Management: Skills, Functions, and Organization Performance,* 2d ed. (Boston: Allyn and Bacon, 1988).
17. Paul H. Thompson, Robin Zenger Baker, and Norman Smallwood, "Improving Personal Development by Applying the Four-Stage Career Model," *Organizational Dynamics* (Autumn 1986), 49–62.
18. Buck Blessing, "Career Planning: Five Fatal Assumptions," *Training and Development Journal* (September 1986), 49–51.
19. Thomas J. Peters, Jr., "The Best New Managers Will Listen, Motivate, Support," *Working Woman* (September 1990), 142–143, 216–217.
20. For related information, see Colin Leinster, "The Young Exec as Superdad," *Fortune.* April 25, 1988, 237–42; Uma Sekaran, *Dual-Career Families* (San Francisco: Jossey-Bass, 1986); F.S. Hall and T.D. Hall, "Dual Careers—How Do Couples and Companies Cope with the Problems?" *Organizational Dynamics* 6 (1978), 57–77.
21. Carol Milano, "Reevaluating Recruitment to Better Target Top Minority Talent," *Management Review* (August 1989), 29–32.
22. Colin Leinster, "Black Executives: How They're Doing," *Fortune.* January 18, 1988, 109–20.
23. James F. Wolf, "The Legacy of Mary Parker Follett," *Bureaucrat* 17 (Winter 1988–89), 53–57.
24. Neil J. DeCarlo and W. Kent Sterett, "History of the Malcolm Baldrige National Quality Award," *Quality Progress* 23 (March 1990), 21–27.

CHAPTER 2

1. James H. Donnelly, Jr., James L. Gibson, and John M. Ivancevich, *Fundamentals of Management* (Plano, Tex.: Business Publications, 1987), 6–8.
2. Harold Koontz, Cyril O'Donnell, and Heinz Weihrich, *Management,* 8th ed. (New York: McGraw-Hill, 1984), 52–69.
3. W. Warren Haynes and Joseph L. Massie, *Management,* 2d ed. (Englewood Cliffs, N.J.: Prentice-Hall, 1969), 4–13.
4. Frederick W. Taylor, *The Principles of Scientific Management* (New York: Harper & Bros., 1947), 66–71.
5. Edward A. Michaels, "Work Measurement," *Small Business Reports* 14 (March 1989), 55–63.
6. Henry L. Gantt, *Industrial Leadership* (New Haven, Conn.: Yale University Press, 1916), 57.
7. Ralph V. Rogers, "An Interactive Graphical Aided Scheduling System," *Computers and Industrial Engineering* 17 (1989), 113–18. For more information on the Gantt chart see: G. William Page, "Using Project Management Software in Planning," *Journal of the American Planning Association* 55 (Autumn 1989), 494–99.

8. Gantt, *Industrial Leadership,* 85.
9. Chester I. Barnard, *Organization and Management* (Cambridge, Mass.: Harvard University Press, 1952). For more current discussion of Barnard's work see: Christopher Vasillopulos, "Heroism, Self-Abnegation and the Liberal Organization," *Journal of Business Ethics* 7 (August 1988), 585–91.
10. Alvin Brown, *Organization of Industry* (Englewood Cliffs, N.J.: Prentice-Hall, 1947).
11. Henry S. Dennison, *Organization Engineering* (New York: McGraw-Hill, 1931).
12. Luther Gulick and Lyndall Urwick, eds., *Papers on the Science of Administration* (New York: Institute of Public Administration, 1937).
13. J.D. Mooney and A.C. Reiley, *Onward Industry!* (New York: Harper & Bros., 1931). With some modifications, this book appeared as *The Principles of Organization* (New York: Harper & Bros., 1939).
14. Oliver Sheldon, *The Philosophy of Management* (London: Sir Isaac Pitman and Sons, 1923).
15. Henri Fayol, *General and Industrial Management* (London: Sir Isaac Pitman and Sons, 1949).
16. Charles A. Mowll, "Successful Management Based on Key Principles," *Healthcare Financial Management* 43 (June 1989), 122, 124.
17. Fayol, *General and Industrial Management,* 19–42. For an excellent discussion of the role of accountability and organization structure see Elliott Jaques, "In Praise of Hierarchy," *Harvard Business Review* 68 (January/February 1990), 127–133.
18. For an interesting discussion of how modern training programs are teaching managers to establish productive authority relationships in organizations see: A. Glenn Kiser, Terry Humphries, and Chip Bell, "Breaking Through Rational Leadership," *Training and Development Journal* 44 (January 1990), 42–45.
19. For detailed summaries of these studies, see *Industrial Worker,* 2 vols. (Cambridge, Mass.: Harvard University Press, 1938); and F.J. Roethlisberger and W.J. Dickson, *Management and the Worker* (Cambridge, Mass.: Harvard University Press, 1939). For more recent discussion of the Hawthorne studies see: Bev Geber, "The Hawthorne Effect: Orwell or Buscaglia?" *Training* 23 (November 1986), 113–14.
20. For additional information, see George C. Homans, *Fatigue of Workers: Its Relation to Industrial Production* (New York: Committee on Work in Industry, National Research Council, Reinhold Publishing, 1941).
21. Homans, *Fatigue of Workers.*
22. C. West Churchman, Russell L. Ackoff, and E. Leonard Arnoff, *Introduction to Operations Research* (New York: Wiley, 1957), 18.
23. Hamdy A. Taha, *Operations Research: An Introduction* (New York: Macmillan, 1988), 1–2.
24. James R. Emshoff, *Analysis of Behavioral Systems* (New York: Macmillan, 1971), 10. For an interesting account of how the scientific method can be applied to studying management problems like information system problems see: Allen S. Lee, "A Scientific Methodology for the MIS Case Studies," *MIS Quarterly* 13 (March 1989), 33–50.
25. C.C. Shumacher and B.E. Smith, "A Sample Survey of Industrial Operations Research Activities II," *Operations Research* 13 (1965): 1023–27.
26. Catherine L. Morgan, "A Survey of MS/OR Surveys," *Interfaces* 19 (November/December 1989), 95–103.
27. Discussion concerning these factors is adapted from Donnelly, Gibson, and Ivancevich, *Fundamentals of Management,* 302–03; Efraim Turban and Jack R. Meredith, *Fundamentals of Management Science* (Plano, Tex.: Business Publications, 1981), 15–23.
28. Harold Koontz, "The Management Theory Jungle Revisited," *Academy of Management Review* 5 (1980), 175–87. For an excellent illustration of how the contingency approach might apply to developing strategies for handling competing firms see: Moonkyu Lee, "Contingency Approach to Strategies for Service Firms," *Journal of Business Research* 19 (December 1989), 293–301.
29. Don Hellriegel, John W. Slocum, and Richard W. Woodman, *Organizational Behavior* (St. Paul, Minn.: West Publishing, 1986), 22.
30. J.W. Lorsch, "Organization Design: A Situational Perspective," *Organizational Dynamics* 6 (1977), 2–4.
31. Louis W. Fry and Deborah A. Smith, "Congruence, Contingency, and Theory Building," *Academy of Management Review* (January 1987), 117–32.
32. For a more detailed development of von Bertalanffy's ideas, see "General System Theory: A New Approach to Unity of Science," *Human Biology* (December 1951), 302–61.
33. L. Thomas Hopkins, *Integration: Its Meaning and Application* (New York: Appleton-Century-Crofts, 1937), 36–49.

34. Joe Schwartz, "Why They Buy," *American Demographics* 11 (March 1989), 40–41.
35. For a discussion of the value of teaching management through these management functions, see Stephen J. Carroll and Dennis A. Gillen, "Are the Classic Management Functions Useful in Describing Managerial Work?" *Academy of Management Review* (January 1987), 38–51.

CHAPTER 3

1. For a good discussion of many factors involved in the modern meanings of social responsibility, see Frederick D. Sturdivant, and Heidi Vernon-Wortzel, *Business and Society: A Managerial Approach,* 4th ed. (Homewood, Ill.: Irwin, 1990), 3–24.
2. Keith Davis and Robert L. Blomstrom, *Business and Society: Environment and Responsibility,* 3d. ed. (New York: McGraw-Hill, 1975), 6. Also see Richard A. Rodewald, "The Corporate Social Responsibility Debate: Unanswered Questions About the Consequences of Moral Reform," *American Business Law Journal* (Fall 1987), 443–66.
3. Peter L. Berger, "New Attack on the Legitimacy of Business," *Harvard Business Review* (September/October 1981), 82–89.
4. Keith Davis, "Five Propositions for Social Responsibility," *Business Horizons* (June 1975), 19–24.
5. Stahrl W. Edmunds, "Unifying Concepts in Social Responsibility," *Academy of Management Review* (January 1977), 38–45.
6. For a worthwhile study on these social responsibility areas, see Vernon M. Buehler and Y.K. Shetty, "Managerial Response to Social Responsibility Challenge," *Academy of Management Journal* (March 1976), 66–78.
7. For extended discussion of arguments for and against social responsibility, see William C. Frederick, Keith Davis, and James E. Post, *Business and Society: Corporate Strategy, Public Policy, Ethics,* 6th ed. (New York: McGraw-Hill, 1988), 36–43.
8. T.G.P. Rogers, "Partnership with Society: The Social Responsibility of Business," *Management Decision* (1987), 76–80.
9. K.E. Aupperle, A.B. Carroll, and J.D. Hatfield, "An Empirical Examination of the Relationship Between Corporate Social Responsibility and Profitability," *Academy of Management Journal* (June 1985), 446–63; J.B. McGuire, A. Sundgren, and T. Schneeweis, "Corporate Social Responsibility and Firm Financial Performance," *Academy of Management Journal* (December 1988), 854–72; Vogel, "Ethics and Profits Don't Always Go Hand in Hand," *Los Angeles Times* (December 28, 1988), 7.
10. For Friedman's current views see "Freedom and Philanthropy: An Interview with Milton Friedman," *Business and Society Review* (Fall 1989), 11–18.
11. Neil M. Brown and Paul F. Haas, "Social Responsibility: The Uncertain Hypothesis," *MSU Business Topics* (Summer 1974), 48.
12. Milton Friedman, "Does Business Have Social Responsibility?" *Bank Administration* (April 1971), 13–14.
13. Eric J. Savitz, "The Vision Thing: Control Data Abandons It for the Bottom Line," *Barron's* (May 7, 1990), 10–11, 22; and Jagannath Dubashi, "The Do-Gooder," *Financial World* (June 27, 1989), 70–74.
14. Sandra L. Holmes, "Executive Perceptions of Corporate Social Responsibility," *Business Horizons* (June 1976), 34–40.
15. Frederick D. Sturdivant and Heidi Vernon-Wortzel, *op. cit.,* 9–11.
16. Harry A. Lipson, "Do Corporate Executives Plan for Social Responsibility?" *Business and Society Review* (Winter 1974–75), 80–81.
17. S. Prakash Sethi, "Dimensions of Corporate Social Performance: An Analytical Framework," *California Management Review* (Spring 1975), 58–64.
18. George Pilo, "Director Readiness for the Big Cleanup," *Directors & Boards* (Spring 1989), 22–27.
19. Frank H. Cassell, "The Social Cost of Doing Business," *MSU Business Topics* (Autumn 1974), 19–26.
20. Donald W. Garner, "The Cigarette Industry's Escape from Liability," *Business and Society Review,* no. 33 (Spring 1980), 22.
21. Meinolf Dierkes and Ariane Berthoin Antal, "Whither Corporate Social Reporting: Is It Time to Legislate?" *California Management Review* (Spring 1986), 106–21.
22. Raymond A. Bauer and Dan H. Fenn, Jr., "What Is a Corporate Social Audit?" *Harvard Business Review* (January/February 1973), 37–48.
23. Condensed from Jerry McAfee, "How Society Can Help Business," *Newsweek* (July 3, 1978), 15. Copyright 1978 by Newsweek, Inc. All rights reserved. Reprinted by permission.
24. Leonard J. Brooks, Jr., "Corporate Codes of Ethics," *Journal of Business Ethics* (February/March 1989), 117–29; James Srodes, "Mr. Diogenes, Call Your Office," *Financial World* Vol. 158, no. 13 (June 27, 1989).

25. Archie B. Carroll, "In Search of the Moral Manager," *Business Horizons* (March/April 1987), 7–15.
26. John F. Akers, "Ethics and Competitiveness—Putting First Things First," *Sloan Management Review* (Winter 1989), 69–71.
27. Thaddeus Tuleja, "Can the Good Guys Finish First?" *Modern Office Technology* (November 1986), 16–20.
28. "Helping Workers Helps Bottom Line," *Employee Benefit Plan Review* (July 1990).
29. Patrick E. Murphy, "Creating Ethical Corporate Structures," *Sloan Management Review* (Winter 1989), 81–87.
30. Touche Ross, *Ethics in American Business* (New York: Touche Ross & Co., January, 1988).
31. Abby Brown, "Is Ethics Good Business?" *Personnel Administrator* (February 1987), 67–74.
32. Alan L. Otten, "Ethics on the Job: Companies Alert Employees to Potential Dilemmas," *Wall Street Journal,* July 14, 1986, 25.
33. Gene R. Laczniak, "Framework for Analyzing Marketing Ethics," *Journal of Macromarketing* (Spring 1983), 7–18.
34. Karen L. Fernicola, "Take the Highroad . . . To Ethical Management: An Interview with Kenneth Blanchard," *Association Management* (May 1988), 60–66.
35. Patricia Haddock and Marilyn Manning, "Ethically Speaking," *Sky* (March 1990), 128–31.
36. Saul W. Gellerman, "Managing Ethics from the Top Down," *Sloan Management Review* (Winter 1989), 73–79.

CHAPTER 4

1. James F. Lincoln, "Intelligent Selfishness and Manufacturing," Bulletin 434 (New York: Lincoln Electric Company).
2. John F. Mee, "Management Philosophy for Professional Executives," *Business Horizons* (December 1956), 7.
3. Paul Psarouthakis, "Getting There by Goal Setting," *Supervisory Management* (June 1989), 14–15.
4. Marshall E. Dimock, *The Executive in Action* (New York: Harper & Bros., 1945), 54. For more on objectives as the central driving force of organizations, see F.G. Harmon and G. Jacobs, "Company Personality: The Heart of the Matter," *Management Review* (October 1985), 36–40.
5. Y.K. Shetty, "New Look at Corporate Goals," *California Management Review* 22 (Winter 1979), 71–79. For more recent evidence that profitability, growth, and market share continue to be the most commonly set organizational objectives see Luiz Moutinho, "Goal Setting Process and Typologies: The Case of Professional Services," *Journal of Professional Services Marketing* (1989), 83–100.
6. Thomas J. Murray, "The Unseen Corporate 'War,'" *Dun's Review* (June 1980), 110–14.
7. Peter F. Drucker, *The Practice of Management* (New York: Harper & Bros., 1954), 62–65, 126–29. For a worthwhile discussion about the constituencies that organizational objectives must serve, see Hal B. Pickle and Royce L. Abrahamson, *Small Business Management* (New York: Wiley, 1986), 211–12.
8. Theodore Levitt, "Marketing Myopia," *Harvard Business Review* (July/August 1960), 45.
9. Mee, "Management Philosophy for Professional Executives," 7.
10. Jay T. Knippen and Thad B. Green, "Directing Employee Efforts Through Goal-Setting," *Supervisory Management* (April 1989), 32–36.
11. For an interesting account of how a mutual insurance company sets financial objectives see Patrick D. Burns, "Objective Setting," *Business Quarterly* (Autumn 1989), 75–79.
12. Joseph G. Louderback and George E. Manners, Jr., "Integrating ROI and CVP," *Management Accounting* (April 1981), 33–39. For a related discussion of financial objectives, see Gordon Donaldson, "Financial Goals and Strategic Consequences," *Harvard Business Review* (May/June 1985), 56–66.
13. Adapted, by permission of the publisher, from "How to Set Company Objectives," by Charles H. Granger, *Management Review* (July 1970). © 1970 by American Management Association, Inc. All rights reserved. See also Max D. Richards, *Setting Goals and Objectives* (St. Paul, Minn.: West Publishing, 1986).
14. Granger, "How to Set Company Objectives," 7. For an interesting example of overall company objectives set for a Japanese bank see "Dai-Ichi Kangyo Aims for Balanced Expansion," *Business Japan* (October 1989), 33–34.
15. Charles H. Granger, "The Hierarchy of Objectives," *Harvard Business Review* (May/June 1964): 64–74. See also Heinz Weihrich, *Management*

Excellence: Productivity through MBO (New York: McGraw-Hill, 1985), 65–84.

16. Edwin A. Locke, Dong-Ok Chah, Scott Harrison, and Nancy Lustgarten, "Separating the Effects of Goal Specificity from Goal Level," *Organizational Behavior and Human Decision Processes* (April 1989), 270–87.

17. Alan Roberts, "Setting Export Training Objectives," *International Trade Forum* (January/February 1989), 24–27.

18. James G. March and Herbert A. Simon, *Organizations* (New York: Wiley, 1958), 191.

19. Drucker, *The Practice of Management;* also Peter Drucker, Harold Smiddy, and Ronald G. Greenwood, "Management by Objectives," *Academy of Management Review* 6 (April 1981), 225.

20. Greta Marie Dixon, "MBO: Tried-&-True Management Tool in a New Setting," *Nonprofit World* (July/August 1988), 26–28.

21. Robert L. Mathis and John H. Jackson, *Personnel: Human Resource Management* (St. Paul, Minn.: West Publishing, 1985), 353–55.

22. Jerry L. Roslund, "Evaluating Management Objectives with the Quality Loss Function," *Quality Progress* (August 1989), 45–49.

23. William H. Franklin, Jr., "Create an Atmosphere of Positive Expectations," *Administrative Management* (April 1980), 32–34.

24. William J. Kretlow and Winford E. Holland, "Implementing Management by Objectives in Research Administration," *Journal of the Society of Research Administrators* (Summer 1988), 135–41.

25. Charles H. Ford, "Manage by Decisions, Not by Objectives," *Business Horizons* (February 1980), 7–18.

26. Kretlow and Holland, "Implementing Management by Objectives in Research Administration," 135–41.

27. E.J. Seyna, "MBO: The Fad That Changed Management," *Long-Range Planning* (December 1986), 116–23.

CHAPTER 5

1. Harry Jones, *Preparing Company Plans: A Workbook for Effective Corporate Planning* (New York: Wiley, 1974), 3.

2. Robert G. Reed, "Five Challenges Multiple-Line Companies Face," *MarketFacts* (January/February 1990), 5–6.

3. Brian Burrows and Ken G.B. Blakewell, "Management Functions and Librarians," *Library Management* (1989), 2–61.

4. C.W. Roney, "The Two Purposes of Business Planning," *Managerial Planning* (November/December 1976), 1–6.

5. Harold Koontz and Cyril O'Donnell, *Management: A Systems and Contingency Analysis of Management Functions* (New York: McGraw-Hill, 1976), 130.

6. "How to Create a New Venture Business Plan," *Agency Sales Magazine* (July 1988), 39–41.

7. George C. Sawyer, "The Hazards of Goal Conflict in Strategic Planning," *Managerial Planning* (May/June 1980), 11–13, 27.

8. For an article emphasizing the importance of pinpointing planning areas see Hans Klauss and Thomas Wolter, "Total Quality at Siemans' Wurzburg Electric Motor Factory," *International Journal of Technology Management* (1990), 114–21.

9. For more detailed information on how strategic planning takes place, see Richard F. Vancil and Peter Lorange, "Strategic Planning in Diversified Companies," *Harvard Business Review* (January/February 1975), 81–90; and William R. King and David I. Cleland, "A New Method for Strategic Systems Planning," *Business Horizons* (August 1975), 55–64.

10. Excerpted, by permission of the publisher, from *1974–75 Exploratory Planning Briefs: Planning for the Future by Corporations and Agencies, Domestic and International,* by William A. Simmons, © 1975 by AMACOM, a division of American Management Associations, 10–11. All rights reserved.

11. Robert Ackelsberg and William C. Harris, "How Danish Companies Plan," *Long-Range Planning* (December 1989), 111–16.

12. Henry Mintzberg, "A New Look at the Chief Executive's Job," *Organizational Dynamics* (Winter 1973), 20–40.

13. Adapted from J.F.R. Perrin, *Focus on the Future* (London: Management Publications, 1971).

14. James M. Hardy, *Corporate Planning for Nonprofit Organizations* (New York: Association Press, 1972), 37.

15. Peter Beck, "Creating a Path to the Future," *Director* (February 1989), 64–66.

16. Milton Leontiades, "The Dimensions of Planning in Large Industrialized Organizations," *California Management Review* 22 (Summer 1980), 82–86.

17. For an interesting discussion of individuals such as consultants who are

outside a company and develop plans for business clients see Donald F. Kuratko and Arnold Cirtin, "Developing a Business Plan for Your Clients," *National Public Accountant* (January 1990), 24–27.

18. The section "Qualifications of Planners" is adapted from John Argenti, *Systematic Corporate Planning* (New York: Wiley, 1974), 126.

19. These three duties are adapted from Walter B. Schaffir, "What Have We Learned About Corporate Planning?" *Management Review* (August 1973), 19–26.

20. Frank Corcell, "How to Identify a Sick Company in Time to Help It," *Practical Accountant* (October 1989), 90–99.

21. Michael Muckian and Mary Auestad Arnold, "Manager, Appraise Thyself," *Credit Union Management* (December 1989), 26, 28.

22. Edward J. Green, *Workbook for Corporate Planning* (New York: American Management Association, 1970).

23. Z.A. Malik, "Formal Long-Range Planning and Organizational Performance" (Ph.D. diss., Rensselaer Polytechnic Institute, 1974).

24. James Brian Quinn, "Managing Strategic Change," *Sloan Management Review* 21 (Summer 1980), 3–20.

25. Kamal E. Said and Robert E. Seiler, "An Empirical Study of Long-Range Planning Systems: Strengths—Weaknesses—Outlook." *Managerial Planning* 28 (July/August 1979), 24–28.

26. George A. Steiner, "The Critical Role of Management in Long-Range Planning," *Arizona Review* (April 1966).

27. Myles L. Mace, "The President and Corporate Planning," *Harvard Business Review* (January/February 1965), 49–62.

28. Paul J. Stonich, "Formal Planning Pitfalls and How to Avoid Them," *Management Review* (June 1975), 5–6.

29. Nigel Piercy, "Diagnosing and Solving Implementation Problems in Strategic Planning," *Journal of General Management* (Autumn 1989), 19–38.

30. Peter F. Drucker, *Management: Tasks, Responsibilities, Practices* (New York: Harper & Row, 1973).

31. Bernard W. Taylor, III and K. Roscoe David, "Implementing an Action Program via Organizational Change," *Journal of Economics and Business* (Spring/Summer 1976), 203–08.

32. William H. Reynolds, "The Edsel: Faulty Execution of a Sound Marketing Plan," *Business Horizons* (Fall 1967), 39–46.

33. Luis Ma.R. Calingo, "Achieving Excellence in Strategic Planning Systems," *Advanced Management Journal* (Spring 1989), 21–23.

34. Stonich, "Formal Planning Pitfalls and How to Avoid Them," 5.

CHAPTER 6

1. Jack W. Duncan, *Decision Making and Social Issues* (Hinsdale, Ill.: Dryden Press, 1973), 1.

2. Abraham Zaleznik, "What Makes a Leader?" *Success* (June 1989), 42–45.

3. Mervin Kohn, *Dynamic Managing: Principles, Process, Practice* (Menlo Park, Calif.: Cummings, 1977), 58–62. For an interesting discussion of slowing down the decision-making process to train managers to be better decision makers see Jack Falvey, "Making Great Managers," *Small Business Reports* (February 1990), 15–18.

4. Herbert A. Simon, *The New Science of Management Decision* (New York: Harper & Bros., 1960), 5–8.

5. Anthony C. LaRusso, "Shutting It Down: A Test for Management," *Business Horizons* (July/August 1989), 59–62.

6. *The D of Research and Development* (Wilmington, Del.: DuPont, 1966), 28–29.

7. Marcia V. Wilkof, "Organizational Culture and Decision Making: A Case of Consensus Management," *R&D Management* (April 1989), 185–99.

8. Charles Wilson and Marcus Alexis, "Basic Frameworks for Decision," *Academy of Management Journal* 5 (August 1962), 151–14.

9. Robert B. Duncan, "Characteristics of Organizational Environments and Perceived Environmental Uncertainty," *Administrative Science Quarterly* 17 (September 1972), 313–27.

10. See Ernest Dale, *Management: Theory and Practice* (New York: McGraw-Hill, 1973), 548–49. This section of Dale's test is based on Erich Fromm, *Man for Himself* (New York: Holt, Rinehart & Winston, 1947), 62–117.

11. "New OCC Guidelines for Appraising Management," *Issues in Bank Regulation* (Fall 1989), 20–22.

12. For an extended discussion of this model see William B. Werther, Jr., "Productivity Through People: The Decision-Making Process," *Management Decisions* (1988), 37–41.

13. These assumptions are adapted from James G. March and Herbert A. Simon, *Organizations* (New York: Wiley, 1958), 137–38.

14. Chester I. Barnard, *The Function of the Executive* (Cambridge, Mass.: Harvard University Press, 1938).

15. For further elaboration on these factors, see Robert Tannenbaum, Irving R. Weschler, and Fred Massarik, *Leadership and Organization: A Behavioral Science Approach* (New York: McGraw-Hill, 1961), 277–78.

16. For more discussion of these factors, see F.A. Shull, Jr., A.L. Delbecq, and L.L. Cummings, *Organizational Decision Making* (New York: McGraw-Hill, 1970).

17. For worthwhile discussion of forecasting and evaluating the outcomes of alternatives see J.R.C. Wensley, "Effective Decision Aids in Marketing," *European Journal of Marketing* (1989), 70–79.

18. F.E. Kast and J.E. Rosenzweig, *Organization and Management: A Systems Approach* (New York: McGraw-Hill, 1970), 385.

19. Steven C. Harper, "What Separates Executives from Managers," *Business Horizons* (September/October 1988), 13–19; Russ Holloman, "The Light and Dark Sides of Decision Making," *Supervisory Management* (December 1989), 33–34.

20. The scope of this text does not permit elaboration on these three decision-making tools. However, for an excellent discussion on how they are used in decision making, see Richard M. Hodgetts, *Management: Theory, Process and Practice* (Philadelphia: Saunders, 1975), 254–66.

21. Richard C. Mosier, "Expected Value: Applying Research to Uncertainty," *Appraisal Journal* (July 1989), 293–96.

22. Peter Boys, "Answers Grow on Decision Trees," *Accountancy* (January 1990), 86–89; and Olen L. Greer, "A Decision-Tree Approach to the Design and Implementation of Accounting and Information Systems for Small Businesses," *Journal of Small Business Management* (January 1989), 8–16.

23. John F. Magee, "Decision Trees for Decision Making," *Harvard Business Review* (July/August 1964).

CHAPTER 7

1. Donald F. Harvey, *Strategic Management* (Columbus, Ohio: Merrill, 1982), 19.

2. Andrall E. Pearson, "Six Basics for General Managers," *Harvard Business Review* (July/August 1989), 94–101.

3. Charles R. Greer, "Counter-Cyclical Hiring as a Staffing Strategy for Managerial and Professional Personnel: Some Considerations and Issues," *Academy of Management Review* 9 (April 1984), 324–30.

4. Yedzi M. Godiwalla, Wayne A. Meinhart, and William D. Warde, "How CEOs Form Corporate Strategy," *Management World* (May 1981), 28–29, 44.

5. Richard B. Robinson, Jr., and John A. Pearce II, "Research Thrusts in Small Firm Strategic Planning," *Academy of Management Review* 9 (January 1984), 128–37.

6. George Sawyer, "Elements of Strategy," *Managerial Planning* (May/June 1981), 3–59.

7. This section is based on Samuel C. Certo and J. Paul Peter, *Strategic Management: Concepts and Applications* (New York: McGraw-Hill, 1991), 3–27.

8. Samuel C. Certo and J. Paul Peter, *Strategic Management: Concepts and Applications* (New York: Random House, 1988).

9. Philip S. Thomas, "Environment Analysis for Corporate Planning," *Business Horizons* (October 1974), 27–38.

10. For more information about several of these examples, see Abraham Katz, "Evaluating the Environment: Economic and Technological Factors," in *Handbook of Business Strategy*, ed. William D. Guth (Boston: Warren, Gorham & Lamont, 1985), 2–9.

11. This section is based on William F. Glueck and Lawrence R. Jauch, *Business Policy and Strategic Management* (New York: McGraw-Hill, 1984), 99–110.

12. D. Stanley Eitzen, *Social Structure and Social Problems in America* (Boston: Allyn & Bacon, 1974), 12–14.

13. Bruce Henderson, "The Origin of Strategy," *Harvard Business Review* (November/December 1989), 139–43.

14. R.S. Wilson, "Managing in the Competitive Environment," *Long-Range Planning* 17 (1984), 50–63.

15. Peter Wright, "MNC—Third World Business Unit Performance: Application of Strategic Elements," *Strategic Management Journal* 5 (1984), 231–40.

16. Discussion in this section is based primarily on Thomas H. Naylor and Kristin Neva, "Design of a Strategic Planning Process," *Managerial Planning* (January/February 1980), 2–7; Donald W. Mitchell, "Pursuing Strategic Potential," *Managerial Planning* (May/June 1980), 6–10; Benton E. Gup, "Begin Strategic Planning by Asking Three Questions," *Managerial*

Planning (November/December 1979); 28–31, 35; L.V. Gerstner, Jr., "Can Strategic Planning Pay Off?" *Business Horizons* 15 (1972), 5–16.

17. This section is based on Arthur A. Thompson and A.J. Strickland III, *Strategy Formulation and Implementation* (Plano, Tex.: Business Publications, 1983), 277–91.

18. For more extended discussion of business portfolio analysis, see Certo and Peter, *Strategic Management,* 102–11.

19. Bruce D. Henderson, *Henderson on Corporate Strategy* (Cambridge, Mass.: ABT Books, 1979).

20. Philip Kotler, *Marketing Management: Analysis, Planning and Control,* 4th ed. (Englewood Cliffs, N.J.: Prentice-Hall, 1980), 76.

21. Harold W. Fox, "The Frontiers of Strategic Planning: Intuition or Formal Models?" *Management Review* (April 1981), 8–14.

22. This discussion of Porter's model is based on chapters 1 and 2 of Porter's *Competitive Strategy* (New York: The Free Press, 1980), and chapter 1 of Porter's *Competitive Advantage: Creating and Sustaining Superior Performance* (New York: The Free Press, 1985).

23. Ian C. MacMillan, Donald C. Hambrick, and Diana L. Day, "The Product Portfolio and Profitability—A PIMS-Based Analysis of Industrial-Product Businesses," *Academy of Management Journal* (December 1982), 733–55.

24. Bill Saporito, "Black & Decker's Gamble on Globalization," *Fortune.* May 14, 1984, 40–48.

25. Doron P. Levin, "Westinghouse's New Chief Aims to Push New Lines, Revitalize Traditional Ones," *Wall Street Journal.* November 28, 1983, 10.

26. Thomas V. Bonoma, "Making Your Marketing Strategy Work," *Harvard Business Review* (March/April 1984), 69–76.

27. For a good discussion of the importance of monitoring the progress of the strategic planning process, see William B. Carper and Terry A. Bresnick, "Strategic Planning Conferences," *Business Horizons* (September/October 1989), 34–40.

28. For a detailed discussion of the characteristics of strategic and tactical planning, see George A. Steiner, *Top Management Planning* (Toronto, Canada: Collier-Macmillan, 1969), 37–39.

29. Russell L. Ackoff, *A Concept of Corporate Planning* (New York: Wiley, 1970), 4.

30. G.E. Tibbits, "Small Business Management: A Normative Approach," *MSU Business Topics* (Autumn 1979), 5–12.

31. "The New Breed of Strategic Planner," *Business Week,* September 17, 1984, 62–67.

CHAPTER 8

1. Charles B. Ames, "Straight Talk from the New CEO" *Harvard Business Review* (November/December 1989), 132–38.

2. Stewart Thompson, "What Planning Involves," American Management Association Research Study no. 54, 1962.

3. Fremont E. Kast and James E. Rosenzweig, *Organization and Management: A Systems Approach* (New York: McGraw-Hill, 1970), 443–49.

4. For discussion on expanding this list of four characteristics to thirteen, see P. LeBreton and D.A. Henning, *Planning Theory* (Englewood Cliffs, N.J.: Prentice-Hall, 1961), 320–44. These authors list the dimensions of a plan as (1) complexity, (2) significance, (3) comprehensiveness, (4) time, (5) specificity, (6) completeness, (7) flexibility, (8) frequency, (9) formality, (10) confidential nature, (11) authorization, (12) ease of implementation, and (13) ease of control.

5. For a discussion of this rule and its difficult enforcement see Sherry C. Hammond, David A. DeCenzo, and Mollie H. Bowers, "How One Company Went Smokeless," *Harvard Business Review* (November/December 1987), 44–45.

6. From "Seize the Future—Make Top Trends Pay Off Now," *Success* (March 1990), 39–45.

7. J. Fred Weston and Eugene F. Brigham, *Essentials of Managerial Finance* (New York: Holt, Rinehart & Winston, 1971), 107; Mark M. Klein, "Questions to Ask Before You Sharpen Your Budget Knife," *Bottomline* (March 1990), 32–37; Pierre Filiatrault and Jean-Charles Chebat, "How Service Firms Set Their Marketing Budgets," *Industrial Marketing Management* (February 1990), 63–67.

8. Kjell A. Ringbakk, "Why Planning Fails," *European Business* (July 1970).

9. For a good discussion on involving people in the planning process see Margaret M. Lucas, "Business Plan Is the Key to Agency Success," *National Underwriter* 94 (March 5, 1990), 15, 17.

10. Walt Yesberg, "Get a Grip on Building Costs," *ABA Banking Journal* 82 (March 1990), 90, 92; Robert Bowman, "Key Logistics Issues in Site Selection," *Distribution* 88 (December 1989), 56–57.

11. Dale S. Beach, *Personnel: The Management of People at Work* (New York: Macmillan, 1975), 220.
12. Henri Fayol, *General and Industrial Management* (New York: Pitman, 1949).
13. William C. House, "Environmental Analysis: Key to More Effective Dynamic Planning," *Managerial Planning* (January/February 1977): 25–29.
14. Olfa Hemler, "The Uses of Delphi Techniques in Problems of Educational Innovations," no. 3499, RAND Corporation, December 1966.
15. For an interesting illustration of how the delphi method works, see Yeong Wee Yong, Kau Ah Keng, and Tan Leng Leng, "A Delphi Forecast for the Singapore Tourism Industry," *International Marketing Review* 6 (1989), 35–46.
16. James E. Cox, Jr. "Approaches for Improving Salespersons' Forecasts," *Industrial Marketing Management* 18 (November 1989), 307–11.
17. N. Carroll Mohn, "Forecasting Sales with Trend Models—Coca-Cola's Experience," *Journal of Business Forecasting* 8 (Fall 1989), 6–8.
18. For elaboration on these methods, see George A. Steiner, *Top Management Planning* (London: Collier-Macmillan, 1969), 223–27.
19. Gilbert Frisbie and Vincent A. Mabert, "Crystal Ball vs. System: The Forecasting Dilemma," *Business Horizons* 24 (September/October 1981): 72–76.
20. Willard Fazar, "The Origin of PERT," *The Controller* (December 1962).
21. Harold L. Wattel, *Network Scheduling and Control Systems CAP/PERT* (Hempstead, N.Y.: Hofstra University, 1964); see also Khaled A. Bu-Bushait, "The Application of Project Management Techniques to Construction and Research and Development Projects," *Project Management Journal* 20 (June 1989), 17–22.
22. R.J. Schonberger, "Custom-Tailored PERT/CPM Systems," *Business Horizons* 15 (1972): 64–66.
23. Avraham Shtub, "The Integration of CPM and Material Management in Project Management," *Construction Management and Economics* 6 (Winter 1988), 261–72.
24. For extended discussion of these steps see Edward K. Shelmerdine, "Planning for Project Management," *Journal of Systems Management* 40 (January 1989), 16–20.

CHAPTER 9

1. Douglas S. Sherwin, "Management of Objectives," *Harvard Business Review* (May/June 1976), 149–60.
2. Lloyd Sandelands and Robert Drazin, "On the Language of Organization Theory," *Organizational Studies* 10 (1989), 457–77.
3. Henri Fayol, *General and Industrial Management* (London: Sir Isaac Pitman and Sons, 1949), 53–54.
4. Burt K. Scanlan, "Managerial Leadership in Perspective: Getting Back to Basics," *Personnel Journal* (March 1979), 168–70.
5. Saul W. Gellerman, "In Organizations, as in Architecture, Form Follows Function," *Organizational Dynamics* 18 (Winter 1990), 57–68.
6. Max Weber, *Theory of Social and Economic Organization,* trans. and ed. A.M. Henderson and Talcott Parsons (London: Oxford University Press, 1947); Stanley Vanagunas, "Max Weber's Authority Models and the Theory of X-Inefficiency: The Economic Sociologist's Analysis Adds More Structure to Leibenstein's Critique of Rationality," *American Journal of Economics and Sociology* 48 (October 1989), 393–400; Foad Derakhshan and Kamal Fatehi, "Bureaucracy as a Leadership Substitute: A Review of History," *Leadership and Organization Development Journal* 6 (1985), 13–16.
7. Richard Bendix, *Max Weber: An Intellectual Portrait* (New York: Doubleday, 1960).
8. Charles Perrow, "The Short and Glorious History of Organizational Theory," *Organizational Dynamics* (Summer 1973), 2–15.
9. George H. Rice, Jr., "A Set of Organizational Models," *Human Resource Management* 19 (Summer 1980), 21.
10. Lyndall Urwick, *Notes on the Theory of Organization* (New York: American Management Association, 1952).
11. For an interesting discussion of a nontraditional organization structure, see John E. Tropman, "The Organizational Circle: A New Approach to Drawing an Organizational Chart," *Administration in Social Work* 13 (1989), 35–44.
12. Sally Helgesen, *The Female Advantage: Women's Ways of Leadership* (New York: Doubleday/Currency, 1990).
13. Tom Peters, "The Best New Managers Will Listen, Motivate, Support," *Working Woman* (September 1990), 142–43, 216–17.

14. Raef T. Hussein, "Informal Groups, Leadership, and Productivity," *Leadership and Organization Development Journal* 10 (1989), 9–16.
15. Gerald C. Werner, "Organizing for Innovation: Does a Product Group Structure Inhibit Technological Developments?" *Management Review* (March 1981), 47–51; for an article arguing in favor of having organizations designed by function, see Jack Cohen, "Managing the Managers," *Supermarket Business* 44 (September 1989), 16, 244.
16. Roderick E. White and Thomas A. Poynter, "Organizing for Worldwide Advantage," *Business Quarterly* 54 (Summer 1989), 84–89.
17. Y.K. Shetty and Howard M. Carlisle, "A Contingency Model of Organization Design," *California Management Review* 15 (1972), 38–45.
18. Adam Smith, *The Wealth of Nations* (New York: Random House, 1937).
19. C.R. Walker and R.H. Guest, *The Man on the Assembly Line* (Cambridge, Mass.: Harvard University Press, 1952). For an excellent example of how technology can affect division of labor see John P. Walsh, "Technological Change and the Division of Labor: The Case of Retail Meatcutters," *Work and Occupations* 16 (May 1989), 165–83.
20. J. Mooney, "The Principles of Organization," in *Ideas and Issues in Public Administration,* ed. D. Waldo (New York: McGraw-Hill, 1953), 86.
21. Bruce D. Sanders, "Making Work Groups Work," *Computerworld* 24 (March 5, 1990), 85–89.
22. George D. Greenberg, "The Coordinating Roles of Management," *Midwest Review of Public Administration* 10 (1976), 66–76.
23. Henry L. Metcalf and Lyndall F. Urwich, eds., *Dynamic Administration: The Collected Papers of Mary Parker Follett* (New York: Harper & Bros., 1942), 297–99; James F. Wolf, "The Legacy of Mary Parker Follett," *Bureaucrat* (Winter 1988–89), 53–57.
24. Leon McKenzie, "Supervision: Learning from Experience," *Health Care Supervisor* 8 (January 1990), 1–11.
25. Gerald G. Fisch, "Stretching the Span of Management," *Harvard Business Review,* no. 5 (1963), 74–85.
26. Harold Koontz, "Making Theory Operational: The Span of Management," *Journal of Management Studies* (October 1966), 229–43; see also John S. McClenahen, "Managing More People in the '90s," *Industry Week* 238 (March 1989), 30–38.
27. V.A. Graicunas, "Relationships in Organization," *Bulletin of International Management Institute* (March 1933), 183–87. For more on the life of Graicunas, see Arthur C. Bedeian, "Vytautas Andrius Graicunas: A Biographical Note," *Academy of Management Journal* 17 (June 1974), 347–49.
28. L.F. Urwick, "V.A. Graicunas and the Span of Control," *Academy of Management Journal* 17 (June 1974), 349–54.
29. Philip R. Nienstedt, "Effectively Downsizing Management Structures," *Human Resource Planning* 12 (1989), 155–65.
30. Robin Bellis-Jones and Max Hand, "Improving Managerial Spans of Control," *Management Accounting* 67 (October 1989), 20–21.
31. Cass Bettinger, "The Nine Principles of War," *Bank Marketing* 21 (December 1989), 32–34; Charles A. Mowll, "Successful Management Based on Key Principles," *Healthcare Financial Management* 43 (June 1989), 122, 124.
32. Henri Fayol, *General and Industrial Administration* (Belmont, Calif.: Pitman, 1949).

CHAPTER 10

1. Andre Nelson, "Have I the Right Stuff to Be a Supervisor?" *Supervision* 51 (January 1990), 10–12.
2. Stephen X. Doyle and Benson P. Shapiro, "What Counts Most in Motivating Your Sales Force?" *Harvard Business Review* (May/June 1980), 133–40. See also G.F. Scollard, "Dynamic Descriptions: Job Descriptions Should Work for You," *Management World* (May 1985), 34–35.
3. Bruce Shawkey, "Job Descriptions," *Credit Union Executive* 29 (Winter 1989/1990), 20–23.
4. Robert J. Theirauf, Robert C. Klekamp, and Daniel W. Geeding, *Management Principles and Practices: A Contingency and Questionnaire Approach* (New York: Wiley, 1977), 334.
5. Deborah S. Kezsbom, "Managing the Chaos: Conflict Among Project Teams," *AACE Transactions* (1989), A.4.1–A.4.8.
6. Robert D. Melcher, "Roles and Relationships: Clarifying the Manager's Job," *Personnel* 44 (May/June 1967), 34–41.
7. For more information on management responsibility guides, see Melcher, "Roles and Relationships."
8. This section is based primarily on John H. Zenger, "Responsible Behavior: Stamp of the Effective Manager," *Supervisory Management* (July 1976), 18–24.

9. Jack J. Phillips, "Authority: It Just Doesn't Come with Your Job," *Management Solutions* 31 (August 1986), 35–37.

10. Max Weber, "The Three Types of Legitimate Rule," trans. Hans Gerth, *Berkeley Journal of Sociology* 4 (1953), 1–11; for a current illustration of this concept see Gail DeGeorge, "Yo, Ho, Ho, and a Battle for Bacardi," *Business Week*. April 16, 1990, 47–48.

11. John Gardner, "The Anti-Leadership Vaccine," *Carnegie Foundation Annual Report*, 1965.

12. Chester I. Barnard, *The Functions of the Executive* (Cambridge, Mass.: Harvard University Press, 1938).

13. Patti Wolf, Gerald Grimes, and John Dayani, "Getting the Most out of Staff Functions," *Small Business Reports* 14 (October 1989), 68–70.

14. Harold Stieglitz, "On Concepts of Corporate Structure," *Conference Board Record* 11 (February 1974), 7–13.

15. Wendell L. French, *The Personnel Management Process: Human Resource Administration and Development* (Boston: Houghton Mifflin, 1987), 66–68.

16. Derek Sheane, "When and How to Intervene in Conflict," *Personnel Management* (November 1979), 32–36; John M. Ivancevich and Michael T. Matteson, "Intergroup Behavior and Conflict," in their *Organizational Behavior and Management* (Plano, Tex.: Business Publications, 1987), 305–45.

17. Robert Albanese, *Management* (Cincinnati: South-Western Publishing, 1988), 313. For an excellent discussion of the role of accountability and organization structure see Elliott Jacques, "In Praise of Hierarchy," *Harvard Business Review* 68 (January/February 1990), 127–133.

18. For an excellent review of the punishment literature, see Henry P. Sims, Jr., "Further Thoughts on Punishment in Organizations," *Academy of Management Review* 5 (January 1980), 133.

19. "How Ylvisaker Makes 'Produce or Else' Work," *Business Week*. October 27, 1973, 112.

20. William H. Newman and E. Kirby Warren, *The Process of Management: Concepts, Behavior, and Practice,* 4th ed. (Englewood Cliffs, N.J.: Prentice-Hall, 1977), 39–40; these steps are also discussed in Jay T. Knippen and Thad B. Green, "Delegation," *Supervision* 51 (March 1990), 7–9, 17.

21. Robert B. Nelson, "Mastering Delegation," *Executive Excellence* 7 (January 1990), 13–14.

22. Jimmy Calano and Jeff Salzman, "How Delegation Can Lead Your Team to Victory," *Working Woman* (August 1989), 86–87, 95.

23. Harold Koontz, Cyril O'Donnell, and Heinz Weihrich, *Essentials of Management,* 8th ed. (New York: McGraw-Hill, 1986), 231–33.

24. H. Gilman, "J.C. Penney Decentralizes Its Purchasing," *Wall Street Journal*. May 8, 1986, 6.

25. Ernest Dale, "Centralization versus Decentralization," *Advanced Management Journal* (June 1955), 11–16.

26. Donald O. Harper, "Project Management as a Control and Planning Tool in the Decentralized Company," *Management Accounting* (November 1968), 29–33.

27. For further discussion on positive and negative centralization and decentralization, see Terence R. Mitchell and James R. Larson, Jr., *People in Organizations* (New York: McGraw-Hill, 1987), 49–50.

28. Information for this section is mainly from John G. Staiger, "What Cannot Be Decentralized," *Management Record* 25 (January 1963), 19–21. At the time the article was written, Staiger was vice president of administration, North American Operations, Massey-Ferguson, Limited.

29. Staiger, "What Cannot Be Decentralized," 19.

30. Staiger, "What Cannot Be Decentralized," 21.

31. Staiger, "What Cannot Be Decentralized," 21.

CHAPTER 11

1. Bruce Shawkey, "Job Descriptions," *Credit Union Executive* 29 (Winter 1989/1990), 20–23; Howard D. Feldman, "Why Are Similar Managerial Jobs So Different?" *Review of Business* 11 (Winter 1989), 15–22.

2. "Job Analysis," *Bureau of Intergovernmental Personnel Programs* (December 1973), 135–52.

3. Gundars E. Kaupins, "Lies, Damn Lies, and Job Evaluations," *Personnel* 66 (November 1989), 62–65.

4. Arch Patton, "The Coming Scramble for Executive Talent," *Harvard Business Review* (May/June 1967), 155–71.

5. Thomas J. Murray, "The Coming Glut in Executives," *Dun's Review* (May 1977), 64. An even more recent article pointing out this trend is "Slackening in Executive Demand," *Personnel Management* 17 (September 1985), 74.

6. Fred K. Foulkes, "How Top Nonunion Companies Manage Employees," *Harvard Business Review* (September/October 1981), 90.

7. John Perham, "Management Succession: A Hard Game to Play," *Dun's Review* (April 1981), 54–55, 58.

8. Walter S. Wikstrom, "Developing Managerial Competence: Concepts, Emerging Practices," *Studies in Personnel Policy,* no. 189, National Industrial Conference Board (1964), 95–105.

9. Patricia Panchak, "Resourceful Software Boosts HR Efficiency," *Modern Office Technology* 35 (April 1990), 76–80.

10. Ray H. Hodges, "Developing an Effective Affirmative Action Program," *Journal of Intergroup Relations* 5 (November 1976), 13. For a more philosophical argument supporting affirmative action see Leo Goarke, "Affirmative Action as a Form of Restitution," *Journal of Business Ethics* 9 (March 1990), 207–13.

11. R. Roosevelt Thomas, Jr., "From Affirmative Action to Affirming Diversity," *Harvard Business Review* 68 (March/April, 1990), 107–17.

12. For more discussion on the stages of the selection process, see David J. Cherrington, *Personnel Management: The Management of Human Resources* (Dubuque, Iowa: Wm. C. Brown Publishers, 1987), 186–231.

13. This section is based on Andrew F. Sikula, *Personnel Administration and Human Resource Management* (New York: Wiley, 1976), 188–90.

14. For information on various tests available, see O.K. Buros, ed., *The 8th Mental Measurements Yearbook* (Highland Park, N.J.: Gryphon Press, 1978).

15. John W. Jones, Philip Ash, Catalina Soto, and William Terris, "Preemployment Testing: An Occasion for Invasion?" *Security Management* 34 (April 1990), 68–72.

16. Robin Inwald, "Preemployment Testing: Those Seven Deadly Sins," *Security Management* 34 (April 1990), 73–76.

17. D.W. Bray and D.L. Grant, "The Assessment Center in the Measurement of Potential for Business Management," *Psychological Monographs* 80, no. 17 (1966), 1–27.

18. Susan O. Hendricks and Susan E. Ogborn, "Supervisory and Managerial Assessment Centers in Health Care," *Health Care Supervisor* 8 (April 1990), 65–75.

19. Barry M. Cohen, "Assessment Centers," *Supervisory Management* (June 1975), 30. See also T.J. Hanson and J.C. Balestreri-Sepro, "An Alternative to Interviews: Pre-employment Assessment Process," *Personnel Journal* (June 1985), 114.

20. For information about strengths and weaknesses of assessment centers, see C.W. Millard and Sheldon Pinsky, "Assessing the Assessment Center," *Personnel Administrator* (May 1980), 85–88.

21. Ann Howard, "An Assessment of Assessment Centers," *Academy of Management Journal* 17 (March 1974), 117.

22. William Umiker and Thomas Conlin, "Assessing the Need for Supervisory Training: Use of Performance Appraisals," *Health Care Supervisor* 8 (January 1990), 40–45.

23. Bass and Vaughn, *Training in Industry*.

24. David Sutton, "Further Thoughts on Action Learning," *Journal of European Industrial Training* 13 (1989), 32–35.

25. For more information on training techniques, see Cherrington, *Personnel Management,* 304–36.

26. Samuel C. Certo, "The Experiential Exercise Situation: A Comment on Instructional Role and Pedagogy Evaluation," *Academy of Management Review* (July 1976), 113–16.

27. For more information on instructional roles in various situations, see Bernard Keys, "The Management of Learning Grid for Management Development," *Academy of Management Review* (April 1977), 289–97.

28. William Keenan, Jr., "Are You Overspending on Training?" *Sales and Marketing Management* 142 (January 1990), 56–60.

29. For more information on the performance appraisal process, see Robert L. Mathis and John H. Jackson, "Appraisal of Human Resources," in their *Personnel: Human Resource Management* (St. Paul, Minn.: West Publishing, 1985), 337–66.

30. Douglas McGregor, "An Uneasy Look at Performance Appraisal," *Harvard Business Review* (September/October 1972), 133–34. For insights on how performance appraisal can motivate employees see Kenneth M. Dawson and Sheryl N. Dawson, "How to Motivate Your Employees," *HR Magazine* 35 (April 1990), 78–80.

31. Harold Koontz, "Making Managerial Appraisal Effective," *California Management Review* 15 (Winter 1972), 46–55.

32. Linda J. Segall, "KISS Appraisal Woes Goodbye," *Supervisory Management* 34 (December 1989), 23–28.

33. William J. Birch, "Performance Appraisal: One Company's Experience," *Personnel Journal* (June 1981), 456–60.

34. George A. Rider, "Performance Review: A Mixed Bag," *Harvard Business Review* (July/August 1973), 61–67; Robert Loo, "Quality Performance Appraisals," *Canadian Manager* 14 (December 1989), 24–26.

35. John D. Colby and Ronald L. Wallace, "The Art of Leveling with Subordinates About Their Performance," *Supervisory Management* (December 1975), 26–29.

CHAPTER 12

1. Rosabeth Moss Kanter, "The New Managerial Work," *Harvard Business Review* 67 (November/December 1989), 85–92.

2. Bridgford Hunt, "Managers of Change: Why They Are in Demand," *S.A.M. Advanced Management Journal* (Winter 1980), 40–44.

3. John S. Morgan, *Managing Change: The Strategies of Making Change Work for You* (New York: McGraw-Hill, 1972), 99.

4. Bart Nooteboom, "Paradox, Identity, and Change in Management," *Human Systems Management* 8 (1989), 291–300.

5. For an interesting discussion of how to handle employee stress that is related to changing a work facility, see: Allen Elkin, "Stress: The FM's Survival Guide," *Facilities Design and Management* 8 (February 1989), 62–65.

6. For a timely discussion of the value of outside change agents see: Robert O. Metzger, "With So Many Consultants, Why Aren't We Better?" *Journal of Management Consulting* 5 (1989), 9–13.

7. Myron Tribus, "Changing the Corporate Culture—A Roadmap for the Change Agent," *Human Systems Management* 8 (1989), 11–22.

8. William C. Giegold and R.J. Craig, "Whatever Happened to OD?" *Industrial Management* (January/February 1976), 9–12.

9. W.F. Glueck, "Organization Change in Business and Government," *Academy of Management Journal* 12 (1969), 440–41.

10. Saul W. Gellerman, "In Organizations, as in Architecture, Form Follows Function," *Organizational Dynamics* 18 (Winter 1990), 57–68.

11. C.J. Middleton, "How to Set Up a Project Organization," *Harvard Business Review* (March/April 1967), 73.

12. George J. Chambers, "The Individual in a Matrix Organization," *Project Management Journal* 20 (December 1989), 37–42, 50.

13. John F. Mee, "Matrix Organization," *Business Horizons* (Summer 1964).

14. Middleton, "How to Set Up a Project Organization," 74; Deborah S. Kezsbom, "Managing the Chaos: Conflict Among Project Teams," *AACE Transactions* (1989), A.4.1–A.4.8.

15. Harvey F. Kolodny, "Managing in a Matrix," *Business Horizons* 24 (March/April 1981), 17–24.

16. John C. Alpin and Duane E. Thompson, "Successful Organizational Change," *Business Horizons* (August 1974), 61–66.

17. This section is based primarily on R. Blake, J. Mouton, and L. Greiner, "Breakthrough in Organization Development," *Harvard Business Review* (November/December 1964), 133–55. For a discussion of other methods for implementing OD change, see William F. Glueck, *Organization Planning and Development* (New York: American Management Association, 1971).

18. Blake, Mouton, and Greiner, "Breakthrough in Organization Development."

19. L.G. Malouf, "Managerial Grid Evaluated," *Training Development Journal* 20 (1966), 6–15.

20. W.J. Heisler, "Patterns of OD in Practice," *Business Horizons* (February 1975), 77–84.

21. Martin G. Evans, "Failures in OD Programs—What Went Wrong," *Business Horizons* (April 1974), 18–22.

22. David Coghlan, "OD Interventions in Catholic Religious Orders," *Journal of Managerial Psychology* 4 (1989), 4–6.

23. Paul A. Iles and Thomas Johnston, "Searching for Excellence in Second-Hand Clothes?: A Note," *Personnel Review* 18 (1989), 32–35; Ewa Maslyk-Musial, "Organization Development in Poland: Stages of Growth," *Public Administration Quarterly* 13 (Summer 1989), 196–214; Eric Frank, "Management and Organization Development in Hungary," *Journal of European Industrial Training* 13 (1989), i–ii.

24. For an interesting discussion of resistance to change from inherited staff see: Margaret Russell, "Records Management Program-Directing: Inherited Staff," *ARMA Records Management Quarterly* 24 (January 1990), 18–22.

25. This strategy for minimizing the resistance to change is based on "How Companies Overcome Resistance to Change," *Management Review* (November 1972), 17–25; see also: Hank Williams, "Learning to Manage Change," *Industrial and Commercial Training* 21 (May/June 1989), 17–20.

26. John P. Kotter and Leonard A. Schlesinger, "Choosing Strategies for Change," *Harvard Business Review* (March/April 1979), 106–13.

27. "How Companies Overcome Resistance," 25.

28. Arnold S. Judson, *A Manager's Guide to Making Changes* (New York: Wiley, 1966), 118.

29. Kurt Lewin, "Frontiers in Group Dynamics: Concept, Method, and Reality of Social Sciences—Social Equilibria and Social Change," *Human Relations* 1 (June 1947), 5–14; Ivan Louis Bare, "The Three Phases of Change," *Quality Progress* 19 (November 1986), 47–49.

30. Edgar H. Schein, "Management Development as a Process of Influence," *Industrial Management Review* (May 1961), 59–76. For a more current discussion of the phases of change see: Dottie Perlman and George J. Takacs, "The 10 Stages of Change," *Nursing Management* 21 (April 1990), 33–38.

31. Newton Margulies and John Wallace, *Organizational Change: Techniques and Applications* (Chicago: Scott, Foresman, 1973), 14.

32. Larry E. Greiner, "Patterns of Organizational Change," *Harvard Business Review* (May/June 1967), 119–30.

33. Edgar C. Williams, "Changing Systems and Behavior: People's Perspectives on Prospective Changes," *Business Horizons* 12 (August 1969), 53.

34. Hans Selye, *The Stress of Life* (New York: McGraw-Hill, 1956).

35. James C. Quick and Jonathan D. Quick, *Organizational Stress and Preventive Management* (New York: McGraw-Hill, 1984).

36. James D. Bodzinski, Robert F. Scherer, and Karen A. Goyer, "Workplace Stress," *Personnel Administrator* 34 (July 1989), 76–80; Richard M. Steers, *Introduction to Organizational Behavior* (Glenview, Ill.: Scott, Foresman, 1981), 340–41.

37. Corinne M. Smereka, "Outwitting, Controlling Stress for a Healthier Lifestyle," *Healthcare Financial Management* 44 (March 1990), 70–75.

38. For more discussion of this area, see Keith Davis and John W. Newstrom, *Human Behavior at Work: Organizational Behavior* (New York: McGraw-Hill, 1985), 469–70.

39. J. Clifton Williams, *Human Behavior in Organizations* (Cincinnati: South-Western, 1982), 212–13.

40. John M. Ivancevich and Michael T. Matteson, "Organizations and Coronary Heart Disease: The Stress Connection," *Management Review* 67 (October 1978), 14–19.

41. Fred Luthans, *Organizational Behavior* (New York: McGraw-Hill, 1985), 146–48.

42. Donald B. Miller, "Career Planning and Management in Organizations," *S.A.M. Advanced Management Journal* 43 (Spring 1978), 33–43.

CHAPTER 13

1. Derek Torrington and Jane Weightman, "Middle Management Work," *Journal of General Management* 13 (Winter 1987), 74–89.

2. See the following articles for insights into and examples of how communication is related to the performance of management activities: Larry Penley and Brian Hawkins, "Studying Interpersonal Communication in Organizations: A Leadership Application," *Academy of Management Journal* (June 1985), 309–26; Richard C. Huseman, Elmore R. Alexander III, and Russell W. Driver, "Planning for Organizational Change: The Role of Communication," *Managerial Planning* 28 (May/June 1980), 32–36; H.M. Shatshat and Bong-Gon P. Shin, "Organizational Communication—A Key to Successful Strategic Planning," *Managerial Planning* 30 (September/October 1981), 37–40.

3. Bernard Reilly and Joseph DiAngelo, Jr., "Communication: A Cultural System of Meaning and Value," *Human Relations* 43 (February 1990), 129–40.

4. Stephen C. Harper, "Business Education: A View from the Top," *Business Forum* (Summer 1987), 24–27.

5. This section is based on the following classic article on interpersonal communication: Wilbur Schramm, "How Communication Works," *The Process and Effects of Mass Communication,* ed. Wilbur Schramm (Urbana: University of Illinois Press, 1954), 3–10.

6. David S. Brown, "Barriers to Successful Communication: Part I, Macrobarriers," *Management Review* (December 1975), 24–29.

7. James K. Weekly and Raj Aggarwal, *International Business: Operating in the Global Economy* (New York: Dryden Press, 1987).

8. Davis S. Brown, "Barriers to Successful Communication: Part II, Microbarriers," *Management Review* (January 1976), 15–21.

9. Sally Bulkley Pancrazio and James J. Pancrazio, "Better Communication for Managers," *Supervisory Management* (June 1981), 31–37.

10. Gene E. Burton, "Barriers to Effective Communication," *Management World* (March 1977), 4–8.

11. John S. Fielden, "Why Can't Managers Communicate? *Business* 39 (January/February/March 1989), 41–44.
12. Lydia Strong, "Do You Know How to Listen?" in *Effective Communications on the Job,* ed. M. Joseph Dooher and Vivienne Marquis (New York: American Management Association, 1956), 28.
13. John R. White, "Some Thoughts on Lexicon and Syntax," *Appraisal Journal* 57 (July 1989), 417–21.
14. Robert E. Callahan, C. Patrick Fleenor, and Harry R. Knudson, *Understanding Organizational Behavior: A Managerial Viewpoint* (Columbus, Ohio: Charles E. Merrill, 1986).
15. For more on nonverbal issues, see I.T. Sheppard, "Silent Signals," *Supervisory Management* (March 1986), 31–33; S. Strecker, "Opening Moves and Winning Plays: An Interview with Ken Delmar," *Executive Female* (January/February 1985), 24–48.
16. Robert S. Goyer, "Interpersonal Communication and Human Interaction: A Behavioral View," paper presented at the 138th annual meeting of the American Association for the Advancement of Science, 1971. For an article that complements this orientation toward feedback, see R. Abrams, "Do You Get What You Ask For?" *Supervisory Management* (April 1986), 32–34.
17. Verne Burnett, "Management's Tower of Babel," *Management Review* (June 1961), 4–11.
18. Reprinted, by permission of the publisher, from *Management Review* (October 1955). © 1955 American Management Association, Inc. All rights reserved.
19. Albert Mehrabian, "Communication Without Words," *Psychology Today* (September 1968), 53–55.
20. For a practical article emphasizing the role of gestures in communication, see S.D. Gladis, "Notes Are Not Enough," *Training and Development Journal* (August 1985), 35–38.
21. Nicole Steckler and Robert Rosenthal, "Sex Differences in Nonverbal and Verbal Communication with Bosses, Peers, and Subordinates," *Journal of Applied Psychology* (February 1985), 157–63.
22. Andrew J. DuBrin, *Contemporary Applied Management* (Plano, Tex.: Business Publications, 1982), 127–34.
23. W. Alan Randolph, *Understanding and Managing Organizational Behavior* (Homewood, Ill.: Richard D. Irwin, 1985), 349–50.
24. Gerald M. Goldhaber, *Organizational Communication* (Dubuque, Iowa: Wm. C. Brown, 1983).
25. Paul H. Pietri, "Organizational Communication: The Pioneers," *Journal of Business Communication* 11 (1974), 3–6.
26. Kenneth R. Van Voorhis, "Organizational Communication: Advances Made During the Period from World War II Through the 1950s," *Journal of Business Communication* 11 (1974), 11–18.
27. Phillip J. Lewis, "The Status of 'Organizational Communication,' in Colleges of Business," *Journal of Business Communication* 12 (1975), 25–28.
28. Paul Preston, "The Critical 'Mix' in Managerial Communications," *Industrial Management* (March/April 1976), 5–9.
29. Arnold E. Schneider, William C. Donaghy, and Pamela J. Newman, "Communication Climate Within an Organization," *Management Controls* (October/November 1976), 159–62.
30. "Upward/Downward Communication—Critical Information Channels," *Small Business Report* 10 (October 1985), 85–88.
31. William V. Haney, "Serial Communication of Information in Organizations," in *Concepts and Issues in Administrative Behavior,* ed. Sidney Mailick and Edward H. Van Ness (Englewood Cliffs, N.J.: Prentice-Hall, 1962), 150.
32. Haney, "Serial Communication," 150.
33. Alex Bavelas and Dermot Barrett, "An Experimental Approach to Organizational Communication," *Personnel* 27 (1951), 366–71.
34. George de Mare, "Communicating: The Key to Establishing Good Working Relationships," *Price Waterhouse Review* 33 (1989), 30–37.
35. Alan Zaremba, "Working with the Organizational Grapevine," *Personnel Journal* 67 (July 1988), 38–42.
36. Stanley J. Modic, "Grapevine Rated Most Believable," *Industry Week* 238 (May 15, 1989), 11, 14.
37. Keith Davis, "Management Communication and the Grapevine," *Harvard Business Review* (January/February 1953), 43–49.
38. Linda McCallister, "The Interpersonal Side of Internal Communications," *Public Relations Journal* (February 1981), 20–23.
39. Joseph M. Putti, Samuel Aryee, and Joseph Phua, "Communication Relationship Satisfaction and Organizational Commitment," *Group and Organizational Studies* 15 (March 1990), 44–52.
40. For an article defending the value of grapevines, see W. Kiechel, "In Praise of Office Gossip," *Fortune* (August 19, 1985), 253–54.

CHAPTER 14

1. David Nadler and Michael L. Tushman, "Beyond the Charismatic Leader: Leadership and Organizational Change," *California Management Review* 32 (Winter 1990), 77–97.
2. Abraham Zaleznik, "Executives and Organizations: Real Work," *Harvard Business Review* 67 (January/February 1989), 57–64.
3. Abraham Zaleznik, "Managers and Leaders: Are They Different?" *Harvard Business Review* (May/June 1977), 67–78.
4. Theodore Levitt, "Management and the Post-Industrial Society," *Public Interest* (Summer 1976), 73.
5. Patrick L. Townsend and Joan E. Gebhardt, "We Have Lots of Managers . . . We Need Leaders," *Journal for Quality and Participation* (September 1989), 18–20.
6. Craig Hickman, "The Winning Mix: Mind of a Manager, Soul of a Leader," *Canadian Business* 63 (February 1990), 69–72.
7. As an example, see R.D. Mann, "A Review of the Relationship Between Personality and Performance in Small Groups," *Psychological Bulletin* 56, no. 4 (1959), 241–70.
8. Ralph M. Stogdill, "Personal Factors Associated with Leadership: A Survey of the Literature," *Journal of Psychology* 25 (January 1948), 35–64.
9. Cecil A. Gibb, "Leadership," in *Handbook of Social Psychology,* ed. Gardner Lindzey (Reading, Mass.: Addison-Wesley, 1954).
10. Eugene E. Jennings, "The Anatomy of Leadership," *Management of Personnel Quarterly* 1 (Autumn 1961).
11. J. Oliver Crom, "What's New in Leadership?" *Executive Excellence* 7 (January 1990), 15–16.
12. For an interesting discussion of followers in a leadership situation see Robert E. Kelly, "In Praise of Followers," *Harvard Business Review* 66 (November/December 1988), 142–48.
13. Robert Tannenbaum and Warren H. Schmidt, "How to Choose a Leadership Pattern," *Harvard Business Review* (March/April 1957), 95–101.
14. William E. Zierden, "Leading Through the Follower's Point of View," *Organizational Dynamics* (Spring 1980), 27–46.
15. Tannenbaum and Schmidt, "How to Choose a Leadership Pattern."
16. This point is elaborated in "The Art of Handling Technical Workers," *Electrical World* 204 (February 1990), 29–30.
17. Robert Tannenbaum and Warren H. Schmidt, "How to Choose a Leadership Pattern," *Harvard Business Review* (May/June 1973), 162–80.
18. Victor H. Vroom and Philip H. Yetton, *Leadership and Decision-Making* (Pittsburgh: University of Pittsburgh Press, 1973).
19. Victor H. Vroom and Arthur G. Jago, *The New Leadership* (Englewood Cliffs, N.J.: Prentice-Hall, 1988).
20. Vroom and Yetton, *Leadership and Decision-Making.*
21. Vroom and Jago, *New Leadership.*
22. Gary A. Yukl, *Leadership in Organizations,* 2d ed. (Englewood Cliffs, N.J.: Prentice-Hall, 1989).
23. Roger M. Stogdill and Alvin E. Coons, ed., *Leader Behavior: Its Description and Measurement,* Research Monograph no. 88 (Columbus: Ohio State University Bureau of Business Research, 1957).
24. "How Basic Management Principles Pay Off: Lessons in Leadership," *Nation's Business* (March 1977), 46–53.
25. Vishwanath V. Baba and Merle E. Ace, "Serendipity in Leadership: Initiating Structure and Consideration in the Classroom," *Human Relations* 42 (June 1989), 509–25; Desmond Nolan, "Leadership Appraisals: Your Management Style Can Affect Productivity," *Credit Union Executive* 28 (Winter 1988), 36–37.
26. Rensis Likert, *New Patterns of Management* (New York: McGraw-Hill, 1961).
27. Andrew W. Halpin, *The Leadership Behavior of School Superintendents* (Chicago: University of Chicago Midwest Administration Center, 1959).
28. Harvey A. Hornstein, Madeline E. Heilman, Edward Mone, and Ross Tartell, "Responding to Contingent Leadership Behavior," *Organizational Dynamics* 15 (Spring 1987), 56–65.
29. Rick Roskin, "Management Style and Achievement: A Model Synthesis," *Management Decision* 27 (1989), 17–22.
30. A.K. Korman, "'Consideration,' 'Initiating Structure,' and Organizational Criteria—A Review," *Personnel Psychology* 19 (Winter 1966), 349–61.
31. P. Hersey and K.H. Blanchard, "Life Cycle Theory of Leadership," *Training and Development Journal* (May 1969), 26–34.
32. Mary J. Keenan, Joseph B. Hurst, Robert S. Dennis, and Glenna Frey, "Situational Leadership for Collaboration in Health Care Settings," *Health Care Supervisor* 8 (April 1990), 19–25.
33. Claude L. Graeff, "The Situational Leadership Theory: A Critical View," *Academy of Management Review* 8, no. 2 (1983), 285–91; Robert P.

Vecchio, "Situational Leadership Theory: An Examination of a Prescriptive Theory," *Journal of Applied Psychology* 72 (August 1987), 444–51; Jane R. Goodson, Gail W. McGee, and James F. Cashman, "Situational Leadership Theory: A Test of Leadership Prescriptions," *Group and Organizational Studies* 14 (December 1989), 446–61.

34. Fred E. Fiedler, "Engineer the Job to Fit the Manager," *Harvard Business Review* 43 (September/October 1965), 115–22. See also Fred E. Fiedler, *A Theory of Leadership Effectiveness* (New York: McGraw-Hill, 1967).

35. Rensis Likert, *New Patterns of Management.*

36. From *A Theory of Leadership Effectiveness*, 255–56 by F.E. Fiedler. Copyright © 1967 by McGraw-Hill, Inc. Used with permission of McGraw-Hill Book Company.

37. Fred E. Fiedler, "How Do You Make Leaders More Effective? New Answers to an Old Puzzle," *Organizational Dynamics* (Autumn 1972), 3–18.

38. Timothy McMahon, "A Contingency Theory: Logic and Method Revisited," *Personnel Psychology* 25 (Winter 1972), 697–710.

39. Robert J. House and Terence R. Mitchell, "Path-Goal Theory of Leadership," *Journal of Contemporary Business* (Autumn 1974), 81–98; Gary A. Yukl, *Leadership in Organizations.*

40. Alan C. Filley, Robert House, and Steven Kerr, *Managerial Process and Organizational Behavior* (Glenview, Ill.: Scott, Foresman, 1976), 256–60.

41. For a worthwhile review of the path-goal theory of leadership see: Gary A. Yukl, *Leadership in Organizations.*

42. Karl W. Kuhnert and Philip Lewis, "Transactional and Transformational Leadership: A Constructive/Developmental Analysis," *Academy of Management Review* (October 1987), 648–57.

43. Bernard M. Bass, *Leadership and Performance Beyond Expectations* (New York: Free Press, 1985).

44. Noel M. Tichy and David M. Ulrich, "The Leadership Challenge: A Call for Transformational Leadership," *Sloan Management Review* (Fall 1984), 59–68.

45. Alan Farnham, "Trust Gap," *Fortune* (December 4, 1989), 56–78.

46. Jack Gordon, "Who Killed Corporate Loyalty?" *Training* (March 1990), 25–32.

47. Craig A. Russell, "Openness and Trust," *Executive Excellence* 6 (December 1989), 12.

48. Fernando Bartolome, "Nobody Trusts the Boss Completely—Now What?" *Harvard Business Review* 67 (March/April 1989), 135–42.

CHAPTER 15

1. Philip A. Rudolph and Brian H. Kleiner, "The Art of Motivating Employees," *Journal of Managerial Psychology* 4 (1989), i–iv.

2. Walter F. Charsley, "Management, Morale, and Motivation," *Management World* 17 (July/August 1988), 27–28.

3. Victor H. Vroom, *Work and Motivation* (New York: Wiley, 1964); Thomas L. Quick, "How to Motivate People," *Working Woman* 12 (September 1987), 15, 17.

4. J. Stacy Adams, "Towards an Understanding of Inequity," *Journal of Abnormal and Social Psychology* 67, no. 5 (1963), 422–36.

5. L.W. Porter and E.E. Lawler, *Managerial Attitudes and Performance* (Homewood, Ill.: Richard D. Irwin, 1968).

6. For more information on intrinsic and extrinsic rewards, see Pat Buhler, "Rewards in the Organization," *Supervision* 50 (January 1989), 5–7.

7. Eric G. Flamholtz and Yvonne Randle, "The Inner Game of Management," *Management Review* 77 (April 1988), 24–30.

8. Abraham Maslow, *Motivation and Personality*, 2d ed. (New York: Harper & Row, 1970). For a current discussion of the value of Maslow's ideas see Edward Hoffman, "Abraham Maslow: Father of Enlightened Management," *Training* 25 (September 1988), 79–82.

9. Robert J. Kelly and Jack Barnathan, "Out on a Limb: Executives Abroad," *Security Management* 32 (November 1988), 117–27.

10. Abraham Maslow, *Eupsychian Management* (Homewood, Ill.: Richard D. Irwin, 1965).

11. Jack W. Duncan, *Essentials of Management* (Hinsdale, Ill.: Dryden Press, 1975), 105.

12. C.P. Alderfer, "An Empirical Test of a New Theory of Human Needs," *Organizational Behavior and Human Performance* 4, no. 2 (1969), 142–75.

13. D.T. Hall and K. Nougaim, "An Examination of Maslow's Need Hierarchy in an Organizational Setting," *Organizational Behavior and Human Performance* 3, no. 1 (1968), 12–35.

14. Hoffman, "Abraham Maslow: Father of Enlightened Management," 1988, Dale L. Mort, "Lead Your Team to the Top," *Security Management* 32 (January 1988), 43–45.

15. Clayton Alderfer, *Existence, Relatedness, and Growth* (New York: Free Press, 1972).

16. Chris Argyris, *Personality and Organization* (New York: Harper & Bros., 1957).

17. Charles R. Davis, "The Primacy of Self-Development in Chris Argyris's Writings," *International Journal of Public Administration* 10 (September 1987), 177–207.

18. David C. McClelland and David G. Winter, *Motivating Economic Achievement* (New York: Free Press, 1969). David C. McClelland, "Power Is the Great Motivator," *Harvard Business Review* (March/April 1976), 100–10.

19. Burt K. Scanlan, "Creating a Climate for Achievement," *Business Horizons* 24 (March/April 1981), 5–9; Lawrence Holp, "Achievement Motivation and Kaizen," *Training and Development Journal* 43 (October 1989), 53–63.

20. David C. McClelland, *The Achieving Society* (New York: Van Nostrand, 1961).

21. Craig R. Hickman and Michael A. Silva, "Individual Fulfillment," *Executive Excellence* 5 (August 1988), 14–15.

22. Edwin Timbers, "Strengthening Motivation Through Communication," *Advanced Management Journal* 31 (April 1966), 64–69.

23. Douglas McGregor, *The Human Side of Enterprise* (New York: McGraw-Hill, 1960). For a current illustration of how Theory X-Theory Y relates to modern business see Kenneth B. Slutsky "Viewpoint: Why Not Theory Z?" *Security Management* 33 (April 1989), 110, 112.

24. W.J. Reddin, "The Tri-Dimensional Grid," *Training and Development Journal* (July 1964).

25. For more discussion on the implications of job rotation in organizations, see Alan W. Farrant, "Job Rotation Is Important," *Supervision* (August 1987), 14–16.

26. L.E. Davis and E.S. Valfer, "Intervening Responses to Changes in Supervisor Job Designs," *Occupational Psychology* (July 1965), 171–90.

27. M.D. Kilbridge, "Do Workers Prefer Larger Jobs?" *Personnel* (September/October 1960), 45–48.

28. This section is based on Frederick Herzberg, "One More Time: How Do You Motivate Employees?" *Harvard Business Review* (January/February 1968), 53–62.

29. Scott M. Meyers, "Who Are Your Motivated Workers?" *Harvard Business Review* (January/February 1964), 73–88.

30. John M. Roach, "Why Volvo Abolished the Assembly Line," *Management Review* (September 1977), 50.

31. Matt Oechsli, "Million Dollar Success Habits," *Managers Magazine* 65 (February 1990), 6–14; J. Barton Cunningham and Ted Eberle, "A Guide to Job Enrichment and Redesign," *Personnel* 67 (February 1990), 56–61.

32. Richard J. Hackman, "Is Job Enrichment Just a Fad?" *Harvard Business Review* (September/October 1975), 129–38.

33. E.G. Thomas, "Flexible Work Keeps Growing," *Management World* 15 (April/May 1986), 43–45.

34. D.A. Bratton, "Moving Away from Nine to Five," *Canadian Business Review* 13 (Spring 1986), 15–17.

35. Douglas L. Fleuter, "Flextime—A Social Phenomenon," *Personnel Journal* (June 1975), 318–19.

36. Lee A. Graf, "An Analysis of the Effect of Flexible Working Hours on the Management Functions of the First-Line Supervisor" (Ph.D. diss., Mississippi State University, 1976).

37. Jill Kanin-Lovers, "Meeting the Challenge of Workforce 2000," *Journal of Compensation and Benefits* 5 (January/February 1990), 233–36.

38. William Wong, "Rather Come in Late or Go Home Earlier? More Bosses Say OK," *Wall Street Journal*, July 12, 1973, 1.

39. B.F. Skinner, *Contingencies of Reinforcement* (New York: Appleton-Century-Crofts, 1969).

40. E.L. Thorndike, "The Original Nature of Man," *Educational Psychology* 1 (1903).

41. Fred Luthans and Robert Kreitner, *Organizational Behavior Modification and Beyond* (Glenview, Ill.: Scott, Foresman, 1985).

42. Richard D. Arvey and John M. Ivancevich, "Punishment in Organizations: A Review, Proposal, and Research Suggestions," *Academy of Management Journal* (January 1980), 123–32; P.M. Padsokaff, "Relationships between Leader Reward and Punishment Behavior and Group Process and Productivity," *Journal of Management* 11 (Spring 1985), 55–73.

43. For another practical discussion on punishment, see Bruce R. McAfee and William Poffenberger, *Productivity Strategies: Enhancing Employee Job Performance* (Englewood Cliffs, N.J.: Prentice-Hall, Spectrum, 1982).

44. Ricky W. Griffin and Gregory Moorhead, *Organizational Behavior* (Boston: Houghton Mifflin, 1986), 183–89.

45. "New Tool: Reinforcement for Good Work," *Psychology Today* (April 1972), 68–69.
46. W. Clay Hamner and Ellen P. Hamner, "Behavior Modification on the Bottom Line," *Organizational Dynamics* 4 (Spring 1976), 6–8.
47. Rensis Likert, *New Patterns of Management* (New York: McGraw-Hill, 1961). For an interesting discussion of the worth of Likert's ideas see Marvin R. Weisbord, "For More Productive Workplaces," *Journal of Management Consulting* 4 (1988), 7–14.
48. These descriptions are based on the table of organizational and performance characteristics of different management systems in Rensis Likert, *The Human Organization* (New York: McGraw-Hill, 1967), 4–10.
49. Robert W. Goddard, "The Healthy Side of Conflict," *Management World* 15 (June 1986), 8–12.
50. Likert, *New Patterns of Management,* 103.
51. "Incentive Pay Plan Replaces Wage Hikes: Lump Sum Bonuses, Profit-Sharing Attract and Maintain Good Workers," *Chain Store Age Executive* (February 1989), 78, 79.
52. Jeffrey P. Davidson, "A Great Place to Work: Seven Strategies for Keeping Employees Committed to Your Company," *Management World* (June/August 1987), 24–25.

CHAPTER 16

1. For an article illustrating the importance of managing groups in organizations see Gregory E. Kaebnick, "Notes from Underground: Walter Corbitt Talks About Monitoring Paperwork for 35,000 Underground Storage Tanks," *Inform* 3 (July/August 1989), 21–22, 48.
2. Edgar H. Schein, *Organizational Psychology* (Englewood Cliffs, N.J.: Prentice-Hall, 1965), 67.
3. George C. Homans, *The Human Group* (New York: Harcourt, Brace & World, 1950), 1.
4. Marvin E. Shaw, *Group Dynamics: The Psychology of Small Group Behavior* (New York: McGraw-Hill, 1971), 10.
5. Dorwin Cartwright and Ronald Lippitt, "Group Dynamics and the Individual," *International Journal of Group Psychotherapy* 7 (January 1957), 86–102.
6. Edgar H. Schein, *Organizational Psychology,* 2d ed. (Englewood Cliffs, N.J.: Prentice-Hall, 1970), 82.
7. For more information on these groups, see Leonard R. Sayles, "Research in Industrial Human Relations," in *Industrial Relations* (New York: Harper & Bros., 1957).
8. For useful guidelines on how to make committees work see Arthur R. Pell, "Making Committees Work," *Managers Magazine* 64 (September 1989), 28.
9. For insights on what causes groups to fail as organizational problem-solvers see Harvey J. Brightman and Penny Verhoeven, "Why Managerial Problem-Solving Groups Fail," *Business* 36 (January/February/March 1986), 24–29.
10. Raymond McLeod, Jr., and Jack W. Jones, "Making Executive Information Systems More Effective," *Business Horizons* (September/October 1986), 29–37.
11. Cyril O'Donnell, "Ground Rules for Using Committees," *Management Review* 50 (October 1961), 63–67. See also "Making Committees Work," *Infosystems* (October 1985), 38–39.
12. These guidelines are taken from "How Not to Influence People," *Management Record* (March 1958), 89–91. For additional guidelines see Peggy S. Williams, "Physical Fitness for Committees: Getting on Track," *Association Management* 41 (June 1989), 104–11.
13. Irving L. Janis, *Groupthink* (Boston: Houghton Mifflin, 1982).
14. Robert B. Reich, "Entrepreneurship Reconsidered: The Team as a Hero," *Harvard Business Review* (May/June 1987), 77–83.
15. Craig Cina, "Company Study: Five Steps to Service Excellence," *Journal of Services Marketing* 4 (Spring 1990), 39–47.
16. Bernard Bass, *Organizational Psychology* (Boston: Allyn and Bacon, 1965), 197–98.
17. Bass, *Organizational Psychology,* 199.
18. Raef T. Hussein, "Informal Groups, Leadership, and Productivity," *Leadership and Organization Development Journal* 10 (1989), 9–16.
19. Keith Davis and John W. Newstrom, *Human Behavior at Work: Organizational Behavior* (New York: McGraw-Hill, 1985), 310–12.
20. Muhammad Jamal, "Shift Work Related to Job Attitudes, Social Participation, and Withdrawal Behavior: A Study of Nurses and Industrial Workers," *Personnel Psychology* 34 (Autumn 1981), 535–47.
21. For the importance of determining such information see Dave Day, "New Supervisors and the Informal Group," *Supervisory Management* 34 (May 1989), 31–33.
22. For a classic study illustrating sociometry and sociometric procedures see Muzafer Sherif, "A Preliminary Experimental Study of Intergroup Relations," in *Social Psychology at the Crossroads,* ed. John H. Rohrer and Muzafer Sherif (New York: Harper & Bros., 1951).
23. Edgar H. Schein, "SMR Forum: Improving Face-to-Face Relationships," *Sloan Management Review* 22 (Winter 1981), 43–52.
24. Homans, *The Human Group.*
25. For an interesting attempt to analyze characteristics of work groups in a small business, see James Curran and John Stanworth, "The Social Dynamics of the Small Manufacturing Enterprise," *Journal of Management Studies* 18 (April 1981), 141–58.
26. W. Alan Randolph, *Understanding and Managing Organizational Behavior* (Homewood, Ill.: Richard D. Irwin, 1985), 398–99.
27. Davis and Newstrom, *Human Behavior at Work,* 218.
28. Don Hellriegel and John W. Slocum, Jr., *Management* (Reading, Mass.: Addison-Wesley, 1986), 539–42.
29. Stanley E. Seashore, *Group Cohesiveness in the Industrial Work Group* (Ann Arbor: University of Michigan Press, 1954).
30. For an excellent critical comment on the quality of research in this area see Peter E. Mudrack, "Group Cohesiveness and Productivity: A Closer Look," *Human Relations* 42 (September 1989), 771–85.
31. O. Jeff Harris, *Managing People at Work* (New York: Wiley, 1976), 122; for an interesting discussion of how employee ownership affects group cohesiveness see Jon L. Pierce and Candace A. Furo, "Employee Ownership: Implications for Management," *Organizational Dynamics* 18 (Winter 1990), 32–43.
32. J.R. Hackman, "Group Influence on Individuals," in *Handbook for Industrial and Organizational Psychology,* ed. M.P. Dunnette (Chicago: Rand McNally, 1976).
33. This section is based primarily on P.C. André De la Porte, "Group Norms: Key to Building a Winning Team," *Personnel* (September/October 1974): 60–67.
34. Peter F. Drucker, "Is Executive Pay Excessive?" *Wall Street Journal,* May 23, 1977, 22.
35. T.N. Whitehead, "The Inevitability of the Informal Organization and Its Possible Value," in *Readings in Management,* ed. Ernest Dale (New York: McGraw-Hill, 1970).
36. This section draws from Samuel C. Certo and J. Paul Peter, *Strategic Management: Concepts and Applications* (New York: McGraw-Hill, 1991), 141–46.
37. Cass Bettinger, "Use Corporate Culture to Trigger High Performance," *The Journal of Business Strategy* (March/April 1989), 38–42.
38. John Hassard and Sudi Sharifi, "Corporate Culture and Strategic Change," *Journal of General Management* 15 (Winter 1989), 4–19.
39. Discussion of these mechanisms is based on Edgar H. Schein, *Organizational Culture and Leadership* (San Francisco: Jossey-Bass Publishers, 1985), 223–43.

CHAPTER 17

1. T.K. Das, "Organizational Control: An Evolutionary Perspective," *Journal of Management Studies* 26 (September 1989), 459–75.
2. L.R. Bittle and J.E. Ramsey (eds.), *Handbook for Professional Managers* (New York: McGraw-Hill, 1985).
3. K.A. Merchant, "The Control Function of Management," *Sloan Management Review* 23 (Summer 1982), 43–55.
4. For an example of how a control system can be used with a formal planning model, see A.M. Jaeger and B.R. Baliga, "Control Systems and Strategic Adaptations: Lessons from the Japanese Experience," *Strategic Management Journal* 6 (April/June 1985), 115–34.
5. Donald C. Mosley and Paul H. Pietri, *Management: The Art of Working with and Through People* (Encino, Calif.: Dickenson, 1975), 29–43.
6. Robert L. Dewelt, "Control: Key to Making Financial Strategy Work," *Management Review* (March 1977), 18.
7. For more discussion on Murphy's Law see George Box, "When Murphy Speaks—Listen," *Quality Progress* 22 (October 1989), 79–84.
8. Robert J. Mockler, ed., *Readings in Management Control* (New York: Appleton-Century-Crofts, 1970), 14.
9. Insights on how such measurements can influence employee performance can be found in Mark K. Hirst, "Accounting Information and the Evalua-

tion of Subordinate Performance: A Situational Approach," *Accounting Review* 56 (October 1981), 771–84.

10. For a discussion of how standards are set, see James B. Dilworth, *Production and Operations Management: Manufacturing and Nonmanufacturing* (New York: Random House, 1986), 637–50.

11. Len Eglo, "Save Dollars on Maintenance Management," *Chemical Engineering* 97 (June 1990), 157–62.

12. Alden M. Hayashi, "GE Says Solid State Is Here to Stay," *Electronic Business* 14 (April 1, 1988), 52–56.

13. Frank Rose, "A New Age for Business?" *Fortune* 122 (October 8, 1990), 156–64.

14. Edward Basset, "Diamond Is Forever," *New England Business* 12 (October 1990), 40–44.

15. David Sheridan, "Getting the Big Picture," *Training* (September 1990), 12–15.

16. Thomas A. Foster and Joseph V. Barks, "The Right Chemistry for Single Sourcing," *Distribution* 89 (September 1990), 44–52.

17. Joseph Conlin, "The House That G.E. Built," *Successful Meetings* 38 (August 1989), 50–58.

18. Robert W. Mann, "A Building-Blocks Approach to Strategic Change," *Training and Development Journal* 44 (August 1990), 23–25.

19. For an illustration of the problem/symptom relationship see Elizabeth Dougherty, "Waste Minimization: Reduce Wastes and Reap the Benefits," *R & D* 32 (April 1990), 62–68.

20. Y.K. Shetty, "Product Quality and Competitive Strategy," *Business Horizons* (May/June 1987), 46–52.

21. Harold Koontz, Cyril O'Donnell, and Heinz Weihrich, *Essentials of Management* (New York: McGraw-Hill, 1986), 454–59.

22. Vijay Sathe, *Controller Involvement in Management* (Englewood Cliffs, N.J.: Prentice-Hall, 1982).

23. James D. Wilson, *Controllership: The Work of the Managerial Accountant* (New York: Wiley, 1981).

24. For other ways in which cost-benefit analysis can be used by managers, see G.S. Smith and M.S. Tseng, "Benefit-Cost Analysis as a Performance Indicator," *Management Accounting* (June 1986), 44–49; "The IS (Information System) Payoff," *Infosystems* (April 1987), 18–20.

25. Amitai Etzioni, *A Comparative Analysis of Complex Organizations* (New York: Free Press, 1961), 4–6.

26. John P. Kotter, "Power, Dependence, and Effective Management," *Harvard Business Review* (July/August 1977), 128.

27. Kotter, "Power, Dependence, and Effective Management," 135–36.

28. Kotter, "Power, Dependence, and Effective Management," 131.

29. For further discussion of overcoming the potential negative effects of control, see Ramon J. Aldag and Timothy M. Stearns, *Management* (Cincinnati, Ohio: South-Western Publishing, 1987), 653–54.

30. Arnold F. Emch, "Control Means Action," *Harvard Business Review* (July/August 1954), 92–98. See also K. Hall and L.K. Savery, "Tight Rein, More Stress," *Harvard Business Review* (January/February 1986), 160–64.

31. James T. McKenna, "Eastern, Maintenance Heads Indicted by U.S. Grand Jury," *Aviation Week & Space Technology* 133 (July 1990), 84–86.

32. Peter F. Drucker, *Management: Tasks, Responsibilities, Practices* (New York: Harper & Row, 1974).

33. W. Jerome III, *Executive Control: The Catalyst* (New York: Wiley, 1961), 31–34.

34. William Bruns, Jr. and E. Warren McFarlan, "Information Technology Puts Power in Control Systems," *Harvard Business Review* (September/October 1987), 89–94.

35. C. Jackson Grayson, Jr., "Management Science and Business Practice," *Harvard Business Review* (July/August 1973), 41–48.

36. For an article emphasizing the importance of management understanding and being supportive of organizational control efforts see Richard M. Morris III, "Management Support: An Underlying Premise," *Industrial Management* 31 (March/April 1989), 2–3.

CHAPTER 18

1. James B. Dilworth, *Production and Operations Management: Manufacturing and Non-Manufacturing* (New York: Random House, 1986), 3.

2. John W. Kendrick, *Understanding Productivity: An Introduction to the Dynamics of Productivity Change* (Baltimore: Johns Hopkins University Press, 1977), 14.

3. Lester C. Thurow, "Other Countries Are as Smart as We Are," *New York Times*, April 5, 1981.

4. W. Edwards Deming, *Out of the Crisis* (Boston: MIT Center for Advanced Engineering Study, 1986).

5. John A. Mearman, *U.S. Industrial Outlook, 1987* (Washington, D.C.: U.S. Department of Commerce), 21–26.

6. Joann S. Lubin, "As Robot Age Arrives, Labor Seeks Protection Against Work Loss," *Wall Street Journal*, October 26, 1981.

7. Jack R. Meredith, *The Management of Operations* (New York: Wiley, 1987), 243–44.

8. For more information on plant layout, see Joseph G. Monks, *Operations Management: Theory and Problems* (New York: McGraw-Hill, 1987), 122–35.

9. Richard B. Chase and Nicholas J. Aquilano, *Production and Operations Management: A Life Cycle Approach* (Homewood, Ill.: Richard D. Irwin, 1981), 4.

10. At this point, it probably would be worthwhile to review the general topic of scheduling and the more specific topics of the Gantt chart and PERT networks.

11. Lester R. Bittle, *Management by Exception* (New York: McGraw-Hill, 1964).

12. Frederick W. Taylor, *Shop Management* (New York: Harper & Bros., 1911), 126–27.

13. These two rules are adapted from *Boardroom Reports* 5 (May 15, 1976): 4.

14. For a clear discussion of more of the intricacies of breakeven analysis, see Lee J. Krajewski and Larry P. Ritzman, *Operations Management: Strategy and Analysis* (Reading, Mass.: Addison-Wesley, 1987), 41–43.

15. Robert J. Lambrix and Surendra S. Singhvi, "How to Set Volume-Sensitive ROI Targets," *Harvard Business Review* (March/April 1981), 174.

16. Chase and Aquilano, *Production and Operations Management,* 516.

17. Krajewski and Ritzman, *Operations Management: Strategy and Analysis,* 573.

18. Krajewski and Ritzman, *Operations Management,* 572–84.

19. A. Ansari and Modarress Batoul, "Just-in-Time Purchasing: Problems and Solutions," *Journal of Purchasing and Materials Management* (August 1986): 11–15.

20. Albert F. Celley, William H. Clegg, Arthur W. Smith, and Mark A. Vonderembse, "Implementation of JIT in the United States," *Journal of Purchasing and Materials Management* (Winter 1987): 9–15.

21. Jack R. Meredith, *The Management of Operations,* 3d ed. (New York: Wiley, 1987), 391–92.

22. Information about companies that have adopted JIT methods appears in Sumer C. Aggarwal, "MRP, JIT, OPT, FMS?" *Harvard Business Review* (September/October 1985): 8–16.

23. John D. Baxter, "Kanban Works Wonders, but Will It Work in U.S. Industry?" *Iron Age*, June 7, 1982, 44–48.

24. Elwood S. Buffa, *Modern Production/Operations Management* (New York: Wiley, 1983), 501.

25. John B. Miner, *Organizational Behavior: Performance and Productivity* (New York: Random House, 1988), 308–16.

26. For an interesting illustration of inspection in a service organization see Robert G. Murdick, Barry Render, and Roberta S. Russell, *Service Operations Management* (Boston: Allyn & Bacon, 1990), 419–20.

27. Roger G. Schroeder, *Operations Management: Decision Making in the Operations Function* (New York: McGraw-Hill, 1985), 597–98.

28. Robert L. Dewelt, "Control: Key to Making Financial Strategy Work," *Management Review* (March 1977), 20.

29. George S. Minmier, "Zero-Base Budgeting: A New Budgeting Technique for Discretionary Costs," *Mid-South Quarterly Business Review* 14 (October 1976), 2–8.

30. Peter A. Phyrr, "Zero-Base Budgeting," *Harvard Business Review* (November/December 1970), 111–21. See also E.A. Kurbis, "The Case for Zero-Base Budgeting," *CA Magazine* (April 1986), 104–05.

31. Linda J. Shinn and M. Sue Sturgeon, "Budgeting from Ground Zero," *Association Management* 42 (September 1990), 45–48.

32. Gregory E. Becwar and Jack L. Armitage, "Zero-Base Budgeting: Is It Really Dead?" *Ohio CPA Journal* 48 (Winter 1989), 52–54.

33. Aaron Wildausky and Arthur Hammann, "Comprehensive Versus Incremental Budgeting in the Department of Agriculture," in *Planning Programming Budgeting: A Systems Approach to Management,* ed. Fremont J. Lyden and Ernest G. Miller (Chicago: Markham Publishing, 1968), 143–44.

34. Chris Argyris, "Human Problems with Budgets," *Harvard Business Review* (January/February 1953), 108.

35. Argyris, "Human Problems with Budgets," 109.
36. This section is based primarily on J. Fred Weston and Eugene F. Brigham, *Essentials of Managerial Finance*, 7th ed. (Hinsdale, Ill.: Dryden Press, 1985).
37. F.L. Patrone and Donald duBois, "Financial Ratio Analysis for the Small Business," *Journal of Small Business Management* (January 1981), 35.
38. Ray Wise, "High Tech's High Debt Worries Financial Community," *Electronic Business* 15 (November 13, 1989), 46–48.
39. For an excellent discussion of ratio analysis in a small business, see Patrone and duBois, "Financial Ratio Analysis," 35–40.

CHAPTER 19

1. Garland R. Hadley and Mike C. Patterson, "Are Middle-Paying Jobs Really Declining?" *Oklahoma Business Bulletin* 56 (June 1988), 12–14.
2. A. Essam Radwan and Jerome Fields, "Keeping Tabs on Toxic Spills," *Civil Engineering* 60 (April 1990), 70–72.
3. Dean C. Minderman, "Marketing: Desktop Demographics," *Credit Union Management* 13 (February 1990), 26.
4. Henry Mintzberg, "The Myths of MIS," *California Management Review* (Fall 1972), 92–97.
5. Jay W. Forrester, "Managerial Decision Making," in *Management and the Computer of the Future*, ed. Martin Greenberger (Cambridge, Mass., and New York: MIT Press and Wiley, 1962), 37.
6. The following discussion is based largely on Robert H. Gregory and Richard L. Van Horn, "Value and Cost of Information," in *Systems Analysis Techniques*, ed. J. Daniel Conger and Robert W. Knapp (New York: Wiley, 1974), 473–89.
7. John T. Small and William B. Lee, "In Search of MIS," *MSU Business Topics* (Autumn 1975), 47–55.
8. G. Anthony Gorry and Michael S. Scott Morton, "A Framework for Management Information Systems," *Sloan Management Review* 13 (Fall 1971), 55–70.
9. Stephen L. Cohen, "Managing Human-Resource Data: Keeping Your Data Clean," *Training & Development Journal* 43 (August 1989), 50–54.
10. David Harvey, "Making Sense of the Data Deluge," *Director* 42 (April 1990), 139–40.
11. Robert Chaiken, "Pitfalls of Computers in a CPA's Office," *Ohio CPA Journal* 46 (Spring 1987), 45–46.
12. John E. Framel, "Managing Information Costs and Technologies as Assets," *Journal of Systems Management* 41 (February 1990), 12–18.
13. Martin D.J. Buss, "Penny-wise Approach to Data Processing," *Harvard Business Review* (July/August 1981), 111.
14. James A. Yardley and Parez R. Sopariwala, "Break-Even Utilization Analysis," *Journal of Commercial Bank Lending* 72 (March 1990), 49–56.
15. Robert W. Holmes, "Twelve Areas to Investigate for Better MIS," *Financial Executive* (July 1970), 24. A similar definition is presented and illustrated in Jeffrey A. Coopersmith, "Modern Times: Computerized Systems Are Changing the Way Today's Modern Catalog Company Is Structured," *Catalog Age* 7 (June 1990), 77–78.
16. This section is based on Richard A. Johnson, R. Joseph Monsen, Henry P. Knowles, and Borge O. Saxberg, *Management, Systems, and Society: An Introduction* (Santa Monica, Calif.: Goodyear, 1976), 113–20.
17. Robert G. Murdick, "MIS for MBO," *Journal of Systems Management* (March 1977), 34–40.
18. F. Warren McFarlan, "Problems in Planning the Information System," *Harvard Business Review* (March/April 1971), 75.
19. David S. Stoller and Richard L. Van Horn, *Design of a Management Information System* (Santa Monica, Calif.: RAND Corporation, 1958).
20. Craig Barrow, "Implementing an Executive Information System: Seven Steps for Success," *Journal of Information Systems Management* 7 (Spring 1990), 41–46.
21. Bertram A. Colbert, "The Management Information System," *Management Services* 4 (September/October 1967), 15–24.
22. Adapted from Henry Mintzberg, "The Manager's Job: Folklore and Fact," *Harvard Business Review* (July/August 1975), 58.
23. William R. King and David I. Cleland, "Manager-Analysts Teamwork in MIS," *Business Horizons* 14 (April 1971), 59–68.
24. Regina Herzlinger, "Why Data Systems in Nonprofit Organizations Fail," *Harvard Business Review* (January/February 1977), 81–86.
25. John Sculley, "The Human Use of Information," *Journal for Quality and Participation* (January/February 1990), 10–13.
26. G.W. Dickson and John K. Simmons, "The Behavioral Side of MIS," *Business Horizons* (August 1970), 59, 71.

27. Steven L. Mandell, *Computers and Data Processing: Concepts and Applications with BASIC* (St. Paul, Minn.: West Publishing, 1982), 370–91.
28. Mark G. Simkin, *Computer Information Systems for Business* (Dubuque, Iowa: Wm. C. Brown, 1987), 299–301.
29. For additional information on these software packages, see *Lotus 1–2–3 Reference Manual* (Cambridge, Mass.: Lotus Development Corporation, 1985); Timothy J. O'Leary, *The Student Edition of Lotus 1–2–3* (Reading, Mass.: Addison-Wesley, 1989); *IFPS User's Manual* (Austin, Tex.: Execucom Systems Corporation, 1984).

CHAPTER 20

1. Alyssa A. Lappen, "Worldwide Connections," *Forbes* 141 (June 27, 1988), 78–82.
2. Lee Smith, "Japan Hustles for Foreign Investment," *Fortune* (May 28), 1984, 163.
3. "Trying to Copy Past Success," *Economist* (February 6, 1982), 70.
4. Ben J. Wattenberg, "Their Deepest Concerns," *Business Month* (January 1988), 27–33.
5. American Assembly of Collegiate Schools of Business, *Accreditation Council Policies, Procedures, and Standards*, 1990–92. St. Louis, Mo.; Sylvia Nasar, "America's Competitive Revival," *Fortune* (January 4, 1988), 44–52.
6. U.S. Department of Commerce, *The Multinational Corporation: Studies on U.S. Foreign Investment*, vol. 1 (Washington, D.C.: Government Printing Office).
7. Robert W. Stevens, "Scanning the Multinational Firm," *Business Horizons* 14 (June 1971), 53.
8. Neil H. Jacoby, "The Multinational Corporation," *Center Magazine* 3 (May 1970), 37–55.
9. Grover Starling, *The Changing Environment of Business* (Boston: Kent, 1980), 140.
10. This section is based primarily on Richard D. Robinson, *International Management* (New York: Holt, Rinehart & Winston, 1967), 3–5.
11. 1971 Survey of National Foreign Trade Council, cited in Frederick D. Sturdivant, *Business and Society: A Managerial Approach* (Homewood, Ill.: Richard D. Irwin, 1977), 425. For an interesting discussion of diversification as an advantage to internationalizing see Jeff Madura and Ann Marie Whyte, "Diversification Benefits of Direct Foreign Investment," *Management International Review* 30 (First Quarter 1990), 73–85.
12. Barrie James, "Reducing the Risks of Globalization," *Long Range Planning* 23 (February 1990), 80–88.
13. Robert O. Knorr, "Managing for World-Class Performance," *Journal of Business Strategy* 11 (January/February 1990), 48–50.
14. "The Bug Comes Back," *Newsweek*, April 4, 1983, 60.
15. Karen Paul, "Fading Images at Eastman Kodak," *Business and Society Review* 48 (Winter 1984), 56.
16. "The Mattress Maker That Woke Up Wall Street," *Fortune* (August 20, 1984), 37. For an interesting discussion of issues to consider when licensing software in Japan see Fred M. Greguras, "Software Licensing in Japan: Checklist for U.S. Licensors," *East Asian Executive Reports* 11 (February 15, 1989), 17–20.
17. Joan Servaas Marie, "Robinson Nugent, Inc.: Working Smarter, Not Harder," *Indiana Business* (June 1983), 4–7.
18. Peter J. Mullins, "Survival Through Joint Ventures," *Automotive Industries* (May 1983), 17–18.
19. Howard V. Perlmutter, "The Tortuous Evolution of the Multinational Corporation," *Columbia Journal of World Business* (January/February 1969), 9–18.
20. Rose Knotts, "Cross-Cultural Management: Transformations and Adaptations," *Business Horizons* (January/February 1989), 29–33.
21. John S. Hill and Richard R. Still, "Adapting Products to LDC Tastes," *Harvard Business Review* (March/April 1984), 92.
22. Geert Hofstede, "Motivation, Leadership, and Organization: Do American Theories Apply Abroad?" *Organizational Dynamics* 9 (Summer 1980), 42–63.
23. Anne B. Fisher, "Peering Past Pepsico's Bad News," *Fortune* (November 14, 1983), 124.
24. Walter Sweet, "International Firms Strive for Uniform Nets Abroad," *Network World* 7 (May 28, 1990), 35–36, 62.
25. R.N. Farmer, "International Management," in *Contemporary Management Issues and Viewpoints*, ed. J.W. McGuire (Englewood Cliffs, N.J.: Prentice-Hall, 1974), 302.

26. Frank Ching, "China's Managers Get U.S. Lessons," *Wall Street Journal,* January 23, 1981, 27.
27. Peter F. Drucker, "Behind Japan's Success," *Harvard Business Review* (January/February 1981), 83–90.
28. "How Japan Does It," *Time,* March 30, 1981, 55.
29. Charles McMillan, "Is Japanese Management Really So Different?" *Business Quarterly* (Autumn 1980), 26–31.
30. Masaru Ibuka, "Management Opinion," *Administrative Management* (May 5, 1980), 86.
31. "How Japan Does It."
32. "Consensus in San Diego," *Time* (March 30, 1981), 58.
33. Lane Kelly and Reginald Worthley, "The Role of Culture in Comparative Management," *Academy of Management Journal* 24, no. 1 (1981), 164–73.
34. Linda S. Dillon, "Adopting Japanese Management: Some Cultural Stumbling Blocks," *Personnel* (July/August 1983), 73–77.
35. Isaac Shapiro, "Second Thoughts About Japan," *Wall Street Journal* (June 5, 1981).
36. William Ouchi, *Theory Z* (Reading, Mass.: Addison-Wesley, 1981).
37. Charles W. Joiner, "One Manager's Story of How He Made the Theory Z Concept Work," *Management Review* (May 1983), 48–53; Mary A. Kiely, "Theory Z May Reduce Turnover," *Nursing Management* 20 (March 1989), 15–20.
38. William Bowen, "Lessons from Behind the Kimono," *Fortune* (June 15, 1981), 247–50.
39. Lee J. Krajewski and Larry P. Ritzman, *Operations Management: Strategy and Analysis* (Reading, Mass.: Addison-Wesley, 1987), 573.
40. Krajewski and Ritzman, *Operations Management,* 572–84.

CHAPTER 21

1. "The Push for Quality," *Business Week,* June 8, 1987, 131.
2. A.V. Feigenbaum, *Total Quality Control* (New York: McGraw-Hill, 1983).
3. From Michael Schroeder, "Heart Trouble at Pfizer," *Business Week* (February 26, 1990), 47–48.
4. For more information on these three contributors, see Charles H. Fine and David H. Bridge, "Managing Quality Improvement," in *Quest for Quality: Managing the Total System,* ed. by M. Sepehri (Norcross, Ga.: Institute of Industrial Engineers, 1987), 66–74.

5. For some of Crosby's more notable books in this area, see Philip B. Crosby, *Quality Is Free* (New York: McGraw-Hill, 1979); *Quality Without Tears* (New York: McGraw-Hill, 1984); *Let's Talk Quality: 96 Questions You Always Wanted to Ask Phil Crosby* (New York: McGraw-Hill, 1989); and *Leading* (New York: McGraw-Hill, 1990).
6. Adapted from fourteen points of W. Edwards Deming, *Out of Crisis* (Cambridge, Mass.: MIT Center for Advanced Engineering Study, 1986). For more discussion of these points, see James R. Evans and William M. Lindsay, *The Management and Control of Quality* (St. Paul, Minn.: West Publishing Company, 1989), 451–53.
7. Ross Johnson and William O. Winchell, *Strategy and Quality* (Milwaukee, Wisc.: American Society for Quality Control, 1989), 1–2.
8. Company Mission Statement, All America Inc., 1991, used by permission.
9. For a discussion supporting how important training can be in a companywide quality effort, see "Dr. W. Edwards Deming," *EBS Journal* (Spring 1989), 3.
10. J. Buckley, "Goal-Process-System Interaction in Management: Correcting the Imbalance," *Business Horizons* 14 (December 1971), 81–89.
11. "Stressing the Systems Approach," *Manufacturing Engineering* (August 1969), 75.
12. Martha McDonald, "Valuing Experience: How to Keep Older Workers Healthy," *Business & Health* 8 (January 1990), 35–38.
13. Robert W. Goddard, "Work Force 2000," *Personnel Journal* 68 (February 1989), 64–71.
14. Tom Lupton, "Efficiency and the Quality of Life," *Organizational Dynamics* (Autumn 1975), 68.
15. George F. Kimmerling, "The Future of HRD," *Training & Development Journal* (June 1989), 50.
16. Gary N. Powell, "One More Time: Do Female and Male Managers Differ?" *Academy of Management Executive* 4:3 (1990), 68–75.
17. Claudia Wallis, "Onward, Women!" *Time* (December 4, 1989), 80–89. Also see Helen Rogan, "Top Women Executives Find Path to Power Strewn with Hurdles," *Wall Street Journal* (October 25, 1984), 35.
18. William A. Henry III, "Beyond the Melting Pot," *Time* (April 9, 1990), 28–31.
19. Joel Dryfuss, "Get Ready for the New Work Force," *Fortune* (April 23, 1990), 165–81.
20. John M. Griffin, "Demographic Opportunities for the '90s and Beyond," *Vital Speeches* 56 (May 1, 1990), 437–40.
21. Loretta D. Foxman and Walter L. Polsky, "Cross-Cultural Understanding," *Personnel Journal* 68 (November 1989), 12–14.

Indexes

Company Name Index

Name Index

Ivancevich, John M., 8, 35
Iverson, F. Kenneth, 431
Izumi, Yoji, 302

Jackofsky, Ellen F., 166
Jackson, Jerry, 518
Jacobson, Allen, 426
Jacobson, Gary, 624
Jacoby, Neil H., 626
Jago, Arthur G., 423–424
Janis, Irving L., 489
Jereski, Laura, 62
Jobs, Steve, 508, 509
Johnson, Robert W., 11
Jones, Jack W., 486
Jones, William, 62
Juran, Joseph M., 662

Kalgoris, Michael E., 188
Karatka, Joseph, 188
Kast, Fremont E., 223
Kates, Henry, 343–345
Katz, Robert L., 14
Kaufman, Steven, 296
Kearns, David, 47, 682–683
Keen, Peter G. W., 169
Keller, Maryann, 442
Kelly, Harold H., 458
Kelly, Phil, 662
Kelly, Thomas, 404
Kemper, Robert E., 100, 128, 250, 278, 308,
    408, 512, 612, 616, 680, 684
Kendall, Donald, 648–649
Kennedy, Robert D., 355
Keyes, Sylvia, 28, 246, 374
Kimbro, Dennis P., 284
King, William R., 144
Kinnear, James, 248–249
Knight, Philip, 269
Koontz, Harold, 8, 35, 135–136, 270, 300
Korman, A. K., 428
Korn, Lester, 410–411
Kotter, John P., 415, 534
Kraar, Louis, 147, 266, 326
Kreitner, Robert, 8
Kroc, Ray, 11, 169
Krok, Arlene, 216–217
Krok, Sharon, 216–217
Krok, Solomon, 216–217
Krushchev, Nikita, 648

LaBonte, C. Joseph, 273
Lager, Chico, 652
Lang, Eugene, 97–98
Lawler, Edward E., III, 452, 531
Lay, Herman, 649
Lear, Norman, 86, 87
Lee, Albert, 443
Leerhsen, Charles, 652
Levering, R., 469
Levitt, Theodore, 114, 415
Levy, John, 510, 511
Lewin, Kurt, 363
Lewis, Edward, 130–131
Lieberthal, Kenneth, 631
Likert, Rensis, 427, 468–470
Lippitt, Ronald, 483
Lipson, Harry A., 74–75
Loden, Marilyn, 342
Lopez, Julie Amparano, 188
Lowenstein, Peter, 308
Luther, David, 47

McAfee, Jerry, 85–86
McAvoy, Eileen, 246–247
McCarthy, Michael J., 348
McClelland, David C., 457
McCurry, Robert B., 228–229
McDonald, Marshall, 680
McDonnell, John F., 251
McGregor, Douglas, 335, 460
McKenney, James L., 169
Mackey, John, 225
McLaughlin, Irene, 566
McLeod, Raymond, Jr., 486
Magee, John F., 176–177
Magin, Roland, 352–353
Maglica, Claire, 617
Maglica, Tony, 616–617
Main, Jeremy, 270
Malone, Thomas, 388, 389
Margulies, Newton, 364
Marshall, Christy, 527
Marszewski, Carl, 390
Martin, John, 348
Maslow, Abraham, 454–455
Massie, Joseph L., 8, 35
Mattox, Jim, 95
Mee, John F., 108, 356
Mehrabian, Albert, 398
Meister, Jeanne C., 652
Michael, John L., 458
Middleton, C. J., 355
Miles, Gregory L., 551, 656
Miles, Raymond E., 264
Milken, Michael, 376
Miller, Annetta, 448, 548
Miller, Doug, 548
Miller, Maggie, 160
Miller, R. S., Jr., 160
Milliken, Roger, 388
Mills, Roderick, 112
Minow, Newton, 209
Mintzberg, Henry, 142
Mitchell, Russell, 426
Moad, Jeff, 602
Mockler, Robert, 520
Monaghan, Thomas S., 437
Mooney, J. D., 41, 268
Moore, Thomas, 293
Morgan, Gareth, 270
Mork, William J., 526
Muchera, Kaaria, 365–366
Murdick, Robert G., 598
Murninghan, J, Keith, 499

Napoleon, 328
Nemetz, Patricia L., 552
Newman, William H., 298
Newport, John Paul, Jr., 233, 366, 558
Nixon, Richard, 489, 648
Norris, F., 349
Norris, William, 68–69

O'Donnell, Cyril, 8, 35, 135–136, 300
Olson, Frank, 544–545
Olsten, Mim, 444
Olsten, William, 444–445
O'Reilly, C. A., III, 404
Osborn, Alex F., 165
Ouchi, William, 641–642

Parilla, Jamie, 633
Paul, Ron, 348
Perot, H. Ross, 443

Perry, Nancy J., 329
Peters, Thomas J., 10, 21, 262, 271
Petersen, Peter B., 56
Plunkett, Ken, 548
Porter, L. W., 452
Porter, Michael E., 205
Posner, Bruce G., 225
Powell, Colin, 612–613
Prahalad, C. K., 189, 631
Prather, Tom, 231
Price, Michael, 157
Pritsker, A. A. B., 240
Pyhrr, Peter, 570
Pyrillis, Rita, 62

Quadracci, Henry, 469

Rath, Bernie, 448
Raven, Bertram, 534
Rawl, Lawrence G., 181–182, 272
Read, Wayne, 584
Reagan, Ronald, 410, 489, 612
Reddin, W. J., 460
Reddy, Helen, 284
Reichert, Linda, 90
Reiley, A. C., 41
Reinemund, Steve, 348
Rhode, John G., 531
Rice, Ron, 30–31
Rich, Robert, 580–581
Richman, Barry M., 634
Ringbakk, Kjell A., 136, 229
Rishman, Louis S., 603
Roberts, Bert C., Jr., 256
Robinson, James, 558
Rodgers, Francis G. (Buck), 11
Rohan, Thomas M., 624
Roney, C. W., 135
Rosener, Judy B., 342
Rosenzweig, James E., 223
Ross, Jerry, 172

Sains, Ariane, 355
Schellhardt, Timothy, 639
Schilit, Warren Keith, 19
Schlesinger, Jacob M., 384
Schmidt, Warren H., 418, 420, 422
Schramm, Wilbur, 390
Schwarzkopf, Norman, 612, 613
Schweitzer, Albert, 86
Scowcroft, Brent, 612
Sculley, John, 508–599
Segal, Joseph, 138
Selye, Hans, 365
Selz, Michael, 106
Sethi, S. Prakash, 75–77
Shad, John, 86
Sheldon, Oliver, 41
Shepherd, Edward, 646
Shepherd, Mark, 11
Shetty, Y. K., 110, 266, 526
Shrader, Charles A., 95
Shulman, Brett, 281
Shulman, Edwin, 280–281
Shulman, Samuel, 280
Shulman, Stanley, 280–281
Simmons, Donald B., 402
Simmons, John K., 603
Sisk, Henry L., 8
Skinner, B. F., 466
Sloan, Alfred P., 135, 442
Slocum, John W., Jr., 350–351

Subject Index

Credits

Chapter 1

Figure 1.2: From Dana Wechsler, "Just Deserts," *Forbes,* May 28, 1990, 208. Excerpted by permission of *Forbes* magazine. © Forbes Inc., 1990. **Table 1.2:** From *In Search of Excellence* (pp. 13–16) by T. J. Peters and R. H. Waterman Jr., 1982, New York: Harper & Row Publishers. Copyright 1982 by Thomas J. Peters and Robert H. Waterman Jr. Reprinted by permission. **Figure 1.6:** From Paul Hersey/Kenneth Blanchard, *Management of Organizational Behavior: Utilizing Human Resources,* 5e, © 1988, p. 8. Reprinted by permission of Prentice-Hall, Inc., Englewood Cliffs, NJ. **Figure 1.7:** From *Careers in Organizations* by Douglas T. Hall, © 1976 Scott, Foresman and Company. Reprinted by permission. **Table 1.3:** From Lynn Slavenski, "Career Development: A Systems Approach," *Training and Development Journal,* (February 1987):58. Copyright 1987, *Training and Development Journal,* American Society for Training and Development. Reprinted with permission. All rights reserved. **Table 1.4:** Reprinted by permission from Paul H. Thompson, Robin Zenger Baker, and Norman Smallwood, "Improving Professional Development by Applying the Four-Stage Career Model," *Organizational Dynamics* (Autumn 1986): 59. © 1986 American Management Association, Inc. All rights reserved. **Table 1.5:** © 1976 by the Regents of the University of California. Reprinted from Ross A. Webber, "Career Problems of Young Managers," *California Management Review,* Vol. 18, No. 4 (Summer 1976): 29, by permission of the Regents.

Chapter 2

Global Highlight: From Anne M. Hayer, "Packaging Solutions at Delta," *Manufacturing Engineering* 103 (August 1989), 69–70. **Table 2.2:** From William R. Spriegel and Clark E. Myers, *The Writings of the Gilbreths* Easton, Pa: Richard D. Irwin, (1953), p. 56. By permission of Hive Publishing Company. **Quality Highlight:** Sources: Jeremy Main, "How to Win the Baldrige Award," *Fortune* (April 23, 1990), 101–116; Christopher W. I. Hart, Christopher Bogan, and Dan O'Brien, "When Winning Isn't Everything," *Harvard Business Review* (January-February 1990) 209–209. **Ethics Highlight:** From Annette Kondo, "Disaster Plans Prove Sound after San Francisco Shake-Up," *Wall Street Computer Review* 17, (December 1989), 6–10. **Case Study:** Peter B. Peterson, "The Pioneering Efforts of Major General William Crozier (1855–1942) in the Field of Management," *Journal of Management,* 15 (1989) 3.

Chapter 3

Quality Highlight: From Alan Halcrow, "Social Service at Xerox," *Personnel Journal* (March 1987), 10–15. **Table 3.1:** Adapted from Terry W. McAdams, "How to Put Corporate Responsibility into Practice." Reprinted by permission from *Business and Society Review* (Summer 1973): 12–13. Copyright 1973, Warren, Gorham and Lamont Inc., 210 South St., Boston, Mass. All rights reserved. **Global Highlight:** From Edgar S. Wollard, Jr., "The 'Soul' Factor in Corporate Growth and Prosperity," *Directors and Boards* (Winter 1989), 4–8. **Table 3.4:** From Sandra L. Holmes, "Executive Perceptions of Social Responsibility," *Business Horizons* (June 1976). Copyright, 1976, by the Foundation for the School of Business at Indiana University. Reprinted by permission. **Figure 3.1:** From Ramon J. Aldag and Donald W. Jackson, Jr., "A Managerial Framework for Social Decision Making," p. 34, *MSU Business Topics* (Winter 1975). Reprinted by permission of the publisher, Division of Research, Graduate School of Business Administration, Michigan State University. **Table 3.5:** © 1975 by the Regents of the University of California. Reprinted from S. Prakash Sethi, "Dimensions of Corporate Social Performance: An Analytical Framework," *California Management Review,* Vol. 17, No. 3 (Spring 1975): 63, by permission of the Regents. **Figure 3.2:** From Kenneth E. Newgren, "Social Forecasting: An Overview of Current Business Practices," in Archie B. Carroll, ed., *Managing Corporate Social Responsibility.* Copyright © 1977 by Little, Brown and Company (Inc.). Reprinted by permission of the author. **Figure 3.3:** Reprinted by permission of the *Harvard Business Review,* from "How Companies Respond to Social Demands," by Robert W. Ackerman (July/August 1973): 96. Copyright © 1973 by the President and Fellows of Harvard College; all rights reserved. **Figure 3.4:** Reprinted by permission from John L. Paulszek, "How Three Companies Organize for Social Responsibility," *Business and Society Review* (Summer 1973): 18, Warren, Gorham and Lamont, Inc., 210 South St., Boston, Mass. All rights reserved. **Table 3.6:** Reprinted by permission from Bernard Butcher, "Anatomy of a Social Performance Report," *Business and Society Review* (Autumn 1973): 29, Warren, Gorham and Lamont, Inc., 210 South St., Boston, Mass. All rights reserved. **Ethics Highlight:** From Bruce Fox, "A&P Staffer Gets Snowball Rolling," *Chain Store Age Executive* (September 1989), 19–20. **Table 3.7:** Reprinted by permission of Johnson & Johnson. **Table 3.8:** Reprinted by permission from "Code of Ethics and Standards of Conduct" (Orlando, Fla.: Martin Marietta, n.d.), p. 3. **Case Study:** Sources: David Bartal, "Volvo's Back-to-the-Future Factory," *U.S. News and World Report,* August 21, 1989, 42. "The Natural Consequence of Doing Things the Volvo Way," *Business Week* November 19, 1990, 128–129. "Taking 'em for a ride." *Time,* November 19, 1990, 85. "Apologies," *U.S. News and World Report,* November 19, 1990, 19. Neal Templin, "U.S. Car Sales Slid Sharply in Nov. 21–30," *Wall Street Journal,* December 5, 1990, A4–A5. Krystal Miller and Jacqueline Mitchell, "Car Marketers Test Gray Area of Truth in Advertising," *Wall Street Journal,* November 19, 1990, B1, B6.

Chapter 4

Figure 4.2: From Jon H. Barrett, *Individual Goals and Organizational Objectives: A Study of Integration Mechanisms,* p. 5. Copyright © 1970 by the Institute for Social Research, The University of Michigan. Reprinted with permission. **Global Highlight:** Based on Kathryn J. McIntyre, "Worldwide Gillette Operations Send Risk Manager Globetrotting," *Business Insurance* (April 18, 1988); and David Wessel, "Gillette Keys Sales to Third World Tastes," *Wall Street Journal* (January 26, 1986), 33. **Ethics Highlight:** From Stacy Shapiro, "Employer Fights AIDS with Education," *Business Insurance* (October 30, 1989), 31. **Figure 4.4:** From Joseph L. Massie and John Douglas, *Managing,* © 1985, p. 244. Reprinted by permission of Prentice-Hall, Inc. Englewood Cliffs, New Jersey. **Table 4.2:** From *Management Concepts and Situations* by Howard M. Carlisle. © 1976, Science Research Associate, Inc. Adapted and reprinted by permission of the publisher. **Table 4.3:** Reprinted by permission from A. N. Geller, *Executive Information Needs in Hotel Companies* (New York: Peat Marwick Mitchell, 1984), p. 17. © Peat Marwick Main & Co., 1984. **Figure 4.5:** From Samuel C. Certo, Stewart Husted, and Max E. Douglas, *Business,* 3d ed. (Boston: Allyn & Bacon, 1990), 205. **Quality Highlight:** From Albert W. Schrader and G. Taylor Seward, "MBO Makes Dollar Sense," *Personnel Journal* (July 1989), 32–37. **Case Study:** Source: Bailey, Jeff and Robert L. Rose, "Ways of a High-Tech Team Didn't Please Many Folks in a Small Iowa Town," *Wall Street Journal,* October 17, 1988, 1, A2.

Chapter 5

Quality Highlight: From Bruce H. Andrews and Henry L. Parsons, "L. L. Bean Chooses a Telephone Agent Scheduling System," *Interfaces* 19 (November/December 1989), 1–9. **Global Highlight:** From Geoffrey E. Duin, "Playing the Flip Side of the Japanese Record Business," *Tokyo Business Today* (January 1990). **Ethics Highlight:** From Thomas G. Donlan, "Still a Lousy Idea: The Odometer Imbroglio Haunts Chrysler," *Barron's* (March 6, 1989), 24–25. **Figure 5.5:** From William R. King and David I. Cleland, "A New Method for Strategic Systems Planning," *Business Horizons* (August 1975): 56. Copyright, 1975, by the Foundation for the School of Business at Indiana University. Reprinted by permission. **Case Study:** Sources: D'Anastasio, "PepsiCo's Pizza Hut Signs Agreement for Soviet Venture; McDonald's Next?" *Wall Street Journal,* September 18 1987, 12; Paul Farhi, "Pizza Rising Fast in Fast Good Market," *Washington Post,* September 20, 1988, E1, E6; "Pizza Hut Outlets to Open in Moscow Under New Pact," *Wall Street Journal,* February 23, 1989; "Pizza Hut Plans Brazil Expansion," *New York Times,* October 19, 1990; "Pizza Huts for Moscow, Beijing," *Wall Street Journal,* September 11, 1990; Charles P. Wallace, "Exotic Dining in Bangkok Means the Pizza Hut," *Los Angeles Times,* August 21, 1990, H4.

Chapter 6

Table 6.1: From Herbert A. Simon, *The Shape of Automation* (New York: Harper & Row, 1965), p. 62. Used with permission of the author. **Figure 6.3:** Republished with permission of E. I. du Pont de Nemours & Company. **Table 6.2:** Reprinted from "Characteristics of Organizational Environments and Perceived Environmental Uncertainty" by Robert B. Duncan. Published by *Administrative Science Quarterly,* Vol. 17, No. 3 (September 1972). By permission of *Administrative Science Quarterly.* **Ethic Highlight:** From Cynthia Starr, "To Sell or Not to Sell Cigarette Products?" *Drug Topics* (May 1988), 28–34. **Global Highlight:** From Ford S. Worthy, "What's Next for Business in China," *Fortune* (July 17, 1989), 110–112. **Quality Highlight:** From Brian Dumaine, "Those High-Flying PepsiCo Managers" *Fortune* (April 10, 1989), 78–86. **Figure 6.8:** Reprinted by permission of the *Harvard Business Review.* An exhibit from "Decision Trees for Decision Making" by John F. Magee (July/August 1964): 130. Copyright © 1964 by the President and Fellows of Harvard College; all rights reserved.

Chapter 7

Table 7.1: (a) and (b) based on E. Meadows, "How Three Companies Increased Their Productivity," *Fortune,* March 10, 1980, pp. 92–101. (c) based on William B. Johnson, "The Transformation of a Railroad," *Long-Range Planning* 9 (December 1976): 18–23. **Figure 7.1:** Adapted from Samuel C. Certo and J. Paul Peter, *Strategic Management: Concepts and Applications* (New York: McGraw-Hill, 1991), p ***. **Table 7.2:** From William F. Glueck and Lawrence R. Jauch, *Business Policy and Strategic Management.* © 1984 McGraw-Hill Book Company, New York. Reprinted by permission. **Ethics Highlight:** From Joshua Levine, "Locking Up the Weekend Warriors," *Forbes,* October 2, 1989, 234–235. **Global Highlight:** From Steven B. Weiner, "The Unlimited?" *Forbes,* April 6, 1987, 76–80. Mast Industries Inc. "The World Without Boundaries," Recruitment Brochure. **Table 7.3:** Adapted from Arvind V. Phatak, *International Dimensions of Management* (Boston: Kent Publishing, 1983), p. 6. © by Wadsworth, Inc. Reprinted by permission of PWS-Kent Publishing Co., a division of Wadsworth, Inc. **Table 7.5:** [1]From the Roy E. Crummer Graduate School of Business Handbook, 1989. [2]From the IBM 1990 Annual Report. [3]From the Federal Express Manager's Guide, 1990. **Table 7.6:** From Arthur A. Thompson, Jr., and A. J.

Strickland III, *Strategy Formulation and Implementation,* 3d ed. Copyright © 1986 Business Publications, Inc. Reprinted by permission. **Quality Highlight:** From "How Harley Beat Back the Japanese," *Fortune,* September 1989, 155–64. **Figure 7.3:** © 1970 The Boston Consulting Group, Inc. All rights reserved. Published by permission. **Figure 7.4:** From Charles W. Hofer, and Dan Schendel, *Strategy Formulation: Analytical Concepts* (St. Paul, MN: West Publishing 1978), p. 32. Copyright © 1978 by West Publishing Company. All rights reserved. **Figure 7.5:** Adapted from Michael E. Porter, *Competitive Advantage: Creating and Sustaining Superior Performance* (New York: The Free Press, 1985), p. 6. Adapted with permission of The Free Press, a division of Macmillan, Inc. Copyright © 1985 by Michael E. Porter. **Figure 7.7:** Reprinted with the special permission of *Dun's Review* form R. M. Besse, "Company Planning Must Be Planned." April 1957, p. 48. Copyright 1957, Dun & Bradstreet Publications Corporation.

Chapter 8

Ethics Highlight: From Michele Galen and Vicky Cahan, "The Legal Reef Ahead for Exxon," *Business Week.* March 12, 1990, 39. **Table 8.1:** Copyright © 1969 by the Trustees of Columbia University in the City of New York. **Global Highlight:** From Larry Armstrong, "The American Drivers Steering Japan Through the United States," *Business Week.* March 12, 1990, 98–99. **Table 8.2:** Reprinted by permission from *Indiana State University Handbook 1969.* Revised in 1970 and in 1972, Terre Haute, Indiana. **Tables 8.3, 8.4:** Adapted from E. S. Groo, "Choosing Foreign Locations: One Company's Experience," *Columbia Journal of World Business* (September/October 1977): 77. Used with permission. **Quality Highlight:** From Bill Stack, "Toyota in Bluegrass Country," *Industry Week,* June 5, 1989, 30–33. William J. Holstein, Peter Engardio, and Dan Cook, "Will Sake and Sour Mash Go Together?" *Business Week,* July 14, 1986, 53–55. **Figure 8.4:** From Bruce Coleman, "An Integrated System for Manpower Planning," *Business Horizons* (October 1970): 89–95. Copyright, 1970, by the Foundation for the School of Business at Indiana University. Reprinted by permission. **Figure 8.6:** From Philip Kotler, *Marketing Management Analysis, Planning and Control,* © 1967, p. 291. Adapted by permission of Prentice-Hall, Inc., Englewood Cliffs, N.J. **Table 8.5:** Adapted, with permission, from W. C. House, "Environmental Analysis: Key to More Effective Dynamic Planning," *Managerial Planning* (January/February 1977): 27, published by the Planning Executive Institute, Oxford, Ohio 45046. **Figure 8.8:** Reprinted by permission of the Sperry Rand Corporation. **Case Study:** Source: Interview by Sylvia Keyes, Bridgewater State College, with Eileen McAvoy, Associate Product Manager, the Gillette Company.

Chapter 9

Ethics Highlight: Carolyn Garrett Cline and Michael D. Cline, "The Gerber Baby Cries Foul!" *Business & Society Review* (Winter 1987), 14–19. **Figure 9.11:** © 1972 by the Regents of the University of California. Reprinted from Y. K. Shetty and H. M. Carlise, "A Contingency Model of Organizational Behavior," *California Management Review,* Vol. 15, No. 1, p. 44, by permission of the Regents. **Quality Highlight:** From Barbra Buell, "Nike Cathes Up with the Trendy Front-runner," *Business Week.* October 24, 1988, 88. **Table 9.2:** From *Principles of Management,* p. 253, by Harold Koontz and Cyril O'Donnell. Copyright © 1972 by McGraw-Hill, Inc. Used with permission of McGraw-Hill Book Co. **Global Highlight:** From Laura Jereski, "Paul Fireman Pulls on His Old Running Shoes," *Business Week.* November 6, 1989, 46–47. **Figure 9.14:** From H. Fayol, *General and Industrial Management,* trans. Constance Storrs (London: Sir Isaac Pitman & Sons, Ltd., 1963), p. 34. Used with permission. **Case Study:** Sedona Fire Department, "Modernizing Current Job Descriptions, Performance Evaluations and Grievance Procedures," *Solicitation for Bid: Sedona Fire Department, Personnel Division,* 1991.

Chapter 10

Quality Highlight: From Phil Niestedt and Richard Wintermantel, "Motorola Restructures to Improve Productivity," *Management Review* 76 (January 1987), 47–49. **Table 10.1:** Reprinted, by permission of the publisher, from "Roles and Relationships Clarifying the Manager's Job," by Robert D. Melcher, *Personnel* (May/June 1967): 35, 38–39. © 1967 American Management Association, New York. All rights reserved. **Table 10.3:** Adapted from ASPA-BNA Survey No. 47, "Personnel Activities, Budgets, and Staffs: 1983–1984," *Bulletin to Management* No. 1785—Part II, June 21, 1984. Copyright 1984 by The Bureau of National Affairs, Inc. Reprinted by permission. **Ethics Highlight:** From Joseph Conlin, "The House That G. E. Built," *Successful Meetings* 38 (August 1989), 50–58. **Table 10.4:** Reprinted with permission of Macmillan Publishing Company from *The New Management* by Robert M. Fulmer. Copyright © 1974 by Robert M. Fulmer. **Figure 10.3:** From David B. Starkweather, "The Rationale for Decentralization in Large Hospitals," *Hospital Administration* 15 (Spring 1970): 139. Courtesy of Dr. P. N. Ghei, Secretary General, Indiana Hospital Association, New Delhi. **Global Highlight:** From Kenneth Silber, "Japan's Banks Decentralized," *Bank Systems & Technology* 27 (February 1990), 28–33. **Case Study:** Sources: George Anders, "Weak Trend: Value Line is Hurt by Low Morale, Slide in Interest in Stocks," *The Wall Street Journal,* August 2, 1989, 1, A2. Value Line Inc. *Compact Disclosure, 1991.*

Chapter 11

Figure 11.2: Reprinted with permission of Macmillan Publishing Company form *Personnel: The Management of People at Work* by Dale S. Beach. Copyright © 1970 by Dale S. Beach. **Table 11.1:** From U.S. Civil Service Commission.

Figures 11.3, 11.4, 11.5: From Walter S. Wikstrom, "Developing Managerial Competence: Concepts, Emerging Practices," *Studies in Personnel Policy* No. 189, pp. 14, 9. Used with permission. **Table 11.2:** From Gene E. Burton, Dev S. Pathak, David B. Burton, "Equal Employment Opportunity: Law and Labyrinth," *Management World,* published by Administrative Management Society, September 1976, pp. 29, 30. **Figure 11.6:** Reprinted by permission from L. C. Megginson, *Providing Management Talent for Small Business* (Baton Rouge, La. Division of Research, College of Business Administration, Louisiana State University, 1961), p. 108. **Global Highlight:** From Anne Ferguson, "Compaq's Personnel Solution," *Management Today* (May 1989), 127–128; Prabhu Guptara, "Searching the Organization for the Cross-Cultural Operators," *International Management* 41 (August 1986), 40–42. **Table 11.3:** From Dale Feuer, "Where the Dollars Go," reprinted from the October 1985 issue of *Training,* The Magazine of Human Resources Development, p. 53. Copyright 1985, Lakewood Publications Inc., Minneapolis, MN (612)333-0471. All rights reserved. **Quality Highlight:** From Kathryn W. Porter, "Tuning in to TV Training," *Training and Development Journal* 44 (April 1990), 73–77. **Figure 11.8:** From George R. Terry and Leslie W. Rue, *Personal Learning Aid for Principles of Management,* p. 138. Copyright © 1982 Dow Jones-Irwin. Reprinted by permission. **Table 11.4:** Compiled from *Personnel Administration and Human Resource Management* by Andrew F. Sikula (New York: John Wiley & Sons, 1976), pp. 208–211. **Ethics Highlight:** From Ken Sternberg, "Mobil Fights a Cover-up Charge," *Chemical Week* 146 (January 3, 1990/January 10, 1990), 10. **Case Study:** *Source:* Marilyn Loden and Judy B. Rosener, *Workforce America! Managing Employee Diversity as a Vital Resource.* Homewood, IL: Business One Irwin, 1991.

Chapter 12

Figure 12.1: From Don Hellriegel and John W. Slocum, Jr., "Integrating Systems Concepts and Organizational Strategy," *Business Horizons* 15 (April 1972): 73. Copyright, 1972, by the Foundation for the School of Business at Indiana University. Reprinted by permission. **Global Highlight:** From James Sasseen, "Change Agent," *International Management* 45 (March 1990), 48–50. **Quality Highlight:** Sources: Ariane Sains, "Carbide Workers Keeping Company Morale High," *The New-Times,* December 13, 1984, 1, 8; James R. Norman, "A New Union Carbide Is Slowly Starting to Gel," *Business Week,* April 18, 1988, 68–69. **Figure 12.4, 12.5:** From John F. Mee, "Matrix Organization," *Business Horizons* (Summer 1964): 71. Copyright, 1964, by the Foundation for the School of Business at Indiana University. Reprinted by permission. **Figure 12.6:** From Richard J. Selfridge and Stanley I. Sokolik, "A Comprehensive View of Organization Development," p. 47, *MSU Business Topics* (Winter 1975). Reprinted by permission of the publishers, Division of Research, Graduate School of Business Administration, Michigan State University. **Figure 12.7:** Reprinted by permission of *Harvard Business Review,* from "Breakthrough in Organization Development," by Robert R. Blake, Jane S. Mouton, Louis Barnes, and Larry Greiner (November/December 1964): 136. Copyright © 1964 by the President and Fellows of Harvard College; all rights reserved. **Figure 12.9:** Reprinted by permission of the authors from Arthur P. Brief, Randall S. Schuller, and Mary Van Sell, *Managing Job Stress* (Boston: Little, Brown, 1981), p. 66. **Ethics Highlight:** From Fraser P. Seitel, "1,000 Points of Banker Light," *United States Banker* 100 (March 1990) 68, 70. **Case Study:** *Sources:* Chris Sauula, "Prime Users Still on Hold," *Datanation,* September 1, 1990; Gary Slutsker, "The Company They Couldn't Sell," *Forbes,* October 2, 1989; Nell Margolis, "Big Overhaul Set at Prime," *Computer World,* December 19, 1988; Interview with Kathleen A. Cote, President and General Manager of Prime Service, by Sulvia Keyes, Bridgewater State College.

Chapter 13

Table 13.1: Reprinted by permission from Stephen C. Harper, "Business Education: A View from the Top," *Business Forum* (Summer 1987): 25. **Quality Highlight:** From Tom Peters and Nancy Austin, *A Passion for Excellence: The Leadership Difference,* Random House (1985), 304–307. Sandra Edwards, "Quality Pays Off at Milliken," *Chemical Engineering* (April 1990), 59–61. **Global Highlight:** From Patricia Crane and James W. Johnson, "A Bright Future for International Teleconferencing," *Satellite Communications* 13 (November 1989), 16a, 18a. **Figures 13.4, 13.5:** From Wilber Schramm, *The Process and Effects of Mass Communication* © 1954 University of Illinois Press, Champaign, IL. Reprinted by permission. **Ethics Highlight:** From Joanne Dillon, "Companies Helping Kids," *Communication World* (October 1989), 31–32. **Figure 13.7:** Reprinted, by permission of the publisher, from "An Experimental Approach to Organizational Communication," by Alex Bavelas and Dermot Barrett, *Personnel* (March 1951): 370. © 1951 American Management Association, Inc. All rights reserved. **Figure 13.8:** Reprinted by permission of the *Harvard Business Review.* An exhibit from "Management Communication and the Grapevine" by Keith Davis (September/October 1953): 45. Copyright © 1953 by the President and Fellows of Harvard College; all rights reserved. **Table 13.2:** From *Human Behavior at Work,* p. 396, by Keith Davis. Copyright © 1972 by McGraw-Hill, Inc. Used with permission of McGraw-Hill Book Company. **Case Study:** *Sources:* Vance H. Trimble, *Sam Walton, Founder of Wal-Mart: The Inside Story of America's Richest Man.* New York: Dutton, 1990. Wal-Mart Stores Incorporated, *Compact Disclosure,* 1991. **Part 4 Integrative Case:** *Sources:* Navajo Arts and Crafts Enterprise, "Personnel Policies and Procedures," July, 1987; Navajo Arts and Crafts Enterprise, "Strategic and Operational Management Guide," July, 1987.

Chapter 14

Global Highlight: From Esther Lee Yao, "Cultivating Guan-Xi (Personal Relationships) with Chinese Partners," *Business Marketing* 72 (January 1987), 62–66.

Sources: Douglas Harbrecht et al, "Managing the War: It Involves Far More than Combat—and Colin Powell Is Much More Than a Warrior," *Businessweek,* February 4, 1991; Mark Lewyn et al, "This Army Marches on Silicon," *Businessweek,* February 4, 1991; Otis Port et al, "The High Tech War Machine," *Businessweek,* February 4, 1991. **Part 5 Integrative Case:** *Source:* Paul B. Brown, "Mag Instruments," *Inc.,* August, 1989.

Chapter 20

Figure 20.1: From "U.S. Direct Investment Abroad: Detail for Position and Balance of Payments Flows, 1987," *Survey of Current Business* 68 (August 1988), 42–68; "U.S. Direct Investment Abroad: Detail for Position and Balance of Payments Flows, 1988," *Survey of Current Business* 69 (August 1989), 62–88. **Figure 20.2:** From "Foreign Direct Investment in the United States: Detail for Position and Balance of Payments Flows, 1987," *Survey of Current Business* 68 (August 1988), 69–83; "Foreign Direct Investment in the United States: Detail for Position and Balance of Payment Flows, 1988," *Survey of Current Business* 69 (August 1989), 47–61. **Ethics Highlight:** From Jang B. Singh and V. Chris Lakhan, "Business Ethics and the International Trade in Hazardous Wastes," *Journal of Business Ethics* 8 (November 1989), 889–99. **Table 20.1:** Excerpted from "The FORBES Foreign Rankings," by permission of *Forbes* magazine, July 19, 1985. © Forbes, Inc., 1985. **Global Highlight:** From Joseph W. Weiss and Stanley Bloom, "Managing in China: Expatriate Experiences and Training," *Business Horizons* 33 (May/June 1990), 23–29. **Figure 20.3:** Reprinted by permission of the author from Richard D. Robinson, *International Management* (Hinsdale, Ill.: Dryden Press, 1967). **Table 20.3:** From Stefan H. Robock and Kenneth Simmonds, *International Business and Multinational Enterprise,* 3d ed. Copyright © 1983 Richard D. Irwin, Inc. Reprinted by permission. **Table 20.4:** Reprinted with permission from Howard V. Perimutter, "The Tortuous Evolution of the Multinational Corporation," *Columbia Journal of World Business* 4 (January/February 1989): 12. **Table 20.5:** From Hugh E. Kramer, "Concepts of Competition in America, Europe, and Japan," in *Business and Society* (Fall 1977). © 1977 Business and Society. Reprinted by permission. **Quality Highlight:** From Carol Hiderbrand, *Computer World,* 100. **Figure 20.6:** From William Ouchi, *Theory Z,* © 1981, Addison-Wesley Publishing Co., Inc., Reading, Massachusetts. Page 58 (adapted figure). Reprinted with permission. **Case Study:** From Walter E. Greene, "The Maquiladora—Japan's New Competitive Weapon," *Business* (October–December 1989), 52–56; "Is Free Trade with Mexico Good or Bad for the U.S.?" *Business Week,* November 12, 1990, 112–113; Jane LeMaster, *A Survey of the Maquiladora Industry in Mexico,* a class term paper at the University of North Texas, Spring, 1990; John P.McCray and Juan J. Gonzales, "Increasing Global Competitiveness with U.S.–Mexican Maquiladora Operations," *San Advanced Management Journal* (Summer 1989) 4–7, 28, 48; "Mexico: A New Economic Era," *Business Week,* November 12, 1990, 102–111.

Chapter 21

Quality Highlight: From R. H. Walklet, "Simultaneous Engineering: A Critical Strategy at Cadillac Motor Car Division and a Highlight of Its Malcolm Baldrige National Quality Award Application." Paper presented to the Society of Automotive Engineers. Anonymous, "Overview of Cadillac Motor Car Division," Malcolm Baldrige National Quality Award Office (December 13, 1990). **Table 21.1:** *Source:* Several of these ideas/comparisons were adapted from Richard J. Schonberger's books: *Japanese Manufacturing Techniques* (New York: Free Press, 1982), 47–82; and *World Class Manufacturing* (New York: Free Press, 1986), 122–43. **Figure 21.1:** From David A. Gavin, "What Does Product Quality Really Mean?" *Sloan Management Review* 26:1 (Fall 1984), 37. Reprinted by permission of the publisher. Copyright 1984 by the Sloan Management Review Association. All rights reserved. **Table 21.3:** From Philip B. Crosby, *Quality without Tears* (New York: McGraw-Hill, 1984), 8–9. Copyright 1984. Reprinted with permission of McGraw-Hill, Inc. **Ethics Highlight:** From Rajendra S. Sisodia, "We Need Zero-Tolerance Ethics Violations," *Marketing News* 24 (March 5, 1990), 4, 14. **Figure 21.2:** Adapted from Robert Handfield, "Quality Management in Japan Versus the United States: An Overview," *Production and Inventory Management Journal* (2d Qtr 1989), 83. Reprinted with permission of The American Production and Inventory Control Society, Inc. **Global Highlight:** From Bruce White, "How Quality Became Job #1 at Ford," *Canadian Business Review,* 17 (Spring 1990) 24–27. **Figure 21.3:** From Philip B. Crosby, *Quality Without Tears* (New York: McGraw-Hill, 1984), 38–39. Copyright 1984. Reprinted with permission of McGraw-Hill, Inc. Figures 21.5, 21.6, 21.7. From Bureau of Labor Statistics. **Figure 21.8:** From Joel Dreyful, "Get Ready for the New Work Force," *Fortune,* April 23, 1990, 165–181. Copyright © 1990 The Time Inc. Magazine Company. All rights reserved. **Case Study:** Adapted from Ellis Booker, "Quality in IS: Managing with Facts, Not Intuition," *Computerworld,* December 11, 1989, 97; Florida Power and Light Company, *Compact Disclosure* (1991); Carol Hildebrand, "The Deming Prize: No Longer a Stranger at Home," *Computerworld,* December 11, 1989, 100; Carol Hildebrand, "Take It from the Top," *Computerworld,* December 11, 1989, 96; "Information Systems Anchor the Entire Organization," *Computerworld,* December 11, 1989, 96; Alan J. Ryan, "For Programmers, a Night's Sleep," *Computerworld,* December 11, 1989, 97; Alan J. Ryan, "Where Quality Takes Command," *Computerworld,* December 11, 1989, 1, 95–100.